OECD Proceedings

Bond Market Development in Asia

OECD

ORGANISATION FOR ECONOMIC CO-OPERATION AND DEVELOPMENT

ORGANISATION FOR ECONOMIC CO-OPERATION
AND DEVELOPMENT

Pursuant to Article I of the Convention signed in Paris on 14th December 1960, and which came into force on 30th September 1961, the Organisation for Economic Co-operation and Development (OECD) shall promote policies designed:

- to achieve the highest sustainable economic growth and employment and a rising standard of living in Member countries, while maintaining financial stability, and thus to contribute to the development of the world economy;

- to contribute to sound economic expansion in Member as well as non-member countries in the process of economic development; and

- to contribute to the expansion of world trade on a multilateral, non-discriminatory basis in accordance with international obligations.

The original Member countries of the OECD are Austria, Belgium, Canada, Denmark, France, Germany, Greece, Iceland, Ireland, Italy, Luxembourg, the Netherlands, Norway, Portugal, Spain, Sweden, Switzerland, Turkey, the United Kingdom and the United States. The following countries became Members subsequently through accession at the dates indicated hereafter: Japan (28th April 1964), Finland (28th January 1969), Australia (7th June 1971), New Zealand (29th May 1973), Mexico (18th May 1994), the Czech Republic (21st December 1995), Hungary (7th May 1996), Poland (22nd November 1996), Korea (12th December 1996) and the Slovak Republic (14th December 2000). The Commission of the European Communities takes part in the work of the OECD (Article 13 of the OECD Convention).

FOREWORD

Although the importance of creating well-developed capital markets in Asia has been recognised for some time, the recent financial crisis in Asia has given us all a strong reminder that the need is now more urgent than ever. In light of this growing importance of capital markets, it is fair to say that the April, 2000 "Round Table on Capital Market Reforms in Asia," co-organised by the OECD Centre for Co-operation with Non-Members and Directorate for Financial, Fiscal and Enterprise Affairs and the Asian Development Bank Institute (ADBI), took place at a very opportune time. The meeting in Tokyo considered future initiatives in capital market reform in the wake of the financial crisis. It followed a first Round Table, also held in Tokyo, in April 1999.

The OECD is very appreciative of the grant from the Japanese government that has made these two Round Tables possible. I would also like to extend our special thanks to Mr. Anthony Neoh, Chief Advisor of the China Securities Regulatory Commission and Professor of Peking University, who was moderator of both these Round Tables and provided us with a number of very useful organizational and substantive suggestions.

Like my colleagues in the OECD, I welcome the recent strong recovery of the Asian economies but recognize that much further progress in reform will still be needed to develop effective capital markets. There are huge investment opportunities in Asia, and we hope that all the parties concerned will work together to promote sustained development of markets in order to enable Asian countries to realise their full potential.

The second Round Table focused on bond markets in Asia. While the building of a vibrant bond market is acknowledged to be one of the highest priorities in building a modern capital market, it is also clear that development of this sector is not an easy task in emerging economies. Though there has been considerable progress in this field, much also remains to be done. It will plainly take more time for thriving bond markets to emerge in Asia. We hope that this Round Table has made some contribution to this long-term process.

This Round Table provided a unique forum, bringing together a broad range of capital markets experts from Asian and OECD countries. While the securities market regulators of IOSCO are the core participants, high-ranking officials from governments, central banks, international organizations, academics, executives from stock exchanges, industries and rating agencies and researchers also participate. Relevant topics were discussed from a range of perspectives, reflecting the diversity of the participants.

This publication contains a summary of the proceedings of the second Round Table, together with papers presented at the meeting and highlights of the discussions by the participants. We hope that this volume will serve as a source of information on capital market reform, particularly on bond market reform in Asia, and constitute a reference source on these topics for policy-makers and experts in both the public and private sectors.

Seiichi Kondo
Deputy Secretary-General

TABLE OF CONTENTS

Introduction

Development of Bond Markets in Asia

OECD AND ADBI NEWS RELEASE

Tokyo, Japan, 12 April 2000

ROUND TABLE ON CAPITAL MARKET REFORMS IN ASIA:

ADB Institute, Tokyo, 11 to 12th April 2000

Organisers: OECD, ADB Institute

Chairman's Statement

The OECD-ADBI Round Table on Capital Market Reforms in Asia was held at the Asian Development Bank Institute (ADBI) in Tokyo on 11th and 12th April 2000. The meeting was chaired by Mr. Anthony Neoh, Professor of Peking University and Chief Advisor to China Securities Regulatory Commission. Professor Neoh is also the former Chairman of the Securities and Futures Commission of Hong Kong Special Administrative Region, People's Republic of China, and the former Chairman of the Technical Committee of the International Organisation of Securities Commissions (IOSCO). The meeting was jointly sponsored by the Organisation for Economic Co-operation and Development (OECD) and the ADBI. Mr. Seiichi Kondo, Deputy Secretary-General, OECD, and Dr. Masaru Yoshitomi, Dean, ADBI, made welcoming remarks.

The Round Table was attended by Chairmen and other top-level representatives of securities market regulatory bodies, as well as high ranking officials of governments and central banks from India, Indonesia, Malaysia, Singapore, Thailand, the People's Republic of China, Hong Kong Special Administrative Region of the People's Republic of China, and Chinese Taipei. Also present were senior officials from securities market regulatory bodies, governments and central banks of OECD member countries and international organisations. Experts in the field from stock exchanges, industry, rating agencies and academic circles also participated in the meeting.

The Round Table was held in co-operation with IOSCO, IMF, the World Bank, ADB and the International Finance Corporation. It provided an important occasion for senior executives of Asian economy regulatory organisations who are members of IOSCO, their colleagues from OECD countries, and experts in the field of capital markets to discuss future initiatives in capital market reforms in Asia.

This Round Table is the second in a series. The first Round Table on Capital Market Reforms in Asia was held in Tokyo in April 1999.

The second Round Table focused on the development of bond markets in Asia and six themes emerged from the presentations and discussions at the conference:

1. The need to develop domestic bond markets to overcome over-reliance on bank financing, particularly short term bank financing.

2. The need to develop robust systems for issuing, trading, clearing and settlement, market surveillance, and enforcement.

3. The need to develop credit enhancement and credit rating systems.

4. The need to create a viable pool of investors.

5. The need to consider using national market development structures.

6. The need to push forward, in tandem with development of domestic bond markets, other financial reforms, particularly banking reforms. Asian economies are likely to have to rely heavily on bank financing in the foreseeable future notwithstanding the development of alternative forms of financing.

There was a consensus that domestic bond markets should be underpinned by a Government Securities Market with multiple maturity structures to create a smooth benchmark yield curve. Even when governments are in budget surplus, there would still be benefit in establishment of a government securities market to set up the benchmark yield curve and to assist in inter-bank financing. Regulatory structures should facilitate the establishment of corporate and asset-backed bond markets.

Robust issuing, trading, clearing and settlement, market surveillance, and enforcement structures are needed to ensure that domestic bond markets can be operated in a fair and transparent manner without causing systemic risk to the financial system. In this respect, a number of participants called on each market to review its bankruptcy regime to ensure that debts of all seniorities are adequately recognised in bankruptcies. The importance of electronic trading systems and internet trading was recognised, as well as the possibility of regional trading, clearing and settlement through the use of such technology.

Credit enhancement was thought to be an important subject requiring further thought. A Regional Credit Enhancement Agency was proposed and discussed at the meeting. Some participants thought that such an agency could be built on the Miyazawa Initiative possibly also with the sponsorship of the Asian Development Bank.

In building an adequate pool of institutional and retail investors, it was thought that each market should review its tax system to facilitate bond investment. Markets should also ensure that transactional costs are reduced and issue procedures are simplified, using perhaps techniques such as shelf registration. Regulations for permissible investments for mutual funds, insurance and pension funds should be reviewed to encourage bond investments.

A National Bond Market Development Committee such as that adopted in Malaysia, involving the Ministry of Finance, the Central Bank, the Securities Commission, and market operators could be used as a potential model to ensure that there is adequate co-ordination among all players for development of a bond market.

Finally, it was agreed that the task of ensuring that financial institutions should have robust risk management systems should be given priority by all governments. The meeting noted efforts by international financial regulatory bodies in promulgating international standards and in encouraging compliance of such standards through seeking self-evaluation by individual jurisdictions and through the use of market discipline. In particular the meeting heard a progress report by a representative of IOSCO on the implementation of the IOSCO Objectives and Principles of Securities Regulation.

The meeting concluded by taking particular note of Dean Yoshitomi's charge to the meeting:

"Many countries still have a long way to go before they could complete their (financial) structural reforms. Therefore, there is no guarantee that there will not be another crisis. Meanwhile, globalisation will continue to speed up and will be accompanied with efficient means of communication such as the internet. Countries in the region will not only have to quickly cope with their homegrown problems of inadequate supervision of financial institutions but also with problems that come from outside".

The summary of the discussions will be available on the following web sites.

OECD: http://www.oecd.org/daf

ADBI: http://www.adbi.org

For further information, contact

OECD: Mr. Fujiki Hayashi, Head, Outreach Unit for Financial Sector Reform, Directorate for Financial, Fiscal and Enterprise Affairs, OECD, tel. (33) 1 45 24 18 38; fax. (33) 1 45 24 18 33

ADBI: Mr. Hitoshi Nishida, Director, Administrative Management & Coordination, Asian Development Bank Institute, tel. (81) 3 3593 5500; fax. (81) 3 3593 5571

TOKYO ROUND TABLE ON BOND MARKET DEVELOPMENT

EXECUTIVE SUMMARY

The 2000 Tokyo Round Table focused on the topic of "Bond Market Development". It was composed of four major sections. In the first, welcome and introductions were provided by **Mr. Seiichi Kondo**, Deputy Secretary-General, Organisation for Economic Co-operation and Development (OECD), and **Dr. Masaru Yoshitomi**, Dean, Asian Development Bank Institute (ADBI). **Professor Anthony Neoh**, Professor at Peking University, Chief Advisor to the China Securities Regulatory Commission, and former Chairman, Securities and Futures Commission, Hong Kong, and Technical Committee, International Organisation of Securities Commissions (IOSCO), was introduced as the Chairman of the Round Table.

Dr. Yoshitomi examined five major topics in his introductory speech. The first was the nature of the Asian financial crisis, the recovery from it, and the future. Dr. Yoshitomi then presented a series of motivations for developing capital markets. Dr. Yoshitomi stressed the importance of good corporate governance, regulation and supervision. The fourth topic Dr. Yoshitomi analysed was the importance of government securities in providing a pricing benchmark for corporate bond markets by offering a yield curve for risk-free assets. Dr. Yoshitomi then briefly discussed the development of domestic bond markets.

In the second section of the Round Table, the progress that countries in Asia had made in reforming their capital markets was discussed. **Mr. Andrew Procter**, Member of the Commission and Executive Director, Securities and Futures Commission (SFC), Hong Kong, discussed two broad topics. He described first the reforms that are currently being undertaken in Hong Kong, and then summarised some developments concerning the implementation of the IOSCO *Principles and Objectives*. **Mr. Devendra Raj Mehta**, Chairman, Securities and Exchange Board of India (SEBI), discussed the current state of the Indian securities markets. **Mr. Herwidayatmo**, Chairman, Capital Market Supervisory Agency (BAPEPAM), Indonesia, discussed the current state of the Indonesian securities markets. **Mr. Ali Abdul Kadir**, Chairman, Securities Commission (SC), Malaysia, analysed the current state of the Malaysian securities markets.

Mr. Kunio Saito, Director, Regional Office for Asia and the Pacific, International Monetary Fund, gave a presentation on the topics of macroeconomic recovery and financial sector reforms in Asia. **Mr. Masamichi Kono**, Director, Planning and Legal Affairs Division, Financial Supervisory Agency, Japan, discussed capital market reform in Japan. **Mr. Prasarn Trairatvorakul**, Secretary-General, Securities and Exchange Commission (SEC), Thailand, spoke about recent developments in Thailand. **Mr. Kung-Wha Ding**, Vice Chairman, Securities and Futures Commission, Chinese Taipei, spoke about developments in the Taiwanese capital markets.

In the luncheon speech **Mr. Haruhiko Kuroda**, Vice Minister for International Affairs, Ministry of Finance, Japan, discussed the future international financial architecture and regional capital market development.

In the third section of the Round Table, a range of topics examining the broad question of the development of bond markets in Asia was analysed. It was divided into five sessions. An introduction was provided in the first session. **Professor Eisuke Sakakibara**, Keio University, Former Vice Minister for International Affairs, Ministry of Finance, Japan, presented a brief overview of the topic of the creation of an Asian bond market. **Professor Shinji Takagi,** Visiting Scholar at the ADBI, examined the topic of developing a viable corporate bond market under a bank-dominated system, focusing on analytical issues and policy implications.

In the next session, the experience in Asia, and the policy issues that need to be addressed, were discussed. **Mr. Noritaka Akamatsu**, Principal Financial Economist, Financial Sector Development Department, World Bank, described the strategy for developing a domestic bond market that Thailand had employed. **Ms. Yeo Lian Sim**, Assistant Managing Director, Capital Markets, Monetary Authority of Singapore, discussed the experience of Singapore in the development of bond markets in Asia. **Mr. Toshio Karigane**, Senior Executive Advisor, Daiwa Institute of Research, Japan, examined the Singaporean experience in bond market development, focusing on the development of the offshore market. **Dr. Gao Jian**, CFO and Chief Economist, China Development Bank, examined the development of the government debt market in China. **Mr. Norman Tak-lam Chan,** Deputy Chief Executive, Hong Kong Monetary Authority, examined the topic of the development of bond markets in Asia, focusing on the Hong Kong perspective. **Mr. Lawrence Fok,** Senior Executive Director, Stock Exchange of Hong Kong, examined the issues to be tackled for the development of the bond market in Hong Kong. **Mr. Ranjit Ajit Singh,** General Manager, Economic Analysis and Financial Policy, Securities Commission, Malaysia, described developments in the Malaysian bond market. **Dr. Yun-Hwan Kim**, Senior Economist, Asian Development Bank, examined the policy agenda for bond market development in Asia. **Mr. Toshio Kobayashi**, Director, International Finance Division, International Bureau, Ministry of Finance, Japan, discussed the development of international bond markets in the region.

In the third session, some lessons from the experience of the OECD countries and other emerging economies were described. **Mr. Hans Blommestein**, Senior Economist, Financial Affairs Division, Directorate for Financial Fiscal and Enterprise Affairs, OECD, talked about eliminating impediments for developing demand in the bond market. **Mr. Hans-Dieter Hanfland**, Division Chief, Ministry of Finance, Germany, discussed developments in the bond markets in Europe. **Mr. Masaaki Shirakawa**, Advisor to the Governor, Financial Markets Department, Bank of Japan, talked about the reforms in the Japanese Government Securities (JGS) market. **Professor Ghon Rhee**, University of Hawaii, discussed the topic of regionalisation of fixed-income securities markets, and asked the question "Is the Tokyo Market Ready?". **Mr. Tadashi Endo**, Senior Capital Markets Specialist, International Finance Corporation, focused on one aspect of the development of corporate debt markets, namely the relationship of the capital market, including the corporate bond market, with public finances and the banking sector.

In the fourth session, the roles of securities laws and securities market regulators in the sound development of bond markets were analysed. **Mr. Giovanni Sabatini**, Head of Market Regulation, Commissione Nazionale per le Societa e la Borsa, Italy, and Chairman of the Working Party 2 of the Technical Committee of IOSCO, presented an overview of the role of regulators in developing government securities markets. **Mr. Rick Shilts**, Acting Director, Division of Economic Analysis, Commodity Futures Trading Commission, discussed the topic of developing bond futures markets. **Mr. David Strachan**, Head of Department, Market Conduct and Infrastructure, Financial Services Authority (FSA), United Kingdom, discussed the topic of bond market regulation in a period of changing market structure, presenting the UK experience. **Mr. Stephen Williams**, Senior Special Advisor, Division of Market Regulation, Securities and Exchange Commission (SEC), United States, gave a presentation on the topic of transparency in the US debt markets. **Ms. Claire Grose**, Director, National Markets Unit, Australia Securities and Investment Commission (ASIC), examined the roles of securities laws and securities market regulators for the sound development of bond markets in Australia.

In the final session, some views from private sector participants on the development of bond markets in the region were presented. **Mr. Kevan Watts**, Executive Chairman, Asia Pacific Region, Merrill Lynch International Inc, presented a list of Ten Commandments for developing local debt capital markets in the internet age. **Ms. Julia Turner**, Managing Director, Moody's Asia Pacific Ltd. talked on the topic of bank reform, as being an essential element of capital market reforms in Asia. **Dr. Warapatr Todhanakasem**, President, Thai Rating and Information Services (TRIS), discussed the topic of a domestic Credit Rating Agency (CRA) in an emerging Asian country, with a perspective from TRIS. **Mr. Fumiyuki Sasaki**, Senior Economist, Economic Research Unit, Nomura Research Institute, Japan, discussed current conditions and developments in Asian domestic bond markets, and the further steps that need to be taken to advance the markets. **Dr. Takatoshi Ito**, Deputy Vice Minister for International Affairs, Ministry of Finance, Japan, and former Professor of Hitotsubashi University, talked on the topic of moving towards deep Asian bond markets.

Professor Anthony Neoh, concluded the proceedings by thanking everybody for their participation, and by identifying six broad themes that had been central to the discussions in the conference. The first was that bond markets could serve as an alternative to over-reliance on bank financing. The second was the need to develop appropriate "systems" at the broadest conceptual level. These included procedures for market-based underwriting of securities, creating a multiplicity of investments, establishing appropriate trading, clearing, settlement and legal structures, and where relevant the construction of appropriate futures markets. The third broad theme traversing the conference was the need to improve the quality of bond issuance - possibly through credit-enhancement schemes or some form of regional cooperation.

The fourth theme identified was the need to focus on investors, and particularly on the incentives they face, and the constraints imposed on them that restrict their developing wider asset allocation policies. The fifth theme was the benefits of establishing a national market development structure in a country so as to take account of all relevant market interests. Finally, Professor Neoh noted that many aspects of Asian financial systems continue to require attention, including risk management, exchange rate regimes, and the recapitalisation and restructuring of banks.

SUMMARY OF PROCEEDINGS

Introduction

Welcome and introductions were provided by **Mr. Seiichi Kondo**, Deputy Secretary-General, Organisation for Economic Co-operation and Development (OECD), and **Dr. Masaru Yoshitomi**, Dean, Asian Development Bank Institute (ADBI). **Professor Anthony Neoh**, Professor at Peking University, Chief Advisor to the China Securities Regulatory Commission, and former Chairman, Securities and Futures Commission, Hong Kong, China, and Technical Committee, International Organisation of Securities Commissions (IOSCO), was then introduced as the Chairman of the Round Table.

Dr. Yoshitomi examined six topics in his introductory speech. The first was the nature of the Asian financial crisis, the recovery from it, and the future. He noted that, while many countries had recovered from the crisis to a significant extent, there was no assurance that a similar crisis would not hit the crisis-affected countries again. This is because of the so-called double mismatch, namely the combination of the maturity mismatch and the currency mismatch, which is more or less inherent in the financial markets in emerging economies that continue to borrow short-term loans dominated in foreign currencies. Poor corporate governance, weak financial regulation, and inadequate monitoring of the financial sector all contributed to the worsening maturity mismatch, namely borrowing short and lending long to too risky investment projects. This was aggravated by borrowing in foreign currencies, largely on an un-hedged basis. These problems, together with those of bad corporate debt, bank restructuring and inadequate bankruptcy laws, will not be solved quickly. There is therefore no guarantee that there will not be another crisis. The speeding up of globalisation, together with enhanced communications technology, may also contribute to problems facing countries in Asia. Dr. Yoshitomi argued that the best way to respond to these problems was by capacity building and training in the region on the complexities of the world's financial system, on understanding both the maturity and the currency mismatches, and on the tools available to mitigate these mismatches.

Dr. Yoshitomi then presented a series of motivations for developing capital markets. The existence of well-functioning securities markets would have reduced the impact of the Asian crisis by enhancing the confidence of international investors, by improving market discipline, by promoting more effective allocation of capital, and thereby reducing the incentives to withdraw from the market. Capital market development might have reduced the heavy dependence on the banking sector and foreign borrowing for project finance. The absence of well-functioning corporate bond markets may have deprived the public of credit information generated by such markets on a continuous basis. The lack of liquidity in the crisis-hit countries was further increased by the low supply of investment-grade paper, the insufficient number of intermediaries, and the high trading costs due to fixed brokerage commissions. Illiquid futures markets may also have limited the hedging opportunities of market participants.

Dr. Yoshitomi stressed the importance of good corporate governance, regulation and supervision, noting the need for efficient use of firms' assets, accurate data, and effective enforcement of corporate laws. He identified the problems of hidden exposures, lack of transparency in accounting and auditing standards, and a widening gap between corporate governance practices in Asia and other parts of the world, including greater shareholder activism. There is also a greater need for enhanced transparency concerning the highly leveraged institutions (HLIs), both because of the potential of HLIs to launch speculative attacks using the securities markets, and because of the potential systemic risk from HLI defaults. Other regulatory and supervisory issues that need addressing include the improvement of the disclosure of exposures in OTC instruments and off-balance sheet items, enhanced prudential capital requirements, and enforcement and supervision of stock exchanges and clearing houses.

The fourth topic Dr. Yoshitomi analysed was the importance of government securities in providing a pricing benchmark for corporate bond markets by offering a yield curve for risk-free assets. They are also useful in hedging interest rate risks, and as collateral for related markets, such as futures and options markets. Practical policy recommendations to develop them include: ensuring an appropriate distribution of maturity and issue frequency through the establishment of large benchmark issues at key maturities; minimising the liquidity-impairing effect of taxes; enhancing the transparency of sovereign issuers and issue schedules and of trading information, while paying due attention to the anonymity of market participants; ensuring the safety and standardisation of trading and settlement practices; and developing futures and options markets.

Dr. Yoshitomi then briefly discussed the development of domestic bond markets. He noted that it is essential that a government strikes a balance between debt management and bond market development, that it supports the market through a sound legal framework, and that it promotes a level playing field for all financial instruments and market participants through consistent economic policies. It is also vital that the debt management and bond market development strategies are consistent with fiscal and monetary policies as well as a country's financial sector development strategy.

A range of other policy measures to develop domestic bond markets were also identified. An effective regulatory and supervisory framework for the bond market, intermediaries, institutional investors and other market participants is necessary. Clear and unambiguous rules and procedures, legal enforceability, a risk management system with rules for various categories of risk, short settlement periods, timely dissemination of information, and suitable contingency arrangements are also important. The promotion of a diversity of market participants, and the establishment of credit-rating agencies are also vital. Dr. Yoshitomi also stressed the important of including banks in the development strategy for a bond market, given their current domination of the markets.

Dr. Yoshitomi concluded by noting that the Round Table would be composed of two parts. In the first, the progress that countries in Asia had made in reforming their capital markets would be discussed. In the second part, a range of topics examining the broad question of the development of bond markets in Asia would be analysed.

Part I   Progress in Capital Market Reforms in Asia

Hong Kong, China

In this first part of the Round Table, a range of topics examining the broad question of the development of bond markets in Asia was analysed. **Mr. Andrew Procter**, Member of the Commission and Executive Director, Securities and Futures Commission (SFC), Hong Kong, China, discussed two broad topics. He described first the reforms that are currently being undertaken in Hong Kong, China, and then summarised some developments concerning the implementation of the IOSCO *Principles and Objectives*.

The legislative reform being undertaken in Hong Kong, China is a consolidation and updating of ten past pieces of legislation. Its aims are to update the objectives of the SFC, to facilitate innovation and competition, to update relevant definitions and concepts, and to promote new ways of delivering financial services. The licensing regime is being simplified, and additional disciplinary powers are being granted to the Commission. A market misconduct tribunal is also being established, which has civil remedies at its disposal, and the availability of criminal remedies as well. The concept of regulatory passports is being developed to allow for the recognition of the quality of regulation abroad, for example to allow well-regulated exchanges access to the Hong Kong, China market. The notion of granting a temporary license is also being considered in some circumstances.

Mr. Procter argued that the SFC would be more accountable as a result of the changes. The creation of the Securities and Futures Appeal Tribunal, to be chaired by an independent judge, will allow most actions and decisions of the Commission to be subject to independent scrutiny, apart from investigations of the SFC. In addition, the establishment of the Process Review Panel, again with independent and external appointees, will allow the decision-making process of the Commission to be challenged.

Mr. Procter identified a range of regulatory issues arising from changes in the operations of the exchanges and clearing houses, particularly their demutualisation, merger, and likely public listing in mid-2000. Such reforms at the exchanges and clearing houses are likely to put pressure on the concept of "self" in self-regulation, as they may well have an incentive to pursue profits at the expense of their regulatory duties. The regulation of members by contract is difficult, and the exchange may also be in competition with its members. The day-to-day supervision of these members has therefore been passed to the Commission. The exchange will still, however, be responsible for the surveillance of trading, risk management by its members, and the listing function.

Implementation Committee of IOSCO Objectives and Principles

Mr. Procter then summarised some developments concerning the implementation of the IOSCO *Principles and Objectives*. He noted that following a decision of the IOSCO Executive Committee in 2/1999, a Committee was established to develop implementation and assessment methodologies for the IOSCO *Objectives and Principles*, and to explore means of offering guidance to the international financial institutions (IFIs) in their use of the principles. The Committee is chaired by the SFC, has 20 other members - drawn from all regions from both developed and emerging markets - and also has participation from the IFIs – in particular, the World Bank, the International Monetary Fund, the OECD, the African Development Bank, the Asian Development Bank, the European Bank for Re-Construction and Development and the Inter-American Development Bank.

The Committee has responded to the first part of its mandate with two exercises. The first, intended to provide a rapid assessment of current implementation among IOSCO members, is a high level self-evaluation based on the entire *Principles* document. At the same time, a more detailed self-evaluation will be performed on discrete sections of the *Principles*. Completion of the high level survey with respect to all the Principles will be an immediate and clear organisation-wide statement of commitment to the document, and will focus the attention of individual regulators upon any areas in need of urgent reform. The more detailed surveys are intended to be much more rigorous inquiries. Over time, it is intended that all aspects of the Principles will be subject to the more detailed assessment.

The documents are drafted so that they may be used for self-assessment by IOSCO Members, as the basis for peer review amongst IOSCO Members, and also by the IFIs. However, there is at present no established procedure or infrastructure to support either peer review, or IOSCO or IFI review of a large number of IOSCO Members to determine the extent of adherence to the *Objectives and Principles*. The most expeditious course of action is to ask every IOSCO Member to undertake a self-assessment. IOSCO has prior experience of such self-assessments and Members are fully aware of their potential limitations in the absence of some external discipline and scrutiny. The result of self-assessments may not be fully reliable. The Committee is considering the possibility of peer review as a complement to self-assessment. It is too early to say whether this will prove viable and acceptable to IOSCO Members. The issues that arise include conflicts of interest, costs, resourcing and transparency.

The IMF and the World Bank are involved in a joint pilot program, the Financial Sector Stability Assessment Program (FSSAP). To the extent that the perceived financial sector vulnerabilities of a country include securities markets issues, the IMF and World Bank have begun to make use of the IOSCO assessment documents in their FSSAPs. It is important to recognise, however, that the IOSCO *Objectives and Principles* were not developed to be used for a "pass" or "fail" grading; rather they are aspirational in nature. Members agree to do what they can to implement them. It is also clear that any particular Principle may be able to be satisfied in variety of ways and, indeed, may reflect the legal and other circumstances of a jurisdiction. That makes it difficult to use the document for assessment purposes.

Members of IOSCO appear to be strongly of the view that IOSCO should remain responsible for the establishment of principles and standards in the securities sector. They also appear willing to remain involved in any work to assist Members in the implementation of those *Principles*. The IOSCO position on continued involvement may be partly a recognition that there is no other organisation that is apparently willing and able to perform the role in the securities sector. It remains to be seen, therefore, to what extent the IMF, the World Bank and others will wish to take on any evaluation role in relation to international standards and principles in the securities sector. If they do contribute to such a role, then there will be resource and skill issues to be addressed. It is clear from their participation in the IOSCO Implementation Committee that there is great potential for the IFIs to work more closely with IOSCO on the resolution of these issues. The IOSCO self-assessments are an important potential foundation for the FSSAPs, and IOSCO Members have the skill sets that are in short supply in the IFIs.

The Financial Stability Forum Working Group on "Offshore Jurisdictions" is considering the need for assessments to be made against internationally agreed standards and principles and has discussed the possibility that organisations such as IOSCO should be asked to expel Members that do not meet those standards or observe those principles. The Report of that Working Group is expected shortly. The other relevant FSF Working Group is on "The Implementation of Standards". The Task Force has met three times and a draft report has been prepared for submission to the next FSF Meeting. The Report is in the form of an "issues paper". The Report identifies the main challenges or obstacles to implementing standards, discusses the key success factors to address these challenges; outlines a strategy for implementation that leverages on the success factors, builds on existing initiatives, highlights areas that need further attention; and sets out options and next steps for the Forum to consider.

India

Mr. Devendra Raj Mehta, Chairman, Securities and Exchange Board of India (SEBI), discussed the current state of the Indian securities markets. As an introduction he presented selected indicators of the Indian economy, a brief outline of the regulatory framework under which SEBI operates, and a few measures characterising the Indian securities markets (including that it has 24 stock exchanges, 300 cities with trading terminals, over 9,000 intermediaries, and over 9,000 listed companies).

Mr. Mehta then discussed the wide range of reforms which had been implemented in the country. In the primary market, he noted that the pricing of all issues was free, that stringent entry norms and track record criteria for issuers, together with initial and continuing disclosure requirements, had been imposed, that issuance procedures had been simplified to reduce costs and time, and that the "book-building" process had been introduced.

Many major reforms had also been implemented in the secondary markets. These included the achievement of market transparency through electronic trading and settlement systems, the imposition of greater disclosure requirements, the timely dissemination of price sensitive information, and the institutionalisation of early warning signals, and actions, through automated systems. Market safety and integrity had been enhanced through setting up depositories, clearing houses, trade/settlement guarantee funds, surveillance systems at both SEBI and the stock exchanges, the establishment of price bands, and the development of a stock-watch system. Market efficiency had been promoted by reducing the settlement cycle from 14 days to a weekly cycle, by introducing a uniform close-out procedure, rolling settlement, and by sanctioning internet trading. In addition, SEBI has introduced a series of rules to protect minority shareholders.

A range of reforms had also been undertaken in the mutual funds arena. Valuation and disclosure norms had been strengthened. Domestic mutual funds had been allowed to invest in overseas markets. A regulation had been imposed requiring that two thirds of the trustees on a board be independent. Restrictions had been placed on investments in securities of group companies of a sponsor, and also on transactions with brokers associated with a sponsor. Mutual funds had been allowed to trade in derivatives and to lend stocks. The amount of funds under management by mutual funds had grown from US $1.5 billion in 1995/6 to US $11.72 billion in 1999/2000.

Mr. Mehta noted that these reforms had had a wide range of effects. They had broadened access to the markets, increased the investor base, reduced transaction costs, made the Indian markets amongst the least volatile, lead to a minimal number of broker defaults, ensured that there had been no halts in trading, guaranteed timely settlement of transactions, promoted prompt detection of market manipulations, lead to efficient risk containment measures, and improved market transparency.

A range of ways in which India was promoting international coordination was described. SEBI is an active member of IOSCO, where India is the Chairman of the Asia Pacific Regional Committee. India hosted a meeting of the Emerging Markets Committee of IOSCO in 11/1999. SEBI has signed an MOU with the American SEC, and is in the process of implementing the IOSCO objectives and principles.

Mr. Mehta concluded by describing the current agenda being pursued in India. It includes spreading the equity cult to 1000 cities by using the internet and VSAT, providing online trading through a single window for both trading and settlement, broadening the reach of the primary market by using the internet, introducing and enforcing a code of corporate governance, aligning domestic accounting standards with international standards, floating new issues through the secondary market, introducing exchange-traded equity-index derivatives, promoting venture capital activity, improving disclosure standards, refining risk management systems, encouraging online book-building and IPOs, developing a vibrant secondary debt market, promoting asset securitisation, and encouraging the listing of foreign companies on Indian exchanges.

Indonesia

Mr. Herwidayatmo, Chairman, Capital Market Supervisory Agency (BAPEPAM), Indonesia, discussed the current state of the Indonesian securities markets. He presented a brief history of the establishment of the Indonesian stock exchanges, of how the market was deregulated in 1987-8, and of how it subsequently grew in the mid-1990s. Details were provided of the growth in the amount of stock and bond issues, the daily average trading volume, and the market capitalisation. The major reforms undertaken in the market were then summarized. These included the establishment of a regulatory system modelled after the US SEC, the change from a merit system to full disclosure for listing, the privatisation of the stock exchange, the shifting of the functions undertaken by BAPEPAM from executive to supervisory activities, and the assignment to the new regulator of enforcement powers.

A range of current priorities were then identified by Mr. Herwidayatmo. The regulator aims to increase the quality of transparency and disclosure by ensuring that domestic accounting and auditing standards are similar to international ones, by requiring listed companies to report financial information promptly, and by responding quickly to complaints regarding disclosure and other actions of issuers. Another goal is to improve a range of rules and regulations, for example by examining proposals to stimulate the expansion of domestic markets, by reviewing tax policy with respect to mutual funds, asset-backed securities, and long-term bonds, and by issuing rules regarding corporate takeovers and reverse stock splits, and the transfer of securities. In order to enhance corporate governance, measures had been recommended to improve the responsiveness of management to the needs of minority shareholders, and recommendations had been proposed to change company law regarding the role of commissioners and directors.

In order to strengthen market institutions, Mr. Herwidayatmo noted it is intended to apply a new Net Adjusted Working Capital rule comparable to international standards. Guaranteed settlement will be initiated as part of a netting process under scripless trading. A new computer for the Central Securities Depository will also become operational shortly, and should provide a reliable settlement mechanism with assured delivery-versus-payment. The government and legislature had approved in principle the reorganisation of the agency in order to promote its independence. The proposed structure is intended to facilitate the coordination of the regulation of securities markets with those of other areas of financial services, including banking, insurance and pensions. Mr. Herwidayatmo identified three primary goals of the regulator: to ensure fair treatment from all issuers and institutions, to protect investors, and to take account of feedback from its primary clients.

Malaysia

Mr. Ali Abdul Kadir, Chairman, Securities Commission (SC), Malaysia, analysed the current state of the Malaysian securities markets. He first presented an economic and market overview. He noted that the Malaysian economy was back on a sustainable growth path driven by a strong external sector with a stable exchange rate. At the same time, the stock market has staged a strong recovery and has been the best performing equity market in the region for the year.

Mr. Kadir then described some recent measures that had been taken to develop the capital markets. During the crisis, the SC had taken a series of tactical steps to maintain stability in the system, to restore market confidence, and to ensure that market intermediaries remained solvent. After the crisis, the SC had moved towards taking more strategic measures and initiatives. A key one was to enhance disclosure and transparency, moving towards a disclosure-based regime, strengthening rules on related-party and interested-party transactions, and requiring quarterly reporting by listed companies.

Great emphasis was being placed on corporate governance and shareholder value. As far as issuers were concerned, efforts were being undertaken to implement recommendations to raise corporate governance standards, disclosure standards were being enhanced, and there was an on-going education campaign. On the investor side, activism by domestic investors was being encouraged, an on-going education and awareness campaign was also being undertaken, and a minority shareholder watchdog group had been established.

A range of recent efforts had been undertaken to strengthen supervision and enforcement. The legislative basis governing the regulation of insider trading had been improved, and the SC had enhanced its enforcement capabilities and capacity. This had lead to a significant increase in the number of cases being filed, and subsequent legal actions. Steps were also being taken to make market intermediaries stronger and more competitive. A new risk-based capital adequacy framework was implemented on 1/12/1999, consolidation of the broking industry was being encouraged, and progressive deregulation was being examined and pursued in commission rates and in the scope of business intermediaries were allowed to undertake.

Technology infrastructure and applications are seen as an important factor going forward. The SC's philosophy is to be proactive and not reactive. It recently released a consultative paper on the framework for e-commerce implementation in the capital markets which proposes recommendations on many areas, including allowing straight-through processing, on-line unit-trust transactions, facilitating the establishment of financial portals, and encouraging the shift towards more paperless processes. A concerted effort is being made to develop the corporate bond market through the forum of the National Bond Market Committee, chaired by the Ministry of Finance, together with participation of the Central Bank and the SC. Mr Kadir concluded that many of these strategies were being incorporated into the Capital Market Master Plan, a plan which aimed to prioritise the immediate needs and chart the long-term growth and direction for the capital market.

IMF

Mr. Kunio Saito, Director, Regional Office for Asia and the Pacific, International Monetary Fund, gave a presentation on the topics of macroeconomic recovery and financial sector reforms in Asia. He noted that few people had expected the Asian economies to recover so quickly and so strongly from the crisis. Growth for 1999 exceeded earlier expectations, and prospects for 2000 are good. Asia's strong growth performance is part of a global economic upturn. The key factors for the improvements were supportive fiscal and monetary policies, rising exports, and a recovery in private investment.

While progress has been made in this area, policy challenges remain to be solved in order to ensure that the ongoing recovery is transformed to high and sustained growth. One serious risk is an abrupt and sharp slowdown of the US economy. Another risk arises from the tentative and fragile nature of the recovery of Japan's economy. Other potentially problematic factors include increases in oil prices, and volatility in key exchange rates. Most importantly, financial policies need to be re-balanced to a more neutral stance and reform and restructuring efforts need to be continued. Fiscal consolidation needs to start soon, and monetary conditions will also need to be tightened to check any inflationary pressures that might arise.

Mr. Saito identified two ultimate goals of financial sector reform and restructuring: to address the existing weaknesses of the financial sector, and to develop mechanisms to ensure that the sector remains strong, healthy, sound, and less vulnerable to another crisis. He noted that considerable progress has been made in addressing weak financial institutions and in establishing mechanisms to alleviate the risks of another financial sector crisis. Measures in five areas were identified: 1) the legal framework has been strengthened; 2) new specialised agencies have been created to deal with financial sector problems, manage nationalised assets, and conduct bank supervision; 3) weak and insolvent financial institutions have been dealt with; 4) measures have been taken to strengthen the remaining solvent institutions; and finally 5) the privatisation of nationalised institutions and assets has begun. Mr. Saito noted some other areas where progress is being achieved. Prudential rules and disclosure procedures have been tightened. A number of international codes and standards have been developed and adopted to ensure that these prudential rules are applied appropriately. The IMF and the World Bank are together undertaking Financial Sector Assessment Programs, and Financial Sector Stability Assessments on member countries.

Mr. Saito concluded that Asian countries have made much progress in implementing financial sector reforms. He maintained, however, that there is no room for complacency, as much remains to be done. Management and operational reforms at the level of individual institutions must continue, and efforts to develop modern market infrastructure need also to be stepped up.

Japan

Mr. Masamichi Kono, Director, Planning and Legal Affairs Division, Financial Supervisory Agency, Japan, discussed capital market reform in Japan. The reforms started in 1996 when the three principles of freedom, fairness, and globalisation were discussed in the so-called "Big Bang" initiative. In 4/1998 foreign exchange controls were completely dismantled, and in 1998 the Financial System Reform Law was passed. Major elements of the reform program for the financial sector included the liberalisation of new products and increased diversity of investment trust schemes, the development of capital markets, the dismantling of barriers between financial sub-sectors, the enhancement of market efficiency, and the creation of rules to prevent unfair transactions.

Mr. Kono identified five key goals of the capital market reforms. The first was to provide greater investment opportunities, and was being promoted by allowing a diversification of investment trust products, letting banks and insurance companies sell investment trusts over-the-counter, by fully liberalising trading in securities derivatives, and by making stock investment more attractive. The second key goal of the reforms was to facilitate corporate financing. New bond products were being introduced, more flexible issuance of bonds was being allowed, the use of special purpose companies was being sanctioned, listing procedures were being made easier, OTC markets were being enhanced, and unlisted share markets were being deregulated.

A third key goal was to encourage the provision of more diversified services. In order to do so, brokerage commissions were liberalised, the licensing of securities companies was replaced by having registration requirements, and other liberalisation measures were taken to allow new entrants into securities-related businesses. The fourth goal Mr. Kono noted was to make markets more efficient. Stock exchange markets were being reformed, the consolidation requirement for order flows of listed securities was abolished, proprietary trading systems were introduced, and both the repo markets and settlement systems were being reformed. The final goal was to ensure fair trading. This was being implemented by establishing fair trading rules for new products, by reviewing the rules concerning short-selling, by strengthening penalties, and by enhancing accounting and disclosure rules. Abolition of the securities transaction tax and the securities exchange tax was also done as of April 1999.

Ongoing reforms include allowing stock exchanges to reorganise themselves as joint stock companies and to demutualise, introducing an electronic reporting and disclosure system, and promoting further diversification of investment trust products. Recent trends include increased participation of individual investors, the establishment of new markets, venture capital activities, mergers and tie-ups between exchange markets, the development of ECNs, and internet trading.

Thailand

Mr. Prasarn Trairatvorakul, Secretary-General, Securities and Exchange Commission (SEC), Thailand, spoke about recent developments in Thailand. He compared first the performance of the Thai stock market with that of the Thai economy. Since the flotation of the Thai baht on 2/7/1997, the Stock Exchange of Thailand index reached its lowest level of 207.31 on 4/9/1998, and highest level of 531.88 on 28/6/1999. Since then the index has followed a downwards trend, with a slight upwards adjustment at the end of 1999. On 3/4/2000, the index was at 399.74, a decrease of 20% from the beginning of the year. In contrast, the Thai economy has shown significant signs of recovery. The last figure of GDP growth in the fourth quarter of 1999 was 6.5% on a year to year basis. Other economic indicators also show evidence of strong economic performance.

In order to answer the question of how the market performance differed so sharply from the overall economic performance, the SEC recently launched a survey of 18 securities firms in Thailand. The sharp decline in stock prices during the last quarter was believed to arise from two main factors: investors' perception that Thai banks and finance companies performed poorly, and the fact that more than one-third of total market capitalisation and one half of market turnover was in stocks in the financial sector. The first factor triggered the selling of bank and finance company stocks, while the second factor made the stock index vulnerable to movements in the prices of stocks in the financial sector. The survey also revealed several other investor concerns: the non-performing loans (NPL) of Thai financial institutions, which are currently about 38.7% of total outstanding loans; the problem of recapitalising the Thai banks and finance companies; the problem of corporate debt restructuring, and the problem of structural reforms in companies in order to restore the long-term competitiveness of the Thai economy.

Most investors appear pessimistic about the NPL problem, assuming it will be a drag on the economy. Mr. Trairatvorakul, however, was rather optimistic, believing that the economy has gained enough momentum to sustain its recovery, and that the NPL problem will be alleviated as corporate performance picks up. He noted that many of the financial reform measures that had been taken also supported his view. These include the capital support facilities for banks and finance companies incorporated in Thailand under the 8/1998 financial reform package, the legal amendments to Thai commercial banking law enabling the establishment of asset management companies (AMCs), and the revision of the bankruptcy and foreclosure laws to facilitate the corporate debt restructuring process.

In the second part of his presentation, Mr. Trairatvorakul examined the micro-level policies affecting the development of the market. He noted that the Stock Exchange of Thailand (SET), with the support of the SEC, is diversifying its activities. Listing requirements are being relaxed to offer more flexibility to firms belonging to both the old and new economy which want to apply for listing on the main board, and a new exchange has been established called the Market for Alternative Investments (MAI). Many state enterprises under the government's privatisation program will soon be listed on the SET. Big corporations in the high-growth economic sectors such as exports will be persuaded to use the capital markets as a source of fund-raising. Small and medium enterprises will be allowed to list on MAI. Thai firms that are listed and traded overseas will be allowed a dual-listing locally.

Mr. Trairatvorakul identified the path of capital market development in Thailand as being composed of three interrelated phases. The first includes the improvement of the basic infrastructure related to products (or securities), intermediaries and the market (or exchange). Reforms at the SET are an example of this. The second phase is to promote liberalisation and pro-competition policies. This stage includes the development of the bond market, the promotion of institutional investors, and the development of liquidity and risk management tools. The third generation is the development of technology to promote Thai competitiveness in the global environment. Internet trading, the liberalisation of securities trading commissions, and group supervision of financial conglomerates will be the focus of this phase. The first and second phases are seen as helping the capital market overcome the problem of "market incompleteness". The goal of the third phase is to help realise both market allocative efficiency, meaning the efficient use of economic resources, and market dynamic efficiency, meaning a resilient market condition capable of coping with a changing business environment.

Mr. Trairatvorakul concluded by arguing that each country has its own unique development path, and that market development will never be ended. He noted that Thailand had just passed through one of the most serious economic crises of its history. Although most listed companies were facing a problem of market under-valuation, he believed that most will be able to survive through this difficult time.

Chinese Taipei

Mr. Kung-Wha Ding, Vice Chairman, Securities and Futures Commission, Chinese Taipei, spoke about developments in the Taiwanese capital markets. He noted that the market had grown over the past year. From 1998 to 1999, the total number of listed companies had increased from 437 to 462, the number of OTC quoted companies had gone from 176 to 264, and the number of publicly held companies had risen from 1,810 to 2,018. Market capitalisation had exceeded US$390 billion, 110% of GDP, and annual turnover had reached US$917.3 billion.

A range of significant events occurred in the year. The excessive cross-holdings of shares, misappropriation of company funds and poor financial management by some listed companies at the end of 1998 and early 1999, resulted in severe problems. The Commission accordingly amended relevant regulations to restrict companies from creating investment vehicles to hold the shares of parent companies, and also strengthened mechanisms to monitor the internal control of publicly held companies. The Commission also increased the responsibility of CPAs in auditing both their financial statements and internal control systems. In order to protect the interests of minority shareholders and creditors of affiliate companies enhance the transparency of the business and financial operations of controlling companies, the Commission issued guidelines for the preparation of consolidated financial statements and operational reports. The Commission also promulgated the "Criteria for Mergers and Acquisitions among Securities Firms" with a view to expanding their operating size and improving their competitiveness. In the wake of the massive earthquake last year, the Commission quickly took a series of measures, including closing the market for four trading days, and adjusting the price-down limit from 7% to 3.5% in order to reduce volatility. No defaults were reported after the natural disaster.

Mr. Ding noted a range of significant measures that had been taken during the last year. The Commission decided to launch a second board market for the shares of smaller firms to be traded on the OTC market. It is expected that this will attract SMEs, start-up technology and internet companies, and also Taiwan Innovative Growing EntrepreneuRs (TIGERs). Listing procedures in floating such shares will be significantly relaxed. At the same time the Commission continues to require a high standard of information disclosure, to place more responsibility on sponsoring underwriters and CPAs, and to require company directors, supervisors, managers, and major shareholders, to deposit their shares with the central depository.

In order to better protect investors, the Commission drafted the "Securities Investors/Futures Traders Protection Bill". It aims to create a fund to compensate the losses of investors in the case of defaults by securities firms or futures commission merchants, and will also introduce the possibility of class legal actions. The Commission encouraged the Taiwan Futures Exchange to increase its product line by introducing contracts on the indices in the electronic, financial and insurance sectors. In order to increase trading in futures contracts, the Commission allowed futures brokers to take orders through the internet, and it also publicised relevant regulations to safeguard the security of on-line trading.

The Commission raised the ceiling of share ownership of any listed or quoted company by foreign investors to 50 percent, and it is expected that the ceiling will be lifted by 1/2001. The Commission also raised the maximum quota for each Qualified Foreign Institutional Investor to invest in Taiwan's securities markets from US$600 million to US$1.2 billion. The Commission proposed amending the law to increase civil and criminal penalties on corporate personnel in the event of insider trading or price manipulation. The Commission required all securities and futures related organisations and public companies to step up their preparation in solving the Y2K problem. Due to the fact that the securities markets in Taiwan are retail-driven and highly liable to the impact of non-economic factors, a stabilising mechanism (the National Stabilisation Fund), was created.

Mr. Ding concluded by identifying three recent developments in the markets. In order to encourage the merger of listed and OTC quoted companies, to safeguard the interests of investors, and to ensure market order, the Commission issued the "Rules governing the mergers of listed and OTC quoted companies" in 2/2000. The Commission instructed the Taiwan Stock Exchange to revise its rules to extend after-hours trading. Finally, in order to meet the trend of on-line trading across international securities markets, the Commission has been considering further extending the daily trading hours. It is expected that this will attract more trading interest and meet the demand of global institutional investors.

Luncheon Speech

Future International Financial Architecture and Regional Capital Market Reforms in Asia

Mr. Haruhiko Kuroda, Vice Minister for International Affairs, Ministry of Finance, Japan, discussed the future international financial architecture and regional capital market development. He noted that a conglomeration of factors – including the Asian currency crisis, the Russian crisis, the Brazil crisis, the collapse of Long-Term Capital Management, and falls in stock prices throughout the world – had lead experts to conclude that these almost simultaneous global currency crises were caused not simply by inherent problems in individual emerging economies, but rather by defects in the international financial system. As a result the international community, with G7 at its core, started to examine reform of this system. These efforts lead to the adoption of the G7 Finance Ministers' Report at Cologne.

Mr. Kuroda examined the progress that had taken place following this Report. He noted first four major developments in the area of strengthening and reforming the international institutions and arrangements. The Board of Governors of the IMF decided last year to transform the IMF's Interim Committee into the International Monetary and Financial Committee and to make it a permanent body. The G20 Finance Ministers and Central Governors was established to provide a new mechanism for informal dialogue in the framework of the Bretton Woods institutional system, to broaden discussion on key economic and financial policy issues, and to contribute to consensus building among its members. The Financial Stability Forum (FSF) which was created last year examined various issues concerning HLIs, capital flows and offshore financial centres. The necessity of streamlining the IMF's facilities was recently emphasized by the US. The essence of the US proposal is that the IMF should be more limited in its financial involvement with member countries, in other words, it should lend selectively and with short maturities.

Mr. Kuroda confirmed that Japan's views about the IMF are: (a) the focus of surveillance and programs should be responsive to potentially abrupt large scale cross border capital movements, (b) involvement of the IMF in structural policies should be limited to cases directly related to crises, and (c) its transparency and decision-making process should be improved. It is also extremely important to secure sufficient resources for the IMF. A key element of IMF reform is to redistribute quote shares to better reflect the changing economic realities of member countries, since the quota is the basis for each member's access limit of IMF resources, as well as a basis for decision-making in the IMF.

Many steps have been taken to enhance the transparency and accountability of the IMF, including the disclosure of IMF discussions, publication of IMF staff papers, and the voluntary disclosure of Article IV consultation papers. Mr. Kuroda maintained, however, that further efforts are still needed. The role of the IMF as one of the core mechanisms for monitoring the implementation of internationally agreed standards and codes for best practices is important. These standards and codes are useful in facilitating rational decision-making by investors, in helping financial markets function effectively, and in promoting responsible and sound policies by governments.

It is vital that emerging economies select an appropriate exchange rate regime in order to reduce their vulnerability to crises. Japan has long expressed its reservations about so-called "two-corner" solutions, which call for either a fixed exchange rate system based on a currency board or some other rigid system, or a freely floating exchange rate system. A consensus has emerged in recent IMF discussions that the appropriate exchange rate regime may vary depending upon the country's circumstances.

Mr. Kuroda argued that the issue of HLIs is particularly important. An international consensus has been reached on enhancing disclosure by all market participants, including HLIs, ensuring counter-party risk management in their transactions, and enhancing appropriate regulatory oversight. In addition, direct regulation should be reconsidered, if these other tools prove inadequate. It is also extremely important to strengthen the involvement of the private sector in preventing and resolving crises. Since it will be difficult to continue to bail-out private investors using public funds, and this also involves moral hazard, there is an international consensus that it is essential to seek the cooperation of all private sector creditors, including bond-holders. However the actual implementation of such efforts is fraught with difficulty.

Mr. Kuroda stressed that strengthening financial institutions and improving the supervision of financial systems are easier said than done. He gave a series of examples to illustrate this point. For the IMF to try to force emerging economies to abide by rules decreed by the Basle Committee, would be difficult given that the Committee's members are all from the industrialised nations. Although it is dangerous for a country to depend on too much short-term capital from foreign countries, there is no simple standard suitable for all countries. For governments to be able to make HLIs including hedge funds disclose information, some form of legal action will be necessary. But most such funds are established in off-shore markets, free from control by outside regulatory bodies. It is also extremely difficult for governments to obtain private sector involvement, as this means asking private lenders to assume responsibility. Although this was achieved in Korea, in most other cases it has not been effective. Similarly, apart from a few exceptions, the restructuring of emerging countries' debts has proved extremely difficult.

Although market intervention, and private sector involvement, may be unavoidable, if the smooth functioning of the global financial and capital markets is to be ensured, Mr. Kuroda argued it will be a very difficult task. Furthermore, market intervention risks hampering the inflow of funds to emerging countries and could delay their economic growth. These funds helped bring about dramatic economic growth in Asia for example. He therefore argued for the exploration of a "third way" to enhance stability.

A crucial first step would be to develop and maintain a market in which international funds, including those going to emerging economies, can flow without impediment. Efforts to help emerging economies to develop their domestic capital markets are particularly important. The establishment of fair accounting standards, settlement systems, and taxation systems, and the removal of unfair market domination are indispensable for the development of capital markets. In emerging Asian economies, loans have been the most common method of raising capital, while stock markets have been widely targeted by speculative investors, and bond markets have been underdeveloped. This is why the New Miyazawa Initiative in the second stage places particular priority on the development of bond markets. The initiative aims to boost financing through bond issuance by guaranteeing bonds issued by Asian countries.

The second step should be for Asia to establish a regional capital market, because capital providers have nationalities and regionalities although funds can move freely across borders. Mr. Kuroda argued that fortunately in Asia there is a large pool of savings that could be effectively used for mutual benefit through a regional capital market. A common mechanism to enhance the credibility of such a regional marketplace, standardized bonds for issuance in the region, and a regional credit-rating agency are measures worth considering to support the distribution of such funds within Asia. It is vital as a third step, to put in place sound macroeconomic, financial and structural policies in Asian countries to enable markets to function smoothly. A regional surveillance system, which has already been adopted under the Manila Framework, should be enforced through various forums. Finally, to enable the financial and capital markets to contribute to the economic growth of the region, exchange rates must be stabilized to reflect the fundamentals of the regional economies.

Mr. Kuroda concluded by noting that ahead of the worldwide reform of the international financial system, and in the wake of the Asian crisis, emerging economies independently introduced various domestic controls and regulations. While it is understandable that they resorted to such countermeasures, he maintained that these are undesirable solutions for the long-term. A shift from the individual nation approach to a coordinated regional strategy may be a practical alternative for emerging economies.

Part II   Development of Bond Markets in Asia

In the second part of the Round Table, a range of topics examining the broad question of the development of bond markets in Asia was analysed. It was divided into five sessions. An introduction was provided in the first session. In the next session, the experience in Asia, and the policy issues that need to be addressed, were discussed. In the third session, some lessons from the experience of the OECD countries and other emerging economies were described. In the fourth session, the roles of securities laws and securities market regulators in the sound development of bond markets were analysed. In the final session, some views from private sector participants on the development of bond markets in the region were presented.

Session 1   Introduction

Overview

Professor Eisuke Sakakibara, Keio University, Former Vice Minister for International Affairs, Ministry of Finance, Japan, presented a brief overview of the topic of the creation of an Asian bond market. He confirmed the widespread view that one of the major causes of the Asian Crisis was a currency and a maturity mismatch. He quoted a statement by Donald Tsang, Financial Secretary of Hong Kong, China, made in 1990: "What Asia lacks, and Europe and the US have, is a deep, liquid and mature debt market where three things can occur. First, governments and corporations can borrow long to invest long, thus eliminating the maturity mismatch inherent in Asia. Second, corporations can issue paper in US dollars, yen or euro, with clearing and settlement in Asian times, thus eliminating currency mismatches and developing a truly deep Asian debt market along the lines of euro-dollar and euro-yen markets. Third, finance ministers in Asian economies can foster a vibrant debt market with adequate risk management by investing their reserves in Asia." Professor Sakakibara noted that even when the Asian crisis was coming to an end, the world bond market was dominated by Europe and the US, and particularly by Euro-currency issues.

He then addressed the issue of what accounts for this dominance. He noted there are a large number of issuers in Asia, but they have not used the markets in Asia. In all the major Asian markets, the authorities have welcomed and encouraged bond issuance by non-residents, and there are no legal restraints on bond issuance. However, there seem to be significant infrastructure problems in these markets. The clearing and settlement systems have been inadequate, requiring much longer transaction times, when compared to London for example. Repo markets have not developed sufficiently. Although there are no direct regulations hampering transactions, such practices as withholding taxes, and the existence of multiple regulatory agencies have discouraged issuers. Also in some countries the number of investors, and particularly institutional investors, has been limited, as has the number of market makers.

Professor Sakakibara confirmed that Asian countries have traditionally relied on indirect financing – bank lending – as a major intermediation mechanism between savings and investment. This system worked well during the 1970s and 1980s when globalisation and market-oriented transactions were relatively limited. Thus the development of debt markets, typically a substitute for bank lending, lagged behind the Western countries significantly. The dramatic globalisation of the world economy by the IT revolution changed all this. Without the existence of effective debt markets in the region, Asian countries were forced to rely on financial intermediation through Euro and New York markets by global market players. This lead to the currency and maturity mismatch.

Authorities in the region have now come to recognise the need to nurture the regional markets and to build necessary infrastructure. There are some who argue the markets should evolve spontaneously, without official intervention, as occurred in the Euro-markets. However, Professor Sakakibara maintained that the necessary infrastructure existed in Europe for the markets to develop. A vicious cycle also stopped further development. Since markets are not developed, the accompanying infrastructure has not emerged, and liquidity as a result is low. But low liquidity means that markets are not developing. He therefore argued that it is appropriate that the regional authorities make a conscious and coordinated effort to nurture markets. In addition to creating an efficient and common settlement mechanism, and other necessary infrastructure, and eliminating tax disincentives, authorities could encourage market participants to start new market practices conducive to increasing transactions in the region.

Professor Sakakibara noted the interesting suggestion for financial institutions to create an Asian-currency based Asian Bond Index to generate greater international and Asian investor interest and demand for Asian bonds. Up to now, bond indices by leading financial institutions have not included any Asian bonds except for JGBs and investors have not had any reliable guidelines for investing in Asian debt instruments. The creation of an Asian Bond Index by a group of prominent Asian or non-Asian financial institutions could be a catalyst to start the process. More extensive use of international credit ratings by Asian issuers would also facilitate investors to assess the risks associated with Asian issuers.

During the initial stage of development, the utilisation of public credit enhancement may be effective in increasing demand for issuers of low ratings. The New Miyazawa Plan provided credit enhancement of sovereign or semi-sovereign issues by Asian countries and such a facility could be expanded to create a permanent regional mechanism to enhance credit and to secure and provide information necessary to create transparent and resilient markets in the region.

Bonds with an artificially created currency basket, including US, Euro, Yen and other Asian currencies could also be listed on plural markets. If authorities come up with a basket consisting of only Asian currencies, it may eventually lead to foreign exchange cooperation among these countries, and finally to the creation of an Asian currency unit. This could be an interesting experiment. However, the current investor demand would be greater for a basket involving US dollars, euro and yen, since such a basket would effectively shield investors from currency risks resulting from the volatile movements amongst these three countries that have been experienced over the past few years.

Developing a Viable Corporate Bond Market under a Bank-dominated System

Professor Shinji Takagi, Visiting Scholar at the ADBI, examined the topic of developing a viable corporate bond market under a bank-dominated system, focusing on analytical issues and policy implications. First, he identified the two key roles of a financial system: to channel savings to productive uses and to provide good corporate governance. Financing and corporate governance are not independent. Asymmetric and imperfect information give rise to adverse selection and to moral hazard, and the presence of these two factors means that the market mechanism does not necessarily lead to an optimal allocation of resources. In the presence of imperfect information, finance matters – there is a positive relationship between financial development and growth. Institutions develop as a way of mitigating informational problems, and there is a role for government policy. The effectiveness of a financial system is therefore largely determined by its ability to overcome the problems of adverse selection and moral hazard.

The nature of corporate finance was analysed by Professor Takagi. He noted that an "agency problem" arises due to the separation of management and control, because investors do not see all the actions of management, and management has information that investors do not possess. Such an agency problem means that the cost of external finance exceeds the cost of internal finance, and that firms generally prefer internal finance to external finance. When external funds must be raised, a credible mechanism of corporate control is needed to reduce the premium over the cost of internal finance.

Professor Takagi summarised the nature of equity and debt. Equity gives a voice to the investor in the direct control of the firm. Debt economises on resources that must be expended for monitoring, while exerting discipline on management. It also increases the risk of bankruptcy. Debt holders' cash flows are fixed to allow efficient investment decision-making by controlling investors. The moral hazard associated with equity finance is minimised by providing ultimate transfer of control in the case of a default. The choice between equity and debt is determined by the marginal cost of diluting control rights relative to the greater risk of default.

There are two major types of debt finance: public debt (directly placed debt and bonds) and intermediated debt (bank loans). Debt economises on resources for monitoring, as such monitoring is required only when the firm fails to make the stated fixed payments. The possibility of liquidation exerts discipline on management. Financial intermediaries exist because of imperfect information, incomplete markets, and non-zero transaction costs. They are useful because they can use their reputation to achieve superior outcomes, they economise by eliminating duplication of information gathering and monitoring, they lower borrowing costs by protecting information, and they allow staged financing and inter-temporal subsidies.

Bank finance and bond finance co-exist because they address different types of informational problems with different degrees of effectiveness, and they have different costs and benefits.

31

Intermediated debt is better suited for mitigating the problems of asymmetric information, while public debt has a superior allocative function by being better able to provide price signals for investment decisions. There is, however, a trade-off between the benefits of bank monitoring and the benefits of financial market information aggregation. The trade-off depends on the monitoring-induced reduction in the costs of funds (relative to the value of rent extraction by banks), the reputation acquisition by firms; financial distress and the possibility of inefficient liquidation, and various institutional and legal requirements.

Professor Takagi concluded by drawing a series of policy implications from his analysis. He argued that bank finance has an advantage of minimising the problems of adverse selection and moral hazard because of its monitoring function. Public debt is better at leading to better resource allocation because of the price signals it provides. For a firm, the choice of which to use thus depends on the magnitude of the information problems it faces, and the informativeness of securities prices. The benefits of bank financing increase with the severity of informational problems and the efficacy of monitoring by banks. The benefits of bond financing increase with the development of financial and legal infrastructures that reduce the cost of information acquisition, raise the informativeness of securities prices, and ensure that covenants are enforced. Bank finance dominates bond finance in countries where accounting and legal systems are not well developed and there are severe informational problems. With financial market development and the maturing of some of the larger firms with long credit histories, more and more firms will migrate to the bond market, if one is available.

Professor Takagi also argued that competition in the banking industry is a double-edged sword. Without enough competition, banks will become too powerful, creating disincentives for management. Without the ability to appropriate surplus from successful projects, banks will not have sufficient incentive to expend the necessary resources on monitoring and information gathering. A corporate bond market allows the firm to escape from a powerful bank that extracts too much rent and provides price signals for investment. Globalisation makes bond market development all the more important because it allows larger firms to bypass inefficient domestic systems, possibly resulting in a large unhedged position in foreign currencies. However the development of a corporate bond market should not undermine the viability of the banking system, which remains the only source of external finance for smaller and younger firms, and for firms with no established reputation. Family, rural and other informal financial systems as well as corporate groups should not be eradicated before they are replaced by an alternative financing mechanism.

Session 2   Experience in Asia and Policy Issues to be Addressed

Thailand

Mr. Noritaka Akamatsu, Principal Financial Economist, Financial Sector Development Department, World Bank, described the strategy for developing a domestic bond market that Thailand had employed. He noted first of all that following the Asian crisis, the country needed to raise a very large amount of money – nearly 10% of the GDP or the assets owned by the banking sector in one year. While this was an enormous challenge, it was also seen as an opportunity to develop the domestic bond market. In order to do this, and recognising that a market was a place of interaction, and therefore that no single party could by itself determine its development process, the Ministry of Finance created the Domestic Bond Market Committee, a forum where all the major interested parties were invited to participate. These included the Bank of Thailand, the Securities and Exchange Commission, the Thai Bond Dealing Center the Thai Securities Depository, and major market intermediaries.

Noting that the Bond Market Committee established nine Task Forces, Akamatsu identified what he believed to be the seven key objectives of these Task Forces as follows: 1) To enhance the treasury/debt management capacity; 2) To enhance the primary market distribution system and secondary market mechanism; 3) To enhance bond settlement systems; 4) To enhance market information systems; 5) To reduce or eliminate impediments to investing in, and trading of, bonds (including tax impediments, regulations on institutional investors); 6) to standardize trading practices (for example yield calculations, and repo master agreements); and, finally, 7) to introduce interest rate futures. The way in which each of these goals were implemented were then summarised.

The key lesson Mr. Akamatsu drew from the Thai experience was that there is normally a need for a coordinated approach in the development of a domestic bond market. This is because there are many goals that need to be realised for the development of such a market, because the implementation and solutions of these goals are closely interdependent, and because it is normally not possible to do everything at once, and therefore strategic sequencing is typically necessary. Sound coordination is required to manage all these various processes.

Singapore

Ms. Yeo Lian Sim, Assistant Managing Director, Capital Markets, Monetary Authority of Singapore, discussed the experience of Singapore in the development of bond markets in Asia. She identified the goals of well-developed Asian bond markets as being to provide a better match for long-term financing, to provide Asian issuers with cheaper costs of funding, to mobilise savings in Asia to invest in Asia, to widen the range of credits and yields, making debt markets an attractive alternative investment choice, and to present a stronger value proposition to attract and retain issuers, investors, and intermediaries in Asia.

In order to foster a vibrant government securities market, Singapore is stepping up the issuance of government securities, extending the yield curve, improving information flow, increasing the number of primary dealers, and developing a repo market. The outstanding amount of government securities increased from Singapore $22.2 billion in 1996 to Singapore $36.1 billion in 1999. The objectives in the arena of corporate issuers are to develop a diversified issuer base with a range of different credits and industries, and a broad range of debt structures. The initiatives being taken to achieve these goals are allowing foreign entities to issue Singapore dollar bonds, encouraging statutory boards, local corporates, and MNCs to issues bonds, and developing the market for asset securitisation.

Another key objective is to promote a diversified investor base, encouraging the participation of foreign as well as domestic participants, and active as well as inactive investors. Most of the existing players are largely institutional investors, but there is an untapped pool of retail investors. The initiatives that are being taken to promote this goal are the development of the asset management industry, the liberalisation of the investments made by the Central Provident Fund, and the creation of tax incentives for bond fund managers and bond investments. Two key elements of the infrastructure need to be implemented: efficient clearing and settlement procedures in order to reduce settlement risk and transaction costs, and linkages to regional and international clearing systems for better foreign investor access.

Moving forward Ms. Yeo argued that the development of national bond markets, collectively, will lead to a wider range of credits and currency denominations. This will attract global investors to hold a long-term portfolio of Asian paper, which will in turn integrate Asian bond markets in the world's bond markets. The key issues that lie ahead are the education of investors, market transparency, corporate governance, harmonisation of conventions, and the electronic and internet revolution.

Singapore – Offshore market

Mr. Toshio Karigane, Senior Executive Advisor, Daiwa Institute of Research, Japan, examined the Singaporean experience in bond market development, focusing on the development of the offshore market. Mr. Karigane examined the reasons for developing bond markets in Asia. He argued the most important one is the urgent need to mobilise large amounts of long-term financing for infrastructure to sustain the present rates of economic growth. Such investments are required in power, transportation and telecommunications, and overall investment must be increased to a percentage of GDP much greater than that in the past. A second critical reason for domestic bond market development in Asia is the changing industrial structure of Asian countries which are shifting from labour-intensive to capital-intensive industries. Investments in these industries normally require a longer-term span to develop, in turn requiring longer-term financing than conventional debt instruments.

The development of domestic bond markets will also help to reduce the currency risk presently faced by companies when they borrow funds internationally in the currencies of the developed countries. Previously, Asian savings tended to be placed with intermediaries outside the region who then invested part of these funds in Asia as bank loans with relatively short maturities. The creation and development of Asian domestic bond markets both negates the need for funds to flow out of the region, and also helps avoid the problems of both currency and maturity mismatches. A further reason for governments to facilitate bond market development is that domestic bond markets can create macroeconomic stability by reducing dependence on volatile international capital flows. They also provide an additional instrument for monetary policy through open-market operations.

Mr. Karigane noted that it will take many years for domestic bond markets to develop. He argued that one of the most effective ways to develop a domestic bond market is to establish an offshore bond market. The development of market infrastructure is a clear advantage. This includes market makers, a clearing system, ratings agencies, and settlement procedures, which are all necessary for both domestic and offshore markets. Other areas where development of an offshore market has positive benefits for a domestic market include the growth of human resources, the improvement of information systems, and the enhancement of the foreign exchange and money markets. Mr. Karigane argued that the establishment of an offshore market does not create a conflict of interest among Asian countries, but is instead complementary. If the goal is to expand the volume and variety of long-term financing available for economic growth in Asia, experience suggests that the best way to mobilise large amounts of funds is through the concurrent maturation of offshore and domestic bond markets.

Mr. Karigane then examined the creation of the offshore bond market in Singapore. It started in 1968 when Singapore allowed non-residents to maintain tax-free foreign currency deposits. Subsequently, after short-term money markets were established, the need arose for long-term funds, primarily from overseas sources. The Asian offshore bond market was differentiated from the dominant Euro market by the physical location in Asia of syndicate members, lawyers and often investors, and by the secondary market and quotation on Asian stock exchanges. Singapore executed the first Asian-dollar bond issue in 1971 when the Development Bank of Singapore issued a ten-million US dollar-denominated bond. Other large Asian borrowers followed throughout the 1970s, followed in the 1980s by the major international organisations, some European and American banks, and several sovereign borrowers. Mr. Karigane noted that the Singapore-dollar denominated domestic bond market has recently developed significantly, and argued that one of the contributing factors to this is Singapore's mature offshore bond market.

Mr. Karigane concluded by stressing the benefits of the New Miyazawa Initiative in this context. He noted that it means that new funds have become available, and that such funds can be used to develop Asian financial markets, and specifically to offer long-term funding through the use of an offshore market. Mr. Karigane argued that not only Singapore and Hong Kong, China, but also the Philippines,

Malaysia and Thailand, countries which have already established short-term offshore bond markets, can make use of the Miyazawa Plan to develop their markets, and particularly offshore yen bond markets in Asia. Mr. Karigane maintained that there is a time for competition and a time for cooperation. He then proposed that the time has come for cooperation in creating healthy Asian bond markets. Individual government money is not enough; it must be supplemented with private funds and efforts, and with intra-regional support.

China

Dr. Gao Jian, CFO and Chief Economist, China Development Bank, examined the development of the government debt market in China. He noted first that economic activity in the People's Republic of China (PRC) is mainly fuelled by indirect financing from banks, which have the country's vast national savings at their disposal. The capital market only commenced in the late 1980s, but has developed remarkably since then. Debt securities issuance has increased substantially, market trading techniques have advanced, and marketable book-entry form securities now account for the majority of securities issued in China. Contemporary tools, such as the tender system for selling, a primary dealer system for securities distribution and market making, and book-entry form for securities have been put in place. The investor base has also been broadened.

Dr. Gao stressed, however, that the underlying market infrastructure still remains fragile. The bond market is currently small, as is its share of the financial market. The bond market includes government, corporate and agency bonds, and financial debentures. Local government bonds and municipal government bonds do not exist. In addition market instruments are still limited, the exchange market is shrinking, the inter-bank bond market is illiquid and savings bonds outweigh marketable securities. Nevertheless, market initiatives will generate new development in the future. One of the signs of the government's recent commitment to developing the financial market is in the legal arena. Steps to establish a legal framework for financial activities are accelerating. Following the Securities Act promulgated in January 1999, the Investment Fund Act is being drafted, and regulations surrounding financial violations are being enacted.

In 1999, the People's Bank of China (PBOC) relied more on open market operations to purse its monetary policy, and it will continue to do so in 2000. Further financial innovations will be adopted in 2000. As the housing market develops, asset-backed securities will be introduced and the assets of state-owned enterprises (SOE) will be securitised. China's big four state-owned commercial banks will continue to focus on limiting risk in 2000 but they are also encouraged to increase their investment in business sector. The shifting of bad loans from their balance sheet to Asset Management Companies (AMC) will reduce the bank burden and restore their confidence.

Government bonds are issued though the MOF for financing the deficit and maturing debt. The PBOC is in charge of distributing securities to individual investors, and acts as the fiscal agent for repayment at redemption. The National People's Congress must approve the total issuing volume, and the State Council sets the coupon rates. The China Securities Regulatory Commission (CSRC) and the PBOC regulates securities firms and other bond market dealers. The MOF and the CSRC regulate government security primary dealer. The Government Security Dealers Associations also exists; it is a self-regulatory body.

The majority of government securities are sold though public offerings. Only special state bonds are sold though private placement to pension funds and insurance funds run by government agencies. In principle, discount securities are priced though uniform prices Dutch auctions, while coupon-bearing securities are priced though multiple-price American auctions. Bidders are mainly primary dealers;

although some non-primary dealer financial institutions participate in bidding process upon MOF's approval. There were 50 primary dealers as of the end of 1999.

Government securities include marketable and non-marketable securities. The marketable securities comprises book-entry form and bearer form securities. Non-marketable securities are savings bonds. Savings bonds and bearer securities have three- and five-year maturities, and target individuals. Bearer securities are also available to other kind of investors, such as SOEs. Book-entry securities have seven- and ten-year maturities, and are only for institutional investors. Maturities for government securities range from three to six months, and one, two, three, five, seven and 10 years.

The main marketplaces are the Shanghai Securities Exchange, and the Shen Zhen Securities Exchange where off-the-run securities are traded. Secondary market trading also takes place in the so-called inter-bank bond market. The two marketplaces are currently separated. The stock exchange market is liquid, whereas the inter-bank bond market is not. In the inter-bank bond market securities are traded at the Shanghai Foreign Exchange Trading Center and settled though the Government Security Depository Trust Company. Daily turnover in 1998 and 1999 was around RMB 10-20 billion, down sharply from RMB300bn in 1996.

Historically, bonds were mainly sold to individual investors. As the market developed, SOEs, banks, pension, insurance and investment funds were permitted to join in and actively subscribed to government securities and corporate bonds. In 1996, institutional investors, financial institutions and SOEs subscribed to 80% of securities. Prior to 1998, banks were discouraged from holding securities. However, as they obtained more liquidity, they were advised to buy securities.

Government agencies and corporations issue bonds, although the market is small vis-à-vis the government bonds market. A credit market has yet to be formulated since there are no internationally recognised rating agencies in the country. Corporate bonds are not priced against a government securities benchmark, as in many other countries. Policy banks, such as the State Development Bank, EXIM Bank and the Agriculture Development Bank issue financial debentures. Financial debentures are the PBOC's most important instrument for open market operations. In 1999, the PBOC bought about RMB100bn government securities and financial debentures from banks to increase money supply.

As in 1998, about one third of government securities were savings bonds that were sold to individuals. Book-entry form securities were placed in the inter-bank bonds market. There were only two issues launched on the Shanghai Securities Exchange. As the State Council set the coupon rates, one issue was welcomed whereas another was not. The CDB was the second largest issuer in the domestic bonds market. The total issuing amount was RMB130 bn. Although CDB's placement was limited to the inter-bank bond market, it achieved the objective of issuing its majority of financial debentures through the market.

Dr. Gao concluded by discussing the outlook for 2000. He maintained that the debt market will be active as the government will continue its fiscal stimulus program and start its West Development Program. The government will streamline the management of the bond market as well. The regulatory authority will shift from PBOC to the State Planning and Development Commission (SPDC) in order to overcome overlapping authority. As in 1999, the majority of book-entry form securities will be sold to the banks in the inter-bank bond market, as banks have tremendous liquidity and they feel it is safer to buy treasury securities than making loans to enterprises. In order to ensure the smooth selling of its securities, the Ministry of Finance has signed an underwriting syndication agreement with a group of banks and non-bank financial institutions. The Ministry of Finance and CDB will also announce a fixed timetable for selling securities.

Hong Kong, China (1) (Hong Kong Monetary Authority)

Mr. Norman Tak-lam Chan, Deputy Chief Executive, Hong Kong Monetary Authority, examined the topic of the development of bond markets in Asia, focusing on the Hong Kong, China perspective. He asked the question why domestic bond markets are still developing at a rather disappointingly slow pace, notwithstanding the widespread agreement about the benefits that can be gained from them, especially after the Asian financial crisis. He then described the conscious efforts that have been taken in Hong Kong, China to develop its bond market since 1990.

The creation of a benchmark yield curve has been seen as an important goal in Hong Kong, China. The Hong Kong Monetary Authority (HKMA) therefore developed, over a period of seven years, a yield curve for Hong Kong dollar debt by issuing Exchange Fund Bills and Notes with maturities ranging from 3 months to 10 years. The major policy challenge stemmed from the fact that Hong Kong, like many other Asian countries, has not been in the habit of running fiscal deficits, and therefore had no fiscal need to borrow from the market. In the absence of a fiscal borrowing requirement, the policy maker must take a view on whether the issuance of government paper for the purpose of developing a reliable benchmark yield curve can be justified in the interest of promoting market development.

A key question is how the government can derive enough income from the investment of the proceeds of issuance to offset the interest costs of the issuance. Given the lack of suitable fixed income securities in domestic currency, many governments have been deterred from issuing long maturity paper, thereby hindering the development of a benchmark yield curve. In Hong Kong, China, Hong Kong dollar interest rate swaps were used to hedge the fixed rate liabilities of the longer term Exchange Fund Notes. Clearly, this hedging technique is only viable, however, when there is a suitably deep and liquid interest rate swap market in existence.

Another vital policy goal is the development of an efficient, reliable and low cost clearing and settlement system. In Hong Kong, the HKMA developed the Central Moneymarkets Unit in 1990, which cleared initially the Exchange Fund Bills and Notes and later, to meet market demand, private sector bonds as well. The system was subsequently enhanced to link up with the Hong Kong dollar interbank payments system so as to provide DVP capability on a real-time basis.

Mr. Chan noted that it is very easy to think that the biggest challenge is the technology required to develop the clearing and settlement systems. However, he maintained that another equally important policy challenge relates to how the authorities perceive their roles vis-à-vis the private sector in the development of such systems. It can be argued that private sector bonds should be cleared by a clearing system developed by the private sector. In Hong Kong, the HKMA regards clearing and settlement systems as an important piece of infrastructure for the financial market, in which the HKMA has the responsibility to ensure its safe and efficient functioning. To leave it entirely to initiatives from the private sector would run the risk of slowing down market development.

Other measures that Hong Kong, China has taken to promote bond market development include offering exemption from profits tax on income derived from Hong Kong dollar bonds issued by multilateral development banks, and other tax measures. The policy challenge of these measures is clearly how one would be willing to grant tax incentives to the bond market without creating an uneven playing field for the other sectors.

Mr. Chan noted several challenges and opportunities for the future, some of which are easier to tackle than others. On the demand side, he stressed that the institutional base for bonds has been fairly narrow. He argued that the situation in Hong Kong, China will improve with the implementation of the Mandatory Provident Fund Scheme in 12/2000, which requires both employers and employees to contribute to the retirement funds at a minimum rate. Such contributions are expected to be an important source of institutional demand for debt securities in the future. Another positive factor is that bonds are yielding a real rate of return as a result of falling inflation. On the supply side, given that international credit has generally shrunk after the Asian financial crisis, there is a practical need for the corporates to diversify their sources of funds. They have thus turned to the bond markets. Moreover, many governments in the region are having real fiscal needs to borrow substantial amounts from the market to finance banking and financial restructuring.

Mr. Chan concluded by identifying two problems, one on the demand side, and one on the supply side, that are quite difficult to resolve. The first problem arises from the generally low credit ratings of sovereigns and corporates in Asia, apart from in Japan and in Singapore. A low credit rating is a negative factor in bond market development. Mr. Chan noted that there is not much that individual economies can do on their own to better their low credit ratings. The establishment of a national rating agency may solve only part of this problem, as it is not easy to build up credibility and confidence overseas. While acknowledging that low credit ratings are a reality that most Asian issuers will have to live with for some time, it seems sensible to consider the idea of setting up a regional credit enhancement and guarantee agency to address investor concern on credit exposure. While the feasibility and viability of this credit guarantee agency idea will require further study, Mr. Chan argued that no matter what form of ownership structure the agency takes, it should be run on prudent commercial principles and be able to price the risks objectively and properly.

The second problem arises from the relatively small size of the Asian corporates. For such small firms, raising funds through bond issues may be more costly than borrowing from banks or listing on the stock markets. This would mean that for many years to come bank lending would remain a major source of funds for the SMEs in the region, as the banks can understand and price the risks of these companies more efficiently than the bond market. Notwithstanding this limitation, there is still enormous room for the Asian corporate bond market to grow with the global trend of financial disintermediation.

Hong Kong, China (2) (Stock Exchange of Hong Kong, China)

Mr. Lawrence Fok, Senior Executive Director, Stock Exchange of Hong Kong, China, examined the issues to be tackled for the development of the bond market in Hong Kong. He first provided some background to the Hong Kong market, noting that two major channels were used for corporate funding: the equity market and the debt market (bank loan/bond issue). He stressed, however, that Hong Kong corporations typically rely on equity market and bank borrowing.

Mr. Fok identified a range of reasons for the slow development of the debt market. There is weak investor demand by retail traders who see a higher return on stock market investments. The banks are also not keen to market debt securities to them, and there is no infrastructure for such investors to access the market. Institutional investors are put off by the small issue sizes, the lack of uniform issues offered at regular intervals, and the existence of only a few benchmark issues. Other obstacles to the development of the debt market include the under-developed settlement and custody system, the continued fiscal surpluses of Hong Kong, China, the lack of enough good quality issuers, insufficient liquidity with associated wide trading spreads, negative real interest rates in the past, credit rating procedures, family ownership/close group control of many Hong Kong corporations, and lastly the ease of raising capital both in the equity market and from the banks.

The major results of these factors have been threefold. The business sector has relied on short-term borrowing, leading to maturity mismatches. The equity market has been overheated. The demand by Asian central banks and financial institutions (including commercial banks, insurance companies, and provident and pension funds) for investing in bonds, has lead them to invest in bonds from outside Asia, and particularly in US Treasuries.

Mr. Fok noted that Hong Kong, China has responded to these issues with a range of policies. It has sought to enhance its financial infrastructure. It established a central clearing and custodian system for debt securities: the Central Moneymarkets Units (CMU), which has formed links with Euroclear, Cedel, and other central securities depositories. It has implemented a Real Time Gross Settlement (RTGS) interbank payment system to reduce settlement and clearing risks, which could also be extended to be a regional system. It is developing a US dollar clearing system for real time settlement of US dollar transactions. This is linked with the Hong Kong dollar payment system to provide real time PVP settlement for US dollar-Hong Kong dollar transactions, and also with the stock and debt securities clearing houses to provide DVP settlement.

A range of government initiatives have also been undertaken. These include: the introduction of the Exchange Fund Bills and Notes Program (EFN) (a market-making system); the creation of a yield curve; granting of permission to use Exchange Fund paper as collateral for trading in futures, index options and stock options; the listing of EFNs on the exchange; building a platform for retail investors to access the debt market; the elimination of stamp duty, the reduction of profits taxes, and the lowering of brokerage charges; the establishment of the Hong Kong Mortgage Corporation, which will purchase mortgage loans with the issuance of unsecured debt securities, and securitise the mortgages into mortgage backed securities; and finally, the implementation of the Mandatory Provident Fund Scheme later this year to stimulate the demand for high quality debt securities.

Mr. Fok drew a range of conclusions from his analysis. You cannot force people to invest in bonds; rather you can encourage retail participation by removing relevant impediments. Listing of major debt issues on an exchange increases awareness about them. And finally, greater demand for investing in bonds may be expected following the implementation of the Mandatory Provident Fund program.

Malaysia

Mr. Ranjit Ajit Singh, General Manager, Economic Analysis and Financial Policy, Securities Commission, Malaysia, described developments in the Malaysian bond market. He focused first on the relationship between the bond markets and the Malaysian economy. Noting that the economy has experienced rapid economic growth for much of the last decade, he stressed that financing has largely been channelled through the banking system. The bond markets have, however, also seen tremendous growth in recent years, driven by several broad factors. There has been a strategic national development agenda since the mid-1980s, in which it has been the policy for the private sector to assume a greater role in economic growth, and to shoulder a greater burden of finance. There has also been privatisation of state corporations in the early 1990s, a large amount of infrastructure development, and much financial liberalisation and development, including the freeing of interest rates, the convertibility of the current account, and the development of the capital markets.

There has also been a specific policy to develop the bond markets for various reasons: to provide an additional avenue for channelling Malaysia's large and rising level of savings, to widen sources of funds thus providing cheaper alternatives, and reducing dependence on the banking sectors; to add breadth to the capital markets; and to remove the maturity mismatch in financing.

A range of development efforts have been undertaken so far. The regulatory framework has been improved in several ways. The Malaysian Central Bank issued a set of guidelines on the issuance and trading of corporate bonds. Discount houses were permitted to underwrite and invest in bonds. The rules governing investment in bonds by banking institutions were relaxed. Unit trusts were allowed to invest in bonds with a minimum BBB rating. The Companies Act was amended to widen the institutional investor base. The government also announced that the Securities Commission will be the sole authority responsible for the regulation of the corporate bond market.

Market microstructure has been enhanced. The Malaysian National Mortgage Corporation was established in 1996. The Rating Agency Malaysia was established in 1990, and a second rating agency, Malaysian Rating Corporation, was set up in 1995. The functionality of SPEEDS (the scripless trading system) was extended to include bonds in 1996. Some Khazanah bonds were issued as benchmarks in 1997. The Bond Information and Dissemination System (BIDS) was created in 1997. SPEEDS was replaced with a real-time gross settlement system in 1999.

Various fiscal incentives have been created, including a waiver of stamp duty for bond issuance and transfer, and exemption of tax on interest earned by individuals on corporate bonds listed on the Kuala Lumpur Stock Exchange. Credit-risk issues are also being addressed by requiring a compulsory rating of bond issues, by establishing investment grade restrictions, and by insisting that ratings for bank-guaranteed issues reflect the rating of the individual guarantor bank.

Despite these efforts, Mr. Singh noted that the corporate bond market still had some way to go for further development. The East Asian crisis also focused attention on the effects of the under-development of bond markets. It meant that companies placed over-reliance on the banking sector, thus exposing them to the risk of credit withdrawal cycles. It gave rise to problems due to maturity mismatches – the lack of long-term financing instruments, and the exposure to roll-over risk. It also meant there was a limited opportunity to diversify portfolio risk, and thus arguably aggravated capital flight.

In order to resolve these problems, a National Bond Market Committee (NBMC) was established to expedite development and growth of the bond market, particularly in light of the crisis. It is composed of representatives from all the key authorities interested in the development of the market, and focuses on regulatory reform, market microstructure, and product and institutional development. The NBMC identified five strategic thrusts that are vital for moving forward.

The first is to lower issuance costs in order to promote the capital market as a cost-effective and competitive source of financing. In order to achieve this, the regulatory approval process will be shortened, asset securitisation will be introduced, a financial guarantee insurer will be set up, issuance guidelines will be deregulated, standardised documentation will be promoted, and tax disincentives will be removed. The second strategic thrust is to encourage a greater breadth of investors, which will allow for different risk appetites and thus encourage more issuers. Institutional investment restrictions need to be removed, bond funds should be promoted, fiscal disincentives need to be eliminated, and regulation should be reformed to improve bond investor protection.

The third strategic thrust is to develop a robust and efficient market microstructure that promotes market integrity and price efficiency, and reduces systemic risk. It is necessary to rationalise and deregulate the clearance and settlement system to allow for OTC trading of listed and unlisted bonds by a wider range of market intermediaries. The fourth strategic thrust is to establish a liquid market for benchmark securities, which is seen as necessary for the efficient pricing of corporate bonds and other instruments. This requires the development of both the primary and the secondary market for benchmark securities. The final strategic thrust is to adopt market-based macroeconomic policies, and this is seen as a necessary prerequisite for a successful corporate bond market. This will require the deregulation of interest rates, reviewing the use of monetary tools, and stopping interventions in the credit market.

Mr. Singh concluded by summarising the key goals the NBMC has announced: the issuance of Malaysian Government Securities (MGS) on a more regular and transparent basis (the schedule for auctions for 2000 has been released); the need to increase secondary market liquidity (restriction on corporate repurchase agreements will be relaxed); the relaxation of the investment rating requirements of new issuers to BB; the introduction of shelf-registration later this year; the formulation of guidelines on asset-backed securities; the relaxation of investment requirements currently set for the Employee Provident Fund to invest in MGS; and lastly, the amendments to the framework for the corporate bond market, with the SC becoming the sole regulator in the second half of 2000.

ADB

Dr. Yun-Hwan Kim, Senior Economist, Asian Development Bank, examined the policy agenda for bond market development in Asia. He summarised, first, the importance of bond market financing. It can address over-reliance on short-term bank borrowing for long-term resources, diversify the sources of industrial and infrastructure financing, alleviate currency mismatches, and reduce financial inflexibility and vulnerability to external shocks. Bond financing will be vital for the huge infrastructure investment in the post-crisis period, and is a way of transforming short-term savings into long-term resources.

Various trends in industrial financing were noted in the crisis economies. The domestic financial systems in four Asian countries (Indonesia, Korea, Malaysia and Thailand) share several characteristics. They each have a large banking sector with a much smaller capital market. In general most have not increased corporate bond financing, although Korea is an exception to this. International bank financing to the four countries peaked in 12/1996 at US$248 billion, and drooped to US$161 billion by 6/1999. However, lending to total developing countries increased over this period – so international investors are rebalancing their portfolios away from Asia. International bond financing by the crisis countries increased sharply. There is a degree of substitutability between bank borrowing and bond issues – however the main bond issuers are government or quasi-government organisations. The increase in bond issues did not replace the reduction in international bank lending, except in Korea.

Dr. Kim then identified the major obstacles to the development of corporate bond markets. One has been that it has been cheaper to finance companies through overseas bank borrowing. In particular, financial liberalisation, significant interest rate differentials and overvalued currencies encouraged unhedged foreign borrowing in yen and US dollar. A second obstacle to the development of corporate bond markets has been that many emerging economies have bank-centred domestic financial systems. A third problem arises from agency problems associated with family-owned corporations. Bank-intermediated finance may be preferred in order to alleviate information asymmetries.

Four obstacles were also identified to the issuance of corporate bonds. The first is the general lack of a benchmark yield curve. The second is the narrow investor base for bonds due to restricted contractual savings systems, undeveloped mutual funds and a focus on bank deposits, over-regulation of the asset-management industry, a limited role for insurance companies, and a lack of awareness among investors of the opportunities and advantages of diversification.

Dr. Kim noted four policy efforts that need to be undertaken to address these issues. The first concerned the importance of developing a treasury bond market. A well-functioning government bond market plays a stepping stone role in fostering corporate bond markets. Its risk-free yield curve facilitates private issuance. Amongst the lessons that can be learned for developing a treasury bond market are the need for a clear and balanced long-term debt strategy and a sound operational strategy, the opening up of the market to foreign investors, a clear division of responsibility between government debt and monetary policy, regular dialogue with markets on debt management objectives and operational strategies, simplicity in the types of government bonds, a benchmark yield curve of at least 10 years maturity, the undesirability of captive investors, a steady supply of new securities to sustain liquidity, an appropriate legal and regulatory framework, and lastly attractive government paper.

The second policy effort needed was on the supply side. It is necessary to provide an enabling environment conducive to financial liberalisation while maintaining international regulatory standards to ensure investor confidence. The reform of corporate governance is also critical. The third group of policy actions relate to the demand side. The role of institutional investors and mutual funds must be strengthened, and private placements should be allowed. Lastly a range of infrastructure improvements must be made. Reliable international credit-ratings must be used, if reputable local agencies are unavailable. Discussions with the data vendors should be held to facilitate the creation of a benchmark yield curve. Regulation should not impose a high cost burden. Settlement systems are subject to scale and scope economies.

New Miyazawa Initiative (Ministry of Finance, Japan)

Mr. Toshio Kobayashi, Director, International Finance Division, International Bureau, Ministry of Finance, Japan, discussed the development of international bond markets in the region. He noted, first, several lessons from the Asian currency crisis. Over-dependence on the banking sector for much of the funding needs for corporate growth and expansion was a contributing factor to the crisis. A mechanism for long-term recycling of funds to the private sector in the region is required. It is crucial that bond markets in the region be developed and deepened. A mature and liquid bond market can improve resource allocation by effectively channelling both local and foreign savings into domestic investments. The growth of issuance and trading in the bond markets would also strengthen corporate governance in the region. Also an increase in the issuance of bonds denominated in Asian currencies would lead to a reduction in exchange rate risk for issuers and investors. Mr. Kobayashi maintained that compared with well-developed markets, most Asian bond markets are underdeveloped. The situation of issuance and trading in the international bond markets in the region has also been unsatisfactory.

Mr. Kobayashi saw the second stage of the New Miyazawa Initiative as a resource mobilisation plan for Asia. In order to ensure that Asian economies are not easily influenced by excessive short-term international capital flows, the New Miyazawa Initiative pointed out that the upgrading and fostering of Asian bond markets is an urgent issue as part of the efforts that need to be taken to establish a stable financial system in the region. It was stressed that the Japanese authorities by themselves will implement measures to revitalise the Tokyo market. Japan will also cooperate with other authorities in the region by fostering and upgrading domestic bond markets in the region, by providing technical and personnel assistance, and by revitalising the regional markets for international bonds.

Mr. Kobayashi argued that the merits of creating regional bond markets are threefold. It would facilitate the mobilisation of a wider range of funds in the region. It would be more convenient for bond issuers and investors in the region. It is a prerequisite for the development of Asian financial business in the 21st century. Three issues need to be addressed in order to develop such markets. Regulatory requirements and market infrastructure need to be reviewed in order to reduce costs and enhance market liquidity. Clearing and settlement systems for cross-border transactions need to be upgraded. Finally, issuers should be encouraged to be rated by credible rating agencies.

Session 3   Lessons from the Experience in OECD Countries and Other Emerging Countries

Emerging Debt Markets

Mr. Hans Blommestein, Senior Economist, Financial Affairs Division, Directorate for Financial Fiscal and Enterprise Affairs, OECD, talked about eliminating impediments for developing demand in the bond market. He noted first that the development of bond markets in different emerging regions has taken very different courses, and is at different stages of development. He compared the relative size of the local bond market with local GDP in different Asian countries, noting that in Malaysia for the first half of the 1990s this figure was in the region of 50-60% whereas in Indonesia for the same period the figure was less than 10%. Another illustration of this was that different regions exhibited different degrees of market liquidity, using bid-ask spreads as a measure for liquidity.

Mr. Blommestein then argued that a common characteristic of most emerging debt markets is a lack of institutional demand. A range of trends and policies could help develop this including deregulation and modernisation of the financial sector, liberalisation of the institutional sector, demography and pension reform, and financial integration. Major obstacles in developing an institutional sector in emerging economies include the lack of a legal base for institutional investor activities, and legislation on a range of activities of investment management, such as their investment objectives and risk profiles, the definition of prudential and fiduciary standards, regulation of self-dealing, fair valuation procedures, and the protection of the integrity of funds' assets.

The obstacles in developing a domestic institutional sector were then discussed. In the mutual funds arena, these include a lack of competition, and the exclusion of mutual funds from the management of pension fund assets. In the insurance industry, problems include limited product innovation, inadequate disclosure of financial information on the solvency and financial performance of insurance companies, the failure to establish an effective system of consumer and investor protection, and excessive portfolio investment restrictions. In the pensions fund arena, problems include the excessive size of public pay-as-you-go systems; the lack of legal frameworks for private pension funds; the absence of a professional asset management industry; excessive portfolio investment restrictions; too restrictive licensing policies, leading to cartelisation of the pension fund business; a lack of freedom for savers to choose among different portfolios of approved retirement products; and high and/or fixed fees of private pension funds.

Mr. Blommestein concluded by noting that in many markets urgent action is needed to improve the regulatory framework, the legal system and property rights, and the financial market infrastructure. Six general impediments for developing the demand for emerging market fixed income investment instruments were also noted: 1) insufficient market sophistication and a lack or insufficiency of local investors as a long-term stabilising factor; 2) a lack of credit quality or credit choice; 3) a lack of liquidity and marketability, arising from a lack or insufficiency of a well functioning secondary market; 4) a lack of reliable information; 5) a lack of variety in the duration of issues (from short to very long term); and 6) a lack of bundling of issues, co-operation of issuers and of public sector guarantees.

European Bond Markets

Mr. Hans-Dieter Hanfland, Division Chief, Ministry of Finance, Germany, discussed developments in the bond markets in Europe. He outlined first some key facts concerning its history. The Euro was introduced on 1/1/1999. New bond issues are already in Euros, old tradeable debt of sovereign issuers is being redenominated, and non-sovereign debtors have to redenominate at latest by end 2001. The circulation of coins and banknotes in Euro will start from 1 January 2002, the legal tender status of national coins and banknotes will be cancelled within a period of two months. After that date, the exchange of national currencies in Euro will be possible.

Several trends in investor behaviour are identifiable. European investors have traditionally had a strong home bias. Now there is a trend to diversify within Euroland, both geographically, and into other asset classes. National bond market indices are being replaced by European equivalents.

There has been a convergence of yields of EMU government bonds. In the government bond markets, there is competitive pressure on national debt management offices, leading to bigger issue sizes, typically with a minimum of Euro 5bn, and benchmark issues having about Euro 20bn. There is a trend towards pre-announced auction calenders, and the enhancement of secondary market liquidity. There has also been more widespread use of the primary dealership model, with an improvement of market making commitments and international representation amongst the primary dealers. Primary dealership exists in several varieties. Liquidity differences in Euro bond markets still remain, and there is a non-unique government bond yield curve unlike in US. German, French and Italian issues are the main components of the yield curve. Different countries are focusing on creating discrete benchmarks in specific market segments, and employing different strategies to create bonds with a benchmark status.

The amount of corporate bonds in the EU is still modest, but issuance increased markedly in 1999. Investors are looking for higher returns, corporates are looking for cheaper funding. The scale of issues is increasing not least associated with merger and acquisition activities. The trend is being stimulated by banks, whose issues dominate the market. The high yield market, the market for asset-backed and structured products is also growing. The German Pfandbriefe market is the oldest and most developed asset-backed market, with 20-25% held outside Germany, large issue sizes, a large number of market makers, and market making obligations. Other EMU-Countries have also set up similar asset-backed products.

Various trends in hedging and bond-related derivatives are evident. There has been a strong increase of euro-bond futures in 1999, with liquidity centred in German Bund contracts at Eurex. The expansion of swap markets is important for fixed income asset management and hedging. There has also been considerable growth of the repo market, but EMU-Banks are less dependent on repos, as they have direct access to central bank liquidity through Lombard facilities.

The development of electronic trading systems has been rapid. They increase efficiency, improve transparency, and are driven by intermediaries' need to cut margins. They are reducing brokerages fees, and simplifying back-offices and securities department structures. Electronic platforms satisfy a need to improve liquidity through concentration of trading volumes, and are attractive for the global players and primary dealers. Notwithstanding the creation of EURO MTS, a pan-European platform for benchmark bonds, human brokerage remains for large block trades, and the creation of market information and research.

Mr. Hanfland concluded by making the following overall assessment. The Euro bond market is definitely more integrated than it was. Sovereign issuers now concentrate on liquidity. The Euro corporate bond market is growing fast, with issue size typically being increased two- to three-fold. The market for high-yield bonds is also developing. Impediments do, however, remain. Integration is not yet completed and there are some remaining barriers, including fragmentation of settlement systems, a lack of clarity and uniformity in bankruptcy laws, and national differences in withholding tax and accounting conventions. There is an EU action plan to promote further integration.

Japanese Government Securities Market (1)

Mr. Masaaki Shirakawa, Advisor to the Governor, Financial Markets Department, Bank of Japan, talked about the reforms in the Japanese Government Securities (JGS) market. He presented an outline of the JGS market showing evidence of increasing outstanding volume, a series of market reforms, and improved market efficiency. He noted, however, that the market still exhibited low market liquidity, with large public sector holdings, and small non-resident holdings. There was therefore a need for market reforms to enhance market liquidity. This would allow a large amount of new issuance to be absorbed, it would enhance the creation of a benchmark yield curve, it would give a resiliency to the system to withstand external shocks, and it would provide fiscal discipline for the government.

Five guiding principles were proposed as a basic strategy to create deep and liquid government securities market. It is necessary to develop a competitive market structure, to create a low level of market fragmentation, to minimise transaction costs, to establish a sound, robust and safe market infrastructure, and to encourage the development of a heterogeneous group of market participants. Five policy recommendations were put forward to implement these principles. It is desirable to establish an appropriate maturity distribution and issue frequency, to minimise the liquidity-impairing effect of taxes, to enhance transparency relating to issuers, the issue schedule and market information, to improve the safety and standardisation of trading and settlement practices, and lastly to develop related markets.

Mr. Shirakawa identified five key issues to enhance the liquidity of the JGS market. Transparency must be improved – relating to the fiscal condition of the government, the debt management policy, and also market information. It is necessary to offer large benchmark issues at key maturities, with regular reopenings, and appropriately distributed original maturities. The effects of adverse taxation must be limited, including the effects of withholding taxes on market liquidity, and of tax-exemption for non-residents. Related markets must be improved, including the futures and repo markets. Finally, straight through processing must be achieved as this is step towards T+1 settlement. Mr. Shirakawa concluded by discussed how the market reforms should be implemented. He saw the role of the authorities as being that of "catalyst", allowing market-makers to implement the market-driven reforms.

Japanese Government Securities Market (2)

Professor Ghon Rhee, University of Hawaii, discussed the topic of regionalisation of fixed-income securities markets, and asked the question "Is the Tokyo Market Ready?". He noted, first, that both Samurai (yen) and Shogun (foreign currency) issuance of bonds in Japan for the past five years has been small. He confirmed also that two measures under the New Miyazawa Initiative are related to regional bond market activities. The first is the acquisition of sovereign bonds issued by Asian countries by the Japan Bank for International Cooperation (JBIC). The second is support for Asian countries in raising funds from international financial markets through the use of credit-guarantees and interest subsidies. The goal is to promote the global and regional role of the Tokyo market by expanding Gaisei Bond issuance. However, of the fourteen JBIC issues made so far, only one has been denominated in yen.

Professor Rhee stressed the cost differences between Samurai and Euroyen bonds, with Samurai bonds being significantly more expensive on a range of measures: the underwriting fees, interest and principal payment commissions, out of pocket expenses, and also requiring a much longer period to be launched.

Professor Rhee then identified two key issues when asking whether the Tokyo market is ready for a regional role in fixed income markets. First, the development of the Gaisai market goes in tandem with the development of the Japanese government bond (JGB) market. Second, without a solid market infrastructure for JGBs and without the participation of foreign institutions, the Tokyo market cannot serve as a regional and global financial centre.

He stressed that the scope and complexity of the capital market-related Big Bang financial reforms has been unprecedented. Cross-border transactions and foreign exchange business have been deregulated. A competitive auction method to issue financing bills has been adopted. The securities transaction tax has been abolished. Brokerage commissions have been deregulated. A legal framework for loan/asset securitisation has been prepared. Off-exchange trading has been allowed. Banks and financial institutions have been allowed to issue bonds. Banks, securities companies, and insurance companies have entered into each other's businesses. Individual stock options have been introduced. The merit-based licensing system has been replaced by a disclosure-based registration system for securities companies.

Professor Rhee argued that the reform process is, however, not completed. He identified several Post-Big-Bang reforms that are still needed for the JGB market. Investment by non-resident investors in JGBs needs to be promoted. As of April last year, the withholding tax on redemption gains and interest income from JGBs was exempted for non-residents. However, tax exemption is not done at the source. So investors first have to pay the tax, and then request for a refund, a cumbersome and long process.

The Ministry of Finance should stop its dual role in the JGB market, and specifically stop being an active buyer in the market. The government is the largest issuer of government debt in the world. At the same time, MOF's Trust Fund Bureau is the largest fund manager in the world, managing the Fiscal Investment and Loan Program (FILP). 19% of FILP's funds are invested in JGBs. MOF's purchase activities of JGBs and its role as a *de facto* underwriter cause two adverse consequences. First, additional uncertainty on long-term interest rates deters investors from investing in JGBs, and, second, intense competition among primary dealers in the primary market cannot be achieved.

MOF should allow easy access to the repo market to foreign institutions. Foreign participation in both the Gensaki and Kashisai repo markets is insignificant. It should introduce a primary dealer system, it should adopt a uniform-price auction method, it should allow when-issued trading, and also introduce separate trading of registers interest and principal of securities (STRIPS).

In order to achieve a regional fixed income market, Professor Rhee advocated the need for a comprehensive study and detailed blueprint. It should examine regional clearing and settlement systems, cross-border securities borrowing and lending mechanisms, cross-border repo transactions, cross-border trading systems, the harmonisation of listing rules and tax treatments, the creation of a common currency for the purpose of issuing sovereign bonds, coordinated regulation, and lastly a regional credit enhancement and guarantee agency.

Corporate Bond Markets

Mr. Tadashi Endo, Senior Capital Markets Specialist, International Finance Corporation, focused on one aspect of the development of corporate debt markets, namely the relationship of the capital market, including the corporate bond market, with public finances and the banking sector. He stressed that mounting pressures on an economy for the consolidation of public finances and diffusion of stresses on the banking system, necessitate the development of a corporate bond market. He drew what he believed to be a critical distinction between major and minor issuers in corporate bond markets, which he thought vital to understand the functions of corporate debt markets, and to lay out a development strategy for debt markets. Very importantly, Mr. Endo maintained that illiquidity for the minor issues never lessens the importance of a corporate bond market to the minor issuers, as evidenced by the observation that of the 400,000 corporate debt issues outstanding in the US in 1996, only 4% of them were traded even once in the year.

The "major" corporate issuers offer a regular, sizable and stable supply of bonds of high quality and uniform characteristics. Their issuance is typically on a cyclical basis and indifferent to market conditions, and therefore not opportunistic. They are typically bought by "impatient" traders with a high demand for immediacy. They meet basic investment needs across a country, are widely held in the market, and are relatively easy to buy and sell. The typical issuers are housing finance companies, infrastructure and utility companies, and development finance companies. In contrast, the "minor" issuers lack the characteristics of the major issuers. They may be highly creditworthy, but only offer irregular issuance for relatively small amounts. They are normally bought by patient traders with a lower demand for immediacy. The minor issuers are opportunistic in terms of their issuance strategies. There is a diverse range of characteristics of the bonds issued by the minor corporations. They are issued to meet specific, short-lived investment needs, and there are few or no trades in their issues after the initial placement. The major issuers typically constitute a small percentage of the total corporate bond issues.

Mr. Endo argued that the primary market for minor issuers plays an enormous role in supplying long-term funds to a country's private sector, and in doing so helps consolidate public finances and diffuse stresses on a country's banking sector. A corporate bond market does not therefore have to have a liquid secondary market to be valuable, and for most minor issues it cannot have a liquid market. Even without a liquid secondary market, however, it is still extremely important.

Session 4   The Roles of Securities Laws and Securities Market Regulators for the Sound Development of Bond Markets

An Overview

Mr. Giovanni Sabatini, Head of Market Regulation, Commissione Nazionale per le Societa e la Borsa, Italy, and Chairman of the Working Party 2 of the Technical Committee of IOSCO, presented an overview of the role of regulators in developing government securities markets. He maintained that deep and liquid financial markets, especially government securities markets, are needed to ensure a robust and efficient financial system as a whole, as highlighted by the recent financial crises. Mr. Sabatini noted three broad sets of factors that affect the development of efficient and liquid government securities markets. The first set, which he did not discuss, were "environmental" factors, including the macroeconomic situation and the creditworthiness of the issuer.

The second set concerned what he called "institutional factors", and related to securities law, regulation, supervision, accounting rules and the tax regime. Key elements of the second set of factors were described by Mr. Sabatini. Securities law depends upon an appropriate legal framework for company law, commercial law, contract law, bankruptcy and insolvency law, competition law, banking law and a dispute resolution system. Regulation is needed to ensure the protection of investors, that markets are fair efficient and transparent, and that systemic risk is reduced. It should facilitate capital formation and economic growth. It should eliminate unnecessary barriers to entry and exit from markets and products, ensure that the market is open to the widest range of participants, consider its economic effects, and ensure that market participants face equal regulatory burdens. Market supervision is needed to ensure market integrity by deterring insider trading, manipulation and other abusive practices; and also to examine market dynamics, such as continuous monitoring of trading, large and concentrated positions, and anomalous market trends in specific securities.

The third set of factors Mr. Sabatini argued were vital for the development of government securities markets concerned market infrastructure. Trading systems for the primary market need to be implemented, specifying the role of specialists, how the auctions work, transparency, and their links with secondary markets. In the secondary markets, issues that need resolution concern whether to use organised or OTC markets, what market microstructure is most appropriate, what level of transparency is desired, and whether to allow alternative trading systems.

Clearing and settlement systems must be established to reduce pre-settlement and settlement risk, to achieve operational reliability, and to sustain liquidity, the reliability of delivery of securities, and confidence in the secondary market. In the event of a default, clearing and settlement systems must limit and contain the effects and consequences of a default to the defaulting entity, and support the continued liquidity of the securities or contracts traded. Central depository systems must promote immobilisation or dematerialisation of financial instruments; broad, direct and indirect industry participation, and a wide range of depository eligible instruments. Other elements of necessary market infrastructure include a market for derivatives, and appropriate mechanisms for repos and securities lending.

In order to illustrate these points Mr. Sabatini outlined the structure of the Italian Government bond markets. He noted that the primary market, through the trading system MTS, had a wide range of securities, was transparent, predictable and liquid. In the secondary market, primary dealers traded an average of 13 billion Euro worth of bonds on a daily basis through MTS. The market is also highly competitive, with the six primary dealers with the highest average volume of transactions accounting for only 35% of the primary dealers' trading activity. This has beneficial consequences for public debt management. In particular it has raised both the duration and average life of debt, thereby reducing the share of Treasury bills and floating rate notes. In addition, bid-ask spreads on Italian government securities are highly competitive, ranging between 3-10 cents, depending on maturity, compared with the spreads on German and French issues, which range from 10-15 cents and from 6-15 cents respectively.

Mr. Sabatini concluded his presentation by quoting from a Third Century B.C. anonymous Latin inscription: "Those who can do, do; Those who cannot do, administrate; Those who cannot administrate, teach; and Those who cannot teach ..... regulate".

Bond Futures Market

Mr. Rick Shilts, Acting Director, Division of Economic Analysis, Commodity Futures Trading Commission, discussed the topic of developing bond futures markets. He noted, first, the difference between a forward contract and a futures contract. Key characteristics of futures contracts include that they are traded on an exchange (a facility for executing trades where buying and selling interests meet); they permit offset of positions prior to contract expiration; most positions in them are liquidated by offset and not settled by delivery; their contract terms are standardised (and set by the relevant exchange); and they are cleared via a clearing mechanism that eliminates counterparty credit risk.

Mr. Shilts identified three economic purposes of futures markets: hedging or risk management – the process of shifting unwanted price risk incidental to business activities to others willing to assume the risk; price discovery – the process of finding market values; and price basing – whereby futures prices are used as a basis for setting cash market transaction prices. Hedging has a range of benefits. It provides protection against adverse price fluctuations for inventories and expected purchases and sales. It provides flexibility in a corporate strategy of buying, selling, and pricing bonds. It can free up working capital used to finance inventories. It can increase the borrowing capacity of a firm. Bond futures markets have various specific economic uses. They provide risk avoidance or insurance hedges of inventories of bonds. They enhance asset allocation. They can be used to alter the duration of a firm's portfolio, to create synthetic securities for yield enhanced, to fix the future rate of return on expected investments, and as a temporary substitute for an expected purchase or sale.

Many elements are required to establish successful derivatives markets. The legal and economic climate should be conducive to commerce and investment. Contractual rights should be enforceable.

There should be potential traders – both commercial users and well-capitalised speculators. There should be equitable access to the financial and legal systems.

Mr. Shilts noted several key points concerning the development of futures markets. It is difficult to predict which new futures markets will succeed, and indeed even under ideal circumstances, most new contracts fail. Success depends on some factors within an exchange's control and others beyond the regulator's or market authority's control, including the legal and economic environment where the exchange is located. Successful futures contracts often have some of the following common features. The instruments should not be subject to significant governmental restrictions. The instruments should have active cash markets. There must be adequate price volatility to sustain active trading. A sufficient base of market users or potential risk shifters to support liquidity should exist. Information should be readily available as to supply, demand, and cash prices of the underlying instruments. The contract must be accepted by key segments of the cash market. Other considerations are whether there is a need for the contract, if firms are able to shift price risk using existing cash market arrangements.

The design of futures contracts is critical to their success. Proper contract design ensures that a contract is less susceptible to manipulation and price distortion. It is necessary to ensure that contract terms are designed to meet commercial risk management needs. A contract should be integrated into the cash market operations of significant commercial sectors likely to use the contract. It should incorporate cash market pricing and delivery systems. A contract size smaller than cash market transactions may appeal to speculative interests to enhance liquidity and allow more precise hedging. IOSCO has developed standards of best practice for contract design and review.

Mr. Shilts noted that market surveillance is needed because even well-defined contracts can be subject to manipulation and abuse. Key purposes of market surveillance are to detect and prevent market abuses (such as manipulation, price distortions, defaults) to assure that the price discovered is a fair representation of actual supply and demand, and to assure that the market operates properly, especially for commercial users, and that the contract terms remain appropriate. There are many elements of an effective market surveillance program. It must be possible: to compare futures prices to cash prices so as to detect artificial prices; to monitor positions and actions of "large" traders; to take action to prevent and detect abuses, including emergency actions, jawboning traders with dominant positions, and forced reductions in position sizes; to have procedures/agreements in place with other affected government regulators; and to be able to assess the deliverable supplies.

Mr. Shilts concluded by identifying three issues of recent importance in the US futures markets. There has been a continued need to monitor the markets. The declining issuance of the US Treasury bonds and notes may raise concerns about the amount of deliverable supply. US Agency notes are now being marketed by Fannie Mae and Freddie Mac (two US government-sponsored enterprises) as substitutes for US Treasuries – and new futures contracts were recently introduced on these instruments.

U.K. Experience

Mr. David Strachan, Head of Department, Market Conduct and Infrastructure, Financial Services Authority (FSA), United Kingdom, discussed the topic of bond market regulation in a period of changing market structure, presenting the UK experience. The sizes of the various UK markets were outlined: there is just under £300bn gilts outstanding (equivalent to some 35% of GDP), but the market for UK domestic corporate bonds is less active than equity markets and overseas counterparts. The international/eurobond market is, however, significant. The UK bond markets are essentially wholesale markets, while there is some on-exchange trading on the London Stock Exchange for cash securities, and on the London International Financial Futures and Options Exchange (LIFFE) for futures. The OTC markets are also very large, both in the international bonds, derivatives and repos. The International Securities Market Association provides facilities for the eurobond market.

On the regulatory side, EU legislation provides a framework relating to public offers of bond issues and listing rules. Its focus is on initial and continuing disclosures. On the trading side, the Financial Services Act and for the future the Financial Services and Markets Bill give the legislative basis, with various rules, guidance and codes also provided by the regulator, and other requirements imposed by the exchanges. A "light touch" approach is used for the regulation of the wholesale markets. For on-exchange business, attention is focused on the market makers and on transparency. For off-exchange business, the FSA has various codes of conduct, and principles, and also monitors market abuse. The industry has also developed codes of conduct, such as the Gilt Repo Code.

Mr. Strachan noted several ways in which the markets were being developed. Institutional roles were changing, a broader product base was being developed, changes were occurring in trading structures and processes, and risk management was being centralised. Three official institutions with an interest in the markets were described: the Bank of England, the Debt Management Office (DMO), and the FSA. Their existence highlighted the issue of whether there is a limit to the number of different functions that a single body can undertake. Given the existence of different bodies, Mr. Strachan noted it is vital to maintain close cooperation between the debt manager and the regulator. He also stressed the inter-relationships between the three broad sectors of the cash, derivatives and repo markets, and thus the necessity for all the interested bodies to communicate. In the UK, the relevant organisations include the FSA, DMO, Bank of England, HM Treasury, the LSE, LIFFE, London Clearing House (LCH), and Crest.

The markets are changing from bilateral dealing via the telephone to a multilateral screen-based trading process, in both the primary and secondary markets. In response, the FSA is interested in transparency, market monitoring, and audit trails. Mr. Strachan concluded by identifying a range of policies that are being pursued to reduce systemic risk. A focus is being placed on credit risk, with the development of central counterparty systems. The LCH is implementing Repoclear. The issues of netting and novation are being examined again, and greater attention is being given to the concentration of risks.

Transparency in the U.S. Debt Markets

Mr. Stephen Williams, Senior Special Advisor, Division of Market Regulation, Securities and Exchange Commission (SEC), United States, gave a presentation on the topic of transparency in the US debt markets. He discussed first the way bond markets are organised in the US, noting that nearly all trading is over-the-counter, and that unlike for equities, there is almost no trading of bonds on registered securities exchanges. Dealers, interdealer brokers, and large institutional investors are principal participants in the markets. Dealers also act as underwriters or distributors. Trades between dealers are normally effected anonymously through the interdealer brokers (IDBs). Most transactions are done by telephone, but electronic trading is growing rapidly and is expected to continue to grow over the next few years.

Mr. Williams defined a transparent market as one that is "open to view", in which the prices of bids, offers and transactions are readily available to all participants. The advantages of transparency include the confidence generated by open processes, and its positive effects on fair and efficient price discovery. When markets aren't transparent, participants with better information have clear advantages over other participants who lack that information. Investors with good information also make better decisions, and that leads to more efficient markets.

The history of the SEC's and Congress's involvement in earlier efforts to bring greater transparency to the bond markets was then examined. Historically, the debt markets have been slow to move toward transparency. While the stock ticker was well established in the US in the 1920s, there was no organised distribution and display of bond prices, even in the Treasury markets, until the 1970's when several IDBs developed screen-based distribution systems to display current bids and offers to their dealer clients. At first, these IDB systems were provided only to primary dealers. Later, one IDB arranged to sell "indicative prices" through a single vendor in an exclusive arrangement. Still later, a major primary dealer made a similar arrangement to distribute its prices through a vendor of which it was a part owner.

By the mid-1980s, some prices for Treasury bonds were available, but not in an open and competitive market. Over the next five years there were two Congressional studies and a growing consensus that government intervention to compel transparency was justified. In 1991, the industry organised a response in the form of GovPX, a private information vendor that distributes both quotation and transaction information for US Treasury bills, bonds, and notes, as well as other information. The quality and timeliness of GovPX information is extremely good, and the Treasury market is now highly transparent. Transparency of this extremely large and liquid market was thus achieved without actual government intervention, but only under the threat of it.

Since then, the Municipal Securities Rulemaking Board, with the encouragement of the SEC, has adopted rules and developed systems for collecting reports of transactions in municipal bonds. The MSRB now publishes, on a next day basis, all transactions in actively traded municipal bonds. The MSRB intends to speed up reporting with a goal of being near real time. The municipal debt market is actually the smallest major segment of the US debt markets, but it happens to be the only one in which individual investors are a major factor. As a result, transparency of that market has been considered especially important from a fairness standpoint since individuals have clearly been at a disadvantage.

Mr. Williams concluded by describing some recent developments concerning transparency in the market for corporate bonds. In the spring of 1998, the SEC's Division of Market Regulation undertook a review of the markets for debt securities with an emphasis on price transparency. Among its principal goals were to identify inadequacies in the availability of pricing information, and to recommend improvements. Overall it found the debt markets to be functioning well, and far more transparent in most segments than they had been 10 years before. Specifically, it found improved transparency in the Treasury market, in municipal bonds, and also for most of the several standardized products in the mortgage-backed securities market. For US domestic bonds, the only category that lacked almost any transparency was that of corporate bonds. Accordingly, the SEC recommended steps to remedy the situation.

In September 1998, Chairman Arthur Levitt called for increased transparency in the corporate debt market. He asked the NASD to do three things: to adopt rules requiring dealers to report all transactions in US corporate bonds, and redistribute prices on an immediate basis; to develop a database of transactions for regulatory purposes; and to create a surveillance program for the corporate debt market utilising the transactions database. In response the NASD began to plan a comprehensive approach to corporate bond transparency.

Following the Chairman's speech, there were Congressional hearings on bond market transparency. Many organisations participated in the testimony, including dealers, major investors, industry associations and others. Almost everyone supported transparent markets in principle, but there were objections to the idea of immediate and comprehensive trade reporting mandated by the SEC or the NASD. Principally, these objections revolved around two points: 1) fear of a negative impact on liquidity, and 2) a preference for an industry-sponsored system such as had been done earlier for government bonds. The liquidity argument arises from a belief that if a dealer who buys a large position in an infrequently traded bond is forced to disclose the price he paid to the world, his ability to resell the bond will be materially hurt. Although Mr. Williams accepted that this is not implausible, he maintained there is another side to the argument as well. This says that transparent markets attract more participants generally, which adds to liquidity, and also that they will attract more participants specifically when they are confident they are being offered a bond at a reasonable price.

Although the hearings didn't reveal a consensus of opinion, they did lead to a bill being passed by the House last year, though not, at least not yet, by the Senate. The House bill, if it becomes law, would extend the requirement for transaction reporting to a much larger group of securities than the SEC has yet considered. The NASD proposal would cover about 30,000 to 40,000 bonds issued by US corporations and a few foreign corporations. The House bill would potentially extend that coverage to nearly all of the approximately one million taxable bonds. The difference, some 900,000 instruments, is primarily made up of mortgage and asset-backed instruments of all kinds, issued or guaranteed largely by public and quasi-public corporations such as GNMA and FNMA. The prospects for this bill becoming law are not considered good.

In the meantime, both the NASD and the industry have been moving forward. There is now an industry-sponsored system that collects reports of trades done between dealers, in investment-grade bonds. The trades are published at the end of the day on at least two web sites and are available free of charge to anyone who has access to the Web. The quality of the information provided is quite good, and includes price, yield, spread to treasuries (at the time of the trade), volume in broad categories, and ratings. Limitations, however, include the limited scope of coverage, the fact that participation is voluntary, the lack of timeliness, and the very small number of transactions reported on a daily basis.

On a slower track, the NASD has developed a much more comprehensive proposal. It covers most ordinary corporate bonds issued in the US, including some issued by foreign corporations, but excluding asset and mortgage backed securities. All NASD members will be required to report transactions with non-members and sales to other members. The scope is much more comprehensive than the industry effort described before, and in particular, it includes all institutional and retail trades. If approved, implementation will begin sometime later this year, and would be phased in over a seven-month period. In addition to its transparency aspects, the NASD proposal also involves providing a new method of bond trade comparison for interdealer trades, which itself is controversial for some participants. This proposal is in the middle of the review process. At this point the SEC has published the proposal for public comment and has received comments back. Among the principal suggestions have been calls for a more carefully structured phase-in period to reduce liquidity risks, and for a more open, competitive approach rather than a regulatory monopoly.

Australian Experience

Ms. Claire Grose, Director, National Markets Unit, Australia Securities and Investment Commission (ASIC), examined the roles of securities laws and securities market regulators for the sound development of bond markets in Australia. She first described the nature of the Australian bond market and the structure of its regulation. The Australian secondary market for government and non-government fixed interest securities is an over-the-counter market conducted by thirteen large investment banks. They operate an interbank market between themselves and offer two-way prices to their wholesale clients. Two brokerage firms provide electronic communication networks to the interbank market which quote prices at which participants in the market are willing to buy or sell government and semi-government bonds and very liquid bank, corporate and foreign bonds. Execution of transactions occurs over the phone.

The regulatory issues that arise in respect of this market can be summarised as: pre-and post trade price transparency and the integrity of the price formation process; agreement on and compliance with market trading rules and conventions; and standards of conduct, training and competence of dealers in the market. The possibility of retail participation in the fixed interest market through electronic facilities is being considered by participants in those markets, and this raises questions of the content and level of detail required in disclosure documents related to the bond issues. Australian retail investors currently have a relatively low level of understanding about the risks of investing in debt securities through secondary markets, as compared with their understanding of the risks in investing in equity securities through secondary markets.

Entities or individuals who carry on a business of dealing in bonds are required to be licensed as securities dealers. Facilities by means of which government and non-government bonds are bought or sold meet the definition of stock market and are required to be authorised as exchanges or declared to be exempt markets. Because dealers in the OTC fixed interest market regularly offer two-way prices, many dealers' activities amount to the conduct of a stock market. However, ASIC has indicated that it does not propose to take action to enforce the prohibition on conducting unauthorised stock markets against dealers in the OTC fixed interest market.

Issues of debt securities are subject to the disclosure provisions of the Corporations Law. However in practice most bond issues do not need disclosure because offers made to sophisticated investors can receive a disclosure exception. Disclosure is needed when the offer is made to retail investors. It has been argued that the disclosure obligations have deterred issuers from large retail bond issues. However, the debenture prospectuses for unlisted finance companies are a case in point of short prospectuses being used for debt issues. Rather, the problem appears to be that issuers who are accustomed to enjoying the benefit of the sophisticated investor exclusion are reluctant to go to the extra trouble of issuing a prospectus to accommodate a retail market which represents only a small percentage of potential demand. Recent amendments to the Corporations Law have clarified the extent to which issuers can issue shorter and less repetitive disclosure documents. If retail participation in the fixed interest market does grow, ASIC may need to provide guidance to issuers on the question of the required level of disclosure for fixed interest securities.

Prohibitions on insider dealing and market manipulation apply to trading in government and non-government bonds to the same extent as they apply to trading in equity securities. However, the prohibitions on insider trading in futures contracts does not apply to trading in futures contracts over government bonds. The prohibitions on market manipulation in the futures market includes trading activities in the government or non-government bond market or the government bond futures market. Because there is no formal self-regulatory organisation or formalised market structure that establishes trading rules and provides for their effective monitoring and enforcement of the OTC dealer market in fixed income securities, ASIC has no formal mechanism for identifying potential contraventions of the insider dealing and market manipulation provisions of the Corporations Law occurring in that market. However because of the sophisticated and concentrated character of the market, market participants are better placed to protect their own interests than is the case in more dispersed, retail markets. Market participants are also likely to complain about suspicious trading to the relevant authorities.

Ms. Grose noted that ASIC's regulation of the OTC fixed interest market has been greatly facilitated by the role played by the industry association, the Australian Financial Markets Association (AFMA). AFMA has taken a number of self-regulatory initiatives applicable to the participants in the fixed interest market, including: 1) the establishment of market committees to address issues associated with the orderly conduct of the OTC fixed interest market; 2) the development of a code of conduct for participants in the fixed interest market; 3) the formulation of accreditation standards for dealers in the fixed interest market and the development of training programs to meet those accreditation standards; 4) the development of protocols for debt securities and the debt capital market; and 5) the collection from fixed interest market participants of information about the volume and prices at which transactions in the fixed interest market were executed and end of the day reporting of those transactions. In addition ASIC and AFMA have undertaken a number of co-regulatory initiatives including arrangements for capital adequacy requirements for fixed interest dealers.

ASIC considers that the timeliness of trade reporting and the dissemination of that price information for the fixed interest market could be improved further. End of the day price reporting and dissemination is of limited benefit to price formation. Real time price information would result in improved price transparency and lower spreads. ASIC is also concerned to improve its ability to identify suspicious trading activity and to reconstruct the audit trail for transactions conducted in the OTC market.

The role of the Reserve Bank of Australia in the bond markets is: 1) to advise the Commonwealth Government on Commonwealth Government debt issues; 2) to conduct government debt issues; 3) to maintain the registry for Commonwealth Government Bonds; and 3) to provide a small sales and purchase facility to manage liquidity and imbalances in supply and demand for Commonwealth Government Bonds.

Ms. Grose concluded by discussing future developments in the Australian bond market. Two electronic communication networks currently service the interbank fixed interest market and the ASX has recently introduced electronic retail exchange trading of fixed interest securities. ASIC is aware of other proposals for the development of electronic facilities which automate the process by which market makers quote two way prices to their wholesale clients, and for retail investors to trade directly with market makers. Change in the structure of the Australian fixed interest market will be given greater impetus by amendments to the Corporations Law contained in the *Financial Services Reform Draft Bill*. The amendments will abolish the current legal distinction between securities and futures markets by introducing the concept of financial products market to include markets for everything from insurance, superannuation and managed investments to securities, futures contracts and other derivative products. Furthermore, the definition of financial products market excludes a facility created by a dealer through which it alone acts as a market maker, and OTC transactions, not through a facility, in which the parties to the transaction accept counter party risk.

Another significant change will be greater flexibility in the regulatory obligations imposed on financial product market licence holders as compared with the existing requirements for regulation as a securities or futures exchange. This will allow regulatory requirements such as operating rules, the need for clearing and settlement facilities, and conditions on the licence and supervisory arrangements, to be tailor-made to the market in question taking into account the financial products to be traded on the market, the size of the market, the participants in the market, the nature of the activities conducted on the market and the technology used in the operation of the market. The draft Bill will also change existing arrangements for regulation of clearing and settlement facilities for financial products. Ms. Grose stressed that the Australian government's timetable for introducing these reforms is short. The rapid changes in the environment of the Australian bond market are likely to hasten as electronic trading systems develop and domestic law reform takes shape.

Session 5   *Private Sector Participation*

Industry (Merrill Lynch)

Mr. Kevan Watts, Executive Chairman, Asia Pacific Region, Merrill Lynch International Inc, presented a list of Ten Commandments for developing local debt capital markets in the internet age.

They are: 1) Thou shalt broaden the base of borrowers; 2) Thou shalt breed more investors; 3) Thou shalt promote secondary market liquidity; 4) Thou shalt establish reliable pricing benchmarks; 5) Thou shalt develop the market for swaps and repos; 6) Thou shalt encourage a proper understanding of credit risk; 7) Thou shalt provide a clear and efficient regulatory framework and tax and settlement system; 8) Thou shalt welcome foreign investors and borrowers; 9) Thou shalt level the level playing field for all participants; and, 10) Thou shalt embrace e-commerce. Mr. Watts then provided the following observations and "food for thought" on each of these Commandments.

First Commandment (concerning borrowers): Issuers have increasingly turned to their domestic bond markets, having learned the risk involved in having currencies mismatched between assets and liabilities. Domestic funding levels and relative spreads have in some cases become significantly cheaper than comparable offshore funding levels. Many borrowers have been looking opportunistically at the differential between onshore and offshore funding levels. Many of the regional governments have been actively promoting the use of their domestic markets. Supranational agencies have been actively issuing in the local bond markets and consequently using the swap markets, promoting confidence and liquidity. Desirable developments might be to facilitate asset-backed or mortgage-backed issuance by making the regulatory and legal environment clearer; to make share repurchases legally easier and more tax efficient to execute to encourage more corporate issuance, and to open the market to foreign issuers.

Second Commandment (concerning investors): A diversity of investor groups with different perspectives and liability structures is necessary for the long-term viability of a market. Domestic banks and financial institutions have been significant investors in their domestic bond markets, often foregoing more traditional types of lending. Countries have had mixed results in developing retail activity in bonds for many reasons. Mutual funds and pension funds will have growing importance as investors increasingly look to outsource investment decisions to professionals. Domestic institutional investors are always looking for new investments and ideas to enhance diversity and yield, but in many cases are faced with limited investment opportunities whether due to regulation or market constraints. Policies to enhance the diversity of investors include: promoting investment activity by insurance companies, pension funds, mutual funds, and other institutional investors, educating retail investors, promoting low-cost online retail trading access, and allowing access to foreign investors, but in a way that is not vulnerable to transient "hot money".

Third Commandment (concerning liquidity): Secondary market liquidity in local markets is important for multiple reasons. Investors in Asia tend to buy and hold bonds until maturity, especially for shorter-dated bonds. Local intermediaries are not as aggressive in providing liquidity as intermediaries in more developed markets. Policies to enhance liquidity might include the following: broadening the mix of investors with different investment orientations and addressing prohibitions on participation from a broader base of participants, such as regulatory hurdles, access to funding in local currency, the ability to hedge the interest rate and currency risks, and disadvantageous tax treatments. Foreign dealers and market makers can bring expertise in book-running.

Fourth Commandment (concerning benchmarks): The existence of reliable benchmarks is paramount to the development of healthy local bond markets. Many countries have a government or quasi-government yield curve up to 10-20 years, however, only some of them are simple or liquid enough to provide real benchmarks for pricing. In several countries, erratic maturity profiles and auction schedules, lack of fungibility, and the use of multiple government bond programs are confusing and overly complicated, making development of a benchmark yield curve extremely difficult. Fiscal budget deficits are not the only driving force behind government bond issuance in many countries. Various policies may improve this situation including the following. Simplify government bond programs, making them reliable, regular, and consistent, develop the repo market and allow market participants to short bonds to enhance secondary liquidity. Establish a floating rate benchmark equivalent to LIBOR. When government aid is needed to recapitalise banks or corporates, the government could borrow directly in the market, thereby putting large benchmark issues into the market, and then inject capital into the banks or the corporates. Foster the development of an interbank swap market.

Fifth Commandment (concerning swaps and repos): An open and liquid swap market allows for easy comparison between local currency bond spreads and those in G7 currencies, and gives investors the ability to hedge currency and interest rate risks. Swap yield curves are easier to "complete" than government yield curves. The availability of repos allows dealers to make liquid two-way prices, thus being able to have both long and short positions when required. It may be worth fostering the development of a swap yield curve, as it is less costly and administratively easier than maintaining a large auction schedule especially for governments without large budget deficits. As swaps are traded OTC, the development of a separate settlement system is not necessary. The development of a reliable floating rate benchmark or fixing, and normal currency systems is, however, necessary. Participants should be exempt from withholding tax on net interest payments on swaps.

Sixth Commandment (concerning credit risk): Many countries have domestic rating agencies. There is a difference in expertise between some of the domestic agencies and the international ones, especially with respect to asset-backed issues. Many domestic agencies are linking up with major international rating agencies. Most Asian countries are already rated by international rating agencies. Many bond issues are priced based on name recognition rather than on their credit worthiness. It might be desirable to encourage the use of ratings for analysis and investment decisions, and to promote better disclosure in financial statements.

Seventh Commandment (concerning regulatory, tax and settlement system): Many countries have already allowed both public and private placement issues and developed procedures governing such issuance. Disclosure requirements in some case may be either inadequate or overly burdensome. There are a number of countries where the tax treatment and/or withholding on interest income and capital gains is different depending on the investor type, the double-tax treaty with the country of the investor, and the bonds the investor holds. Domestic settlement systems appear to work adequately, but there is no regional clearing systems. It would be desirable to develop an issuance "standard" practice for different types of issues, to speed up the turnaround time for regulatory documentation review and to ensure confidentiality in the process, and to create a regional settlement system using Euroclear or Cedel as models.

Eighth Commandment (concerning foreign investors and borrowers): There are only a small number of local currency markets that allow foreign issuers and investors free access. Domestic institutional investors range from comprising relatively small to relatively large percentages of the investment community within Asian countries. Some countries have taken significant steps towards opening stock markets and the anticipation is they will take similar measures with local debt markets. The foreign investor community can add breadth and depth to the market. It can bring new issues and investment as well as know-how. While tax incentives can encourage some foreign asset and investment managers to set up operations onshore, opening up capital markets to some degree could be more effective in attracting foreign participation. Policy makers could develop interim measures that are acceptable from the currency control perspective.

Ninth Commandment (concerning level playing field): Taxation and withholding taxes can be inconsistent from investor to investor, especially if the investors are foreign. Funding costs are higher for non-bank borrowers relative to comparably rated banks because of differences in treatment on the balance sheet according to capital adequacy guidelines. Capital controls make participation illegal or economically impractical in many countries. Desirable developments might be to make access to funding more equitable and competitive, to exempt withholding tax or make it equal for all investors.

The best environment for a local currency market to develop properly is one where everyone is operating on a level playing field.

Tenth Commandment (concerning e-commerce): The advent of e-commerce will enhance the services that intermediaries provide to their issuing and investing clients by reducing the cost of distributing securities, potentially broadening the investor base and facilitating the information flow between an issuer and investor. The various trading portals that are being developed will facilitate secondary market trading in bonds once introduced and adapted to local markets. Some countries are already allowing the use of the internet to facilitate trading. A desirable development might be to improve access and information quality, and thereby help investors understand the credit quality of an issuer and the value of the securities which they hold. Regulators and governments should also begin to anticipate and prepare the structural and regulatory framework desired in governing the use of electronic distribution methods.

Rating Agency (1) Moody's

Ms. Julia Turner, Managing Director, Moody's Asia Pacific Ltd. talked on the topic of bank reform, as being an essential element of capital market reforms in Asia. She first reiterated Moody's support for financial market reform, stressing that the allocation of financial capital at prices that reflect the riskiness of an investment is at the heart of healthy, sustainable economic development. Moody's analysts recently noted that restructuring and reform were critical elements for any further upgrade of the ratings on several sovereign credits in Asia. Regulation is important for sustainable capital allocation. Financial disclosure and transparent practices are two of the most potent tools that regulators have at their disposal. They are far more effective than regulations designed to direct either the source or user of financial capital.

However, bond market reforms alone are inadequate to spur capital market development. Moody's has observed a number of regulatory regimes evolve that were, and are, designed to promote domestic bond markets. In some countries, the monetary authorities and economic managers are anxious to develop an alternative source of financial capital, having watched the damage done to their banks by the last financial crisis. Nonetheless, in most countries, banks continue to be the primary source, and in some cases still the only source, of debt capital. And, as long as borrowers have the option to borrow at uneconomic rates from their bankers, without disclosing the true state of their financial health, not even the most enlightened reform of capital market regulation will be sufficient to motivate them to borrow in the public debt markets.

For that reason, Moody's believes that the proposals from the Basle Committee are a large step in the direction of a more durable market financial framework. As the barriers between market sectors are inevitably, if slowly, destroyed, Ms. Turner argued that motivating bankers to reflect the relationship between risk and return will increase the opportunities for a broader array of non-bank lenders to enter the markets at more realistic prices. This process will, however, work slowly, since one can hardly underestimate the resistance to change that characterises these economic and financial systems -- not necessarily change to a Western system, just any change.

Moody's sees the Basle Committee's proposals as another step forward in the development of an efficient and globally consistent approach to bank supervision. The proposed new framework recognises that credit risk management practices are undergoing a technology-driven transformation and that each regulated bank has a unique pattern of risks and capabilities. Ms. Turner stressed, that in Moody's view, regulatory capital is not the key determinant of capital strength or credit quality. However, to the extent that national regulators implement the proposals in a way so as to strengthen economic capital, banks systemic credit quality should improve. Not only will their capitalisation be stronger, their profitability should be less volatile because of fewer earnings surprises. This will not apply to all banks within a given system. However, Moody's expect that banks with strong management, strong credit cultures, good asset quality and adequate profitability will be the beneficiaries of the proposed accords, emerging as winners over the banks whose lending practices have depended on regulatory forbearance.

Moody's agrees with the Committee's position that an internal ratings-based regime can provide a more accurate assessment of risk for sophisticated banks than the current Basle capital adequacy framework. The supervisors' responsibilities will be particularly challenging, given the Committee's desire to achieve consistency across a wide variety of banks and nations. In this regard, Moody's expects that external risk assessments, including credit ratings and related risk management services will prove valuable as both direct inputs to banks' internal rating systems and as tools for benchmarking and validating those systems. The proposal also sets challenges for the bankers, who need to develop and/or demonstrate to investors and regulators a system for loan risk evaluation that 1) is clear, coherent and credible to regulators in all the jurisdictions in which a bank operates; 2) does not place a wholly uneconomic burden on risk underwriting costs; and 3) reflects a given bank's specific approach to its target market. Ms. Turner suggested that this may be one of those scenarios where "what doesn't kill you makes you stronger". Moody's expectation that stronger banks will emerge from the effects of the proposals reflects its belief that the future of risk-adjusted regulatory capital lies with internal risk-scoring and credit assessment technology, rather than with external ratings.

Nevertheless, Ms. Turner argued that not all banks or regulators are yet ready to put an internal ratings-based system into operation. While it seems feasible to design an external ratings approach that, in transition to a fully internal system, would represent an improvement over the current regulatory capital framework, Moody's believes the external ratings approach has a number of shortcomings that need to be addressed. In particular, at present external credit ratings cover only a small portion of most bank's portfolios, nor are they economically practical. Implementation could raise a moral hazard problem in the ratings industry – frankly Moody's believes that relying solely on external ratings agencies to fulfil regulatory requirements would encourage rating shopping. In order to allow market discipline to increase the consistency among ratings, Moody's recommends that ratings eligible for use in regulation should be made public and subject to market scrutiny, and that regardless of whether an issuer requested a rating, regulators should consider all ratings that have been assigned to a given issuer by recognised agencies.

Regulators have somehow to reconcile the advantages of internal ratings with the claims of smaller banks that have not yet developed them. A regime that clearly and systematically discriminates in favour of large and/or multinational banks is likely to be politically unpalatable for most national bank regulators. The world's most sophisticated financial institutions have, for some years, been developing a battery of tools, such as scoring models for the extension of consumer credit. In recent years, an increasing level of analytic technology and expertise has been focused on credit risk management. The financial crisis raised the level of awareness among market participants – some of who really did not seem to believe that such a risk still existed. The regulatory changes proposed in the Basle accords have intensified the interest, and it seems likely that third party providers will accelerate the process by which the technology spreads to a broad array of banks, large and small, sophisticated and less sophisticated.

Ms. Turner concluded with the following observations. Improved risk management techniques are likely to support what Moody's regards as the primary goal of capital market reform, which is the efficient allocation of capital. Risk management technology is available, will improve rapidly, and will spread to a wide array of users. By improving asset quality and supporting sound lending practices, it will strengthen bank capital and profitability of well-managed banks. Moody's expects winners and losers among the banks in this process, but believes that overall banking systems will be strengthened.

Since banking systems remain a critical component of financial markets, Moody's expects the Basle accords may, if sensibly implemented, contribute significantly to capital market reform and development.

Rating Agency (2) (Thai Rating and Information Services)

Dr. Warapatr Todhanakasem, President, Thai Rating and Information Services (TRIS), discussed the topic of a domestic Credit Rating Agency (CRA) in an emerging Asian country, with a perspective from TRIS. He provided, first, a description of the development of local CRAs in southeast Asia. At present nearly all Asian developing countries have at least one rating agency, such as Indonesia, the Philippines and Thailand, Malaysia has two, and India and Korea have three. The Asian economic crisis brought much attention both to the internationally operated credit rating agencies, and to the local ones. Some of the major CRAs have reviewed and fine-tuned their methodologies, and the domestic CRAs have also learned a series of valuable lessons.

Dr. Todhanakasem identified a series of impacts the economic crisis had on domestic bond markets and credit rating agencies. The development of local CRAs relates closely to the development of domestic bond markets: the bigger the bond market grows, the more clients a local CRA obtains. Evidence from different members of the ASEAN Forum of Credit Rating Agencies (AFCRA) confirms this. By the end of 1998, Rating Agency Malaysia Berhad had more than 220 customers, while TRIS, even during its best year in 1996 had just 61 clients. One reason for this is that Malaysia has the biggest bond market in AFCRA. Apart from the fact that investors in larger capital markets tend to be more aware of risk than investors in smaller ones, government incentives and statutory requirements regarding credit ratings also have a significant influence on the demand for credit ratings. Requiring all corporate debentures in Malaysia to be rated significantly increased the demand for credit ratings since the measure was implemented in 1992. Thailand did not implement a similar requirement until 3 April 2000.

The Asian economic turbulence hit credit rating businesses hard. Few credit ratings were initiated during the crisis, because almost all new investment plans were postponed and few financial instruments were launched. After successive negative alerts followed by rating downgrades, almost all Asian credit rating agencies saw the number of rating clients significantly reduced. This was particularly true in countries with immature capital markets where no statutory rating requirements existed to limit ratings avoidance and withdrawals. The Thai financial crisis left TRIS with merely 10 company ratings and 12 issue ratings in 1997, compared to 23 company ratings and 38 issue ratings by the end of 1996. In 1998, TRIS did not gain any new credit rating clients. At the end of the year, after 12 downgrades and 12 withdrawals, TRIS had merely 11 rating clients which was the same level of business as the first year it opened.

However, TRIS took this crisis as an opportunity to review and develop its rating process and methodology to prepare for future developments. New rating services were studied, including a rating methodology for structured finance securities, and mortgage-backed securitisation. TRIS staff participated in the development of institutional financial infrastructure in Thailand, and provided assistance to the Financial Sector Restructuring Authority. A representative of TRIS also participated in the development of the state-owned Secondary Mortgage Corporation. By the end of 1998, it appeared that the Thai economy was beginning to recover. In 1/1999, Thai Farmers Bank issued the first hybrid equity-debt instruments in Thailand, called SLIPS, for Stapled Limited Interest Preferred Shares. This was followed by a series of bond issues by commercial banks and major companies – but all were private placements and needed no ratings. In 10/1999, TRIS announced the rating for its first new customer since 1997, a satellite company. Two more companies, one a former client that had cancelled a rating-contract in 1997, signed contracts with TRIS by the end of 1999, and business has been picking up since then.

Dr. Todhanakasem argued that the economic crisis put credit rating agencies under the spotlight. A number of international rating agencies made sharp adjustments of sovereign credit ratings for many emerging markets. Concerns were raised about the transparency of the credit rating process and the accuracy of rating assignments by the major international rating agencies. Domestic credit rating agencies were also criticised. Many were in worse situations than their international counterparts because of their short track records. Dr. Todhanakasem stressed, however, that being local is sometime advantageous, as domestic credit rating agencies are able to detect problems in local industries at their early stages. What is critical is to build a reputation for independence and capability. A key factor is the necessity to safeguard their rating activities from intervention of any party. To promote transparency, the major international rating agencies typically disclose their rating methodologies and processes both to the public and to their customers. TRIS has followed this example.

International rating agencies have an important role to play in the development of local credit rating agencies. Relationships between local and international agencies can take many forms. Some are merely marketing partnerships, some receive technical training in return for some kind of compensation, and some participate as equity shareholders. Analytical support and capital from the big credit rating agencies are important reasons that local credit rating agencies need cooperation with international ones. TRIS is a wholly Thai company. Nonetheless, during its initial three years of operation (1993-1996), TRIS received technical assistance from Standard & Poor's. In mid-1997, it formed a strategic partnership with Fitch Investors Service. However, the economic crisis in Thailand two months later affected the development of the capital market, and nullified the benefits that might have occurred from this agreement.

A range of both external and internal factors are critical in determining a domestic credit rating agency's performance. The major external factors are the country's culture, quality of information and disclosure standards, and the size of the bond market. The key internal factors are the quality of rating analysts and its rating methodology. The socio-cultural context can be either an obstacle or a support to the development of credit-rating agencies. It is difficult for local rating agencies to grow in Asia where people like to maintain anonymity and avoid evaluation. Asian companies are also not accustomed to disclosing information or being rated by a third party. Comparisons with competitors, and especially downgrades, are not liked. The quality of information that a rating agency gathers is an important factor determining the relative accuracy of its ratings. Asian rating agencies struggle with the problems of inadequate and unavailable information. Realising this, TRIS has been actively promoting transparency and good corporate governance in Thai businesses. Disclosure standards in Thailand have improved significantly, and accounting standards have also been reviewed. Another difficulty for domestic credit rating agencies is the small size of the domestic debt markets. Without actual practice, it is hard for analysts to develop their rating skills.

The key internal factor leading to the successful operation of a credit rating business is the quality of its human resources. During the boom period, rating agencies had to compete for high quality and experienced financial analysts who could demand much higher salaries in the market. Dr. Todhanakasem noted that to improve rating services, domestic rating agencies have cooperated on a regional basis for joint training and other exercises.

Dr. Todhanakasem concluded by raising a series of questions that arise as a result of the recovery in the Asian economies: Will the Asian bond markets return to growth rates seen prior to the crisis? Will the growth be sustainable? Will domestic credit rating agencies benefit from the potential bond market? He noted that there was a dramatic recovery in the Thai bond market in 1999, but that this had not yet had a significant impact on TRIS. Notwithstanding any regulatory requirement for bonds to have a compulsory credit rating, Dr. Todhanakasem argued that the most powerful factor motivating issuers to seek a credit rating is to maintain their credibility and reliability in the eyes of investors.

Research Institute (Nomura research Institute)

Mr. Fumiyuki Sasaki, Senior Economist, Economic Research Unit, Nomura Research Institute, Japan, discussed current conditions and developments in Asian domestic bond markets, and the further steps that need to be taken to advance the markets. He first examined the supply side, and identified three steps that need to be taken to enhance development. 1) There needs to be a sustainable supply of government bonds: a balance needs to be maintained between having sufficient bonds outstanding while keeping fiscal discipline, and public enterprises' bonds should act as quasi-government securities. There will be demand for infrastructure investments which will add to the supply of bonds. 2) The liquidity requirements for banks need to be deregulated as they are an obstacle to the development of secondary markets. 3) The importance of ratings agencies should be recognized.

On the demand side domestic institutional investors need to be fostered. Their presence will help prevent financial instability. Mr. Sasaki argued that the promotion of the bond markets is necessary now for two important reasons. It will provide an alternative funding channel to banking systems, and it will offer an alternative asset class for investors, thus enhancing their diversification opportunities.

Key characteristics of a government bond market are that it provides a benchmark with a risk-free asset and it offers instruments with big sizes, and large liquidity. Liquidity is vital for many reasons: to ensure that bonds can be used to hedge interest rate risk, to fund foreign currencies in a time of financial turmoil, to reduce issuance costs, to encourage the development of the market for other issuers, to let market players control their risks, and to facilitate monetary policy. There are many types of government bonds that can be issued – including fixed and floating rate notes, discount bonds, and inflation-indexed bonds. A range of maturities should be issued to build up a yield curve, and benchmarks should be issued relatively frequently. The establishment of an auction system for the primary market, an inter-dealer market, and also a repo market, will all help development of the markets.

A corporate bond market can be more flexible and less costly compared to bank borrowing. For example a medium term note program can be used many times, once the initial registration and approvals have been obtained. Corporate bonds can enhance returns for investors, with appropriate risk premiums.

In the secondary market, a dealer or OTC market is much more popular than an agency auction market on an exchange. Licensed primary dealers operate in the primary auction market, and make two-way quotes in the secondary market. A repo market provides a funding channel for leverage and for taking long positions, a vehicle for borrowing bonds and taking short positions, facilitates arbitrage and speculation, and provides a mechanism for the operation of monetary policy. It enhances the liquidity of a bond market, and has a close relationship with both the derivatives and foreign exchange market.

Mr. Sasaki concluded his speech by examining the relationship between a government bond market and monetary policy. He argued that indirect measures should be used for monetary policy, more particularly open market operations using repos. Mr. Sasaki defined "direct" measures as being when prices and quantities are set by regulation, or when a limit is set on credits. He defined "indirect" as being when monetary policy is carried out by influencing demand and supply through the market. He argued that development of the indirect channel promotes financial market structure, such as a settlement and book-entry system. Open market operations are more flexible than reserve requirements. A transition to indirect measures can, however, only be made under the conditions of stability of the macro economy and a sound fiscal policy, with developed financial markets, when macro conditions are not far from a balanced level, when interest rates are not far away from a balanced level, and when there are incentives for saving, intermediation, and setting an appropriate real interest rate.

Discussant

Dr. Takatoshi Ito, Deputy Vice Minister for International Affairs, Ministry of Finance, Japan, and former Professor of Hitotsubashi University, talked on the topic of moving towards deep Asian bond markets. He, first, identified the major types of capital flows: bank loans, bonds (short- or long-term, sovereign or corporate), subordinated corporate debts, equities (portfolio investment), and equities (direct investment). In order to avoid a future crisis he argued that the last type of flows should be encouraged, rather than short-term liabilities. Dr. Ito drew three key lessons from the Asian crisis: a dollar peg is dangerous, weak financial institutions cause and deepen a crisis, and too many external liabilities cause a crisis. He maintained that the presence of more bond financing would not have stopped the crisis – it is not a "silver bullet". The exchange rate regime, the dollar peg, was a key culprit for the crisis, as it lead to a misalignment in exports and imports, and exacerbated the "free lunch" problem for capital flows.

A critical question is how to structure a financial system for growth, namely how to channel savings (both domestic and foreign) to investment. Should it be via bank loans, bond financing or equity financing? Dr. Ito maintained that different answers are required for different stages of development. Policy makers should not fool themselves that because banks have many problems, bond financing is the answer. Infrastructures and investor bases need to be more sophisticated for the development of capital markets. With only a small amount of human capital, bank loans may be the appropriate first step. The main requirement to have a financial system operating through bank loans is the presence of competent bankers who can monitor their loans. Bond financing requires both market infrastructure and diverse investors. Equity financing requires market infrastructure and risk capital investors.

The different financial structures have different merits in crisis prevention. Bank loans are prone to sudden withdrawals (as in Korea), in contrast, FDI and long-term bonds are more stable. Short-term loans are similar to bank loans (as seen in Mexico and Russia). Foreign-currency denominated bonds may cause a currency crisis (as in Mexico), however, local-currency denominated bonds can do the same thing (as in Russia). Equities are less likely to lead to a sudden withdrawal, but are still not perfect (as in Hong Kong, China and Malaysia).

The different financial structures also have different merits in crisis management. Bank loans are easier to restructure (as there are typically only a limited number of creditors for a particular emerging market). The presence of bank loans can, however, cause a credit crunch (as occurred in Thailand and Indonesia). Bond financing is difficult to restructure, as there may be many investors who are not easy to contact and marshal. Default may result (as in Russia). Equity financing places the responsibilities on investors for crisis management.

Dr. Ito summarised his views stating that bond markets need to be developed, coexistent with bank loans, that long-term bonds have to be promoted, and that crisis management has to be planned. Bond market infrastructure, choice of exchange rate regime, and currency denomination are all important. There are countries that need bank financing. Long-term bond financing may be good for crisis prevention. Crisis management may, however, be more difficult with bond financing than with bank loans.

In order to develop bond markets, three principles need to be pursued: investor protection, efficient and trouble-free trading systems, and the prevention of systemic risk. Appropriate infrastructure needs to be implemented to achieve these principles. While a government bond market may provide benchmark securities, in the past prudent fiscal policies have prevented government bond market development. Amongst the pitfalls to appropriate development are that market integrity may be compromised, or there may be market imperfections. Respective remedies include education and training of market participants, and information asymmetry corrective measures. Desirable bond market infrastructure include: an appropriate trading system, well functioning securities firms, securities exchanges and a rating service; market monitoring to prevent corruption, fraud, and insider trading; a sound clearing and settlement system (with a central depository, RTGS, and DVP), collective action clauses; a bankruptcy court and liquidation procedures; and a role for government guarantee.

Dr. Ito concluded by discussing the merits of regional cooperation. This could include a region-wide rating service, and information sharing among regulators and securities exchanges. measures to encourage regional investors to remain in the region (rather than channelling their funds to US bonds for US investors, which then place their money in Asian risk assets), and lastly cooperation between exchanges that could lead to deeper markets.

Conclusion

Professor Anthony Neoh, concluded the proceedings by thanking everybody for their participation, and by identifying six broad themes that had been central to the discussions in the conference. The first was that bond markets could serve as an alternative to over-reliance on bank financing. The second was the need to develop appropriate "systems" at the broadest conceptual level. These included procedures for market-based underwriting of securities, creating a multiplicity of investments, establishing appropriate trading, clearing, settlement and legal structures, and where relevant the construction of appropriate futures markets. The third broad theme traversing the conference was the need to improve the quality of bond issuance - possibly through credit-enhancement schemes or some form of regional cooperation.

The fourth theme identified was the need to focus on investors, and particularly on the incentives they face, and the constraints imposed on them that restrict their developing wider asset allocation policies. The fifth theme was the benefits of establishing a national market development structure in a country so as to take account of all relevant market interests. Finally, Professor Neoh noted that many aspects of Asian financial systems continue to require attention, including risk management, exchange rate regimes, and the recapitalisation and restructuring of banks.

INTRODUCTION

BIS Tulle

WELCOME REMARKS

by
Dr. Masaru Yoshitomi

(asia) G12
G18
O16 G30
O19 G21
G28

Distinguished Delegates; Distinguished Speakers, Distinguished Colleagues from the OECD, Paris, and the International Organization of Security Commissions (IOSCO), Ladies and gentlemen.

A very good morning to you all. Let me join Mr. Kondo in welcoming you to this Round Table. Also, welcome to the ADB Institute, and welcome to Tokyo, this is the best time of the year in Tokyo, particularly when Sakura -- Cherryblossom -- are in full bloom.

Ladies and Gentlemen, as Mr. Kondo said, this is the second time that the ADB Institute, and OECD have organized a Round Table like this, and the theme of the Round Table, this time, is Capital Market Reforms in Asia. The collaborators of this Round Table are IOSCO, the World Bank, the International Monetary Fund and the Asian Development Bank.

Let me also say, such Round Tables and seminars form a part of the financial sector program of the ADB Institute, which are aimed at disseminating knowledge and helping governments in the region to build robust and sustainable financial systems. The ADB Institute would be happy to co-organize such events in the future as well.

Ladies and gentlemen, for the rest of my welcome remarks, I would like to briefly touch upon the (i) the Asian Crisis, recovery and the future; (ii) background to the motivation for capital market development; (iii) the issue of governance, regulation and supervision; (iv) government securities; (v) domestic bond market development; and (vi) the coverage of the Round Table.

The Asian Crisis, Recovery and the Future

Now, many countries in the region have been recovering from the recent Asian crisis to a considerable extent. However, there is no assurance that similar crises will not again hit the crisis-affected economies and also newly emerging economies like People's Republic of China, and South Asia in general.

This is because of the so-called double mismatch. That is, the combination of maturity mismatch and currency mismatches are more or less inherent in the financial markets in emerging economies which continue to borrow short-term loans dominated in foreign currencies. Poor corporate governance, weak financial regulations and inadequate monitoring of the financial sector all contributed to worsening maturity mismatch, namely, borrowing short and lending long to too risky investment projects. These problems were also responsible for aggravating currency mismatch of borrowing in foreign currencies, which are largely un-hedged. The region's problems of unregulated banks and financial corporations are not going to be cleaned up anytime soon. Even for the advanced economies, it took decades to strengthen their prudential regulations in a timely and adaptive manner. It would thus be unrealistic for us to expect that the region will be able to solve its own problems of bad corporate debt, bank restructuring and inadequate bankruptcy laws in a relatively quick manner. Many countries have still a long way to go before they will be able to complete their structural reforms. Therefore, there is no guarantee that there will not be another crisis.

Meanwhile, globalization will continue to speed up, accompanied by the availability of fast and efficient means of communication such as the Internet. Countries in the region will have to quickly cope with their homegrown problems of inadequate supervision of financial institutions as well as with external problems.

How can we in the region be better prepared to solve our homegrown problems, as well as externally generated problems, in an efficient manner? In my view, building capacity in the region and training personnel to comprehend the following three considerations is the first important step to help the region in averting another crisis.

First, to better understand the complexities of the world's financial system. Second, to comprehend better the occurrence of maturity mismatch and to introduce better maturity transformation to mitigate this mismatch. And, third, having the appropriate tools to reduce currency mismatch problems.

Background to the Motivation for Capital Market Development

It may be said that better functioning securities markets would have reduced the impact of the Asian crisis (e.g., by providing increased confidence of international investors, improved market discipline, more effective allocation of capital, and thereby less incentives to withdraw from market). On the other hand, capital market development could have reduced heavy dependence on the banking sector and foreign borrowing for project finance.

It is also argued that the *absence of well-functioning corporate bond markets* deprived the Asian financial systems of the public domain credit information generated by such markets on a continuous basis. Some suggest that local corporations have been reluctant to issue public debt because they feared disclosure requirements and negative ratings.

The *lack of liquidity* in the crisis-hit countries was further increased through the low supply of investment-grade paper, an insufficient number of intermediaries and high trading costs from fixed brokerage commissions. The heavy *reliance on the banking system* as provider of finance led to a slow development of market breadth in many of the Asian securities markets. *Illiquid futures markets*, limiting the hedging opportunities of market participants and also the inadequate understanding of the uses and trading of derivatives hindered the development of a sound derivatives industry in the Asian countries.

Governance, Regulation and Supervision

Corporate governance is one important area. There is the need for an efficient use of firms' assets, accurate data and an effective enforcement of corporate laws. However, there are problems of hidden exposures, lack of transparency in accounting and auditing standards and a widening gap between corporate governance practices in Asia and other parts of the world. Let me also say that there is wide recognition of the need for greater shareholder activism in the Asian countries. Among others, the study undertaken by our Institute and the ADB support these arguments[1].

Related to corporate governance is the issue of transparency in market activity. Transparency concerns regarding highly leveraged institutions (HLI) have been increased since the onset of the Asian crisis. There are two main reasons for this: first, the potential of the HLI to launch a speculative attack using the securities markets; and second, the potential systemic risk of HLI defaults.

Another related issue is the call to improve the disclosure of exposures in OTC instruments and off-balance sheet items. Ideally, the transparency principles should not differ greatly between countries, as gaps between the standards could lead to regulatory arbitrage. Cross-border trade in very different assets makes effective enforcement a question of concerted international effort.

There are regulatory and supervisory standards which need to be maintained at the international level. Important issues on the scope for improvement are e.g. prudential capital standards (which are not high enough); a forward-looking framework for the dynamic nature of markets and a constant review mechanism; and enforcement and "front-line" supervision of capital market institutions like stock exchanges, clearing houses, etc.

Government Securities

Government securities markets are considered the "most natural" candidate for liquid markets, as the yield curve for government securities, virtually being free from credit risk, could serve as a benchmark in pricing other financial assets. As a result, government securities are often used by dealers as a major hedging tool for interest rate risk, and as underlying assets and collateral for related markets such as the futures and options markets. May I also add, an alternative to government securities in the case of an insufficient supply could be private instruments, such as interest-rate swaps.

Let me refer to a recent BIS paper[2]. According to this paper, there are five inter-related guiding principles for policy recommendations concerning liquid markets: (i) maintaining (or rather creating) a competitive market structure ("contestable markets"-idea); (ii) reaching for a low level of fragmentation (higher liquidity through a larger trading supply of securities; (iii) trade-off between a liquid large-volume market of homogeneous products and a less liquid, but specific need-adjustable heterogeneous product market); (iv) minimizing transaction costs; (v) encouraging the heterogeneity of market participants (especially through attracting non-resident investors); and ensuring a sound and safe market infrastructure.

Accordingly, the practical policy recommendations would be: (I) ensuring an appropriate distribution of maturity and issue frequency through establishing large benchmark issues at key maturities; (ii) minimizing the liquidity-impairing effect of taxes; (iii) enhancing the transparency of sovereign issuers and issue schedules and of trading information, while paying due attention to the anonymity of market participants; (iv) ensuring the safety and standardization in trading and settlement practices; and (v) developing futures and options markets.

---

[1] Corporate Governance of Family Businesses in Asia, by Haider A. Khan, ADBI Working Paper 3; A Study of Corporate Governance and Financing in Selected DMCs, Draft Final Report, ADB.

[2] How Should We Design Deep and Liquid Markets - the case of government securities, BIS, September 1999.

Furthermore, it may also be noted that Central Bank activities have an impact on market liquidity through the monetary policy decisions, the dissemination of information, direct market transactions, and the role of a provider of clearing and settlement. The knowledge of the dynamics of market liquidity is still limited.

Domestic Bond Market Development

The government is considered to be the key actor in various possible roles such as an issuer, regulator, facilitator, promoter and catalyst. Government bond market is expected to be the foundation for the broader domestic bond market. However, it is essential that the government strike a *balance between debt management and bond market development*, that it support the market through a sound *legal framework*, and that it promotes a level playing field for all financial instruments and market participants through *consistent economic policies*. Besides, it is very important that the debt management and bond market development strategy are *consistent with fiscal and monetary policies* as well as with the *financial sector development* strategy.

An *effective* regulatory and supervision framework for the bond market, intermediaries, institutional investors and other market participants should provide for adequate *investor protection and sound business practices*. A recent study[1] of APEC, for example, explicitly names a range of transparency-enhancing *disclosure requirements* as well as internationally accepted *accounting standards* as important features for a market. In this context, an objective criteria-based differentiation between public offering and private placement, as well as between institutional and private investors, is deemed helpful. Other aspects are an *appropriate supervisory and regulatory authority*, clear definitions and responsibilities under a comprehensive legal and regulatory framework, and different *governance* aspects.

Clear and *unambiguous rules and procedures*, legal enforceability, a risk management system with rules for the various categories of risk (principal, liquidity risk etc.), short settlement periods, timely dissemination of information and suitable contingency arrangements are also important. Certainty about a *reliable pricing for bonds* in the domestic market encourages investors and intermediaries to participate in the market. A *competitive trading structure* and efficient, reliable, and standardized *trading and settlement processes* enhance liquidity while minimizing transaction costs.

The establishment of reliable *benchmark yield-curves,* through a number of measures (e.g. regular issuance of bonds along the entire maturity curve, etc.) together with different transparency and information requirements, is critically important. It may also be said that the *heterogeneity of market participants* and the development of the derivatives market and facilities are also supposed to increase liquidity and trading activities.

Furthermore, effective risk management by both the issuers and the investors is deemed important in fostering the development of domestic bond markets. Some simple rules can be derived from a range of *risk management frameworks;* e.g. the asset and liability management approach, using static as well as dynamic risk management techniques.

Credit rating agencies play an important role in bond market development through enhancing transparency and objectivity. It is important to conduct a *risk audit* of governments, as well as private

---

[1]   Compendium on Sound Practices - Guidelines to Facilitate the Development of Domestic Bond Markets in APEC Member Countries, APEC, September 1999.

issuers, in order to identify the exposure of the respective bond program, and liquidity, maturity, currency mismatch and government guarantee risks. A carefully designed and fully understood *hedging strategy* (using derivatives, etc.) can help to limit exposure and risks.

It is also often suggested that governments should *avoid setting minimum credit rating requirements* for bond issuers in order to avoid a drift of issuance activities into risky unregulated channels. *Credit rating agencies* should be encouraged to maintain and improve their credibility and reputation by avoiding conflict of interests in their ownership, staffing, revenue structure, and decision-making process.

Last but not the least, one issue on which we are brainstorming at the moment here at the Institute is the desired role of banks in the development of bond markets. The issue emanates from the very fact that financial markets in Asia and the Pacific are dominated by the banks. Given this, could a bond market develop without their involvement?

The Round Table

Ladies and gentlemen, let me now turn to the of this Round Table subject. It appears that many countries in the region are already involved in, or considering, reform of their capital markets. A consensus is emerging on the motivation for domestic bond market development. However, the task is arduous. On the other hand, many countries in the region also suffer from a lack of trained personnel for regulating and monitoring the financial markets and for developing the securities market in particular. You may agree with me in saying that the markets are almost always many steps ahead of the regulators. Unless our regulators' skills match those of the market players, it is very difficult to discipline them to ensure that they will not cause widespread disruption to the markets. This is because the so-called serious information asymmetry between the borrowers and lenders is unique to the financial market.

For the interest of those who did not attend the Tokyo Seminar last week, let me give you this information that we just completed at the Tokyo Seminar. The seminar focussed on regulatory issues relating to recent developments in securities market, such as, cross-border securities transaction, online securities, and de-mutualization of exchanges.

The Round Table for which we are gathered here is organized in two parts. The first Part will focus on the progress in capital market development in Asia in general. The second Part will look at the development of bond markets in selected emerging economies in Asia. The second part will also review the issues related to regional bond markets in Asia, the experience of OECD countries, and the roles of security laws and regulators.

Let me also say that we are very fortunate to have distinguished speakers from national agencies such as securities commissions, securities boards and financial supervisory agencies, as well as academia.

We also have resource speakers from the ADB who have been involved in undertaking detailed country-level studies on capital market development, and government bond market development. We also have our research scholar, from the ADB Institute, who has been working on the issue of sequencing of financial market development, to make a presentation in this regard.

I am sure the Round Table will be productive in terms of generating and exchanging useful ideas.

I wish you a very good deliberation on the issues tabled and a fruitful discussion on each of them.

FUTURE INTERNATIONAL FINANCIAL ARCHITECTURE
AND REGIONAL CAPITAL MARKET DEVELOPMENT

by
Mr. Haruhiko Kuroda

First of all, I would like to thank you for giving me this opportunity to speak before such a distinguished audience. Taking advantage of this opportunity, I would like to express my personal views on the future international financial architecture and regional capital market development.

I.   Background and Necessity of Strengthening the International Financial Architecture

The Asian currency crisis began in the summer of 1997 in Thailand and instantly spread to Indonesia, Korea, and eventually all over Asia. During the crisis, about $100 billion worth of funds reportedly flowed out of Asia. A year later, Russia was hit by a currency crisis and at the end of 1998, it was Brazil's turn. During this 18-month period, many emerging economies had either been directly hit or at least affected by their worst crisis since World War II. These developments caused experts to conclude that these almost simultaneous global currency crises were caused not simply by inherent problems in individual emerging economies, but rather by defects in the international financial system.

II.   G7 Finance Ministers' Report on Strengthening the International Financial Architecture

Thus, with the Group of Seven major countries at its core, the international community started to examine reform of the international financial system. At the Cologne summit last June, the G7 leaders welcomed the report prepared by their Finance Ministers on strengthening the international financial architecture.

In fact, the G7 countries had once reviewed the international financial system after the Mexican currency crisis of late 1994 to early 1995. However, at that time, they concluded only that the transparency of each country's economy should be increased and that the International Monetary Fund's financial resources should be strengthened.

Even immediately after the outbreak of the Asian currency crisis, the lack of transparency inherent in the public and private sectors of Asian economies, often dubbed "crony capitalism," was criticized sharply.

The G7 Finance Ministers' report eventually adopted at the Cologne summit was unprecedented in that the G7 leaders, taking fully into account the recent worldwide currency crisis, agreed to a comprehensive reform of the international financial architecture. Their report provides many useful and important principles and prescriptions to strengthen the international architecture.

III.　Progress in Strengthening the International Financial Architecture

Now, I would like to review developments that have taken place in several areas since the G7 Finance Ministers' report was issued.

1.　*Strengthening and reforming international institutions and arrangements*

There have been four major developments in the area of strengthening and reforming international institutions and arrangements

First, at the IMF's annual meeting last year, the Board of Governors decided to transform the IMF's Interim Committee into the International Monetary and Financial Committee, and to make it a permanent body.

Second, the Group of Twenty Finance Ministers and Central Governors, the so-called 'G20', was established to provide a new mechanism for informal dialogue in the framework of the Bretton Woods institutional system, to broaden discussions on key economic and financial policy issues, and to contribute to consensus building among its members. The inaugural meeting of the Group was held last December in Berlin.

Third, the Financial Stability Forum (FSF), which was created last year, has examined issues concerning highly leveraged institutions (HLIs), capital flows, and offshore financial centers. Final reports on the three topics were just released.

Fourth, the necessity of streamlining the IMF's facilities was recently emphasized by the United States. The essence of the U.S. proposal is that the IMF should be more limited in its financial involvement with member countries, in other words, it should lend selectively and with short maturities.

Concerning reform of the IMF, Japan has long expressed its views that (a) the focus of surveillance and programs should be responsive to potentially abrupt large-scale cross- border capital movements, (b) the involvement of the IMF in structural policies should be limited to cases directly related to crises, and (c) its transparency and decision- making process should be improved. These views are basically in line with the U.S. view that the IMF's lending should focus on coping with crises.

In order to provide appropriate and adequate international financial support for economies in crisis, it is extremely important to secure sufficient resources for the IMF. In this context, we have to continue to pay due attention to strengthening the financial base of the IMF.

Another imperative element of IMF reform is to redistribute quota shares to better reflect the changing economic realities of member countries since quota is a basis for each member's access limit to IMF resources as well as a basis for decision-making in the IMF.

2.　*Enhancing transparency and promoting best practices*

Let me now turn to the area of enhancing transparency and promoting best practices.

Major steps have been taken to enhance the transparency and accountability of the IMF through disclosure of the content of IMF discussions, publication of IMF staff papers, and the voluntary disclosure of Article IV consultation papers. These developments are certainly welcome, but further efforts are needed.

The implementation of internationally agreed upon standards and codes is important in facilitating rational decision-making by investors, in helping financial markets function effectively, and in promoting responsible and sound policies by governments. Therefore, it is necessary to disseminate international standards and codes steadily, with due consideration for the specific circumstances of each country.

The IMF has decided to become a core mechanism for monitoring the implementation of standards and codes. This process will be carried out on a modular basis covering a wide range of standards and codes, with the IMF responsible for its core areas of expertise and other institutions such as the World Bank, the OECD, and the Basel Committee, taking responsibility for other areas.

3. *Strengthening financial systems in emerging economies*

It is vital that emerging economies select an appropriate exchange rate regime in order to reduce their vulnerability to crises. Concerning the type of exchange rate regime that should be adopted by emerging market economies, Japan has long expressed its reservations about the so-called 'two corner solution', which calls for either a fixed exchange rate system based on a currency board or some other rigid system, or a freely floating exchange rate system. A consensus has emerged in recent IMF discussions that the appropriate exchange rate regime would vary depending upon the country's circumstances. For example, for an open emerging economy, one option could be to aim at stabilizing the currency's value by adopting as a reference a basket of currencies of its major trade and investment partners.

4. *Response to highly leveraged institutions (HLIs)*

The issue of highly leveraged institutions is particularly important. In international discussions to date, a consensus has been reached on enhancing disclosure by all market participants, including HLIs, ensuring appropriate counter-party risk management in their transactions, and enhancing regulatory oversight as recommended by the FSF Working Group's final report on HLIs. Achieving progress in putting in place and implementing the necessary measures in this respect is certainly important. In addition, as the FSF's meeting last March emphasized, direct regulation should be reconsidered if, upon review, the implementation of the report's recommendations do not adequately address the concerns identified.

5. *Private sector involvement for crisis prevention and resolution*

It is extremely important to strengthen the involvement of the private sector in preventing and resolving crises. Since it would be difficult to continue the bail out of private investors using public funds, and this also involves moral hazard, there is an international consensus that it is essential to seek the cooperation of all private sector creditors, including bondholders. However, the actual implementation of such efforts is fraught with difficulty. I will touch upon this issue later.

IV.   Regional Capital Market Development

Strengthening financial institutions and improving the supervision of financial systems are easier said than done. When it comes to supervising banks, there is an established international organization -- the Basel Committee on Banking Supervision (BCBS) -- however, its members are all from industrialized countries. If the IMF were to try to force emerging economies to abide by the rules decreed by the Basel Committee, such a move might be resisted.

Though it is dangerous for a country to depend on too much short-term capital from foreign countries, there is no simple standard suitable for all countries. The negative effects of regulating capital inflow also need to be considered.

Even if industrialized countries reinforced the risk management of financial institutions that lend money to HLIs, simply raising the risk weights required by the BCBS-set Basel Capital Accord would not be sufficient. It is also necessary to strengthen the risk-management capability of the financial institutions themselves.

For governments to be able to make HLIs, including hedge funds, disclose information, some form of legal action will be necessary. But there is a problem with this. Most hedge funds are established in offshore markets, where transactions are free from control by outside regulatory bodies. Also, given that most hedge funds are managed from the United States, whether the U. S. Congress accepts such a measure would be critical.

It is extremely difficult for governments to obtain private sector involvement, as this means asking private lenders to assume responsibility. When Korea was hit by a currency crisis in late 1997, the G7 countries asked their banks to rollover their loans to Korean banks. This drastically alleviated a critical situation. By complying with the moral suasion of their governments, the banks of G7 countries benefited and the self-sustained flow of funds was recovered. However, in most other cases, such measures have not been effective.

As regards the outstanding bonds issued by emerging countries, though Pakistan and Ukraine have recently succeeded in restructuring their debts without a contagion effect on other economies, generally speaking, restructuring emerging countries' debts has proved extremely difficult. Though various coercive measures have been discussed, including the forcible restructuring of debts through the so-called standstill approach or the imposition of restrictions on capital outflow, in the worst case, none of the measures would be easy to implement.

In short, although some intervention in the market, including financial supervision and private sector involvement, may be unavoidable if we are to ensure the smooth functioning of the global financial and capital markets, it will be a very difficult task.

Furthermore, market intervention risks hampering the inflow of funds to emerging countries could delay their economic growth. We have to remember that the massive capital flow into Asian countries between the mid-1980s and the mid-1990s brought about dramatic economic growth in the region, although in retrospect the inflow could be deemed excessive. In any event, we should not ruin the whole by trying to correct a small fault. The smooth inflow of funds to emerging countries needs to be secured by utilizing the functions of the global financial and capital markets. I believe that we have to explore 'a third way' to enhance stability.

To this end, the first crucial step would be to develop and maintain a market in which international funds, including those going to emerging economies, can flow without impediment. Efforts to help emerging economies develop their domestic capital markets are particularly important.

Since the saving ratio is as high as 30 to 40 percent in emerging Asian economies, their growth could have been largely achieved without overseas borrowing as far as the total amount of funds is concerned. However, when a substantial part of these savings was channeled overseas, short-term funds were imported in larger amounts to feed the economies, resulting in the Asian financial crisis and its global reverberations.

The most pressing need therefore is to develop capital markets in each emerging economy to facilitate the adequate flow of funds to where they are needed. The establishment of fair accounting standards, settlement systems, and taxation systems, and the removal of unfair market domination are indispensable for the development of capital markets.

In emerging Asian economies, loans have been the most common method by far of raising capital, while stock markets have been widely targeted by speculative investors, and bond markets have been underdeveloped. This is why the New Miyazawa Initiative in the second stage places particular priority on the development of bond markets. The initiative aims at boosting financing through bond issuance by guaranteeing bonds issued by Asian countries.

The second step should be for Asia to establish a regional capital market, because capital providers have nationalities and regionalities although funds can move freely across borders. Such reasoning is the main factor behind Europe's great efforts to set up a regional capital market. Likewise, U.S. capital has been invested primarily in the United States and Latin America because ordinary investors have a greater understanding and trust of their own countries and neighboring countries.

Fortunately, in Asia, there is a large pool of savings that could be effectively used for mutual benefit through a regional capital market. A common mechanism to enhance the credibility of such a regional marketplace, standardized bonds for issuance in the region, and a regional credit-rating organization are measures worth considering to support the distribution of such funds within Asia.

It is vital, as a third step, to put in place sound macroeconomic, financial, and structural policies in Asian countries to enable markets to function smoothly.

A regional surveillance system, which has already been adopted under the Manila Framework, whose members include Australia, Japan, other key Asian countries, and the U.S., should be enforced through various forums. Also worth considering is the establishment of a safety net, linked to the surveillance system, to support the financial market.

Finally, to enable the financial and capital markets to contribute to the economic growth of the region, exchange rates must be stabilized to reflect the fundamentals of the regional economies.

Even though currently it would be difficult to set up a global mechanism to stabilize foreign exchange rates, a regional mechanism is possible and may be necessary. For example, many northern, central, and eastern European countries peg their currencies to the euro. In Latin America, a few countries peg their currencies to the dollar. It would be difficult for the yen in its own to play a role similar to that of the euro and the dollar; however, the region could start with a basket composed of the yen, the euro, and the dollar before imagining a common currency for Asia.

Ahead of the worldwide reform of the international financial system, and in the wake of the Asian crisis, emerging economies independently introduced various domestic controls and regulations. It is understandable that they resorted to such countermeasures; however, it is an undesirable solution for the long term. A shift from the individual nation approach to a coordinated regional strategy may be a practical alternative for emerging economies.

PROGRESS IN MACROECONOMIC STABILITY AND CAPITAL MARKET REFORMS IN ASIA

by
Mr. Kunio Saito

I. Introduction

I would like to deviate slightly from the theme of this session. I will certainly talk about progress, but in "Macroeconomic Recovery and Financial Sector Reforms in Asia".

I make this deviation for three reasons: (i) almost three years after the crisis, policy focus is now on economic recovery, rather than stabilization; (ii) reform and restructuring efforts in the last three years have involved the entire financial sector, and not just the capital markets; and (iii) perhaps most importantly, I believe that in this way, my presentation can provide a broader and more useful background to today's and tomorrow's discussions of capital market reforms. I must also admit that there are many other people here who are more qualified than I am to talk about capital markets.

II. Economic Recovery

My conclusions on the first broad topic—macroeconomic recovery—are twofold:

- In most Asian countries, economic recovery has begun. Growth outturns for 1999 exceeded earlier expectations, and prospects for 2000 are good. Progress has certainly been made in this respect.

- Nevertheless, policy challenges remain to ensure that the ongoing recovery is transformed into high and sustained growth. Most importantly, financial policies need to be rebalanced to a more neutral stance and reform and restructuring efforts need to be continued.

To elaborate, I will first review developments in 1999 and the outlook for 2000, and then discuss risks to this outlook and policy challenges to deal with them.

Developments in 1999 and prospects for 2000

I think it is fair to say that at the beginning of 1999, not many of us expected that the Asian economies would recover so quickly and so strongly from the crisis. There were of course some indications—financial stabilization had been achieved, and stock markets had been staging a strong recovery since mid-1998. Nevertheless, many of us were talking about a slow U-shaped recovery and were projecting negative growth for almost all Asian economies. For example, the IMF's World Economic Outlook published in December 1998 projected that growth in 1999 would be minus1 percent for Korea, minus 3 percent for Indonesia, minus 2 percent for Malaysia, and 1 percent for Thailand. I must add that the IMF was not the only institution forecasting these negative growth rates. Other institutions were similarly pessimistic, as were the governments and central banks of the region.

As the year went on, however, economic and financial conditions have improved progressively and dramatically. And growth projections were revised upwards several times during the year—a process which was exactly the opposite of what had happened in 1998. Just as we underestimated the severity of the crisis in 1998, we underestimated the speed and strength of the recovery in 1999. (Table 1)

The growth outturn in 1999, as estimated now, was impressive. Korea's growth is estimated to have been close to 10 percent. China's growth was around 7 percent, while growth rates of Malaysia, Thailand, Singapore, Hong Kong SAR and Taiwan POC were in the range of 3-6 percent. Growth in the Philippines and Vietnam are likely to have been slightly below that range, while Indonesia's growth was close to zero, a substantial improvement compared with a contraction of over 10 percent in 1998.

For 2000, growth prospects are good. The IMF's earlier projections published last October, showed that the growth of most Asian countries will range between 4 and 7 percent. These projections are now being revised, taking into account the strong Q4 performance in some countries. And it is likely that more countries will have their projected growth rates in the upper half of the 4-7 percent range.

Asia's strong growth performance is a part of a global economic upturn. According again to the IMF's last WEO, global growth was estimated to be 3 percent for 1999 and 3.5 percent for 2000. These numbers represent the result of a few rounds of upward revisions during 1999. And they are likely to be revised further, again, upward. The most important factor underlying these upward revisions and the continuation of strong global growth are the continued impressive expansion of the US economy. Japan's economic turnaround, (where growth for 1999 was originally projected to be minus 0.5 percent but turned out to be close to one percent, positive), and Europe's stronger growth (than had been anticipated) were also important factors. Of course, the strong recovery in Asia and elsewhere also contributed.

What were the key factors responsible for the dramatic economic improvements in 1999? What explains the strong growth momentum that is continuing into 2000?

- In my view, the first impulse for the recovery in crisis-hit Asian countries came from policy factors—supportive fiscal and monetary policies and progress in structural reforms. These policies played a crucial role in restoring confidence and supporting the resumption of growth in domestic demand.

- Asia's economic recovery, then, gained momentum from rising exports. The stronger global growth that I just mentioned played a crucial role in raising Asia's exports to industrial countries, as well as to other trading partners, especially in the region.

- More recently, the rising exports, and the recovery in domestic consumption, seem to have given rise to a recovery in private investment. The return of FDI and progress in corporate restructuring also helped this investment recovery. Although the situation differs considerably among countries, Asian growth in 2000 is thus likely to be more broadly based.

Risks and Policy Challenges

Let me now turn to the next topic—the risks to the projected continuation of Asian recovery and policy challenges to address such risks. Notwithstanding the improved outlook, the ongoing Asian recovery may be derailed by a number of factors, both external and domestic. I will discuss four of them.

First, one of the external factors that may have a far reaching impact on the Asian recovery is an abrupt and sharp slowdown of the US economy. This hard-landing scenario may materialize if, for example, a sudden and substantial correction in stock prices were to occur, or through a resurgence of inflationary pressures that requires a significant tightening of monetary policies. Accordingly, the US Fed has raised interest rates in several steps, and some people argue that, as shown in the recent weakening of some stock prices, these interest rate increases are showing their effects, and a soft-landing of the US economy is quite possible. But many people argue otherwise and there is no hard evidence that domestic demand is slowing from a level many people consider unsustainable. It is therefore important, I think, that US policies, especially monetary policy be kept tight.

Second, another risk to the Asian outlook is Japan's recovery which has so far been tentative and fragile and perceived so widely. The weak Q4 GDP number, released recently, did not help change this perception. However, many analysts point to a number of positive indicators especially private investment, and argue that Japan's recovery is now more robust than earlier projected. Nevertheless, it would be prudent, I think, that financial policies—especially monetary policy—remain supportive of the recovery.

Third, there are a number of other external factors that may adversely affect Asia's economic outlook. For example, a sharp increase in international market prices of oil, as indicated from the trend over the last 12 months, could have a considerable negative impact on the growth of many Asian countries, but the situation seems to have improved recently reflecting OPEC's decision to increase oil production. Also, the exchange rates of key currencies may continue to be a source of concern. Recently, some people have expressed concern about the strength of the dollar vis-à-vis euro, while some others, especially the Japanese authorities, have been worried about a premature weakening of the dollar vis-à-vis the yen. There are also related risks that investors suddenly become unwilling to continue to finance the large US deficit at current exchange and interest rates. These concerns can be addressed by attaining a better balanced-pattern of growth among industrial countries. That, in turn, requires the asymmetric adjustments of monetary policies in the US, Japan and Europe that I mentioned earlier.

Fourth, among domestic factors, a key challenge confronting many Asian countries is to transform the ongoing recovery into high and sustained growth. This will require rebalancing financial policies to a more neutral stance. The supportive fiscal policy that has been in place for the last two years needs to be moderated, and fiscal consolidation must start soon. Monetary conditions will also need to be tightened to check inflationary pressures that may arise. This tightening could be provided by greater exchange rate flexibility, as interest rates may have to be kept at relatively low levels partly to facilitate financial and corporate sector structuring. As you recall, a combination of high interest rates and an inflexible exchange rate arrangement was one of the causes of the Asian crises. And one should not repeat the same mistake.

Fifth, another domestic factor that may derail ongoing recovery is the risk that restructuring and reform efforts may be slowed down or even abandoned completely. This may happen because of reform fatigue or complacency arising from the economic recovery. Some people argue that while bank recapitalization and corporate debt restructuring are essential in restoring growth, management and operational reforms are not. They also point out that reforms come with increased unemployment which can dampen consumption. However, recapitalization and restructuring can not be attained without reforms. Reform may not boost growth in the short run, but it is crucial to strengthen the economy and sustain growth over the longer-term.

III.   Financial Sector Reforms

This brings me to my second broad topic—progress in financial sector reform and restructuring. My conclusions are, again, twofold.

Considerable progress has been made in addressing weak financial institutions and in establishing mechanisms to alleviate the risks of another financial sector crisis.

However, there is no room for complacency, as much remains to be done in both areas. Also, management and operational reforms, at the level of individual institutions, must continue, and efforts to develop modern market infrastructure need to be stepped up.

I will now elaborate on these points by going over the reform objectives and what has been done to pursue these objectives.

Reform Objectives

But let me first go back to late 1997 when reforms started under crisis conditions. As we all know, financial sector weaknesses were at the root of the Asian crisis and market attention was focused on weak institutions. At the initial stage of reform, the authorities' priority was to address market concerns over weak financial institutions, restore confidence, and thereby contain the crisis. They did not have the luxury of time to prepare a carefully designed reform plan or to follow proper sequencing. However, as the crisis was arrested, the reform agenda was broadened, with clearer reform objectives.

These objectives—or the ultimate goals of the reform—have been (i) to address the existing weaknesses of the financial sector, and (ii) to develop mechanisms to ensure that the sector remains strong—healthy, sound, and less vulnerable to another crisis. To pursue these two goals, many new policies have been introduced and many actions have been taken.

Strengthening the financial system

So, what have been done to pursue the first reform goal—of addressing existing financial sector weaknesses? Quite a lot. I will now list the key measures in five areas.

(i)   The legal framework has been strengthened. Legislation has been introduced and clarified to empower governments to intervene private businesses—including to suspend or close them. To support government interventions, arrangements have been made to provide guarantees to depositors and, in some cases, creditors of closed institutions, as well as to provide public funds when deemed appropriate. Also, rules concerning loan classification, provisioning, capital adequacy requirements etc. have been tightened. Disclosure rules have been extended to cover these variables and, in general, made more strict. Also, bankruptcy and foreclosure laws have been, or are being, updated in many countries.

(ii)   New specialized agencies have been created to deal with financial sector problems, manage nationalized assets, and conduct bank supervision. These institutions—which are known by such acronyms as FRA (in Thailand), IBRA (Indonesia), KAMCO (Korea), Danaharta and

Danamodal (Malaysia)—are expected to be more independent of other branches of the governments and are thus more objective in their operations.

(iii)   Weak and insolvent financial institutions have been dealt with. You will still remember the announcements made in late 1997 regarding the closures of 58 finance companies in Thailand, 16 banks in Indonesia, and 24 merchant banks in Korea. Those were just the beginning, as more closures have taken place subsequently. Also, a large number of banks have been nationalized or brought under government control, and are currently going through a process of rehabilitation (including finding new owners). Although unavoidable, reform in this context has been very deep and wide-ranging. In the extreme case of Indonesia, almost two-thirds of financial institutions have been closed, nationalized, or otherwise, brought under government control.

(iv)   Measures have also been taken to strengthen the remaining solvent institutions. This has involved recapitalization of these institutions, which was supported by public funds when the institutions concerned were considered to have credible plans for management and operational reforms. It has also involved disposal of non-performing loans and related restructuring of corporate debts. There is, of course, a close link between recapitalization of financial institutions and the disposal of their non performing loans. In some countries financial institutions have now begun raising capital in the markets (with or without government support), and moving ahead with strategic mergers and alliances (often with government encouragement). Clearly, these moves—and management and operational reform of individual institutions—must continue.

(v)   Beyond these developments, financial sector reform will involve the privatization of nationalized institutions and assets, including sales of these assets to foreign entities. This process has begun, but, again, much remains to be done.

Developing better mechanisms for bank supervision

What has been done with regard to the second reform goal—of developing mechanisms to strengthen bank supervision and to help avoid future financial sector problems? Four points are worth making.

(i)   As mentioned earlier, prudential rules (on loan classification, provisioning, and capital adequacy requirements) and disclosure procedures have been tightened. And specialized agencies have been created to oversee the compliance with these rules and procedures and to ensure that financial institutions remain healthy and sound.

(ii)   Internationally, a number of codes and the standards have been developed and are being adopted to ensure that these prudential and disclosure rules are applied appropriately. These international codes and rules include the "Basel Core Principles on Bank Supervision", IOSCO's, "Objectives and Principles of Securities Regulation", and the IMF's "Code of Transparency on Monetary and Financial Sector Policies".

(iii)   Also, the IMF, and the World Bank are now tasked to conduct FSAP/FSSA exercises on member countries. This exercise aims to assess the strength of the country's financial sector, including by looking at how fully it is complying with various international codes and standards. More importantly, the exercise calls for the staff of the Fund and other institutions to work with the country authorities on resolving any financial sector problems that have potential to become a source of instability—if and when such problems are found. This may involve technical assistance from the Fund and other international agencies.

(iv)   In short, it is fair to say, I think, that the mechanisms for alleviating the risks of financial sector problems have been developed. The remaining challenge is to put them firmly in place and implement them.

Progress in financial sector reforms

As I just mentioned, a number of new policies have been introduced, and governments have intervened in many cases of weak financial institutions, and spent a considerable amount of public funds. Two questions can be asked at this stage.

The first question is: have Asian countries made progress in implementing financial sector forms? My answer is positive. I think it is fair to say that considerable progress has been made in many respects. Reform actions—such as the closing of some weak financial institutions and the recapitalization of some others—represent an important step towards strengthening the financial sector. Implementing these reform measures is an achievement in itself.

The second question is: have reform efforts been effective in achieving their goals? Have financial sectors in Asian countries been substantially strengthened? Is Asia now less vulnerable to another crisis? I hesitate to answer positively to these questions. But I will quickly add that it is premature to make judgement, as many important reforms are still continuing. Notwithstanding the progress made so far, much still remains to be done to achieve the ultimate reform goals—of strengthening financial sectors and establishing mechanisms to keep them strong.

There are, of course, considerable variances among countries regarding how far they have progressed in their reform process. Some countries—like Korea—are well ahead in the process, while some others—like Indonesia—are behind. In Korea, statistics on non-performing loans and compliance with capital adequacy requirements have improved and are now close to international standards. Banks have started extending credit to the private sector again, while following more stringent post-crisis prudential rules. We all know that the situation in Indonesia is, unfortunately, quite the opposite, and the other Asian countries fall somewhere between these two extremes.

IV.   Conclusion

In concluding, I should link up the two broad topics I have been discussing so far—economic recovery and reforms. In my view, progress in reform has helped reestablish confidence in markets and thus provide a basis for economic recovery. Obviously, reform is essential to strengthen the economic structure and transform the recovery into high and sustained growth over the medium term. Nevertheless, continuation of reform now appears at risk, as complacency arising from ongoing recovery may slow the reform effort. So, I will end my presentation by reiterating what has now become the IMF's motto—complacency must be avoided, and reform efforts must continue.

THE ACTIVITIES OF THE IMPLEMENTATION COMMITTEE ON IOSCO OBJECTIVES AND PRINCIPLES

by
Mr. Andrew Procter

F33 O16 G12 G24
G19 G18 G28 (asia)

Introduction

Following the decision of the Executive Committee in February 1999, a Committee was established to implement a mandate to:

a) Develop implementation and assessment methodologies for the IOSCO *Objectives and Principles*;

b) Explore means of offering guidance to international financial institutions in their use of the *Principles*.

The Committee is chaired by the Securities and Futures Commission, Hong Kong. There are 20 other members, drawn from all regions and from both developed and emerging markets.

Consistent with the second part of the mandate, on cooperation with IFIs, The World Bank, The International Monetary Fund, The OECD, The African Development Bank, The Asian Development Bank, The European Bank for Re-Construction and Development and The Inter-American Development Bank also participate in the work of the Committee.

Work Program

The Committee has responded to the first part of its mandate with two exercises. The first exercise, intended to provide a rapid assessment of current implementation among IOSCO members, is a high level self-evaluation based on the entire *Principles* document. At the same time, a more detailed self-evaluation will be performed on discrete sections of the Principles

Completion of the high level survey with respect to all Principles will be an immediate and clear organization-wide statement of commitment to the document and will focus the attention of individual regulators upon any areas in need of urgent reform. (IOSCO Members have resolved to use their best efforts within their jurisdiction to ensure adherence to the *Principles*. This commitment extended to seeking changes to legislation, policy or regulatory arrangements that may impede adherence to the *Principles*.) The more detailed surveys are intended to be very much more rigorous inquiries. Over time, it is intended that all aspects of the Principles will be subject to this more detailed assessment.

Principles relating to The Regulator and Principles for Issuers are the first two discrete sections of the Principles that have been selected for more detailed evaluation. These two areas are of great relevance to the stability of the international financial system.

Principles relating to the Regulator include principles for self-regulation and principles for enforcement of securities regulation (Principles 1 – 10), and cover subjects relating to the responsibility, independence, accountability, processes and powers of regulators.

The Principles for Issuers (Principles 14 – 16) address issues of market transparency, accounting and auditing standards, and the fair and equitable treatment of shareholders. In addition to the importance of these subjects to the strength of the international financial architecture, this work will complement the work done by the OECD on the Draft Principles of Corporate Governance.

The three surveys have been prepared both to allow for an assessment of current levels of adherence to the *Objectives and Principles* and also to seek information on movement towards adherence. Members are expected to provide their self-assessment answers by 30 April 2000.

The documents are drafted so that they may be used:

a) for self-assessment by IOSCO Members;

b) as the basis for peer review amongst IOSCO Members (discussed below);

c) by international financial institutions (IFIs) (discussed below).

Self Assessment by IOSCO Members

There is, at present, no established procedure or infrastructure to support, on a timely basis, either peer review or IOSCO or IFI review of a large number of IOSCO Members to determine the extent of adherence to the *Objectives and Principles*.

In the circumstances, the most expeditious course of action is to ask every IOSCO Member to undertake a self-assessment using the documents that have been prepared or that are under preparation by the Committee.

IOSCO has prior experience of such self-assessments and Members are fully aware of their potential limitations in the absence of some external discipline and scrutiny. The result of self-assessments may not be fully reliable.

The Committee is considering the possibility of peer review as a complement to self-assessment. It is far too early to say whether this will prove viable and acceptable to IOSCO's Members. The issues that arise include conflict of interest, costs, resourcing and transparency. Conflict of interest is a more acute issue in the highly competitive securities markets than in, for example, the banking sector or in the FATF peer reviews on money laundering.

The work of the International Financial Institutions

The IMF and the World Bank are involved in a joint pilot program, The Financial Sector Assessment Program. To the extent that the perceived financial sector vulnerabilities of a country are expected to include securities markets issues, the IMF and World Bank have begun to make use of the IOSCO assessment documents in their FSAPs. Senior staff from IOSCO Members have also contributed their expertise to the assessments themselves.

It is important to recognize that the IOSCO *Objectives and Principles* were not developed to be used for a "pass" or "fail" grading. The *Objectives and Principles* are recognised to be aspirational. Members agree to do what they can to implement them. It is also clear that any particular Principle may be able to be satisfied in variety of ways and, indeed, that may reflect the legal and other circumstances of a jurisdiction. That makes it difficult to use the document for assessment purposes. A sophisticated understanding of the issues is required.

Members of IOSCO appear to be strongly of the view that IOSCO should remain responsible for the establishment of principles and standards in the securities sector. They also appear willing to remain involved in any work to assist Members in the implementation of those *Principles*.

The IOSCO position on continued involvement may be partly a recognition that there is no other organisation that is apparently willing and able to perform the role in the securities sector. When he spoke at the 1999 Annual Conference of IOSCO, the then Managing Director of the IMF in addressing this issue said:

> "In executing these new tasks, it is quite evident that the IMF will have to enhance and supplement its in-house expertise by relying heavily on the skills, resources, and advice of the many agencies engaged in defining standards. But, even more, we would look to the standard-setting agencies to play an active role in developing methodologies for assessing observance of their standards. We shall have to develop with IOSCO and organizations like it a high degree of collaboration. As we proceed, the most pressing needs will be for technical assistance in countries adopting new standards, and the human resource constraints may well be the largest challenge we face, since in some areas, there are simply not enough people with adequate skills to go around. An uncommon degree of cooperation among the many international bodies and national agencies is now essential to meet this challenge."

It remains to be seen, therefore, to what extent the IMF, the World Bank and others will wish to take on any evaluation role in relation to international standards and principles in the securities sector. If they do contribute to such a role, then there will be resource and skill issues to be addressed.

It will be a key issue for the coming period to determine what role the IFIs (and the IMF and World Bank, in particular) should play in the implementation of IOSCO's *Principles* and standards in general.

If, as seems likely, there is a growing international consensus that the IFIs are to play a key role in implementation, then the question of their resourcing needs to be addressed.

It is clear from their participation in the IOSCO Implementation Committee that there is great potential for the IFIs to work more closely with IOSCO on the resolution of these issues. The IOSCO self-assessments are an important potential foundation for the FSAPs and IOSCO Members have the skill sets that are in short supply in the IFIs.

The Financial Stability Forum

The Financial Stability Forum Working Group on Offshore Jurisdictions is considering the need for assessments to be made against internationally agreed standards and principles and has discussed the possibility that organisations such as IOSCO should be asked to expel Members that do not meet those standards or observe those principles. The Working Group reported in March 2000.

The other relevant FSF Working Group, on The Implementation of Standards is chaired by Andrew Sheng, Chair of the Hong Kong Securities and Futures Commission. IOSCO is represented by its Secretary-General.

The Task Force has met three times and a draft report has been prepared for submission to the next FSF Meeting. The Report is in the form of an "issues paper" and is expected to be available shortly from the FSF web site. The Report:

- Identifies the main challenges or obstacles to implementing standards, and discusses the key success factors to address these challenges;

- Outlines a strategy for implementation that leverages on the success factors, builds on existing initiatives, and highlights areas that need further attention; and

- Sets out options and next steps for the Forum to consider.

The Report is positive about the work of IOSCO in articulating principles and in "setting standards". The Report is also positive in its discussion of the type of self assessment being undertaken by IOSCO.

The Report identifies the need for further work in areas including:

- The development of incentives (including market incentives);

- The role of the IFI's (especially the IMF and World Bank) and the availability of skills and resources to undertake assessments.

DEVELOPMENT OF BOND MARKETS IN ASIA

Session 1

Introduction

A BRIEF OVERVIEW: CREATION OF ASIAN BOND MARKET

by
Professor Eisuke Sakakibara

Distinguished participants, ladies and gentlemen. It is indeed an honor for me to have this opportunity to speak to you this afternoon.

It has been widely recognized by now that one of the major causes of the so-called "Asian" crises was a currency and maturity mismatch. As early as December, 1990 Donald Tsang, Financial Secretary of Hong Kong called for the creation of a regional debt market to try to avoid such a mismatch. "What Asia lacks, and Europe and the U.S. have, is a deep, liquid and mature debt market where three things can occur. First, governments and corporations can borrow long to invest long, thus eliminating the maturity mismatch inherent in Asia. Second, corporations can issue paper in U.S.-dollar, yen or euro currencies, with clearing and settlement in Asian times, thus eliminating currency mismatches and developing a truly deep Asian debt market along the lines of Euro-dollar and euro-yen markets. Third, finance ministers in Asian economies can foster a vibrant debt market with adequate risk management by investing their reserves in Asia."[1]

According to BIS, in the first quarter of 1999, the Euro-dollar bond market accounted for 70.5 percent of total bond issues of 766.7 billion U.S. dollars. If we combine Euro-dollar, European currency denominated, and Euro-yen bonds, they reach 93.0 percent of the total. If you add 2.8 percent for the Yankee bond and 2.0 per cent for the Swiss franc bond in each of these domestic markets, the sum would reach 97.8 percent.

Samurai bond, Hong Kong-dollar, Singapore-dollar, Australian-dollar denominated bonds, in their respective markets together only account for 1.4 percent of the total. Issuance of Shogun bond was nil during the period when the Hong Kong market foreign currency denominated bond was 0.4 percent of the total. Thus, even at the time when the "Asian" crisis was coming to an end, the world bond market was dominated by Europe and the U.S., particularly by Euro-currency (Euro-dollar, Euro-euro and Euro-yen) issues.

What accounts for this dominance? There are a large number of issuers in Asia, but somehow they have not used markets in Asia. In all of the major Asian markets, (Hong Kong, Singapore, Sydney and Tokyo) authorities have welcomed and encouraged bond issuance by non-residents and there are no legal constraints for bond issuance. However, there seem to be some significant infrastructure problems in these markets. First, the settlement and clearing system has been inadequate, requiring a much longer transaction time as compared to London, for example. Second, repo markets have not developed sufficiently. Third, although there are not direct regulations hampering transactions, such practices as withholding taxes, or the existence of multiple regulatory agencies has discouraged issuers. Also, in some countries the numbers of investors, particularly institutional investors in debts

---

[1]   "The Asian Debt Market", Asiaweek, Dec. 19, 1997.

instruments, have been somewhat limited. As a result of all these factors, the liquidity in Asian markets has been low and there have not been sufficient numbers of market makers.

Asian countries have traditionally relied on indirect financing, or bank lending, as a major intermediation mechanism between savings and investment. The system worked well during the seventies and eighties when globalization and markets oriented transactions had been relatively limited. Thus, the development of debt markets, which is a substitute for bank lending, lagged behind western countries significantly. Neither authorities nor banks had an incentive or the motivation to develop markets until quite recently. Developments of debt markets meant the loss of loan business by banks.

However, dramatic globalization of the world economy driven by the IT revolution during the decade of nineties, has fundamentally altered the scene. Without the existence effective debt markets in the region, Asian countries were forced to rely on financial intermediation through Euro and New York markets by global market players. The result was the maturity and currency mismatch mentioned earlier.

Authorities in the region have now come to recognize the need to nurture the regional markets and to build necessary infrastructure. There are some who argue that markets should evolve spontaneously, without official intervention. Indeed, the Euro-markets, for example, developed without endorsement of authorities, or rather, as ways to circumvent regulations that restricted market transactions. However, it needs to be recognized that necessary infrastructure was there, for example, in London. Also, it should be noted that the chicken and egg type situation does exist here in the region. Since markets are not developed, the accompanying infrastructure has not emerged and the liquidity as a result is low and vice versa. Therefore, it is probably quite appropriate that authorities in the region make a conscious and coordinated effort to nurture markets. In addition to creating an efficient and common settlement mechanism and other necessary infrastructure, or eliminating tax disincentives, authorities could encourage market participants to start new market practices conducive to dramatically increase transactions in the region.

One interesting suggestion which has been floating around is for financial institutions to create an Asian currency based Asian Bond Index to generate greater international and Asian investor interest and demand for Asian bonds. Up to now, bond indices by leading financial institutions have not included any Asian bonds except for JGBs and investors have not had any reliable guidelines for investing in Asian debt instruments. The creation of an Asian Bond Index, by, say, a group of prominent Asian or non-Asian financial institutions could be a catalyst to start the process. In the same vein, more extensive use of international credit rating by Asian issuers would facilitate investors to assess risks associated with Asian issuers. During the initial stage of development, the utilization of public credit enhancement may be effective in increasing demand for issuers of low ratings. The New Miyazawa Plan provided credit enhancement of sovereign or semi-sovereign issues by Asian countries and such facility could be expanded to create a permanent regional mechanism to enhance credit and to secure and provide information necessary to create transparent and resilient markets in the region.

Also, bonds with an artificially created currency basket including U.S. dollar, Euro, Yen and other Asian currencies could be listed at plural markets, say, Hong Kong, Singapore, Sydney and Tokyo. To start the process, Australian, Japanese, or Singapore governments might consider floating government bonds in such new currency baskets. If authorities come up with a basket consisting of only Asian currencies, it may eventually lead to foreign exchange cooperation among these countries and finally to the creation of an Asian currency unit. This could be an interesting experiment. However, the current investor demand would be greater for a basket involving U.S. dollar, Euro and Japanese yen since such basket would effectively shield investors from currency risks resulting from somewhat volatile movement among these three currencies that we have experienced during the past few years.

Let me say that I heartily welcome the keen interest generated in the creation of regional debt markets. Some analytical work and policy dialogue has already been initiated. I sincerely hope that these efforts by international organizations, research institutions and policy authorities will lead to some concrete actions. Having participated in international discussion on such topics as international financial architecture, I have become somewhat cynical about the recent process of international dialogue which results in the creation of numerous papers and the holding of many international conferences and policy meetings but falls short of agreement on any significant concrete actions. Having become an academic, I should probably not say this but papers, particularly, papers on policies are not only useless but even harmful if they are used as excuses by authorities for not doing what they should be doing. I am sure that the Japanese and other authorities are eager to pursue the issue and that they will eventually take some action. In order to do that, the discussions with the private sector in identifying their needs and supporting their endeavors in the market seems to be extremely important. Since governments are issuers of the key debt instrument, government bills notes and bonds, they are, in a sense, a part of the market and the collaboration with the market is all more important.

In concluding, let me express my sincere hope that this round table will become a major milestone in the creation of effective and deep Asian debt markets in the near future which should serve as one of the key deterrents to the possible international financial crisis that might hit us sooner or later, again.

DEVELOPING A VIABLE CORPORATE BOND MARKET UNDER A BANK-DOMINATED SYSTEM - ANALYTICAL ISSUES AND POLICY IMPLICATIONS

by
Professor Shinji Takagi

(asic)

G12
G18 O16 G21
G28

1.   Introduction

This paper will review some of the major analytical issues that are involved in the development of a viable corporate bond market in a bank-dominated system of the type observed in much of developing or emerging Asia. This topic is particularly relevant today as the recent Asian currency crisis of 1997-98 has brought to our attention the potential danger of a bank-dominated system. Some have argued, for example, that the crisis was in part caused by a poorly supervised banking sector which, given some distorted incentive structure, had acquired mismatched balance sheets in terms of maturity, currency and sectoral allocation. As corporate financing was heavily dependent on the banking sector, the argument goes, the initial currency depreciation set in motion a downward spiral on the economy, as the resulting deterioration in the balance sheet led to a contraction of bank credit to the corporate sector, which had little alternative to bank borrowing. In other words, in a bank-based system, everything tumbles once the banking sector gets into difficulty. Hence, the call for the development of viable corporate bond markets in post-crisis Asia.

It goes without saying that a sound financial system is a prerequisite for economic recovery and sustained development. There is a large empirical literature that suggests a positive relationship between different measures of financial development and economic growth (see Levine 1997 for a survey). Moreover, this positive association does not appear to depend on how financial development is measured, whether it is defined in terms of bank liabilities, stock market capitalization or stock market trading volume, and appears independent of the particular financial structure of a country, be it bank-based or market-based. It may be, therefore, not productive to consider taking specific measures to favor either a bank-based or market-based system over the other. A more productive approach may be to consider banking sector development and securities market development as complementary, and to make sure that quality financial infrastructure is in place. Levine (2000) has called this interpretation of the empirical evidence the "financial services view" (as opposed to the bank-based or market-based view). Strengthening of the banking sector and the development of securities markets, including bond markets, must go hand in hand. This paper is an attempt to provide an analytical framework for thinking about these and other financial development issues, particularly related to the corporate bond market.

The rest of this paper is organized as follows. Section 2 will present some preliminary concepts that are useful in thinking about financial market issues, principally related to corporate finance under imperfect information. Section 3 will discuss the role of debt finance, without explicitly distinguishing public debt (or directly placed debt) from intermediated debt (or bank loans), although some particular issues may be more relevant to one type of debt than the other. Section 4 will discuss the features of intermediated debt, which is the principal vehicle of corporate financing in much of

Asia. Section 5 will then discuss the conceptual issues involved in choosing between public debt and intermediated debt in terms of resource allocation and moral hazard. Section 6 will discuss additional conceptual issues involved in the choice of bond and bank finance. Finally, in Section 7, all these issues are brought together to yield some policy implications.

2.   Preliminaries

(i)   The role of a financial system

A financial system serves an important role in an economy by (1) channeling savings to productive uses and (2) providing corporate governance. The "financing" role and the "corporate governance" role of the financial system, however, cannot be independent. For instance, when a potential investor believes that the funds will be misused by a firm, he will be reluctant to make that investment, so that otherwise profitable projects will not be funded. In other words, there must be an effective monitoring or corporate governance mechanism to minimize the problem of moral hazard (whereby the firm will shirk efforts once the funds are provided) before an adequate inflow of funds can be expected into the corporate sector.

On the financing side, the presence of asymmetric information between firms and investors (whereby the firms possess more information about the profitability of an investment project) will give rise to adverse selection, a phenomenon by which a higher interest rate would attract riskier projects, so that some cannot obtain financing at any interest rate. The market mechanism does not necessarily lead to an optimal allocation of resources in this environment. The empirically positive influence of financial development on economic growth can then be explained by the fact that a more developed financial system can better overcome these problems of moral hazard and adverse selection, so as to allocate capital to the highest value use at a minimum transactions cost.

(ii)   Finance under imperfect information

Finance matters for growth for the very reason that financial transactions are necessarily characterized by imperfect information. In fact, in an Arrow-Debreu-McKenzie world of perfect information with complete markets and no transactions cost, two firms faced with the identical investment opportunity would make an identical decision. In such a world, there would be no role for financial institutions or financial intermediaries, and the choice of debt and equity would make no difference by virtue of the Modigliani-Miller theorem. The world we live in, however, is quite different. In our world, information is imperfect, markets are incomplete, and transactions are not frictionless. In such an environment, institutions develop as a way of reducing transactions cost or mitigating the informational problems, and there is a role for government policy (Greenwald and Stiglitz 1986).

In his pioneering work on the economics of imperfect information, Akerlof (1970) explained the controlling role of "managing agencies" in Indian industrial enterprises as a solution to the problem of asymmetric information, which is particularly severe in developing countries. Likewise, we find large industrial groups and informal financial arrangements, such as family-based or rural financial systems, in may of the countries of Asia. We can consider these economic institutions, too, as a response to the problems of asymmetric information within the environments of inadequate accounting and legal rules. In considering the development of financial markets and institutions, it is important to bear in mind that the effectiveness of a financial system is largely determined by its ability to overcome the problems of adverse selection and moral hazard resulting from imperfect and asymmetric information.

(iii)   *Some corporate finance issues*[1]

Within the context of corporate finance, imperfect or asymmetric information manifests itself as what is called an "agency problem", which results from the separation of management and control. Agency problems between management and the investor arise from two sources of imperfect information, namely, the hidden action problem (i.e., the investor does not see all the actions of management) and the hidden information problem (i.e., management has information that the investor does not possess). In the extreme case where the agency problem becomes prohibitively serious, no funds will be raised. For example, if the investor believes that management will take the money for consumption, otherwise profitable projects will not be funded. Because of the agency problem, the cost of external finance necessarily exceeds the cost of internal finance, whereas these costs should be identical in a perfect market. A wedge between the two costs may stifle profitable investments (Stulz 2000).

It is for this reason that a firm generally prefers internal finance, which is cheaper under the presence of asymmetric information. In fact, large firms are known to make a predominant use of internal finance. Corporate mergers and acquisitions can also be interpreted as an informal way of using internal funds; with mergers and acquisitions, information is internalized and informational asymmetry is mitigated (Allen and Gale 1995). Corporate groups may also act as an informal market for internal funds.

Not all firms are so lucky. When external funds must be raised, the premium over the cost of internal finance ideally need to be reduced by a credible mechanism of corporate control. One of the devices used for this purpose is equity, which gives voice to the investor in the direct control of the firm. In this context, concentrated ownership may be better able to discipline management by raising the equity holder's stake in the firm and hence minimize the free rider problem inherent with diversified equity holding. At the same time, concentrated shareholding may lead to a situation where decisions are made to benefit the large shareholder at the expense of smaller ones (Stulz 2000). In contrast, debt provides less binding control on management, particularly when the maturity is long. In the case of long-term zero coupon bonds, for example, there would be virtually no monitoring of management. For shorter-term maturity bonds, however, each possible rollover becomes an opportunity for the bondholders to monitor management.

In terms of this characterization, a pecking-order theory of governance structure has been suggested in which the firm first wants to start with internal funds, then long-term and short-term debt, followed by equity, which gives full control to the investor. However, if the firm issues debt to avoid the prospect of greater direct control from equity holders, there are the risk of default and the danger of losing control to the creditors in that eventuality. The more debt is raised, the higher is the risk of bankruptcy. Thus, the firm must choose between debt finance and equity finance by weighing the marginal cost of diluting its control rights to new shareholders against the marginal costs of debt and default (Aghion and Bolton 1992). The upshot of this is that the optimal financial structure of an externally financed firm must be some mixture of debt and equity.

3.   The Role of Debt Finance

(i)   *Debt versus equity*

As may be inferred from the preceding argument, debt and equity together contribute to efficient investment decisions through their joint distribution of cash flows and control rights. Zender (1991)

---

[1]   See Shleifer and Vishny (1997) and Stultz (2000) for excellent surveys of these and other corporate finance issues.

has considered a world inhabited by active and passive investors, where the active investor holds equity, hence the control of the firm, and the passive investor holds debt. Disagreements may arise between the two investors because of asymmetric information. In this environment, the debtholder's cash flows are fixed in order to ensure optimal decision making by allowing the controlling investor to realize the marginal product of investment. The potential for moral hazard (i.e., under-investment or excessive risk taking, given the fixed payment schedule) is offset by the ultimate transfer of control in case of default (Zender 1991). Moreover, repaying as much as possible in bankruptcy states allows the fixed repayment in non-bankruptcy states to be minimized, thus minimizing the probability of bankruptcy and hence the costs (Gale and Hellwig 1985).

(ii)   *The optimality of debt*

More generally, debt has the advantage of being able to economize on resources that must be expended to monitor the borrowing firm because as long as the firm is making the stated coupon payment, there is no need for monitoring. In a class of what is called costly state verification models (in which verification is costly and the agents have limited wealth), the optimal contract is shown to be a simple debt contract, which requires a fixed repayment when the firm is solvent, requires the firm to be declared bankrupt if this fixed payment cannot be made, and allows the creditor to recoup as much of the debt as possible from the firm's assets.

In these models, debt is optimal in the following way. In an alternative scheme, for example, if the payment to outside investors varies with the reported cash flows, the firm may have incentives to misrepresent its cash flows. If there is no way of verifying the true cash flows, the firm will always underreport its cash flows and the investor will not recover the capital he contributes. Debt is a way of solving this problem by designating certain levels of reported cash flows as being subject to verification. If a low cash flow report results in a verification (i.e., default or bankruptcy), the firm with a high realized cash flow may not want to underreport.

The potential for deception is limited by two factors. First, if the firm falsely underreports to the point of requiring verification, it is sure to be found out because the contract requires the investor to observe the state. Second, in order for the investor to be deceived, he must receive the same income as if the announced state had actually occurred. If that is the case, it must be that the firm is able to pay this income from the actual revenues (Gale and Hellwig 1985). This feature of a debt contract that encourages truthfulness on the part of the firm is called "incentive-compatibility". In other words, with debt, the borrowing firm has no incentive to lie about the true state, even though the contract is made contingent, not on the true cash flows, but on the reported cash flows.

Moreover, debt exerts a disciplinary effect on management, to the extent that a default would give the creditor the option to force the firm into liquidation. Thus, there is an incentive, on the part of management, to try to avoid that eventuality by making sound investment decisions. If the cost of bankruptcy is low, high leverage works particularly well as an incentive and monitoring device, because liquidation becomes a real possibility in the event of mismanagement. Management that makes mistakes will not be able to repay the debt, and ends up yielding the control of the firm to the creditors (Harris and Raviv 1990; and Stulz 2000).

In sum, debt is optimal because (1) it dispenses with the need for costly verification in good states, (2) because management receives nothing when verification takes place, it tries to minimize the probability of verification taking place, and (3) it is incentive-compatible (Townsend 1979; Williamson 1987; Chang 1990; and Dowd 1992).

(iii)   *The information content of debt*

Debt also generates information that can be used by investors to evaluate the major operating decisions of a borrowing firm. The information role of debt is twofold. First, the mere ability of the firm to make its contractual payments provides information about the viability of its operations. Second, in case of default, management must placate creditors to avoid liquidation, either through informal negotiations or through formal bankruptcy proceedings. This process disseminates otherwise unavailable information to the investors (Harris and Raviv1990).

(iv)   *The collateral requirements of debt*

An important feature of debt is that it requires the availability of collateral. When debt does not explicitly require collateral, it is collateralized by the value of the whole firm. Because of this feature of debt, some have argued that debt finance is not conducive to economic growth, particularly when it involves the development of innovative activities (such as R&D) which do not necessarily yield collateral. Hence, equity finance is essential as a way of financing intangible assets, including growth opportunities.

Rajan and Zingales (1999) have observed that equity financed industries tend to have few hard assets and, with the development of accounting and legal standards, equity financed industries tend to use less fixed capital. In other words, the intangible assets that they typically possess in abundance become easier to finance. In contrast, in financially less developed economies, there is a greater use of debt finance, and this tends to distort asset holdings towards fixed capital.

(v)   *Equilibrium credit rationing*

A debt market may be characterized by equilibrium credit rationing, because the probability and expected cost of monitoring increase with the interest rate, through two channels: (1) the adverse selection effect, whereby the average riskiness of borrowers increases with the interest rate; and (2) the incentive effect, whereby firms will undertake projects with lower probabilities of success but higher payoffs when successful because the return on successful projects declines with the interest rate (Stiglitz and Weiss 1981).

This means that those willing to borrow but cannot at the prevailing interest rate will not be able to bid the funds away from those receiving them by offering a higher interest rate. Moreover, as the cost of monitoring increases, the possibility of equilibrium credit rationing also increases. Williamson (1986) has shown that, with costly monitoring, asymmetry in the payoff functions between the lender and the borrower alone can generate equilibrium credit rationing, without resorting to moral hazard and adverse selection.

4.   Financial Intermediaries

Up to this point, we have not made an explicit distinction between public debt (or directly placed debt) and intermediated debt (or bank loans) or, in the words of Rajan (1992), between arm's-length debt and informed debt. Here, we will discuss intermediated debt, which is the principal vehicle of corporate financing in much of Asia, before moving on to discuss the issues involved in choosing between the two in the next two sections.

(i)   *Transactions cost, imperfect information, and incomplete markets*

Even under perfect information, the presence of transactions cost would be a sufficient ground for the emergence of financial intermediaries. With transactions cost, investors with short-run liquidity needs may want to keep their assets in the form of deposits, while banks will mobilize them for longer-run investment. This maturity transformation and aggregation roles of financial intermediaries are well recognized.

In a world of imperfect information and incomplete markets, there are more reasons for financial intermediaries to exist. A powerful argument for the existence of financial intermediaries is based on the incompleteness of financial contracts, which is caused by the difficulty of fully specifying all contingencies. Institutions then emerge to use reputation to bond themselves, and achieve negotiated outcomes that are superior to those that can be obtained through direct transactions in the market (Rajan and Zingales 1999).

(ii)   *The cost saving argument for intermediaries*

With many investors per firm, there are potential economies to be gained from not duplicating each other's information gathering activity. The unit cost (per firm) of delegating verification to an intermediary falls to zero in the limit, as the number of borrowing firms expands. An intermediary has a gross cost advantage in collecting information because the alternative is either duplication of effort (if each lender monitors directly) or a free rider problem, in which case no monitoring takes place.

(iii)   *Delegation costs and the optimality of two-sided debt contracts*

If we think of the financial intermediary as a delegated monitor, it has then an incentive problem of its own. The problem of providing incentives for delegated monitoring has been termed in the literature "delegation costs". Then, the delegation costs of providing incentives to the intermediary must be netted out from any cost savings in information production. In this environment, optimal contracts must be designed to ensure simultaneously that the firm report truthfully to the intermediary and that the intermediary reports truthfully to the investor (Krasa and Villamil 1992). Here, it turns out that there is a remarkable similarity to the earlier argument on the optimality of debt as an incentive device.

Several authors have addressed this issue. For example, Diamond (1984) has shown that a financial intermediary has a net cost advantage over direct transactions because of diversification within the intermediary. This follows from the fact that the per-firm cost of providing incentives to the intermediary is reduced as it contracts with more firms with independently distributed projects, which increases the probability that the intermediary has sufficient loan proceeds to repay a fixed debt claim to the investors (depositors), even though the intermediary is not being monitored by them (Diamond 1984; also Williamson 1986). With a diversified loan portfolio, it is easier to assess bank management's performance (which presumably depends more on macroeconomic or aggregate signals) than to assess the performance of management in an undiversified firm. Moreover, the short-term nature of bank deposits exerts discipline on bank management (Diamond 1984; and Stultz 2000).

Krasa and Villamil (1992) have considered the relative performance of "one-sided contracts" (i.e., direct trade between the investor and the firm, where each investor monitors each firm in case of bankruptcy) and "two-sided contracts" (i.e., financial intermediation between the intermediary and each firm, and between the intermediary and the investor, where the investors elect a monitor to perform the costly verification task), and shown that (1) two-sided simple debt contracts with delegated monitoring dominate direct lending and borrowing in an economy with default risk, and that

(2) simple debt is the optimal contract for both the intermediary-borrower and the intermediary-lender sides of the contract in terms of minimizing monitoring costs. In other words, for the lower end, a deposit with bankruptcy penalties provides the intermediary with incentives for both payment to the depositors and for monitoring the borrower (see also Diamond 1984; Williamson 1986; and Dowd 1992).

(iv)   The information role of intermediaries

Certain types of information (e.g., about patents) cannot be communicated to the public without reducing firm value. In this case, intermediated debt is the preferred way of raising funds at a lower cost. Likewise, a bank may obtain information about the firm in the course of lending, which cannot easily be supplied in any other way. In this sense, financial intermediaries are producers of information.

As inside debt, bank loans provide positive signals to the market. James (1987) has shown that the cost of reserve requirements on CDs is borne by borrowers, and not CD holders, and that significant positive abnormal returns accrue to the stockholders of firms announcing new bank loan agreements. Moreover, negative abnormal returns are associated with the announcement of private placements and straight debt issues used to retire bank debt.

Emphasizing the role of intermediaries as sellers of information, Allen (1990) has a different theory of financial intermediation based on the exploitation of the unclaimed value of information due to lack of credibility. When information cannot be directly verified and risk aversion is unobservable, an information seller can only capture a portion of the value of his information. If the seller cannot obtain the full value of information because of lack of credibility, an intermediary can arise to capture some of the unclaimed value. An intermediary, who intermediates between an initial seller of information and its ultimate buyer, can signal its informed status by investing its wealth in assets about which it has special knowledge.

(v)   The Japanese main bank system

The effectiveness with which Japan's so-called main bank system (in which a bank maintains a long-term stable relationship with a client firm) has performed its role both as a mechanism of monitoring the firm and as an institution that mitigates the problem of asymmetric information between the lender and the borrower has extensively been studied. Emphasizing the role of banks as corporate monitors who bear the cost of becoming informed about their client firms and who ensure that they make efficient business decisions, Hoshi, Kashyap and Schafstein (1991) have shown that liquidity is more binding for investment by independent firms than for investment by bank-affiliated firms. They took this evidence to conclude that long-term stable bank relationships can mitigate information problems in the capital market, such that profitable projects get funded regardless of liquidity (see also Weinstein and Yafeh 1998).

5.   Bond and Bank Finance in Terms of Resource Allocation and Moral Hazard

(i)   The price signaling effect of public debt

Given these and other features of intermediated debt, what are the contrasting features of public debt, and what considerations should govern the choice between the two types of debt? In short, bank finance and bond finance coexist because they address different types of informational problems with different degrees of effectiveness. In broadest terms, intermediate debt is better suited for mitigating the problems of asymmetric information (including monitoring to reduce adverse selection and moral hazard), while public debt has a superior allocative function by being better able to provide price signals.

In terms of providing price signals that are useful for decision making, public debt is by far superior to bank finance, although it is dominated by the more complex informational content of equity. With a financial market, there is information feedback from equilibrium market prices to the decisions of firms, which in turn affect those market prices (Boot and Thakor 1997). In contrast, particularly in relationship-based banking, there are no price signals to guide investment decisions, so that the effective cost of financing can deviate substantially from the true risk-adjusted cost (Rajan and Zingales 1999).

Consequently, firms that rely on more complex technologies have more to gain from the feedback role of market prices and should prefer public debt. In this context, in the United States, because a significant number of firms are covered by financial analysts, the US stock prices are more likely to reflect much more information of relevance to managers. Boot and Thakor (1997) argue that this greater information context of price signals (hence, the usefulness of public securities issues) explains why more US firms raise funds in the bond market.

(ii)   Other allocative issues

Resource allocation is also affected by incentives. While bank finance may be flexible, that flexibility may involve an element of revenue sharing. For example, banks may be able to provide intertemporal subsidies by lending at lower interest rates to young firms in exchange for higher interest rates later; banks may use their bargaining power to extract rents when the investment turns out to be profitable (see the next section). In these cases, management's incentives to exert effort will be reduced, as it can no longer claim all of the marginal product of investment. In contrast, public debt would allow the firm to realize the marginal product of investment. For this reason, public debt may give higher incentives to exert effort (Rajan 1992).

As a related point, a financial intermediary has incentives to discourage risk taking, because the value of debt falls as risk increases. Consequently, the intermediary evaluates additional investment decisions differently from the firm. To put it differently, banks care more about being repaid than maximizing firm value. This tendency of intermediated finance to lead to a suboptimal allocation of resources, however, is mitigated by allowing banks to hold equity (Stulz 2000).

The generally superior ability of public debt to effect better resource allocation should be conditioned by the observation that public debt does not provide the flexibility to modify its covenants in accordance with the realization of different contingencies. Bond covenants are written in terms of readily observable but noisy indicators of the firm's ability to repay. As the covenants are based on imperfect information, default policies based on these covenants are inefficient, by either allowing unprofitable projects to continue or allowing profitable projects to be terminated. In other words, public debt lacks the ability of bank debt to respond to different contingencies in a flexible manner so as to effect better resource allocation (Berlin and Loeys 1988).

(iii)   The moral hazard attenuation role of bank loans

Although bank finance does not provide adequate price signals, it is superior in resolving asset substitution moral hazard. Thus, the choice between intermediated debt and public debt is effectively a tradeoff between a more efficient attenuation of moral hazard and improved real decisions associated with feedback from market prices.

Boot and Thakor (1997) have considered a theoretical model to conceptualize this tradeoff by assuming two types of investors (traders), called discretionary and liquidity traders. Discretionary traders must pay a fixed cost to become either an informed trader or a monitoring trader. The financial market consists of informed traders, uninformed discretionary traders, and liquidity traders, where the presence of liquidity traders makes prices noisy and sustains the ex post trading profits of informed traders. Banks consist of monitoring agents and non-monitoring depositors. The financial market is ineffective in deterring borrowers from investing in an unprofitable project. The bank, on the other hand, specializes in deterring borrowers from investing in unprofitable projects, but it learns nothing about the firm-specific piece of information which is conveyed by the market signal.

In this environment, it is shown that the firm chooses a combination of bank finance and bond finance by optimally balancing the benefits of bank monitoring and financial market information aggregation. If asset-substitution (post-lending) moral hazard is severe, a firm is likely to choose considerable bank funding to induce sufficient monitoring. If moral hazard is low, the firm can better exploit the information aggregation benefits of financial markets by borrowing more by public bond issues. This prediction is consistent with the observation that firms in industries with substantial state verification (hence, little need for additional monitoring) use financial markets, while firms in industries that require a lot of monitoring use banks (Boot and Thakor 1997).

6.   Additional Issues in the Choice of Bond and Bank Finance

(i)   *The higher cost of bank loans*

When informational problems are severe, bank finance can be a cheaper way of external financing than bond finance. In practice, however, banks may exploit their monopolistic position to extract rents from the borrowing firm. Weinstein and Yafeh (1998) show that, prior to the financial market liberalization of the 1980s when Japanese firms began to enjoy greater access to bond financing, firms with a main bank had lower profits and lower growth rates than their industry peers,[1] and argue that the conservative investment strategies motivated by the bank's position as a major debtholder may have inhibited firm growth by discouraging risky yet profitable investments.

In this interpretation, the main bank captures most of the rents through higher interest payments and through pressure on clients to use large quantities of bank-financed capital inputs. For this reason, when capital markets are underdeveloped and entry into the banking sector is restricted, close bank-firm relationships may lead to a redistribution of rents away from the manufacturing sector to the financial sector. The net benefit of bank debt, therefore, must be assessed by comparing the monitoring-induced reduction in the cost of funds against the value of rent extraction.

---

[1]   The main results are: (1) the share of capital used by main bank clients was significantly higher than that of independent firms prior to 1980, but the difference in capital use virtually disappeared since; (2) the transfer of rents from client firms to main banks often took the form of higher interest payments; (3) main bank client firms grew no faster than independent firms; and (4) main bank client firms did not outperform their independent peers in terms of growth and profitability (Weinstein and Yafeh 1998).

(ii)   ***Reputation acquisition by the firm through bank loans***

Reputation can to some extent mitigate the problems caused by asymmetric information. Diamond (1989) has analyzed the joint influence of adverse selection and moral hazard on the ability of reputation to eliminate the conflict of interest between borrowers and lenders about the choice of risk in investment decisions. If there is initially widespread adverse selection (i.e., a large proportion of borrowers with undesirable characteristics), reputation effects are too weak to eliminate the conflict of interest for borrowers with short track records.   Adverse selection becomes less severe as time produces a longer track record, and a good reputation can eventually become strong enough to eliminate the conflict of interest for borrowers with a long record of repayment without a default. If adverse selection is initially not substantial, reputation can begin to work immediately.

Because reputation requires time to develop, new borrowers face more severe incentive problems and would be most likely to utilize costly methods for dealing with such problems, such as restrictive covenants in bond indentures, and additional monitoring by a financial intermediary. The incentive problem is that debt contracts may encourage risky and less valuable projects. With a long time horizon, the reduced interest rates for a borrower who does not default imply that the present value of the borrower's rents for any constant investment decision rises over time. The value of a good reputation rises over time, as does the cost of a default. Therefore, over time, the payoff of the risky project declines relative to a safe but profitable project. The reputation itself becomes a valuable asset, and a single default causes a large decline in its value (Diamond 1989).

In a separate paper, Diamond (1991) has shown that borrowers with intermediate credit ratings tend to rely on bank loans. On the other hand, for very low rated borrowers, monitoring does not provide incentives because they have little to lose by default. For them, monitoring only serves to screen out borrowers who are caught taking self-interested actions. Monitoring that only screens borrowers is less useful, and it may not be worth its cost for these lower-rated borrowers. As a result, many new borrowers will be turned down for credit (Diamond 1991).

If moral hazard is sufficiently widespread, new borrowers will begin their reputation acquisition by being monitored by a bank and later switch to issuing directly placed debt. A borrower's credit record acquired when monitored by a bank serves to predict future actions of the borrower when not monitored. Directly placed debt is a contract with terms and loan granting decisions that depend only on public information. A bank loan uses this information plus information from costly monitoring of a borrower's actions to condition the decision to grant a loan or to condition the loan's covenants (Diamond 1991).   Firms build reputation by taking on costly bank-monitored debt, and those that acquire good reputations then switch to publicly traded debt to save monitoring costs.

(iii)   ***Financial distress***

When a firm gets into financial distress, it may be because of the poor quality of its projects (in which case, the firm should be liquidated) or for reasons unrelated to project quality (in which case, the firm should not be liquidated but debt be renegotiated, as continuation value is greater than liquidation value).   Lenders are unable to distinguish between the two kinds of situations without devoting additional resources to evaluation.

 Financial distress can be costly if free-rider problems and information asymmetries make it difficult for the firm to renegotiate with creditors, when it is in fact solvent. The free-rider problem is that while an individual creditor bears the full cost of renegotiation, all creditors share the benefits, so that no renegotiation will take place. Because there is no long-term relationship between the borrower and the investors with public debt, there will be less likelihood that an otherwise solvent firm will be bailed out, whereas the likelihood is higher with intermediated debt because the intermediary can internalize the stream of future benefits that result from the firm remaining in business (Rajan and Zingales 1999).

As a related point, the cost of collective action for creditors is much higher for public debt than for intermediated debt. With public debt, ownership is generally diversified, increasing the cost of negotiation in case of default. In contrast, the ownership of non-public debt is more concentrated, so that it is relatively easy to negotiate with management (Stulz 2000). On this account, too, intermediated debt outperforms.

This tendency is further strengthened by the intermediary's desire to acquire a reputation for "financial flexibility" and making the "right" renegotiation vs. liquidation decision, which provides an incentive to devote a larger amount of resources than bondholders toward such evaluations. A bank is able to use reputation as a commitment device to promise the borrowing firm credibly that it will devote more resources toward evaluating the firm and thereby make better renegotiation vs. liquidation decisions if the firm is in financial difficulty. In equilibrium, bank loans dominate bonds from the point of view of minimizing inefficient liquidations (Chemmanur and Fulghieri 1994).

Hoshi, Kashyap and Schafstein (1990) have used a sample of Tokyo Stock Exchange listed firms to show that bank group-affiliated (keiretsu) firms invest more and sell more than independent firms in the years following the onset of financial distress. Moreover, independent firms that receive a greater fraction of debt financing from their largest lender bank invest more and sell more following the onset of financial distress. On this basis, they conclude that relationship banking reduces the cost of financial distress, by minimizing the free rider problem and the problem of informational asymmetry.

To the extent that this aspect of intermediated finance is an insurance, it comes with a cost. Thus, we would expect firms with a lower probability of financial distress to have less reason to choose bank loans over public debt. In contrast, those with a higher assessed probability of being in financial distress would find it more advantageous to use bank loans, despite the fact that banks may charge a higher interest rate compared to publicly traded debt. Borrowers are willing to pay higher interest rates for loans from banks with greater reputations for flexibility in dealing with firms in financial distress (Chemmanur and Fulghieri 1994).

(iv)   Financing for young or small firms

Bank finance may be better suited for financing young firms because of its greater ability to provide "staged financing". Under staged financing, a firm may start on a scale that allows investors to learn about the project and stop funding it if found unprofitable (Stulz 2000). With public debt, it is also possible to provide staged financing by rolling over a series of short-term debt. Short-term debt mitigates adverse selection problems because those who would accept contracts of this form more willingly are those who have greater confidence in their venture; short-term debt also mitigates conventional agency problems, because there must be refinancing at short intervals (Dowd 1992). With public debt, however, the cost of renegotiation is not trivial, diminishing its value as a vehicle of staged financing.

If bank financing needs to be staged, the bank must expend resources to assess the project at each stage. It then follows that some restrictions must be placed on competition among financial intermediaries, in order to allow them to extract rents from successful projects, thereby justifying the expenditure of resources on projects to increase their probability of success. Some ability to extract rents is necessary for relationship banking (Stulz 2000).

There is some evidence to show that in concentrated banking markets, more credit is available to young firms that are more credit rationed, so that relationship-based systems seem to do a better job of ensuring that value-adding projects get funded (Rajan and Zingales 1999). Banks are also capable of providing intertemporal subsidies, whereby lower interest rates (relative to the market rate) at an early stage are offset by the higher interest rates at a later stage, which may appear to be a transfer of rents from the firm to the intermediary. This type of intertemporal subsidies cannot be provided by bond finance.

Bank finance is also better suited for financing small to medium-sized firms, because it reduces the agency cost associated with lending to entities for which the cost of information acquisition is large. The bank first screens prospective clients. Later, by threatening to cut off credit, it provides the firm with the incentives to take the right investments. As a result of the diminished adverse selection and the reduced moral hazard, the bank has the capacity to provide cheap informed funds, as opposed to costly arm's length funds (Rajan 1992)

(v)   Institutional requirements of public and intermediated debt

Public debt and intermediated debt have different levels of institutional requirements. Public debt relies heavily on legal enforcement. Without the rigorous and speedy enforcement of contractual terms, a market for public debt cannot be viable. In contrast, relationship-based systems can function even if laws are poorly drafted and contracts not enforced. Likewise, market-based systems require transparency as a guarantee of protection, whereas relationship-based systems are designed to preserve opacity, which has the effect of protecting the relationships from the threat of competition (Rajan and Zingales 1999).

In fact, some restrictions on competition and disclosure are necessary for relationship banking to thrive. With too much competition and disclosure, hence with the reduced ability to appropriate rents, there is little incentive for financial intermediaries to invest in resources in project evaluation, in which case they do not develop expertise, unprofitable projects may be started or continued, or fewer profitable projects would be started. On the other hand, with too little competition, if the intermediary becomes too powerful and their ability to extract rents increases, the payoff to the firm from its innovative activities falls, making it less likely that profitable projects will be undertaken (Rajan 1991; and Stulz 2000).

7.   Policy Implications for Bond Market Development

The conceptual issues discussed so far can be brought together to yield the following policy implications for bond market development.

1. Bonds are loan contracts with covenants but no monitor, while bank loans are loan contracts that are enforced by a monitoring specialist. In general, bank finance has advantage in minimizing the problems of adverse selection and moral hazard because of its monitoring function, while public debt is better at effecting better resource allocation because of the price signals it provides. Thus, for a firm operating in a particular country, the choice between bank finance and bond finance depends on the magnitude of informational problems as well as on the informativeness of securities prices, both of which are in part affected by the country's regulatory policies.

2. The benefit of bank finance increases with the severity of informational problems and the efficacy of monitoring by banks, for which there is an important issue of delegation costs. On the other hand, the benefit of bond finance increases with the development of financial and legal

infrastructure, which reduces the cost of information acquisition, raises the informativeness of securities prices, and ensures that covenants are enforced.

3. These considerations suggest that bank finance should dominate bond finance in countries where accounting and legal systems are not well developed and there are severe informational problems. These situations may characterize some of the emerging, transition, and other developing countries. With a large moral hazard premium, monitored debt is a cheaper way of external finance. With financial market development and the maturing of some of the larger firms with long credit histories, more and more firms will migrate to the bond market, if it is available.

4. Competition in the banking industry is a double-edged sword. With too little competition, banks will become too powerful and their ability to extract rents from borrowers will increase, creating disincentives for management to exert effort and causing some profitable investments not to be funded. On the other hand, without the ability to appropriate some surplus from successful projects, banks will not have sufficient incentive to expend the needed resources on monitoring and information gathering.

5. Developing a corporate bond market is important because it allows the firm to escape from a powerful bank that extracts too much rent and provides the firm with price signals that can be used for investment decisions. Globalization of finance makes bond market development all the more important because it allows larger firms to bypass the inefficient domestic system, if they perceive the benefits of bond finance to be large. This can be an undesirable development because international bond issues are typically made in a handful of major currencies, so that the country may end up accumulating large long-term unhedged liabilities in foreign currencies.

6. It is thus important to develop a corporate bond market in a way that does not undermine the viability of the banking system. One way to accomplish this may be to allow banks to participate in bond underwriting syndicates. Keeping the banking system viable is important because bank finance continues to be the only source of external finance for smaller and younger firms, or firms with no established reputation. Likewise, family, rural and other informal financial systems as well as corporate groups are also important. They are not the vestiges of prehistoric times, but are institutions endogenously developed to cope with the acute informational problems prevalent in developing societies. The pace of financial liberalization as well as the application of transparency and disclosure rules should be carefully timed to make sure that these informal institutions not be eradicated before they are replaced by an alternative financing mechanism.

REFERENCES

Aghion, Philippe and Patrick Bolton, "An Incomplete Contracts Approach to Financial Contracting", Review of Economic Studies 59, July 1992, 473-494.

Akerlof, George A., "The Market for 'Lemons': Quality Uncertainty and the Market Mechanism", Quarterly Journal of Economics, August 1970, 488-500.

Allen, Franklin, "The Market for Information and the Origin of Financial Intermediation", Journal of Financial Intermediation 1, March 1990, 3-30.

Allen, Franklin and Douglas Gale, "A Welfare Comparison of Intermediaries and Financial Markets in Germany and the US", European Economic Review 39, 1995, 179-209.

Berlin, Mitchell and Jan Loeys, "Bond Covenants and Delegated Monitoring", Journal of Finance 43, June 1988, 397-412.

Bhide, Amar, "The Hidden Costs of Stock Market Liquidity", Journal of Financial Economics 34, August 1993, 31-51.

Boot, Arnould W. A. and Anjan V. Thakor, "Financial System Architecture", Review of Financial Studies 10, Fall 1997, 693-733.

Boyd, John H. and Edward C. Prescott, "Financial Intermediary-Coalitions", Journal of Economic Theory 3, April 1986, 211-232.

Chang, Chun, "The Dynamic Structure of Optimal Debt Contracts", Journal of Economic Theory 52, October 1990, 68-86.

Chemmanur , Thomas J. and Paolo Fulghieri, "Reputation, Renegotiation, and the Choice between Bank Loans and Publicly Traded Debt", Review of financial Studies 7, fall 1994.

Diamond, Douglas W. , "Financial Intermediation and Delegated Monitoring", Review of Economic Studies, 1984, 393-414.

Diamond, Douglas W., "Reputation Acquisition in Debt Markets", Journal of Political Economy 97, August 1989, 828-862.

Diamond, Douglas W., "Monitoring and Reputation: The Choice between Bank Loans and Directly Placed Debt", Journal of Political Economy 99, August 1991, 689-721.

Dowd, Devin, "Optimal Financing Contracts", Oxford Economic Papers 44, 1992, 672-693.

Gale, Douglas and Martin Hellwig, "Incentive-Compatible Debt Contracts: The One-Period Problem", Review of Economic Studies 52, October 1985, 647-663.

Greenwald, Bruce C. and Joseph E. Stiglitz, "Externalities in Economies with Imperfect Information and Incomplete Markets", Quarterly Journal of Economics, May 1986.

Harris, Milton and Artur Raviv, "Capital Structure and the Informational Role of Debt", Journal of Finance 45, June 1990, 321-349.

Hoshi, Takeo, Anil Kashyap and David Scharfstein, "The Role of Banks in Reducing the Costs of Financial Distress in Japan", Journal of Financial Economics 27, September 1990, 67-88.

Hoshi, Takeo, Anil Kashyap and David Scharfstein, "Corporate Structure, Liquidity, and Investment: Evidence from Japanese Industrial Groups", Quarterly Journal of Economics, February 1991, 33-60.

James, Christopher, "Some Evidence on the Uniqueness of Bank Loans", Journal of Financial Economics 19, December 1987, 217-235.

Krasa, Stefan and Anne P. Villamil, "Monitoring the Monitor: An Incentive Structure for a Financial Intermediary", Journal of Economic Theory 57, June 1991, 197-221.

Levine, Ross, "Financial Development and Economic Growth: Views and Agenda", Journal of Economic Literature 35, June 1997, 688-726.

Levine, Ross, "Bank-based or Market-based Financial Systems: Which is Better?", University of Minnesota, 2000.

Rajan, Raghuram G., "Insiders and Outsiders: The Choice between Informed and Arm's-length Debt", Journal of Finance, September 1992, 1367-1400.

Rajan, Raghuram G. and Luigi Zingales, "Financial Systems, Industrial Structure, and Growth", University of Chicago, 1999.

Shleifer, Andrei and Robert W. Vishny, "A Survey of Corporate Governance", Journal of Finance 52, June 1997, 737-783.

Stiglitz, Joseph E. and Andrew Weiss, "Credit Rationing in Markets with Imperfect Information", American Economic Review 71, June 1981, 393-410.

Stulz, Rene M., "Does Financial Structure Matter for Economic Growth? A Corporate Finance Perspective", Ohio State University, January 2000.

Townsend, Robert M., "Optimal Contracts and Competitive Markets with Costly State Verification", Journal of Economic Theory 21, October 1979.

Weinstein, David E. and Yishay Yafeh, "On the Costs of a Bank-Centered Financial System: Evidence from the Changing Main Bank Relations in Japan", Journal of Finance, April 1998, 635-672.

Williamson, Stephen D. , "Costly Monitoring, Financial Intermediation, and Equilibrium Credit Rationing", Journal of Monetary Economics 18, September 1986, 159-179.

Williamson, Stephen D., "Costly Monitoring, Loan Contracts, and Equilibrium Credit Rationing", Quarterly Journal of Economics, February 1987, 135-145.

Zender, Jaime F., "Optimal Financial Instruments", Journal of Finance 46, December 1991, 1645-1663.

Session 2

Experience in Asia and Policy Issues to be Addressed

DEBT MARKET DEVELOPMENT IN SINGAPORE

by
Ms. Yeo Lian Sim

016 G32
G12
G21

Introduction

The Asian financial crisis has highlighted the dangers of relying too heavily on short-term financing and bank credit, and, conversely, the benefits of having strong debt markets which provide a better funding match for longer-term expenditure needs. Although bond markets are relatively underdeveloped in Asia, compared to equities markets, Asian governments have taken positive initiatives to develop their domestic bond markets, including creating local bond yield benchmarks. There have also been various efforts among governments to develop the Asian debt markets under regional and international fora, including at the APEC and ASEAN Grouping levels.

The prognosis for the Asian bond market is healthy. The economic recovery in Asia has increased bond investors' confidence in Asian issues. This is evidenced by a remarkable rebound in the ability of Asian debt issuers to tap the international markets, with about 80% year-on-year increase in issuance volume to US$16 billion in 1999 (non-domestic currencies). Spreads on all sovereign & corporate bonds have also narrowed, a further sign of international investors' returning confidence.

Equally, if not more importantly, coupled with low interest rates and healthy domestic demand, Asian borrowers have also started to shift their borrowing to local markets. In 1999, while about US$16 billion was raised overseas, another US$25 billion was raised by non-government borrowers in domestic markets[1]. With further developments in Asia's domestic bond markets, we can expect to see more Asian borrowers returning to raise funds domestically.

The bond market is also a promising area of potential growth for Singapore's financial industry. An active bond market will add breadth to Singapore's capital markets and complement the development of the equities market as well as enhance existing Treasury activities, ACU operations and other financial services. It will also offer investors a wider range of liquid instruments to invest in. Bonds can be sold to a broad range of investors, diversifying risks in the financial system over the long-term. Consequently, Singapore has taken several initiatives to develop its nascent bond market, as part of its overall efforts to develop the financial sector.

This paper outlines the main measures taken by Singapore to develop its debt market, and examines issues that we believe are relevant to the continuing development of Asian domestic bond markets.

Debt market development

The Monetary Authority of Singapore ("MAS") embarked in late 1997 on a fundamental review of its policies in regulating and developing Singapore's financial sector. MAS worked closely with industry players and other government agencies to review the regulatory framework and improve financial infrastructure that would encourage growth in specific industries in the financial services sector. A series of reforms were announced in February 1998.

The reforms are designed to intensify the development of the financial services sector in Singapore over the next five to ten years, making Singapore a world-class financial centre. MAS' strategic approach is two-fold: to create a regulatory environment more conducive to Singapore's development as an international financial centre, one that is well-supervised but also encourages innovation; and, to adopt a more active role in promoting the industry.

One component of the broad strategy is the development of a deep and broad capital market. Singapore's traditional strengths are in foreign exchange, money markets and syndicated loans, while the capital markets have been less vibrant. Our equity market has been relatively small and domestically focussed and the bond market has not been 'blessed' by imperative need of government budget deficit financing.

The development of a debt market adds to the spectrum of financial services we offer, to serve market needs. Foreign funds present in Singapore could channel their investments alternatively into fixed income securities, instead of only equities. A more vibrant bond market would also satisfy the needs of investors who prefer to hold a portfolio of diversified issues, and encourage investors to hold strategic, long-term investments in Asian issues. A number of initiatives have been taken to develop Singapore's debt market, and they are focused on the following key elements:

- a more active Singapore Government Securities ("SGS") market with a yield curve responsive to demand and supply conditions;

- a conducive environment for domestic and global bond issuers;

- a diverse investor base; and

- a strong talent pool with expertise and experience in debt origination, trading and sales.

Singapore Government Securities Market

Trading in book-entry Singapore Government Securities (SGS) revolving around a system of primary dealers had been in place since 1987. But, while inter-dealer spreads were reasonably narrow and market practices well established, interest in the SGS market was not widespread and investors tended to be buy-and-hold rather than active managers. The SGS market needed to be enlivened to provide the underpinnings of a vibrant bond market and towards this end, various measures were undertaken at the beginning of 1998.

Initiatives Implemented

Increased Issuance

The government decided in mid-1998 to increase the issuance of SGS to raise the tradeable float above what was required by banks to fulfil regulatory minimum liquid asset requirements. More SGS were issued in 1998 than any other year. The net increase in the issue of Treasury bills and Government bonds in that year amounted to $1.6 billion (US$0.9 billion) and $4.9 billion (US$2.8 billion), respectively. The increase in supply of SGS bolstered trading activities in the secondary market. Liquidity in the inter-bank market also improved when two broking houses commenced operations as SGS brokers.

Extension of the Yield Curve

The SGS yield curve was extended from 7 to 10 years, with MAS' issuance of the first 10-year SGS bond (issue size S$1.5 billion (US$0.9 billion)) in July 1998, to create a benchmark for long-dated corporate debt.

Improving information flow to the market

To reduce uncertainty about market supply, MAS has announced an annual issuance calendar in more detail, indicating the maturity and date of issue. In addition, to raise market awareness and improve information flow to investors, MAS also publishes information on historical SGS prices and yields on the MAS website.

Primary Dealership

Primary dealers underpin liquidity in the market by quoting two-way bid and offer prices under all market conditions. They are also important for underwriting the success of auctions by marketing new issues to final investors. Primary dealers are also the conduit for all bids for securities at SGS auctions. MAS holds regular meetings with the primary dealers to discuss market-related issues directly.

The pool of primary dealers has risen to 9 currently, from 7 in 1998. However, this number is still small and there is room for increase. A larger number of primary dealers would be positive to the development of the SGS market eg sustaining liquidity during adverse market conditions, and increasing liquidity in the repo market.

Developing the Repurchase Market

A well functioning repurchase ("repo") market contributes to developing liquidity in the cash market. The ability to borrow bonds allows traders to go short when prices shoot up, providing more depth to the market. To encourage more depth and activity in the SGS market, MAS has removed totally a previous cap on repo done by non-residents.

Impact of Liberalisation Measures on the SGS Market

Outstanding SGS

The outstanding amount of SGS has risen from S$25.4 billion (US$14.9 billion) in mid-1998 to S$36.1 billion (US$20.6 billion) at the end of 1999. This comprised S$12 billion (US$7 billion) in T-bills and S$24 billion (US$14 billion) in book-entry/scripless bonds, and represented a 33.5% increase over the total SGS outstanding as of 1 July 1998, when MAS issued the first 10-year government bond.

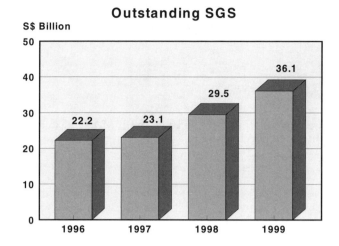

Outstanding SGS

S$ Billion

Turnover

Considerable increases in trading volumes were seen in the 5 months following our inaugural 10-year bond issue in July 1998. Average daily turnover increased to S$874 million (US$510 million) in 1998 compared to S$534 million (US$310 million) in 1997. However, this fell 31% to S$602 million (US$350 million) in 1999, as trading adjusted to more sustainable volume. Banks' Y2k moratorium on trading activities closer to the year's end also contributed to the lower trading volumes.

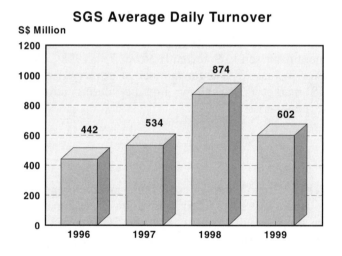

SGS Average Daily Turnover

S$ Million

SGS as a Benchmark Yield Curve

The increased issuance and higher turnover in the SGS market has raised the usefulness of the SGS yield curve as a benchmark. The spreads between long-end SGS and the interest rate swap ("IRS") yields have narrowed to a relatively stable level. In addition, the correlation between 7- and 10-year SGS and IRS yields appears to have improved markedly. As correlations rise, this is likely to improve the usefulness of SGS as a hedge for market players in the IRS market, raising interest in the SGS market.

Issuer Base

Traditionally, property development companies had been the main bond issuers in Singapore. To build critical mass and diversity of issues, a number of initiatives have been taken to encourage issuance in the market.

Increased Bond Issues by Statutory Boards

Public sector statutory boards were encouraged to tap the bond market and be subjected to market discipline in raising their funds rather than to wholly rely on the government for their funding needs. They are encouraged to issue more debt securities to finance infrastructural projects, which would enlarge the pool of tradable Singapore-Dollar bonds.

The Jurong Town Corporation was the first to tap the market following the new initiatives, issuing a S$300 million (US$ 176 million) 10-year bond in October 1998. This was followed by the Housing and Development Board's inaugural offer of a S$300 million (US$176 million) issue in February 1999. To date, S$2.6 billion (US$1.5 billion) has been raised by three statutory boards since October 1998.

Foreign Entities S$-Denominated Bond Issuance

Singapore's policy on the internationalisation of Singapore dollar was liberalised in August 1998 to allow foreign entities/non-residents of good credit standing to issue S$ bonds. The S$ proceeds are swapped into foreign currencies as most of the issuers ultimately require foreign currency to use outside Singapore. Credit ratings are not compulsory for such bond issues. Unrated foreign issuers, as they are not well known to the general public, offer their bonds only to sophisticated investors.

With the relaxation, we hope to open up an avenue for Asian issuers, which traditionally have not had the practice of being rated, to tap the S$ bond market. Unrated blue-chip Asian companies which find difficulty in reaching global investors in developed markets would have an opportunity to reach Asian and emerging market investors based in Singapore and the rest of Asia.

Market participants have responded positively to the policy changes, designed to better serve Asian issuers' needs. The International Finance Corporation launching the first supranational bond issue in October 1998, a triple A-rated Singapore dollar issue. This was followed by GE Capital Corporation in January 1999, the first foreign corporate to issue a Singapore dollar bond. To date a total of S$3.6 billion (US$2.1 billion) have been issued by 23 foreign entities, which are largely supranationals, and US and European corporates and financial institutions. Cheung Kong Holdings also became the first Asian issuer in Singapore dollars in March 2000.

Volume of Total Debt Issuance in 1999

Boosted by the package of initiatives, the non-government debt market recorded good growth in 1999. A total of S$21.1 billion (US$12.4 billion) worth of debt papers were issued in 1999, compared with S$8.7 billion (US$5.1 billion) in 1998. Of the total issues, 44% or S$9.2 billion (US$5.4 billion) were denominated in Singapore dollar. By issuer type, 75% of the issues were launched by local corporates while 15% were issued by foreign entities. The remaining 10% of the issues were raised by statutory boards.

Issuance of Non-Government Debt

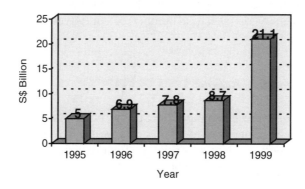

Investor Base

At present, our investor base is largely institutional, dominated by insurance companies while other financial institutions (banks/finance companies/merchant banks) and fund managers are also fairly active. Our retail investor base is small. In view of this, several initiatives have been taken to develop the asset management industry in Singapore, as well as liberalise investments of the Central Provident Fund ("CPF"), Singapore's compulsory retirement saving scheme.

Development of Fund Management Industry

The quantum of funds managed in Singapore has grown significantly over the years. Total assets under management were about S$12 billion (US$7 billion) in 1989. This had grown to S$204 billion (US$120 billion) as at 30 June 1999, representing a 17-fold increase over the 10-year period. The number of asset management companies in Singapore has also grown from 44 in 1989 to 189. As at end 1998, only 16% of funds under discretionary management was invested in fixed income securities, suggesting potential for greater demand for the debt market. MAS and the Government of Singapore Investment Corporation (GIC) have also been placing out a total of S$35 billion (US$21 billion) of funds to external fund managers. This will act as further seed money to grow the Singapore fund management industry.

Singapore has a high savings rate of over 40% of GDP, attributable in part to compulsory savings in the CPF. CPF membership totalled 2.8 million accounts and members' balance amounted to S$88.6 billion (US$52 billion) as at 30 September 1999. CPF members can manage the investment of their CPF savings in excess of stipulated minimum sums under the CPF Investment Scheme. Thus, in addition to balances remaining with the CPF, CPF members had made net investments of S$14.9 billion (US$8.8 billion) as at 30 September 1999.

Bond investment being new and unfamiliar to the retail investing public, CPF members are now encouraged to have their investible funds managed by professional asset managers on a discretionary basis or investing in approved funds, including fixed income unit trusts. There is also a greater choice of fund managers, with a widening of qualifying criteria by the CPF Board. New investment guidelines for CPF-approved unit trusts allow fund managers more flexibility to invest in a wider range of assets, including high-grade bonds. Recognising the need to improve distribution for direct retail investment in bonds as well, ATM systems can be used for primary purchase of statutory board and government bonds.

Tax Incentives

To further encourage the development of the bond market, We have also provided various tax incentives for bond fund managers and bond investments since February 1998. These incentive allows financial institutions and companies to be granted:

- Tax exemption on fee income earned from arranging, underwriting and distributing qualifying debt securities;

- Concessionary tax rate of 10 per cent on interest income from holding qualifying debt securities arranged in Singapore;

- Concessionary tax rate of 10 per cent on income earned from trading in debt securities; and

- Withholding tax exemption on interest from qualifying debt securities arranged in Singapore payable to non-residents.

Intermediaries

Approved Bond Intermediary (ABI) Scheme

Apart from issuers and investors, Singapore need to more intermediaries to nurture the bond market. These are financial institutions which can provide expert advice to borrowers and launch their bond issues successfully, and professionals who have the expertise and experience to promote, trade and create new products for their customers. Taking this into account, MAS implemented in March 1999 the Approved Bond Intermediary (ABI) scheme, under which debt securities lead managed by an ABI are treated as qualifying debt securities for tax purposes.

Infrastructure

As part of basic infrastructure, bond market participants expect an efficient custody and settlement system. Singapore has made further strides in enhancing the capabilities and sophistication of its clearing and settlement systems, including linkages for cross-borders transactions.

Improvement of Securities Clearing and Settlement Systems

Singapore Government Securities

The clearing of Singapore Government Securities trades are carried out through the Singapore Government Securities Book-Entry System (BES) maintained by MAS. The BES came into operation in 1987. All banks, primary dealers and approved dealers in the government securities market may open securities account with MAS.

More recently, MAS Electronic Payment System (MEPS) was introduced on 13 July 1998 and propelled Singapore into the ranks of developed financial markets that have implemented real time gross settlement systems. BES is linked to MEPS to provide delivery-versus-payment with finality for SGS transactions, contributing to the reduction of settlement risk in SGS transactions. MEPS employs state-of-the-art cryptography and smartcard technology to protect the transactions; and achieve end-to-end security between the front-end system at the banks and the host settlement system in MAS.

The settlement of an SGS transaction is effected one day after the trade date (T+1) of the transaction (regular trade). Cash trades in SGS, ie for same-day settlement (T+0) is also available, assisting banks and other financial institutions in their liquidity management.

Corporate Debt Securities

In 1998, The Central Depository (Pte) Ltd[2] (CDP) introduced the Debt Securities Clearing and Settlement System (DCSS), an electronic book-entry system for the custody and settlement of Singapore dollar denominated bonds. In line with international convention, the settlement period is T+3 days. All debt securities listed on the Singapore Exchange Securities Trading Limited are settled through the DCSS on a gross trade-for-trade, real-time basis.

The CDP system is also linked with MEPS and has full delivery-versus-payment settlement capability for Singapore dollar-denominated bonds. CDP also have indirect linkages with Euroclear and Cedel, which allow for cross border trades for both S$ and non-S$ bonds. Euroclear and Cedel can use their CDP account via depository agents in Singapore to custodise Singapore dollar bonds on behalf of their international investors.

Working with the Industry

MAS has benefited from considerable public and private sector interaction in reforming the Singapore debt market. In September 1998, 14 professionals formed an ad-hoc Debt Capital Market Working Group (DCMWG) and provided comments and recommendations to MAS in June 1999. Most of the 17 recommendations have been effected or are being considered by the Government. The effort of the DCMWG is only a beginning and we believe in continued dialogue. Openness will serve us well in fostering concerted commitment from all market participants to develop a vibrant Asian bond market.

Concluding Remarks - Issues for the Asian Bond Market

Securities regulators and central banks in Asia are all taking initiatives to develop their national bond markets. Our common objective should be the collective growth of the Asian market. A single country's bond market can be an attractive investment proposition for a time but not forever. Individual countries or markets may fall in or out of favour with investors and speculators but we could endeavour to secure funds that remain committed to the region.

The market is richer for a variety of credits and a range of yields. Varied sector exposure and a portfolio of instruments would serve to make the Asian market more attractive to global investors. A single country cannot supply all the components, certainly not in one or two years. But Asian countries, collectively, can do it.

There remain many issues in the path of Asian bond market rising to international prominence, and we would like to highlight some of the key issues for discussion at the Round Table session.

Investors Education

Asian investors have traditionally been more accustomed to property and equity investments, even when bond investments offered better returns. Even when bond returns would have been lower than equities, the improvements to risk-adjusted return from diversification into bonds were ignored. Apart from Japan where investment in bonds is more widespread, we need to educate Asian investors to the bond asset class and provide them with a full range of assets with which to build robust investment portfolios.

Transparency in Corporate Bond Market

The corporate bond market does not possess the same degree of price transparency as the equities market, or even the public debt market. The question of price transparency was raised by SEC Chairman Mr Arthur Levitt on 9 September 1998[3], who noted that investors in the US corporate bond market had less access to information than a car or home buyer. He called for increased transparency, as this would help investors make better decisions and increase confidence in the fairness of the markets. If this is true of the US with its developed bond market, we in emerging markets would do well to take note.

To argue that the bond market is largely serving institutional investors is probably not fully justified. With time, technology and changes in business models, information can move speedily to even small investors. There is a strong linkage between transparency and investor confidence, one good reason to for us in Asia to consider the issue as we develop the Asian bond market.

Harmonisation of Bond Conventions

The question of transparency leads to another issue. Taking a lesson from Europe, harmonisation of bond convention would be one effort that could work to Asia's collective advantage. As Asia shifts from traditional bank financing to new bond markets, we would do well to resist the tendency to perpetuate existing individual conventions and move towards preferred practices and align our bond conventions and market practices to the best that prevail in international bond markets. Our prospects of doing this would be greatly enhanced by continuing existing efforts to improve corporate governance, standards of information disclosure and financial law.

Electronic and Internet Revolution

Electronic Trading Platform

Technological advances are reshaping the dynamics of international bond markets. In Europe, the introduction of the unified market and single currency had given impetus to the development of electronic platforms to trade government bonds. One such system is the EuroMTS, which has gained prominence over the past 8 months. Across the Atlantic, Brokertec, a company originally formed by 6 big US banks – Citibank/Salomon Smith Barney, Goldman Sachs, Credit Suisse First Boston, Lehman Brothers, Merrill Lynch and Morgan Stanley Dean Witter – together with Deutsche Bank, has been created as a world wide electronic platform to trade cash bonds, repo and other securities. Apart from the US banks, US bond brokers Cantor Fitzgerald has developed a wholesale trading system named E-speed, which was also launched in Europe in July 1999.

Apart from trading, we also witnessed the World Bank, Freddie Mae and Fannie Mae using the internet to market and sell their bond offerings. Municipals in the US have bypassed brokers and offered direct online auctions in the past 2 years, reaping cost savings in fees and charges. Many companies in the US are also getting ready to issue debt online, although fear of reprisals by dealers has delayed a quick rush to the internet.

In summary, the Asian bond markets, though in relatively nascent stages of development, would not be immune to the electronic revolution in trading. Such innovation will soon find its way to our shores. We should prepare ourselves speedily to utilise the new technology and remain relevant in the new age bond market place. On the regulatory front, we must also keep pace with these market developments by formulating appropriate regulatory regimes tailored to the e-commerce/e-finance era.

NOTES

1. IFR Thomson Financial Database

2. The CDP is a subsidiary of the Singapore Exchange Limited. It began operations in 1987 as the central depository for Singapore securities market. Since June 1994, it has provided electronic book transfer for clearing and settlement of all share transactions in Singapore listed companies.

3. Speech at Media Studies Center, New York

G12 G21
G16 G32

SINGAPOREAN EXPERIENCE IN BOND MARKET DEVELOPMENT

by

Mr. Toshio Karigane

Introduction

Daiwa Securities Group has been involved, since 1971, in developing the Asian financial markets, especially the offshore bond market in Singapore. The latest commitment of Daiwa Group in this field was developing the offshore bond market in the Philippines.

There are many ways to develop domestic bond markets in Asia. One of the most effective ways is to establish offshore bond markets.

Singapore and Hong Kong already have well established offshore markets (both short-term and long-term markets). The Philippines, Malaysia and Thailand have short-term offshore markets. As for long-term offshore markets, the Philippines has just started development, while Malaysia and Thailand have not yet begun the process .

The major impact of the Miyazawa plan is that new funds have become available which can be utilized for developing Asian offshore bond markets, particularly the Asian yen bond market.

The establishment and development of offshore bond markets in the above-mentioned Asian countries should not create a conflict of interest among the countries involved, but instead, should be complimentary. The development of each individual market will accelerate the development of Asian bond markets as a whole.

The necessity for Asian bond markets

What are the reasons for developing bond markets in Asia? The most important reason is the urgent need to mobilize large amounts of long-term financing for infrastructure in order to sustain the present rates of economic growth. If we exclude the recent temporary economic downturn, we find that today's levels of infrastructure investment are inadequate to support the high rates of economic growth that Asia has enjoyed over the past many years.

Major investments are required, especially in power, transportation, and telecommunications. Overall investment must be increased to a percentage of GDP much greater than that in the past. It is difficult to estimate precisely how much will be needed in the coming years, but it is certain to be a tremendous amount.

A second important reason for domestic bond market development in Asia is the changing industrial structure of Asian countries. Most economies of East and Southeast Asia are shifting from labor-intensive to capital-intensive industries. Investments in these industries normally require a longer time span to develop. Consequently longer-term financing than conventional debt instruments offer is needed.

Many Asian companies raise debt funds internationally, and these funds are denominated in the currencies of developed countries, such as US dollars. However, because infrastructure projects normally generate revenues in local currency, external financing creates potential currency mismatches and generates exchange risk. The development of domestic bond markets would help to reduce this particular risk.

Domestic bond markets in Asia, however, will not necessarily take the place of bank loans. Domestic bond markets can complement bank loans and equity markets, which are more appropriate in a project's earlier stages. Bank financing is especially desirable during construction periods because a company can draw on resources as needs arise, instead of raising the whole lump sum at once, which a bond issue requires. But as a project comes on stream and as a steady cash flow becomes available, a bank loan can be refinanced with a bond issue.

A further reason for governments to facilitate bond market development is that domestic bond markets can create macroeconomic stability by reducing dependence on volatile international capital flows. They also provide an additional instrument for monetary policy through open-market operations.

It is interesting to note that international bond markets have grown rapidly in recent years. The volume of traditional Eurobonds has grown along with the issuance of global bonds, a significant number of bonds have been issued by Asian borrowers. Because access to Asian domestic bond markets has been limited for international investors, Asian issuers must go to Europe or the United States to raise funds.

I would like to mention the past tendency of Asian savings to be placed with intermediaries outside the region – who then invested part of these funds in Asia as bank loans with shorter maturities. The creation and development of Asian domestic bond markets can tackle this problem in two ways. First, it can negate the need for funds to flow out of the region. Second, it can help to avoid the problem of currency and maturity mismatches in the future.

How offshore bond markets assist domestic bond market development

It will take many years for domestic bond markets to develop. One of the most effective ways to develop domestic bond markets is to establish offshore bond markets. There are several ways in which the development of an offshore bond market can have an especially significant impact on the evolution of domestic bond markets in a region. The case of Singapore is a good example of how experience in developing the offshore markets was transferred to developing the domestic markets.

Market infrastructure is the most obvious beneficiary in the process. Market infrastructure, such as market makers, a clearing system, ratings agencies, and settlement procedures, are all necessary for both domestic and offshore markets. Furthermore, offshore bond market makers must maintain inventories and thus fund through repo transactions, which can easily also be used by domestic markets. Disclosure standards are enhanced because international investment banks require the standard due diligence for transactions. Accounting rules, regulatory enforcement, and benchmark yield curves for offshore issues can all be developed in the offshore markets and then adopted to develop the domestic market.

Human resources is another obvious area where development of an offshore bond market has a spill-over into the domestic bond market. Foreign banks that establish a presence in offshore markets take it upon themselves to train local workers or to establish joint ventures with local banks. A new class of local financiers and local institutional investors with greater experience in a wide range of investment techniques and vehicles will emerge. They can apply their skills to domestic as well as offshore markets.

Information systems for the domestic market will be improved. Besides employment, the technical transfer of information systems and computers will extend the technical capabilities of local banks and investors. The sophistication of dealers, brokers, and customers in the offshore bond market will have positive benefits also for domestic players.

Foreign exchange and money markets will also benefit. The offshore bond market will also help to expand the sophistication of foreign exchange markets and international money markets, along with interest rate hedging tools, in order to cope with offshore investor and issuer demand. This has recently been especially relevant.

It should be obvious that the establishment of offshore bond markets does not create a conflict of interest among Asian countries, but is instead complimentary. If the real goal is to expand the volume and variety of long-term financing available for economic growth in Asia, experience suggests that the best way to mobilize large amounts of funds is through the concurrent maturation of offshore and domestic bond markets.

The Offshore Bond Market in Singapore

The Asian offshore market originated in Singapore in 1968 when Singapore allowed non-residents to maintain tax-free foreign currency deposits. Later, after short-term money markets were established, the need arose also for long-term funds, primarily from overseas sources. Thus emerged the Asian offshore bond market, differentiated from the dominant Euro market by the physical location in Asia of the syndicate members, lawyers and often investors, and by the secondary market and quotation on Asian stock exchanges.

Singapore executed the first Asian-dollar bond issue in 1971 when the Development Bank of Singapore issued a ten-million U.S. dollar-denominated bond. The issue was lead managed by Daiwa Securities. A joint venture company was established in Singapore between Daiwa and the Development Bank of Singapore to provide the necessary secondary market infrastructure, including market making facilities, which had not existed until that time.

Throughout the 1970s, other large Asian borrowers followed the successful issue of the Development Bank of Singapore, including Keppel Shipyard, Singapore Airlines, and several Singapore subsidiaries of Japanese companies. Later, in the 1980s, international organizations, European and American banks, and several sovereign borrowers, including major Asian countries, issued bonds for amounts as much as US$300 per issue, which tapped a diverse variety of currencies including the Japanese yen. The market continued to deepen in the 1990s as the variety of issuers and number and amount of issues outstanding continued to expand at a healthy pace. The Singapore-dollar denominated domestic bond market has recently developed significantly. Apart from the Singapore government and Singapore issuers, foreign issuers have also been utilized in this domestic market. I believe that one of the contributing factors to this development is Singapore's mature offshore bond market.

I would like to mention the case of the Philippines, which has had a short-term offshore market since the mid-1970's. In 1997, the Development Bank of the Philippines issued an Asia-yen bond in the

Philippines offshore market under the lead management of Daiwa Securities. The idea was very similar to the case of the Development Bank of Singapore in the 1970s, with Daiwa establishing a joint venture company with the issuer -- called DBP-Daiwa Securities Philippines, Incorporated - to ensure the fulfillment of secondary market needs in the Philippines. The issue was solely targeted at Asian investors, and was underwritten by a group of Asian investment banks. We hope this issue will raise interest in the market and eventually help lead to the development of the domestic bond market in the Philippines.

The Miyazawa Plan could result in further growth of the offshore bond market, particularly the Asian offshore yen bond market.

The main features of the Miyazawa Plan (officially the new Miyazawa Initiative) are:

-   a $3 billion guarantee fund in the Asian Development Bank,

-   27.5 billion yen or $230 million to subsidize interest payments

-   the Export-Import Bank of Japan (now Japan Bank for International Cooperation) can guarantee sovereign bonds issued by emerging economies, or purchase them directly.

With these new instruments, it is expected that a total of 2 trillion yen or approximately US$17 billion, of long-term sovereign debt could be raised from the markets. Although there have been some significant withdrawals of Japanese bank loans from the region in recent years, I expect a large amount of Japanese money, primarily from institutional investors, to flow back to Asia through these long-term debt instruments which could be issued in the region.

To summarize,

-   the major impact of the Miyazawa Plan is that new funds have become available

-   the funds can be utilized for developing Asian financial markets, that is, for long term funding through the use of an offshore bond market.

I believe not only Singapore and Hong Kong, but also the Philippines, Malaysia and Thailand, which have already established short-term offshore markets, can make use of the Miyazawa Plan to develop their financial markets, particularly offshore yen bond markets in Asia.

There is a time for competition and there is a time for co-operation. Ladies and gentlemen, I propose that the time has come for co-operation in creating healthy Asian bond markets. Individual government money is not enough. It must be supplemented with private funds and efforts, and with intra-regional support. This will make the global financial system work in a more stable and balanced manner and help to prevent a repetition of the Asian currency crisis.

P34 G21 G20
G16 G12
G32
P31

DEBT MARKET IN CHINA

by
Dr. Gao Jian

Economic activity in the People's Republic of China (PRC) is mainly fuelled by indirect financing from banks, which have the country's vast national savings at their disposal. The capital market only commenced in the late 1980s, but has developed remarkably since then. Debt securities issuance has increased substantially. Market trading techniques are advanced. Marketable book-entry form securities account for the majority of securities issued in China. Contemporary tools, such as the tender system for selling, a primary dealer system for securities distribution and market making, and book-entry form for securities have been put in place. Furthermore, the investor base has been broadened. China's bonds market has grown in a remarkably short period of time.

Still, the underlying market infrastructure remains fragile. The bond market is currently small, as is its share of the financial market. Total bonds issued by government, government agencies, banks and state-owned enterprises (Sows) from 1981 to 1999 amounted to RMB 2,800bn, and only RMB1,800bn remained outstanding as of the end of 1999, compared to total bank assets of RMB1, 000bn. The bands market includes government, corporate and agency bonds, and financial debentures. Local government bonds and municipal government bonds do not exist.

Debt Market Development in China

The government security issuance can be traced as early back as the 1950's, soon after the founding of PRC. The first government debt was incurred in 1953 to finance the government's economic recovery program. The repayment was calculated in terms of volume of crops, due to persistent inflation at that time. As the government had tided over the difficult period time and entered into economic construction stage the government started to issue construction bonds to support its economic development program. From 1954 to 1958 there were five issues, once a year. Between 1958 and 1981 there was no central government bonds due partly to the predominant philosophy of no debt and balanced budget at that time and partly to the decentralization move of central government. As a result, the issuance authority was delegated to the local government. In 1962 all government debt was repaid and there was a period of time without debt in China's economy.

China resumed to issue government debt in 1981 two years after the economic reform program was commenced. Since then China has never suspended its issuance of government securities. The total issuing amount was RMB 2172 billion as of the end of 1999. 1000 billion remains outstanding, around 12.5% of GDP.

Until 1988 there was no government securities market. The bonds were mainly targeted towards individual investors at the issue. Individuals were forced to buy treasury notes or informed to deduct from their wages or salary for payment. Except those priced through auction, the State Council sets coupon rates.

A government securities market was established in 1988 when the government allowed the securities held by individuals to be traded over-the-counter in securities firms or banks. In 1991, the Ministry of Finance organized the first underwriting syndication to subscribe part of its issuing amount. This represented a fundamental change from administrative placement to market-oriented approach. At the same time government security future's market was introduced by the Ministry of Finance and the Shanghai Security Exchange, the first derivatives market in government securities. Futures were traded not only in stock exchanges but also in Zheng Chou commodity exchange.

To develop the wholesale markets in government securities, the MoF set up a primary dealer system in 1993. Primary dealers played a very important role in subscribing government securities at the issue and distributing them to the investors. The futures market was very active in 1994, which created tremendous demand for the new issue. A government securities collateralised Repo market was also created in the second half of 1993 which provided non-bank financial institutions with a useful instrument for accessing financial resources. Also in 1993, the first book-entry form paperless security was issued and subscribed to the primary dealers. To support book-entry form security, and to make paper security physically tradable, the MOF, in collaboration with the People's Bank of China (PBOC), set up the Government Security Depositary Trust Company for the custody, clearance and settlement of bonds transactions.

The government securities market changed significantly in 1996. Government securities were sold through auction and a number of new instruments were introduced, such as discounted three-month treasury bills and seven-and 10-year coupon-bearing treasury bonds. As treasury securities were priced through a bidding process that reflected the yield in the secondary market, sentiment in the market was very positive.

In 1997, MOF took steps to improve auction techniques. Multiple prices and changeable differential method were introduced to the bidding process. These innovations improved fair competition. However, the auctions were only conducted for two-year zero-coupon treasury notes and 10-year maturity treasury bonds. As market-oriented reforms aroused individuals' interest and their desire to buy government securities, the government decided to issue more savings bonds.

In 1998, the government bonds issuance increased substantially. Of total issue, 200 billion is for financing the deficit and maturity debt; 100 billion is for fiscal stimulus program, and 270 billion for bank recapitalazation. Most bonds were subscribed by the banks or placed though savings bonds. There was no new instrument traded in the securities exchange. MOF has return to international capital market by a successful global bonds issue. As deposit rate were cut by the government three times, individuals are tend to buy savings bonds because the coupon rates are 1% higher than deposit rates. Banks were also very active to hold government security to improve their assets quality. As interest was on the decline, the bonds market staged several rallies since the end of 1998.

A government effort to curb overheating stock market banks was required to cut the fund flow from banks to the stock market. As a result, banks have to trade the securities they hold among themselves. This is called the inter-bank bonds market.

In addition, there was no new issue in the stock exchange in 1998. This gave rise to a reduction of the number of instruments traded in the stock exchange market.

Overall, the bond market in the PRC has undergone profound changes since it was established. Given its short history, the progress so far is remarkable. However, the market-oriented approach remains inconsistent, bank deposit and lending rates have not been unliberalized and there are conflicts between features of the new regime and the old system.

Whether government securities should target individual investors or institutional investors also remains controversial. In addition, market instruments are still limited, the exchange market is shrinking, the inter-bank bond market is illiquid and savings bonds outweigh marketable securities. Nevertheless, market initiatives will generate new development in the future.

Impact of Recent Finanacial Environment

One of the signs of the government's recent commitment to developing the financial market is in the legal arena. Steps to establish a legal framework for financial activities are accelerating. Following the Security Act promulgated in January 1999, the Investment Fund Act is being drafted, and regulations surrounding financial violations are enacted.

Because of the recent Asia financial crisis and liquidity crunch, banks and financial institutions are implementing strict disciplinary measures such as internal supervision and cross-examination of banks' performance by reviewing major indicators. The closure of GITIC at the end of 1998 reflects the government's determination to deal with bankruptcies.

As the PBOC's monetary policy ease sets the tone for the 1999 financial environment, bond markets are looking increasingly favorable. Against the backdrop of the central government's fiscal stimulus program of 1999 and the fact that some window issuers who were granted the borrowing statue by State Council in 1989 are refraining from entering the international capital market and are instead turning to the domestic bonds market, the market anticipates more supply of securities in the pipeline.

In 1999, the PBOC relied more on open market operations to purse its monetary policy, it will continue to do so in 2000. The financial innovations will develop further in 2000. As the housing market develops, asset-backed securities will be introduced and the assets of state-owned enterprises (SOE) will be securitised. China's big four state-owned commercial banks will continue to focus on limiting risk in 2000 but they are also encouraged to increase their investment in business sector. The shifting of bad loans from their balance sheet to Assets Management Company (AMC) will reduce the bank burden and restore their confidence.

Government bonds market

Government bonds dominate the bond market. Total outstanding debt was RMB1, 100bn or about 13% of GDP in 1999. Although this figure is relatively small compare to that in other countries.

Legal framework

China's economic activities are mainly maintained by indirect financing through the banking system, which pumps the vast national savings into the economic system. The capital market was started only as recently as the late 1980s, but there has been remarkable development since then. The bonds market was still insignificant in size and in its share in the financial market. China has only public debt. The bonds market includes government bonds, corporate bonds and agency bonds. There are no local government bonds and municipal government bonds.

Government bonds are issued though the MOF for financing the deficit and maturing debt. The PBOC is in charge of distributing securities to individual investors, and acts as the fiscal agent for repayment at redemption. The National People's Congress must approve the total issuing volume, and the State Council sets the coupon rates. The China Securities Regulatory Commission (CSRC) and the PBOC regulates securities firms and other bond market dealers. The MOF and the CSRC regulate government security primary dealer. The Government Security Dealers Associations also exists; as a self-regulatory body.

Issuing format

The majority of government securities are sold though public offering. Only special state bonds are sold though private placement to pension fund and insurance fund run by government agencies. Before 1990, government securities were sold though administrative placement. Between 1991 and 1996 government securities were placed though underwriting syndication. In 1996 and 1997, government securities were mainly placed though tender. In 1998 the tap method (whereby bonds are sold over a period of time rather than at one time) was widely used for selling savings bonds.

In principle, discount securities are priced though uniform prices Dutch auctions, while coupon-bearing securities are priced though multiple-prices American auctions. Some innovations, such as changeable price differecials, and double calculations of weighted average method, are used to improve the competitiveness, fairness and consistency against secondary market yield. Bidders are mainly primary dealers, although some non-primary dealer financial institutions participate in bidding process upon MOF's approval.

When the primary dealers system was established in 1993, 19 security firms, banks and trust investment companies were selected as primary dealers based on "The Regulation on Government Security Primary Dealers". MOF and PBOC must approve the member of institutions and the number of primary dealers varies, depending on how many qualified institutions are available. Membership status is subject to periodic examination. There were 50 primary dealers at the end of 1999.

Instruments and tenor

Government securities include marketable and no-marketable securities. The marketable securities comprise book-entry form and bearer form securities. Non-marketable securities are savings bonds. Savings bonds and bearer form securities have three- and five-year maturities, and target individuals. Bearer securities are also available to other kind of investors, such as SOE's. Book-entry securities have seven- and ten-year maturity, and are only for institutional investors. Maturities for government securities range from three to six months, and one, two, three, five, seven and 10 years. For 1996 issues, only three-month and seven year maturities are available, and only 10-year maturities for 1996 and 1997 issues. In 1998, the MOF issued 30-year bonds for the first time. They targeted banks, and the proceeds were used for bank recapitalisation. Ten-year bonds were also sold to the banks.

There was a tendency of diversification of maturity profile in 1994 and 1996 with a view to smooth out the payment peak and increase instruments for trading as well as for formulating a yield curve.

Secondary market

The main marketplaces are Shanghai Securities Exchange Shen Zhen Securities Exchange where there are seven off-run securities traded (not very active). Secondary market trading also takes place in the so-called inter-bank bond market. The two marketplaces are currently separated. The stock exchange market is liquid, whereas the inter-bank bond market is not. In the inter-bank bond market security are traded at the Shanghai Foreign Exchange Trading Center and settled though Government Security

Depositary Trust Company. Daily turnover in 1998 and 1999 was around RMB 10-20 billion, down sharply from RMB300bn in 1996.

Three- and six-month and one-year bills are sold as discount securities, and paid at full face value. Day count for calculation of yield to maturity is on a 30/360-day basis. Two-, three- and five-year maturities are zero-coupon, and simple interest is calculated on seven-and10-year maturities for coupon-bearing securities. Coupon payments are made on a yearly basis. Bearer form securities are demobilised and dematerialised before being traded on the securities exchanges, where trading is computerised. Bearer form securities are also available on the over-the-counter market. Three-, seven-, 14-and 28-day repos are traded very actively with securities firms as active borrowers.

Security firms are borrowers though repo markets. Banks and SOE's were mainly lenders in repo market. As banks walked out from the exchange in 1997, only non-bank institutions act as moneylender. In 1999, central bank allowed some securities firms to participated in inter-bank market and borrows money in the market.

Foreign debt issues

Foreign debt is all public debt. The total outstanding foreign debt was $143 billion as of the end of 1999. Government foreign debt includes the debt incurred by agencies that the central government is committed to repay and the debt incurred by the MOF for financing maturing government foreign debt. The outstanding government debt is about US$6 billion. Since the end of the 1980s, in addition to the World Bank loans and other bilateral and multilateral loans, new government debt has been incurred through public offering in international capital markets. The debut issue in 1987 was for 300 million Deutsche Mark, which was lead-managed by Dresdner bank. After suspension for six years, the MOF resumed international borrowing after Moody's upgraded its rating from Baa1 to A1. The MOF has 12 bond issues all together, including an Euro yuan issue, and dragon, samurai, Yankee and globe bond issues.

Market participants

Historically, bonds were mainly sold to individual investors. As the market developed, SOE's, banks, pension, insurance and investment fund were permitted to join in and actively subscribed to government securities and corporate bonds. In 1996, institutional investors, financial institutions and SOEs subscribed to 80% of securities. Prior to 1998, banks were discouraged from holding securities. However, as they became more liquid, they were advised to buy securities.

Primary dealers played an important role in subscribing to government securities in the primary market and making market (i.e. quoting bid–offer prices) in the secondary market. Currently, there are 50 primary dealers: security firms, banks and some institutional investors. Some local security firms and government security trading centers function as distributors and paying agent for redemption.

Other debt securities

The corporate bonds market

Government agencies and corporations issue corporate bonds, although the market is small vis-a-vis the government bonds market. By the end of 1998, only RMB28.5bn was outstanding.

Corporate bond issuance is subject to approval of State Planning and Development Commission and PBOC. The coupon rate is set by SPDC. The quotas for total annual issue control the size of corporate bonds. The quotas were about RMB4bn between 1994 and 1997. A credit market has yet to be formulated since there are no internationally recognized rating agencies in the country. Corporate bonds are not priced against a government securities benchmark, as in many other countries.

Financial debentures

Policy banks, such as State Development Bank, EXIM Bank and Agriculture Development Bank issue financial debentures. Until 1997, they were issued through administrative placement to commercial banks and postal savings institutions. Since the latter half of 1998, financial debentures have been placed through a bidding process. Bidders are mainly banks, although since the end of 1998 some insurance companies have been allowed to participate in the bidding process. At the end of 1999, total outstanding financial debentures were about RMB600bn. Financial debentures are the PBOC's most important instrument for open market operations. In 1999 alone, the PBOC bought about RMB100bn government securities, financial debentures from banks to increase money supply.

Tax and fee

Government security holders are exempted from income tax but subject to capital gain tax if securities are traded in the market. Corporate bonds holders are subject to 40% withholding tax as well as capital gains tax.

Market performance in 1999

In 1999, the government's macro-economic policy was focused on public investment. Government spending played important role in achieving the government's 7% growth target. In addition to RMB430bn financing program in the initial budget, the National People's Congress endorsed RMB60bn investment earmarked to infrastructure projects.

As in 1998, about one-third of government securities were savings bonds that were sold to individuals. Book-entry form securities were placed in the inter-bank bonds market. There were only two issues launched in Shanghai Securities Exchange. As the State Council set the coupon rates, one issue was welcomed whereas another was not.

The CDB was the second largest issuer in domestic bonds market. The total issuing amount was RMB130bn. Although CDB's placement was still limited in the inter-bank bonds market, it achieved the objective of issuing its majority of financial debentures through market-oriented method.

To cater to the market need, CDB introduced floating rate notes in the inter-bank bonds market and created a new instrument in China's bonds market. The spread was decided through a bidding process on one-year maturity bank deposit rates. With FRN issues, CDB successfully issued 10-year maturities financial debentures and extended the duration of its debt portfolio.

CDB also improved its selling method by experimenting the multiple-price auction in selling its five-year maturity.

However the secondary market trading remained inactive in both inter-bank bonds market and securities exchange market.

CDB also conducted a globe bonds transaction in international capital market raising USD500mn. The deal was lead-managed by Merrill lynch and Solomon Smith Barney. This was the only issuance by Chinese issuer the market.

Outlook for 2000

Debt capital markets will be active as the government continues its fiscal stimulus program and starts its West Development Program. The government will also streamline bonds market management. The regulatory authority will be shift from PBOC to SPDC, to overcome overlapping authority.

The budgetary revenue for 2000 is expected to rise 7.9 per cent, reaching 690.4 billion yuan [US$83.18 billion], while expenditure will total 920.3 billion yuan [US$ 110.88 billion] an increase of 12.3 percent.

China will issue bonds worth RMB438bn [US$ 52.77 billion] this year to finance the maturing debt and deficit.

As in 1999, the majority of book-entry form securities will be sold to the banks in the inter-bank bonds market as banks have tremendous liquidity and they feel it is safer to buy treasury securities than to give loans to enterprises, as the demand for money remain to be weak.

CDB will issue RMB200bn in the market to finance infrastructure project. Some other issuers like Railway Ministry will also return to the market.

To get a smooth selling of securities, the Ministry of Finance has signed a contract with a group of banks and non-bank financial institutions on underwriting syndication agreement.

The Ministry of Finance and CDB will announce a fixed timetable for selling securities. MOF will launch its medium- and long-term securities at the third week of every month while CDB will auction its financial debentures on the second week of every month.

DEVELOPMENT OF BOND MARKETS IN ASIA: THE HONG KONG, CHINA PERSPECTIVE

by
Mr. Norman Chan

Introduction

There are numerous studies and literature on bond market development in Asia and why it is relatively underdeveloped. There has also been little disagreement amongst the policy makers and regulators in Asia on the desirability of developing their domestic bond markets. The advantages of a mature bond market are numerous and such advantages have become even more self-evident after the latest Asian financial crisis. Yet, despite this consensus, the question still remains: why is it that domestic bond markets are still developing at a rather disappointingly slow pace, notwithstanding the benefits an economy can gain from them?

This question has been discussed in many forums such as this particular Round Table. There are of course many impediments to the development of a mature, deep and liquid bond market in Asia. These are the usual supply side and demand side problems, which I do not need to repeat here. It may be useful, however, if I share with you Hong Kong's experience in tackling some of these impediments during the process of developing our bond market. In so doing, I would like to offer some general observations on the policy challenges or dilemmas that may be relevant to other economies which intend to step up their efforts in bond market development.

Hong Kong's Experience

Hong Kong has been making conscious efforts to develop its bond market since 1990. In the last ten years or so, we have come a long way. The amount of outstanding debt securities has increased 40 times from US$1.3 billion or 1% of GDP to US$54 billion or 34% of GDP. It would be useful to look back and examine what we have done so far to come to where we are now.

Development of Benchmark Yield Curve

A mature bond market must have a reliable benchmark yield curve to enable proper pricing of bond issues. Without a benchmark yield curve, it is difficult for the bond market to develop. So the first thing the HKMA did was to develop a benchmark yield curve for the Hong Kong dollar debt by issuing Exchange Fund Bills and Notes. We started from scratch and extended the maturity of the Bills and Notes all the way from 3 months to 10 years over a period of 7 years.

The *policy challenge* here stems from the fact that Hong Kong, like many other Asian economies, has not been in the habit of running fiscal deficits and has therefore had no fiscal need to borrow from the market. In the absence of a fiscal borrowing requirement, the policy maker must take a view on whether the issuance of government paper for the purpose of developing a reliable benchmark yield curve can be justified in the interest of promoting market development. In this analysis, there is the key question of how the government can derive enough income from the investment of the proceeds of issuance to offset the interest costs of the issuance. Given the lack of suitable fixed income securities in domestic currency, many governments have been deterred from issuing long maturity paper, thereby hindering the development of a benchmark yield curve. In Hong Kong, we overcome this problem by using Hong Kong dollar interest rate swaps to hedge the fixed rate liabilities of the longer term Exchange Fund Notes. But clearly this hedging technique is only viable when there is a suitably deep and liquid interest rate swap market in existence.

Clearing and Settlement System

In introducing the Exchange Fund Bills and Notes Programme, we knew for sure that if we wanted the Programme to be successful, we needed to have an efficient, reliable and low cost clearing and settlement system. This is not a special requirement in Hong Kong, as almost all governments with a regular bond issuance programme must grapple with this problem. In Hong Kong, the HKMA developed the Central MoneyMarkets Unit in 1990, which cleared initially the Exchange Fund Bills and Notes and later, to meet market demand, private sector bonds as well. We then further enhanced the system to link it up with the Hong Kong dollar interbank payment system so as to provide Delivery Vs Payment capability on a real time basis. Outstanding debt securities amounting to around US$30 billion are presently lodged with the CMU.

It is very easy to think that the biggest *challenge* here is the technology required to develop the clearing and settlement systems. However, it seems to me that another equally important policy challenge relates to how the authorities perceive their roles vis-à-vis the private sector in the development of clearing and settlement systems. It can be argued that private sector bonds should be cleared by a clearing system developed by the private sector. For example, US Treasuries are cleared by the New York Fed whereas private sector bonds are cleared by private sector run clearing systems. In Hong Kong, the HKMA regards clearing and settlement systems as an important piece of infrastructure for the financial market, in which the HKMA has the responsibility to ensure its safe and efficient functioning. To leave it entirely to the initiatives from the private sector would run the risk of slowing down market development.

Tax Incentives and Other Measures

In addition, Hong Kong has introduced a number of other measures to promote bond market development. These include offering exemption for profits tax on income derived from Hong Kong dollar bonds issued by multilateral development banks and concessionary tax rate on other private sector Hong Kong dollar bonds with 5-year maturity or longer. The *policy challenge* of these measures is clearly how one would be willing to grant tax incentives to the bond market without creating an uneven playing field for the other sectors. The HKMA also set up the Hong Kong Mortgage Corporation (HKMC) in 1997 to help promote the debt market and secondary mortgage market. The HKMC has since then become an important issuer of bonds and a leading force in mortgage securitization in Hong Kong.

Looking Ahead: Challenges and Opportunities

Given what we have done, are we very happy with our achievements and how do we see the prospects of Hong Kong's bond market in the future? As indicated earlier, Hong Kong's debt market capitalisation to GDP ratio is 34%, which is low comparing with 167% in the US and 137% in Japan

(Table 1). More importantly, the primary market issuance is dominated by the Government, banks and multilateral development banks which together accounted for 80% of the total outstanding Hong Kong dollar debt at end-1999. Local corporates (excluding statutory bodies) accounted for only 9% of the total (Table 2). At the same time, there is quite a narrow investor base on the demand side. At end-1999, banks and financial institutions held around US$11 billion or 84% of the Exchange Fund paper and around US$16 billion or 43% of the private sector paper, mainly for liquidity and collateral management purposes (Table 3). The rest of the paper is held by a few institutional investors, such as the public funds and pension funds.

So Hong Kong is not totally immune to the usual supply and demand side bottlenecks that its neighbours are experiencing. There are many challenges that lie ahead, some of which are easier to tackle than the others.

On the **demand side**, the institutional investor base for bonds has been fairly narrow. However, the situation will improve with the implementation of the Mandatory Provident Fund Scheme in December this year, which requires both employers and employees to contribute to the retirement funds at a minimum rate of 5% of an employee's salary. Contributions from the Mandatory Provident Fund Scheme, together with other voluntary retirement fund schemes, will become an increasingly important source of institutional demand for debt securities in the future.

Another factor that is presently favourable to the demand for fixed income in Asia is that for the first time in the past decade or so bonds are yielding a real rate of return as a result of falling inflation, if not deflation, in the region. In the case of Hong Kong, the real rate of return on 5-year Exchange Fund Notes increased from around minus 3% at end-1995 to around 11% at end-1999 (Table 4).

On the **supply side**, given that international credit has generally shrunk after the Asian financial crisis, there is a practical need for the corporates to diversify their sources of funds. They have thus turned to the bond market. Statistics of selected Asian economies show that new corporate debt issuance in the region has increased significantly in 1999 (Table 5). Moreover, many governments in the region are having real fiscal needs to borrow substantial amounts from the market to finance banking and financial restructuring. All these are conducive to the development of domestic bond markets.

There are two problems that are quite difficult to resolve: one on the demand side and one on the supply side,. The first problem arises from the generally low credit ratings of sovereigns and corporates in Asia. The second relates to the small size of corporates in Asia.

With the exception of Japan and Singapore, most Asian governments and corporate issuers receive **relatively low credit ratings** from the international rating agencies. While I do not intend to embark upon a debate on the objectivity and reliability of the ratings and the rating process itself, it is important to point out that low credit rating is a negative factor in bond market development in the region. For example, while official reserves collectively held by Asia amounted to a staggering figure of US$945 billion at end-1999, I imagine that most official reserve managers in Asia would be constrained in investing in Asian bonds as they can only invest in bonds with ratings above certain thresholds. Similarly, prudent fund managers and private sector investors would also have concerns on low credit ratings of Asian issuers.

So, what can we do about the low credit rating problem? There is not much that individual economies can do on their own. The setting up of national rating agencies may only solve part of the problem as it is not easy to build up credibility and confidence overseas. While acknowledging that a low credit rating is a reality that most Asian issuers have to live with for some time, it seems sensible to consider the idea of setting up a regional credit enhancement and guarantee agency to address investor concern on credit exposure. While the feasibility and viability of this credit guarantee agency idea will require further study, I believe that no matter what form of ownership structure the agency takes, it should be run on prudent commercial principles and be able to price the risks objectively and properly.

The second problem arises from **the relatively small size of the Asian corporates**. Although more and more Asian companies have become bigger over the years, whether through natural growth or mergers, one must recognise that Asian corporates cannot match the size of the corporate sector in the US and Europe. For example, Microsoft, before its stock price crashed, had a capitalisation of around US$580 billion which was almost the combined annual GDP of Korea, Hong Kong and Singapore (Table 6). For the smaller Asian firms, raising funds through bond issues may be more costly than borrowing from banks or listing on the stock markets. This would mean that that, for many years to come, bank lending would remain a major source of funds for the small- and medium-sized enterprises in the region, as the banks can understand and price the risks of these companies more efficiently than the bond market. While acknowledging this limitation arising from the small size of Asian companies, there is enormous room for the Asian corporate bond market to grow in the years ahead in line with the global trend of financial disintermediation.

Table 1: **Bond Market Sizes and Savings Rates** (Percentage Points)

	Hong Kong	**Japan**	**USA**
Bond Market[1]/ Stock Market[2]	9	118	90
Bond Market/ Bank Loans[3]	26	143	304
Bond Market/ GDP[4]	33	137	167
Domestic Savings[5]/ GDP	30	29	19

1. Bond market - HK: end-1999; Japan & USA: end-June 1999.
2. Stock market - HK, Japan & USA: end-1999.
3. Bank loans - HK, Japan & USA: end-1999.
4. GDP - HK, Japan & USA: 1998.
5. Domestic savings - HK, Japan & USA: 1998.
Source: HKMA, IMF, BIS, Bloomberg and CEIC.

Table 2: **Outstanding HK$ Debt by Issuers**

	End – 1990		End – 1999	
	Amount (HK$ mn)	**Share (%)**	**Amount (HK$ mn)**	**Share (%)**
Authorised Institutions	350	4	173,556	41
Exchange Fund	7,540	72	101,874	24
MDBs*	1,600	15	60,537	14
Local Corporates	750	7	36,461	9
Other Overseas Borrowers**	208	2	27,209	7
Statutory Bodies	0	0	20,692	5
Total	**10,448**	**100**	**420,329**	**100**

* Multilateral development banks, including ADB, IBRD, IFC, EIB, EBRD, IADB, NIB, AfDB, Council of Europe and European Company for the Financing of Railroad Rolling Stock.
** Excluding MDBs.
Source: HKMA, Bloomberg, Basisfield.

Table 3: **Holders of HK$ Debt Securities at End-1999** (HK$ million)

Debt Securities Issued by	Debts Held By		
	Financial Institutions	**Non-Financial Institutions**	**Total**
Authorised Institutions	92,192	81,364	173,556
Exchange Fund	85,811	16,063	101,874
MDBs	17,512	43,025	60,537
Local Corporates	16,758	19,703	36,461
Other Overseas Borrowers	1,843	25,366	27,209
Statutory Bodies	8,931	11,761	20,692
Total	223,047	197,282	420,329

Source: HKMA, Bloomberg, Basisfield.

Table 4: **Real Rate of Return of 5-year Exchange Fund Notes** (Percentage Points)

	Yield (a)	**CPI* (b)**	**Real Rate of Return (a) – (b)**
1995	6.3	9.0	-2.7
1996	6.7	6.3	0.4
1997	9.3	5.8	3.5
1998	6.2	2.8	3.4
1999	7.1	-4.0	11.1

*Year-on-year changes in Consumer Price Index.
Source: HKMA and IMF

Table 5: **New Corporate Bond Issuance in Selected Asian Economies** (In US$ million)

	1995	1996	1997	1998	1999
Australia	1,797	4,751 (+164%)	6,171 (+30%)	8,574 (+39%)	12,375 (+44%)
China	90	820 (+811%)	2,731 (+233%)	769 (-72%)	100 (-87%)
Hong Kong	2,280	3,096 (+36%)	6,977 (+125%)	2,444 (-65%)	7,617 (+212%)
Indonesia	1,674	5,007 (+199%)	8,271 (+65%)	254 (-97%)	80 (-69%)
Japan	890	842 (-5%)	1,179 (+40%)	2,102 (+78%)	17,464 (+731%)
Korea	2,815	3,349 (+19%)	6,668 (+99%)	1,656 (-75%)	2,689 (+62%)
Malaysia	2,783	3,121 (+12%)	9,337 (+199%)	2,722 (-71%)	5,600 (+106%)
Philippines	1,025	1,545 (+51%)	3,034 (+96%)	838 (-72%)	1,889 (+125%)
Singapore	1,844	2,490 (+35%)	2,593 (+4%)	2,093 (-19%)	2,078 (-1%)
Thailand	538	952 (+77%)	1,268 (+33%)	1,645 (+30%)	3,004 (+83%)

Note: Percentages in brackets represent percentage increases or decreases in issuance over the previous year.
Source: Basisfield

Table 6: **GDP of Selected Asian Countries in 1998**
(US$ billion)

China	965
Hong Kong	164
India*	398
Indonesia	117
Japan	4,284
Korea	373
Malaysia	75
Pakistan	60
Philippines	68
Singapore	85
Thailand	125

*The GDP figure for India is applicable to the year from 1 April 1997 to 31 March 1998.
Source: IMF

POLICY AGENDA FOR BOND MARKET DEVELOPMENT IN ASIA

by
Dr. Yun-Hwan Kim

I.   Introduction

The Asian financial crisis suggests many policy tasks not only to its worst hit economies but also to other developing countries. One of them is the need to diversify bank borrowings as the main source of industrial financing. The crisis countries[1] relied for their long-term development resources on short-term external borrowings, both from domestic and foreign as a result of bank-centered financial systems. Although this kind of financial system has contributed to the high-economic growth outcomes since it could monitor more effectively financial environments characterised by asymmetric information in underdeveloped financial markets, it has also resulted in the industrial sector's overreliance on short-term borrowing. In the case of Indonesia, immediately after the break of the crisis in July 1997, of the total corporate sector foreign debt (US$ 64.6 billion) two-thirds were short-term, with the average maturity of all private sector debt (occupying about 80 percent of the country's debt) being roughly 18 months only. This kind of industrial financing behavior has caused two critical financial mismatches: a maturity mismatch and a currency mismatch. First, the maturity mismatch was the consequence of their unhealthy financing practices, which were characterized by large long-term investments under the financing of short-term bank borrowings.[2] Second, the practice involved a serious currency mismatch without a proper currency hedging arrangement. In fact, the currency mismatch was implicitly protected by overvalued exchange rates, which were the result of foreign exchange misalignments in these countries.

The crisis economies have achieved much less successful development in the financial sector than in the real sector. Financial sector weaknesses are deep-seated and have been posing problems in the overall economy. These countries have not addressed these weaknesses in a vigorous manner during their high growth period over the last four decades. The real sector growth in these countries has been successful but the financial sector development has lagged behind. Real sector strengths have been clearly evidenced by low inflation, high growth, fiscal discipline, and significantly advanced manufacturing capacity. By contrast, the financial sector remains weak largely due to the government's intervention in the operation and management of financial institutions, direct fiscal support for a significant number of special-purpose banks, government's implicit guarantees about banks' operations, and an improper financial sector development strategy downplaying the role of capital markets. In view of this underlying situation, the Asian crisis is perceived as a liquidity crisis rather than a macroeconomic crisis.

Until now, the crisis countries' restructuring policy has focused on the stabilization of financial markets (particularly banking and foreign exchange markets), recapitalization of viable banks, workout of heavily indebted corporations, reform of corporate governance, and resolution/management of non-performing loans. Except for Indonesia where the restructuring is sluggish, the crisis countries' efforts have generally been successful, making substantial contributions

141

to the recent fast economic recovery. Particularly in the Republic of Korea and Malaysia, where the governments are playing the leading role, the speed of the restructuring is fast, although the ongoing effort leaves the country with many remaining tasks including the accumulation of huge bad assets in the hands of asset management companies (AMCs), injection of large public funds for bank recapitalization, and related nationalization of several banks.

While the crisis economies need to maintain the ongoing restructuring efforts on the one hand, they must start to deliberate the post-crisis policy agenda in order to prevent recurrence of similar financial crises as well as to lay a stronger foundation for sustainable long-term development. An important agenda in this context would be to diversify the source of industrial financing through the development of deeper capital markets, particularly bond markets, which remain underdeveloped in these countries. It is also desirable to actively tap international bond markets to finance long-term industrial projects.

In the post crisis period, the industrial corporations in Asian developing economies, including those in the crisis economies, will see some significant changes in the financing environment in the sense that foreign as well as domestic banks will be extremely cautious about providing credits.[3] This will result in bank disintermediation, as in the US and, to a lesser extent, Japan and European countries,[4] though for different reasons. Given that bank intermediated finance still forms the single most important source of industrial funds in Asian developing countries, this change reinforces the need to develop direct financing in the developing countries. The potentialities for developing domestic bond markets are great given these countries have the worlds highest savings rates.

Effective capital markets may play several positive roles: first, there will be greater diversification of financing and a smaller concentration of financial risks; second, the markets may check and screen financial risks more efficiently than bank credit departments, based on swift flows of various information; and third, deepen the financial base which has far-reaching positive implications for development resource mobilization in developing countries.

II.   Trends of Industrial Financing in the Asian Crisis Economies

2.1   Domestic Financing

The financial systems of the four crisis economies display very different characteristics. The two economies of Indonesia and Thailand are easily characterized as bank-centric financial systems where banks are required to exert a significant monitoring role arising from both equity as well as debt exposures. Malaysia with a more developed equity market should facilitate arm's length bank financing. On the other hand, the Republic of Korea, through its chaebol structure, displays a web of interconnected corporate cross-holdings. Overlaid onto the corporate control processes that emerge from these systems are the separate influences from the state, small groups of founding families and finally shareholders that are usually poorly organized and lacking in political influence. The mitigation of these agency factors and the different degrees of development of institutional infrastructure have affected the structure of the respective bond and equity markets in the crisis economies.

Table 2.1 **Bank Loans, Corporate Bonds, and Equities
in Asian Crisis Countries and the U.S., End-1998**
(Percent of GDP)

	Outstanding Bank Loans	Outstanding Corporate Bonds	Equity Market Capitalization
Indonesia	60.2[1/]	1.5	16.2
Republic of Korea	43.5	27.3	30.7
Malaysia	148.4	5.1	134.4
Thailand	108.7	2.6	26.3
U.S.	38.8	43.2	158.1

1. At the end of 1997
Source: Countries' Monetary Authorities and Bloomberg Investor Services.

The size of bond and equity markets and domestic bank lending in the crisis economies is shown in Table 2.1. All crisis economies have significantly larger banking sector and much smaller bond and equity markets. It clearly shows that these countries' domestic financing has traditionally heavily relied on the banking sector. By country, Malaysia has the largest market for bank loans and equity market capitalization in relation to gross domestic product (GDP), while Republic of Korea has the largest corporate bond market. As of the end of 1998, Republic of Korea had the highest rate of outstanding corporate bonds to GDP (27.3 percent), followed by Malaysia (5.1 percent), Thailand (2.6 percent), and Indonesia (1.5 percent).

These economies reliance on bank intermediated finance is evident when compared to the large and integrated financial market in the U.S. [5] where bank lending and corporate bond markets are of a similar magnitude (38.8 percent and 43.2 percent). Thus the ratios suggest that Republic of Korea has the most disintermediated debt market whereas Indonesia has the least. On the other hand Malaysia has an equity market whose capitalization is comparable in GDP terms to that of the U.S. Since intermediation via traditional financial institutions, and direct securities market processes compete with one another on efficiency criteria, the key issue is to identify those factors that have dissuaded the development of non-intermediated forms of financing in the crisis economies.

The three-year trends from 1996 to 1998 in Table 2.2 suggest that only Republic of Korea has increased corporate bond financing over that period, from 18.2 to 27.3 percent with the three other countries remaining generally unchanged despite year-to-year fluctuations. By comparison the U.S., assisted by the on-going recycling of bank loans through various securitization vehicles, shows evidence of ongoing disintermediation with levels of bond financing increasing over the three year period from 37.1 to 43.2 percent. This comparison shows that the bond markets in the crisis countries remain at a modest level. In Republic of Korea, upon the eruption of the financial crisis, commercial banks became extremely cautious about new lending and eager to withdraw old loans in order to meet the Bank of International Settlement (BIS) capital adequacy ratio. This led industrial corporations to tap bond markets. In Malaysia, the banking sector was well capitalized, with capital–asset ratios exceeding 10 percent, before the crisis. Therefore Malaysian banks did not drastically cut their loans to the industrial sector. Thailand and Indonesia also did not reduce bank loans in a significant manner. However, Indonesia, Malaysia, and Thailnd have all been keen to develop corporate bond markets, with their enthusiasm being strengthened after the crisis.

Table 2.2 **Outstanding Corporate Bonds in Asian Crisis Countries and the U.S.**
(Percent of GDP)

	Dec 1996	Dec 1997	Dec 1998
Indonesia	1.9	2.5	1.5
Korea, Republic of	18.2	21.4	27.3
Malaysia	6.1	7.1	5.1
Thailand	2.8	2.8	2.6
U.S.	37.1	39.6	43.2

Source: Countries' Monetary Authorities and Bloomberg Investor Services.

2.2 *International Bank Financing*

The levels of international lending to the crisis economies from 1996 to 1999 are provided in Table 2.3. This Table provides a summary of levels in lending to the crisis economies and the Asia-Pacific region generally, while more specific details and key facts of lending to individual countries are provided in Appendix B. Lending peaked at US$247.9 billion by December 1996 dropping significantly to US$160.7 billion by June 1999. In nominal terms though this appears to be linked to a withdrawal from lending to Asia generally. In percentage terms, Thailand (50%) and Republic of Korea (37%) experienced the largest reduction in bank lending over the period. This suggests that following the Asian crisis international bank lending to the crisis economies was characterized by the rebalancing of investor portfolios away from the Asian region.

Table 2.3 **International Bank Lending to Crisis Economies**
(US$ billion)

	December 1996	December 1997	June 1998	December 1998	June 1999
Total Developing Countries (TD)	692.6	891.7	860.7	842.7	809.6
Total Asia (TA)	367.1	378.8	319.6	299.4	287.0
Indonesia	55.5	58.0	48.4	45.0	43.8
Korea, Republic of	100.0	93.7	71.6	65.6	63.5
Malaysia	22.2	27.3	22.8	20.9	18.6
Thailand	70.2	58.5	46.4	41.2	34.7
Total Crisis Countries (TC)	247.9	237.5	189.2	172.7	160.7
(TA/TD) %	53.0	42.5	37.1	35.5	35.4
(TC/TD) %	37.8	26.6	22.0	20.5	19.8
Average Maturity (Crisis Economies)					
Less than 1 and 1 year (%)	61.2	60.5	51.7	50.3	50.1
Average Maturity (Total Asian Economies)					
Less than 1 year and 1 year (%)	61.5	60.3	53.0	52.5	51.4

Notes:
(i) Asia includes Afghanistan Bangladesh, Bhutan, British Overseas Territories, Brunei, Cambodia, PRC, Fiji, French Polynesia, India, Indonesia, Kiribati, North and South Korea, Laos, Macao, Malaysia, Maldives, Mongolia, Myannar, Nauru, Nepal, New Caledonia, Pakistan, Papua New Guinea, Philippines, Solomon Islands, Sri Lanka, Taipei, China, Thailand, Tonga, Tuvalu, US Pacific Islands, Vietnam, Wallis-Futuna Islands, Western Samoa. Singapore and Hong Kong, China are treated as offshore banking centres and are not included.
Source: BIS (1999) "*Consolidated International Banking Statistics for End-June 1999*" November and BIS (1997) "*The Maturity, Sectoral and Nationality Distribution of International Bank Lending: Second Half 1996*" Basle July.

Whereas in 1996 Asia enjoyed a privileged position as being the main focus of international lending to the developing world (53.0% of lending in 1996), this changed quickly as the contagion of the Asian Crisis unfolded such that by June 1999 it accounted for only 35.4%. Simultaneously the amount of this lending that was directed to the crisis economies also was reduced from 37.8% in December 1996 to 19.8% in June 1999. That is, not only was lending redirected away from the Asian region to other developing economies (mostly Eastern Europe), but also of those funds allocated to Asia a reducing amount has been directed towards the crisis economies.

This situation has arisen due to two factors. First, there is evidence of a structural shift away from bank intermediated lending originating from Japan[6] owing to the domestic crisis confronting that economy and an aversion to yen denominated loans by regional borrowers. Specifically, Thailand and Republic of Korea have experienced the least reduction in loans from Japan while Indonesia and Malaysia have experienced the greatest reduction[7]. However, while the reduction in lending from Japan has been partly offset by lending from European banks, the absolute quantity of loans has reduced. Second the reduction in lending reflects a reassessment on the part of lenders from the developed world to the creditworthiness of the Asian region and the crisis economies in particular. The risk reassessment has been manifest as higher (credit) spreads on bank intermediated loans and higher yields on bonds trading in secondary markets. Though the price of debt has risen, the significant reduction in lending has been entailing liquidity concerns for the region.

Information on the average maturity of lending to Asia and to the crisis economies is provided in Table 2.3. At the peak of lending in 1996 most loans to Asia (61.5%) and the crisis economies (61.2%) had a maturity of less than or equal to one year. Though the maturity of loans has been subsequently extended, at June 1999 the crisis economies still borrowed 50.1% of loans as short maturities. However this figure disguises the true situation that the increase in the average loan maturity is more a function of the non-rollover of short-term loans.

Though not recorded in Table 2.3, the majority of international lending over the period was directed towards the banking sector in the case of Republic of Korea (from 65.9% in December 1996 to 57.4% in June 1999), while in the other three crisis economies lending was directed towards the private sector (an average of 62.5% in December 1996 to 69.2% in June 1999). The anomalous situation in the Republic of Korea is likely to be due to the concentration of the banking market and the arrangements in place between the Korean chaebols. The levels of lending to the public sector in preference to the other industry sectors also have shown an increase in recent years. Also a feature of lending to the region was that capital inflows through banks were not sensitive to the movements in interest rate differentials such that banks increased their domestic lending once they had borrowed unhedged from abroad[8].

2.3   *International Bond Issues*

2.3.1.   *Recent Trends*

International bond issues comprise bonds issued in Eurobond markets or in foreign domestic bond markets such as in the U.S., Japan or the U.K. Details of these issues are provided in the following Table 2.4. In total, in 1999 international bond issues by crisis economies (US$77.7 billion) were significantly smaller than the intermediated finance offered by international banks (US$ 160.7 billion). However it would be expected that these markets compete with one another on efficiency criteria. The larger size of the intermediated finance market is consistent with a higher entry or cost structure and may well inhibit the ability of Asian crisis economies tap this market as a debt alternative.

International bond financing by the crisis economies has increased from US$30.9 billion in 1995 to US$77.7 billion in 1999 (an increase of 128% over the period). The Republic of Korea has been the largest issuer, while the level of international bonds issued by Japan has fallen; a function of the well documented "Japan premium" that reflected the higher yields demanded by investors holding yen bonds in offshore markets. The international issues from the crisis economies have largely focused on bond issues in the U.S. market (termed Yankee bond issues) by quasi-government or sovereign borrowers. Though these securities have to be registered[9] with the Securities and Exchange Commission (SEC), declining issuing and compliance costs, and the withdrawal by international banks to the region following the Asian crisis (the reduction in lending was -4% in 1999 and –21% in 1998) has encouraged borrowers to bypass national banking systems and pursue direct security market processes. Also the SEC discourages the sale of Eurobonds to U.S. citizens, although there are provisions which enable the sale and subsequent trading of Eurobonds as private placements.

Thus, on the one hand, U.S. investors have emerged as the largest buyers of crisis economy bonds, while on the other hand U.S. financial intermediaries have historically demonstrated a lack of interest in pursuing intermediated bank lending business to crisis economies. This apparent anomaly is explained by the sanctity of the U.S. financial system and its ability to better solve the information asymmetries that exist between crisis economy borrowers and potential investors than are financial intermediaries operating in the home environment.

Despite the non-investment grade status of most of these domestic U.S. issues, investors can take comfort from their quasi-government or sovereign status. Historically, few non-government or quasi-government issuers have tapped these markets since they have little or no issuance history and they lack the marketability of a sovereign issue. The interest rate spreads of unknown or new issuers demanded by the markets has also been wider than demanded by similarly rated European or U.S corporations in recent years and may have discouraged borrowers.

Table 2.4   **International Bonds Issued by Asia-Pacific Economies**
(US$ billion)

Countries	Mar-94	Mar-95	Mar-96	Mar-97	Mar-98	Mar-99
Australia	42.1	50.1	53.7	88.5	80.4	86.9
China	9.6	13.0	12.0	13.0	14.8	13.9
Hong Kong, China	10.9	14.7	12.4	17.5	20.1	22.3
India	3.0	3.3	3.7	4.6	5.9	5.7
Indonesia	1.4	3.1	3.9	5.6	5.8	4.5
Japan	279.8	276.6	226.2	188.4	145.5	127.9
Korea, Republic	0.0	19.4	23.4	40.6	48.1	48.3
Malaysia	17.7	4.4	5.9	10.1	12.1	12.5
New Zealand	6.5	5.9	5.4	6.3	7.9	7.0
Philippines	0.0	2.0	2.2	6.4	8.0	9.9
Singapore	1.2	1.0	1.2	2.5	3.2	5.7
Taipei, China	3.3	2.4	2.8	3.8	5.7	6.5
Thailand	0.3	4.0	5.4	9.9	11.5	12.4
Total: Crisis Economies	19.4	30.9	38.6	66.2	77.5	77.7
Total: Developed Economies	329.6	333.6	286.5	285.7	237.0	227.5
Total: All Economies	375.8	399.9	358.2	397.2	369.0	363.5

Notes: Nepal, North Korea, Pakistan, and Vietnam are excluded from the Table since there were no international bond or note issues recorded. "Crisis Economies" are Indonesia, Malaysia, South Korea and Thailand. " Developed Economies" are Australia, Japan, New Zealand and Singapore.
Source: BIS, *International Banking and Financial Market Developments* (various issues), Table 13 "International Bonds by Nationality".

The attractive feature of the Yankee market is that it is available to the non-investment grade issuers (credit rating lower than BBB) representative of sovereign issuers in the crisis economies (see Table 2.5 below). Emerging market issuers are generally unable to tap the international Eurobond market[10], which has a preference for investment grade issues, and is also largely a U.S. denominated market[11]. However from the borrowers' perspective the degree of substitutability of these different markets ultimately is a function of cost. For example there were significant increases in the level of offshore issues in the period prior to 1995 largely associated with the decline in spreads of issues over U.S. Treasuries of similar maturity. Following the Asian crisis there was an increase in spreads which discouraged international issues in favour of domestic issues and loans from international banks[12].

Table 2.5   Credit Ratings of Crisis Economies
(at March 10, 2000)

Country	Standard & Poor's Sovereign Long Term Debt Rating	
	Foreign Currency	Domestic Currency
Indonesia	CCC+	B-
Korea, Republic of	BBB	A
Malaysia	BBB	A
Thailand	BBB-	A-

International bond issues by crisis economies were also undertaken against a background of ongoing change in the risk transformation capability, through the use of forwards, futures and options, of the region. Key to this has been the changing role of Singapore and Hong Kong following the handover to China. Many international transactions are now being booked through Singapore instead of Hong Kong. For example foreign exchange turnover in Singapore is now US$139 billion per day compared with Hong Kong's US$78.6 billion (BIS 1999).

Risk transformation capability is crucial when the bulk of both intermediated finance and international bonds are denominated in non-local currencies. For example apart from some offshore issues denominated in Hong Kong and the new Taipei dollars, regional borrowers usually issue securities in USD. To avoid potential translation losses arising from the revaluation of foreign currency denominated bonds, issuers would normally undertake a foreign currency swap into local currency and an interest rate swap from fixed to floating rate coupons. The absence of these derivatives in a local market would effectively restrict the hedging alternatives available to a corporation.

There have been a number of transactions in 1999, which have highlighted the ability of Asian issuers to tap international markets. Specific transactions include:

(i)   Federation of Malaysia's US$1 billion sovereign bond issue priced at 330 basis points;

(ii)   Development Bank of Singapore's US$750 million issue priced at 200 basis points (2%) above U.S. Treasuries;

(iii)   Globe Telecom and Bayan Telecom from the Philippines of US$220 million and priced at 709 basis points over U.S. Treasuries; and

(iv)   Republic of Korea US$3 billion fixed rate 10 year bond issue priced at 300 basis points.

The key features of each of these transactions which encouraged high-yield investors were the size of the issue, which ensured liquidity, the size of the spread which compensated investors for the risks of holding emerging market bonds and the marketing of the issues which included government and central banker representation during the international promotion or "roadshow" prior to the actual issue arranged by high-profile and credible bookrunners[13]. Also, each of the issues had a simple fixed rate pricing structure and were quasi-government if not sovereign issues. It is doubtful if a more complex structure (for example having a call feature) would have found favour with investors, or if smaller tranches offered over a range of maturities would have satisfied the markets desire for liquidity[14] since smaller issues fragment the distribution of bonds. However the key features of very large ("jumbo") Eurobond issues by prime name corporations is that they are all simple fixed rate U.S dollar denominated securities.

2.3.2. Implications

The replacement of intermediated finance with international bond issues suggests there is a degree of substitutability between these two forms of financing. However the prevalence of issues by quasi-government or sovereign issuers reflects reluctance by international investors to hold non-sovereign paper suggesting that substitute forms of financing are only available to high quality issuers. This reluctance, at this point in time, effectively caps the quantity of debt that could be placed into the international bond markets. Alternately the markets may display a crowding out effect of corporate issuers by the public sector, or be unable, rather than unwilling to price corporate debt since appropriate infrastructure is not available (such as benchmark yield curves).

Table 2.6   **A Comparison of International Bank Lending and International Debt Securities of Crisis Economies, 1996 - 1999**

Country	Change in Levels of Bank Lending (Dec 1996 to June 1999)	Change in levels of International Bond Issues (Mar 1996 to Mar 1999)
Indonesia	-11.7	+3.1
Korea, Republic of	-36.5	+48.3
Malaysia	-3.6	-5.2
Thailand	-35.5	+12.1

While bond issues and intermediated finance may be substitutes for some risk classes of borrower it is evident from Table 2.6, which provides a comparison of the changes in international bank lending and bond issues in the period following the Asian crisis, that increases in international bond issues have not adequately replaced the reduction in the levels of international bank lending in Indonesia, Malaysia and Thailand.

Only the Republic of Korea has been able to successfully tap international bond markets for additional funding. While each country's experiences have been different, from the regional perspective, the reduction in funding by international lenders is part of a much larger withdrawal of private sector funds from the region (see Table 2.7.) It is the liquidity aspect of the Asian crisis, which may be addressed by increasing the number of long-term financing options through the development of more viable domestic bond markets in crisis economies, and improving the access by these borrowers to international bond markets.

148

Table 2.7   **Financial Flows to Emerging Market Economies by Region**
($US Billion)

	1996	1997	1998	1999
Private Flows, Net	327.9	265.7	147.8	148.7
Latin America	97.3	107.7	97.5	68.8
Europe	50.4	74.5	35.1	31.9
Africa/Middle East	3.8	15.7	9.4	8.7
Asia/Pacific	176.3	67.9	5.8	39.3
Five Asian Economies	108.1	-0.2	-36.4	-3.7
Official Flows, Net	7.6	38.9	52.8	11.9
Latin America	-10.5	-2.6	15.7	5.5
Europe	11.2	6.1	8.1	3.0
Africa/Middle East	1.8	-1.3	-2.2	-1.0
Asia/Pacific	5.0	36.7	31.2	4.3
Five Asian Economies	-1.6	29.9	26.9	1.4

Source: The Institute of International Finance, Inc. (1999)
Note: The Five Asian Economies include South Korea, Indonesia, Malaysia, Thailand and Philippines.

III.   Major Obstacles to Development of Domestic Corporate Bond Markets

3.1   *Traditional Negligence of Domestic Bond Markets*

The traditional negligence of domestic corporate bonds by the industrial sector in the crisis economies is largely due to the following three reasons:

(i)   Cheaper financing through overseas bank borrowing;

(ii)   Bank dominated domestic financial systems; and

(iii)   Agency problems arising from family–owned corporations.

These reasons are discussed in turn.

(i)   *Cheaper financing through overseas bank borrowing*

Most of the crisis economies had long taken a series of measures to liberalize their financial sectors, and immediately before the crisis their domestic financial markets were virtually fully open to foreign capital. In the case of Indonesia, Republic of Korea and Thailand, domestic banks, finance companies/merchant banks, and large conglomerates could borrow foreign funds without much regulatory restrictions or supervisory screening. Foreign borrowings were sometimes encouraged by the financial authorities to fill expeditiously the domestic financing gap. Under the circumstances, domestic financial institutions and industrial corporations had borrowed huge foreign funds, whose maturity was generally short. (It was possible to extend or roll-over their borrowing terms). The most important factors that accelerated such borrowings were a substantial difference between domestic and foreign interest rates and a rigid foreign exchange policy causing a significant appreciation of local currencies[15].

Before the crisis, domestic lending rates were much higher in Indonesia and Thailand than the one-year LIBOR rates on US dollar lending, while the gap between domestic and overseas rates was moderate in the Republic of Korea and Malaysia. The gap between two rates in the early 1990s before the crisis was as high as 12 – 16 percentage points per annum in Indonesia, and 5 – 8 percentage points per annum in Thailand. In the first two countries, domestic lending rates were generally roughly two to five times higher than LIBO rates each year. Under the circumstances, together with the misalignment of exchange rates as discussed below, domestic banks and corporations, as rational economic entities, must have made best efforts to maximize their borrowing from international financial markets.

Table 3.1 Comparisons of Domestic and Overseas Interest Rates[1/]
(Percent p.a., period average)

	1993	1994	1995	1996	1997	1998	Oct 1999
Indonesia	20.6	17.8	18.9	19.2	21.8	32.2	22.8
Korea, Republic of	8.6	8.5	9.0	8.8	11.9	15.3	9.0
Malaysia	9.1	7.6	7.6	8.9	9.5	10.6	6.8
Thailand	11.2	10.9	13.3	13.4	13.7	14.4	8.3
LIBOR[2/] (US$)	3.64	5.59	6.24	5.78	6.08	5.53	5.7(Jul)

1. Commercial bank lending rates, unless otherwise stated.
2. For one year
Sources: ADB, Key Indicators, and IMF, International Financial Statistics, various issues.

Table 3.2 Purchasing Power Parity of Crisis Economies' Currencies (1990 = 100)

	1990	1991	1992	1993	1994	1995	1996
Indonesia							
Relative price (I)	100	104.9	109.6	119.7	128.0	135.7	140.6
Exchange rate(II)	100	105.8	110.2	113.3	117.3	122.0	127.1
PPP(II/I)	100	100.9	100.5	94.6	91.6	89.9	90.4
Korea							
Relative price (I)	100	104.9	108.1	110.0	113.9	115.8	118.1
Exchange rate(II)	100	103.6	110.3	113.4	113.5	109.0	113.7
PPP (II/I)	100	98.8	102.0	103.1	99.6	94.1	96.3
Malaysia							
Relative price (I)	100	100.2	101.8	102.4	103.5	106.0	106.7
Exchange rate(II)	100	101.7	94.2	95.2	97.0	92.6	93.0
PPP(II/I)	100	101.5	92.5	93.0	93.7	87.4	87.2
Thailand							
Relative price (I)	100	101.4	102.4	102.8	105.4	108.4	111.5
Exchange rate(II)	100	101.4	101.8	101.0	99.6	100.1	101.5
PPP(II/I)	100	100	99.4	98.2	94.5	92.3	91.0

Sources: IMF, International Financial Statistics, Yearbook 1998.

First, the domestic interest rates in the crisis economies before the crisis were much higher than international interest rates. Table 3.1 provides the trends of interest rates in the crisis economies as well as in international financial markets.

Table 3.2 shows the purchasing power parity (PPP) indexes in the 1990s in the crisis economies. The indexes were calculated in the manner that a currency's nominal exchange rate against the US dollar (an index for which 1990 = 100) is compared with a relative consumer price index (CPI) which is the local CPI divided by the US CPI. If it is 100, the currency's value against the US dollar, as of 1990, remains unchanged. If it is lower (higher) than 100, the currency is overvalued (undervalued) compared to the level as of 1990. It is a simplified PPP index in that only the US CPI, not all major trading partners', is used. Nevertheless, it could provide the general trend of the real value of each currency in the 1990s before the crisis. The table suggests that all countries' currencies had been overvalued in the 1990s, with Indonesia, Malaysia and Thailand being most significantly.

Combining the interest rate gap and the PPP index makes it clear that foreign borrowing was a profitable financial method in the crisis countries before the crisis. The international interest rates were always cheaper than the local rates, encouraging domestic firms and financial institutions to borrow from abroad. The borrowing has been further protected by the exchange rate regime that has continued the overvaluation of the local currency, which made foreign loans even cheaper.

(ii)   Bank centred domestic financial systems.

These countries have generally attached higher policy priority to the banking sector than to the capital market. Although capital market development has not been neglected, the banking sector was treated as the most important financial sector for various reasons. In the process of seeking a high growth strategy since the early 1960s, the banking sector served as the main supplier of financial resources, which were mobilized from both domestic and foreign markets. Capital markets remained underdeveloped, which prevented them from financing industrial projects through diversified sources. As stated above, corporate bond markets are particularly lagging behind in all these countries, while Republic of Korea has achieved significant progress only in recent years after the crisis.

Bank-centred financial systems also have favoured the high-economic growth outcomes of many developing economies since they provide more effective monitoring in financial environments characterised by asymmetric information due to opacity in financial information.

Under these circumstances a case may be argued that banks are better able to ration scarce resources to priority sectors, though there is evidence that these decisions may be both influenced by outside parties (e.g. the decision by four Indonesian state banks to lend US$2.7 billion to then President Suharto's son, Bambang Trihatmodjo, to build the Chandra Asri petrochemicals plant), or family-members in first-family owned banks and corporations. In the latter case family members are able to influence managerial objectives such that resources are not allocated optimally. These outcomes reflect poor governance structures which fail to address the underlying agency problems[16].

(iii)   Agency problems arising from family–owned corporations

Industrial firms in developed economies generally rely upon debt financing rather than issuing new equity since issuing equity dilutes control and exacerbates agency problems. The choice of financing has been shown to follow a "pecking order" (Myers 1984) where first choice is given to internal sources of funds (e.g. retained earnings), then external sources in the form of additional debt or equity, in both private and public markets. Mitigating agency concerns and those problems arising from asymmetries in information (usually the opacity of financial information) appear to dictate the choice between the various combinations of debt and equity instruments.

Many emerging countries lack the financial and technical infrastructure to enable the satisfactory development of public security markets. Traditional firm financing then is largely through banks that assume a vital corporate governance role as part of their intermediation activities. However the governance function may be affected by the significant ownership of lending institutions by entrepreneurs and their families, who may also occupy prominent management positions, or the significant cross-ownership between financial intermediaries and corporate borrowers.

The ownership structures of both banks and other financial intermediaries and large private sector firms in the crisis economies may be categorized as examples of the "family-state model" where either a small group of founding families, or a pervasive state plays an important role[17]. These structures vary from the nominally privatised and largely state-owned Korean banks (with non-bank intermediaries generally privately owned) to the largely family–owned banks of Malaysia (which directly control many of the non-bank intermediaries)[18].

Apart from the Korean nationwide banks, the domestic financial institutions in the other crisis economies are generally small by world standards so the contagion effects of imprudent lending to local firms can be more extreme. There is also pressure from the government (e.g. Malaysia) for specific intermediaries to consolidate to gain efficiencies while still maintaining a local character, since the banks play an important role in understanding the co-operative dimensions that exist between family, kin and the community. In effect, local banks are required to solve the potential information opacity and asymmetry problems between firm borrowers and providers of funds that have arisen due to poor disclosure and accounting standards.

Though not generally discussed in the empirical literature, in addition to concerns over equity dilution, the capital structure choices of firms (both financial and non-financial) may also be made on the basis of maintaining the asymmetries in information that exist between and within family owners, and non-family owners and managers. For example there has been an on-going debate in the economic development literature on the expected behaviour of family members in family-owned firms when additional funds are required for the firm's expansion. These arguments centre upon the information asymmetries between family members and may be seen as an extension of theories popular in the development literature where kinship (family) links are seen as an obstacle to economic development. Family members, in family owned firms, may be reluctant to provide additional savings to support new investment, since this signals information on individual wealth to other family members, who will then attempt to free ride on the effort of their wealthier kin. Firm managers may be able to avoid this source of conflict and borrow directly from financial intermediaries, thus avoiding ancillary problems of equity dilution or equity readjustment within family groups.

However, in recent years banks have come to rely upon negative pledges, which may confer proprietary rights to the lender. To overcome this equitable lien, firms will prefer to issue securities if it cost effective to do so. However the decision to do so may depend upon the relationship between the firm-managers and the main group of shareholders. Non-owner managers may resolve the information asymmetries that exist between family and non-family owners by the issuance of debt securities or through stock listings. Whether owner-managers would be reluctant to do so is an outstanding empirical question. However, this would heavily rely on the funding costs (loan rates and bond rates): in crisis countries, loan rates have been lower than bond rates, discouraging bond issues.

The capital structure of the smaller firms, which are majority in these countries except Republic of Korea, is also time varying, suggesting that at an aggregate level firm financing preferences may be a function of the business cycle. Thus, small innovative start-up firms (high-risk, high growth) are mostly reliant upon the entrepreneur's (or family's) equity. As these firms become larger they are able to obtain a variety of loans from financial institutions and suppliers. Occasionally some firms obtained equity participation called "angel finance" from wealthy individuals not related to the entrepreneur at the commencement of the firm's activities. Alternately lower risk, lower growth firms tend to access debt. Without collateral or a financial track record, information opacity will prevent these firms from obtaining finance from bond markets.

3.2   *Major Obstacles to Bond Issuance*

The general negligence of the bond market is a broad factor for the underdevelopment of the corporate bond market. Several technical obstacles are discussed below.[19]

(i)   *Lack of a benchmark yield curve*

A major impediment to the development of corporate bond markets in the crisis countries has been the lack of interest rate benchmarks for bond pricing. Usually benchmark yield curves are constructed by market participants from the suite of outstanding government bond across a range of maturities. Mathematical interpolation enables a continuous curve to be constructed which then serves as a "benchmark" for the revaluation of existing portfolios and also for the pricing of corporate issues. Market convention is to add a time-varying spread to the risk-free government rate to establish the yield of a corporate security. This form of construction requires accurate bond prices to be available in liquid secondary bond markets. Where markets for government securities are not liquid or where certain maturities of bonds are not available, then market participants must construct these curves from a variety of alternate securities such as implied yields in long-term forward markets or the rates implied by the fixed rate leg of an interest rate swap.

Given the implied parity relationships between different financial products it is essential that deep OTC or exchange traded markets co-exist along with bond markets to ensure pricing accuracy. Daily turnover in foreign exchange and interest rate derivatives markets in the Asia-Pacific region is described in the following Table 4.3 which is based on Bank for International Settlements survey data. There was no interest rate derivative data collected for Indonesia or Thailand though other market sources suggest that turnover does exist though is very small. Republic of Korea and Malaysia also display very small levels of daily turnover even relative to small developed economies such as New Zealand. Another method of zero-curve construction is through the implied zero rates from long-dated forward contracts or currency swaps. The daily turnover of these instruments is also very small with Indonesia, Malaysia, and Republic of Korea having approximately US$1 billion of daily turnover, while Thailand has US$2.3. This volume in total is less than daily turnover in New Zealand. It is clear that the use of alternate sources for the construction of benchmark curves will be difficult due to the lack of liquidity in the underlying instruments.

Despite these difficulties, attempts have been made by the crisis economies to solve these problems. In Indonesia, a market for short-term central bank certificates (SBIs) has existed since 1983[20], but it has not played any meaningful role in providing a useful benchmark for long-term debt securities. Therefore, various proxies have been attempted: (i) the rates of 3-6 month time deposit plus a premium (generally 1-4 percentage points per annum) and (ii) a yield curve with maturities of up to 30 years from the Indonesian swap offer rate (IRSOR) quoted by investment banks on the Yankee bonds issued by the Government of Indonesia (GOI). However, none of these could be a perfect substitute for a government bond-based yield curve. A major reason for the GOI's disinterest in developing government bond market was its strong preference for a balanced budget policy.

In Republic of Korea, three-year bank-guaranteed corporate bonds have been used as benchmark facilities for the entire bond market. Government bonds involve a range of problems, including arbitrarily set low interest rates and mandatory purchase requirements in some cases (e.g., housing bonds and telephone bonds), and lack of coordination between government ministries concerning issuance and administration of their bonds, which prevent government bonds from becoming benchmark facilities. Besides the guaranteed corporate bonds, there are a few other bonds which are of low risk, such as Type I National Housing bond, five-year Regional Development bond, three-year Land Development bond, and 364-day Monetary Stabilization bond, serve also as quasi-benchmark bonds. However, a reliable yield curve cannot be established because all these bonds involve different types of problems. Even the guaranteed bond faces the possibility that guaranteeing banks themselves may go bankrupt. Another problem is the increasing reluctance of banks to provision of guarantees after the Asian crisis.

Table 3.3 Derivatives Turnover in Selected Asia Pacific Countries

(a) Foreign Exchange Derivatives Daily Turnover in Select Countries April 1998		
Country	Total	Local
Australia	28.75	16.50 (57.4%)
China	-	-
Hong Kong	48.94	13.53 (27.6%)
Indonesia	1.04	0.76 (73.08%)
India	1.29	0.90 (69.8%)
Japan	91.65	77.04 (84.06%)
Malaysia	0.80	0.54 (67.5%)
New Zealand	4.97	3.75 (75.5%)
Philippines	0.40	0.28 (70.0%)
Singapore	85.40	5.23 (6.1%)
Korea	1.05	0.32 (30.4%)
Taipei	1.52	0.37 (24.3%)
Thailand	2.28	1.93 (84.6%)
U.K.	468.26	77.07 (16.5%)
U.S.	235.37	220.02 (93.50%)

Note: 94.47% of World Average FX Derivatives Turnover is specified against the US$. Turnover includes OTC forwards, FX swaps, currency swaps, options
Source: BIS Survey

(b) Interest Rate Derivatives Daily Turnover in Select Countries April 1998		
Country	Total	Swaps
Australia	2.830	1.272 (44.9%)
China	-	-
Hong Kong	2.437	1.939 (79.5%)
Indonesia	-	-
India	-	-
Japan	31.623	17.612 (55.7%)
Malaysia	0.001	0.001 (100.0%)
New Zealand	0.421	0.101 (24.0%)
Philippines	-	-
Singapore	5.347	4.183 (78.2%)
Korea	0.007	0.007 (100.0%)
Taipei	0.116	0.115 (99.0%)
Thailand	-	-
U.K.	122.928	68.754 (55.93%)
U.S.	58.441	31.368 (53.67%)

Note: 58.5% of World Average IR Derivatives Turnover are swaps, 28.1% are FRAs, 13.4% are options. Turnover includes OTC, FRAs, swaps, and options
Source: BIS Survey

Also in early October 1999, the Thai BDC developed the Thai Government Bonds Benchmark/Yield Curve. It is derived from average bid prices quoted by nine counter-parties of the Bank of Thailand. The Thai BDC publishes the yield curve at the end of each trading day. Benchmark bonds must have remaining maturities of approximately one, two, five, seven, or 10 years, and amounts outstanding of at least THB 20 million.

(ii)   Narrow investor base

The investor base is narrow in most countries. These are associated with (a) the restricted contractual savings system and its over-regulation, (b) underdeveloped mutual funds, (c) over-regulation of the asset management industry, and (d) a limited role for insurance companies in capital markets. Subjecting bond markets to nonmarket forces, such as the practice of forcing captive investors to purchase bonds at below-market yields, also restricts demand. In the bank-dominating financing system, major clients of banks have also inclinations to put their surplus funds in bank deposits rather than in bond markets. Such a bank-client relationship has been a contributing factor for the narrow investor base. Lack of understanding of bonds by investors is another factor. High savings have been channeled mostly into banks in those countries which provide only short-term financial instruments.

(iii)   Limited supply of quality bond issues

The limited number of quality bond issues impedes the liquidity and construction of benchmark instruments. There are few viable debt instruments because of (i) the poor credit standing of issuing corporations, (ii) statutory restrictions and financial regulations on the issuance of bond instruments, and (iii) repressive regulatory processes. First, most corporations in these countries were excessively leveraged by bank loans and foreign borrowing, which resulted in poor financial status. Poor corporate governance, in particular the lack of transparency in financial transactions and unsatisfactory accounting practices, have further aggravated investors' confidence in corporate bonds. In most of the countries surveyed, laws governing the bond markets can barely cope with the demands of trading and regulation of sophisticated financial transactions. Where laws do appear to be adequate, regulators are unable to enforce rules and regulations. This renders investments in the bond markets more uncertain, reduces overall demand for such investments, and makes the markets even shallower.

Further deterioration of the credit standings of issuing corporations as a result of the Asian crisis also reduces the supply of quality bonds. Governments must also be aware that undue legal restrictions on the amount of bonds that corporations can raise, or on the number of eligible issuers, interfere with the proper operation of market forces in bond markets (and hence unduly limit supply).

(iv)   Inadequate bond market infrastructure

The inadequate bond market infrastructure in the DMCs is due to the absence of (a) competitive auctions, (b) a secondary market trading system where real-time price and volume information is readily available, (c) an advanced clearing and settlement system for bonds, (d) a stronger role for credit-rating agencies, and (e) hedging instruments for long-term and short-term interest rate risk. High transaction costs are also a major impediment.

Bond market development requires mechanisms to ensure that the market value of securities reflects correct market perceptions of relative borrower risk and other fundamentals. For this purpose, bond markets should be competitive and have efficient access to information. All participants should have access to information to help them value securities correctly. To this end, an economy must have a stable, consistent, and accessible framework for the timely and accurate analysis and interpretation of information about issuers and securities. Exhaustive, objective, and independent research by credit rating agencies, investment banks, and other financial service institutions is also essential for bond market development. Some countries, such as India, Republic of Korea, and Malaysia, have allowed the establishment of credit-rating agencies to foster competitive ratings. However, with low demand for ratings due to shallow bond markets, the efficacy of such a step is questionable.

High transaction costs resulting from such factors as stamp taxes, which curtail liquidity in both primary and secondary bond markets, may also hold back bond market development. Most of the countries levy transaction taxes, such as stamp taxes and capital gains taxes, on the trading of bonds and other securities in the financial markets. To stimulate liquidity in their domestic bond markets, Malaysia and Thailand have eliminated stamp taxes to lower transaction costs and encourage trading of securities. Regulations that require institutional investors (especially banks or insurance companies) to set aside a proportion of their investments in bonds as regulatory capital or reserves also increase bond market transaction costs. Such requirements, though essentially prudential in nature, impose an opportunity cost on investors that reduces the demand for bonds and other securities.

IV.   Strategies for Development of Domestic Corporate Bond Markets

Developing viable corporate bond[21] markets needs continued and consistent policy efforts over a sustained time period. The policy efforts should deal with both demand and supply side impediments as well as infrastructure problems. While banks account for up to 80 percent of financial assets in Asia, they do less than 25 percent in the US. This suggests that capital markets, including bond markets, have a promising future in Asia if proper policies are pursued. The following are the most important issues which deserve government's vigorous policy efforts.

4.1   Importance of Treasury Paper Market

A well-functioning government bond market may play a stepping stone role in fostering corporate bond markets. Its risk-free yield curve facilitates private issuance. It would be unrealistic if any country wanted to develop corporate bond market and derivative markets without a satisfactory treasury paper market. In light of this, in Asia, the Australian government and the Hong Kong government, in particular, have been committed to preserving a liquid treasury paper market although there is no immediate funding need from the market. The Australian government paper market provides currently a yield curve of 12-13 year maturity, while the Hong Kong treasury paper market provides a 10-year long yield curve.

The following are the lessons for developing countries:

- To develop a meaningful government bond market, there should be a clear and balanced long-term debt strategy and a sound operational capacity.

- Three courses of actions are advisable to minimize the cost of government debt securities. They are: first, tap the pool of global capital, in other words, open the government debt market to foreign investors; second, there should be clear division of responsibility between government debt management and monetary policy; and third, primary and secondary market infrastructures should be satisfactory.

- Regular and substantive communication and dialogue with markets on debt management objectives and operational strategies is essential. The rationale for debt management operations should be transparent and the operations are reasonably predictable. When-issued trading is recommended to minimize price and quantity uncertainties.

- Too many different types of sovereign bonds are not desirable, but simplicity is better.

- There seems to be a broad consensus that a benchmark yield curve of at least ten years is meaningful.

- Selection of primary issue arrangements should consider the development stage of the government bond market. Generally the open auction system is preferable, while smaller and less liquid markets may benefit from a dealer panel arrangement. In any case, a primary dealer system is essential to ensure market competition among participating dealers, efficiently distribute government securities and increase the liquidity of the securities.

- A captive or obligatory investor arrangement, such as required holding of specified proportions of financial institutions' assets in the form of government securities, is not desirable. In Australia, one consequence of the captive arrangement was only a very limited secondary market in government securities.

- Markets require a steady supply of new securities to sustain liquidity. Secondary market liquidity should be ensured by deliberate policy measures of the authorities.

- The uniform price, sealed bid auction is advocated in general.

- A coupon stripping, which splits bond income streams into coupon interest and principal repayment is desirable.

- Reliable and real-time clearing and settlement arrangements are equally critical to efficient operations.

- It is important to ensure a regulatory regime that provides both legal certainty and a level playing field, and remains responsive to the changing requirements of the market.

- Government bonds must be attractive to investors.

- There is the need to create a single regional central securities depository (CSD) to perform safekeeping, clearance, and settlement functions for all securities available in the region.

4.2   Strategies for Development of Corporate Bond Markets

Supply-Side Strategies

(i)   Providing enabling environment: financial liberalization, maintaining adequate exchange rate policy and regulatory standards

The capital regime in most Asian economies has been significantly liberalized allowing flows of foreign funds across countries. This trend will be accelerated due to the ongoing globalization process and fast development in information technology. As a result, domestic industrial sector and financial institutions will increasingly vigorously seek the funds with the cheapest interest rate at home as well as abroad. In this foreseeable situation, domestic interest rates and foreign exchange rates will play a critical role in determining the real effective price of those funds. If the local currency remains overvalued, *ceteris paribus*, foreign borrowing will become attractive, and vice versa. As discussed earlier, crisis countries had long kept the overvaluation of their currencies before the crisis, providing a significant incentive to foreign borrowing. Financial liberalization needs to be continued and an adequate exchange rate policy must be put in place to facilitate both development of domestic financial markets, including bond markets, and achieve other macroeconomic goals.

Also while Government's must provide an enabling environment conducive to financial liberalization, central banks are duty bound to maintain tight regulatory standards and enforcement procedures to ensure that investor confidence in the financial system is maintained. Critical to this process is the independence of the central bank and its success in money policy management and the risk management practices of financial firms[22].

Recent examples of regulatory improvement include:

- Improvements in the supervision of finance companies in Thailand;

- Improved asset-quality norms in Republic of Korea (Korean banks accrue interest on loans past due for one month whereas international standards are 3 months);

- General acceptance that central banks subscribe to the Special Data Dissemination Standard (SDDS)[23] which details what data can be published and when (The Bank of Korea and the Korean Ministry of Finance now publish material through a webpage, though the quality and timeliness of the data from the Bank of Thailand is poor).

Any public sector bond should not receive privileged treatment such as lower prices or rates. Prices of all bonds should be determined by market forces. In some developing countries, governments issue a large amount of bonds to finance special projects and budget deficits at lower prices through forcing financial institutions to purchase or providing tax incentives to investors. Such practices distort the overall bond markets, while discouraging corporate bond market.

(ii)   Reforming corporate governance

Good corporate governance enhances the protection of the legitimate interests of all stakeholders including the holders of corporate bonds. Many Asian corporations have been blamed for weak and unsatisfactory corporate governance in the areas of anti-corruption, transparency in financial transactions, accounting methods satisfying international standards, and ownership structure. These problems caused, among others, the erosion of investor confidence in corporations' financial documents and accordingly the bonds issued by them.

Before the crisis, in Republic of Korea, mutual payment guarantee arrangements between companies inside the group of chaebol were made frequently, and chaebol-affiliated financial institutions provided loans to their associated corporations in a manner lacking transparency and these undermined the confidence in financial documents of the concerned corporations and financial institutions. In many countries, accounting methods were changed in an ad hoc manner. While the crisis countries have redressed these practices, reforming accounting methods to adopt the best practices should be expanded to broader areas. Improved corporate governance will enhance the quality of corporate bonds. Investor perceptions of intangibles such as corporate integrity, prevention of asymmetric availability of corporate information, and enforcement capabilities of securities market regulators are a key factor determining the quality of corporate bonds and capital market dynamism.

Although corporate systems differ across countries, they can be grouped into two contrasting models: outsider and insider models.[24] The U.S. and the U.K are adopting the former, while other countries the latter. The former may be termed as a "market-based model," and the other a "board-based model." In case of the former, widely dispersed investors own and control the company. If management neglects shareholder value, investors react by selling the shares. In the board-based model, members of the board represent the interest of identifiable groups and are in charge of disciplining management. It is the general trend that Asian countries are shifting their board-based model to a market-based model. However, the market-based model requires sufficient disclosures, a good flow of information, rigorous trading rules, and well-developed investor protection systems.[25]

Demand-Side Strategies

(iii)   Strengthening the role of institutional investors and mutual funds

The role of institutional investors (pension funds and insurance companies) and mutual funds is particularly important in developing countries for expanding the investor base because individual investors in developing countries are not much familiar to bond markets and this results in reluctance to their investments in corporate bonds. In those economies, which have been successful in developing bond markets, the role of institutional investors and mutual funds is pronounced in the purchasing and selling of various bonds and creating attractive asset portfolios by utilizing those bonds.

In Asia, the Republic of Korea and Malaysia are relatively successful in this context. In the Republic of Korea, establishment of mutual funds was significantly deregulated in 1998 and the provision of tax benefits to foreigners investing in domestic fixed income securities is being considered. In Malaysia, tax exemptions on bond market gains only apply to individual investors, not to institutions. However, there is still a strong need to strengthen the capacity of institutional investors by increasing pension funds (e.g., corporate and banking sector employees) and mutual funds, broadening funding sources, and improving fund management skills. Providing consistency in the *tax exemptions* available to investors and the encouragement of purchases of bonds by other financial institutions[26] will also assist the development of this market.

In Indonesia, only institutional investors, the banking sector, and the newly emerging mutual funds purchase domestic bonds (including government bonds). Before the crisis, foreign investors' holdings of rupiah bonds accounted for 10-20 percent of new bond issues, concentrated in highly liquid ones with good credit standing such as PLN (the state-owned electricity company) and BTN (a state bank). Pension funds' composition of investments before the crisis was: about 50-55 percent in time deposits; 10-15 percent in stocks; 10-15 percent in bonds and promissory notes; and 15-30 percent in others including real estates. Insurance companies' composition of investments before the crisis was: about 45-50 percent in time deposits; 4-6 percent in stocks; 12-15 percent in money market instruments (SBI); 8-10 percent in bonds and promissory notes; and 19-30 percent in others including real estates. Bond holding of these companies was not noticeable.

The mutual funds, which emerged in 1996, grew fast: in 1997 before the crisis their investment portfolio assets recorded Rupiah 7.2 trillion. Their portfolios in 1997 comprised 25 percent of money market instruments, 15 percent of equities, 50 percent in bonds and promissory notes, and the balance in cash. This clearly exhibits the large investment of mutual funds in domestic bonds. Indonesia needs to expand the role of institutional investors and mutual funds by developing pension funds and mutual funds, developing human resources, and broadening funding sources.

International investors have also been encouraged to purchase Asian bonds following the establishment of broader benchmark indexes, which offer the advantage of risk diversification. For example, JP Morgan has updated the "Emerging Market Bond Index" (EMBI Global) to have a greater weighting on Asian issuers and now includes three of the crisis economies[27].

Also robust legal frameworks for perfecting and enforcing security interests are important in encouraging investors. In Thailand, new bankruptcy legislation is hoped to increase bank lending to business by ensuring that banks are able to recover future bad debts. However, Senate amendments set the minimum threshold level at double the proposed levels (debts need to exceed Thai bhat 1 million for individual bankruptcy, and 2 million bhat for corporations) with bankruptcy status able to be lifted after 3 years instead of the proposed 10 years. These developments appear to have helped secondary market bond turnover with more than half of total turnover now due to corporate bonds[28].

(iv)   Private placement

Private placement of corporate bonds has advantages, particularly in developing countries where the overall bond market is underdeveloped. Securities privately placed are exempt from registration with the SEC because their issuance does not involve a public offering. Corporations and investment banks may find potential buyers of bonds through various means and decide issuing conditions without involving official procedures. It shares some characteristics with bank loans.

In the case of the US, even the trading of privately placed corporate bonds has been allowed since 1990 through the adoption of SEC Rule 144A and it has brought major changes in the market. Consequently there are now two types of private placement markets: the market for 144A bonds and the traditional market that includes non-144A bonds. In the US, Rule 144A private placement is now underwritten by investment banks on a commitment basis like the case of publicly offered securities. The following Table 5.4 provides an idea on the importance of the private placement in the US as a source of corporate financing:

During the period of the 1970s to the early 1990s, private placed corporate bonds accounted for about 40 percent of total issuance of corporate bonds in the US, which is significantly large. A noteworthy development is the increase in percentage of private placed bonds from 1986-91 and this was partly attributed to by the adoption of SEC Rule 144A in 1990.

Table 4.4   **Issuance of Publicly Offered and Privately Placed Bonds by Non-financial Corporations in the U.S., 1975-1991**
($ Billion, annual rate)

Type of Bonds	1975 - 1980	1981- 1985	1986 - 1991
Public	21.0 (58.8)	35.6 (64.3)	87.6 (57.4)
Private	14.7 (41.2)	19.8 (35.7)	64.8 (42.6)
Total	35.7 (100.0)	55.4 (100.)	152.4 (100.0)

Source: Frank Fabozzi and Franco Modigliani (1996), Capital Markets (second edition), Prentice Hall, p 530.

Developing Infrastructure

(v)   Reliability in credit rating

Each country has few domestic credit rating agencies which provide rating services free of charge or are receiving service fees. In Indonesia, PEFINDO was established in 1994 by an initiative of Ministry of Finance and Bank of Indonesia under a partnership agreement with Standard & Poor's (S&P's). Another new agency, Kasnik Duff and Phelps was licensed in 1997 but is not operational. PEFINDO has rated some 200 companies involving about 250 debt securities (including CP). Requirements for rating of listed bonds and CP have increased the demand for the services. PEFINDO's partnership contributed to gaining international credibility. In the Republic of Korea three local agencies are in operation: Korea Management Consulting and Credit Rating Corporation (KMCRC), Korea Investors Service (KIS), and National Information and Credit Evaluation Corporation (NICE). All publicly issued non-guaranteed bonds are required to be rated by at least two credit rating agencies, and those corporations rated A or higher may issue non-guaranteed bonds.[29] However, the dominance of guaranteed bonds in Republic of Korea, which do not need a credit rating, has restricted the development of rating services.

In general, local rating agencies suffer low reliability of their ratings due to problems associated with rating skills and techniques, limited source of information, and inadequate accounting practices of corporations. Partnership agreement with internationally reliable agencies such as Standard & Poor's or Moody's, like the case of Indonesia, will significantly increase the reliability of local rating agencies. In small countries, it would be advisable to use those international agencies rather than to set up local agencies in view of large fixed costs for operating the agencies.

(vi)   Creating a benchmark yield curve

The establishment of benchmark yield curves is essential for the pricing of non-government securitie, since investors traditionally price these securities based on a spread over the equivalent risk-free or government security with the same maturity. Specifically, normal procedure is to interpolate the yield for a particular bond maturity based on spread over a stripped benchmark yield curve derived from a series of on-the-run government bullet bonds.

Except for a few economies such as Hong Kong, China and Malaysia, mid- and long-term benchmark government bonds have never existed in Asian developing economies. There are only short-term benchmark government bonds (including central bank issues) or quasi benchmark bonds like guaranteed corporate bonds in the Republic in Korea. However, no substitute can replace government bonds given their low risks. Traditionally, the high growing Asian developing countries have generally maintained balanced or surplus fiscal positions and this has discouraged the issuance of any government bonds to finance current fiscal expenditures, although various special purpose government bonds have been issued. There has also been prevailing opposition to creating benchmark treasury bonds based on the fear of accumulation of government debts.

By contrast, Hong Kong, China, one of the successful economies in minimizing the adversity of the Asian crisis, made continued efforts even before the crisis to develop the Exchange Fund Bills (EFBs) and the Exchange Fund Notes (EFNs) (termed hereafter as the Exchange Fund paper or EFP), and has significantly strengthened them in the aftermath. As Hong Kong, China's fiscal status has generally been in surplus. The main objective of the EFP program was to facilitate the development of the local debt market by increasing the supply of high quality bonds and creating a reliable benchmark yield curve for Hong Kong dollar debt instruments. The EFP program was introduced in March 1990 with the issuance of 91-day bills. Over the ensuing years, the program expanded both in terms of size and tenor. The 182- and 362-day bills were launched in October 1990 and February 1991, respectively, followed by two-year notes in May 1993, three-year notes in October 1993, five-year notes in September 1994, seven-year notes in November 1995, and 10-year notes in October 1996. The EFP has been very well received by the market and provide a reliable Hong Kong dollar benchmark yield as a result of regular issuing of EFP with varying maturity, developing an effective market making mechanism.

The Hong Kong case offers a good example for developing a benchmark government bond market in developing economies, although Hong Kong, China has been in a much better situation in terms of financial and economic conditions. Recently, the Republic of Korea and Thailand have also initiated benchmark government bond programs. The benefits from a benchmark bond market are much larger than the costs incurred from government debts, which justifies the need to create a government bond-based yield curve. It is essential that benchmark government bonds be highly liquid through the offering of sufficient government bonds across a range of maturities. This facilitates the correct interpolation of yields for non-benchmark maturities and also helps to prevent distortion of the yield curve through illiquidity induced volatility.

These issues have recently been addressed by Thailand, which identified the establishment of a benchmark yield curve as a priority policy area in its overall bond market reform package. Since there is now an ample supply of government bonds arising from the financing of fiscal deficits and the restructuring and recapitilisation of financial intermediaries it is now been possible to establish a market yield curve. Two curves are currently available: the market yield curve based on same day trading is provided by the Thai Bond Dealing Centre, and a yield curve based on yields as of settlement date is provided on the Bank of Thailand website[30].

(vii)   Regulatory Framework[31]

Although regulatory authorities should make best efforts to avoid discouraging market innovation through their regulatory measures, an effective and sound regulatory and supervision framework for a bond market, intermediaries, institutional investors and other market participants are critical for adequate investor protection and sound business practices or codes of conduct that reduce systemic risks. This requires clearly defined market rules, a high degree of transparency, and rigorous prudential standards and governance principles. It is also essential to ensure a combination of internal and external checks and surveillance to monitor compliance with the regulatory framework.

Transparency and clarity in the responsibilities, roles, and objectives of the regulatory authorities is essential for maintaining a high level of effectiveness of and public confidence in the regulatory framework as well as avoiding regulatory gaps and duplications. To this end, it is important to ensure clear legal definitions of supervisory actions, close coordination and cooperation between different regulatory authorities, and precisely defined regulations for various market participants (diversity of bank and non-bank participants) and financial instruments.

(viii)   Settlement Systems

The transaction costs associated with trading and issuing securities are subject to economies of scale and scope. Technology improvements and the establishment of Asia-wide settlement systems would assist the long-term viability of domestic bond markets. The establishment of uniform procedures would provide a first step in this direction. At the specific country level there are policy efforts which provide some guide to the challenges ahead. For example, in Thailand the real-time delivery versus payment project (DVP) was started in April 1998 and is due to be completed by the third quarter of 2000. And a real time bond price quotation system to news wire services has been established to improve information flows and pricing mechanisms. Thailand also has a "Master Plan" to serve as an internal guideline for policy implementation and coordination between agencies such as the Thai Bond Dealing Centre, Securities and Exchange Commission and the Ministry of Finance

V.   Conclusions

It would be the diversification of industrial financing methods which the Asian crisis countries should vigorously pursue to increase financial resources for development projects and accelerate financial sector development in the post-crisis period. The industrial financing in these countries has long been excessively bank-based, which has revealed several dangers such as an extremely inflexible financing mechanism, a dominant portion of short-term financing, and the vulnerability to external shocks. Bank disintermediation has already been emerging in terms of the extremely guarded lending policy of commercial banks for Asian developing countries. To diversify funding methods, bond market, which has been neglected, should receive a policy priority. The negligence has been due to the cheaper financing through overseas borrowing, bank dominated domestic financial systems, and agency problems arising from family-owned corporations.

The paper makes several policy suggestions to develop bond market in the crisis countries, which cover supply and demand side policies and infrastructure development issues. They include: (i) providing enabling environment; (ii) reforming corporate governance; (iii) reliability in credit rating; (iv) creating a benchmark yield curve; (v) strengthening the role of institutional investors and mutual funds; (vi) expanding private placement; (vii) real time delivery system; and (viii) strengthening the regulatory framework. The paper has also discussed how to tap international bond markets: the Asian countries need to provide enabling regulatory environment, ensure corporate governance, establish international benchmark yield curves, and have internationally acceptable risk management and regulatory standards.

However, all these issues require substantial time to be satisfactorily implemented. Admitting that a developing bond market cannot be accomplished in a short period of time, these countries should take phased and consistent steps under a well designed mid- and long-term bond market development strategy. Also, it is advisable to increase bond issuance in international financial markets to ensure financing diversification and minimum funding cost.

APPENDIX A

International Bank Financing by Asian Crisis Economies

1. *Indonesia*

– The level of international lending to Indonesia peaked in 1997 (US$58 billion) but fell 25% to US$43.8 billion by June 1999;

– Indonesia's share of total lending to Asia has been relatively constant (around 15.0%);

– the average maturity of bank lending has been rising, so that by June 1999 49.6% of loans had a maturity of less than one year;

– lending to the non-bank private sector has been consistently near 70.0% of total loans, though the balance reflects a reallocation to the public sector and a withdrawal from lending to banks; and

– though Japan stills remains a significant lender (31.9% in June 1999), European banks have increased their share of total loans from 30% in 1996 to 40% in 1999.

Table A.1   **Summary of International Bank Lending to Indonesia** (1996 to 1999)

1.	December 1996	December 1997	June 1998	December 1998	June 1999
Total Asia (US$ Billions)	367.1	378.8	319.6	299.4	287.0
Total Indonesia (US$ Billions)	55.5	58.0	48.4	45.0	43.8
(TI/TA)%	15.1	15.3	15.1	15.0	15.3
Maturity					
Less than 1, and 1 year (%)	61.7	60.5	54.1	52.8	49.6
Over 1 year (%)	34.1	36.2	42.6	43.5	46.6
Sector					
Banks (%)	21.2	19.8	13.7	11.8	10.1
Public Sector (%)	12.5	11.8	15.7	14.8	21.0
Non-Bank Private Sector (%)	66.2	68.4	70.7	73.4	68.8
Nationality of Reporting Banks					
Euro-Area Banks	30.4				39.6
U.K. Banks	6.9				7.8
U.S. Banks	9.5				8.5
Japanese Banks	39.7				31.9
Other	13.5				12.2

Notes: (i) Maturity and Sector percentage does not sum to 100%. (ii) Source BIS "Consolidated International Banking Statistics for End-June 1999" November 1999 and BIS "The Maturity, Sectoral and Nationality Distribution of International Bank Lending: Second Half 1996" Basle July 1997.

2. *Republic of Korea*

- The level of international lending to Republic of Korea peaked in 1996 (US$100 billion) but fell 36.5% to US$63.5 billion by June 1999;

- Republic of Korea's share of total lending to Asia has fallen from 27.2% in 1996 to 22.1% in June 1999;

- the average maturity of bank lending has been rising, so that by June 1999 53.7% of loans had a maturity of less than one year;

- lending to the bank sector has been reduced from 65.9% of total loans in 1996 to 57.4% in June 1999, though the balance reflects a reallocation to the public sector and a withdrawal from lending to the non-bank private sector; and

- though Japan stills remains a significant lender (23.7% in June 1999), European banks have increased their share of total loans from 28.8% in 1996 to 31.9% in 1999.

Table A.2   **Summary of International Bank Lending to South Korea**
(1996 to 1999)

	December 1996	December 1997	June 1998	December 1998	June 1999
Total Asia (US$ Billions)	367.1	378.8	319.6	299.4	287.0
Total South Korea (US$ Billions)	100.0	93.7	71.6	65.6	63.5
(TSK/TA)%	27.2	24.7	22.4	21.9	22.1
Maturity					
Less than 1, and 1 year (%)	67.5	62.8	45.1	45.3	53.7
Over 1 year (%)	20.0	23.4	39.4	38.2	28.7
Sector					
Banks (%)	65.9	59.3	56.6	57.0	57.4
Public Sector (%)	5.7	4.2	6.8	8.3	8.2
Non-Bank Private Sector (%)	28.3	36.4	36.6	34.4	33.9
Nationality of Reporting Banks					
Euro-Area Banks	28.8				31.9
U.K. Banks	5.6				7.3
U.S. Banks	9.4				10.1
Japanese Banks	24.3				23.7
Other	31.9				27.0

Notes:
(i) Maturity and Sector percentage does not sum to 100%.
(ii) Source BIS "Consolidated International Banking Statistics for End-June 1999" November 1999 and BIS "The Maturity, Sectoral and Nationality Distribution of International Bank Lending: Second Half 1996" Basle July 1997.

3. *Malaysia*

- The level of international lending to Malaysia peaked in 1997 (US$27.3 billion) but fell 31.9% to US$18.6 billion by June 1999;

- Malaysia's share of total lending to Asia has been reduced slightly from 7.2% in 1997 to 6.5% in June 1999;

- the average maturity of bank lending has been rising, so that by June 1999 42.3% of loans had a maturity of less than one year;

- lending to the non-bank private sector has been increasing slightly from 61.7% of total loans in 1996 to 64.3% in June 1999, though the balance reflects a reallocation to the public sector and a withdrawal from lending to the bank sector; and

- though Japan stills remains a significant lender (32.5% in June 1999), U.K. banks have increased their share of total loans from 6.4% in 1996 to 11.1% in 1999.

Table A.3   **Summary of International Bank Lending to Malaysia**
(1996 to 1999)

	December 1996	December 1997	June 1998	December 1998	June 1999
Total Asia (US$ Billions)	367.1	378.8	319.6	299.4	287.0
Total Malaysia (US$ Billions)	22.2	27.3	22.8	20.9	18.6
(TM/TA)%	6.1	7.2	7.1	7.0	6.5
Maturity					
Less than 1, and 1 year (%)	50.3	52.8	48.2	44.7	42.3
Over 1 year (%)	36.1	37.8	41.9	44.0	45.8
Sector					
Banks (%)	29.3	35.3	30.8	27.7	21.7
Public Sector (%)	9.0	6.4	6.6	8.8	13.8
Non-Bank Private Sector (%)	61.7	58.2	62.5	63.4	64.3
Nationality of Reporting Banks					
Euro-Area Banks	35.2				35.4
U.K. Banks	6.4				11.1
U.S. Banks	10.5				5.7
Japanese Banks	36.9				32.5
Other	11.0				15.3

Notes
(i) Maturity and Sector percentage does not sum to 100%.
(ii) Source BIS "Consolidated International Banking Statistics for End-June 1999" November 1999 and BIS "The Maturity, Sectoral and Nationality Distribution of International Bank Lending: Second Half 1996" Basle July 1997.

4.   *Thailand*

–   The level of international lending to Thailand peaked in 1996 (US$70.2 billion) but fell 50.6% to US$34.7 billion by June 1999;

–   Thailand's share of total lending to Asia has been reduced from 19.1% in 1997 to 12.0% in June 1999;

–   the average maturity of bank lending has been rising, so that by June 1999 54.9% of loans had a maturity of less than one year;

–   lending to the non-bank private sector has been increasing significantly from 59.6% of total loans in 1996 to 74.4% in June 1999, though the balance also reflects a reallocation to the public sector and a withdrawal from lending to the bank sector; and

–   Japan remains a significant lender (52.7% in June 1999), though European banks have increased their share of total loans from 22.3% in 1996 to 30.9% in 1999.

Table A.4   **Summary of International Bank Lending to Thailand**
(1996 to 1999)

	December 1996	December 1997	June 1998	December 1998	June 1999
Total Asia (US$ Billions)	367.1	378.8	319.6	299.4	287.0
Total Thailand (US$ Billions)	70.2	58.5	46.4	41.2	34.7
(TT/TA)%	19.1	15.4	14.5	13.8	12.0
Maturity					
Less than 1 and 1 year (%)	65.1	65.8	59.3	58.3	54.9
Over 1 year (%)	30.2	30.7	36.5	37.1	39.4
Sector					
Banks (%)	36.9	29.9	26.1	22.0	19.4
Public Sector (%)	3.2	3.1	4.3	4.7	6.2
Non-Bank Private Sector (%)	59.6	66.9	69.6	73.2	74.4
Nationality of Reporting Banks					
Euro-Area Banks	22.3				30.9
U.K. Banks	4.5				4.3
U.S. Banks	7.2				3.6
Japanese Banks	53.5				52.7
Other	12.5				8.5

Notes:
(i) Maturity and Sector percentage does not sum to 100%.
(ii) Source BIS "*Consolidated International Banking Statistics for End-June 1999*" November 1999 and BIS "*The Maturity, Sectoral and Nationality Distribution of International Bank Lending: Second Half 1996*" Basle July 1997.

NOTES

1. The crisis economies in this paper refer to the worst hit countries, namely, Indonesia, Republic of Korea, Malaysia, and Thailand.

2. The best international practice as well as banking laws suggests that a commercial bank, which is generally entitled to receive only short-term deposits up to one year, should not provide any loans for longer than one year.

3. During the period 1996-1999, the levels of international bank lending to Asian developing countries decreased significantly. See Chapter II for details.

4. International portfolio diversification and yield-seeking behavior of globalised investors has increased the opportunity cost of bank deposits, and this has led to bank disintermediation and a broadening of securities markets in many advanced countries. For example, the total market value of assets managed by US mutual funds (roughly $5 trillion) and invested in securities markets surpasses the total value of deposits in US banks. Japan and European financial markets are largely in the process of following the US trends, though slower. (Garry J. Schinasi and R. Todd- Smith (December 1998), "Fixed-Income Markets in the United States, Europe, and Japan: Some Lessons for Emerging Markets," IMF Working Paper.)

5. Given the large difference in historical backgrounds and underpinning frameworks between financial systems, it is not advisable to directly compare these countries with the U.S. However, because the U.S. has the most advanced capital market, it may serve as a comparator country in discussing bond market.

6. Japanese banks at June 1999 only accounted for 26.1% of US$287 billion claims to Asia, compared with 30.3% of US$378.8 billion at December 1997 (BIS, 1999, Table 2).

7. Details of international bank lending to each of the crisis economies are provided in the Appendix A.

8. Mashiro Kawai and Ken-Ichi Takayasu (1998) "The Banking and Financial System in Thailand", ADB Report, make this point concerning Thailand, though it may be generalised to other crisis economies.

9. Domestic bond issues in the U.S. must be registered with the SEC (U.S. Securities Act of 1933).

10. Bond credit rating agencies categorise corporate bond issuers into nine major classes according to perceived credit quality. These ratings classes include investment grade issuers: AAA, AA, A and BBB, and non-investment grades: BB, B, CCC, CC, and C. Bonds with ratings below C are bonds in default or of bankrupts. The two major agencies use slightly different notation to refer to equivalent credit risk categories. Standard & Poor's use upper-case capitals (e.g. AAA), while Moody's Investor Services use an upper case first character and have any remaining characters lower case (e.g. Aaa). This paper uses the Standard & Poor's notation.

11. The US dollar is the most frequent currency of issue with US$1673.4 billion, then the Japanese Yen US$407.1 billion, the Deutsche Mark US$369.4 billion, the Pound US$308.3 billion, the French Franc US$191.3 billion, the Swiss Franc US$141.5 billion, the Italian Lire US117.9 billion, the Dutch

Guilder US$105.3 billion, the ECU US$99.3 billion, and finally the Luxembourg Franc with US$37.8 billion in outstandings (BIS, 1998 Table 13B).

12. See Chart 5, Kamin and von Kleist (1999:17) for graphical evidence of the decline in spreads (1991 to 1997). Lenders favoured Asian issues (eg spreads on Latin American issues with the same characteristics as Asian issues were 39% higher). This may be due to: (a) Latin American and Eastern European countries exhibited greater volatility than Asian Economies (K and VK :18) and/or (b) Greater supply since Latin American countries issue more bonds Asian countries (Eichengreen and Mody (1997). But as K and VK note Asia, while not issuing bonds, tends to take out more loans. This suggests economic stability is the key factor for deciding spreads.

13. Capital Data Bondware (Euromoney) generally list the following firms as the major bookrunners of emerging market bonds: JP Morgan, Merrill Lynch, CSFB, Union Bank of Switzerland and Lehman Brothers.

14. It is difficult to assess what issue size is necessary to maintain adequate liquidity. One of the world's largest Eurobond issuers (Federal Home Loan Mortgage Corporation or Freddie Mac) suggests one bullet maturity issues of at least US$4 billion every quarter is necessary (Euromoney June 1998: "Borrowers, A Mad Rush for Liquidity").

15. An expectation that the local currency will not depreciate more than the interest rate differential between the two countries will encourage unhedged foreign currency borrowing. International parity relationships predict that over time interest rate differentials equal the actual depreciation or appreciation of floating-rate currencies.

16. Agency problems were originally investigated by Jensen and Meckling (1976).

17. See Nestor and Thompson's (1999) discussion of the different systems of corporate governance which vary from the outsider model (in the U.S. and the U.K), to the insider model, of which the family/state model is a sub-category.

18. Casserley and Gibb (1999: Exhibit 11.3) estimates significant family ownership of the 15 largest banks in Thailand (27% of stock), Indonesia (47% of stock), Malaysia (59% of stock) and the Philippines (60% of stock) at year end 1997.

19. See Kim (1999).

20. In 1983, Indonesia took several measures to liberalize the financial sector including interest rate deregulation and initiation of the central bank certificates.

21. In terms of medium- to long-term industrial financing, corporate bond and medium-term note (MTN) may be comparable. However, an MTN is different in that it is issued directly to investors without the use of agent and there is no secondary market for MTNs.

22. Note the Institute of International Finance Task Force on Risk Assessment Report (2000:January) that specifies best risk management practice for the private sector.

23. Note the Institute of International Finance report (1999:March): "Report of the Working Group on Emerging Markets Finance" also recommended that this information include the off-balance sheet positions of reporting institutions. See this report for further details on data transparency and disclosure.

24. Thompson (1999).

25. Specific policy concerning the enhancement of the governance structures in crisis economies has also been analysed by a number of ADB studies.

26. The manner in which Indonesian banks hold their reserves is specified under the Banking and Financial Institutions Act. Procedures could be established which facilitate the holding of bonds as bank reserves.

27. EMBI Global has a weighting of South Korea 7.5%, Philippines 2.9% and the new additions of Malaysia 2.5%, China 1.6% and Thailand 0.4% (Source: Asiamoney, September 1999). Other examples include the Strategic Income Fund of Chase Manhattan.

28. The Nation (11/1/2000) reported that in December 1999 BHT18.6 billion of BHT35.4 billion was attributable to corporate bond turnover.

29. The rating categories of these agencies are similar to S&P's.

30. opcit Meecharoen (1999)

31. APEC Collaborative Initiative on Development of Domestic Bond Markets (August 1999), Guidelines to Facilitate the Development of Domestic Bond Markets in APEC Member Economies.

REFERENCES

(BIS) Bank of International Settlements, Quarterly Review: International Banking and Financial Market Developments, various issues.

Benzie Richard, (1992), The Development of The International Bond Markets, Bank for International Settlements, Monetary and Economic Department, Basle.

Berger, Allen and Gregory Udell, (1998), 'The Economies of Small Business Finance: The Roles of Private Equity and Debt Markets in the Financial Growth Cycle', Journal of Banking and Finance (22): 613-673.

Eichengreen, Barry and Ashoka Mody, (1997), "What Explains Changing Spreads on Emerging-Market Debt: Fundamentals or Market Sentiment" Mimeo, International Monetary Fund.

Emery Robert F., (1997), The Bond Markets of Developing East Asia, Westview Press Boulder, Colorado.

Euromoney, (June 1998), "Borrowers a Mad Rush for Liquidity".

(IIF) Institute of International Finance, Inc., (1999), Report of the Task Force on Risk Assessment, March (see: http://www.iif.com/public.htm).

(IIF) Institute of International Finance, Inc., (2000), Capital Flows to Emerging Market Economies Report, January (see: http://www.iif.com/public.htm).

Jensen, Michael C. and William H. Meckling, (1976), 'Theory of the Firm: Managerial Behaviour, Agency Costs, and Ownership Structure', Journal of Financial Economics, 3 (October): 305-360.

Kamin, Steven and Karsten von Kleist, (1999), "The Evolution and Determinates of Emerging Market Credit Spreads in the 1990s" BIS Working Paper No. 68, May.

Kawai, Mashiro and Ken-Ichi Takayasu, (1998), The Banking and Financial System in Thailand, Asian Development Bank Report.

Kim, Yun-Hwan, (1999), Creating Long-Term Mortgage-Backed Bond Markets in Asian Developing Economies – A Postcrisis Agenda, Asian Development Bank.

Myers, Stewart C., (1984), 'The Capital Structure Puzzle', Journal of Finance, July: 575-592.

Nestor, Stilpon and John Thompson, (1999), "Corporate Governance Patterns in OECD Economies: Is Convergence Under Way?" Conference on "Corporate Governance in Asia: A Comparative Perspective" OECD Seoul, 3-5 March.

Schinasi, Gary J. and R. Todd Smith, (1998), "Fixed Income Markets in the United States, Europe, and Japan: Some Lessons for Emerging Markets" IMF Working Papers December.

Thompson, (1999), "Alternative Systems of Corporate Governance in OECD Countries: Strengths and Weaknesses," ADB-ADBI capacity Building Workshop on Corporate Governance in Asia, 22-26 Nov 1999.

White, William R., (1999), "Evolving International Financial Markets: Some Implications for Central Banks" BIS Working Papers No. 66-April.

Nasial

DEVELOPMENT OF INTERNATIONAL BOND MARKETS IN THE REGION – NEW MIYAZAWA INITIATIVE -

612 516
615

by
Toshio Kobayashi[*]

Lessons from the Asian Currency Crisis

The Asian Currency Crisis taught us several lessons. One of the important lessons is that over-dependence on the banking sector for much of the funding needs for corporate growth and expansion was a contributing factor to the 1997 crisis. (Graph 1) One way to protect against the risks and volatility of short-term capital movements is to reduce the dependence on bank loans. This will require a mechanism for long-term recycling of funds to the private sector in the region in order to enable it to meet its financing needs. This mechanism is required not only in each economy in the region, but also within the region.

The East Asian region as a whole is in capital surplus. Yet, before the crisis many capital deficit countries in the region were financing their development with short-term loans. This requires an effective mechanism for long-term recycling of funds from the surplus countries in the region to the deficit countries. Therefore, it is crucial that bond markets in the region be developed and deepened.

Importance of the Bond Markets

A mature and liquid bond market can improve resource allocation by effectively channeling both local and foreign savings into domestic investments and can diversify the investment channels for investors. Greater diversification of financing and investment channels is beneficial to the stability of financial markets.

There seems to be a growing consensus that deep and liquid financial markets are needed to ensure a robust and efficient financial system as a whole.

Vitalization of issuance and trading in the bond markets would also strengthen corporate governance in the region. Compared with banking loans, fund-recycling through bond markets means spreading risks from the banking sector to a wider sector of the public. This, therefore, requires more transparency in the financial conditions of issuers, which is an urgent element for the restructuring of the corporate sector.

Furthermore, if the issuance of bonds denominated in Asian currencies increases, this would have the merit of enabling reduction in exchange risk for issuers and investors.

---

[*] The author wishes to emphasize that the content and opinions expressed in this paper are entirely his own and do not represent the official position of the Ministry of Finance of Japan.

Current Situation of the International Bond Markets in the Region

I would like to very briefly look at the current situation of the Asian-Pacific bond markets.

Compared with well-developed markets, most Asian bond markets are underdeveloped. (Table 1) The size of bond market outstanding against GDP is less than 50% in most economies of this region. The share is 42% in South Korea, and only around 25% in other economies, such as HK, Thailand, and the Philippines. In Indonesia, the share is a low 5%.

The situation of issuance and trading in the international bond markets in the region has also been unsatisfactory. For foreign currency-denominated bonds, the Eurobond market is dominant. Over 90% of international bond issues are raised in the Euro-market. As regards domestic currency-denominated bonds issued by non-residents, only the Yankee bond and Swiss franc bond markets are active. The share of the Samurai bond market is small, and other regional international bond markets are tiny.

There is much room to develop and improve the functions of the bond markets in the region for international bond offerings.

Second Stage of the New Miyazawa Initiative - Resource Mobilization Plan for Asia (Appendix)

Taking into account these challenges, the Japanese Government made public its policies in May 1999, in a package called the Second Stage of the New Miyazawa Initiative, in order to mobilize domestic and foreign private-sector funds to achieve a full-scale, vigorous recovery in these economies. To ensure that Asian economies are not easily influenced by excessive short-term international capital flows, it will be necessary to promote the influx of good-quality and long-term funding.

Along these lines, the New Miyazawa Initiative pointed out that the upgrading and fostering of Asian Bond Markets is an urgent issue in establishing a stable financial system in the region.

To that end, Japanese authorities should by themselves implement measures to vitalize the Tokyo market, for such measures to promote the issuance of Samurai bonds, and to improve its settlement and clearing system.

Besides that, the Initiative states that Japan will cooperate with other authorities in the region to tackle the following issues:

– Fostering and upgrading domestic markets in the region by providing technical and personnel assistance
– Vitalizing the regional markets for international bonds

The former issue concerning the development of domestic bond markets is very important and urgent, and has been dealt with in the previous sessions. Here I would like to touch upon the latter issue of vitalizing the regional international bond markets.

Necessity and Merits of Regional International Bond Markets

(1)   Mobilizing funds in the region on a wider range

Developing the domestic bond markets in the region might take time, especially taking into account the fact that a market with sufficient depth needs a broad base of institutional investors. In addition, even well-developed domestic markets have their limits in volume and fund availability. For the effective recycling of funds within the region, it would be desirable to further develop international bond markets.

(2)   *More convenient for bond issuers and investors in the region*

Even in the Asian-Pacific region, institutional investors have recently grown or are expected to grow. Investors in the region have many opportunities to gain a far greater knowledge of regional bond issuers, and therefore can take higher risks. This means that we have the foundation to vitalize markets where mainly Asian investors can make their own pricing in the Asian time zone.

Having well-developed international bond markets in the region has merits both for issuers and investors in the region.

(3)   *Prerequisite for the development of Asian financial business in the 21st century*

The rapid progress of the financial system and technology caused by the IT revolution has aroused concerns that Asia could be left behind in the 21st century. Further developing regional international bond markets by collecting financial-related knowledge and information is a vital element for the development of the financial service sector in the region.

Issues to be Addressed

We are now exchanging views and opinions with market participants and authorities in the region in order to find measures to vitalize international bond markets in the region.

The basic direction is that we should establish markets where non-residents can issue bonds smoothly and cost-effectively and national or international investors can easily obtain necessary information on issuers for their investment decisions.

From this point of view, the following issues need to be addressed:

- Review of regulatory requirements and market infrastructure to reduce costs and enhance market liquidity

- Upgrading of the clearing and settlement system for cross-border transactions

- Role of credit enhancement

    (Ref)   Japan expressed its readiness to provide credit guarantees for public bonds issued by Asian countries via JBIC and the Asian Currency Crisis Support Facility of the ADB.

- Encouragement for issuers to be rated by credible rating agencies, etc.

The authorities cannot solve all these issues. The private sector should lead some of them. Both the public and private sectors have to tackle the challenges for having well-developed and functioning international bond markets in the region.

Session 3

Lessons from the Experience in OECD Countries and other Emerging Economies

(OECD, LDCs)

KEY POLICY ISSUES IN DEVELOPING FIXED INCOME SECURITIES MARKETS IN EMERGING MARKET ECONOMIES

016

by
Mr. Hendrikus Blommestein

G12 F32

I. Introduction   H63

The government has a key role to play in the development of the fixed income debt market, through regulation and supervision, and as a key market participant, by virtue of it often being the largest issuer. Through regulation and supervision, the government provides key parts of the payment system, removes functional dislocations, and undertakes measures to deepen money and bond markets. Governments also contribute to the development of trust or confidence in financial markets through high disclosure standards to promote transparency, and the enforcement mechanism that prevents the use, or abuse, of private information in the market. As the largest issuer, the government establishes the benchmark which provides the "risk-free" rate which is used as the basis for pricing all securities, assures a regular supply of debt through planned auction schedules, introduces fixed-income securities trading and promotes the development of investment culture. Public debt instruments also serve as collateral and hedging vehicles. The government also needs to increase the demand for fixed-income securities by, first, focusing on encouraging institutional demand and, subsequently, retail demand, as well as promoting the supply of liquid securities by undertaking regular, transparent issuance through auctions of its own securities.

The adverse consequences of underdeveloped fixed-income securities markets demonstrate clearly why there is an important public policy role for the financial authorities in developing these markets. Underdeveloped markets entail infrastructure risk in addition to investment risk. The higher level of uncertainty associated with such markets could discourage capital investment or raise the cost of capital formation. The international financial crisis in 1997-1998 has brought sharply into focus the risks and costs associated with underdeveloped fixed-income securities markets, in particular, that *underdeveloped* markets have encouraged excessive reliance on foreign and domestic bank financing.

The experience with debt management and development of government bond markets in the more advanced OECD markets provide sovereign debt managers from emerging debt markets with important insights on best practices in this policy area. OECD debt managers made important progress in the development of more market-oriented and more sophisticated debt management procedures and techniques. In doing so, they also contributed to the development and strengthening of domestic capital markets.

This article provides a concise overview of the key issues and policy actions related to the development of fixed-income securities markets. It includes an overview and analysis of OECD fixed-income securities markets as well as fixed-income securities markets in emerging economies, including obstacles faced by them. Special attention will be paid to the role of the Asian bond market in the 1997-98 financial crises. The role of cross-border capital flows in the development of domestic bond markets, as well as the contribution of government securities markets and public debt management to the development of corporate securities markets, will be highlighted. The final part of the paper presents conclusions on best practices and suggest actions in key policy areas.

II.   The Importance of Fixed-Income Securities Markets in Advanced OECD Countries – Overview and Analysis[1]

Capital markets constitute the place where securities are issued and traded. They channel local and international savings into local or international investments. They provide a price discovery mechanism to ensure that capital is valued realistically and allocated efficiently. An important part of capital markets is fixed-income securities markets. The yield curve associated with government securities markets is important for the correct pricing of corporate bonds. Fixed-income securities differ from equity with respect to maturity and the extent of liability. Concerning the latter aspect, each fixed-income security specifies how much, and when, coupon and principal would be paid and, in the event of default, the security holder could ask for bankruptcy of the security issuer. In the case of bankruptcy, the debt outstanding is usually subordinated.[2] If a debt issuer is successful in its business, the debt holder will receive, as a maximum, the amount specified in the debt agreement.[3] Thus, debt holders have a smaller stake in a business than shareholders. This makes the role of rating agencies – distributing information about business prospects – vital for the successful performance of fixed-income securities markets.

Almost all advanced OECD countries have developed their fixed-income government securities markets pressed by the necessity of financing fiscal deficits. Many of the largest economies have government bond markets approaching or exceeding US$1000 billion (Table 1). The 1980s trend in OECD countries to improve the depth and liquidity of government debt instruments has continued during the 1990s. This trend is in large part due to the internationalisation of domestic markets and investor bases (Table 2) that is also affecting emerging market economies. The presence of foreign investors improves competition, liquidity and transparency in local markets but it is less clear whether it increases price volatility. Table 3 presents some indicators of market liquidity in the largest economies.

Table 1. **A comparison of the size of some important bond markets**
(USD billion, end-1998)

US government[a]	3 355.5
Japanese government	2 590.4
US non-financial corporates	1 621.8
US government-sponsored enterprises[b]	1 273.6
German government	1 110.2
German Pfandbriefe[c]	1 073.2
US asset-backed securities issues	1 012.8
Italian government[d]	959.6
French government[d]	654.4

a)   Total marketable interest-bearing Federal debt.
b)   Securities issued by Federal Home Loan Banks, Fannie Mae, Federal Home Loan Mortgage Corporation (Freddie Mac), Farm Credit System, the Financing Corporation, the Resolution Funding Corporation, and the Student Loan Marketing Association (Sallie Mae), not including mortgage-backed securities (MBS).
c)   Hypotheken Pfandbriefe and Öffentliche Pfandbriefe.
d)   Excluding Treasury bills.
Sources: Board of Governors of the Federal Reserve System, *Flow of Funds Accounts of the United States*; Bank of Japan, *Financial and Economics Statistics Monthly*; Deutsche Bank (1999), Owens-Thomson(1999).

Table 2. **Non-Residents' Holdings of Public Debt**

	United States	Japan	Canada	Italy
1983	14.9	..	10.7	..
1984	15.4	..	11.3	..
1985	15.2	3.7	12.4	..
1986	16.1	3.3	16.1	..
1987	16.6	3.3	15.5	..
1988	18.4	2.0	15.7	..
1989	20.8	3.0	16.3	..
1990	20.1	4.4	17.4	4.4
1991	20.1	5.8	19.0	5.2
1992	20.4	5.5	20.2	6.2
1993	22.2	5.4	21.8	10.1
1994	22.8	5.9	22.6	12.2
1995	28.3	4.3	23.3	13.2
1996	35.0	4.3	23.8	15.9
1997	40.1	..	23.1	..

Source: Schinasi, G.J. and R.T. Smith (1998), "Fixed-Income Markets in the United States, Europe and Japan: Some Lessons for Emerging Markets", IMF Working Paper, 98/173.

Table 3. **Liquidity indicators for major OECD countries' government bond markets**
(As of 1997)

	United States	Japan	Germany	France	Italy	United Kingdom	Canada	Sweden
Bid-ask spread:								
On-the-run issues[a]								
2 years	1.6	5	4	4	3	3	2	4
5 years[b]	1.6	9	4	5	5	4	5	9
10 years	3.1	7	4	10	6	4	5	15
30 years[b]	3.1	16	10	24	14	8	10	27[c]
Off-the-run issues[a,d]								
5 years[b]	6.3	11	4	6	8	4	12.5	..
10 years	6.3	7	5	6	8	4	15.5	..
30 years[b]	12.5	19	10	10	14	12	18.5	..
Volume outstanding (a)[e]	3 457	1 919	563	551	1 100	458	285	35
Yearly trading volume (b)[g]	75 901	13 282	..	18 634[f]	8 419	3 222	6 243	125[f]
Turnover ratio (b)/(a)	22.0	6.9	..	33.8	7.7	7.0	21.9	3.6

a) Bid-ask spreads in one-hundredth of a currency unit for the face amount of 100 currency units.
b) For Japan, 6-year bonds are used in the place of 5-year bonds and 20-year bonds are used in the place of 30-year bonds for Japan.
c) For the 22 year bond.
d) Bid-ask spreads for off-the-run issues having similar remaining maturity as the on-the-run issues. Some of the spreads are indicative rather than definitive.
e) The figures are for end-1997, in billions of US dollars, converted at the exchange rates of end-1997.
f) Figures may include trading other than outright transactions; such as repos or buy/sell backs.
g) The figures are for the 1997 calendar year.
Source: BIS

By the late 1990s, longer-term, fixed rate instruments accounted for a large part of government debt. (Tables 4 and 5) as debt managers sought to minimise re-financing risk as well as interest risk. Moreover, with the deepening of secondary markets, the impact of market interest rates from issuance activity in primary markets appears to have been considerably reduced. Another interesting feature during the last few years is that a number of large governments (USA, France) have joined the relatively small number of OECD countries that issue index-linked bonds. These instruments may be attractive for a wide range of investors but in particular those with longer term liabilities such as pension funds in developed and emerging economies.

Table 4. **Features of the maturity profile for central government debt** (As of 1997)

Country	Maturity distribution[a] (as a percentage of total volume outstanding) (In years)				Average term to maturity	Duration	Original maturities (m = months, y = years)	Number of original maturities	Number of benchmarks
	1 or less	1-5	5-10	Over 10	(Years)				
United States	21	62		17	5.2	n.a	3, 6 m; 1, 2, 5, 10, 30 y	7	7
Japan	5	8	78	9	n.a.	n.a.	3, 6 m; 2, 4, 5, 6, 10, 20 y	8	1
Germany	2	32	61	5	n.a.	n.a.	6 m; 2, 4, 5, 10, 30 y	6	4
France	10	27	53	10	6.2	n.a.	3, 6 m; 1, 2, 5, 10, 15, 30 y	8	7
Italy	17	32	48	3	4.7	2.4	3, 6 m; 1, 1.5, 2, 3, 5, 7, 10, 30 y	10	5
United Kingdom[b]	7	29	34	30	9.7	6.5	3 m; 5, 10, 20, 30 y	5	3
Canada	32	29	27	12	5.8	5.1	3, 6 m; 1, 2, 5, 10, 30 y	7	7
Belgium	19	6	43	32	4.4	3.4	3, 6 m; 1, 5, 10, 15, 30 y	7	2
Netherlands	4	10	74	12	5.9[c]	4.1	3, 6 m; 1, 5, 10, 30 y	6	2
Sweden	n.a.	n.a.	n.a.	n.a.	n.a.	n.a.	n.a.	n.a.	12
Switzerland	27	23	13	37	n.a.	n.a.	3, 6 m; 5, 7, 9, 10, 11, 12, 13, 14, 15, 20 y	12	7

a) Distribution by original maturity, excluding older issues out of the regular issuance cycle and index-linked securities.
b) Maturity distribution by remaining maturity.
c) Excluding Dutch State Treasury Certificates.
Sources: BIS and OECD .

Table 5. **Central government securities by type of instrument**
(In per cent of total, end-1997[a])

	Fixed	Floating	Indexed	Zero coupon[b]	Short term[c]
United States	77.9	-	1.0	-	20.7
Japan	94.2	-	-	0.5	5.2
Germany	95.8	1.9	-	-	2.0
France	78.2	5.6	-	6.2	9.9
Italy	39.4	29.1	-	8.2	15.5
United Kingdom	84.4	3.1	11.3	-	-
Canada	59.7	-	2.1	-	28.1
Belgium	74.2	5.8	-	0.6	19.5
Netherlands	96.1	-	-	-	3.6
Sweden	73.3	-	10.3	-	16.4
Switzerland	72.6	-	-	-	27.4

a) Any difference between 100 and the sum of displayed percentage shares comprise other, non-classified marketable issues.
b) Zero coupon issue with original maturity above one year.
c) Zero coupon issue with original maturity up to one year.
Source : BIS .

An important recent development is that many OECD governments managers (with the notable exception of Japan) have been running budget surpluses, which have reduced their net borrowing needs and have led to a reduction in the supply of securities on issue. Thus, in some cases, strong demand has encountered reduced supplies, which has resulted in shortages of selected bonds with the usual pricing anomalies. Forecasts for many governments call for further reductions in the supply of bonds from current levels, so debt managers are likely to continue to face complications arising from a declining debt environment and these may intensify.

A major new challenge is that OECD debt managers are facing the policy implications of lower liquidity in traditional benchmark markets in view of the projections of a rapidly diminishing gross debt. Issuing strategies have to be adjusted. Also the potential impact of a low or zero gross debt on the functioning of financial markets needs to be assessed.

A market requires products to be traded, participants to trade, and a trading system. Various trading systems have been developed and are in operation in advanced markets. The trading systems in use differ depending on the kind of participants that use them, the products that are traded on them, and the size and structure of the market. A key issue related to market structure is that of the balance between "on exchange" and "off exchange" transactions. On the one hand, it could be argued that consolidation of these transactions would enhance liquidity and transparency of the transactions and thereby be beneficial for an efficient price discovery process. On the other hand, there seems to be a trend in advanced market economies to place more importance on the benefits of competition between markets. Information technology is the key driving force in shaping the outcome of this competition.

An important recent development, in this context, is the impact of new electronic trading systems on debt management and government securities markets. Various types of Electronic Trading Systems (ETS) can be distinguished, including dealer-based ones, matching systems, competitive bidding and auction systems. Three types of primary market systems are usually distinguished: competitive bidding systems (issuer to dealers), online selling systems (dealer to clients), and direct primary issuance systems (issuer to clients). And two types of secondary trading systems : single and multiple (co-mingled) dealer systems (to clients), and cross-matching systems (between dealers and client to client).

This is an extremely fast-moving area in which it was not clear which business model will succeed. The number and types of fixed-income ETSs are growing rapidly. Markets and governments will have to adapt to this new reality. Several driving forces for the greater use of ETS can be distinguished. The first is technological change. This is forcing globalisation of the markets, and allowing the creation of new cheaper communications networks. It is enhancing pricing engines and security, and also making the transfer of information cheaper and more timely. A second driving force is transparency. Previously, fixed-income markets were not highly transparent as dealers preferred having privileged access to information. ETS improve access to information, reduce information asymmetries, and allow market-wide integration of real-time trading information. A third important driving force is cost-reduction. ETS cut resource costs of all parties -- sales, trading and back-office. They are most attractive in commoditised securities markets such as those for government bonds. Access can be offered at minimal costs.

The advance of ETS is inevitable and will reshape the fixed income markets. They could improve national markets by extending access to, and awareness of, the markets. Two risks are that emerging markets could be left behind, and that major dealers could dominate them. While transparency is critical, and will naturally improve, it may need public support. Intermediation will also remain important as ETS are not a substitute for committed dealers. Primary dealers need to be involved. When choosing a system, issues to consider include participation, market-making obligations, vendors, and international alliances. Lastly, there will be regulatory concerns about transparency and access, member and market rules, and market soundness, namely the reduction of systemic and credit risks.

The establishment of an appropriate infrastructure is not sufficient for the development of liquid capital markets. A vibrant capital market also requires active players. Players include institutional and individual investors, as well as brokers and dealers. Investors that conduct arbitrage trading (e.g. hedge funds) are important for enhancing the activity, the efficiency and liquidity of capital markets. In advanced markets, institutional investors play a significant role by trading considerable amounts of financial assets; they have also stimulated the development of the proper infrastructure for capital markets.[4]

Attractive products are also indispensable for capital market development. Three central factors that determine the attractiveness of a financial product are risk, return and liquidity. Transparency and disclosure about the products are also a key factor in attracting investors in order to enable them to make satisfactory assessments of return and risk. Government securities possessing these attractive features have been instrumental in encouraging the development of OECD capital markets more generally, in particular corporate fixed-income securities. The contribution of government securities markets and public debt management to the development of corporate securities markets will also be studied.

III.   Overview of Fixed-Income Securities Markets in Emerging Economies

The development of bond markets in different emerging regions has taken very different courses, and is at different stages of development (Chart 1 provides an illustration for Asian markets). While in Latin America and Eastern Europe, government bonds have spear-headed the establishment of the markets, in Asia, often the private sector has led the development (e.g. decrease and cessation of government bonds in Malaysia and Thailand before the Asian financial crisis, paralleled by an increase in the bond issues by Malaysia's Cagamas, and Thailand's government enterprises). Another relevant characteristic that differentiates East Asian from Latin American emerging market economies is the higher saving propensity in East Asian countries.

Regions exhibit different degrees of market liquidity. It is often argued that Latin American securities markets are characterised by high liquidity because they have an active money market. By the same token, while Asian markets are larger, they could be less liquid owing to a lack of money markets and limited trading of government bonds, often held as part of reserve requirements. Central and Eastern Europe have generally been credited with the establishment of relatively liquid markets in a fairly short time. However, the quantitative evidence derived from indicators of market liquidity is, at best, mixed (Chart 2).

A common characteristic of most emerging debt markets is a lack of institutional demand.[5] Nevertheless, considerable contractual savings reform has taken place in Latin America, particularly in Chile, in the early 1980s, and in Argentina and Mexico. Private pension funds have been introduced recently in several other Latin American countries – the Chilean model serving as the starting point for these pension reforms. The change from a pay-as-you-go system to pre-funded pension schemes has served as an important catalyst for the development of deeper and more liquid debt and equity markets.

Macroeconomic stability is a prerequisite for the development of domestic fixed-income markets. Robust fixed-income securities markets, in turn, can contribute to financial market stability. In contrast, excessive reliance on bank financing and lack of development of the domestic debt market, especially medium to long-term fixed rate instruments, have been identified as important causes of the Asian financial crisis.

Chart 1

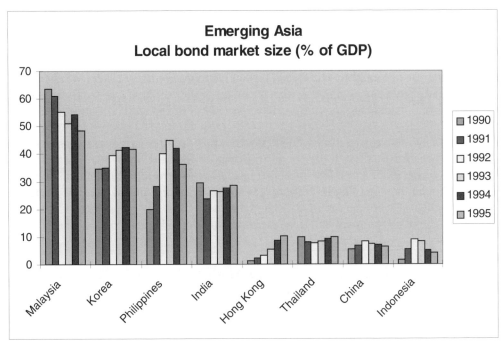

Source: Financial Times.

Chart 2

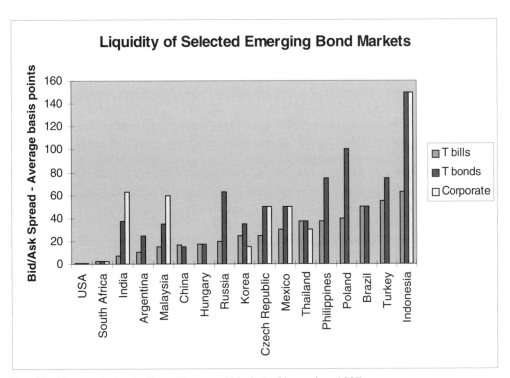

Source: The J.P. Morgan Guide to Emerging Local Markets, November 1997..

Governments are the dominant issuers in all local debt markets. In Asia, maturities of active instruments are focused on one year; exceptions are some corporate instruments in Korea and Malaysia. Treasury bills dominate in Central Europe. In Latin America, only Chile has longer-term maturities. In Asia, fixed-rate instruments are the most common, while floating rate instruments proliferate in Central Europe and Latin America.

On the demand side, institutional investors are key. Pension reforms in Latin America have boosted institutional demand. In many countries, the dominant role of banks, restrictions on institutional investor operations and inadequate regulations have hampered the growth of institutional demand.

Inflation-indexed bonds have sometimes been promoted as an alternative instrument for economies with high inflation records, although this is not necessarily the best solution. Furthermore, it is not enough just to introduce this instrument, it is also necessary to develop the demand from institutional investors, in particular pension funds. Some countries have introduced foreign currency-indexed bonds to support their private sector in their hedging activities. It is recognised that this can be particularly risky for the government and total exposure should be kept small.

IV. Contribution of Government Securities Markets and Public Debt Management to the Development of Corporate Securities Markets

The focus on debt management and the upgrade of debt management capabilities, establishment of interest rate, liquidity and currency benchmarks has helped to improved the transparency, predictability, and liquidity of fixed income debt markets in OECD countries. The increase in the prominence of the debt office has revolutionised, starting in the mid-1980s, how OECD governments finance themselves, and the critical role that fixed-income securities markets play in the financial sector. An effective debt management policy is always accompanied by a developed fixed-income market.

Public debt management and government securities market operations have a direct effect on the securities markets as a whole. The government is simultaneously a supplier of financial instruments and a regulator of the market. Suppliers of fixed-income instruments include the central government, municipalities, housing finance institutions, infrastructure project financiers and the corporate (mainly industrial) sector. On the other side, we have the investors that operate in the wholesale markets such as institutional investors (banks, pension funds, insurance companies, mutual funds and hedge funds) and large non-financial corporations with financial surpluses, and those belonging to the retail sector such as small firms, co-operatives and private individuals. The development of strong institutional demand is a key factor for a strong government and corporate fixed-income securities market, and has to be addressed by looking at the tax and regulatory dimensions of encouraging the holding of fixed-income securities by institutions. Finally, financial intermediaries exist between suppliers and investors: banks as underwriters and advisers, primary dealers, brokers, etc. They operate alongside other "market builders" such as rating agencies.

A central proposition in the literature on market microstructure (the study of the process as well as the results of exchanging assets under explicitly specified trading mechanisms) is that the pricing of assets cannot be determined independently from the institutional structure of the market. Consequently, public debt managers are responsible for developing the appropriate structure for trading government securities that will minimise the cost of raising funds in the market subject to a desired level of risk. In this regard we can also identify the authorities' objectives to regulate, to provide infrastructure, and to promote the establishment of efficient securities markets in general. It is often emphasised that the development of an efficient market structure (i.e. beyond setting-up the basic regulatory and supervisory framework) cannot be left solely to the private sector. First, vested interests of intermediaries may support less than efficient market structures. Second, the costs of certain elements of market infrastructure, such as electronic trading networks, clearing and settlement systems as well as information systems may prove too costly for market participants to develop spontaneously.

The impact of the electronic revolution on trading is an important, recent example of this public policy consideration. As shown in section II, Electronic Trading Systems (ETS) could have a potentially significant market impact by improving the transparency, liquidity and efficiency of markets. They will attract trading activity and a wider range of investors. Higher transaction volumes may in turn reduce dealer-spreads and issuer costs. Their impact will be affected by the actions of governments, dealers and investors. Governments can champion ETS or they can leave it to the market.

Thus, the task of the public authorities may comprise several or all of the following components: (i) defining market structure; (ii) defining the type of intermediaries and their role and obligations *vis-à-vis* the market and the public; (iii) selecting the intermediaries; (iv) designing, managing and providing the trading system; (v) providing the physical location of the market. Furthermore, in the context of encouraging the transition from emerging to well-developed markets, the authorities can establish transitional supporting arrangements aimed at promoting the efficient functioning of markets: the public debt manager could take direct roles such as establishing or sponsoring dealer firms, possibly as a direct shareholder; acting as a market-maker through a separate window to promote secondary market liquidity; acting as an interdealer broker through brokering transactions of market participants and displaying price information. Transitional price stabilisation measures are also an option as are indirect support arrangements, for example, through credit lines.

From the work of organisations such as the OECD, there is now agreement about a number of important issues involving government securities markets and debt management.[6] Government securities market development should be step-by-step, focusing on the introduction of essential regulations and institutions. The major reasons for creating and maintaining this market are: to cover the government's borrowing needs; to facilitate monetary management by the central bank; and to provide a benchmark for a risk-free rate. The design of a programme of government debt instruments should take into account a number of considerations such as adhering to selling arrangements that are market-based, with flexible and competitive interest-rate determination; developing the medium- and long term bond market so as to provide a more stable funding of the public sector debt, as well as to offer opportunities for financial investments by the private sector; promoting liquidity in the market by avoiding any policy that could segment the market. The goal of development of medium- and long term bond markets can be difficult in a highly volatile and/or highly inflationary environment. Index-linked bonds are a solution in this type of environment; for example Chile and Israel with a two-digit inflation level tradition now offer 20 year government bonds. More recently, with inflation down to single-digits, Israel has started to offer fixed-income government securities. However, negative consequences, such as the indexation of the economy, which may come with excessive use of indexed instruments, should be kept in mind.

As mentioned above, also in some advanced markets with low inflation governments are now issuing index-linked securities. However, as a general rule, the market for index-linked bonds is less developed than that for conventional bonds. Indexed instruments have low liquidity — arising from relatively low issue volumes and the buy and hold strategy of important categories of investors (e.g. pension funds).

To achieve the goal of liquidity,[7] it is essential to possess well-functioning secondary markets, which additionally enable investors to continuously observe interest variations (price discovery) as a basis for their decisions. Moreover, secondary markets support interest rate liberalisation, as the government can rely on competitive money and interbank markets to set interest rates in line with supply and demand conditions. It is very instructive to study the behaviour of markets when liquidity is being reduced, also in the more advanced financial markets. After the Russian financial crisis in August 1998, investors began fleeing from any securities with risk.[8] In the United States, investors were willing to trade only the most liquid assets – United States Treasury bonds. With liquidity problems, the spread[9] increases and with it the cost of financing. For example, in the market for bonds from emerging-market governments and companies, not only did the bid-offer spreads triple in late October 1998 with respect to July of that year for most emerging-market bonds, but also the volume was almost non-existent in many bond types. Daily trading volume for Brazilian Capitalisation bonds, the government sector's benchmark, decreased from $315 million early in 1998 to about $80 million at the beginning of November 1998. This episode illustrates vividly how important liquidity is for well-functioning capital markets.

In sum, governments play a key role in supporting the development of fixed-income securities markets. Governments are usually the largest supplier of this kind of instrument and they are also the regulators of the market. Transparency and adequate disclosure requirements are important elements of the financial infrastructure. The pricing of assets cannot be determined independently from the institutional structure of the market and, therefore, this structure will affect the development of government and corporate securities markets.

V. The Role of the Asian Bond Market in Recent Financial Crises

The lack of developed fixed-income securities in Asia has been identified as an important factor exacerbating the crisis, and making recovery more difficult. Underdeveloped bond markets, characterised by the absence of a "risk-free" bench-mark, such as a high-volume liquid treasury instrument, prevented the accurate assessment and pricing of the credit risk of borrowers. This, coupled with the ability of large corporations to get cheap loans, and issue debt internationally, led to a high leverage (more than 150% for Thai and Korean companies). The collapse of these highly-leveraged firms increased rapidly the non-performing loans of banks, all of which contributed to creating the full-blown financial crisis. Although the depth of local money markets in Asia, particularly in Indonesia and Thailand, had increased in 1996, they remained poorly developed due to the lack of a clear legal infrastructure and sufficient secondary market trading. Owing to inadequate monitoring by the authorities and rating agencies, there was considerable uncertainty about the size of external liabilities of domestic residents (e.g. the foreign holding of bills of exchange in Thailand, and corporate commercial paper in Indonesia), which added to general financial market uncertainty, as the financial crisis developed.

The lack of development of Asia's local debt market exacerbated the crisis, as during the financial crisis, there was an abrupt loss of international market access. In the aftermath of financial turbulence in Hong Kong, China in October 1997, spreads increased sharply for Asian emerging market debt, fuelled by the worsening regional outlook and sharp sovereign downgrades by international credit agencies, such as Korea's fall to below investment-grade status.

Several Asian economies are facing growing fiscal deficits because of the crisis, and they will need to develop their fixed-income bond market to finance them. High priority should therefore be given to the development of fixed-income securities with maturities that exceed one year in order to reduce vulnerability to such financial shocks and to minimise refinancing risk.

VI.   The Role of Cross-Border Capital Flows in the Development of Domestic Bond Markets

The problems related to the massive inflows of foreign capital, followed by abrupt reversals, have initiated a debate as to whether cross-border capital flows – in particular in the form of short-term portfolio investment and bank loans – constitute a proper major source of external financing for emerging markets. Some are advocating the use of capital controls to alter the volume and composition of capital inflows. In this context, Chile's capital controls have been viewed by some observers as the type of instrument that can be used to manage short-term flows. Chile has been pursuing a semi-open capital account where capital inflows of less than one year are taxed. However, it is of interest to note that in response to the most recent international turbulence, Chile has chosen to lower its barriers to capital inflows. On the other hand, Malaysia's response to the recent financial crisis was to impose draconian controls.

Opponents of capital controls have argued that controls will lead to higher funding costs, a misallocation of investment and other distortions, unequal access to international capital markets by large and small companies, and an encouragement of corruption. Over time, controls are increasingly being evaded. The role of financial engineering in undermining the effectiveness of controls seems to have become more important. Financial engineering also leads to a blurring of the distinction between short-term flows and long-term flows. More generally, the view that controls can be imposed on a temporary basis, while an economy stabilises, and then simply removed again, gives insufficient weight to the serious imbalances that will emerge as a result of controls. For those countries already committed to capital account convertibility, there are great dangers in appearing to backtrack.

Moreover, short-term capital flows are needed to accommodate longer-term flows such as FDI. The ability of domestic capital markets to intermediate longer-term funds is to a large part dependent on the presence of liquid markets in short-term funds. Also risk management activities such as hedging of forex positions can generate large short-term capital flows. Attempts to cut-off short-term maturities, may therefore increase the welfare costs of controls much more than is normally assumed by its proponents.

Emerging equity and bond markets have developed so far in an environment of decreasing capital controls. International securities houses and investment banks have opened up shop in emerging markets, only when the open capital regime has guaranteed them the opportunity to be a full player. This has caused knowledge transfer to local market players, and upgraded regulatory, prudential and general business practices. The share of foreign investors in trading volume and market capitalisation has been very large, e.g. the foreign share in trading in Indonesia, Malaysia, Brazil and Philippines has been 75%, 50%, 35% and 50% respectively. When emerging market entities have been issued abroad, made possible by the open capital regime, they have learnt the structuring of instruments and market strategies which can subsequently be introduced to the local market. Restrictions on cross-border flows will reduce such market-developing effects.

In a globally integrated environment, domestic markets in emerging market economies must compete with advanced financial markets. This means improving the local market in areas such as market infrastructure so as to reduce delays and failed trades, strengthening property rights including those of minority shareholders, and increasing transparency and fairness of markets, which is affected by insufficient disclosure of information.

As most international flows in emerging markets are intermediated by the banking system, prudential measures that restrict certain cross-border activities and regulate banks' open foreign positions can have similar effects to restrictions to capital movements. However, these prudential provisions can be expected to be less distorting than outright controls. Well-designed prudential regulations complemented by modern risk management systems constitute a superior way of protecting the financial system from capital flow swings than crude, outright controls on cross-border capital flows.

More generally, the existence of well-developed domestic fixed-income markets with appropriate risk valuation systems is important for the reduction of the risk associated with the rapid movements of short-term capital flows, or "hot money". Moreover, more financing can be raised from these domestic markets, thereby reducing the dependency on external hot money. There is a broad consensus that open regimes for cross-border capital flows are vital for the deepening of local markets.

VII.   Obstacles Faced by Emerging Fixed-Income Securities Markets

There are many regulatory impediments in emerging fixed-income markets. For example, regulatory restrictions on investment, portfolio allocation and trading of bonds and contractual savings institutions, accounting rules for mark-to-market, recognition of capital gains and losses, withholding tax on interest, taxation of capital gains and amortisation of losses, accounting for repo transactions and bond lending, and non-standardised rules for calculation of yields and accrued interest. In some Asian countries, there are major restrictions on investment allocations for pension funds and insurance companies. There is a relatively high withholding tax in most countries in the regions of Asia, Eastern Europe and Latin America. These regulations often discourage investment in bonds and limit the ability of the investor to assume risk. In many countries, conflicts of interest are generated by ownership, e.g. when a bank owns an investment fund leading to perverse management incentives.

There are also problems with standardisation of fixed-income instruments. In many countries the supply of debt by the government is not planned or regular, which limits secondary market trading and the ability of the dealer to go short, as future supply is not assured. Asian countries, with little experience of budget deficits, are the most backward in this regard. The lack of liquidity in the secondary market is also due to a lack of market makers, which in turn stems from their inability to fund positions through short-selling and repos. Very few countries have well-functioning inter-dealer broker and trading systems. The lack of a yield curve is a feature common to most emerging financial markets.

Finally, there has been concern about the macroeconomic stability and consistency of government policies in emerging countries, which has spooked markets. Rules have been changed too frequently by governments, e.g. concerning auctions, often based on opportunistic, immediate market considerations, which have prevented investors from taking the medium-to-long term view on their investments, and forces them to focus on the short-term view.

Although in Asia, domestic bond markets may be large, such as in Korea (54 per cent of GDP in 1996), they do not function as deep and liquid markets, with a full yield curve extending from a month to several years. Most of the countries have been running a surplus for several years, and hence have a very small government bond market. But also deficit countries such as Thailand concentrate most of their issues in less than one year maturities. Only the Philippines has a fairly complete yield curve extending to 20 years, though liquidity in certain issues may be problematic. Another major problem is non-market pricing, which is caused by the requirements by governments for banks to hold government securities as a part of reserve requirements. This creates a captive market, and forces the banks to hold government securities to term, as the secondary markets are illiquid and cannot provide assurance that the securities will be available at a competitive price. Yields are further depressed by governments forcing the banks to buy the government securities at sub-market rates.

In Eastern Europe, the local debt markets are fairly liquid, but only in the short term, hence it can be said that a money market exists, but not a bond market. Some markets have introduced derivatives:

the Czech Republic has forwards, forex and interest rate swaps and options up to one year; Hungary has a non-deliverable forwards market up to 6 months; and Poland has forwards up to 6 months and non-deliverable forwards up to 1 year.

In Latin America, Argentina and Chile's fixed-income markets contain only government securities, while Brazil and Mexico also have a presence of private securities.   Argentina has introduced a new series of government securities which are standardised and fungible, but is still working at increasing the depth of the market. Many Latin countries such as Argentina,   Mexico and Colombia had announced their decision to extend the length of the yield curve, but adverse market conditions in 1998 slowed this process.

In sum, obstacles in emerging financial markets include:

- the lack of a benchmark, which would enable the pricing of bonds

- missing auction-based systems to sell bonds, operated on the basis of internationally accepted principles

- the lack of a concentration of debt instruments in a small set of standardised and liquid benchmark issues

- the need to strengthen domestic money markets, such as the market for repos or asset-backed securities

- the necessity of establishing futures contracts on government debt

- the need to encourage the establishment of broker-dealer networks

- the need for stronger, more active intermediaries

- the absence of large and active domestic institutional investors

- inadequate clearing and settlement systems

- the absence of credible and well-functioning credit agencies

- the need to establish a simplified tax regime for securities. A complex tax code limits the development of financial markets. Stamp and withholding taxes and related registration fees can discourage new issuance and trading on the secondary market. Differences in tax treatment of residents and non-residents, institutions and individuals, treasury and corporate securities, and interest and capital gains can discourage market development. High corporate taxation can also discourage trading and limited deductibility can raise the cost of carrying bond portfolios

- the absence of a consistent legal and regulatory framework, including Company Law, Securities Law, Tax Law and Criminal Law

- the need to introduce modern investment guidelines for contractual savings entities, which would increase their ability to purchase longer-term securities;

- lack of clearly defined regulations on negotiable instruments, collateral, mortgages on moveable and immovable property and on foreclosure and bankruptcy

- lack of competition in domestic financial markets, which can be created by wide participation by banks, securities firms, mutual fund companies, venture capitalists, insurance companies, pension funds and investment banks. This creates incentives for development of a system with low unit costs and professional management.

An important concern is therefore how to overcome these obstacles in extending the yield curve and how to generate demand for their government instruments in their local markets. Moreover, a common characteristic of many countries is the presence of an entrenched dominant banking system with interests counter to that of the public debt manager.

VIII. Conclusions and Policy Actions

Recent policy meetings at the OECD on the development of fixed-income securities markets indicated broad support for the following main conclusions:[10]

- Transparency and disclosure are vital for the development of fixed-income securities markets. The role of rating agencies, adequate disclosure requirements and internationally acceptable accounting standards are essential for wide and rapid information dissemination.

- All financial market participants should perceive the financial market infrastructure as safe and reliable.

- Improving access for foreign investors and building a base for institutional investors are two key measures for reinforcing domestic fixed-income securities markets.

- Implementing a proper institutional arrangement for the efficient co-ordination between central bank and debt management office is part of the basic infrastructure for developing fixed-income markets.

- Well-functioning government securities markets and market-oriented public debt management practices are essential contributions to the development of corporate securities markets.

- Efficient primary markets for government securities are characterised by the following best practices:

- issuing strategy based on regular auctions;

- the issuance of benchmarks;

- abolition of privileged access by governments;

- a transparent debt management framework;

- a primary dealer framework with the capacity to develop markets.

- Efficient secondary government securities markets are characterised by the following features:

–   liquid markets with a large stock of outstanding benchmark issues and repo market financing;

–   safe and sound clearing and settlement systems;

–   transparent and equitable regulatory and supervisory framework;

–   a market-making structure based on primary dealers.

–   Debt managers should possess sufficient capacity to manage volatility and risk. Finance theory has developed concepts and techniques that have been successfully used in risk management systems by the finance industry.

–   A well-developed repo market and short selling possibilities are important features of liquid fixed-income securities markets.

–   Tax incentives can help to reduce the excessive stock of public debt instruments in the hands of banks, thereby reducing market risk and, in extreme cases, systemic risk.

–   The strengthening of domestic fixed-income securities markets is an important part of the strategy for reducing excessive reliance on bank financing.

NOTES

1. This section is based on the third OECD Green Book : "Public Debt Management and Government Securities Markets in the 21st Century", OECD, forthcoming.

2. In the case of bankruptcy, older debt has priority of payment over new debt, and if there is something left, the shareholder would receive the rest. This characteristic of stocks has finance theorists assimilate its payoff structure with a call option, where the strike price is the amount of debt outstanding (the typical hockey stick shape) and without expiration date.

3. New debt instruments have been introduced in advanced OECD countries. It is now possible to find debt instruments whose payoff is a function of different variables like company profits, performance of a market(s) index(es), etc. Financial engineering played a key role in this development.

4. H.J. Blommestein (1998), "Impact of Institutional Investors in Financial Markets", in *Institutional Investors in the New Financial Landscape*, OECD.

5. H.J. Blommestein (1998), "Institutional Investors, Pension Reform and Emerging Securities Markets", in *Capital Market Development in Transition Economies*, OECD.

6. Rhee, Ghon, 1993, *Emerging Bond Markets in the Dynamic Asian Economies*, OECD Publications, Paris; V. Sundararajan, P. Dattels and H.J. Blommestein, eds., 1997 *Co-ordinating Public Debt and Monetary Management: Institutional and Operational Arrangements*, IMF, Washington DC; G. Bröker, 1993, *Government Securities and Debt Management in the 1990s*, OECD.

7. The ability to move from securities to cash, and vice versa, with little delay and at reasonable cost.

8. See OECD *Financial Market Trends,* No. 71, November 1998.

9. Here, the spread is the difference between the prices at which the security can be bought or sold.

10. The principal policy forum is the OECD Working Party on Public Debt Management. This Working Party initiated in 1990 a policy dialogue with transition countries. Since then, the Working Party has held every year, a workshop on policy issues related to public management and government securities market operations in emerging financial markets, in particular transition countries. The first OECD/World Bank Workshop on the Development of Fixed-Income Securities Markets in Emerging Market Economies, held in Paris on 14-16 December 1998, marked the beginning of a parallel policy forum for bringing together policy makers from all emerging financial markets.

G-12 G21
G-18 F34

DEVELOPMENTS IN EUROPEAN BOND MARKETS

by
Dr. Hans-Dieter Hanfland

During the last years the European bond markets have been influenced by several factors:Obviously, the introduction of the euro was the main, if only one of the reinforcing factors that determined European bond market developments.

Other more structural factors included:

- the consolidation trend in the banking industry;

- the drive to an efficient use of banks' capital and balance sheets;

- increased merger and acquisition activity financed by corporate bond issues;

- and the integration of financial markets in the EU area.

If I may recall, the euro was introduced on 1 January 1999 and the conversion rates of EMU currencies were irrevocably fixed.

- From that date all new sovereign bonds were issued in euro.

- The old tradable debt of sovereign issuers was redenominated in early 1999.

- Non-sovereign debtors will have to denominate new issues and redenomi-nate old issues at latest by the end of 2001.

- Circulation of coins and banknotes in euro will start from 1 January 2002.

- The cancellation of their legal tender status will be within a period of two months.

- After that date, however, the exchange of national currencies into euro is still possible.

On the whole, reconventioning and redenomination have gone very smoothly and are no longer an issue for market participants.

In my presentation I would like to elaborate on

- the structure of euro bond markets

- the trends in investor behaviour following the introduction of the euro; and the geographical diversification of bond portfolios and diversification into other asset classes.

- Observations concerning the trends in capital market supply and the behaviour of major issuers

- the government bond market is the biggest market, but the corporate sector and other

- market sectors as asset-backed products rapidly increasing

Then some remarks on

- trends in hedging and bond-related derivatives; and

- electronic trading systems and

Finally, the overall assessment.

The introduction of the euro as single currency has created a euro bond market the size of the Japanese bond market.

The market for government and state agencies, that is the public bond market is by far the largest segment of this market.

This market can now be described as a single market in as much as all government bonds are issued in one currency rather than in eleven different currencies.

The second largest segment of the euro bond market is the market for commercial bank issues and the private mortgage and the Pfandbrief market, also a mortgage-backed securities market.

In comparison with the US market, the corporate bond market sector and the asset-backed security market are relatively small but they are increasing very rapidly.

In fact, the euro launch has had a greater impact on corporate bonds than on government bonds. It appears that the trend towards "crowding in" of the private sector in the euro area is now well under way, bringing the market structure more into line with the US markets.

What trends in investor behaviour can be observed in the course of the past years and particularly, since the introduction of the euro?

Traditionally, European investors have had a strong home bias in their fixed-income investment, partly because

- they were familiar with their domestic market;

- they feared exchange rate risks;

- or because there were legal impediments, such as currency-matching rules, for instance for insurance companies.

However, as early as the mid-90s, with increasing European integration, a tendency to diversify can be observed among European institutional investors, largely confined to government bonds.

A remarkable feature of the recent diversification in euroland is that investors have not only changed the country allocation of their fixed-income portfolio, but also the distribution over various asset classes.

Investors in smaller countries seem to have diversified their portfolios more quickly than in larger ones. Yet some segments of the bond markets – mainly those that are less liquid – have remained largely national.

The strategic repositioning of investment portfolios following the introduction of the euro is clearly reflected in the change of indices that institutional investors use as benchmarks; widely-used national benchmark bond market indices have been replaced by European equivalents.

Investors started as early as the mid-90s to invest more heavily in high-yielding European government bonds.

The convergence of fundamental economic policy in accordance with the Maastricht Treaty and the increasing prospects of monetary union led to significant decreases in interest-rate spreads of government bonds.

After the introduction of the euro the spreads narrowed to between 0 – 30 basis points and became established in this range.

The remaining spreads are due to issuers' different ratings, the liquidity of the bonds and the efficiency of individual markets (that is: transparency, hedging possibilities, repo markets etc.).

So in general euroland finance ministries have benefited from the integration of national capital markets. Funding costs have come down considerably in a number of countries.

There has also been remarkable convergence in the maturity structure of sovereign debt in the bond market. The average maturity has increased to 6 years. This is especially true for Member States where it has been traditionally shortest.

The convergence of yields in the unified euro bond market has also heightened the competitive pressure on EU Member States' debt management.

To increase issuance efficiency and liquidity of individual bonds, the national ministries have raised the average volume of their issues. A nominal amount of 5 bn euro per issue seems to be a minimum and the size of benchmark issues is about 20 bn euro.

Sovereign issuers try to improve market transparency by pre-announced auction calendars. Issuing programmes with regular issue dates are now commonplace.

In order to attract more investors and to secure a smooth and diversified placement of debt a number of governments have changed their issuance procedure; there is a trend to more widespread use of primary

Dealership, also to improve market-making commitment for banks and to enhance secondary market liquidity.

Primary dealership exists in several varieties in the euro area. In Germany the commitments of the members of the "bond auction group" refer only to an adequate participation in the auction, while in other countries this commitment is more specific.

Liquidity in the secondary market is managed in some countries by primary dealer banks, in others by fiscal agents (thus in the case of Germany by the Bundesbank).

In order to reach a larger group of investors special emphasis has been placed on internationalisation of the primary dealership.

Liquidity and credit differences between the sovereign issuers in euroland will remain and will result in a non-unique government bond yield curve.

In this respect the European bond market differs from the US market, where Treasuries provide a unique yield curve.

It appears that at the 10-year maturity, German government bonds are probably now regarded as the benchmark. In many other maturities, French issues have the benchmark status. At the lower end of the yield curve, Italian issues have a strong position.

Given the importance of the three big issuers, competitive pressure has risen considerably for smaller sovereign borrowers.

They focus the issue of government bonds on individual segments of the maturity range to ensure the necessary market liquidity.

Ireland for instance has restructured its outstanding debt into a few liquid benchmark issues. The Netherlands and others have also converted old, less-liquid bonds into new benchmark bonds.

Especially since the launch of the euro we observe different strategies:

- The larger countries appear to be aiming for a presence at all maturities, with a full range of liquid instruments.

- The smaller states have opted to increase liquidity in "niche areas" in a smaller number of issues.

In comparison with the US corporate bond market the euro area is still way behind as far as market completeness and liquidity are concerned. The corporate issuance, however, increased markedly in 1999 and represented 20% of the total bond issues in the first half of 1999.

A number of mutually reinforcing factors in the corporate bond market can be identified:

- In a low-yield environment for government bonds, investors turn to higher-yielding corporate bonds.

- Corporates can fund themselves more cheaply in the bond market than via bank loans.The scale of issuance is increasing in the much bigger euro market also due to merger and aquisition activity financed by bond issues.

- Finally corporate issuance tends to be stimulated by banks; their capital can be better utilised in more profitable activities than bank loans.

So far, banks dominate the market to refinance their loans and other activities. The non-bank market remains less developed, also due to not wide-spread rating. There are mostly big industrial companies in the market.

But there are differences between European countries. As of mid-1999 in France, for instance, the securitised debt of enterprises (including funds raised via foreign financial subsidiaries) came to about 14 % (in the UK 20 %) of the gross domestic product compared with 3 % in Germany. Conversely, the share of bank debt securities in Germany was much higher.

However, we can observe that an increasing number of relatively smaller and lower-rated companies are taking the step of joining the corporate euro-denominated bond market and have issued bonds that offer relatively high yields.

The growth of the high yield market has been strong. However, its relative import-ance is still far below that of the US market.

Market participants, therefore, foresee that corporates will be increasingly inclined to apply for ratings.

The increased focus of banks in Europe on their balance sheet use has also been a major impetus for the asset-backed markets. "Securisation" is a major theme in the European banking community.

Mortgage portfolios tend to be the first type of bank assets to be sold off to investors.

One of the oldest markets in this respect is the German Pfandbrief (mortgage) market, the liquid so-called "Jumbo market", in particular being very popular with national and international investors.

This type of mortgage bond is perceived as an extremely safe investment vehicle, being covered by mortgage real estate liens or government guarantees and underpinned by a close regulatory framework.

Currently 20 – 25% of this segment is held outside Germany.

This success can be attributed

- to the large issue size starting at 500 m euro, and

- to a large number of market-makers and market-making obligations.

Other European countries have set up similarly successful ABS products.

As to the location of euro-bond trading, this is hard to determine as business is mostly conducted OTC or is screen based. London is well ahead of the other European financial centres. More than 80 % of all bond dealers are located there.

Turning to trends in hedging and bond-related derivatives.

The trading volumes of euro-denominated bond futures have increased dramatically in 1999, indicating a high level of turnover in this market.

While short-term interest-rate futures are dominated by contracts on Liffe in London, liquidity for bond futures is centered on the German Bund contracts of the German/ Swiss derivatives exchange

Eurex. They are the cheapest way to hedge and are used as a hedging vehicle for all euro-denominated issuance.

The launch of the euro and the increase in corporate bond issuance has also led to an expansion of swap markets in euroland. Interest rate swaps are increasingly used for fixed income asset management and hedging purposes.

Market participants also observe a considerable growth of the repo market in euroland sovereign issues, an important factor to increase liquidity and in the pricing of bonds.

However, as European banks generally have direct access to central bank liquidity through Lombard facilities, they are less dependent on the repo market for financing purposes than US banks. It might therefore take some time before a European repo market comes close to the US market.

One of the most visible changes in the euro bond market is the development of electronic trading systems.

The new trend to screen-based trading, which increases the efficiency of fixed-income operation and improves market transparency, is driven by intermediaries' need to cut margins due to strong competition between banks and cost awareness among investors.

This means

- reducing brokerage fees

- simplifiying back offices and securities department structures.

On the other hand, the concentration of trading volumes into a single computerised system where major participants can meet would improve liquidity.

The pan-European platform for trading euro-denominated European government bonds electronically – the EUROMTS –, developed in Italy, is considered one of the most successful. The system is partly owned by big banks and investment banks.

Although electronic trading systems will become more dominant, human brokerage is expected to remain for large block trades, additional market information and research.

So to give an overall assessment:

More than one year after the introduction of the euro major structural changes begin to appear. They could bring the European bond market closer into line with the US market.

- The euro bond market is definitely more integrated due to the introduction of the euro.

- Sovereign issuers concentrate on the liquidity of their debt by improving transparency, concentrating on bigger issues.

- The corporate market is growing very fast, size of corporate issues has increased two- or three-fold. However it is still dominated by financials.

The market for high-yield bonds is relatively small, but also growing.

But integration is not yet complete.

Some remaining barriers are for instance:

- Fragmentation of national settlement systems impeding cross border repo transactions

- Legal impediments, the lack of clarity and uniformity in bankruptcy law

- Withholding tax in some countries is an issue

- Also some differences in accounting conventions have been mentioned.

We are working on these issues.

A European action plan contains more than 40 measures to promote the integration of a single wholesale financial market, the opening of cross-border retail financial services and the strengthening of prudential regulations. The implementation of this plan is intended to be completed in 2005

THE REFORMS OF THE JAPANESE GOVERNMENT SECURITIES MARKET

by
Mr. Masaaki Shirakawa

G-12
G-18   H63

Introduction

I would like to address the issues related to the reforms in the Japanese government securities market from the perspective of the central bank. It is my hope that my presentation will provide food for thought in the discussions aimed at further reforms in the Japanese government securities market. I would also be very happy if my remarks stimulate thinking in other markets.

In my remarks, after outlining the characteristics of the market, I will touch on why market liquidity needs to be enhanced. Next, I will outline the basic strategy to improve market liquidity. And finally, I will discuss key issues in pursuing market reforms in Japan and how such reforms could be implemented. Please note that the views presented in this speech are my personal ones, and so they do not necessarily represent the views of the Bank of Japan.

Outline of the JGS market

The Japanese government securities market (hereafter I call it the JGS market) is the largest government securities market in the world. The volume outstanding is US$ 3.4 trillion (359 trillion yen) as of the end of 1999, and is increasing, contrary to the trend in most industrial countries. Total issues in fiscal 2000 will be around US$ 800 billion (86 trillion yen), reflecting the growing fiscal deficit. Chart 1, drawn from the OECD Economic Outlook, clearly shows Japan's fiscal conditions. JGSs will account for as much as 36% of the global government securities outstanding as of the end of 2001, according to an estimate by JP Morgan. As a result of the trend, as illustrated in Chart 2, the OECD forecasts the ratio of outstanding volume of government debt to gross domestic product will hit 122% in the year 2001, which will be the largest among the G7 countries. The growing fiscal deficit is a bad sign, but it can be a driving force for market reform.

Pushed partly by the need to absorb a large amount of new issues and partly by the need to respond to financial market globalization, several reforms have been implemented in the JGS market. As to taxation, the securities transaction tax was abolished in April 1999. The coupon bearing JGSs held by non-residents were exempted from withholding taxes under certain conditions from September 1999, though there still remains a problem concerning the use of non-resident custodians and International Central Securities Depositories (ICSDs), which I will mention later. As to product design, the issuance of 1-year TBs, 5 and 30-year coupon bearing bonds started in fiscal 1999 and public tender of FBs, which are financing bills issued for cash management purposes, started in April 1999. As to settlement practices, the settlement lag was shortened to T+3 in 1997, and the Real-Time Gross Settlement of JGSs will start by the end of this year.

In fact, the efficiency of the JGS market seems to have improved. For example, as indicated in Chart 3, the smoothness of the yield curve, a proxy of market efficiency, has improved significantly.

Nevertheless, further reforms seem to be required in many areas, given the fact that, as shown in Chart 4 and 5, the liquidity of the JGS market is low compared to other major markets. According to the report of the study group on market liquidity, which I chaired, under the Committee of the Global Financial System of the G10 central banks, the liquidity of the JGS market is the lowest in the major countries, in the sense that the bid-ask spreads are the largest in Japan and the turnover ratio is the lowest in Japan among G7 countries.

Another salient feature of the JGS market is who holds the securities. As seen in Chart 6, in Japan, more than half of the outstanding JGSs is held by the public sector, which is composed of the government and the central bank. On the other hand, the share of non-resident holdings is marginal. These features may have diminished market liquidity since the volume of trading supply, which is a pool of tradable securities, is smaller and the profile of market participants is less heterogeneous. These figures seem to imply the need for further reforms in the JGS market.

Need for market reforms to enhance market liquidity

Before elaborating on specific market reforms in Japan, I would like to briefly touch on why it is important to enhance liquidity of the JGS market.

First of all, improved market liquidity will help absorb the large amount of new issues. In a more liquid market, investors would demand smaller additional yield to buy more securities, because they can liquidate their holdings immediately. If market reforms could halve the bid-ask spreads, the decline in liquidity premium could enable the Japanese government, and eventually taxpayers, to save as much as US$ 30 million per year for the issuance of 10-year bonds.

In addition, a liquid JGS market will be a key factor in developing a whole range of fixed income markets including an efficient corporate bond market. This is because the yield curve of government securities, which are virtually credit risk free, serves as the benchmark of pricing other financial products. In this sense, the lack of a reliable JGS yield curve across maturities can be considered as one of the reasons why the corporate bond market is not well developed in Japan in comparison with the United States.

Furthermore, a deep and liquid JGS market could make the Japanese financial system as a whole more resilient to external shocks, especially in cases where the creditworthiness of individual financial institutions were questioned, as happened in the autumn of 1997. This is because non-resident investors can put their money in the JGS market as a haven, which facilitates smooth capital flow across markets.

Finally, a liquid JGS market with a more heterogeneous holding pattern would help maintain fiscal discipline, since international investors might be more sensitive to the risk-return profile of government securities of other countries than domestic investors who tend to have a bias to buy their home country's assets. Therefore, if a considerable portion of JGSs was held by non-residents, the government would need to explain its fiscal conditions to investors, both at home and abroad, creating incentives to maintain fiscal discipline.

Basic strategy to create a deep and liquid government securities market

The next question is how can one enhance market liquidity. To begin with, the study group of the Committee on the Global Financial System, which I mentioned earlier, identified a set of interrelated guiding principles to formulate practical policy recommendations for deep and liquid markets. Please take a look at the Appendix. On the left side, there are five guiding principles, although these principles should be tailored in a way to fit the financial environment of each country. Those are;

1. A competitive market structure should be maintained;

2. A market should have a low level of fragmentation;

3. Transaction costs should be minimized;

4. A sound, robust and safe market infrastructure should be maintained; and

5. Heterogeneity of market participants should be encouraged.

Based on these guiding principles, five practical policy recommendations are shown on the right side of the Appendix. Those are;

1. Regarding desirability of coherent debt management policies, an appropriate distribution of maturities and issue frequency should be ensured as a means of establishing large benchmark issues at key maturities;

2. The liquidity impairing effect of taxes should be minimized;

3. Transparency of sovereign issuers and issue schedule should be ensured to encourage active participation and trading activity. Also, transparency of trading information should be encouraged, with due attention being paid to the anonymity of market participants;

4. Safety and standardization in trading and settlement practices should be ensured; and

5. Related markets, such as repo and futures markets should be developed in a consistent manner.

The same caveat applies in that these recommendations should be tailored depending on the characteristics of the market.

Key issues in enhancing the liquidity of the JGS market

Since it is difficult to discuss market reforms common to every country, I would like to talk about the reforms in the JGS market as a case study from the viewpoint of how these guiding principles and policy recommendations apply. I hope that you would distill possible lessons from the Japanese experiences. I will touch on transparency, large benchmark issues, taxation, related markets, and straight through processing.

Transparency

Transparency in this context has three facets; transparency of fiscal conditions of the government; transparency of debt management strategy, and transparency of market information.

From the viewpoint of the transparency of fiscal conditions of the government, it is important for the government to explain its fiscal conditions to the public in a clear and understandable manner. This is particularly the case when the fiscal deficit of the government is large. In this regard, recent initiatives to enhance transparency can be regarded as a welcome sign.

Next, it is important for the government to express its basic debt management strategy. For example, maturity distribution is an important component of debt management strategy. In formulating strategies, it is important to make sure that decisions are made in a transparent way so that it is predictable to market participants. Talking about debt management strategy, it is an important step forward that the government started to announce an indicative quarterly issue schedule from March 1999. Nevertheless, at this moment, it is difficult to conduct when-if-issued trading, that is trading conducted between auction announcement day and auction day. This is because redemption dates could not be determined before the auction day. If when-if-issued trading is available, more market players could participate in bidding since the true prices of the securities are well tested before auction.

Transparency of market information should not be ignored. While real-time price and trade information of JGSs is available to dealers to a great extent, the information available to investors is very limited at this moment. Only the closing prices are published by the Japan Securities Dealers Association and some individual interdealer brokers. In this regard, the initiatives in the United States and Canada are interesting. In the case of the United States, GovPx, which is a joint venture of primary dealers and interdealer brokers, was established in 1992. GovPx releases real-time price and trade information to investors, which is said to have further increased the liquidity of the U.S. Treasury market.

Large benchmark issues at key maturities

The next issue is to create large benchmark issues at the key maturities of yield curve. To this end, one could consider conducting regular reopenings, whereby an identical security is offered in several consecutive auctions, rather than being supplied in a single auction. Regular reopenings allow issuers to create a large issue while paying lower premia to dealers, as dealers do not have to bear financing costs incurred by subscribing to large amounts of securities at once. For example, one could consider conducting reopening of 10-year bonds, which are currently issued every month.

In addition to reopenings, one could consider smoothing out issue amount across the yield curve. Currently, JGSs are issued at maturities of 3 and 6 months, 1, 2, 4, 5, 6, 10, 20, and 30 years. While it is a progress that the government started to issue 1 year TBs and 5 and 30-year coupon bearing bonds in fiscal 1999, in the sense that the lineup of original maturities would cover most of different investment horizons of investors, as you can see in Chart 7, the issuance volume is still heavily skewed to 10-year bonds. Also, one could argue that 4 and 6 year bonds could be merged to create a large 5-year benchmark, and 20 and 30-year bonds for a large 30-year benchmark.

Taxation

In terms of taxation, several measures have been taken. Above all, the abolishment of the security transaction tax in April 1999 was a great improvement for the market. Nevertheless, there is some room for further improvement.

The largest remaining issue is withholding taxes. At this moment, as to coupon bearing JGSs held by taxable entities, 20% of coupon payment is withheld by the government. The withholding tax adversely affects market liquidity in several ways. For example, the tax increases transaction costs by imposing opportunity costs to holders in the form of lost interest income on coupons. In addition, the tax fragments the market between taxable bonds and non-taxable bonds, thereby making the trading supply of an issue smaller. In such an environment, the bid-ask spread tends to be larger, since it is more costly to make markets for an issue with smaller trading supply. Furthermore, given the existing taxation scheme, the tax could discourage active participation of non-residents to the new style of repo transactions currently under discussion among market participants, if the gap between the start price and end price is considered an interest on a loan, and thus subject to withholding taxes.

As mentioned previously, coupon bearing JGSs held by non-residents are tax-exempt if non-residents deposit them to a domestic office of financial institutions that are participants of the JGS bookentry system, and if their identity is certified by the head of the domestic office. Generally speaking, international investors usually hold government securities of various countries under one account at global custodians and ICSDs which may not have domestic offices in Japan. Given this, the conditions to be tax-exempt are costly for such investors to fulfill.

Needless to say, when it comes to revamping the withholding tax, it is necessary to consider several ramifications. Collecting taxes is also an important policy objective of the government. Having understood the difficulty in reconciling the needs of the tax authority and the global financial market, many countries have tried to find practical solutions. Japan, too, is required to endeavor to find such a solution.

Related markets

If hedging, arbitrage and speculative transactions can be conducted easily, market liquidity as a whole is enhanced. In this regard, the importance of "trilogy", where cash, repo, and futures prices are simultaneously and interdependently determined, was highlighted at the experience in the JGS market of the last summer. To this end, I believe the development of related markets such as repo and futures markets is important. Repo transactions enable dealers to finance long positions and cover short positions, allowing them to respond to customers' needs quickly. A well-structured futures market reduces hedging costs, and thus makes it easier to take cash market positions. In this sense, it is important to continue efforts to develop these markets, such as improving the existing master agreement to the one for the new-style repo transaction which conform to the prevailing practices in major markets, as well as revamping product design of futures contracts in terms of theoretical coupon rate, etc.

Straight through processing

Safety in trading and settlement is a prerequisite for the existence of deep and liquid markets. A shift to T+1 settlement from the current T+3 settlement is an important step in this regard. Also, a decrease in transaction costs leads to enhanced market liquidity. To achieve T+1 settlement practice and to reduce transaction costs, it is important to effect straight through processing by streamlining both front and back office operations.

As to front office operations, the introduction of electronic trading could be an important step forward. Electronic trading, where buyers and sellers can execute a transaction with a click on computer screen, enables both trading parties to eliminate trade confirmation process that is necessary under telephone-based trading. At present, several institutions are endeavoring to set up an electronic trading platform for the JGS market. As to back office operations, it is important to prepare a sound infrastructure to process information after execution and before settlement. There are several ongoing initiatives in the areas of trade confirmation and settlement instruction confirmation. At this moment, it is hardly predictable which initiatives would receive overwhelming support from market participants. In any case, since straight through processing is likely to enhance financial market liquidity and efficiency, it is important that market participants including central banks promote the moves to straight through processing.

How should the market reforms be implemented?

As a concluding remark of my presentation, I would like to emphasize two points concerning successful market reform. First, the role of a "catalyst" in the process of market reform. While all financial market participants, as well as the economy as a whole, enjoy the benefits of high market liquidity, the very nature of externality means that each of them individually, on occasion, may lack the proper incentives to initiate market reforms. This suggests a role of a "catalyst". By the word "catalyst", I mean somebody, either the private sector or the public sector, who identifies liquidity-impairing factors and explain in a clear language the need for reform.

Second, the role of market makers in implementing market-driven reforms. When it comes to conducting market reforms, the role of market participants is important. In particular, the role of market makers, who in most cases provide liquidity and are rewarded for providing this service to the market, is crucial. Market makers have, or at least ought to have, insights on desirable market reforms based on their know-hows on the market mechanisms including settlement procedure and legal and accounting treatments. At the same time, governments and central banks should pay keen attention to the market intelligence provided by such market participants in the private sector. In this sense, the collaboration between the private sector and the public sector should be fostered. I believe that my colleagues at the Bank of Japan as well as myself should be willing to play an active role in this process.

REFERENCES

Bank for International Settlements, "CGFS issues recommendations for the design of liquid markets", paper by the Committee on the Global Financial System, November 1999

Bank for International Settlements, "Market Liquidity: Research Findings and Selected Policy Implications", paper by the Committee on the Global Financial System, May 1999

Chart 1 General Government Financial Balances

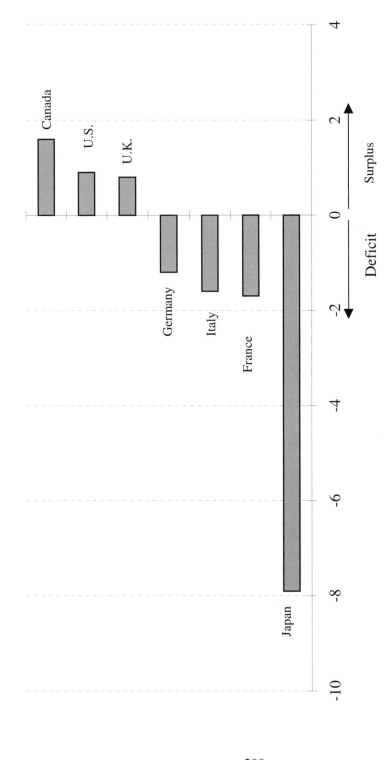

Notes   Surplus or deficit as a percentage of nominal GDP.
Source OECD, "OECD Economic Outlook Vol. 66", 1999

Chart 2 **General Government Gross Financial Liabilities**

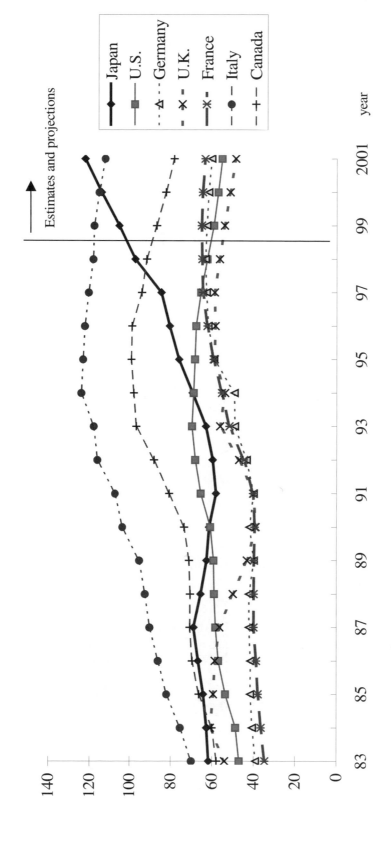

Notes As a percentage of nominal GDP.
Source OECD, "OECD Economic Outlook Vol. 66", 1999

Chart 3 Divergence from Fitted Yield Curve

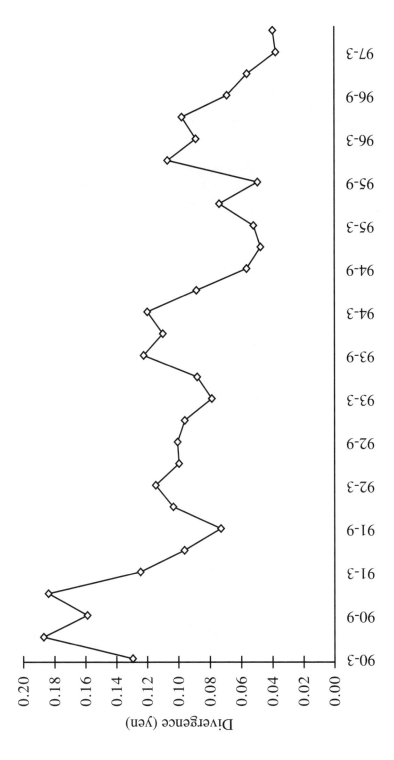

Notes   Divergence from the fitted yield curve of 10-year bonds, using cubic spline function.
Source Miyanoya, Inoue and Higo, "Microstructure and Liquidity of the Japanese Government Securities Market", Bank of Japan Financial Markets Department
        Working Paper 99-J-1, 1999 (Japanese version only)

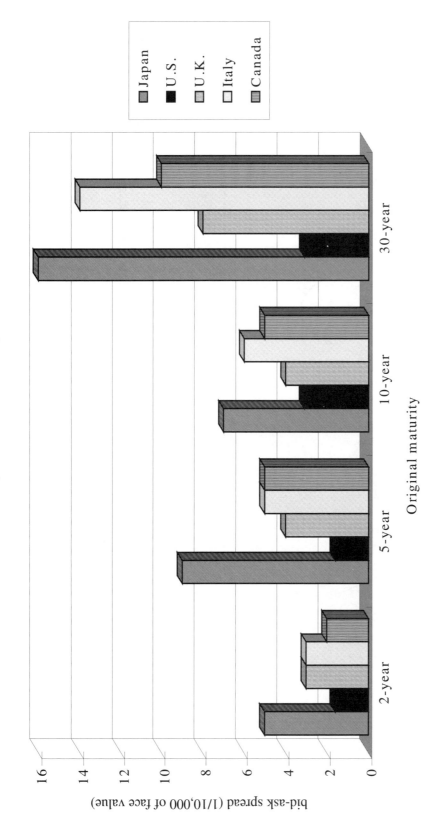

Chart 4 **Comparison of bid-ask spread**

Legend: Japan, U.S., U.K., Italy, Canada

bid-ask spread (1/10,000 of face value)

Original maturity: 2-year, 5-year, 10-year, 30-year

Notes   The spreads for 5 and 30-year JGSs are those of 6 and 20-year bonds.
Source BIS, "Market Liquidity: Research Findings and Selected Policy Implications", 1999

Chart 5 Turnover ratios

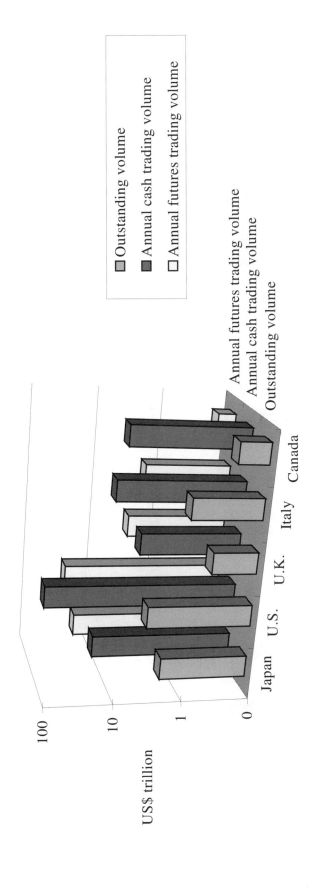

	Japan	U.S.	U.K.	Italy	Canada
Cash turnover ratio	6.9	22.0	7.0	7.7	21.9
Cash/futures ratio	0.7	2.7	1.0	4.1	33.7

Notes   As of 1997. Cash turnover ratio = trading volume (two-way basis) / outstanding volume, Cash/futures ratio = cash trading volume / futures trading volume.
Source   BIS, "Market Liquidity: Research Findings and Selected Policy Implications", 1999

213

Chart 6 Holding Pattern of Government Securities

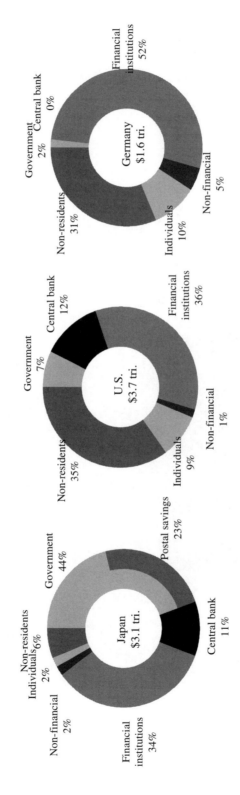

Notes As of March 1999 for Japan and U.S. As of end-1997 for Germany. Outstanding volume is converted at rates of US$1=110 yen=DM2. FBs are not included in the Japanese figures.

Sources Japan - Bank of Japan, "Flow of Funds Accounts", 1999, U.S. - FRB, "Flow of Funds Accounts", 1999, Germany - Bundesbank, "Securities Deposits", 1998.

Chart 7 **Composition Ratio by Original Maturity**

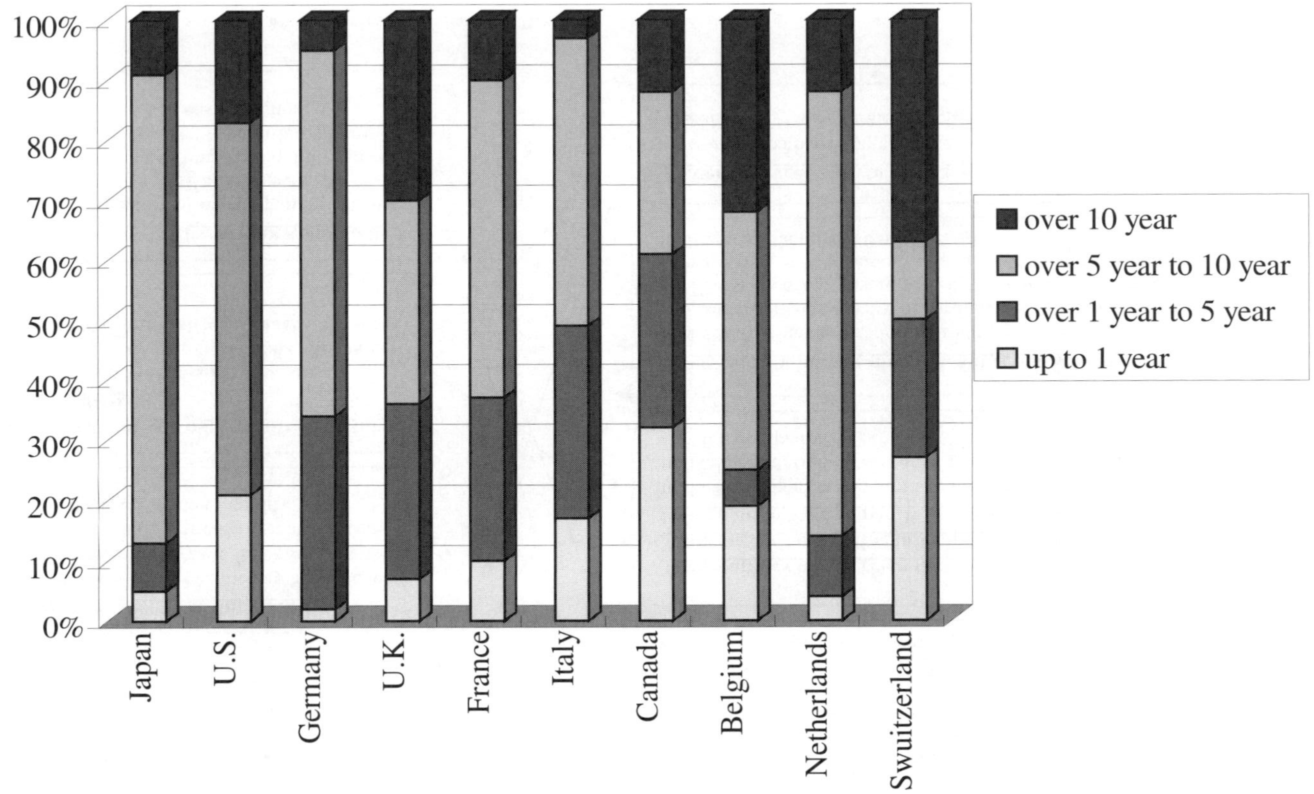

100%
90%
80%
70%
60%
50%
40%
30%
20%
10%
0%
Japan
U.S.
Germany
U.K.
France
Italy
Canada
Belgium
Netherlands
Switzerland
over 10 year
over 5 year to 10 year
over 1 year to 5 year
up to 1 year

Notes As of end-1997. Breakdown not available for 1-10 year segment for the U.S. Breakdown for the U.K. is based on remaining maturity.
Source BIS, "Market Liquidity: Research Findings and Selected Policy Implications", 1999

Appendix

Basic Strategy to Create Deep and Liquid Government Securities Market

Guiding Principles

Policy

An appropriate distribution of maturities and issue frequency should be ensured as a means of establishing large benchmark issues at key maturities (related to Guiding Principles 2 and 5) Issue sizes should be enlarged to enhance market liquidity, which can be realized by regular reopenings, by appropriately distributed original maturities, and by appropriate frequency of new issues. Introduction of stripping facility may increase heterogeneity of market participants.

The liquidity impairing effect of taxes should be minimized (2, 3 and 5) It is appropriate for the government to weigh the potential increase in tax revenue against the potential decline in market liquidity. Abolishing withholding taxes can decrease transaction costs and market fragmentation between taxable and non-taxable bonds. Exempting withholding taxes on the holdings via global custodians can enhance heterogeneity of market participants.

Transparency of sovereign issuers and issue schedule should be ensured. Transparency of trading information should be encouraged with due attention being paid to the anonymity of market participants (1 and 4) Transparency in trading information can promote competition among trading platforms and confidence in market integrity. Transparency of issuers and issue schedules can also facilitate active participation.

Safety and standardization in trading and settlement practices should be ensured (2,4 and 5) Standardization in trading practices can decrease market fragmentation and enhance heterogeneity of participants. Shortening settlement lag and promoting DVP settlement can ensure security of transactions. Rules for delivery fails can contribute to smooth settlement and market integrity. Introduction of electronic trading may facilitate standardization.

Related markets, such as repo and futures markets, should be developed (2 and 4) Ensuring smooth arbitrage among the cash, repo, and futures market would facilitate price discovery at any time, thereby increasing market liquidity.

1) A competitive market structure should be maintained A competitive market structure between trading platforms (dealers, exchanges, etc.) can heighten liquidity by increasing pressure for a narrowing of bid-ask spreads.

2) A market should have a low level of fragmentation High substitutability of products (or low level of fragmentation of markets) means a larger trading supply. A large trading supply facilitates matching of transaction demands, resulting in increased market liquidity.

3) Transaction costs should be minimized When transaction costs, i.e., the gap between the effective price received by the seller and that paid by the buyer, are small, it is easy to match orders, resulting in enhanced market liquidity.

4) A sound, robust and safe market infrastructure should be ensured A sound, robust and safe market structure promotes active participation and make the market more resilient to external shocks, thereby enhances market liquidity.

5) Heterogeneity of market participants should be encouraged Heterogeneity of market participants in terms of transaction needs, risk assessments, and investment horizons enhances market liquidity, since heterogeneous participants may react differently to new information, resulting in easy matching of transaction demands.

Source Based on BIS, "How should we design deep and liquid markets? The case of government securities", 1999.

216

G12 H63
G18 G15

FURTHER REFORMS AFTER THE "BIG BANG": THE JAPANESE GOVERNMENT BOND MARKET

by
Professor Ghon Rhee [*]

I.   Introduction

At the end of 1999, Japanese government bonds (JGBs) issued by the central government reached ¥359 trillion (US$3.30 trillion), exceeding the United States in outstanding Treasury securities balance of $3.28 trillion. In fiscal year 2000 alone, Japan's Ministry of Finance (MOF) plans to raise a gross amount of ¥85.87 trillion through the issuance of JGBs, while the U.S. Treasury paid down $140 billion in debt over last two years and plans to do so further. As a result, Japan is expected to remain the largest issuer of government debt in the world in the foreseeable future. As summarized in Table 1, Japan's government debt is expected to reach 137% of GDP in year 2000, whereas the United States and United Kingdom are expected to achieve debt levels of 53% and 61% relative to their respective GDPs.

Table 1 **Government Debt and Fiscal Deficit**

	Japan	United States	United Kingdom
A. Government Debt /GDP(%)			
1997	101.1	65.9	65.8
1998	117.9	62.1	65.8
1999	127.8	57.7	62.6
2000	137.2	53.2	61.0
B. Fiscal Deficit /GDP(%)			
1997	-3.4	0.4	-2.1
1998	-5.3	1.3	0.3
1999	-7.3	1.6	-0.4
2000	-7.1	2.0	-0.6

Source: IMF, World Economic Outlook (October 1999)

This is bad news for Japan's economy and future credit rating of JGBs. Even though it sounds far-fetched at present to discuss the risk of runaway inflation given the deflationary trend of the Japanese economy, the latent threat of inflation cannot be overlooked in the presence of ever-increasing fiscal deficits in the Japanese government budget. According to the International Monetary Fund's prediction, Japan's fiscal deficit will reach 7.1% of its GDP in year 2000, while the United States will gain a surplus of 2% as presented in Panel B of Table 1. Furthermore, international credit rating agencies such as Moody's and Duff and Phelps issue warnings about possible down-grading of yen-denominated debt rating.

---

[*]   I am grateful to Hiroshi Yoshida for research assistance and to Masahiro Yoshikawa and Rosita Chang for serving as a sounding board on various issues identified in the paper.

The fact that Japan will remain the largest issuer of government debt securities is important news for further development of the JGB market because the MOF will be forced to heed the cost minimization of JGBs.[1] Any reform measures necessary to attain this goal will be adopted more expediently and decisively than ever before.

This paper reviews key steps for further development of the JGB market in aligning its infrastructures with those of the U.S. and U.K. government securities markets. The remainder of this paper is divided into three sections. In Section II, we assess if Japan's MOF is able to minimize the cost of JGBs given the current status of the market. In Section III, we identify numerous reform measures to create a more effective and efficient JGB market. The last section touches upon particularly urgent policy issues on the regional level for the progression of the JGB market to better serve global and regional constituencies.

II.   How to Minimize the Cost of Government Debt Securities?

Schinasi and Smith (1998) recommend three courses of action to minimize the cost of government debt securities: first, tap the pool of global capital; second, grant greater independence to government debt management from monetary policy; and, third, reform primary and secondary market infrastructures to appeal to institutional investors. When the cost minimizing effort is assessed against the above three criteria, Japan's MOF does not earn a good mark.

A.   *Tapping the Pool of Global Capital*

Inonue (1999) reports that non-residents hold approximately 10% of JGBs, while non-resident holdings of U.S. and U.K. government debt amount to 36.9% and 14.4%, respectively. Schinasi and Smith (1998), however, report a smaller percentage in the order of 4%-5% for Japan, citing the Bank for International Settlements source. This suggests that further internationalization of the yen is necessary to tap the pool of global capital. Although some concerns have been expressed regarding the delay of implementing reform measures in the areas of pension system, bank re-capitalization, and deposit insurance scheme, the MOF should be credited for its Big Bang reforms in internationalizing the yen. As of April 1999, the withholding tax on redemption gains and interest income from JGBs were exempted for non-residents and foreign corporations.[2] The impact of eliminating withholding taxes in Japan has yet to be assessed, but it is expected to have a significant and lasting effect on non-resident holding of JGBs.[3]

B.   *Granting Greater Independence to Government Debt Management Program from Monetary Policy*

As far as the management of government assets and liabilities is concerned, central banks are responsible for assets management while ministries of finance maintain operational authority over liabilities management. As Cassard and Folkerts-Landau (1997) espouse, such separation of responsibilities is necessary considering the potential conflicts of interest between monetary policy and debt management. In Japan, however, MOF violates the simple rule of separating assets and liabilities management because of the activities of its Trust Fund Bureau (TFB). The TFB is the largest fund manager in the world, managing a total asset of ¥440 trillion, which is known as the Fiscal Investment and Loan Program (FILP).[4] As presented in Table 2, the primary sources of the FILP fund are comprised of postal savings (58%) and employee's and national pension deposits (32%). On the asset side of the balance sheet, the fund is invested in government-owned organizations (27%), general and special accounts (23%), JGBs (19%), municipal governments (15%), etc.

Table 2 **Fiscal Investment and Loan Program** (As of February 2000)

A. Assets	Unit: ¥Billion	
	Amount	%
Long-term government Bonds	¥83,302	18.8
Treasury and Financial Bills	999	0.2
General Account and Special Accounts	102,145	23.0
Government-owned Organizations	117,850	26.5
Local government	66,042	14.9
Special Companies	69,821	15.7
Bank Debentures	1,278	0.3
Others	1,533	0.3
Cash/Deposits	1,100	0.3
Total	¥444,069	100.0
B. Liabilities		
	Amount	%
Postal Savings and Postal Transfer Deposits	¥256,268	57.5
Postal Life Insurance Deposits	4,587	1.0
Employee's Pension Deposits	130,942	29.5
National Pension Deposits	10,772	2.4
Other Deposits	36,238	8.2
Others	5,262	1.2
Total	¥444,069	100.0

Source: Ministry of Finance, http://www.mof.go.jp/english/mr-tfb/e1c014ao.htm

Although MOF considers FILP an extension of its fiscal policy, its purchase activities of JGBs are perceived critically important by market participants in predicting the direction of long-term interest rate movement. For example, the TFB announced in the latter part of 1999 that it would suspend ¥200 billion ($1.91 billion) bond purchases in the open market each month. This announcement triggered the prices of JGBs to decline sharply, raising their yields to as high as 2.7%. After the resumption of the purchase activities by TFB, however, the yield level stabilized to the current level of around 1.8% (10-year JGBs).[5] With FILP's holdings accounting for over one-third of JGBs outstanding, the MOF is effectively the largest seller and buyer of JGBs. This dual role executed by MOF is an explicit violation of the rule of separation between government debt management and monetary policy. Commingled management of assets and liabilities, especially FILP's inadvertent influence over monetary policy, not only causes the cost of government-issued debt to increase but also creates serious impediments to the development of the JGB markets as discussed below.

C. Unfinished Primary and Secondary Markets Infrastructures

Recognising the growing importance of capital-market-based financing, the Big Bang program implemented numerous reform measures to improve the primary and secondary markets infrastructure since November 1996. These measures include: (i) deregulation of cross-border transactions and foreign exchange business; (ii) adoption of competitive auction method to issue financial bills; (iii) abolition of securities transaction tax; (iv) deregulation of brokerage commissions; (v) preparation of legal framework for loan/asset securitization; (vi) deregulation of off-exchange trading; (vii) entry by banks, securities companies, and insurance companies into each other's business; (viii) introduction of individual stock options; and (ix) replacement of merit-based licensing system with a disclosure-based registration system for securities companies. As summarized in Table 3, the scope and complexity of the reform programs were unprecedented. The coordinated effort among various government agencies was exemplary in implementing these Big Bang reform measures.

219

Table 3

(April 2000)

Schedule for Financial System Reform

I. Expansion in means of asset investment

	Fiscal 1997	Fiscal 1998	Fiscal 1999	Fiscal 2000	Fiscal 2001
1. Enhancements to investment trusts					
1) Introduction of general securities accounts (CMA)	Made necessary deregulation and introduce on October 1.	Further improvements in product attractiveness (salary/amendment concerning salaries effected September 10			
2) Introduction of company-type investment trusts		Establish the general institutional framework (Investment Trust Law) (law took effect on December 1)			
3) Introduction of privately-placed investment trusts		Stipulate privately-placed investment trusts in law (Investment Trust Law) (law took effect on December 1)			
4) Introduction of over-the-counter sales of investment trusts by banks and other financial institutions	Store space lent for "direct sales by investment trust companies" (Introduced on December 1 after sales rules was finalized)	Sales by banks themselves (Securities and Exchange Law) (law took effect on December 1)			
2. Full liberalization of securities derivatives	Tokyo Stock Exchange and Osaka Stock Exchange Introduction of options on individual stocks (on July 18)	Introduce over-the-counter securities derivatives (Securities and Exchange Law) (Law on Foreign Securities Law Firms) (law took effect on December 1)			
3. Enhance attractiveness of stocks	Expanding use of stock options (law took effect on June 1) Promoting share buy-backs as a means of writing down profits (law took effect on June 1)				
4. Smaller minimum investment lots for stocks	Have already articulated how the Commercial Code is to be interpreted regarding conditional changes in the Articles of Incorporation (July 31)				
5. Streamlining of foreign equity listing by using DRs	Introduced DR-based trading in listed foreign equities (June 1)	Designate DRs as securities (Securities and Exchange Law) (law took effect on December 1) Revision of listing standards (December 1) (Tokyo Stock Exchange)	....	....	▶
6. Improved access to trading and quotation information	Eliminated the system that gives access to real-time information only to branches in the vicinity of the market (October 1)	Tokyo Stock Exchange: Enhancement of market information (November 30)			

II. Facilitation of corporate fund-raising

	Fiscal 1997	Fiscal 1998	Fiscal 1999	Fiscal 2000	Fiscal 2001
1. Introduce new corporate bond products	Perpetual bonds (clarified interpretation of the Commercial Code) (July 31)	Introduce bonds linked to share-price indexes (enhanced laws related to over-the-counter derivatives on securities) (law took effect on December 1)			
2. Expand use of ABS		Review issues concerning protection against third party claims and established of SPC (enhanced laws related to SPC) (law took effect on September 1)			
3. Promote use of MTN	Measures taken (Clarified that boards could delegate representative directors, and improved system for registering issues) (May 30)				
4. Facilitate listing and initial public offering	Introduced book-building method (modified association and exchange rules) (September 1)	Move to after-the-fact notifications for equity listings (Securities and Exchange Law) (law took effect on September 1)			
5. Revision of listing standards		December 1 (Osaka Stock Exchange) January 1 (Tokyo Stock Exchange) February 1 (Nagoya Stock Exchange)			
6. Strengthen registered over-the-counter market functions.	Introduced share lending system (modified association rules) (July 1)	Alter the characterization of registered over-the-counter market as a "supplement" (Securities and Exchange Law) (law took effect on December 1)			
	Introduced margin trading and date-of-issue trading (October 27)	Introduction of market maker system (alteration of association rules) (December 1)			
		Revision of OTC registration standards (alteration of association rules) (December 1)			
7. Deregulation unlisted and unregistered equities market					
1) Permit securities companies to handle unlisted and unregistered equities	Ban lifted (modified association rules) (July 1)				
2) Permit investment trusts to investment in unlisted and unregistered equities	Ban lifted (amended ministerial ordinance and enhanced association rules) (September 1)				

III. Provide a wider variety of services

	Fiscal 1997	Fiscal 1998	Fiscal 1999	Fiscal 2000	Fiscal 2001
1. Eliminate restrictions on the range of business open to securities companies	General securities accounts (introduced October 1)	Eliminate compartmentalization (Securities and Exchange Law) (Law on Foreign Securities Firms) Introduce wraparound accounts (Securities and Exchange Law) (Law on Foreign Securities Firms) (law took effect on December 1)			
2. Liberalize brokerage commissions		Reduce to in excess of ¥50 million (April 1)	Full libera-lization (Financial System ref-orm Law) (October 1)		
3. Reform of the rating organization system		Eliminate the obligation for member insurer of the rating organization to use premium rates calculated by the rating organization (Law Concerning Non-Life Insurance Rating Organization) (law amended July 1)			
4. Strengthen asset investment business	Permitted investment trusts to invest in unlisted and unregistered equities (amended ministerial ordinance and enhanced association rules) (September 1)	Introduce outside consignments (Investment Trust Law) (Law for Regulating Securities Investment Advisory Business) Review business regulations (Investment Trusts Law) (Law for Regulating Securities Investment Advisory Business) Switch from approvals to notifications for investment trust deeds (Investment Trust Law) (law took effect on December 1)			
5. Expand the range of fund raising for banks			Allow banks to issue straight bonds (Financ-ial System Reform Law) (October 1)		
6. Expand the range of fund-raising for finance companies (Allowing to issue bonds for financing funds for lending)			Law on Bond Issuance for Financial Companies (May 20)		
7. Reform market-entry regulations					
1) Switch from licensing to registration system for securities companies		(law took effect on December 1)			
2) Switch from licensing to authorization for investment trust companies		(law took effect on December 1)			
3) Promote competition across sectorial walls					
Expand range of business permitted securities subsidiaries and trust-banking subsidiaries	All business except equities-related (October 1)		Eliminate all regulations (Financial System Reform Law) (October 1)		
Permit cross-sectorial competition between insurance companies and other financial institutions		Entry of insurance companies into securities business and securities companies into insurance business accelerated [Insurance Business Law, Banking Law] (laws took effect on December 1)	Entry of insurance companies into banking business (Financial System Reform Law) (October 1)	Entry of banks into insurance business (October 1)	
8. Over-the-counter sale of insurance by banks					Lift ban on handling of certain products (April 1)
9. Utilization of holding companies (HCs)	Enacted two laws on HCs (December 5), took effect on March 11				

IV. Create efficient markets

	Fiscal 1997	Fiscal 1998	Fiscal 1999	Fiscal 2000	Fiscal 2001
1. Improve exchange trading and review exchange market operations	Improved trading systems within the exchange (November 14)	Formulate merger rules for securities exchanges (Securities and Exchange Law) (law took effect on December 1) Improvement of trading systems within the exchange for amortization of company's own stock (December 1, 1999)			
2. Abolish requirement of consolidation of order-flow for listed securities		Abolish the requirement of consolidation of order-flow for listed securities (Formulate fair trading rules) (Securities and Exchange Law) (law took effect on December 1)			
3. Strengthen the functions of the registered over-the-counter market (repeat)					
4. Deregulate unlisted and unregistered equities market (repeat)					
5. Introduce proprietary trading systems (PTSs)					
6. Create share-lending system		Review rules on margin rates (Securities and Exchange Law) (law took effect on December 1)			
7. Enhance clearing and settlement system	Expanded and enhanced system trading (August 4) Bond delivery and settlement system (JB-NET) (December 22) Same-day cash delivery (December 1)	Formulate rules for share lending (December 1) Enhance notifications from custodial and registrar institutions to issuing companies of actual shareholders (Equity Custody and Transfer Law) (law took effect on December 1)	·······················▶		
8. Promote reduction of Settlement risk		Clarify the legal validity of close-out netting contracts (Close-out Netting) (law took effect on December 1)			

V.　Assure fair trading

	Fiscal 1997	Fiscal 1998	Fiscal 1999	Fiscal 2000	Fiscal 2001
1. Formulate and enhance fair trading rules		Formulate fair trading rules for new product introductions (Securities and Exchange Law) (law took effect on December 1) Review rule for short selling (Securities and Exchange Law) (law took effect on October 23)	·····················►		
2. Strengthen punitive measures	Strengthened punitive measures against insider trading etc. (Enacted Law on Punitive Measures for Financial Matters on December 3; took effect on December 30)	Formulate rules for forfeiture of illicit profits from insider trading etc. (Securities and Exchange Law) (law took effect on December 1)			
3. Formulate regulations to prevent conflicts of interest		Formulate rules against conflicts of interest (Securities and Exchange Law) (Law on Foreign Securities Firms) (Investment Trust Law) (Law for Regulating Securities Investment Advisory Business) (law took effect on December 1)			
4. Enhance disputes-settlement system		Enact arbitration procedures (Sécurities and Exchange Law) (law took effect on December 1)			
5. Expand and enhance the definition of securities	Have taken steps for the beneficiary certificates for financial-institution loan-asset trusts (amended government ordinance, effective June 1)	Designate DRs covered warrants and ABSs by SPCs as securities (Securities and Exchange Law) (law took effect on December 1)	·····················►		
6. Enhance disclosure system 1) Switch to consolidated reporting	Published opinion paper on reviewing consolidated financial statements (June 6) Published opinion paper on setting standards for the creation of interim consolidated financial statements and consolidated cash flow statements (March 13)	Phased in from the business year beginning April 1	Move to full implementation		
2) Formulate accounting standards for financial products		Accounting standards for tax effect accounting (January 1, 1999 (voluntary))	Achieve all objectives from the business year started on April 1, 1999		
		Published opinion paper on accounting standards for research and development costs	Achieve all objectives from the business year started on April 1, 1999		
		Accounting standards for retirement allowances (June 16) Accounting standards for financial instrument		To be phased in from the business year starting on April	Achieve all objectives

VI. Ensure soundness of intermediaries and prepare system for dealing with failures

	Fiscal 1997	Fiscal 1998	Fiscal 1999	Fiscal 2000	Fiscal 2001
1. Review capital adequacy requirements		Review in conjunction with expansions in range of business (Securities and Exchange Law) (Law on Foreign Securities Firms) (law took effect on December 1)			
		Formulate clear withdrawal procedures if below a set ratio (Securities and Exchange Law) (Law on Foreign Securities Firms) (law took effect on December 1)			
2. Enhance financial-institution disclosure		Enhance disclosure requirements on banks and others (Banking Law etc.)			
		Obligate disclosure by securities companies (Securities and Exchange Law) (Law on Foreign Securities Firms) (law took effect on December 1)			
3. Prepare rules of bank and insurance subsidiaries		Clarify the scope of subsidiaries (Banking Law) (Insurance Business Law) Review rules on margin rates (law took effect on December 1)			
4. Prepare framework to protect customers in the event of failure					
1) Thorough separation of accounts	Enacted for futures and options trading (October 29)	(Securities and Exchange Law) Enhance overall legal system (Securities and Exchange Law) (Law on Foreign Securities Firms) (law took effect on December 1)			
2) Creation of Investor Protection Fund		Incorporate under the Securities and Exchange Law, establish and expand system (Securities and Exchange Law) (law took effect on December 1)			
3) Enhancement of bankruptcy procedures		Create special procedures for securities company bankruptcies and reorganizations (Law for Improving the Reorganization and Bankruptcy Procedure for Financial Institutions) (law took effect on December 1)			
4) Creation of Policy-holders Protection Corporation		Creation of Policy holders Protection Corporation in order to protect policy-holders (Insurance Business Law) (law took effect on December 1)			

	Fiscal 1997	Fiscal 1998	Fiscal 1999	Fiscal 2000	Fiscal 2001
Review securities taxation		Reduce the rate of the securities transaction tax and the bourse tax (April 1)	Elimination of the securities transaction tax and the bourse tax on (April 1)		

Notes
1. Shading indicates measures that are not taken.
2. Underlines indicate measures requiring amendments to laws.

With the aim of identifying the unfinished reform areas for the JGB market, however, Japan may want to consider the U.S. government securities market as a role model. In retrospect, four major developments signify the underlying forces that rapidly expanded the U.S. government securities markets in the 1980s. These developments are: (i) active trading of Treasury securities on a when-issued basis which assisted in minimizing the underwriting risk by reducing price and quantity uncertainties; (ii) introduction of financial futures and options written on Treasury securities which provided necessary vehicles for hedging of interest rate risk; (iii) expansion of REPO and reverse REPO transactions which supported the increase of market liquidity and short-term investment activities; and (iv) introduction of the Separate Trading of Registered Interest and Principal of Securities (STRIPS) which facilitated hedging of reinvestment risk through coupon stripping.

Presently, when-issued trading is illegal in Japan. STRIPS has yet to be introduced. Although localized variations of REPO markets such as the *Gensaki* market and the *Kashisai* market emerged in Japan, their developments were inhibited by tax-related impediments (*Gensaki* market) and interest rate ceiling on the cash collateral (*Kashisai* market). For example, as *Gensaki* is recognized as a form of bond trading, they were subject to securities transaction tax. Therefore, the majority of *Gensaki* transactions were implemented using Treasury bills and financing bills that were exempted from securities transaction tax.[6] However, stamp duties on bills could not be avoided. In contrast, transactions on the *Kashisai* market have not been subject to securities transaction taxes. Legal and operational modalities of the two markets, however, reflected a hybrid form of American-style classic REPOs and European-style sale-and-buyback contracts. As a result, the two markets could not fully develop. The Japanese futures market (with equity index and long-term bond as underlying assets) has earned an unfortunate reputation of an "over-regulated" market because of stringent regulatory policies including margin requirements and circuit breakers.

III.   Post-Big Bang Reform Measures

In terms of GDP, Japan's economy is about one-half the size of U.S. economy while it is about twice as large as Germany's economy. As Japan's capital market development emulates past experiences of the U.S. counterpart, the above four areas should be an interesting point of departure in assessing further reforms for the JGB market. Since the JGB market has matured in its own historical, macroeconomic, and institutional framework, it faces its own unique blend of capital market policy issues. Therefore, this section will introduce some capital market policy issues that are unique to the JGB market as well as the policy issues in light of U.S. market experiences.

A.   *Lack of the Primary Dealer System*

One idiosyncratic feature of the JGB market is the lack of the primary dealer system. This may be attributed in large part to the role played by TFB as a de facto underwriter in the primary market. With TFB serving as an active buyer of newly issued JGBs (usually under a buy-and-hold investment strategy), purely competitive public auctions must have been difficult to implement. Naturally, underwriting by a syndicate has been the standard in the JGB primary markets, especially for the benchmark 10-year bonds, with a specific goal of absorbing the full amount of new issues. Although competitive auction features were built into the current syndicate underwriting, their utilization has been limited. Public auction systems (based on the multiple-price auctions) were introduced later for the maturities of 2-, 4-, 6-, and 20-year bonds, but syndicate underwriting and non-competitive auctions remain the major vehicle to absorb new issues of JGBs. As a result, a primary dealer system providing competitive bidding at primary market auctions did not find its position in the JGB market.

With respect to international investors' primary concerns regarding low liquidity and large spread between bid and ask prices on the JGB market, the introduction of a primary dealer system is definitely a viable alternative that deserves serious consideration.[7] Primary dealer systems are designed to attain at least three goals in the government securities market: first, efficient price discovery through intense competition among participating dealers; second, provision of liquidity through market-making; and third, distribution of government-issued securities. In addition, primary dealers serve as the counterparts to central banks in open market operations. Most of the advanced economies adopted the primary dealer system with the exception of Japan and Germany, where both economies are historically known for their bank-based financial systems as opposed to the U.S. and U.K.-style capital-market-based financial system.

Table 4 **Government Securities Markets**

	Japan		United States	United Kingdom
Turnover Ratio		6.9	22.0	7.0
Bid-Ask Spread				
10-Year On-the-Run Issues		7.0	3.1	4.0
10-Year Off-the-Run Issues		7.0	6.3	4.0
Maturity Distribution				
< 1 Year		5%	21%	7%
1-5 Year		8%	62%	29%
5-10 Year		78%	0%	34%
>10 Year		9%	17%	30%
Average Issue Size ($Billion)		8.2	13.9	5.6
Government/Central Bank Holding (%)		46.3	13.1	3.6
Non-Resident Holding (%)		10.0	36.9	14.4
Settlement		T+3	T+1	T+1
DVP-Basis Settlement	• 67.6% of registered JGBs and 42.7% of book-entry JGBs • All JGBs through BOJ-NET		100%	100%
No. of Primary Dealers		None	37	16
No. of Dealers		501	1,700	16

Source: Inoue (1999)

The major impediment to the adoption of the primary dealer system in Japan is MOF's role as a buyer of JGBs. Therefore, it is a blessing in disguise that the MOF expects a large shortfall in FILP funds amounting to approximately ¥35 trillion as fixed 10-year deposits in the national postal savings system mature in 2000 and 2001.[8] This expected shortfall forces MOF to review structural reforms in the funding method and the management of FILP agencies with the implementation target in 2001. Given the sheer magnitude and scope of FILP activities, the complexity of FILP reforms is beyond comprehension.[9] However, the overall direction of FILP reform is not difficult to define no matter how complicated the process is. First, FILP agencies should be corporatized to gain complete autonomy, while MOF should adopt a "hands-off" policy. This "hands-off" policy will facilitate the separation between management of government assets and liabilities. Second, the MOF should not meddle with the JGB market as an active buyer. The MOF's direct involvement should be limited to issuer's function in the capacity of the manager of government debt.

B. *Introduction of the Uniform-Price Auction Method*

In an MOF publication, entitled *Guide to Japanese Government Bond 1998*, the uniform-price auction method is introduced as a "non-competitive" bidding method executed at the average price paid in the competitive auction undertaken concurrently. This is not a generic definition of the uniform-price auction but a Japan-specific interpretation. Under the conventional uniform-price auction (also known as the "Dutch" auction), all bidders whose tenders are accepted pay the same price for a given security. This is either the lowest of the accepted prices or the highest of the accepted yields. Therefore, some of the successful bidders may pay a lower price than they actually bid. In contrast, under the multiple-price auctions (also known as the "discriminatory" auction), participants submit sealed bids and pay the prices they bid. The government accepts the bids at gradually lower prices until the price at which the auction is fully subscribed.[10] As a result, successful bidders for a security may pay different prices for that security. These multiple-price awards result in the "winner's curse," which means that the highest bidder wins the auction by paying the highest price, only to find that another bidder pays a lower price. In the presence of this curse, bidders tend to shade their bids below the maximum that they are actually willing to pay.[11] Since Salomon's "short squeeze" scandal uncovered in mid-1991, the multiple-price method has been criticized for failing to minimize financing costs to the U.S. Treasury and for encouraging manipulative behavior in the marketplace. As an alternative, the "uniform-price, sealed-bid" auction is advocated.[12]

Australia, France, and New Zealand now utilize multiple-price (or multiple-yield) auctions to sell marketable securities, while Canada, Belgium, Italy, and the Netherlands use it for some portions of marketable securities. Uniform-price, sealed-bid auctions are employed in Denmark, Switzerland, and the United Kingdom. Beginning in 1992, the US Treasury experimented with uniform-price auctions for 2-year and 5-year notes. Malvey, Archibald, and Flynn (1995) and Malvey and Archbald (1998) indicated that these auctions produced marginally greater revenue on the average for the US government. Nyborg and Sundaresan (1996) report that when-issued market volume is higher under uniform- as compared to multiple-price auctions, which indicates a higher information release. The information release, in turn, reduces the pre-auction uncertainty, the winner's curse, and the probability of short squeeze. Feldman and Mehra (1993) report that uniform-price auctions become readily accepted because of their administrative simplicity, economic efficiency, and revenue-enhancing potential. A plethora of academic research papers provide empirical evidence in support of this perception.[13]

As summarized in Table 5, Japan's MOF never adopted uniform-price auctions, whereas the U.S. and U.K. employ these auctions for index-linked bonds and some bonds with specific maturities (2- and 5-year bonds in the United States).[14] The U.S. Treasury is considering expanded use of uniform-price auctions for all Treasury issues in the near future.

Table 5 Auction Methods for Government-Issued Securities

	Japan	United States	United Kingdom
Uniform-Price Auction	None	☐ 2-and 5-Year Notes ☐ 10- and 30-Year Index-linked Bonds	☐ Index-linked Bonds
Multiple-Price Auction	All JGBs ☐ 20-Year Bond: Competitive Auction Only ☐ 2-, 4- and 6-Year Bond: Both Competitive and Non-competitive Auction ☐ 5- and 10-Year Bond: Syndicated Underwriting	☐ 10- and 30-Year Bonds ☐ 3-, 6-and 12-Month Bills	☐ All Securities other than Index-linked Bonds

Source: Asia-Pacific Financial Markets Research Center, University of Hawaii

C. *Lack of When-Issued Trading*

Among the developed government securities markets, Japan represents the only exception that considers when-issued trading illegal. In most of the advanced markets including the United States, however, trading during the period between the time a new issue is announced and the time it is actually issued (ranging from one- to two-weeks) is allowed and the issue is said to trade "when, as, and if issued."[15] When-issued trading functions like trading in a futures market, in which long and short positions are taken prior to the settlement date which is the issue day of the security traded. Prior to auctions, when-issued securities are quoted for trading on a yield basis because a coupon is not determined until after an auction is completed. Subsequent to auctions, they are quoted on a price basis. The most important benefit of when-issued trading is the minimization of price and quantity uncertainties. As trading on a when-issued basis facilitates the price discovery and distribution, the risk of underwriting becomes smaller and potential revenue from the new issue increases for the government. By not allowing when-issued trading, the MOF foregoes these benefits.

D. *REPO Market*

A REPO represents the sale of securities by the borrower to the lender (investor) with an agreement to repurchase the securities at a specified date and price. It is a combination of spot sale and forward purchase of the securities. The difference between the selling and repurchasing prices represents the interest on the transaction. The borrower's REPO is the lender's reverse REPO. The REPO market serves numerous purposes. It allows primary dealers to cover their short positions, institutional investors to maximize their investment income by lending their securities, and foreign investors to reduce currency risk through money market hedging.[16] It also facilitates clearing and settlement transactions and enhances market liquidity. Without an active REPO market, the primary and secondary markets cannot develop to their full potentials.

The *Kashisai* market (now patterned after the U.S.-style REPO market) is basically a cash-backed bond lending market with the same effect as that of the *Gensaki* market. However, *Kashisai* transactions differ from *Gensaki* transactions in that they are marked-to-market on a daily basis like the U.S.-style REPOs. *Kashisai* transactions steadily increased since the shift to rolling settlement in October 1996.[17] The *Kashisai* market witnessed a major impediment eliminated when the upper limit on the interest rate charged on the cash collateral was lifted in 1996. In addition, market participants in the *Gensaki* REPO market are exempted from payment of securities transaction tax in 1999. With these positive developments, one would expect the *Kashisai* market and the *Gensaki* market to take off. No drastic changes in market activities have been reported so far. This puzzle surrounding the *Gensaki* and the *Kashisai* markets warrants a careful review.

E.   *Introduction of STRIPS*

At present, Japan does not allow "coupon stripping" which splits bond income streams into coupon interest and principal repayment. The coupon stripping was devised in 1982 by Merrill Lynch and Salomon Brothers to serve bond investors who were concerned about reinvestment risk. Beginning in 1985, the Treasury introduced the Separate Trading of Registered Interest and Principal of Securities (STRIPS) program to formalize the stripping of designated Treasury securities. The main appeal of STRIPS is to provide the market with highly liquid zero-coupon Treasury bonds and notes, thereby expanding the bond investor base. The strip market also generates arbitrage activities. Primary dealers continuously check the price of strippable bonds against the sum of the stripped parts (the "whole" versus the sum of "parts"). The existence of zero-coupon yield curve allows a better pricing of traditional coupon bonds. In developing a very active government securities market from an insignificant and illiquid market, the French authorities, for example, introduced a set of well-sequenced reform measures. As shown below, the introduction of STRIPS and the creation of legal and institutional framework for the REPO market were the last set of reform measures implemented in France:

- Bond futures market (1986)

- Primary dealer system (1987)

- Interdealer broker network (1987)

- Purely competitive auctions (1987)

- Interdealer broker network (1987)

- REPOs (1991)

- STRIPS (1991)

Given the U.S. experience with STRIPS and more recent experiences in the French government securities market, the MOF should expedite the introduction of STRIPS.

Internationalization of Yen: Implications for the Creation of a Regional Bond Markets

Under the new Miyazawa Initiative, a total of $30 billion was pledged by Japan and one-half of this amount was made available for the medium- to long-term financing needs for Asian economies affected by the Asian financial crisis. At least two measures under the Initiative are directly related to regional bond market activities. They are: (i) acquisition of sovereign bonds issued by Asian countries by the Export-Import Bank of Japan and (ii) support for Asian countries in raising funds from international financial markets through the use of guarantee mechanisms. These measures are important vehicles to promote the global and regional role of the Tokyo market by expanding the *Gaisai* market. *Gaisai* is a general term assigned to all foreign- and yen-denominated bonds issued in

Japan by non-residents. Yen-denominated bonds are called "*samurai*" bonds while foreign-currency-denominated bonds are known as "*shogun*" bonds. The capital-market-related funding programs of the New Miyazawa Initiative were expected to provide the Tokyo financial markets (both on- and off-shore) with a critical momentum to reaffirm itself as a global and regional financial center. Unfortunately, no details have been made available from the MOF regarding the implementation of the above two measures, in addition to the fact that the underlying reasons for the unavailability are not clear. As presented in Table 6, the amount of *Gaisai* bonds issued does not exhibit any substantial increases over the 5-year period, 1995-1999.

Table 5
Auction Methods for Government-Issued Securities

	Japan	**United States**	**United Kingdom**
Uniform-Price Auction	None	☐ 2-and 5-Year Notes ☐ 10- and 30-Year Index-linked Bonds	☐ Index-linked Bonds
Multiple-Price Auction	All JGBs ☐ 20-Year Bond: Competitive Auction Only ☐ 2-, 4- and 6-Year Bond: Both Competitive and Non-competitive Auction ☐ 5- and 10-Year Bond: Syndicated Underwriting	☐ 10- and 30-Year Bonds ☐ 3-, 6-and 12-Month Bills	☐ All Securities other than Index-linked Bonds

Source: Asia-Pacific Financial Markets Research Center, University of Hawaii

As an international financial center, the Tokyo market must compete with other financial markets including the eurobond market. As shown in Table 7, the difference in all-in-cost to sovereign borrower of ¥20 billion between *samurai* bonds and euro-yen bonds amounts to 7 basis points or ¥14 million. The difference between time-lengths required for bond issuance in both markets differs substantially (6-7 weeks vs. a few days). With a recording system still in place, the clearing and settlement processes in the *samurai* bond market is far more cumbersome than the eurobond market where Euroclear and Cedel are readily available and utilized. In order for the Tokyo market to serve global and regional customers more efficiently at the least cost, concerted efforts must be made.

Table 6
Volume of *Gaisai* Bond Issuance

Unit: ¥ trillion

	1995	1996	1997	1998	1999*
Samurai Bonds	¥1.6	¥3.9	¥2.1	¥0.3	¥0.5
Shogun Bonds**	0	0	0	0	0

Notes: *   Including the first 10 months only.
**   Last *shogun* bonds were issued in 1994.

Table 7
Cost Differential between *Samurai* and Euroyen Bonds

Assumptions			
Issuer:	Sovereign Borrower		
	Issue Amount: ¥20 billion		
	Term:	5 years	

	Samurai Bonds	Euro-Yen Bonds
Underwriting Fee	40 bp (upfront)	25 bp (upfront)
Commissioned Bank Fee/		
Recording Fee	3 bp (upfront)	n.a.
Interest Payment Commission	20 bp	nil
		(of each payment)
Principal Payment Commission	10 bp (at maturity)	nil
Out-of-Pocket Expenses	¥15 million	¥8 million
	(upfront)	(upfront)
All-in-Cost to Issuer	2.03% (s.a.)	1.961% (s.a.)
Time-Length of Launch	6 to 7 weeks	A few days
Clearing and Settlement	Recording System	Euroclear and Cedel

Source: Industrial Bank of Japan Securities Co. (1998)

Numerous reform measures were undertaken to internationalize the yen and promote foreign investments in the Tokyo financial markets. A legal framework for the promotion of cross-border transactions is in place with the revision of Foreign Exchange Law in April 1998; yet, much more has to be done to facilitate actual transactions. For example, clearing and settlement have to be revamped to introduce delivery versus payment (DVP). At present, 67.6% of registered JGBs and 42.7% of book-entry JGBs are settled on the DVP basis, whereas all JGBs processed through the Bank of Japan Financial Network System (BOJ-Net) rely on the DVP settlement. In contrast, the U.S. and U.K. government securities are all settled on the DVP basis. Additionally, JGBs are not eligible for clearing through international clearing houses such as Euroclear and Cedel, whereas U.S. and UK government securities are all eligible. Furthermore, no regional clearing network has been created to link the Tokyo clearing system with the region's financial centers such as Hong Kong, Singapore, and Sydney. A T+3 settlement period for JGBs is longer than T+1 cycle for U.S. and U.K. securities. Real-time-gross settlement systems (RTGS) must also be completed to bring Japan's practices in line with U.S. and U.K. systems.[18] No publicly accepted practice exists for failures of deliveries in Japan unlike the U.S. and U.K. markets.[19]

So much work has yet to be done for the harmonization of cross-border listing, trading, clearing and settlements, securities borrowing and lending, REPO markets, etc. A study of inter- and intra-region portfolio capital flows must precede the implementation of the above cross-border infrastructures. In his own assessment of the Japanese debt market serving the Asia-Pacific region's financing needs, Sakakibara (1999) noted that the JGB market still lagged substantially behind London and New York in terms of market infrastructure. Therefore, in addition to building domestic market infrastructures, Japan should intensify its effort to assume a leadership role in creating regional bond market infrastructures in Tokyo and other financial centers in the region. One of key projects for the regional bond market infrastructures should focus on the creation of a single regional central securities depository (CSD) to perform the safekeeping, clearance, and settlement functions for all securities available in the Asia-Pacific region.[20]

NOTES

1. The ratio of government bond issues to total government expenditures in the fiscal year 2000 budget will be 38.4%. Refer to a Fiscal Policy Speech by Finance Minister Kiichi Miyazawa at the 147th Session of the National Diet in January 2000.

2. Campbell (1997) forcefully illustrates how the counter-party risk was unnecessarily created by the lack of ownership registration to avoid the withholding taxes and how unnecessary "churning" prior to coupon payment dates added costly transaction costs as non-resident investors switch out of their JGB holdings before the Big Bang financial reforms were implemented.

3. Germany eliminated withholding taxes on interest income from domestic government bonds held by non-residents in October 1984. As a result, the percentage of German government bonds held by foreign investors jumped from 10% in 1984 to 38% in 1988. This information is drawn from the Tokyo-Mitsbushi Securities Company's web site.

4. This amount is equivalent to approximately 80% of Japan's GDP.

5. Refer to "Bond Plan Key to Halting Rise in Japan Interest" *Asian Wall Street Journal* (November 30, 1999).

6. Financing bills are issued on a discount basis like Treasury bills. Because the discount rate remained below prevailing short-term market interest rate, virtually all issues had to be subscribed by the Bank of Japan (BOJ). Under the Big Bang reform programs, Treasury financing bills, food financing bills, and foreign exchange fund bills are all integrated into single financing bills and they are issued under a competitive auction system.

7. Refer to Table 4 "Government Securities Markets."

8. Refer to "Japanese turn to 'zaito' to boost finances" (*Financial Times*, March 13, 2000).

9. Refer to an MOF web site, http://www.mof.go.jp/english/zaito/zae054a.htm, for "Fundamental Reform of the Fiscal Investment and Loan Program (FILP)."

10. In some countries, minimum cut-off prices are imposed by ministries of finance or fiscal agents conducting auctions, which may distort truly competitive bidding process because: (i) the bidders try to second-guess cut-off prices rather than assessing the demand and supply of the securities to be issued; or (ii) the cut-off prices may set the yields higher than market conditions warrant. At the time of writing this report, it is not known to the author whether this practice is used in multiple-price auctions in Japan.

11. For details, refer to the *Joint Report on the Government Securities Market* (1992) prepared by the Department of the Treasury, the Securities and Exchange Commission, and the Board of Governors of the Federal Reserve System.

12.   Refer to Friedman (1991 and 1960), Chari and Weber (1992), and Umlauf (1993).

13.   Refer to Umlauf (1993), Nyborg and Sundaresan (1996), and Heller and Lengwiler (1998).

14.   Because the uniform-price auction is a legitimate competitive mechanism, the Japanese version of a "non-competitive" uniform-price auction is a misnomer. Non-competitive bids specify quantity only, while competitive bids specify both price (or yield) and quantity. In Japan, the price used for settlement for a non-competitive bid is the weighted average price from the competitive auction conducted concurrently. By design, this "non-competitive" method should be restricted to small transactions intended for small investors and should remain as an insignificant supplement to multiple-price auctions.

15.   Refer to Appendix A "Background on the Treasury Securities Market" in the *Joint Report on the Government Securities Market* (1992), A1-A19.

16.   Bossard (1998) reports that the newly developed REPO market in 1991-1993 was essential to foreign participation in the French government securities market. At present, one-third of the French government securities are held by non-residents.

17.   Refer to Executives' Meeting of East Asia and Pacific Central Banks and Monetary Authorities' *Financial Markets and Payment Systems in EMEAP Economies* (1997).

18.   The target date of adopting RTGS for JGBs is the latter part of 2000.

19.   Refer to Appendix "Table of Questionnaire Results" to Bank for International Settlements, 1999, Market Liquidity: Research Findings and Selected Policy Issues (May).

20.   For the regional and global level clearing and settlement, refer to Rhee (2000) and Morgan Guaranty Trust Company (1993).

REFERENCES

Bank for International Settlements, 1999, Market Liquidity: Research Findings and Selected Policy Issues, Report of a Study Group Established by the Committee on the Global Financial System of the central banks of the Group of Ten countries (May).

Brossard, Philippe, 1998, The French Bond Market: Enhancing Liquidity, A paper presented at a World Bank Workshop on the Development of Government Bond Markets, June 11-12, Seoul, Korea.

Campbell, William D., 1997, Toward a More Professional Yes Fixed Income Market, in *Issues Facing Japanese Government and Corporate Bond Markets* (Tokyo: Nomura Research Institute), 259-286.

Cassard, Marcel and David Folkerts-Landau, 1997, Risk Management of Sovereign Assets and Liabilities, *IMF Working Paper* WP/97/166.

Chari, V. V. and R. Weber, 1992, How the U.S. Treasury Should Auction Its Debt, *Quarterly Review of Federal Reserve Bank of Minneapolis* (Fall), 3-12.

Department of the Treasury, Securities and Exchange Commission, and Board of Governors of the Federal Reserve System, 1992, *Joint Report on the Government Securities Market* (January).

Executives' Meeting of East Asia and Pacific Central Banks and Monetary Authorities' *Financial Markets and Payment Systems in EMEAP Economies* (1997).

Feldman, Robert A. and Rajnish Mehra, 1993, Auctions: Theory and applications, *IMF Staff Paper* 40, 485-511.

Freidman, Milton, 1960, *A Program for Monetary Stability* (New York: Fordham University Press).

Friedman, Milton, 1991, How to Sell Government Securities, *Wall Street Journal* (August 28).

Heller, Daniel and Yvan Lengwiler, 1998, The Auctions of Swiss Government Bonds: Should the Treasury Price Discriminate or Not?, Board of Governors of the Federal Reserve System Working Paper.

Inonue, Hirotaka, 1999, The Structure of Government Secdurities Markets in G10 Countries: Summary of Questionnaire Results, in Report by Bank for International Settlements and the Committee on the Global Financial System of the central banks of the Group of Ten countries (May).

Ministry of Finance, *Guide to Japanese Government Bond 1998*, (Tokyo: Ministry of Finance, The Japanese Government, 1998).

Malvey, Paul F. and Christine M. Archbald, 1998, Uniform-Price Auctions: Update of the Treasury Experience, Office of Market Finance, U.S. Treasury.

Malvery, Paul F., Christine M. Archbald, and Sean T. Flynn, 1995, Uniform-Price Auctions: Evaluation of the Treasury Experience, Office of Market Finance, U.S. Treasury.

Miyazawa, Kiichi, 2000, Fiscal Policy Speech at the 147th Session of the National Diet (January).

Morgan Guaranty Trust Company, 1993, *Cross-Border Clearance, Settlement, and Custody: Beyond the G30 Recommendations* (Brussles, Belgium: Euroclear Operations Centre).

Nyborg, Kjell G. and Suresh Sundaresan, 1996, Discriminatory versus Uniform Treasury Auctions: Evidence from When-Issued Transactions," *Journal of Financial Economics* 42, 63-104.

Rhee, S. Ghon, 2000, Risk Management System in Clearing and Settlement, forthcoming in *Asian Development Review*.

Rhee, S. Ghon, 2000, *Rising to Asia's Challenge: Enhanced Role of Capital   Markets* (Manila, Philippines: Asian Development Bank, 2000).

Sakakibara Eisuke, 1999, The Lessons of the Financial Crises of 1994 to 1998, A Paper presented at an OECD/ADBI Round Table on Securities Market Reforms, April 8, 1999 in Tokyo, Japan.

Schinasi, Gary J. and R. Todd Smith, 1998, Fixed-Income Markets in the United States, Europe, and Japan: Some Lessons for Emerging Markets, IMF Working Paper WP/98/173.

Umlauf, Stephen, 1993, An Empirical Study of the Mexican Treasury Bill Auction, *Journal of Financial Economics* 33, 313-340.

CORPORATE BOND MARKETS DEVELOPMENT

by
Mr. Tadashi Endo [*]

1.   Introduction

Expectations have been growing that, given the limitations of the banking systems and public finances in developing countries, corporate bond markets will be critically conducive to the economic development in those countries at macroeconomic as well as microeconomic levels. Only a very small number of selected corporate bond issuers ("major" corporate issuers) in a developing country can enjoy a liquid secondary market of their bonds under a properly designed policy framework for supply and demand of bonds. The rest of corporate bond issuers ("minor" corporate issuers) will hardly have it. Despite the illiquidity on the secondary market, minor corporate bond issuers can substantially benefit from opportunistically raising long-term funds on a deregulated primary market. An aggressive deregulation policy, in conjunction with market infrastructure building, is central to the development of an efficient primary market. In addition, macroeconomic constraints may not permit some developing countries to have a large, liquid government bond market to form a benchmark yield curve. In such a case, one of major corporate issuers may as well be chosen to form an approximation of the benchmark yield in their debt markets. A corporate nature of such a *de facto* benchmark issue raises special policy issues in connection with liquidity needs, which will also be discussed in this chapter.

In the following section, this paper will start with outlining what macroeconomic as well as microeconomic roles the corporate bond markets is expected to play in an development economy in comparison with the stock market and the bank loan market. In Section 3, we will comparatively overview characteristics of corporate bond markets in selected developed and developing countries, and will identify policy implications of these characteristics. Section 4 will present a conceptual distinction between "major" and "minor" corporate bond issuers in order to elucidate the limited liquidity of the corporate bond market and help formulate realistic policies for corporate bond market development. In Section 5, we will examine rationales for the centricity of the primary market in corporate bond market development in light of institutional investors' behavior, and it will be recommended that policy focus for corporate bond market development should rest on aggressive deregulation of the primary market. In Section 6, we will analyze key developmental components of the corporate bond market including disclosure system and information, credit rating system, securities registration, and bankruptcy laws. The last two sections, Sections 7 and 8, will be devoted to point out a macroeconomic policy dilemma that developing countries may be trapped in when they work for

---

[*]   The author gratefully acknowledges the comments of Alison Harwood, Michele Lubrano, Jack Glen and Debra Perry at IFC, and Clemente Luis Del Valle and Christopher Juan Costain at IBRD. In addition, the author is gratefully indebted to Michele Lubrano for the section of securities laws in this chapter. The author also thanks Mari Ishii and her Bond Database project team at IFC for valuable data and insights on the emerging bond market, and Peter Taylor for excellent research assistance. The views here are those of the author and do not necessarily reflect the views of either IFC or IBRD.

public finance consolidation as recommended by the IMF/World Bank, to propose to develop some major corporate issues into *de facto* benchmark issues, and to examine institutional characteristics of the corporate bond market conducive to enhancing the liquidity of their secondary market.

2.   Expected Roles of Corporate Bond Markets

Objectives of the government bond market are not limited to financing a country's fiscal deficit. One of the objectives of the development of a government bond market in a developing country is to facilitate the development and functioning of a corporate bond market in the country, for example, by establishing a benchmark yield curve for pricing non-benchmark bonds, including corporate bonds.

2.1.   *Macroeconomic roles*

To begin with, why do we ever more desire to have a corporate bond market in a national economy? The rationale for it is twofold: (i) a satisfactory pace of economic growth will not be warranted without debt capital; and (ii) both banking lending and public finances in developing countries largely failed to provide long-term debt in a sound and/or efficient manner.

A corporate bond market is generally expected to play the following roles:

- to diffuse stresses on the banking sector by diversifying credit risks across the economy,

- to supply long-term funds for long-term investment needs,

- to supply long-term investment products for long-term savings

- to lower funding costs by avoiding a liquidity premium,

- to provide products the flexibility to meet the specific needs of investors and borrowers, and,

- to reallocate capital more efficiently.

Figure 1: Increasing Roles of Corporate Bond Markets in Economic Development

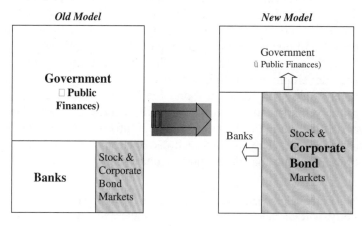

Public finances and bank loans increasingly give way to capital markets.

Among these roles of a corporate bond market, the most commonly known one is its provision of long-term funds for long-term investments. Economic development in today's world requires capital-intensive production technologies in the private sector, which entail long-term investment risks (Demirgüç-Kunt, 1995). Long-term investment risks can be better managed when the investments are matched by long-term capital. A corporate bond market is supposed to intermediate between long-term investment needs and long-term capital for private sector activities. These roles of a corporate bond market are commonly seen in developed economies and sought for as part of financial market reforms in developing economies.

Then, why is the corporate bond market, rather than bank lending or public finances, now considered crucial to developing economies? Two major factors have been leading a corporate bond market to have an increasingly important place in developing economies. They are (i) the reducing roles of bank loans and (ii) public finances in developing economies (schematically illustrated in Figure 2).

First, the recent Asian financial crisis unveiled the limitation of a banking system in financing industrial investments, even if the banking system had been reasonably regulated, supervised, capitalized and managed. The banking system's primary role is to create and maintain liquidity to finance production in the form of own liabilities, and act with in a short-term horizon (Bossone, 1998). It cannot finance investments with longer-term horizon without making the economy dangerously vulnerable to external shocks.

Second, structural reform programs, led by multilateral institutions including the World Bank Group and IMF, have been expanding the role of the private sector in developing countries. Though the public sector's role in economic development continues to be substantial, it has been widely realized that private sector enterprises have been considered more appropriate in the areas where efficiency is the highest priority. In addition, the World Bank Group, in conjunction with the IMF, has been promoting the consolidation of public finances in developing countries. These trends have been relatively reducing the role of a government bond market and increasing that of a corporate bond market in financing infrastructure building in developing countries.

Figure 2: Major Sub-markets of Corporate Bond Market

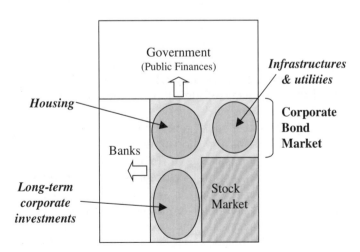

Infrastructures, utilities, housing and long-term corporate investments, among other things, are increasingly expected to be financed by corporate bond issuance.

Consequently, the corporate bond market will provide debt capital to the areas that have been ill served by either public finances or bank lending, on top of equity capital supplied through the stock market. The major sub-markets of the corporate bond market will conceivably include: (i) infrastructures and utilities, (ii) housing, and (iii) long-term corporate investments (See Figure 2).

2.2.   *Microeconomic comparisons*

2.2.1.   *Comparison with equity*

The economy will generally grow faster with corporations being financially leveraged. A corporation's growth pace and potential will be significantly hampered unless debt capital is efficiently available to corporations. The reasons for this include (i) fear of ownership dilution through equity financing, and (ii) expensiveness of equity capital relative to debt capital.

While their financial resources are not unlimited, controlling shareholders in general do not want to dilute their equity stake in corporations, let alone lose it, by raising additional equity capital for expansion from outside the existing shareholders. If banks' lending capacity is constrained, the existing shareholders may choose not to make additional investments for the corporation's future. Furthermore, as has been discussed in Section 2.1. "Macroeconomic roles" if banks recklessly accommodate corporations' long-term investments with their short-term liabilities, that is, deposits, the banking system of the country will become vulnerable to external shocks.

Equity capital is usually costlier than debt capital to a corporation. This is attributable to at least two factors. First, equity investment is by definition riskier than debt investment, and, therefore, the equity investor demands a higher return than the debt investor. Second, interest expenses on debt are usually tax-deductible at a corporate level, whereas corporate profits are usually taxed before dividends on shares are paid to shareholders or internally retained.

2.2.2.   *Comparison with bank loans*

Private enterprises have usually two ways to issue debt: taking loans from banks and issuing bonds in a capital market. These two debt-financing avenues are termed indirect financing and direct financing. Besides each avenue's unique role in a macroeconomic picture as briefly discussed above, their differences can been seen at a corporate level. Table 1 below compares the typical characteristics of publicly offered bonds and bank loans in a well-developed capital market.

This quick comparison suggests that bonds generally serve better for long-term, sizable and opportunistic financing while bank loans for short-term, small-sized and constant financing. On a company's balance sheet, bonds are more suitable to finance its fixed asset accounts and investments, whereas bank loans are more suitable to support its current asset accounts, such as inventories.

It is worth noting that bond financing normally requires its issuer to have better cash management skills at a corporate level in order to reap its intended benefits of cost effectiveness. An irregular pattern of cash flows arising from a company's long-term project inevitably does not match a regular pattern of bond cash flows, namely, issue proceeds, interest payments and principal redemption. Project cash flows tend to be highly complex, whereas bond cash flows are normally very simple. As such, it is the company's treasury department that undertakes an on-going task of optimally managing a series of the cash flow deviations through tactical investment or borrowing on a short-term basis. Ineffective management of the short-term cash flow deviations would significantly defeat the purpose of long-term bond financing. Therefore, the development of corporate finance knowledge and skills on the part of issuing corporations is indispensable for the development of corporate bond markets.

Table 1: Publicly Offered Bonds vs Bank Loans

	Publicly Offered Bonds	Bank Loans
Size of financing	Substantially large. No particular limit. A smaller issue size is impractical.	Smaller unless syndicated. Limited by a credit line available to a borrower, industry, country and other category to which the borrower belongs
Term	Usually one year or longer	Usually shorter and rolled over. Limited by credit policy of a bank
Repayment	Bullet or limited prepayment patters. Generally inflexible.	Generally flexible.
Interest rate	Fixed or floating rates	Floating rates for long maturities
All-in cost	Normally cheaper, depending on market conditions. Very cheap for opportunistic deals.	Normally more expensive.
Swap	Available	Available
Structured financing	Widely available	Limited
Credit analysis	Standardized rating by rating agencies	Proprietary credit analysis by a bank
Security	Normally unsecured	Normally secured
Use of proceeds	Normally not restricted	Normally restricted
Listing	Either listed or non-listed	Non-listed
Creditors	"Unspecific, many" investors, including individuals, corporations, banks, insurance companies, pension funds, mutual funds, etc.	A small number of banks and some other financial institutions
Transferability & Liquidity	Readily transferable, and limited liquidity except for "major" issuers	Not transferable, and no liquidity

Note: Each individual bonds and loans may have characteristics different from the generalized descriptions above.

3.   Overview of Corporate Bond Markets

3.1.   *Developed countries*

Corporate bond markets in developed countries have some salient characteristics that may be different from common perceptions about them. The salient characteristics are summarized as follows:

1. The corporate bond market in the United States is far larger, presumably due to the historical background of the country's financial system;

2. Corporate bond markets in non-US developed countries, which have been on the increase, are dominated by issuance by financial institutions rather than non-financial ones;

3. Liquidity of secondary markets for corporate bonds in developed countries is generally marginal except for a limited number of "major issues" (as will be discussed in detail later); therefore, corporate bond market activities in developed countries are centered on the primary market;

4. Institutional investors, rather than individual investors, are ascendant in corporate bond markets in developed countries; and,

5. Historically, the development of corporate bond markets in developed countries was preceded by that of government bond markets, which had been long preceded by years of capital accumulation through industrial developments.

Among developed countries, the United States has distinct features with respect to its corporate bond market. First, it has a unique historical background for development of the corporate bond market. Second, its debt market as a whole is far larger than those in Western European countries and Japan.

Business of commercial banks in the United States had been long confined within their states. Moreover, nearly half the states required a bank to do all its business from one location under so-called unit banking rules. Interstate banking was legalized in 1994[1]. Therefore, banks' lending capacity had been so limited that banks had not been able to sufficiently meet funding needs of companies that nationally expanded their business, let alone their long-term capital. As a result, the corporate bond market in conjunction with the stock market developed as a mechanism through which to raise capital from across the country as well as from abroad.

The debt securities markets in Western European countries and Japan are much smaller than those in the United States, not only in dollar amount, but also in terms of percentage of their GDPs (see Table 2). Table 3 illustrates that bonds issued by financial institutions were also predominant in non-US developed countries. This is typical of Germany. According to Table 2, the outstanding amount of corporate bonds in Germany accounted for 55.1% of the total debt securities outstanding, as compared to 40.9% in the United States. However, it is evident from Table 4 that most German corporate bonds were those issued by financial institutions, namely, banks, and non-financial corporate bonds were miniscule. Non-financial corporate debt issues in Japan were second to the United States, and were steadily rising relative to financial corporate debt issues, remained at about half that of the United States, in terms of the percentage.

Table 2: Selected Industrial Countries –

Domestic Debt Securities by Nationality of Issuers (1997)

(In US$ Billion)

	France	Germany	Italy	Japan	The Netherlands	UK	USA	Total
GDP	1,392.5	2,089.9	1,139.0	4,197.4	362.6	1,312.3	8,110.9	18,604.6
Total Debt Securities	1,113.2	1,730.0	1,471.7	4,433.7	227.8	767.8	12,414.6	22,158.8
Against GDP	*79.9%*	*82.8%*	*129.2%*	*105.6%*	*62.8%*	*58.5%*	*153.1%*	*119.1%*
Public Sector	647.4	777.5	1,123.4	3,116.8	177.5	465.4	7,337.1	13,645.1
Against GDP	*46.5%*	*37.2%*	*98.6%*	*74.3%*	*49.0%*	*35.5%*	*90.5%*	*73.3%*
Against Total Debt Securities	*58.2%*	*44.9%*	*76.3%*	*70.3%*	*77.9%*	*60.6%*	*59.1%*	*61.6%*
Private Sector	465.8	952.5	348.3	1,316.9	50.3	302.4	5,077.5	8,513.7
Against GDP	*33.5%*	*45.6%*	*30.6%*	*31.4%*	*13.9%*	*23.0%*	*62.6%*	*45.8%*
Against Total Debt Securities	*41.8%*	*55.1%*	*23.7%*	*29.7%*	*22.1%*	*39.4%*	*40.9%*	*38.4%*

Source: Table 1 in Schinasi and Smith (1998) and World Economic Outlook database

Table 3: Debt Securities Financing by Non-Financial Firms in Selected Industrial Countries

(As a percentage of total funds raised in financial markets)

	Germany	Italy	Japan	The Netherlands	USA
1990	0.0%	0.2%	14.2%	3.4%	48.6%
1991	0.0%	1.0%	10.4%	-2.5%	33.5%
1992	0.1%	0.2%	4.6%	-0.1%	18.2%
1993	0.0%	-6.5%	7.1%	12.0%	10.6%
1994	0.0%	-2.9%	11.5%	-	27.7%

Source: Table 3 in Schinasi and Smith (1998). Original sources: OECD, *Financial Statistics*: Non-Financial Enterprises Financial Satements (Part III); R. Todd Smith, "Markets or Corporate Debt Securities", IMF, Working Paper No.95/67; Deutsche Bank, *KapitalMarket Statistik* Notes: For Germany, does not include international issues of bonds. For Italy and the Netherlands, does not include commercial paper.

Table 4: Debt Securities of Non-Financial Corporate Sector Relative to Financial Sector

	Germany	Japan	USA
1992	0.3%	34.7%	119.0%
1993	0.2%	33.9%	107.0%
1994	0.2%	37.1%	97.7%
1995	0.2%	40.1%	89.4%
1996	0.2%	41.3%	81.5%

From Table 5 in Schinasi and Smith (1998). Originally from Federal Reserve Bulletin; Deustche Bundesbank Monthly Report; Bank of Japan, Economic Statistics. Note that non-financial sector debt securities include bonds and commercial paper outstanding, and financial sector debt securities include bonds an short-term paper.

As will be analyzed later in Section 4. "Major" and Minor" Corporate Issuers" and Section 5. "Primary Corporate Debt Markets", the majority of corporate bonds, once they are purchased and settled in institutional investors' portfolios, upon issuance or during a short period of time after issuance, do not change hands until their maturities. Even in the US market, more than 95% of corporate bond issues outstanding have no trade at all in the secondary market. Nonetheless, corporations raised US$ 663.1 billion and 861.3 billion in 1997 and 1998 respectively in the US corporate bond market[2].

Corporate bonds issued in developed countries are mainly bought by institutional investors such as insurance companies, pension funds and mutual funds. The holdings of corporate bonds by households in the United States and Japan both accounted for 12.2% of the total amounts outstanding at end of 1998; and those by non-financial corporations in the United States and Japan accounted for only 1.5% and 6.9%, respectively[3]. This is because investment of long-term debt funds idling in households and corporations can generally achieve better risk/return tradeoff through institutional investors who specialize in collecting and managing funds of specific characteristics.

3.2. *Developing countries*

3.2.1. *Different economic context*

In developed countries, the development of corporate bond markets was preceded by that of government bond markets, which in turn had been preceded by years of capital accumulation through industrial developments. If developing countries were to repeat this historical process to see their local bond markets, the current efforts to develop corporate bond markets would be irrelevant to most developing countries unless they have already achieved a relatively high level of economic development. In fact, they have not.

We should realize that we are now trying to weave a corporate bond market into developing countries' economy at an earlier stage of economic development, that is, under an economic context different from that of developed countries. For example, the economy in developing countries for which we formulate and implement a strategy for their corporate bond markets is generally much smaller in size than that in developed countries. This suggests that a strategy for a developing country's corporate bond market might differ from the historical process that corporate bond markets in developing countries have been going through in certain aspects such as the design of market framework and infrastructures, and in the sequence of institutional building.

3.2.2. *Comparison with developed countries*

Most corporate bond markets in developing countries are fledgling and small, even relative to their own GDPs. Table 5 shows how marginal local corporate bond markets are in comparison with other financial markets, and Figure 3-B illustrates the developing countries' anomalous dependence on bank loans. Out of the ten developing countries from which IFC has been able to collect reliable statistics on their debt markets, only Malaysia and Korea exceed 10% of their GDPs in the relative size of their corporate bond markets. In Korea, a majority of corporate bond issues, though the issuers were reasonably diverse[4], had guarantees from commercial banks[5], and, therefore, they can be regarded as another kind of bank loan. Another example of commercial banks' significant involvement in a corporate bond market is the Czech Republic, where bonds issued by commercial banks account for 77% of all corporate bonds issued from February 1997 to October 1999[6].

A picture of corporate bond markets in developing countries gets clearer when we compare them with those in developed countries. Therefore, an attempt will be made here to illustrate some conceivably salient characteristics of corporate bond markets in selected developing countries in comparison with those in developed countries despite some limitations and inconsistency of the data[7]. Table 5 was compiled from various data sources to show the 1998 nominal GDPs, their common logarithms, the US dollar amounts and percentages of GDPs for equities and bonds outstanding in selected developing and developed countries[8] for 1998 or at the end of 1998 with some exceptions.

Table 6 shows correlation coefficients between the relative sizes of corporate bonds on one side and, equities, bank claims on the private sector (as a proxy for bank loans to corporations) or government bonds on the other, on the basis of the data in Table 5. The coefficients of correlation were calculated separately for the developed countries, the developing countries and all the countries. In Figure 3 are scatter diagrams of the same variables.

244

Table 5: GDPs, Equities, Government Bonds, Corporate Bonds in Selected Developing and Developed Countries

(US$ Bil., % of GDP)

Country	GDP	Log10	Total Equities		Bank Claims on Private Sector		Total Bonds		Government Bonds		Corporate Bonds	
Czech Republic	$56.0	1.75	$12.05	21.5%	$35.20	62.9%	$6.62	11.8%	$2.33	4.2%	$3.72	6.6%
Hungary	$48.0	1.68	$14.03	29.2%	$8.26	17.2%	$12.04	25.1%	$11.80	24.6%	$0.24	0.5%
India	$372.0	2.57	$105.19	28.3%	$98.79	26.6%	$108.88	29.3%	$63.07	17.0%	$16.49	4.4%
Indonesia	$92.0	1.96	$22.10	24.0%	$63.37	68.9%	$1.70	1.8%	$0.00	0.0%	$1.00	1.1%
Korea	$321.0	2.51	$114.59	35.7%	$264.67	82.5%	$277.78	86.5%	$178.46	55.6%	$99.32	30.9%
Malaysia	$72.0	1.86	$98.56	136.9%	$74.92	104.1%	$37.78	52.5%	$19.74	27.4%	$15.13	21.0%
Philippines	$65.0	1.81	$35.31	54.3%	$32.71	50.3%	$9.26	14.2%	$7.87	12.1%	$1.26	1.9%
Poland	$158.0	2.20	$20.46	13.0%	$30.84	19.5%	$12.63	8.0%	$12.63	8.0%	$0.00	0.0%
Slovak Republic	$20.0	1.30	$0.97	4.8%	$8.92	44.6%	$3.39	16.9%	$2.78	13.9%	$0.51	2.6%
Thailand	$113.0	2.05	$34.90	30.9%	$144.44	127.8%	$21.02	18.6%	$9.67	8.6%	$3.46	3.1%
France	$1,455.0	3.16	$991.48	68.1%	$1,121.82	77.1%	$1,209.90	83.2%	$731.30	50.3%	$478.60	32.9%
Germany	$2,123.0	3.33	$1,093.96	51.5%	$2,672.98	125.9%	$2,005.90	94.5%	$865.90	40.8%	$1,140.00	53.7%
Italy	$1,186.0	3.07	$569.73	48.0%	$740.64	62.4%	$1,579.90	133.2%	$1,215.60	102.5%	$364.30	30.7%
Japan	$3,787.0	3.58	$2,495.76	65.9%	$5,046.28	133.3%	$5,213.60	137.7%	$3,700.50	97.7%	$1,513.10	40.0%
The Netherlands	$378.0	2.58	$603.18	159.6%	$468.73	124.0%	$243.60	64.4%	$199.40	52.8%	$44.20	11.7%
UK	$1,399.0	3.15	$2,374.27	169.7%	$1,690.47	120.8%	$852.80	61.0%	$464.30	33.2%	$388.50	27.8%
USA	$8,511.0	3.93	$13,451.35	158.0%	$5,412.90	63.6%	$13,973.20	164.2%	$8,002.40	94.0%	$5,970.80	70.2%

Sources: JPMorgan, *World Financial Markets*; Institute of International Finance (IIF); IFC, *Emerging Stock Markets Factbook 1999*; IMF, *International Financial Statistics*; IFC, Emerging Markets Information Center Bond Database; BIS, *International Banking and Financial Market Developments*.

Notes:
1) GDP figures are Nominal GDP for 1998 from JPMorgan's *World Financial Markets* (except Slovakia).
2) GDP figure for the Slovak Republic is Nominal GDP for 1998 from the Institute of International Finance (IIF).
3) Equities figures are for December 1998 and are from IFC's *Emerging Stock Markets Factbook 1999*.
4) Bank claims on the private sector are from the IMF's *International Financial Statistics* and are for end-1998 (except France and the Netherlands, end-first quarter 1999, and Hungary, end-third quarter 1996). The amounts shown are US$ equivalents for local currency denominated bank claims. Bank claims are the closest available proxy for bank loans, although claims could also other claims, such as, equity securities. Claims on the private sector, therefore, should approximate to loans to the private sector.
5) Bond figures for the ten developing countries include only debt securities with initial maturities of at least one year and are from IFC's Emerging Markets Information Center Bond Database. All data as of December 1998, except India (March 1998) and the Philippines (December 1997). Figures for the Slovak Republic are estimates. The amounts shown are US$ equivalents for local currency denominated bonds.
6) Bond figures for the seven developed countries are debt securities of all maturities, not just bonds, and are for December 1998 from BIS's *International Banking and Financial Market Developments*.

Using the same data, Table 7 shows correlation coefficients between the common logarithms of the 1998 nominal GDPs on one side and, equities, bank claims on private sector, total bonds (government plus corporate bonds), government bonds or corporate bonds on the other. In Figure 4 are scatter diagrams of the same variables.

The table and figure reveal very interesting relationships of the absolute size of a country's GDP with different financial sub-markets. First, the logarithmic size of the GDP has little relationship with the relative sizes of equity or bank loans, except with the inverse relationship between bank loans market in developed countries. This also supports a corporate bond market's partial substitutability for a bank loan market. Second, the size of a country's corporate bond market relative to its GDP is directly correlated to its logarithmic size of the GDP, and, it may be more so as the economy gets larger. This may be interpreted to imply that economic development will be accompanied by an increasing role of a corporate bond market, and also that a larger population of a country will likely make the relative size of a corporate bond market larger. In other words, a country with a small population may not have potential for a sizable corporate bond market unless its per capita income increases drastically.

245

Table 6: Correlation Coefficients between Market Sizes – Corporate Bonds vs Equities, Bank Loans, or Gov't Bonds

	Corporate Bonds as % of GDPs of Countries		
% of GNPs for	All	Developed	Developing
Equities	0.5038	-0.1099	0.5108
Bank Claims on P/S	0.4235	-0.3195	0.4694
Gov't Bonds	0.7749	0.3163	0.8477

Figure 3: Market Sizes – Corporate Bonds vs Equities, Bank Loans, or Gov't Bonds

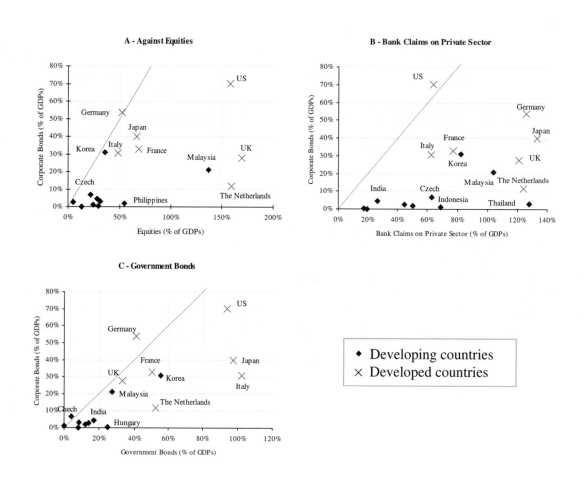

Summing up the analyses above, Table 8 outlines policy implications of each possible interpretation of the data for the development of corporate bond markets in developing countries.

Figure 4: Market Sizes – Equities, Bank Loans, Total Bonds, Gov't Bonds, or Corporate Bonds vs Common Logarithm of GDPs

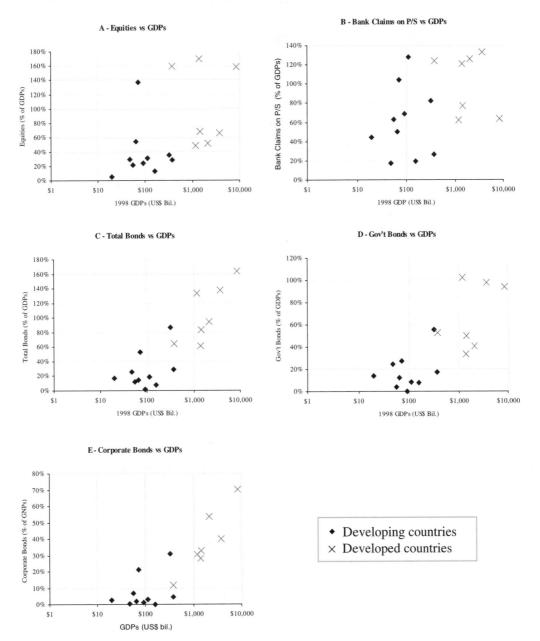

Table 7: Correlation Coefficients between Market Sizes – Equities, Bank Loans, Total Bonds, Gov't Bonds, or Corporate Bonds vs Common Logarithm of GDPs

% of GNPs for	Common Logarithm of GDPs of Countries		
	All	Developed	Developing
Equities	0.4998	-0.0770	0.0107
Bank Claims on P/S	0.4184	-0.2678	0.0544
Total Bonds	0.8713	0.7788	0.4373
Gov't Bonds	0.7899	0.4622	0.3690
Corporate Bonds	0.8685	0.9161	0.3797

Table 8: Policy Implications for Corporate Bond Market Development

Possible Interpretations of the Data	Policy Implications
A country's financial system in general and the government bond market in particular need to be at a certain level of development prior to corporate bond market development, especially at an earlier stage of economic development.	Corporate bond market development should be introduced in a bid later stage, but preemptively geared into the whole financial market development. It should timely follow the developments of commercial banking and a government bond market.
The corporate bond market in a country can substitute part of the bank loan market, and is potentially able to relieve the stressed banking system in a developing country of unbearable burden.	Corporate bond market development should be designed into restructuring of the banking system. An incentive mechanism should be devised to alleviate resistance from the commercial banking sector against a rapid development of a corporate bond market.
Economic development will be accompanied by an increasing role of a corporate bond market.	Unlike the developed countries that completed their capital accumulation process in a pre-open economy era, the underdevelopment of the corporate bond market in a developing country may risk the country's economic development itself in the environments of an open economy.
A larger population of a country will likely make the relative size of a corporate bond market larger. (A country with a small population may not have potential for a sizable corporate bond market unless its per capita income increases drastically.)	Economic unification may enhance the potential for corporate bond market development. Though it is a politically challenging task, an example is UEMOA (Union économique et monétaire ouest-africaine) in the West Africa.

248

There are some direct relationships between the relative size of the corporate bond market in a country and the relative size of the equity, bank loan, or government bond markets[9] in the same country. The three markets are usually instituted ahead of a corporate bond market. Furthermore, the direct correlation coefficients are considerably higher in the developing countries than the developed countries (0.5108 against -0.1099, and 0.8477 against 0.3163). These may imply that a country's financial system, including equity, bank loan and government bond markets, needs to be at a certain level of development prior to corporate bond market development, especially in an earlier stage of economic development. The leading role of the government bond market is more patent.

The relationship between the bank loan and corporate bond markets in developed countries is invert (-0.3195), while that in developing countries is direct (0.4694). This suggests the substitutability of corporate bonds for bank loans probably in a longer end of the yield curve, and supports the potential ability of a corporate bond market to relieve the banking system in a developing country of unbearable burden.

4.   "Major" and "Minor" Corporate Issuers[10]

It is essential to distinguish between "major" and "minor" issuers of corporate bonds in apprehending the functions of corporate bond markets, especially in the context of developing countries. The distinction presumably makes it easier for policymakers in developing countries to lay out the development strategy for a debt market as a whole in a country. The two categories of issuers and their bonds substantially differ from each other in their evolving process and subsequent roles in a country's bond market. Major corporate issuers can enjoy a liquid secondary market of their corporate bonds, depending on the actual microstructure of the market and the portfolio investment demand available for their bonds. The trading volume of their bonds on the secondary market may get large enough for the bonds' secondary market prices to form a benchmark yield curve. In contrast, bonds issued by minor issuers will hardly be liquid. However, their inherent illiquidity on the secondary market will in no way lessen the importance of a corporate bond market to minor issuers as a long-term funding source. Both major and minor issuers benefit from the corporate bond market. We have every reason to have a corporate bond market developed for both major and minor issuers.

4.1.   Major corporate bond issuers

"Major" corporate bond issuers mean those issuers who provide the investors with a regular, sizable and stable supply of bonds of high quality and uniform characteristics through public offerings. They are "impatient traders" with a high demand for immediacy. They issue their bonds almost on a regular basis, say, every week, every month, or every quarter, so that the investors can reasonably anticipate when the bonds will be available for sale. Their issue timing is basically cyclical and somewhat indifferent to ever changing market conditions so that they can meet funding needs that are constantly arising from their business operations. They are not opportunistic. Under normal circumstances, their issue size is large enough to universally meet the demand for the bonds across the market. Their issue sizes are relatively stable; and they should not surprise the investors with unexpectedly large or small issues. They are financially strong and competently manage their business operations so that their ability to pay interest and principal on their bonds in a timely manner is well trusted by the investors. The high quality is conveniently expressed with a rating symbol such as "AAA" or "Aaa". Their different issues, which hit the market one after another, have the same legal claim, coupon type and maturity. For instance, they are always unsecured, fixed coupon rate, straight 3-, 5- or 10-year bonds. Ideally, some of them should be made fungible[11] by reopening outstanding issues at consecutive auctions.

As a result, major corporate bonds will be widely held in the market. The chances are high that, when one investor holding specific major bonds wants to sell them, there is another investor who is willing to buy them, and once the both parties agree upon the price, quantity of the bonds and other terms, a trade occurs. They are likely to be actively traded on the secondary market if the market is properly designed and maintained.

Suitable candidates for major corporate issuers are (i) infrastructure and utility companies, (ii) housing finance companies, and (iii) development finance companies. All the three kinds of companies are those strategic enterprises that are first needed for social and industrial developments in developing economies. Furthermore, they tend to have a regular, sizable and stable demand for long-term funds. Properly structured and operated, therefore, they will likely be able to provide investors with a regular, sizable and stable supply of bonds of high quality and uniform characteristics through public offerings. Their suitability as a major corporate issuer will be further analyzed later in Section 8.1. "Likely candidates for major corporate issuers".

4.2. *Minor corporate bond issuers*

"Minor" corporate bond issuers lack the characteristics of "major" bond issuers. For example, they may be of high quality in terms of creditworthiness but tap the bond market only irregularly. Their bond issues tend to be either small in size or opportunistic in timing, or both. This is probably because their long-term funding needs are not constant and arise only sporadically, which allows them to be patient and opportunistic. They may be termed as "patient traders" with a lower demand for immediacy. Opportunistic issuers' bond issues may be diverse in characteristics of the bonds, because such issuers hit the bond market only when a very attractive financing window opens to meet specific, short-lived investment needs of a specific type of investors. Their bonds are unlikely to trade frequently on the secondary market after they are initially placed on the primary market, not because the market infrastructures are not properly in place but simply because they themselves are fundamentally short of those prerequisites that "major" bonds have for being actively traded.

Many developing countries, which are faced with weak banking systems and constrained public finances, consider financing construction projects of badly needed social infrastructures by issuing asset-backed bonds in their capital markets. For example, these bond issues, if structured to recourse only, or primarily, to the project cash flows and assets (non- or limited recourse financing), will likely be minor issues.

Even in the US capital market, only 4 percent of about 400,000 corporate issues outstanding in 1996 traded even once that year[12]. This striking reality provides us with two insights into corporate bond markets. First, only a handful of corporate issuers in the market are likely to fall in the category of "major" issuers, and the rest belong to the category of "minor" issuers. Second, in spite of the inherent illiquidity of minor corporate bond issues, the primary market of minor issuers has been playing an enormous role in supplying long-term funds to a country's private sector.

5. Primary Corporate Debt Markets

5.1. *Primary-market-centric minor corporate issues*

An immediate issue with respect to most corporate debt issues in developing countries is how to facilitate their bond issuance in the primary market, but not to develop their liquid secondary market as is often perceived. This is because the "buy and hold" strategy is reasonably legitimate for investments in corporate debt securities.

5.1.1.   Buy and hold

It is obvious that most corporate bond issuers, or their issues, cannot meet the stringent criteria for "major" corporate bond issuers or issues. Hence, they are "minor". The term "minor" no way means that such issuers are marginal in their country's economic development. Simply, their financing patterns in the debt market do not qualify for "major" corporate issuers or issues. Typically, their individual issues are too small in size for exactly identical debt securities to be extensively distributed among a wide range of investors across the economy, and frequently change hands.

Figure 5: Liquid/Illiquid Parts of Investment Portfolio

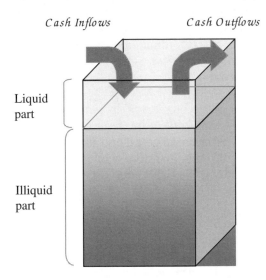

Money that frequently inflows and outflows is marginal to the whole investment portfolio. The rest does not need to stay liquid at all

The "buy and hold" strategy is generally legitimate for corporate debt securities. Institutional investors usually buy them usually in a large lot through public offerings and/or in the secondary market, and hold them to maturity. A substantial part of the institutional investor's investment portfolio does not need to be kept liquid all the time. Money that frequently inflows and outflows is marginal to the whole portfolio. The rest or residual part is relatively illiquid funds at least in a certain period of time, if not forever. Its actual size varies and fluctuates, depending on investment objectives, restrictions, strategy of the fund, the outlook for market conditions, and other factors (see Figure 5). As for this illiquid part of the portfolio, the institutional investor would be better off investing in higher yield bonds, that is, minor corporate bonds, at the expense of their liquidity and credit quality to the extent that its risk tolerance parameters, or other investment restrictions, permit. Minor corporate bonds are basically illiquid and tend to be of a lower credit quality, and yield higher returns than either government bonds or major corporate bonds to compensate for these disadvantages. If the investor tries hard to sell them in the secondary market, its market impact will get larger (in other words, its selling price will get lower) than major corporate bonds of the same amount due to their relative illiquidity, and will likely result in a lower realized rate of return. This risk would further discourage the investor to sell them prior to maturity and encourage it to hold them to maturity.

Only when a country's capital market development reaches a highly sophisticated level, where institutional investors are systematically pressed for better fund management performance, major corporate debt issues and some minor corporate issues will be frequently traded in the secondary market. Until that time, most corporate debt securities are just transferable when badly needed to trade, but not liquid most of the time. Consequently, the efficiency of the primary market is the single most critical issue for corporate debt market development in developing countries except in the case of major corporate issues, including benchmark debt securities.

5.1.2. *Specific investment needs, specific types of issues*

There is no question that, ideally, all corporate bond issues should have their liquid secondary markets. However, as has been repeatedly emphasized, it is far from realistic. Only a few corporate bond issuers can be "major" corporate bond issuers whose bonds are frequently traded in the secondary market. The factor most responsible for illiquidity of most corporate bond issues is that their individual issues are small in size. Nevertheless, small issue sizes are convenient to effectively fulfill specific investment needs of investors.

Different investors operate under different settings in terms of investment objectives, preferences, capacities, constraints and others. A single event inside or outside the market will affect the investors' portfolios in different manners, to different degrees, and in different timings. Some events will bring about widely different impacts on different investors, while some others will give a relatively uniform effect across the universe of investors. A wide variety of responses to a series of events inside and outside the market will result in a whole range of investment needs. Each investor will also sporadically have internal events that are independent of its externalities but affect its investment stance. In addition, the market will continue to remain somewhat imperfect, despite all policy initiatives. As a result, some investment needs may be very unique or delicately different, though some others may happen to be pretty alike. Interestingly, very unique investment or funding needs are often driven by motives for tax savings and/or accounting window-dressings.

All these phenomena will create a row of different and short-lived opportunities where shrewd corporate issuers can selectively exploit with best-matching products. In some cases, investors are willing to pay some premium for their very particular needs to be satisfied. Conversely, issuers will also be faced with unique or delicately different funding needs from time to time, and some of them are ready to pay some premium for their very specific needs to be met. Evidently, most of such deals are not very large in size. Because they are particular in characteristics, they will poorly substitute for other issues. Once they are bought by particular investors at particular times, they are most likely to be held until maturity. Their liquidity is naturally low.

No matter how rare it is to have a liquid secondary market for these "minor" corporate bonds, their primary pricing should be made in reference to the prevailing yield of the benchmark issue (the "on-the-run" issue) with a comparable maturity, rationally adjusted for particular characteristics of funding or investment needs. It is this principle that makes the whole primary market activities coherent and their economies measurable.

In order to meet these particular needs arising from either temporary or long-lasting market imperfections of various kinds, investment banks have been inventing a wide range of debt instruments, in addition to fine-tuning parameters of individual instruments for specific clientele. Some instruments are long established and well accepted in the market. Some others sound very exotic. These include commercial paper, certificates of deposits, floating rate notes, zero-coupon bonds, deep-discount bonds, perpetual bonds, secured or unsecured bonds, convertible bonds, bonds with equity warrants, mortgage-back securities, asset-backed securities, index-linked bonds, medium-term notes, dual-currency bonds, reverse dual currency bonds, and catastrophe bonds.

The variety of debt instruments means that each bond issue has unique contractual features. Some of them are also complex and will expose investors to unique risks. This gives rise to the importance of accurate and comprehensible disclosure of product information in the case of debt issues[13].

Through these issuing and investing activities mainly in the primary market, investors and issuers will continuously match up each other's long-term financial needs in a practical and rational way. All in all, an efficient primary market of corporate bonds, even though their trading in the secondary market is miniscule, still makes unparalleled contributions to the developing economies. Their contributions encompass (i) alleviating stresses on the banking system by diversifying credit risks in the economy, (ii) procuring long-term debt capital for long-term investments, and (iii) reallocating capital efficiently.

5.1.3. *Incessant competition*

Investors and corporate issuers, major or minor alike, are actively generating, or passively being faced with, specific investment and financing needs under quickly changing business environments including financial market conditions. Developing economies have been more or less financially integrated with the international markets, and are constantly interacting with them. As such, most opportunities are generally short-lived, limited by time and size. In the primary market, therefore, investors are competing with each other for better but finite opportunities, for investment provided by issuers. They are also racing against time. The reverse holds true for issuers. This competitive situation in the primary market is illustrated in Figure 6.

It is under the incessantly competitive circumstances that investors and issuers are required to make investment or financing decisions. As such, anything that hampers their clear-eyed and nimble decision-making will undermine their confidence in the primary market.

5.2. *Impediments to primary market development*

5.2.1. *Statutory restrictions*

Ironically, the primary market is more subject to governmental interference than the secondary market, because it is the entry point of securities into the market and thus the very first checkpoint for investor protection. The statutory restrictions are usually imposed around either the market participants' eligibility or product features, or both. Such government inference often ends up with a merit regime[14].

Figure 6: Incessant Competition for Better Opportunities

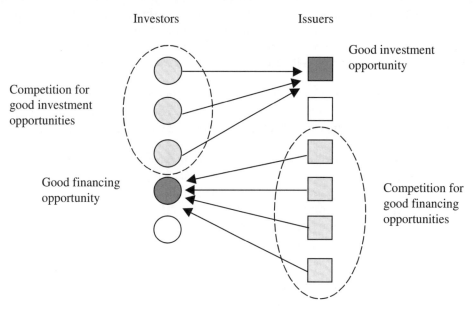

In a marketplace, investors are competing with each other for better investment opportunities provided by issuers, and issuers are also competing with each other for better financing opportunities provided by issuers.

Table 9 summarizes (i) some typical restrictions that the government in a developing country often imposes on the primary market of corporate bonds, (ii) possible, hidden motives behind the restrictions, and (iii) possible negative impacts of the restrictions on debt market development. Usually, all these statutory restrictions have plausible but ostensible policy objectives, which often disguise their true intentions and/or negative effects. Possible motives behind those statutory restrictions can be categorized as follows:

- protection of vested interests of market intermediaries,

- preservation of the existing tax base,

- capital control, and,

- bureaucratic inefficiency.

Table 9: Examples of Statutory Restrictions Impeding to Primary Market Development

Restrictive areas	Restrictions	Possible, Hidden Motives behind the restrictions	Possible Negative Impacts on Debt Market Development
Product features	No short term	Shorter-ends are not allowed to avoid conflicts with banking products.	No reliable/natural anchor for the yield curve, and will distort the yield curve
	Cap on coupon rates	Keep the general level of interest rates low	Will hamper the formation of a yield curve
	No floating rate	Limited competition with bank deposits	Limited hedging tools against interest rate risks
	No/restrictive unsecured bonds	Unsecured bonds may undermine banks' demand for collateral to their loans.	Disadvantageous to new, fast growing companies and non-capital intensive companies
	No forex-linked bonds	Capital control	Will limit hedging tools against interest rate risks
Issuer's eligibility	Credit rating-linked eligibility for bond issuance	To avoid conflict with banks in a lucrative mid-market.	Will limit free risk/return tradeoff; disadvantageous to low-rated companies
	Cap on debt issue amount Queuing system	Bureaucratic investor protection in the absence of a well-accepted rating system. Banks may benefit from this restriction.	Will limit free risk/return tradeoff
Underwriter's eligibility	Too strict or no license for new entrants including commercial banks and/or foreign underwriters	Protection of vested interests of existing	Will limit competition and innovation
Taxation	Withholding tax Stamp duties	Conflict or dilemma with a weak tax collection system	Will fragment the market and limit the liquidity
Others	Ban on swap Ban on futures & options	Bureaucratic investor protection in the absence of financial expertise and well-organized risk management systems at regulatory and corporate levels.	Will limit hedging tools against interest rate risks, and arbitrage activities

The development of corporate bond markets may erode some part of business interests of banks. Commercial banks have often grown into such heavy-duty market powers that they are politically powerful by the time a corporate bond market is eventually given birth. Mistakenly feeling threatened by the securities industry, they are tempted to politically defend their turf in the "old garden". However, we have already discussed the macroeconomic as well as microeconomic necessities of corporate bond markets to defuse potentially unbearable stress on the financial system in a developing country, and complement the banking industry for the country's more efficient economic development. Policymakers in a developing country should be aware of the risks of administering compromise policies in this regard.

Another possible concentration of market power that may impede the primary market of corporate bonds can be found in a country's securities industry itself. Existing intermediaries like investment banks and brokerage houses may have built up significant vested interests through a banking/brokerage segregation policy like the Glass-Steagall Act in the United States. They may resist changes to existing market structures and environments that have effectively barred new entrants such as commercial banks and foreign investment banks from posing strong competition to them.

Taxes on securities transactions are another common impediment. If the country cannot repeal them in the short run, harmonization efforts of tax obligation across the investment community may be a practical solution; and, policymakers may find that the actual and potential investment community is much more dispersed (and fragmented) than they initially assumed.

Lengthy vetting of filed securities registration statements is in all likelihood not an intended restriction. It is a by-product of a statutory action to effectuate disclosure requirements. Nonetheless, the inefficient regulatory action virtually turns out to be a *de facto* statutory restriction in that it actually prohibits issuers from expeditiously grabbing short-lived financing opportunities. In addition to making vetting operation at the regulatory authority efficient through staff training and other means, a shelf registration system[15] may as well be instituted.

5.2.2.   Lack of Market Infrastructures

Besides statutory restrictions, there are vital market infrastructures whose absence, deficiency or inefficiency in a country may practically impede the country's primary market development. They include (i) disclosure and information system, (ii) credit rating system, (iii) intermediaries, (iv) institutional investors, (v) trading system and (vi) clearing and depository system. These topics will be discussed later in Section: 6; Development Components".

5.2.3.   Distraction by an equity boom

An equity market binge in a financially immature country, coupled with insufficient understanding of modern corporate finance principles, may easily deviate the country's corporate debt market development from its planned course. In a booming economy in a developing country, for instance, the majority of investors, being fascinated by handsome capital gains potential, will get overly indifferent to risks inherent in equity investments and zealously buy up stocks. Corporate managers, being naïvely lured by a super-low interest rate and/or dividend yield, will lavishly float equity or equity-linked securities such as common shares, convertible bonds, and bonds with equity warrants to raise superficially low-cost capital, by ignoring hidden, ultimately expensive, costs to their shareholders. Few market participants will bother to contemplate financing with or investments in straight debt securities. Cool-headed capital structure selections all will pale into insignificance beside stock market euphoria. No serious need for the primary market of corporate debt will be felt.

In the worst case, corporate managers entrusted with more-than-needed equity capital under loose corporate governance will be liable to make lax risk assessments and poor investments. Losing their traditional clients to the equity market, banks will become imprudently aggressive in lending loans. All this will most likely end up with overbuilt capacity, massive bad loans, and finally, economic crisis.

It has been pointed out earlier that the development of corporate finance knowledge and skills on the part of issuing corporations is indispensable for the development of corporate bond markets. Additionally, if education can tame greed, systematic education on the rational relationship of equity, loans and bonds --- a theory of corporate capital structure and investment --- will be desirable to reduce the distracting impact of a booming equity market on the development of primary markets for corporate debt securities. The recent equity market boom in the United States has never distracted the issuance of corporate debt securities.

6. Developmental components

Developmental components for a corporate bond market are those market infrastructures that are so essential that their absence, deficiency or inefficiency in a country may practically impede the market development and/or substantially impair the functioning of the market. They include but are not limited to (i) a disclosure and information system, (ii) a credit rating system, (iii) bankruptcy laws, (iv) intermediaries, (v) institutional investors, (vi) a trading system and (vii) a clearing and depository system. Out of these developmental components, a disclosure and information system, a credit rating system, and bankruptcy laws are peculiar to non-government bond markets in general and a corporate bond market in particular. The other components are relevant to a corporate bond market, too. However, they will have to be properly established for a highly liquid market of government bonds or *de facto* benchmark bonds that are usually antecedent to the development of a corporate bond market. Therefore, our discussion on them in this section will be limited to a few aspects of those components that are worth noting in connection with corporate bond market developments.

6.1. Disclosure system and information

There is no question that fair disclosure about the issuer and the securities it is offering to the public is vital to fund raising through securities issuance in the capital market. If our memory is not short, we should remember that some arbitrary, incomprehensive, unsystematic and cherry-picking disclosure practices on the part of the issuer, and undemanding, compromising, imprudent and unanalytical investment practices on the part of the investor helped form a basis for the Asian Crisis and finally led almost every market participant to pay the price. In addition, it is essential to view disclosure issues in a broader perspective for the sake of corporate bond market development: (i) disclosure system vs merit system, (ii) the enforcement of regulatory or statutory disclosure, (iii) the promotion of voluntary disclosure, and (iv) the development of information service professions.

6.1.1. Disclosure system vs merit system

Our emphasis on economic development through private sector investments unequivocally demands efficient allocation of financial resources. This generally requires a socio-economic framework in which optimal behavior of many, unspecific investors with diverse views and objectives is basically assured. A disclosure system is one of key pillars to support such a socio-economic framework.

The antithesis of a disclosure system is a merit system[16]. A merit system or its elements extant in a developing country's disclosure system has a fundamental root in the mixture of (i) a policy-based development strategy, (ii) two elements latent in a capital market mechanism, *i.e.,* a direct exposure of inventors to issuer's risks and a socially broad base of fund contributors (investors), and (iii) a populist inclination of democratic political process. The combination of these factors has been long posing an enormous amount of difficulties in shifting some countries' securities market regulation from a merit system to a disclosure system. However, it is worth noting that there can be no "100% pure" disclosure system as there is a government. The point is a matter of relativity with a "pure" disclosure system and a "pure" merit system at the extreme ends of the spectrum. An ideal system is one that is reasonably close to a pure disclosure system.

A merit system, which is operated by a limited number of regulators, does not warrant the accountability of the regulators for their decisions, and induces moral hazards among market participants including investors. Hence it will protract and ultimately defeat the development of a sustainably efficient market mechanism.

A merit system in corporate bond markets is exemplified by a queuing system, a coupon rate control, eligibility criteria for issuers, restrictions on bond term, etc.

It is useful to recognize that the backdrop of populist pressures for a merit system is weaknesses in key market infrastructures that many developing countries share as impediments to capital market development. They include (i) weak law-enforcement and court system, (ii) unsophisticated/immature investors, (iii) weak intermediaries, (iv) weak credit rating system, (v) weak accounting standards and auditing system, and (vi) weak corporate governance. The balanced strengthening of these market infrastructures will ensure the materialization or "upgrading" of a disclosure system in a corporate bond market.

6.1.2. Enforcement of regulatory disclosure

The degree of regulatory disclosure requirements for debt instruments may vary by the issuing history of issuer and the scope of targeted investors. The existence of an equity market is practically a prerequisite for debt market development for disclosure practice purposes. International Accounting Standards are a good model to alleviate accounting ambiguity for regulatory disclosure. Nevertheless, the willpower and capability in a country is a key to the effectiveness of regulatory disclosure. Disclosure on debt instruments should focus on the issuer's creditworthiness rather than prosperity, and on product information.

Varying degree of required disclosure

The most fundamental regulatory disclosure practice for fund raising through a capital market is the filing of securities registration statements with the relevant authority in a country. The degree and form of required disclosure through a securities registration statement usually varies, depending on whether the securities are equity or debt (the type of securities), whether the issuer is seasoned or unseasoned in the capital market (the issuing history of issuer), whether the issue is public or private (the scope of targeted investors). Conventionally, disclosure required for a publicly offered equity by a new comer (an initial public offering) is the most stringent, and that for a privately placed debt by a repeater is the simplest. More issues surrounding the securities registration statements of corporate bond issues will be explored separately in Section 6.3. "Securities Registration system".

Equity market as a prerequisite

Listing of the issuer's stock is a continuing disclosure mechanism not only for the listed stock itself but also the issuer's corporate bonds, regardless of whether the bonds themselves are listed or not. The development of an equity market is evidently a prerequisite to that of a corporate bond market in a country. Through the initial public offering process, a company discloses its operations, financial statements and other required information to the public, and lists its shares on an exchange. Generally under its securities laws and/or, more specifically, under the listing agreement, the listed company is generally committed to make regular and periodic disclosures, as well as occasional disclosures, on the occurrence of any material events to the issuer. This statutorily and/or contractually bound flow of information in reference to the issuer's stock listing is practically the basis for the information required for investments in the issuer's debt securities. It is extremely important that disclosure requirements under the listing agreement should be adequate and duly complied with; and that, if they are not complied with, the stock exchange should be competent enough to enforce them[17].

International Accounting Standards

Typical sources of ambiguity, misunderstanding, misleading or misrepresentation with regard to the issuer's accounting information under developing country settings include: (i) consolidation of subsidiaries; (ii) related party transactions; (iii) contingent liabilities; (iv) unrealized gains and losses from securities investments and forward, swap or futures positions; (v) segment information; and (vi) leasing (finance lease). In this respect, the efforts by International Accounting Standards Committee (IASC) to set a comprehensive body of principles for enterprises undertaking cross-border offerings and listings are valuable for developing countries with capital markets to undertake the full process of preparing internationally acceptable accounting standards.

Actual willpower and capabilities

Setting high-quality accounting standards in a country is essential, but no more than the first step toward credible disclosure. The accounting standards must be rigorously interpreted and applied. The real key issue is the actual level of willpower and capacities for compliance and enforcement available in the country. It encompasses not only regulators but also auditors in the private sector. Everybody in the real business world knows that it is quite simple to fabricate business transactions and financial positions for dressing-up purposes under an ineffective and lenient auditing system.

Credit focus and product information

Disclosure for debt issuance differs from that for equity issuance in some aspects: (i) prosperity focus vs credit focus, and (ii) product information.

First, an equity investor focuses more on the issuer's potential for and likelihood of future growth and prosperity. A debt investor is more concerned with the issuer's capacity and willingness to meet its obligations. In case of asset-backed securities, the characteristics of the assets backing securities' cash flows need to be disclosed extensively so that investors can evaluate their credit risks. Credit ratings and reports from rating agencies supplement the disclosure through a listing system.

Second, the product information of debt issuance is more complex than that of equity issuance, and varies from issue to issue. Except derivatives such as equity warrants, equity issues are usually those of common shares whose characteristics are generally well stipulated in the country's company laws or commercial codes. By contrast, there is a wide range of debt instruments as discussed in Section 5.1.2. "Specific investment needs, specific types of issues". New debt products may be introduced. Each issue has a number of unique parameters such as coupon rate, issue price, maturity, early redemption, etc. In other words, each bond issue has unique contractual features. Some of them are complex and will expose investors to unique risks such as reinvestment risk, liquidity risk, tax liability risk, currency risk, credit risk besides normal market risk.

For instance, investors are naively attracted to a nominally high coupon rate of a bond without being able to evaluate risks arising embedded in that bond. A exotic feature of a bond, though legally transferable, may practically eliminate its liquidity so much that an initial investor in the bond would have to hold it to maturity or realize a substantial capital loss to induce a reluctant purchaser.

Therefore, accurate and comprehensible disclosure of product information of debt issues is imperative for a risk and return tradeoff of a bond to be correctly and easily recognized. Unreasonable damage of investors' interests as a result of inadequate, incorrect or incomprehensible disclosure on product features would hamper the development of a corporate bond market.

6.1.3. *Promotion of voluntary disclosure*

On top of regulatory disclosure, there is enormous room for making the corporate bond market more efficient through voluntary disclosure. Policymakers in developing countries should be aware of the important role that voluntary disclosure activities have been playing in the smooth functioning of developed capital markets, and should promote and facilitate such proactive information dissemination activities driven by private sector initiatives. If it is not made mandatory in a country, a credit rating system will be an indispensable part of voluntary disclosure for debt financing through bond issuance. There are three major areas identified for voluntary disclosure: (i) corporate governance, (ii) public relations through media, and (iii) investor relations.

In 1999 the OECD published the OECD Principles of Corporate Governance. These benefited from broad exposure to input from non-OECD countries, the World Bank, the International Monetary Fund, the business sector, investors, trade unions, and other interested parties. [18]

The issuer can conduct public relations through conventional mass media (press, radio and TV), international electronic media like Reuters and Bloomberg, and internet websites. Despite the importance of a cool-eyed assessment of risks and returns of investments, it is very true that investment banks generally find it easier to place bonds of a well-known issuer (a household name), and that the issuer's yield tends to be lower than an unfamiliar name. A writer-driven nature of internet[19] has made it possible for the issuer to make itself known articulately, economically, and nationally, even globally. Now, the issuer can instantaneously disseminate the contents of its annual reports including financial statements, and current event reports intact to almost every investor who is interested in the issuer's bonds.

Many issuers in developed capital markets hire in-house or outside investors relation professionals to systematically meet and communicate with the investment community, and proactively address issues that the community is concerned with, with a view to maximizing the value of their securities in the marketplace. They design and carry out regular investors relation programs and roadshows on the occasions of its securities issuance, domestically and/or internationally. The programs are targeted mainly for institutional investors but not necessarily.

6.1.4. Development of information service professions

It is commonly recognized that capital market activities demand an array of professionals such as investment bankers, lawyers, accountants, and research analysts. For the improvement of disclosure system and information quality, there are two elements whose significance should be more emphasized and whose professions should be more developed: (i) corporate accountants, and (ii) research analysts. In this connection, it is worth noting the important role of vernacular languages in developing countries.

Corporate Accountants

Information available in emerging markets is unfortunately more often inaccurate or imprecise than that available in developed markets. Why is that so? Let's compare information to an egg. In order to enjoy an egg on your dining table, the egg has to be fresh and attentively picked up at a henhouse, carefully transported on the way, and nicely cooked in a kitchen. Under the circumstances prevailing in some developing countries, information may not be new, sufficient or carefully prepared at source. Information may be damaged in the communication process, since it is so fragile and perishable that its handling requires some skill and care. Information may not be professionally analyzed and processed at a brokerage house.

Corporate accountants means those accountants who work in accounting-related areas of the bond issuer's office but do not necessarily qualify as public certified accountants (CPAs). They are responsible for day-to-day accounting operations of the issuer, and probably support a few inhouse or outside CPAs in collecting and processing accounting information at source. They may also take charge of passing the information to outside auditors, bankers, and financial analysts. It is often observed in developing countries that there is a wide gap of professional quality between a small number of prestigious CPAs and a large number of corporate accountants. They appear to be one of the weakest links in the information chains, and are significantly responsible for persistently less-reliable and inefficient flows of financial information in developing countries.

Research analysts

Research analysts at brokers, underwriters, institutional investors and credit rating agencies, perform a valuable function for the maintenance of an efficient, orderly, and informed securities market. They gather, analyze, and process information on securities, their issuers, their industries and other relevant subjects in a way useful to investors for their investment decisions. Their information products are routinely disseminated in various forms such as research reports, media comments, internet web sites or face-to-face meetings with investors. Their expert opinions, which are often diverse and conflicting, drive investors and traders to buy and sell particular securities for better performance in their investment and/or trading. Investors directly or indirectly purchase their analyses and opinions. They are professional "cooks" for investment information. In a sense, all disclosure information that is regulatorily or voluntarily made available is just raw materials, and will remain almost meaningless to the market without their skillful "cooking".

They are professionally trained and, in some cases, privately qualified for the profession. Many of them are educated in business administration including economics, finance, accounting, marketing or operations research. Some of them have engineering or other technical backgrounds to analyze the issuers' technological competence. Usually, they are not directly, but indirectly, regulated as part of brokerage houses or investment banks, unless they are independent of such institutions. They often form a professional association for the promotion and maintenance of professional standards and ethical practice in financial analysis and investment management.

Vernacular languages

A means of communicating financial market information is another issue of disclosure system and information in light to corporate debt market development. Quite a few developing countries presumably need to develop vernacular terminology for financial market activities and promote a broader use of it for (i) efficiency of financial information dissemination, (ii) effectiveness of policy implementation, and (iii) political support to capital market mechanisms.

Heavy reliance on the languages of developed countries in communicating financial information in a developing country may make it more efficient to take in financial information and practices straight from developed capital markets. However, communication of financial information in the country's vernacular language(s) must be far more efficient in sharing the information widely across the economy on the assumption that the language(s) is developed enough to professionally express financial activities. Similarly, the policy implementation for the development of capital markets in general, and corporate debt markets in particular, must be domestically more effective if it can be done in the country's vernacular language(s). This is because the use of vernacular language(s) ensures wider and deeper participation by the rank and file in the country.

Capital market activities affect and involve a broader spectrum of society in a country. Though visible players in corporate bond markets are institutional investors, most   ultimate stakeholders of institutional investors are households if institutional investors are normally developed in a country. Households' better understanding of and support of the activities of regulators and marker participants will eventually facilitate smooth flows of financial resources for more efficient use.

6.2.   Credit rating system

6.2.1.   Role of credit rating system

A credit rating system is essential for the well-functioning of a corporate bond market in the long run. It (i) provides the measurement of the relative risk of bonds in question, (ii) is conducive to the efficient allocation of financial resources, (iii) affords bond issuers an incentive for financial improvements, (iv) augments the quality and quantity of information on issuers, and (v) alleviates a loss of liquidity due to security fragmentation.

The purpose of credit ratings is primarily to provide investors, through a simple symbol system, with objective and independent opinions of relative credit risk of the rated financial instruments, mainly bonds. They measure the relative risk of a given debt issuer's ability and willingness to make full and timely payments of principal and interest over the lifetime of the rated financial instruments (Pinkes, 1997).

Thus, a credit rating system facilitates the transferability of corporate bonds.

Investors will demand a higher interest rate, commonly known as a risk premium, to compensate for investing in debt issues with a lower rating, reflecting higher credit risk. This differentiation of interest rates on the basis of risk should have two beneficial effects: (i) the efficient allocation of resources by investors; and (ii) the encouraging of companies to improve their financial structures in order to obtain better ratings so that they have cheaper borrowing costs.

A credit rating system also encourages greater transparency, increased information flows, and improved accounting and auditing. A rational, efficient and continuous reallocation of debt capital through a securities market hardly becomes possible without reliable credit agencies.

In addition, the simple system of a limited number of creditworthiness symbols alleviates security fragmentation[20] of bonds and, to some extent, enhances their liquidity to some extent. The system bundles up bond issues of the same, or fairly close, degree of creditworthiness into a single category from among the universe of the bond issues that are rated by the same credit agency. This creates the ground for interchangeability of bond issues by different issuers and facilitates arbitrage activities, which in turn make the bond market more liquid. The credit rating system compensates for a loss of liquidity because of security fragmentation.

6.2.2. *Chicken and egg situation*

Not only is a credit rating system essential for the development of a well-functioning corporate bond market, but more than one credit rating agency is needed in a bond market to induce competition among the agencies, which bring efficiency and professional quality and allows users of credit ratings to compare different rating judgments that are subjective by nature; and that to be disinterested, credit rating agencies should be independent. However, IFC's experience[21] indicates that it is not an easy job to make even a single credit rating agency in a developing country commercially viable. A critical mass of corporate bond issues is most needed for the commercial viability of a credit rating agency. A reliable rating agency is badly needed to build up the critical mass. Thus, we run into a chicken-and-egg situation.

Attributable to this sticky situation are: (i) a thin fee rate for rating services[22]; and (ii) a long lead-time to reach a critical mass of corporate bond issues. A credit raging agency usually cannot charge a flat fee, given its passive role in materializing bond issues. Otherwise financing through bond issues would become economically unattractive to corporations. To make matters worse, a corporate bond market usually takes years to reach the level of critical mass. A lead-time of five to ten years would not be unusually long after the government has launched a corporate bond market development program.

As such, it is not uncommon that credit rating agencies in nascent corporate bond markets have a financially hard time and, consequently, may well be subject to the perception that their professional credibility might be compromised. The Asian Financial Crisis reinforced this kind of perception in a blatant manner.

6.2.3. *Development of rating agencies*

Success requirements

Despite a generally difficult start-up, some rating agencies have been successful in establishing themselves in their corporate bond markets. Their success requirements would include (i) credibility of the rating agency in terms of independence, objectivity and reliability of its opinions, (ii) existence or development of a corporate bond market of sufficient size for the sustenance of a rating agency, and (iii) interest rate differentials for perceived investment risks (Shah, 1991 and 1993).

The second and third requirements, which are basically beyond the control of a rating agency or its promoters, indicate the importance of the timing of a market entry. The timing should not be too early to minimize a money losing period after the start up and it should not be too late to hinder a corporate bond market from developing.

A proactive part of launching a credit rating agency is the first one, *i.e.* the establishment of credibility, which is rather subjective and a matter of perception management, because the rating would have no track record to show. To this end, the steps to be taken are (i) to create awareness of concept and benefit of credit rating amongst investors, borrowers, regulators and market intermediaries, (ii) to win credibility, confidence and trust of its constituents; and (iii) generate rating business that would gradually snowball in volumes (Shah, 1991 and 1993).

The most logical target of a credit rating awareness campaign would be financial institutions. This is because they would be the first in using ratings for their business.

Business models

Three business setting alternatives, as possible solutions to the chicken-and-egg situation, can be suggested as follows:

- To encourage a local credit agency to expand into other business lines and have them cross-subsidize credit rating operations;

- To set up a credit rating agency to cover a regional group of countries; or,

- To set up a credit rating agency as a department of the national stock exchange or some government branch, but not the securities commission.

For instance, in Turkey and the Philippines, local credit rating agencies provide local banks with ratings in order for them to establish corresponding or credit-line relationships with foreign banks. Other revenue sources include non-rating activities, such as, financial information services. Whether or not this solution works in a country depends on various factors prevailing in the country.

A regional rating agency will be set up to cover issuers across national markets in a certain region. In addition to relative ease in achieving a critical mass of rating business, it is more likely to provide more comparable companies to determine relative creditworthiness of companies. A developing country often has only one company in certain industries such as oil refining, airlines, and telecommunications. Healthy rivalry among the regional countries may encourage corporations and regulators in the region to compete in conforming to the "global standards". This scheme may make better sense in a region that has achieved a certain level of economic and/or unity. Examples of this concept are Inter-Arab Rating Company (IARC) which covers Egypt, Tunisia and Jordan, and DCR Centroamericana which covers the Central American countries and the Dominican Republic. A basic drawback of this is that political rivalry in the region may not allow assigned ratings to be objectively accepted among the countries.

The third solution is a public agency approach to the problems. This raises a question right away on whether or not the public agency can be efficient, competent and fair without market-based competition. However, we usually do not rule out the national stock exchange or the securities commission for lack of market-based competition. The development process of local rating agencies in developing countries may be arguably different from rating agencies in developed countries.

Measures that may be effective in ensuring the efficiency, competence, fairness and transparency of a public-sector credit rating agency include:

- To make public the rating methodology and data;

- To publish individual ratings and their rationales in a timely manner;

- To subject the agency to annual audits or evaluations by more than one internationally reputed rating agency, accounting firm, or consulting firm in terms of its efficiency, competence, and fairness;

- To publish the results of annual audits or evaluations;

- To disclaim any liabilities arising from ratings; and

- To incorporate a sunset clause in the agency's charter.

These measures will make differences between a public and a private sector credit rating agency, which is currently conventional. A striking difference will be, if the above measures are adopted, that ratings by a public sector credit rating agency will not be based on any non-public or confidential information. By contrast, conventional ratings rely partly on non-public information that is supplied in confidence primarily by the issuers, and is kept confidential from the public even after ratings have been assigned and publicized.

The departure from the conventional rating in this respect is unlikely to critically undermine the credibility or usefulness of credit ratings in local corporate bond markets. The quantity, quality and dissemination efficiency of corporate information that is supposed to be public are a primary concern in many developing countries. The limitation of rating basis to public information, *ex ante facto* or *ex post facto*, would also alleviate the concern over the liability that may arise from ratings.

Internationally reputable rating agencies are often hesitant to participate in local rating agencies. Their involvement in local bond markets just as a rating practice auditor may facilitate their contribution to the development local corporate bond markets[23]. Hence, a channel for technology transfer will be practically secured.

6.2.4   *International Brands of Credit Ratings*

Besides indigenous efforts to develop rating agencies, the evolution of the credit rating industry in some developing countries may take a course towards international networking under internationally prominent brands. Similarly, many local accounting and auditing firms all over the world have become affiliated with internationally prominent accounting firms. The international networking may take the form of subsidiaries, franchising or their variations.

The international or global networking of the credit rating industry will likely make sense for the following purposes:

- To achieve economies of scale in rating;

- To accelerate technology transfer;

- To facilitate foreign investors in a local bond market; and,

- To facilitate issuers' access to international capital markets.

Apart from distinctive features that require some country-specific rating approaches, there are concurrently a great deal of features that are common across countries, markets, industries and issuers. This will allow rating works to get significantly standardized in cross-border rating institutions. Consequently, international comparison of issuers, which helps make ratings more objective, will get less burdensome and less costly. Therefore, international economies of scale are achievable in the rating industry.

Global financial integration and innovation keep pouring new financial products and technologies into local corporate bond markets. New financial products and technologies often require novel approaches to risk analyses and assessments. A typical example of this trend is asset-backed securities, which have been rapidly spreading into emerging markets and have required a new rating technology. Technology transfer within the same institution is generally much faster and smoother.

Foreign investors, especially foreign institutional investors from developed countries, can play a significant role in fostering the development of a local corporate bond market, though they tend to stick to highly liquid, high credit quality issues only. The size of their financial resources can easily help create a critical mass of demand. They feel definitely comfortable with ratings assigned by internationally recognized rating agencies or their local affiliates with global perspective.

Issuers in developing countries that are capable of tapping international capital markets for debt capital or ambitious to do so may find it convenient and economical to get rated by credit rating agencies with a well-recognized international network, even for domestic purposes. The issuers will be more quickly and better understood by a group of internationally accepted rating analysts. This will expand the issuer's funding alternatives which, in turn, lowers its funding costs.

A caveat is that international rating networks will hardly cover every developing country, and every issuer even in a developing country where they have operations. Nonetheless, the countries and the issuers that are left over by international rating agencies are "entitled" to grow economically through a capital market mechanism and are actually, or potentially, capable of contributing to economic development. International rating agencies are basically owned by shareholders mainly in developed countries. Their ultimate objective is to maximize profits within risk tolerance and preference parameters that are acceptable to the shareholders, and are inevitably different from those acceptable to people in developing countries. Therefore, the local presence or affiliation of international names will not substitute indigenous rating agencies but will complement them.

6.2.5   Issues with a mandatory rating system

In most developing countries with credit rating agencies, mandatory rating has been introduced. A mandatory rating system usually requires (i) public debt issues to be rated a certain grade or higher and/or (ii) certain institutional investors to purchase securities a certain grade or higher. This is inevitably accompanied by a system under which the regulator designates or licenses eligible credit rating agencies.

A primary rationale for a mandatory rating system is to administratively ensure the objectives of a credit rating system, namely, (i) to provide the measurement of the relative risk of bonds in question, (ii) to conduce to the efficient allocation of financial resources, (iii) to afford bond issuers an incentive for financial improvements, (iv) to augment the quality and quantity of information on issuers, and (v) to alleviate a loss of liquidity due to security fragmentation. In the context of the chicken-and-egg situation, the system is also often designed to generate a certain level of demand for credit rating services in the local corporate bond market.

The arguments against a mandatory rating system are that it may compromise ratings' accuracy or objectivity for lack of investor-driven competition; that investors naively believe that government sanctions assure the quality of a rating agency's opinions; that it may entice issuers into shopping around a favorable rating while it may temp credit rating agencies to inflate their ratings in favor of issuers; and that artificially created revenue streams may upset the delicate balance for rating agencies that have been operating as private, profit-oriented institutions in unregulated markets (Pinkes, 1997). These arguments appear generally legitimate. In fact, it is occasionally observed that some credit rating agencies undercut each other by implicitly selling favorable, lax ratings to meet the regulatory benchmark of rating.

However, they are less likely to provide a local corporate bond market with a practical solution to its chicken-and-egg situation. The historical evolution process of corporate bond markets in developed countries is presumably responsible for the legitimacy of the arguments against a mandatory rating system. Most developing countries are not repeating the same process of corporate bond market evolution.

6.3. *Securities registration system*

Securities registration is an administrative process through which to register with the relevant authorities securities to be publicly offered, sold and traded to investors. A securities registration system is designed to provide investors in new and seasoned issues of securities with information regarding the issuer for their investment decisions, and to prevent fraud in the sale of securities. Under a pure disclosure system as opposed to a merit system, the regulatory authority administering the securities registration system neither explicitly nor implicitly passes on the investment merits of the issue. Besides these aspects in common with equity markets, corporate bond markets differ from equity markets in (i) having actually or potentially several distinct sub-markets, and (ii) functioning as an incentive mechanism for better disclosure practices.

6.3.1. *Distinct markets*

In a given country, there are likely to be in fact several distinct markets in debt securities, with different instruments, players and market mechanisms. The types of markets for corporate debt instruments divide up differently across countries. They normally divide up by maturities of debt, characteristics of investors or issuers, and product features. Securities registration should be flexible enough to adjust for each difference to better serve its goals.

It is typical to see (i) money markets in which short-term instruments such as commercial papers (CPs) and certificate of deposit (CDs) are traded principally or exclusively among banks and other financial institutions; (ii) markets in which both individual and institutional investors are purchasers; and (iii) markets in which only institutional investors or other large-scale investors are active. Government debt markets are distinct markets by nature of the issuer[24]. Regulators need to recognize this, and the goal of a securities registration system should be to put in place and enforce appropriate frameworks for each market, recognizing that the cost/benefit analysis of regulation will be different in each of them.

Money market instruments whose maturities are less than a certain period, typically 9 months to 12 months, are generally exempt from securities registration, subject to credit ratings of an investment grade. In the private markets where only institutional investors or other large-scale investors are active, securities are also exempt from securities registration in exchange for strict restrictions on their distribution.

Another set of attributes that may divide up debt markets are new product features. For instance, mortgage-backed securities may require, for better protection of investors, information other than typically required for conventional corporate bonds, such as prepayment information of house mortgages. A rigid securities registration system may fail in effectively protecting investors or impede market innovation by preventing new products from evolving only because they do not fit into conventional categories.

6.3.2. Incentive mechanism

The much lower market risk of corporate bonds relative to the same issuer's shares, the seasoned nature of corporate bond issuers, and the consideration for a cost/benefit tradeoff together give rise to an incentive mechanism for better disclosure and higher efficiency in the capital market as a whole.

Debt issuers are generally well "seasoned" on the market. In practice, hardly does the corporate bond market in a country develop without an equity market having already developed in the country; and rarely does a corporate bond issuer publicly issue bonds without having publicly-traded shares. It is more than likely, therefore, that general requirements for securities registration statements are already in place by the time corporate bond market development is seriously implemented. Most debt issuers also are already reporting companies and subject to the full panoply of disclosure rules.

Securities registration as a means for disclosure is a costly affair for an issuer, though the protection of investors is in the public interest. Excessively costly and/or burdensome registration would discourage corporations from raising debt funds in a corporate bond market. Consequently, a securities registration system is generally subject to a cost/benefit tradeoff. In addition, an average issuer is likely to tap the capital market more often by debt issues than by equity issues. In designing the system for a corporate bond market, policymakers should carefully weigh them so as to strike the optimal balance in light of the objectives of the securities regulations.

As such, registration requirements for corporate issues should be worked out to be simpler than those for initial public offerings and subsequent equity offerings as a reward for seasoned issuers with a good disclosure track record in the capital market. The simpler registration requirements usually take the form of, for instance, the following:

- A simpler and/or shorter form of registration;

- Incorporation by reference of information documents into a registration statement;

- A shorter waiting period for the effectiveness of a filed registration statement; and,

- Shelf registration[25].

For granting a registrant issuer such preferential treatments in respect of an issue to be registered, regulators typically take into account factors such as:

- The length of the period reporting under a country's securities laws;

- The quality of reporting materials filed;

- Timely filings of all materials required; and,

- Credit rating (usually an investment grade) of the debt issue.

A proven track record of satisfying these criteria is reasonably considered to verify the issuer's integrity for the purposes of securities laws. In turn, the issuer is rewarded with less expensive, less time consuming and less burdensome compliance with the regulations and laws. Criteria for special facilities under which securities, including debt securities, can be issued solely to qualified institutional investors without securities registration may also be linked to the compliance with the similar factors.

6.4. Bankruptcy laws

Bankruptcy laws are another cornerstone of corporate bond markets development, though they relate to the down side of corporate finance activities. Non-government bonds, typically corporate bonds, may default, whereas government bonds denominated in the local currency do not default, at least in theory. Default risks distinguish non-government bonds from government bonds. Most events of default on bonds occur when the issuer goes bankrupt or both the issuer and the guarantor go bankrupt in the case that the bonds are guaranteed.

The issuer's obligation to pay interest and repay the principal in a timely manner should not be at the issuer's disposal. The investor is able to rationally assess the risk of investing in bonds only if the limit of the investor's legal ability to force the bankrupt issuer to repay its obligations, and the procedures for going to that limit, are clearly defined. It is bankruptcy laws that define the limit and the procedures. In other words, a mechanism for efficient reorganization is vital to a smooth functioning of corporate bond markets (Hakansson, 1999) in that it establishes the inventor's right to recover investments and the right's priority or subordination to other creditors in the worst case.

The investor's ability to force the bankrupt issuer to repay its obligations can be generally classified into three classes, according to its security type: (i) secured or collateralized bonds, (ii) senior bonds, and (iii) subordinated bonds. Holders of secured or collateralized bonds have a charge against a particular piece of the bankrupt issuer's asset. This asset (or proceeds from its sale) must be used to satisfy the bankrupt issuer's obligation to the bondholders before it can be used to satisfy debts to other creditors. Holders of senior bonds have a statutory priority interest, and the obligations must be paid before other debts when the issuer becomes insolvent. Holders of subordinated bonds have neither a charge against the bankrupt issuer's asset nor are the subject of a statutory priority. Some countries may have just two categories: secured and unsecured bonds, instead of the three. These classifications of bonds by security ranking would be apparently meaningless without a reliable bankruptcy mechanism in place.

However, a deal-breaker often arises during bankruptcy proceedings when bondholders are involved as debtors, unless a country's laws, such as bankruptcy or company laws, have been tailored to bonds' legal structure. When an issuer becomes insolvent, the issuer's assets are rarely liquidated from the beginning. More often, the issuer tries hard to rehabilitate itself by first filing for protection from creditors while undergoing reorganization under the relevant provisions of the bankruptcy laws. The issuer's management negotiates a debt-restructuring plan with all outstanding creditors, including bondholders. Bondholders are unspecific and many, as compared with bank creditors, under defaulted syndicated bank loans. Given this diversified nature of bondholders, it is controversially argued that majority-vote, instead of unanimity-vote, will make it easier to negotiate a debt rescheduling (Adler, 1999).

6.5.   *Trading System*

What does the integration process of the corporate bond market into the national debt market of a developing country look like? How does it affect the trading system or market structure of the country? We will first examine those characteristics to help identify a trading system suitable to a particular national market.

For discussion purposes, we decompose the institutional characteristics of the corporate bond market along three dimensional axes: (i) investors, (ii) issuers, and (iii) intermediaries. They virtually form a cubic space as illustrated in Figure 7-A. Each axis represents the following characteristics:

(i)	Investors:	Demand for trading immediacy
		Institutionalization
(ii)	Issuers:	Demand for trading immediacy
		Number of issues per issuer
(iii)	Intermediaries:	Capitalization
		Sophistication.

The degree of each characteristic increases as you move along the axis outwards, and each axis is divided into two parts: the lower-scale and the higher-scale parts. The division of the scale on each axis makes eight combinations of the institutional characteristics represented by eight sub-spaces in the cubic space, namely, Sub-Spaces 1-8 (see Figure 7-A). A set of institutional characteristics in each sub-space determines a specific market structure or structures suitable for that sub-space.

Sub-Space 1 typifies a well-developed market of government bonds or major corporate bonds (see Figure 7-B). In this type of market, investors are highly institutionalized and have a higher demand for trading immediacy (impatient traders); issuers also have a higher demand for trading immediacy (impatient traders) and a larger number of issues; and market intermediaries, mainly dealers, are better capitalized and sophisticated. A dealer market or quote-driven market is generally suitable for this type of market. The reasons for this will be later discussed in detail in Section 8.2.2. "Transaction modes".

Sub-Space 8 represents a nascent market of either government or non-government debt securities (see Figure 7-C). In this kind of market, investors are scantily institutionalized and have a lesser demand for trading immediacy (patient or opportunistic traders), issuers also have a lesser demand for trading immediacy (patient or opportunistic traders) and a smaller number of issues, and market intermediaries are inadequately capitalized and sophisticated. A bond market in this sub-space may well start with a rudimentary form of market structure such as periodic markets[26] or a call auction market. As the market develops within the same sub-space, however, the growing trading volume, and/or the increasing needs for market efficiency and transparency, will likely cause the market to shift to an electronic order-driven market under today's technological environments even within this sub-space.

Once the corporate bond market comes into play, the national market made up of the government and the corporate bond markets is expected to take the form of (i) a dealer market (a quote-driven market), or (ii) a dual market system of a dealer market and an electronic order-driven market.

After the highly liquid government bond market or the *de facto* benchmark major corporate issue market has established itself in the form of a dealer market, the corporate bond market will dovetail into the existing dealer market. Major corporate issues may be traded by virtue of market-making by selected dealers. Minor corporate bonds will be practically neglected for trading except in the primary market. As such, the national debt market will function as a dealer market under the institutional environments represented by Sub-Spaces 1to 4 (see Figure 7-D). It is reasonable to assume that this market, though quote-driven, will be more and more electronically automated.

If the corporate bond market gets far larger, additional efforts to make the debt market more efficient may result in the polarization of the national debt market into Sub-Space 1 where highly liquid bonds are traded in a dealer market and Sub-Space 8 where relatively illiquid corporate bonds, probably together with subnational government bonds and privately placed bonds[27], are traded in an electronic order-driven market (see Figure 7-E). This dual market system will be a hybrid of the market structures suitable to the sets of institutional characteristics shown in Figures 7-B and 7-C.

In an economic situation where the institutional characteristics for the government, or *de facto* benchmark bond market remain in Sub-Space 8, those for the corporate bond market will probably be much less favorable in the same sub-space. Corporate bonds will, in all likelihood, trade in an auction market only occasionally, it not at all.

7.   Policy Dilemma and An Alternative Solution

The macroeconomic constraints that many developing countries are faced with do not, or will not, permit them to develop and/or maintain a large, liquid government bond market just to form a benchmark yield curve. One of major corporate issuers may be a choice as the benchmark issuer in their domestic bond markets.

7.1.   *Policy dilemma*

In developed economies, benchmark issues in their bond markets are usually the most heavily traded government debt securities, with maturities ranging from as short as a week to as long as 10 years, 20 years or even 30 years. They have the highest credit rating in the country, substantial liquidity, and an efficient and transparent issuing procedure. Their actual trade prices are used to calculate yields on the bonds, which in turn are used to construct the benchmark yield curve. The benchmark yield curve is a basic benchmark for pricing other government or non-government bond issues of comparable maturities across the yield curve on the primary market as well as the secondary market.

There is no doubt that government bonds fit in best as benchmark issues. However, what happens if a country does not have a government bond market deep and liquid enough to reasonably constitute a benchmark yield curve? Should a developing country issue a sufficient amount of government bonds so that the country can create a benchmark yield curve before it tries to develop a corporate bond market in order to achieve its economic development through private sector activities?

Figure 7: Institutional Characteristics and Trading System

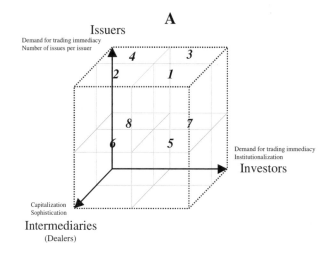

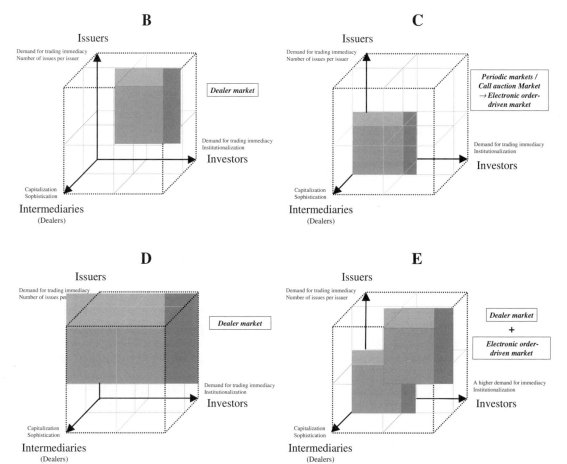

Hong Kong and the Republic of Singapore, which have graduated from being developing countries for many years, began to actively issue government bonds in 1990 and 1998, respectively, to develop a benchmark yield curve and consequently a debt securities market in general in the city-states[28]. Is this policy viable for developing countries in general? Probably not for many developing countries, because Hong Kong and Singapore began to develop their debt securities markets after they had reached a formidable level of economic development. But many developing countries will develop their debt securities market for more efficient economic development through private sector investments.

A key macroeconomic policy question for these countries is whether or not it is possible for the government of a country which lacks sustainable export power and domestic supply capacity to keep issuing government debt without worsening its current-account position or getting its currency depreciated in the long run under the open economy environments[29]. If a country has substantial export power to keep its current-account in surplus, it can generally afford to run fiscal deficits that are financed by issuing government bonds. Without adequate domestic supply capacity, however, excessive government spending, like one under a populist policy, would likely cause uncontrollable inflation or would simply deteriorate the country's current-account position through import of foreign goods and services. Either inflation or deteriorating current-account position would possibly build up downward pressures on the country's currency, leading the country to external instability. Macroeconomic instability would certainly discourage investors, foreign and domestic alike, from investing in the country, especially on a long-term basis. In addition, market-based investments are by and large more efficient than public investments. This is one of the reasons why the World Bank/IMF have been persistently encouraging developing countries to consolidate their public finances.

Hong Kong and Singapore are obviously not in such a macroeconomic dilemma for their debt market development. They have been running current-account surpluses for many years. Moreover, they do not run budgetary deficits. Issuance of government debt did not expose the then British colony and the city-state to external instability. What they are doing by issuing government bonds is mainly to transform a part of the existing contractual savings into liquid assets and a part of the existing bank deposits into long-term assets.

7.2. *An alternative solution – an approximation of benchmark issues*

Given the historical backgrounds in many developed countries, it has made sense to have their government bond markets take the lead in developing their fixed income markets as part of their efforts to make their capital reallocation process more efficient. However, today, most developing countries have not yet gained sufficient export power, and many of them have already been in the open economy situation under the floating exchange rate regime. Therefore, it may be not economically viable for quite a few developing countries to start their debt market development with massive issuance of government bonds as the developed countries did.

Such developing countries are in a chicken-egg situation. They need to have efficient government bond markets to develop economically. However, they cannot afford to have efficient government bond markets before they have achieved a certain level of economic development.

How can a developing country get out of this chicken-egg situation? How can a developing country in a macroeconomic framework significantly different from the one that developed countries once were in construct a benchmark yield curve in its bond market? Government agency issues or major corporate issues may substitute for government bonds with some limitations in forming a benchmark yield curve for developing a fixed income market as a whole. Adoption of some government agency issues, or major corporate issues as an approximation for benchmark issues, can be a practical policy choice for some developing countries.

Another possibility is that a swap curve will substitute for the benchmark yield curve of government bonds. Interest and currency swaps are usually quoted on the basis of average banks' implied rating of AA. In fact, a swap curve is often employed as the benchmark for pricing corporate bonds in developed countries where the government bond benchmark yield curve is imperfect. However, this choice is barely practical in most developing countries. Most developing countries seldom have an active, deep, long-term credit market in place, which is definitely prerequisite for a swap curve being a benchmark to price long-term bond issues. The swap curve can be volatile in response to the funding and/or credit positions of a small number of, say, several swap providing banks, whose community is much smaller than that of bond investors.

8.   De Facto Benchmark Issues

In this section, we will take a look at how to qualify major corporate issues for an approximation of benchmark issues in two aspects if a country's macroeconomic circumstances warrant such a policy choice: (1) likely candidates for major corporate issuers in development economies and (2) possible policy measures to make their secondary market liquid enough to be *de facto* or substitute benchmark issues. As you will see, the line between government agency issuers and major corporate issuers gets blurred for the purpose of policy implementation.

Most discussions below on how to qualify major corporate issues for an approximation of benchmark issues are not limited to a benchmark corporate bond issuer. In fact, they are applicable to major corporate bond issues in general to the extent they need liquidity on their secondary market to achieve lower funding costs, regardless of whether or not one of her major corporate bond issuers is chosen to be the *de facto* benchmark bond issuer.

8.1.   *Likely candidates for major corporate issuers*

Likely candidates for major corporate issuers in developing economies include:

- infrastructure and utility companies,

- housing finance companies, and,

- development finance companies (DFCs).

What is common among these three kinds of companies is that they tend to have a regular, sizable and stable demand for long-term funds. Once they are properly structured and operated, therefore, they will likely be able to provide the investors with a regular, sizable and stable supply of bonds of high quality and uniform characteristics through public offerings.

8.1.1.   *Infrastructure and utility companies*

Infrastructure and utility companies include companies engaged in power (*e.g.* generation, distribution), transportation (*e.g.* roads, railways, airlines, sea and air port facilities), telecommunications, water supply, and sanitation, out of which power and telecommunications companies are very likely candidates for major corporate issuers. Demand for infrastructure in developing countries is pressing and massive. Infrastructure is badly needed to boost productivity and improve standard of living. Overall quality of infrastructure in a county is also one of key factors for attracting foreign private investment. Foreign financial aid, which used to be one of vital sources for infrastructure building in developing countries, has been on the decline. To make matters worse, as discussed earlier, many developing country governments are constrained to raise funds from the market on their own credit.

Hence, infrastructure and utility companies have been increasing their presence in the capital markets. Existing government branches for infrastructure and utility operations have been spectacularly privatized. More and more new projects are left to the private sector. Private participation in infrastructure projects in developing countries increased at an average annual rate of 33.9% in real terms from 1990 to 1997. Even after a downfall of infrastructure investment in 1998 due to the Asian Financial Crisis in 1997, the real growth rate was 25.4% over the period from 1990 to 1998[30]. The enormous rate of the demand growth is evident from these figures, as compared to the average real GDP growth rates of 6.4% for the developing countries over the period from 1990 to 1997[31]. The percentage of project costs estimated to be locally financed by debt in developing countries is 10-20 percent[32].

Infrastructure and utility companies' operations are highly capital intensive and highly financially leveraged. The upfront cost of an infrastructure project easily amounts to more than a hundred million US dollars. Even if its finance is sliced into phases of bond issuance, an issue will be sizable in the local bond market. Since their funding demand is massive and continuous, they will tap the market on a regular basis. They generally cannot afford to be too opportunistic in terms of issue timing. If they want to minimize the average funding cost of a series of their bond issues, a wise strategy is to break the whole into pieces of such a similar size that the market can swallow each piece without any resistance from investors, and to feed the pieces into the market one by one over time. Funding needs range from short-term to long-term. Investments in production facilities are of a long-term nature. Operations require short- to medium-term funds. Credit quality is generally high, because they are usually oligopolistic, if not monopolistic, regulated and supervised, and often have direct or indirect support from their governments for the sake of public interests.

You may have already noticed that non- or limited-recourse financing such as build-operate-transfer (BOT) or build-own-operate-transfer (BOOT), which are innovative and popular, does not fit in as a major corporate issue. This is because that type of financing is project-specific and stops short of satisfying the key criteria for being major corporate issues. Centralized financing and financing on a company's balance sheet are another two prerequisites.

8.1.2. Housing finance companies

Housing finance has the makings of the centerpiece of a fixed income market in a developing country, despite its technical hurdles. Housing needs are so basic to every individual that an aggregate demand in an economy is constantly huge. This holds up especially in developing countries that are going through a rapid urbanization process. Housing investment is estimated to be 2% to 8% of GNP. House building creates an additional demand of 5% to 10% of GNP through its broad supporting industries (World Bank, 1992; Lea, 1999). Since a house or apartment flat is as expensive to an individual as multiple times his or her annual income, it inevitably induces a prospective house owner to save on a long-term basis as well as an expected or current buyer to borrow on a long-term basis. It continuously creates long-term financial assets and debts in the economy. By collateralizing its bonds with house mortgages underlying house loans, a housing finance company can issue bonds of high quality under a proper legal and regulatory framework.

Among several models available for housing finance, a centralized liquidity facility, which purchases housing loans with recourse to their originators for its own portfolio and finances the purchase by issuing general obligation bonds of a simple bullet type, not only most probably works well as a major corporate issuer, but also appears suitable to a developing country where the housing finance industry is in its initial stage (Lea 1998). There could be variations, depending on actual conditions of a country.

A strong legal framework and certain operations skills, among other things, is requisite for smooth functioning of a housing finance company on a national scale, even in a developing country. The legal framework includes a land registry system, an effective bankruptcy law, and efficient foreclosure procedures through the court system. Standardized property appraisal and valuation procedure, mortgage loan underwriting, and modern technology in loan processing and servicing are also needed.

8.1.3. Development finance companies

DFCs are by definition financial intermediaries specializing in long-term finance primarily for industrial development. As compared with infrastructure and utility companies and housing finance companies, they are logically simpler to become major corporate issuers in terms of their sizable, regular and stable supply capacity of bonds.

Their institutional necessity for industrial development has been long conceived and widely accepted. As a result, they have been in operation for decades in many developing countries. Nonetheless, most of them have not been successful in their financial independence. They are rife with lackluster performance. This is probably not because they are fundamentally illegitimate for economic development, but because they have been long subjected to previous policy mistakes and inability of governments and multilateral development institutions. Learning from its own lending and investment activities for DFCs, IFC identified as causes for their disappointing track records the following elements: lowering commercial standards for the sake of "development", lack of cool-eyed assessment of commercial viability, undue influence of governments on lending, lack of their access to local currency long-term funding, and dependence on external and/or government-guaranteed funding. (Berger, 1998).

IFC's empirical analysis strongly indicates that it is DFCs that need well-functioning corporate bond markets in order to play their initially intended roles in economic development of developing countries. High credit quality of their bond issues derives from nowhere but commercial prudence in their lending operations.

8.2. Policy measures for de facto benchmark issues

De facto benchmark issues must have a liquid secondary market. Furthermore, in an ideal case, their secondary market will be expected to be so deep and liquid that the market can accommodate even the government's open market operations at a reasonable cost to the government. Why does liquidity matter? It is because liquidity is an important determinant of the bid/ask spread of a bond (Chakravarty, 1999) and the market impact[33]. The more fluid the market is, the narrower the spread is and the smaller the market impact is. The commission or fee (if any) is also likely to be smaller. As a result, the total transaction cost[34] will be cheaper.

Various factors that critically contribute to liquidity of debt securities can be grouped into four categories: (1) characteristics of a bond issue and its issuer, (2) transaction modes, (3) transaction environments, and (4) portfolio investment demand. Out of these four groups, only the discussions, which will follow below, about characteristics of a bond issue and its issuer are unique to *de facto* benchmark issues because they are corporate, not government, bonds. The discussions about the other three groups of factors for liquidity are largely indifferent to characteristics of a bond issue and its issuer.

Though the four groups of factors are important for the liquidity of *de facto* benchmark issues, the fundamental sources of liquidity are a critical mass of supply and demand. In that sense, "characteristics of a bond issue and its issuer" and "portfolio investment demand" matter first. "Transaction modes" and "transaction environments" consist of the microstructure of debt securities markets, which connects the existing supply and the existing demand but never generate the supply and the demand themselves.

8.2.1. Characteristics of a bond issue and its issuer

In this section, we will discuss the characteristics of a bond issue and its issuer that significantly affect the bond issue's liquidity in terms of (1) its credit quality, (2) the transparency of the issuer's operations, and (3) the simplicity and consistency of the bonds. The endogenous and exogenous factors responsible for the issuer's credit quality will be looked into separately.

High credit quality

Credit quality, among others, is a key factor to liquidity of a bond issue (Chakravarty, 1999). The salient characteristics of a bond issue to qualify as a *de facto* benchmark issue have been discussed above by stipulating likely candidates for major corporate issuers. To be liquid on the secondary market, *de facto* benchmark issues must be of high credit quality, and their supply to the market must be regular, sizable, and stable. All these characteristics other than high credit quality are generally embedded in the three types of businesses that the issuers are engaged in, namely, infrastructure-utility, housing finance, and development finance. However, credit quality of a bond issue is issuer-specific (more precisely issue-specific), but not industry-specific. It basically reflects creditworthiness of its issuer adjusted for the specific structure of individual issues. An issuer's creditworthiness can be endogenously built up and exogenously reinforced.

Practically, *de facto* benchmark bond issues have the highest rating by one of reputable rating agencies. A *de facto* benchmark corporate bond issue is different from a benchmark government bond issue in this respect. Government bonds denominated in the country's currency are, at least theoretically, free from a default risk, because the government has ultimate taxation power and ability to print notes to repay its debt, irrespective of its fiscal soundness.

What are endogenous factors for the high credit quality of the issuer or its bond issues? The most fundamental is sustainable profitability of the issuer's business operations. It is the first step in building up and supporting the issuer's highly credible financial position. In order to keep its operations sustainably profitable, the issuer must strictly adhere to market-based, commercially prudent operations, and must be free from "policy investments" that compromise the bottom line of the issuer. Any one of the three likely candidates for major corporate issuers is susceptible to such commercially unjustifiable investments. This is more likely in the context of developing countries, because (i) infrastructure-utility, housing and development finance directly affect the people's welfare and involve substantial business interests, and (ii) they are usually given a monopolistic or quasi-monopolistic status and other types of preferential treatments by the government.

The credit quality can be also exogenously reinforced in an implicit or explicit form.

Implicit forms of credit enhancement for fostering the benchmark issuer from among major corporate issuers include (i) government ownership or (ii) board representation. It would be preferable to keep government ownership or board representation to a minority position. This will allow the issuer to keep a private sector culture in itself so as to be efficient, quick and flexible enough to adjust itself for ever changing market conditions, customers' needs and other business environments. Such implicit forms of credit enhancement may be also accompanied by additional arrangements such as:

- a privileged status of the issuer to borrow directly from the government,

- participation in the monetary authority's open market operations,

- eligibility of the issues as an instrument for the open market operations and/or as a collateral for direct borrowing from the monetary authority,

- a preferential tax status of the issuer or its issues,

- exemption from the requirement of obtaining the central bank's approval, or

- exemption from normal securities registration requirements for the issuer's securities issuance,

- exemption from statutory reserve, or,

- recognition of the issues as liquid assets for the purpose of capital adequacy ratio calculation.

It should be noted that some of these preferential treatments for credit implications might adversely affect the liquidity of the securities. This is because a preferential treatment creates a pocket of demand by inducing a specific category of investors to invest in the securities at an off-market price. It may fragment the market for the securities. Examples are exemption from statutory reserve and recognition as liquidity assets for capital adequacy ratio purposes. This exemption will create demand for the issues from banks that are subject to statutory reserve requirements or whose assets are subject to capital adequacy rules. The problem with this is that only banks will benefit from the preferential treatment and most of the issues will get stuck in banks' portfolios. This is how CAGAMAS bonds, which are bonds issued under a highly successful housing finance scheme in Malaysia, failed to have a liquid secondary market (Rhee, 1999). Bonds of the Industrial Finance Corporation of Thailand, though they are currently not intended as benchmark bonds at all, have been facing an illiquidity problem due to the similar special treatment.

Guarantees for bond issues from governments or multilateral institutions, or bond insurance from private sector insurers, are explicit forms of credit enhancement. These guarantee schemes hardly work as credit enhancement tools for *de facto* benchmark issues. A potential threat posed by government guarantees is that an excessive governmental credit commitment would build up the government's contingent liabilities and consequently defeat the purpose of the government's fiscal consolidation if a country chooses to foster the benchmark issuer from among major corporate issuers, instead of government bond issues, due to its fiscal constraints. On the other hand, multilateral institutions' guarantees under the current scheme are too expensive to support a series of benchmark issues on a regular basis[35]. Private bond insurance is also too costly.

The *de facto* benchmark bond issuer would be viewed as a "government-sponsored enterprise" (GSE) to the extent that it gets support with credit implications from its government implicitly or explicitly with a view to creating an efficient and fluid secondary market. The protected nature of a GSE status tends to pose some policy issues: (i) a moral hazard, and (ii) a threat to taxpayers. The GSE status of the issuer provides its management with weaker incentives to good investment and competitive production, potentially resulting in inefficient selection of investments. It also allows the issuer to potentially grow to such an enormous size of presence in the capital markets that its failure would be unaffordable and could be avoided only by taxpayers' money. In order to minimize such risks, the following measures should be considered:

- to keep the issuer's preferential status at a minimal possible level,

- to establish a governmental oversight agency and/or institute congressional oversight,

- to establish regulatory standards such as minimal risk-based capital standards, and,

- to institute "sunset provisions" to phase out the privileged status in the future.

Nevertheless, the mixed private/public nature of a GSE status causes conflicts of interest on the part of the government as well as the issuer's management: (i) a regulator versus an advocate on the former, and (ii) maximizing profit for the shareholders versus ensuring the public mission on the latter. The tradeoff of public mission and costs to taxpayers should be well recognized, and a careful balance should be struck as the tradeoff changes over the time.

Transparency about the issuer

The second characteristic of a bond issue and its issuer that presumably contributes to a *de facto* benchmark issue's liquidity is transparency of its issuer's operations[36]. The transparency is particularly important, because the issuer is a corporation, not the government. Not only does the issuer comply with disclosure requirements for public offering and listing of its equity shares and bonds, as will be discussed later, but also should more proactively make its operations, including their results and future implications, known to existing and prospective investors and capital market practitioners. Continuous flow of information on the issuer's operations will help generate trading demand for its securities. This is especially important when foreign investors are part of liquidity source. Desirable transparency enhancement programs include:

- compliance with internationally accepted corporate governance rules such as the OECD Principles of Corporate Governance[37],

- compliance with internationally accepted accounting principles,

- listing of its equity shares on a stock exchange in an international capital market,

- public relations through conventional mass media (press, radio and TV), international electronic media like Reuters and Bloomberg, and internet websites,

- domestic as well as international regular investors relation programs[38], and

- extensive roadshows on the occasions of its securities issuance.

These activities will help alleviate unnecessary skepticism about the issuer's operations, increase the credibility of the issuer's management, and gain more confidence in its creditworthiness from investors. It is worth noting that investors usually discount the ambiguity about the issuer or its securities by demanding a premium for it, which generally results in a higher rate return, wider bid-ask price spreads and lower liquidity with respect to the issuer's bonds.

It would be wise to incorporate some incentive mechanism in the issuer's corporate workings to motivate its managers and staff to achieve those endogenous factors for higher liquidity of the issuer's bond issues.

Simplicity and consistency

The last characteristic of the bond issue contributing to a *de facto* benchmark issue's liquidity is the simplicity and consistency of the obligations. The simplicity and consistency satisfy the greatest common factor of investors' needs across the marketplace and over the time, and thus capture the highest liquidity. The simplest form of a bond is conventionally referred to as "straight bond" or "plain vanilla". Detailed characteristics of a straight bond is summarized as follows:

- No early redemption of the principal except for rare and material cases (a "bullet" maturity),

- Redemption at par,

- Conventionally accepted terms to the maturity such as 1, 3, 5, 7 or 10 years,

- Issue price at par or at a smallest possible premium or discount to par,

- Constant fixed coupon rate or spread over an interest rate index like LIBOR[39],

- No change in seniority of bondholders' claim on the issuer's assets, and,

- No varying tax treatments on the interest and principal payments.

As will be discussed later, there are a wide variety of types of corporate bonds. A particular type of corporate bond comes to the market with a lot of variations. Some of them are considerably sophisticated and consequently complex, in their structure to seize on a short-lived opportunity to achieve aggressive cost savings. That should not be the case with a de facto benchmark issue that needs liquidity.

8.2.2. *Transaction modes*

Transaction modes of bonds both on the primary and secondary markets are part of the microstructure of the country's debt market as a whole, and affect the liquidity of corporate bonds as well as the market efficiency. If the demand and supply for the bonds are compared to gasoline for a car, transaction modes would be lubricant to the engine. Lubricant does not drive a car but is indispensable for smooth and economical driving.

OTC vs exchange

The majority of seasoned bonds are traded over-the-counter through telephone connections among dealers and institutional investors rather than on the exchange, even if the securities are listed. This is because bond trading involves some negotiations before a trade is done. Investment parameters of the mainstream fixed-income investors who are institutional investors are generally too complex and diverse to trade mechanically on the exchange. This leads most institutional orders to the OTC market.

Fist of all, there are a much greater number of bond issues outstanding in a market in a smaller issue amount for each issue, as compared with listed common stocks, since most bond issuers make multiple issues over time ("security segmentation"). In picking up a particular issue of bonds, or a particular portfolio of bonds for trade, the bond investor or trader essentially looks at the coupon rate, price, coupon payment dates, maturity, yield, liquidity, and credit risk of bonds, and often has flexibility in some of these parameters. In a usual case, the investor or trader has no strong reason to stick to a specific issue as long as his or her investment parameters are satisfied. Many different but comparable bonds are often interchangeable ("nearly perfect substitutes" for each other), thanks to arbitrage activities. There can be at least a few alternatives to his or her choice, and the investor or trader usually negotiates the terms of a trade before he or she trades.

Some countries may claim that the majority of bonds publicly issued in their countries are traded on their exchanges. A statement of this kind is misleading, if not incorrect. It is not unusual that those trades recorded in the exchanges were mostly negotiated over the phone and then registered with the exchanges only for reporting and/or clearing purposes; and that very little order matching actually goes on in the exchanges.

Quote-driven market vs order-driven market

Bond transactions on the OTC market are quote-driven[40], and those on the exchange are usually order-driven. Automated trading systems for debt securities can be either quote-driven or order-driven. Execution costs of equity securities on the OTC market tend to be higher than on the quote-driven auction market, since dealer pricing is less transparent. It is inferred that the same tendency exists with respect to execution costs of debt securities (Chakravarty, 1999).

Then, should bonds be transacted on the exchange or a more cost-efficient automated trading system, instead of over the counter, for savings on the transaction costs? The total transaction cost would generally increase at the current level of technology. The market impact of an institutional order, if executed in an order-driven market, would outweigh possible savings on an execution cost by a switchover from a quote-driven market. It is often the largest component of the total transaction cost. As long as dealers' flexibility in dealing with complex and diverse orders is of value to investors and provides much higher liquidity, the OTC market remains cheaper to institutional investors in terms of the total transaction costs.

However, it is reasonable to assume that the rapid advancement in technology will sooner or later make an order-driven automated trading system increasingly intelligent as well as flexible, and that more and more complex orders will be automatically executable. This is more likely the case with highly homogeneous instruments like *de facto* benchmark bonds and other major corporate bonds. This trend will be contingent partly upon the degree of comprehensiveness and sophistication of the centralized clearance, settlement and depository systems for securities in a country.

Until then, a policy focus of debt market regulation will be on how to effectively regulate the quote-driven or dealers' market for enhancement of the market efficiency. The dealers' market is prone to unfairness or even collusion at the expense of investors. Minor corporate bonds, if traded on the secondary market, are more so due to less liquidity and a smaller number of dealers who are willing to trade them. Prevailing bid/offer spreads for trading fairly reflect the degree of market efficiency. An enhancement of pricing transparency (quote transparency) has been empirically effective in narrowing bid/offer spreads. The following measures are suggested to enhance price transparency:

- Low entry barrier into bond dealership,

- Reporting requirement of actual trade prices,

- Establishment of an electronic database of the trade prices,

- Dissemination of the trade price data to investors and the public by easy and affordable means, and,

- Electronic surveillance of dealers' trading practices.

The trade price reporting does not need to be on a real-time basis. *Ex post facto* reporting, if its contents are meaningful enough, will exert significant pressure on dealers to be fair and honest to investors. The price reporting and trading practice surveillance systems may be linked to the centralized clearance, settlement and depository systems.

Dealers, market makers and primary dealers

One firm can simultaneously be a dealer, a market maker and a primary dealer in the debt market. However, the three terms represent slightly different concepts in the order of a more general concept to a more specific one. In generic parlance, the dealer is a firm that professionally sells and buys securities for its account as a principal of transactions. The market maker is a dealer that is voluntarily or statutorily committed to making a market of specific securities. The primary dealer[41] is a market maker that is officially designated for government debt securities or, in our case here, *de facto* benchmark issues.

The market maker's role as a liquidity provider in the bond market is well recognized. The trading volume of a cash securities market is considerably asymmetric: the volume swells and shrinks as the security prices rise and decline. By quoting bids or offers for specific debt securities against the prevailing market trend, it provides the specific debt securities with more liquidity and, as a result, makes their price movements orderly.

It is also well-known that the dealer trades for its own account, too. It may bet simply on the direction of interest rate (bond price) movements or, more moderately, on widening or narrowing of yield spreads. It may try to arbitrage anomalies in the market in a sophisticated way.

However, it is also important to realize that the dealer's role as an investment advisor and a portfolio assemble/dissembler for the investor is a main source of liquidity in relatively developed debt markets. As has been discussed earlier, the investment needs of a debt investor, especially those of an institutional investor, are generally not issue-specific. Other parameters such as the coupon rate, price, coupon payment dates, maturity, yield, liquidity, and credit risk of bonds are more relevant to its investment decision. The institutional debt investor, unless betting on the direction of interest rate movements, usually trades to align part of its large portfolio to adjust for new cash flow needs or new market conditions. Eventually, the investor buys and sells partial portfolios of debt securities.

The dealer advises the investor on the best way to meet its investment objectives by discussing the current market conditions and an outlook for the market, and proposing the investment strategies that it professionally believes best for the investor. These investment strategies will be materialized by buying or selling particular sets of debt securities. The dealer assembles a desired portfolio for the client by picking up component bonds straight from its existing inventory or by buying them selectively from the market in its inventory, and then sells the completed portfolio to the client as a new part of its investment portfolio. It finances its inventory by short-term funding including repurchase agreements (repos). When the investor wants to sell a sub-portfolio of specific bonds from its investment portfolio, the dealer's function is principally reverse. The dealer buys the sub-portfolio in its inventory first, and may or may not resell the component bonds later, depending on the actual demand from other investors, and other factors.

This role of the dealer in the debt market as an investment advisor and a portfolio assembler/dissembler is particularly important to generate liquidity in the corporate bond markets where a wide variety of bonds are outstanding. Only experienced and competent dealers are able to convince their clients of selling or buying particular bonds to assemble or dissemble portfolios for contemplated transactions.

These dealing activities impose a substantial financial burden on the dealer, and expose it to a significant amount of market risks. Therefore, the dealer must have sufficient financial capital to not only support its inventories but also cushion fluctuations in values of the inventories. In order to mitigate risks associated with dealership and lower its operating costs as possible, it also needs to possess highly sophisticated expertise in trading and managing risks through financial tools like short-selling, interest or currency swaps, futures and options.

The role of the market maker is relevant particularly in the context of primary issues of debt securities or their underwriting. Issuers, when appointing their lead-underwriters (lead managers) for their bond issues, often demand their would-be lead-underwriters to maintain "aftermarket trading" of their newly issued bonds. Thereby, the underwriters are required to make a market throughout the lives of the issues, but practically until the bonds finally end up in "firm hands" (end-investors who buy the bonds for investment purposes rather than for trading purposes, and are likely hold them to maturity). This is because issuers whose bonds have a liquid secondary market will likely be able to achieve lower financing costs for the next issues, to the extent their liquidity premiums are smaller. This is also an additional source of liquidity in the corporate bond market.

The primary dealers are the designated group of government debt securities distributors or, in our case, *de facto* benchmark corporate debt securities distributors that maintain a certain threshold of activity in the secondary market for the securities. They are usually among the best-capitalized securities dealers in the market, and are privileged to exclusively participate in auctions of the benchmark issuer's debt securities. No other dealers and investors are entitled to bid for the newly issued debt securities. As will be discussed in the following section, the benchmark issuer should issue its debt securities through auctions rather than underwritten placements in order to reflect articulately the actual demand and supply relationship of debt capital in the economy. However, a pure form of an auction, which is open to the public, will subject the benchmark issuer to uncertainties not only in the price of the new securities but also in their volume, or make the price highly volatile if the predetermined auction volume is maintained. This is because it reflects only the snapshot relationship of demand and supply at the point of the auction. The participation of the best-capitalized dealers as the primary dealers in the auction, and their ability to hold part of the auctioned-off securities and sell them off gradually in the secondary market, will smooth out the demand and supply relationship over the intervals between regular auctions, and thus make the price and/or volume less volatile.

The exclusivity of auction participation granted to an issuer-appointed group of the primary dealers theoretically limits the competition in the primary market of the benchmark issuer's debt securities. This privilege is arguably granted in exchange for the primary dealer's obligation to maintain a secondary market of the securities, by means of its capital and trading expertise. It is a practical incentive mechanism for the smooth functioning of the market. Therefore, the primary dealership for the benchmark issuer's debt securities is a commonly accepted practice in well-developed capital markets.

From the general description of the dealer's activities in a relatively developed debt market above, it follows that the liquidity providing function of dealers including market makers and primary dealers will be significantly constrained without the following conditions:

- A highly liquid money market including a repo market;

- An upward-sloping yield curve;

- Low transaction costs;

- Risk/return-tradeoff-conscious institutional investors;

- Availability of risk management tools;

- Ability to sell short; and,

- Trading and risk management expertise.

Some developing countries have already instituted the system of market makers or primary dealers. Not all of them have seen the existence of market makers assisting in improving market liquidity (OICV-IOSCO, 1999)[42]. The influence of market markets is disappointing in some countries, probably because their markets lack some of the above conditions.

Auction vs. underwriting for new issues

Issuance of the *de facto* benchmark corporate bonds into the primary market on an auction basis would be more appropriate for efficient pricing of new issues than syndicated underwriting. The latter is used where there is some uncertainty about the complete placement of bonds to be issued, because the underwriters in the syndication of an issue severally guarantee for fee to place their allocated bonds with investors at an offering price or take unsold bonds for their accounts. Most corporate bonds are underwritten at an offering price that underwriters determine in reference to the actual yield of a benchmark issue of a comparable maturity, and other factors such as the credit risk of the issuer and the prevailing market conditions.

Since benchmark yields are inevitably referred to for rationally pricing non-benchmark issues, the benchmark issues cannot be benchmarks in a strict sense unless they are auctioned freely, reflecting the equilibrium supply and demand for the benchmark issues in the market. However, an issuer with unchallengeable authority, like the government, the central bank or the *de facto* benchmark issuer, are occasionally tempted to have its issues underwritten by syndicate members such as commercial banks, insurance companies, and investment banks, and/or to force its captive investors such as the country's contractual savings institutions to buy the bonds for their portfolios. This is likely to occur when the market of the benchmark issues is still in its infancy, or when the benchmark issuer attempts to issue more bonds than the market can absorb at the time of issuance. The following dangers that are associated with underwritten placements of benchmark issues should be recognized:

- The benchmark yield curve will be distorted to an artificially lower level or will not be positively sloped;

- Capital losses arising from sales of seasoned benchmark bonds prevent initial investors to sell them in the secondary market;

- A negative carry or an unreasonably thin spread between long- and short-term interest rates due to artificially lower yields on long-term bonds discourages market makers to carry an inventory of the bonds for resale in the secondary market, which is funded usually with short-term borrowing;

- The development of a liquid secondary market will be hindered;

- A reasonable level of profitability of the country's major institutions will be hampered;

- The accumulating balance of benchmark bonds underwritten or bought at an off-the-market yield will crowd out non-benchmark issuers from the debt market;

- Rational and efficient reallocation of the country's capital will be impeded;

- The country's major financial institutions, many of whom are funded with short-term liabilities such as deposits, become unbearably vulnerable to external shocks; and,

- This will, in turn, increase systemic risks of the country's financial system.

In order to reduce its interest cost of its bonds on the long run, the *de facto* benchmark issuer is suggested to undertake auctions of its bond issues in the following manners:

- The bonds are issued on a regular basis by having a stable schedule for auctioning bonds with specific maturities and publicly announcing specifics of each auction well in advance;

- Auction amounts should be kept as stable as possible, and any unusual amounts should be known to the market well in advance with reasons for them;

- The auction process should be designed to invite bids from as broad a spectrum of investors as possible (*e.g.* participation of foreign investors is preferable, and noncompetitive bids may be permitted to tap non-professional investors' demand); and,

- Detailed auction results should be promptly announced to the public.

8.2.3. Transaction environments

Trading environments for debt securities should be investor-friendly in order to enhance liquidity in the secondary market. Most issues involved in enhancement of investor-friendly trading environments are common between government and non-government debt securities including corporate debt securities. They are summarized in Table 10, but detailed discussion will be left to another occasion.

Table 10: Measures for Trading Environments Improvement	
Objectives	Specific measures
Reduction of transaction costs	Lower entry barriers into dealership (more competition)
	An electronic bond information dissemination system
	Abolition of or exemption from the withholding tax and the stamp duty
	Book-entry, registered form of bond (dematerializaion)
Enhancement of reliability of transactions	Book-entry, registered form of bond (dematerializaion)
	A single automated depository, clearing and settlement system
	A single combined system for cash and securities settlement
Avoidance of market segmentation or fragmentation	Harmonization of tax treatments across provincial states/ subdivisions and investor categories
	Reduction of investment restrictions on different categories of institutional investors
Efficient and rational price discovery mechanism	Short-selling
	Securities lending
	Futures and options
	Interest rate and currency swap
Availability of risk management tools	Short-selling
	Securities lending
	Futures and options
	Interest rate and currency swap
Ease of inventory funding	Money market including a repo market
	Upward-sloping yield curve
	Dealers' access to the discount window
	A group of dealers with a strong capital base
Generation of demand for debt securities	Institutional investors
	Capital account convertibility
Enhancement of investors' confidence and trust in the market	Well-coded regulations
	Competent, corruption-free and well-motivated regulators
	Enforcement ability of regulators

There can be also some tradeoffs between independently appropriate policy measures. For instance, the entry barriers into dealership such as dealership eligibility criteria should be low to encourage competition in the market. To protect the market from any systemic risks, the dealer must have ethical, competent, qualified professionals, and a strong capital base. A lower bar for entry into the industry may allow malicious or incompetent elements to infiltrate into the system and, as a consequence, inflate regulatory costs or endanger the financial system. A balance should be struck, and the balance may shift over time.

Among the policy measures stated above, short-selling, which must be accompanied by securities lending facilities, and futures and options often face strong resistance against their introduction into the market from policymakers and/or existing market participants, even though they are an integral part of an efficiently functioning debt market. They are not just risk-management mechanisms. They are also essential "price discovery" tools. In a market without these means, market participants can make profits only by buying low and then selling high; and, no market participants can initiate paired transactions by selling high and then buying low and be economically motivated to correct overprices of securities. This will tend to lead market participants to bidding up the most heavily traded issues until the whole market comes to realize that they are really overvalued, and the market for the securities collapses. As a result,

      – one or two specific issues will be overpriced and the rest underpriced;

      – liquidity will unproportionately concentrate on the specific issues;

      – the benchmark yield curve will be intolerably distorted;

      – the market's ability to discover the right prices[43] of individual debt securities will be crippled; and,

      – more market participants will be financially damaged to a greater extent.

The objectives of the debt market as an efficient and rational mechanism for capital reallocation will be significantly defeated. Short-selling as well as futures and options enable and, more importantly, motivate smarter or more cautious market participants to continuously correct overpricing, and help increase the overall liquidity in the market.

The resistance to these financial instruments is not necessarily baseless. However, their benefits are too valuable to forego for the development of a debt market. It is more constructive to pay more attentions and devote more resources to preventive measures against risks associated with them.

8.2.4. *Portfolio investment demand*

Institutional investors such as pension funds, mutual funds, insurance companies, or foreign institutional investors are unquestionably a key to the development of a debt market, especially to mobilize long-term capital. Nonetheless, they invest in corporate bonds, but are unlikely to trade them in the secondary market. This is truer with what we call here minor corporate bond issues. We focus our discussion on the policy implications of such a behavior of institutional investors that are likely to be more acute in developing countries.

The institutional investor in general does not need to keep its entire investment portfolio liquid all the time. Money that frequently inflows and outflows is marginal to the whole portfolio. The rest is relatively illiquid funds, at least for a certain period of time, if not forever. Its actual size varies, depending on investment objectives, restrictions and strategy of the fund, and the outlook of market conditions. With respect to this residual part, therefore, it is reasonable that the institutional investor invests a substantial amount of funds in minor corporate bonds for higher yields at the expense of liquidity, and holds them to maturity.

Demographic trends in developing economies tend to weaken investment disciplines. New money tends to flow continuously into investment portfolios under the management of institutional investors in the developing countries where the population and per capita income are growing. Moreover, the population is younger, which demands less cash outflows from the portfolios for the years to come. These demographic trends, common to developing economies, help mask the true investment performance of the portfolios. As a result, they help relax pressures on the institutional investor to elaborately manage the relatively illiquid portions of its portfolios in order to maximize their return on investments by optimally adjusting the portfolios for ever-changing market conditions and by shrewdly seizing on better investment opportunities.

In order to alleviate the negative situation more typical of growing economies, the following policy measures should be considered:

- To privatize the asset management business and introduce competition in the industry;

- To make the performance of institutional investors and/or their fund managers transparent to the public; and,

- To set up their performance measures controlling for demographic factors.

NOTES

1. The Riegle-Neal Interstate Banking and Branching Efficiency Act. This act is applicable to national-chartered banks only. State-chartered banks need to be permitted interstate business by their state legislatures.

2. BIS, *International Banking and Financial Market Development* (Quarterly publication), November 1999

3. FRB, *Flow of Funds Accounts of the United States 1998* (released on March 12, 1999), and Bank of Japan, *Shikin Junkan Kanjo 1998* (Flow of Funds Accounts 1998). The corporate bonds in Japan are "industrial securities" (straight bonds, convertible bonds, and bonds with equity warrants) and bank debentures.

4. The distribution by sector of corporate bonds issued from February 1997 to October 1999 in Korea is as follows: electric & electronic equipment: 33%; transportation equipment: 21%; whole sale trade: 15%; petroleum and chemical 8%; metal: 6%; communications: 5%; machinery: 4%; construction: 3%; and miscellaneous: 5%. (IFCs bond database)

5. In 1996 and 1997, 93% and 87% of corporate bonds were guaranteed, with the remaining 7% and 13% non-guaranteed, respectively. In 1998 these proportions had altered drastically with 33% guaranteed and 67% non-guaranteed. (The Bank of Korea and, Korea Securities Dealers Association, KSDA).

6. The distribution by sector of corporate bonds issued from February 1997 to October 1999 in Czech Republic is as follows: banking: 77%; electric, gas and sanitary: 9%; metal: 7%; communications: 3%; oil, gas, petroleum: 2%; and miscellaneous: 5%. (IFCs Bond database)

7. Though corporate bond markets already exist in one way or another in many developing countries, it is highly problematic to gather reliable statistical data on their corporate bond markets. More surprisingly, reasonable data of the corporate bond markets in developed countries consistent across countries is not available. For example, bond data for the developed countries was taken from *BIS Quarterly Review*, where as that for the developing countries were taken from IFC's bond database, but not from the BIS source. This is because BIS data does not have amounts of domestic debt securities in some of the developing countries such as Indonesia, Philippines, Slovakia and Thailand, and has amounts different from the IFC data for the other developing countries. Therefore, there are some differences in definitions of corporate bonds or debt securities issued by corporate issuers.

8. Korea is no longer usually considered to be a developing country. However, since the Asian Financial Crisis in 1997, Korea has again become a World Bank Group client country eligible for World Bank and IFC programs. As such, it is included in IFC's bond database and is here categorized as a developing country.

9. As will be discussed later, it is appropriate in this context to broaden the concept of a government bond market to include a market of major corporate bond issues whose secondary market is liquid enough to substitute the function of a government bond market.

10. The terminology of "major" and "minor" issuers or "major" and "minor" bonds is not common in the securities industry. It is arbitrarily coined here to present a conceptual framework for devising a strategy for debt market development in a developing country.

11. Interchangeable. Fungible bonds are bonds issued by the same issuer in several tranches with the same nominal coupon rate as well as identical dates for the payment of coupons and for repayment of the principal at maturity; therefore, they can be substituted for purposes of trading, clearing, settlement, coupon payments, repayment, etc. The fungibility of bond ensures the depth and continuous liquidity of the market.

12. Mr. Micah S. Green, Executive Vice President of The Bond Market Association in New York, as quoted in the June 27, 1999 issue of the New York Times. This was found by Ms. Lori A. Trawinski, Director, Policy Analysis and Research, The Bond Market Association, through her PhD desertion research work.

13. See Section 6.1.2. "Enforcemnet of regulatory disclosure"

14. See Section 6.1.1. "Disclosure system vs merit system"

15. A shelf registration system allows for the sale of securities on a delayed or continuos basis. Once it registers for an amount that may reasonably be expected to be sold for a predetermined period (say, two years) after the initial date of registration, the issuer and its underwriters are allowed the flexibility to sell the registered securities when they think market conditions are most favorable during that period.

16. A merit system is one in which the regulatory authorities review the substantive merits of a proposed capital market issue in order to ensure that investors are protected and that the issue is compatible with the national development scheme. Pursuant to laws, decrees, or directives, the authorities determine the participants who may enter the market and the terms of this involvement, including but not limited to the type of instrument that may be used and the substantive terms of the instrument (e.g., timing and pricing of the issuance). This gives regulators the ability to exercise tremendous power over market outcomes. (Wong, 1997)

17. In this connection, it is logical that some countries require companies aspiring to publicly issue bonds to have listed their shares on a national stock exchange. However, rules of this kind prevent a project-specific company from publicly issuing bonds to finance its project, because the company often is a special-purpose company but not a public company, and, therefore, disqualifies for listing of its stock. Bonds collateralized with the assets and cash flows without recourse to the issuer would also disqualify for public issuance. These bond structures are of great value to infrastructure and other development projects. Therefore, the rules need some exemptions to facilitate the innovative debt financing techniques that development countries may need for their social infrastructure building.

18. The five basic principles are: (1) The Rights of Shareholders: The corporate governance framework should protect shareholders' rights. (2) The Equitable Treatment of Shareholders: The corporate governance framework should ensure the equitable treatment of all shareholders, including minority and foreign shareholders. All shareholders should have the opportunity to obtain effective redress for violation of their rights. (3) The Role of Stakeholders in Corporate Governance: The corporate governance framework should recognize the rights of stakeholders as established by law and encourage active cooperation between corporations and stakeholders in creating wealth, jobs, and the sustainability of financially sound enterprises. (4) Disclosure and Transparency: The corporate governance framework should ensure that timely and accurate disclosure is made on all material matters regarding the corporation, including the financial situation, performance, ownership, and governance of the company. (5) The Responsibilities of the Board: The corporate governance framework should ensure the strategic guidance of the company, the effective monitoring of the management by the board, and the board's accountability to the company and the shareholders."

19. The internet platform is writer-driven than reader-driven or watcher-driven. The traditional media, such as TV, radio, and hard copy publication, are basically either reader-driven or watcher-driven. This means that unless you or your intermediary are like a publisher, commercially sure that you can attract a critical mass, you cannot present your views and ideas to the public. Moreover, you have to rely on a host of professionals to have your information disseminated. Because the traditional media's fixed and marginal variable costs of transmitting information are substantial, and are almost prohibitive to individuals. The internet world has revolutionarily changed the economic equation of disseminating facts, opinions, views or thoughts. Moreover, you have in principle full control on the contents and the way they are presented.

20. One issuer issues bonds of different coupon rates, maturity dates, interest payment dates, security arrangements though distinct issuers and/or tranches. This fragments one issuer's fixed income securities into less interchangeable and less substitutable securities even though they are issued by the same issuer.

21. Since 1994, IFC has invested in eight rating agencies in developing countries and has several projects to invest in rating agencies in pipeline.

22. Only a few basis points of a principal mount for straight corporate bonds on an annualized basis.

23. Duff & Phelps Credit Rating Co. provides a commercial bank with services of assessing the bank's overall credit administration process (Orabutt , 1999). What is proposed above can be an extension of this kind of services.

24. Government debt instruments, regardless of their maturities and target investors, are generally exempt from securities registration due to the "risk-free" creditworthiness of the government.

25. Shelf-registration was initiated in the US, but similar mechanisms have been tried elsewhere. Its process is designed to permit issuers to access the public markets quickly, without sacrificing on the adequacy of information to the public. Generally, qualified issuers may register a prospectus that does not include certain aspects of the final terms of the debt security to be issued (usually, the tenor and interest rate). This prospectus is then reviewed and approved by the supervisor. For a set period of time, during which the information in the prospectus is assumed to be current, the issuer is then permitted to offer securities under this prospectus without further registration. Eligible users of this must usually be reporting companies, with good credit records and the types of debt instruments that may be the subject of shelf registration may be limited to straight debt.

26. In periodic markets, trading occurs at periodic (discrete) intervals. At the specified time of the call auction, accumulated orders are executed in a multilateral transaction (batch) at a uniform (single) price that balance demand with supply. (Dattels, 1995)

27. The distribution of privately place bonds is likely to be restricted.

28. In 1990, the Hong Kong Government launched its debt market development strategy by introducing a government debt program of Exchange Fund Bills and Notes, a robust and efficient clearing and settlement system, a market-making system to enhance secondary market liquidity, high quality, marketable debt issues by private sector, and tax concessions on profits arising from debt securities investments (Lee, 1999). The Republic of Singapore has been issuing her government bonds. However, most issues of the government bonds were, for many years, placed with its Central Provident Fund, the State contractual savings system. They were not intended to actively trade on the secondary market. The first attempt was made to create a risk-free yeild curve with the largest ever issueance of the government bonds worth S$30.3 billion in 1987. In early 1998, the Republic launched a series of financial sector reforms, including bond markets. Its bond market reforms included (i) increased government debt issues and announced a regular calendar of issues, (ii) issuance of 10-year Singapore Government Securities, and (iii) increased bond issues by its Statutory Boards. (The Monetary Authority of Singapore)

29.   A macroeconomic identity that accounts for these relations is:

$$X + R - M \equiv S - I + T - G$$

where X = Export, R = Transfer, M = Import, S = Saving, T = Tax less domestic transfer and G = Government Spending.

30.   Calculated from The World Bank PPI Project Database (Roger, 1999)

31.   IMF, *International Financial Statistical Yearbook 1998*

32.   According to the data on the 115 IFC-financed private infrastructure projects from 1967 to 1996 (Carter, 1996), the financial structure of the projects were as follows: debt:equity = 58%:42%; local:foreign =33%:67%. If the debt and equity shares were the same in the foreign and local shares, the local debt share would be 19.4% (58% x 33%). The actual shares of local debt (local commercial banks) and local equity in 1996 were 10% and 26%, respectively. The range of 10-20% was estimated from the 19.4% and 10% figures.

33.   The effect of the positions bought or sold on the price paid or received for a security. If an order lot is large relative to the actual liquidity, the order will be executed only at a price low or high enough to meet the required volume of demand for or supply of the security. The difference between the executed and initially quoted prices is called the market impact or price impact. Market impact is often the largest component of trading cost for a large transaction and for a large investor.

34.   The transaction costs include commissions and fees, market makers' bid/offer spreads and opportunity costs associated with not transacting when a trade is not executed at the initially quoted market price (the market impact).

35.   IFC, as a multilateral institution, provided emerging market issuers with guarantees to encourage issuance of local currency, medium- and long-term bonds. "Since markets find IFC grantees expensive, this vehicle has been most successful in poorer, less stable markets where generous spreads can cover the costs of the guarantee." (Berger 1998).

36.   There is a positive relationship between equity issuance in emerging markets and the level of accounting standards (Ayward, 1999). In developing markets, large firms become more leveraged as the stock market develops; and, stock trading on an exchange aggregates information about the prospect of the issuers and makes it publicly observable by the issuer's creditors and investors (Demirgüç-Kunt, 1995). Legal and accounting reforms that strengthen creditor rights, contract enforcement, and accounting practices can boost financial intermediary development and thereby accelerate economic growth (Levine, Loayza & Beck, 1999).

37.   See Footnote 18.

38.   Major companies with substantial global networks which render investor relations services are: Thomson Financial Investor Relations (New York), Hill and Knowlton (New York), Shandwick International (London), Burson-Marsteller (New York), The Carson Group (New York), to name but a few.

39.   Floating rate bonds are excluded from "straight bonds" in some cases.

40.   "Quote-driven" means that the prices of securities are determined principally by bid/offer quotations that dealers in the securities make at their own risk. The dealers are "market makers" for the securities. A quote-driven market is also referred to as a "dealers' market". It includes NASDAQ in the United States, the London Stock Exchange, and the Bombay Stock Exchange in India. "Order-driven" means that bids, offers and prices (matched bid/offer prices) are determined principally by the

terms of orders arriving at a central market place, and market makers such as "specialists" are secondary to the impact of orders arriving from the public. Most stock exchanges in the Unites States, most futures exchanges worldwide, the Tokyo Stock Exchange in Japan, the National Stock Exchange of India, are examples of order-driven markets.

41.   In Hong Kong's government bond market, for example, the registered dealer corresponds to the market maker in our terms here, and the market maker to the primary dealer.

42.   The International Organization of Securities Commissions conducted a survey on the influence of market makers in the creation of liquidity by sending a questionnaire to all its emerging market committee members. Replies were received from 18 jurisdictions.

43.   They will conceivably be closer to their intrinsic values.

BIBLIOGRAPHY

Adler, Michael, 1999, "Emerging Market Investment: Problems and Prospects", in *Financial Markets & Development*, edited by Alison Harwood and others, Brookings Institution Press, Washington, D.C.

Aylward, Anthony, and Jack Glen, 1999, "Primary Securities Markets: Cross Country Findings", Discussion Paper Number 39, International Finance Corporation

Barry, John S., 1996, "Why Congress Should Privatize Fannie Mae and Freddie Mac -- A Special Report to the House Banking and Financial Services Committee", Committee Brief, The Heritage Foundation

Berger, Teressa C., 1998, "Financial Institutions" (Lessons of Experience; No. 6), International Finance Corporation

Bossone, Biagio, 1998, "Circuit theory of finance and the role of Incentives in Financial Sector Reform", Policy Research Working Paper 2026, The World Bank

Carter, Laurence W., and Gary Bond, 1996, "Financing Private Infrastructure" (Lessons of Experience; No. 4), International Finance Corporation

Chakravarty, Sugato, and Asani Sarkar, 1999, "Liquidity in U.S. Fixed Income markets: A Comparison of the Bid-Ask Spread in Corporate, Government and Municipal Bond Markets"

Chiquier, Loïc, 1999, "Secondary Mortgage Facility: Case Study of Cagamas Berhad in Malyasia", Study for the World Bank Capital Markets Development Department

Dattels, Peter, 1995, "The Microstructure of Government Securities Markets", IMF Working Paper WP/95/117, International Monetary Fund

Demirgüç-Kunt, Asli, and Vojilav Maksimovic, 1995, "Stock Market Development and Firm Financing choices", Policy Research Paper 1461, The World Bank

Hakansson, Nils H., 1999, "The Role of a Corporate Bond Market in an Economy --- and in Avoiding Crises", Working Papers RPF-287, Institute of Business and Economic Research (IBER), University of California at Berkeley

Gatti, James F. and Ronald W. Spahr, The year unknown, "The Burden of Government-sponsored Enterprises: The Case of the Federal Home Loan Mortgage Corporation", CATO, http://www2.thebooktree.com/usp/lr/articles/gov_enterprise.htm

Hong, Gwangheon, and Arthur Warga, 1998, "An Empirical Study of Bond Market Transactions", The Bond Markets Association

Inoue, Hiroshi, 1999, "G7 Shokoku no Kokusai Shijou --- Shijou Ryudousei no Kanten kara Mita Nihon Shijou no Tokuchouten", Working Paper Series 99-J-2, The Bank of Japan

Klock, Mark, and D. Timothy McCormick, 1998, "The Impact of Market Maker Competition o Nasdaq Spreads", NASD Working Paper 98-04, National Association of Securities Dealers

Kriz, John, Devid Levey, and Vincent Truglia, 1998, "Rating Methodology: Government-Sponsored Enterprises (GSEs)", *Global Credit Research*, Moody's Investors Service

Lea, Michael J, 1998, "Models of Secondary Mortgage Market Development", in *New Deirections in Asian Housing Finance: Linking capital markets and housing finance*, edited by Masakazu Watanabe, International Finance Corporation, Washington, D.C.

Lea, Michael J, and Loïc Chiquier, 1999, "Providing Long-term Financing for Housing: The Role of Secondary Markets", United Nations Development Programme

Lee, Esmond K. Y., 1999, "Debt Market Development in Hong Kong", Presentation to The World Bank Group

Levine, Ross, and Sara Zervos, 1996, "Stock Market Development and Long-Run Growth", Policy Research Paper 1582, The World Bank

Miyanoya, Atsushi, Hitotaka Inoue, and Hideaki Higo, 1999, "Nihon no Kokusai Shijou no Microstructure to Shiou Ryuudousei", Working Paper Series 99-J-1, The Bank of Japan

Orabutt, Chuck J., 1999, "A New Framework for Capital Adequacy --- Preliminary Comments", (written in response to the BIS proposal on capital adequacy guidelines published in May 1999), Duff & Phelps Credit Rating Co.

OICV-IOSCO, 1999, "The Influence of Market Makers in the Creation of Liquidity", Report by the Emerging Markets Committee of the International Organization of Securities Commissions

Pinkers, Kenneth, 1997, "The Function of Ratings In Capital Markets", *Global Credit Research*, Moody's Investors Service

Rhee, S. Gho, 1998, Institutional Impediments to the Development of Fixed-Income Securities markets: An Asian Perspective", OECD/World Bank Workshop on the Development Of Fixed-Income Securities Markets in Emerging Market Economies

Roger, Neil, 1999, "Recent Trends in Private Participation in Infrastructure", *Private Sector/Viewpoint*, Note No. 196, The World Bank, September, 1999

Schinasi, Garry J., and R. Todd Smith, 1998, "Fixed-Income Markets in the United States, Europe, and Japan: Some Lessons for Emerging Markets", IMF Working Paper WP/98/173, International Monetary Fund

Shah, Pradip, 1991, "The CRISIL Experience: Building a Rating Agency in a Developing Country", a presentation note at the US SEC's International Institute for Securities Market Development in Washington, DC, The Credit Rating Information Services of India Limited

Shah, Pradip, 1993, "Introducing and Establishing a Credit Rating System: The Case Study of India", a presentation note at the Asian Credit Rating Conference in Denpasar, Bali, Indonesia, The Credit Rating Information Services of India Limited

Taylor, Peter, 2000, "Review of IFC Investments in Credit Rating Agencies", IFC Working Document

U.S. Securities and Exchange Commission, 1997, "Report to Congress: The Impact of Recent Technological Advances on the Securities Markets"

Wong, Nancy L., 1996, "Easing down the merit-disclosure continuum: a case study of Malaysia and Taiwan", *Law and Policy in International Business*, Fall/1996

Session 4

THE ROLES OF SECURITIES LAWS AND SECURITIES MARKET REGULATORS FOR THE SOUND DEVELOPMENT OF BOND MARKETS

299- 312

G12 H63
G18

THE ROLE OF REGULATORS IN THE DEVELOPMENT OF GOVERNMENT SECURITIES MARKETS: AN OVERVIEW

by
Mr. Giovanni Sabatini

In my presentation today I would like to outline which are the areas of interest for regulators in the development of liquid and efficient markets for government Bonds. Strictly speaking, I should talk about the role of "securities regulator", but I rather prefer to use the more generic term "regulator" since in different jurisdictions some of the functions that could be performed by a securities regulator are allocated elsewhere (Central bank, Ministry of Finance, SROs, etc) and vice-versa.

I will start with some broad concepts about the basic conditions that should be met in order to provide a sound legal and regulatory framework for the development of efficient and liquid Government Bond Markets; I will then move to the issues related to market structure and I will end up with some reference to the Italian Wholesale Government Bond Market which is a good example of effective co-operation among the Italian Treasury, Consob, Bank of Italy and market participants.

Recent financial crises have highlighted the need for the development of domestic bond markets. Extensive literature has shown that deep and liquid financial markets, especially government bonds markets, are needed to ensure a robust and efficient financial system.

The importance of the development of government securities markets

- The need for the development of domestic bond markets has been highlighted by recent financial crises.

- "Deep and liquid financial markets, especially government securities markets, are needed to ensure a robust and efficient financial system as a whole.".
  ("How should we design deep and liquid markets? The case of government securities" CGFS Oct. 1999)

Characteristics of Government Bond Securities

GS have some intrinsic characteristics that make them different from other types of securities and that affect the market structure and liquidity. First, prices for GS are dependent on macroeconomic factors; this type of information is eminently public. This contrasts to equities markets, in which private information play a role in the agents trading behaviour.

The market maker's behaviour in GS markets will be then influenced by its inventory management rather than by the concern of trading against a better informed counterpart (i.e. an insider). (consequence: it is important to identify measures to reduce the inventory cost of market makers); Secondly, GS have finite maturity. There will be investors that will adopt a "buy and hold till maturity strategy" hence reducing the amount of securities available for trading. (consequence: ensure sufficient liquidity to each issue, e.g. regular re-openings of the same issue);

Third, being virtually free from credit risk, the yield curve for GS serves as benchmark in pricing other financial assets. Therefore GS are used by dealers as a major hedging tools for interest rate risk and as underlying assets or collateral for related markets as repo, futures and options markets.

Characteristics of government securities

- Price driven by public information
  (statistical announcement, central bank policy actions)
- Finite maturity
- Benchmark for other securities and financial claims
- Underlying/collateral for futures, options and repo markets

---

The development of efficient and liquid markets is affected by several "external" factors:

- "Environmental factors", such as the macroeconomic situation and the creditworthiness of the issuer;

- "Institutional factors", such as securities law, regulation, supervision, tax and accounting: the existence of a sound legal environment is a conditio sine qua non of effective capital markets;

- "Market Infrastructure", including trading systems for cash and derivatives products, clearing and settlement systems, central depository systems.

In the slide, I marked with a tick the areas where regulators may play an active role in providing a sound and efficient framework for the development of liquid government bond markets. In the following slides I will discuss the issues regulators should address, particularly focusing on issues related to market infrastructure.

```
┌─────────────────────────────────────────────────────┐
│          Factors affecting the development of         │
│            efficient and liquid G.S. markets          │
│                                                       │
│   • Environmental Factors    • Market Infrastructure  │
│      – macroeconomic                                  │
│        situation                – trading systems  ✓  │
│      – issuer creditworthiness  – clearing and        │
│                                   settlement  ✓       │
│   • Institutional Factors                             │
│                                 – CSDs  ✓             │
│      – securities law  ✓        – repo and securities │
│                                   lending  ✓          │
│      – regulation  ✓                                  │
│                                                       │
│      – supervision  ✓                                 │
│      – accounting rules                               │
│      – tax regime                                     │
└─────────────────────────────────────────────────────┘
```

Regulation is necessary to ensure the achievement of the three core objectives and should facilitate capital formation and economic growth. However, the benefits of competition should also be recognized: inappropriate regulation can impose an unjustified burden on the market and inhibit market growth and development.

To strike an efficient balance between regulation and competition has become more and more fundamental in the last decade, in parallel to the increased and now superior importance of markets (vs intermediaries) [to fulfill the functions traditionally attributed to efficient financial markets: (i) allocation of funds, (ii) management of risk, etc.]

```
┌─────────────────────────────────────────────────────┐
│        Institutional Factors - Regulation             │
│                                                       │
│   • Regulation                                        │
│      – is necessary to ensure:                        │
│         • the protection of Investors                 │
│         • that markets are fair, efficient and        │
│           transparent                                 │
│         • the reduction of systemic risk              │
│                                                       │
│      – should facilitate capital formation and        │
│        economic growth;                               │
│                                                       │
└─────────────────────────────────────────────────────┘
```

Regulators therefore should:

- avoid unnecessary barriers to entry and exit from markets and products,

- favour the widest participation in markets from those who meet the specified entry criteria,

- consider the economic impact of the requirements imposed,

- ensure an equal regulatory burden on all market participants providing similar services.

```
┌─────────────────────────────────────────────────┐
│          Institutional Factors - Regulation       │
│                                                     │
│    ·  no unnecessary barriers to entry and exit     │
│       from markets and products;                    │
│    ·  market open to the widest range of            │
│       participants;                                 │
│    ·  consider the economic impact of               │
│       regulation;                                   │
│    ·  equal regulatory burden.                      │
│                                                     │
└─────────────────────────────────────────────────┘
```

Market Surveillance

Effective regulation should be supported by adequate market surveillance, but because of time constraints, I will not spend much time on this issue. I have just listed as a reminder some items to be taken into account in order to deliver an effective market surveillance.

```
┌─────────────────────────────────────────────────┐
│              Institutional Factors -               │
│                   Supervision                      │
│                Market Surveillance                 │
│                                                     │
│   • Market Integrity        • Market Dynamics      │
│     – insider trading,        – continuous         │
│     – price manipulation,       monitoring of      │
│     – other abusive             trading,           │
│       practices.              – large and          │
│                                 concentrated       │
│                                 position,          │
│                               – anomalous market   │
│                                 trends in specific │
│                                 securities.        │
└─────────────────────────────────────────────────┘
```

Market Infrastructure - Trading Systems: Primary market

Given the special features of the Italian secondary and primary markets for GS, in commenting the next two slides (nn. 9 and 10) I will constantly refer to those markets.

The efficiency of the primary market is affected by the **Role of Primary Dealers (PDs). These** market participants also provide **a** crucial link between the primary and secondary market.

To facilitate the placement of GS the so called "primary dealers system" has been adopted in several countries, where a group of dealers, designated as PDs by the Treasury (or the central Bank), have been attributed special rights and obligations. The former include: (i) greater access to primary market auctions, (ii) being counterparts in open market operations. The latter include: (i) active participation in primary auctions, (ii) market making in the secondary market with a certain degree of tight bid-ask spreads. Because of the obligations in the secondary market, the PD system can help enhance market liquidity.

In the Italian system, the PDs are market-makers selected by MTS, the firm managing the Official wholesale Secondary market for Treasury Securities, on the base of specific prerequisites concerning their patrimonial stability and the volume traded on that market.

The Department of the Treasury selects the **Specialists in Italian Government Bonds among** the PDs and requires them to participate meaningfully in both the primary and the secondary market of Treasury securities. As a reward, Specialists are entitled to participate to specific auctions reserved to them. They get an average of 60-70% of total nominal amount of Treasury securities issued.

Primary markets for GS function as Auctions.

A second feature that affects the efficiency of the primary market is the mechanism through which the securities are auctioned. In Italy Treasury securities are issued according to two types of auctions: the *multiple price auction* (also called *competitive* or *American auction)* for T-bills ('BOT') and the *uniform price auction* (also called *Dutch auction)* for medium-long term bonds ('BTP', 'CCT' and 'CTZ'). Both types of auctions are not subject to a minimum price.

In the *multiple price auction* each bid is satisfied at the price offered. The first bids to be accepted are those with the highest price and then all the others are satisfied in descending order until the quantity of accepted bids reaches the amount tendered by the Treasury.

In the *uniform price auction* all the requests are auctioned at the same price, the so-called "marginal price", which is determined by satisfying bids starting from the highest price until the total amount of bids accepted equals the amount offered. The price of the last successful bid is the "marginal pnce

In both types of auction a "threshold price" is calculated according to the prices offered in order to limit bidders' speculative behaviour. The algorithm used to obtain the "threshold price" is well known by the auction participants and it has not been changed since 1992, the year of its introduction.

After the auction is announced, but before it takes place, investors begin trading the yet-to-be-issued security in what is called the **when-issued-market.**

Transactions in this market are agreements to exchange securities and funds on the day the new security is settled (although a considerable portion of when-issued positions are unwound before the issue date). The when-issued market allows new Treasury issues to be efficiently distributed to investors and provides useful information to potential bidders about the prices the Treasury may receive at the upcoming auction.

In order to increase the **Transparency** of the primary market, the Treasury releases an **Annual Auction Calendar** and a **Quarterly Issuance Program.** The first contains the announcement, the auction and the settlement dates concerning the issuance program of the following year. The second is intended to announce the newsecurities to be issued in the following quarter. It contains all the relevant characteristics of these securities as well as the minimum issue size, i.e. the minimum quantities to be issued overtime.

Market Infrastructure - Trading Systems Secondary market Organized Markets VS OTC

One of the main differences between GS markets and equities markets is the degree of centralization of trading. Equity trading generally occurs on centralized(organized) markets, while trading on GS occurs in OTC markets.

For the purpose of this presentation, I differentiate between decentralized and centralized markets by the degree of information being available to the public (customer and dealers alike) on a consolidated basis, where "consolidated basis" means that price and trade data from the spectrum of dispersed dealers is available on a single screen.

GS markets (and fixed-income markets more generally) typically are multiple dealer markets but they tend not to be linked up electronically. Investors in GS markets cannot easily ascertain what is the best, most recent bid-ask spread being offered by the population of dealers.

In principle, the only way for an investor to ascertain which dealer has the best quotation in a decentralized market, would be to directly contact each dealer.

Therefore, given the decentralized nature of GS markets, it is possible for simultaneous transactions to occur at different prices and, more importantly, at prices other than the best available price across a spectrum of market-makers.

The lack of "openness in the price-setting process is considered one of the main point of "friction" (i.e. dealers profits) in the bond market. Market liquidity depends on the ease with which market participants can carry out transactions. Thus, otherthings being equal lower transaction costs contribute to higher market liquidity. Therefore there is a strong incentive towards more centralization. This could be obtained through either a regulated market (this is the case for Italy, where GS are dealt in two different regulated market: the MTS, which is the wholesale GB market and the MOT which is the retail market) or an electronic-computer network (ECN).

Transparency

The degree of transparency which market participants observe in the trading process is also important, although the content of the appropriate set of information will differ from one market to another, depending on their specific characterisics.

Generally speaking, in a dealer market, the dissemination of prevailing prices to a broader trading community, including end users, will help to enhance market liquidity.

Two examples are BondExpress and **GovPX.** BondExpress provides a database of US bond quotations to traders (now the service is available through the Internet). GovPx is the main service providing US Treasury bond quotations. They sell them through Bloomberg, Bridge, Reuters and Dow Jones on a subscription basis. This step is said to have further enhanced the liquidity of the US Treasury bond market.

By contrast the disclosure of information on specific orders which might endanger the anonymity of market participants would require careful consideration, as it might discourage dealers from making markets. For instance a move towards anonimity of market makers in the MTS in 1997 was found to have led to narrower bid-ask spread and smaller market impact of large trades.

Dealer markets vs auction markets

Broadly speaking, two types of trading system exist in the secondary market for GS:dealer markets and auction-agency markets. In the latter, buy-orders and sell-orders are matched by a centralized auction agency. Therefore, they are called "order-driven markets (the MTS is an example). In the former, dealers supply immediacy of trade by continuously providing bid and/or ask quotations. In this sense, they are called "quote-driven markets" (the MOT is an example). In order for the dealer system to be transparent and efficient, dealers must compete with each other for the order flow. Posted quotes must be firm and "preferred clients" practices must be forbidden.

Market Infrastructure - Alternative Trading Systems

As previously mentioned, because of the inefficiency of OTC markets in GS, the fastest growing area of ATS is believed to be within the bond market, at least in Europe. ATS offer:

- broader execution choice: continuos auction, limit order book, crossing and profile order market models;

- lower costs: lower commission and narrower spreads

- anonymous dealing: reduced market impact of large trades;

- efficient execution and processing: immediate price and transaction confirmation.

- extended trading hours/24 hour trading;

- smaller "tick-sizes" (minimal price change), which enable more precise limit orders;

- higher liquidity in certain securities through specialization.

In this light I would like to mention the success of EuroMTS, a UK company, founded in October 1998 and authorized by the SFA as inter-dealer-broker. Euro MTS manages a trading system for the European Benchmark Securities (Germans, Italian, French, and others). EuroMTS is a key example, in Europe, of this move from OTC bilateral transactions in GS markets towards a multilateral trading system operated by an ATS.

In the US, volume traded electronically is estimated at 1 to 3 percent of total volumein the wholesale bond market.

Market Infrastructure - Trading systems

- Alternative Trading Systems in Bond Markets:
  - Bloomberg BondTrader,
  - Brokertec,
  - Coredeal,
  - Cantor e.speed system,
  - Euro MTS,
  - Instinet Fixed Income,
  - Web.ET.

Clearing and Settlement

Market integration and globalisation have brought enormous increases in market efficiency: markets are deeper and more liquid and provide a wider range of products to end users at lower costs than in the past.

However, these trends have also some drawbacks because of the greater speed and virulence with which financial turmoil can spread. This implies, amongst other things, making clearance and settlement systems, along with payment systems, as robust as we can, since they constitute the infrastructure that tie markets and participants together.

There is a direct link between markets liquidity and the efficiency of clearance and settlement systems. In situation of market stress, the liquidity of markets is reduced and the volatility of asset prices increases. If settlement systems are perceived by market participants as a possible source of additional risks (i.e. risks other than those arising from their investment decisions) they may be reluctant to trade and the overall market liquidity may be further reduced.

Increasing the efficiency of clearance and settlement systems, allows market participants to optimise the use of liquidity and contributes to minimize the risk of market disruption and systemic risk.

Therefore, arrangements for clearing and settling transactions should ensure the reduction of pre-settlement and settlement risks along with operational reliability, should sustain liquidity and reliability of delivery of securities.

Market Infrastructure - Clearing and Settlement

- General objectives of clearing and settlement systems on an ongoing basis are:
  - to reduce pre settlement and settlement risks (replacement risk, liquidity risk, principal risk) [e.g. STP, (T+3), DVP]
  - to achieve operational reliability; and
  - to sustain liquidity, reliability of delivery of securities, and confidence in the secondary market supported by the system.

In the event of a default, the system should limit and contain the effects and consequences of the default to the defaulting entity and support the continuing liquidity of the securities or contracts traded.

On this issue, I would like to remind that JOSCO Technical Committee and CPSS have recently started a joint project to promote the implementation by securities settlement systems of measures that can enhance international financial stability, reduce risks, increase efficiency, and provide adequate safeguards for investors. A Joint Task Force co-chaired by Mr. Patrick Parkinson and myself has been set up to develop recommendations for the design, operation, and oversight of clearance and settlement systems. The recommendations will cover both individual systems and links between systems.

The Task Force will develop recommendations for domestic settlement systems, identifying the minimum requirements that these systems should meet in order to minimise risks for the domestic and international financial stability, including recommendations addressing the additional issues raised by their cross border settlement activity, such as cross border linkages between settlement systems.

Market Infrastructure - Clearing and Settlement (2)

- At the highest level, in the event of a default, the objectives of the system are:
  - to limit and contain the effects and consequences of the default to the defaulting entity;
  - to support the continuing liquidity of the securities or contracts traded;

Central Depository Systems

A key role in an efficient SSS is played by **CSDs.** The slide lists some of the most important issues to be addressed:

- immobilisation or dematerialization of financial instruments,

- effective and fully developed central securities depository,

- broad direct and indirect industry participation,

- wide range of depository eligible instruments.

Market Infrastructure - Central Depository Systems

- immobilisation or dematerialization of financial instruments,
- effective and fully developed central securities depository,
- broad direct and indirect industry participation,
- wide range of depository eligible instruments.

Derivatives

The demand for Treasury securities is also affected by the markets for derivatives. Derivative markets offer the following list of functions on which I will not comment:

- hedging-arbitrage strategy
- additional liquidity
- improve market completeness
- increase market efficiency (informational).

> ### Market Infrastructure - Derivatives
>
> - hedging-arbitrage strategy
> - additional liquidity
> - improve market completeness
> - increase market efficiency (informational)

Repo and Securities Lending

The repo market allows participants to exchange funds and securities on a temporary basis, i.e. borrowing and lending using Treasury securities as collateral.This market allows investors to deliver securities that they sold short by "reversing in" the securities repeatedly, until they decide to cover the position by purchasing the securities outright. On the other side, investors frequently rely on the repo market to finance their long positions in Treasury securities by "repoing out" those securities. Partly as a result of these activities, trading volume in the repo market is heavy: MTS reported about 20 billion Euro of lending and borrowing in the repo market.

To facilitate transactions in the repo market, the Italian Treasury will start a securities lending program that allows primary dealers to borrow individual Treasury securities from the Treasury portfolio.

> ### Market Infrastructure - Repo and Securities Lending
>
> - Cash-driven market (e.g. GC repo)
>   - dealer financing, secured lending eg central banks, flexible money market instrument
> - Securities-driven market
>   - settlement fails, market maker short positions, arbitrage strategies, custody add-on, institutional income
> - Enhanced liquidity

MTS

Finally, I would like to conclude with some remarks on the effects of the development of the MTS which, as already said, is the Regulated Wholesale Secondary Market for Italian Government Securities. This brings us to chart n. 2, 3 and4.

• **The Italian Government Bond Market - MTS**

- **Primary Market**

  - **Wide range of securities**
  - **Transparent**
  - **Predictable**
  - **Liquid**

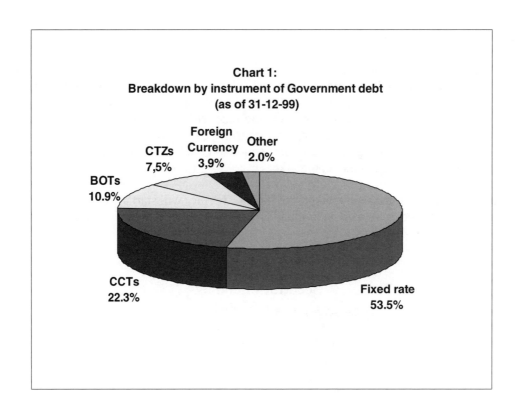

Chart 1:
Breakdown by instrument of Government debt
(as of 31-12-99)

CTZs 7,5%
Foreign Currency 3,9%
Other 2.0%
BOTs 10.9%
CCTs 22.3%
Fixed rate 53.5%

Chart 2 shows the evolution of Italian Government debt stock composition. In six years (1993-1999), the percentages of short term and fixed rate notes has completed reverted: in 1993 fixed rate notes were only *35%* of total Government debt stock; in 1999, the same percentage was *65%*.

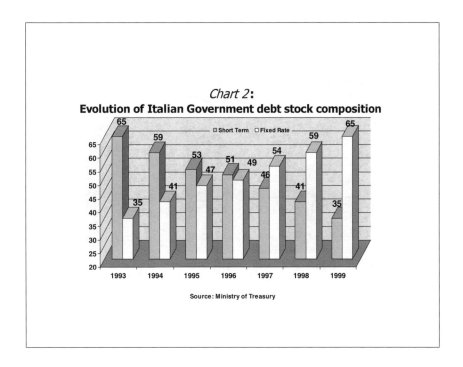

The same tendency is evident in **Chart 3** in terms of duration and average life: in 1993 duration was a bit more than *1.5* years, while in 1999 it was about 3.5 years.

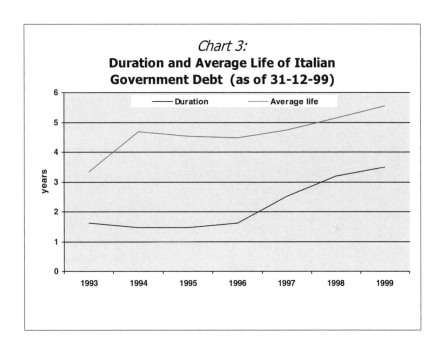

Chart 4 shows a comparison among the MTS, the French and the German GS markets in terms of efficiency, as measured by the bid-ask spread on the 10 and 30 year maturity.

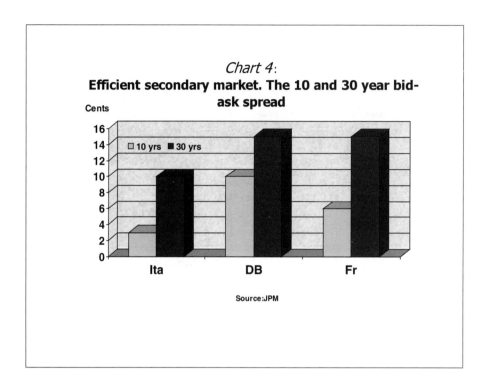

Expectedly, the 1 Gy segment is more efficient for all markets considered. More importantly for our purpose, bid-ask spreads for Italian GS range from 3 to 10 cents, while French and German GS ones range from 6 to 15 and 10 to 15 cents respectively.

Bond Market Regulation in a period of Changing Market Structure: The U.K. Experience

by
Mr. David Strachan

G12

G18 H63

Introduction

Our theme in this session is regulation in a period of changing market structure. In the case of the UK, we have been experiencing not only changes in the markets but also, in the case of the government bond market, in what I will call the market management structure. On top of all this, we are nearing the end of a process of fundamental re-organisation of the regulatory structure for financial services.

My plan is to focus on four aspects of market development that have been uppermost in our minds in the UK. Some of them may seem rather parochial, but I think that they all raise issues of universal relevance and will probably strike chords with most of you. First, though, it will probably be useful if I give you a very brief overview of the UK markets and the regulatory framework in which they sit.

The UK bond markets

Although the UK government is currently balancing the books, it is no different from other governments in having been a major borrower over time. At the end of last year, the nominal value of outstanding government securities, commonly known as gilt-edged securities or gilts, was just under £300 billion, equivalent to roughly 35% of GDP. For the most part, initial maturities range from 5 to 30 years.

Unlike the government, UK companies have not been great users of the bond markets, or certainly of the domestic sterling bond markets. For the most part, they have tended to place far greater reliance on equity financing. In part, this reflects the fact that the UK has had a well-developed equity market for a very long time. But it was due to the fact that for long periods of the 1970s and 1980s high levels of inflation, followed by lingering inflationary expectations, left the nominal costs of longer term debt finance unattractively high. Even now that we have returned to lower nominal long-term financing costs than for many years, the real cost of sterling borrowing is not especially low. And in 1999, only 43 UK companies listed bond issues on the London Stock Exchange (LSE), raising around £1.5 billion. By contrast, the UK is a major centre for international bond trading. London based book runners issued roughly 70% of all Eurobonds in Q1 1999 and London averages around 60% of all Eurobond issues. London is estimated to account for 75% of all secondary market Eurobond trading.

Those are the main markets. A few words now on market structure. The first thing to say is that bond markets in the UK are essentially wholesale markets. Retail interest in bonds is relatively small.

Trading venues vary. The cash gilt market, in particular, is largely on-exchange, in part because the debt issuer continues to require primary dealers to be market makers on the LSE. There is a significant interest rate futures market on the London International Financial Futures Exchange (LIFFE), and an even larger OTC market in interest rate contracts. The repo market is wholly OTC.

Core trading of eurobonds is mainly the domain of the major banks, either direct with one another or through brokers. Most of the participating firms are members of The International Securities Market Association (ISMA).

Clearing and settlement arrangements for domestic bonds, including gilts, is now centred on CRESTCo, which also settles equities; exchange derivatives settle in the London Clearing House (LCH); and international securities are normally cleared and settled via the international clearing and settlement depositories, such as Euroclear.

The regulatory framework

I will now move on to describe, briefly, the broad regulatory framework for the debt markets. The two core elements here are the regulation of issuance and the regulation of the secondary markets.

First, issuance. Broadly speaking, regulation of issuance in the UK, as elsewhere in the EU, stems from EU legislation governing the public offering of securities. Securities to be publicly offered are subject in the UK to the Public Offer of Securities Regulations. If they are to be 'listed' on a stock exchange they are also subject to the listing rules set by the UK Listing Authority – currently a public function discharged by the London Stock Exchange but one which the government will be transferring to the FSA next month. The emphasis of this regulation is essentially on initial disclosure about the issuer and continuing disclosure of information likely to impact on an investor's valuation of a security.

Second, there is the regulation of trading. This is captured within the regulatory framework constructed by the Financial Services Act – shortly to be superseded by the Financial Services and Markets Act - and addresses trading activity in a number of ways. In particular, the legislation:

– specifies debt securities as investments, therefore making them qualifying instruments for regulatory purposes;

– provides for the FSA to establish rules, guidance and codes for authorised firms that address their trading of debt instruments;

– imposes a requirement on exchanges, supervised by the FSA, to operate proper and orderly markets

What does this mean in practice in the bond markets? Basically, very 'light touch' regulation in what are generally wholesale markets populated by knowledgeable investors. That is certainly true in the OTC arena, but it is also largely the case in respect of exchange traded debt instruments. For example, exchange market trading of bonds has been conspicuously less transparent – if that is not a contradiction in terms -- than, say, on-exchange trading in equities. In the case of gilts, for instance, market makers are obliged to make continuous prices, but their quotes are not published, simply supplied on request. Currently, post-trade publication applies only to gilts trades of up to £50,000 – a key protection for retail investors and the means of establishing whether a broker has delivered best execution.

The regulation of OTC trading takes a number of forms. These include a small number of direct rules on firms, and several codes of conduct. At the moment, we are in the process of merging two existing codes into a single new code, to be known as the Inter-Professionals Code ("IPC"). We plan to put this out for public consultation some time next month. Basically, the IPC will set out our guidance on how we will interpret the FSA's high level Principles in respect of dealings between "professionals" in the wholesale markets. It will therefore inform the market as to the standards of behaviour and practice which we view as good, and by implication explain when lapses from good practice might be in breach of the Principles.

In addition, the FSA is currently working on a new financial penalties framework to tackle market abuse –insider dealing, the dissemination of false or misleading information and market manipulation. The key point here is that the scope of the regime will cover most of the core instruments traded on an exchange. So if a bond is admitted to trading on an UK exchange, it may well become a 'designated' security. The scope of the framework will extend to any abusive activity in respect of that instrument, whether or not the abusive behaviour occurs on or off exchange, or in or outside the UK.

Finally, we are very supportive of specific sectors of the financial services industry developing their own codes of good practice to cover conduct in more specialist areas. A good example of this is the Gilt Repo Code, developed by the Securities Lending and Repo Committee ("SLRC"), a committee of industry practitioners chaired by the Bank of England. The SLRC drafted the Gilt Repo Code in 1995, ahead of the launch of the gilt repo market in the UK. The Code sets out general, high level standards that are expected of all repo market participants and the preliminary steps, such as establishing systems and controls, which participants should address before undertaking repo activity. It then goes on to describe 'know your counterparty' checks, the roles of agents and name-passing brokers, the need for appropriate legal documentation, and it gives guidance on margin, custody, default and confirmation issues. A number of annexes to the Code define terms commonly used in the market and set out standard conventions, including repo calculations, and a schedule of key times in the gilt repo trading day.

The Code therefore provides a comprehensive guide for repo market participants and serves as a useful benchmark for issues concerning good market practice. It has served the market well, particularly during the development stages of the gilt repo market and will, I am sure, continue to be the primary reference point for that market.

Market development

That is the background. I want to spend the rest of this talk focusing on the evolution of the regulatory approach in the UK in the light of market developments. I will cover four developments in particular which, to varying degrees, are inter-related. These developments are:

- the modification of institutional roles;

- the broader product base and the regulation of interacting product groups;

- changes in trading structures and processes;

- the centralisation of risk management.

- In sum, the main core market issue for the FSA in its brief life has been how to ensure that there is an appropriate regulatory approach when:

- the government has decided to alter the institutional structure of the market;

- the product base has broadened and becomes more complex;

- the trading process is changing rapidly; and

- the management of risk figures ever higher in both firm and regulatory priorities.

Institutional roles

First, institutional roles. Here I am referring to the changes that have been taking place in the UK over the past couple of years in the organisation – or what I earlier referred to as the management -- of the government securities market. For many years the Bank of England performed multiple roles in the gilt market, not only as central banker but also managing the issue process, general market oversight and even the prudential oversight of some of the players, particularly the primary dealers and inter-dealer brokers. Then the government decided to grant the Bank independence in determining monetary policy. From that decision followed a chain of changes which has seen issuance and day-to-day cash management pass to a new government agency, the Debt Management Office (DMO), and remaining supervisory responsibilities for firms pass to the FSA. In short, the DMO now looks after issuance, the Bank looks after monetary policy (and financial stability), and the FSA has responsibility for regulation.

Point number one, then, is the recognition that there are probably limits to the number of functional responsibilities you can concentrate in a single organisation without creating a degree of potential conflict of interest that may start to undermine investor or market confidence. But how does this new separation of roles between the operation of monetary policy, the issuance of debt and the regulation of firms and the marketplace work in practice? In particular, how does the market regulator interact with the government's issuer, who does after all retain a very strong interest in the operation of the secondary market.

I think there are two main points worth making about our experience to date. Number one is that while we have a shared interest in the orderliness of the market, our primary concerns about any disorderliness in the market are somewhat different. The DMO's primary objective is to rectify any disorderliness that occurs and restore the market to an orderly state as quickly as possible. Hence, its focus on measures such as special repo facilities to alleviate squeezes. But in this situation, the FSA's objective will be to pursue those abusing the market and, by doing so, to deter further abuse. But ultimately, such differences are more apparent than real since our interests coincide in the need for orderly markets and the two institutional objectives are not incompatible.

Point number two is that it is essential and in their respective best interests for the issuer and the regulator to maintain a good working relationship. That does not mean a cosy relationship without barriers. The DMO, quite deliberately, is not within the regulatory loop in the UK. But that does not preclude us from maintaining the kind of relationship in which we can discuss, on both a regular and an ad hoc basis, market developments and issues of concern. And that is exactly what we do; with no formal framework but with a clear understanding of our respective roles and responsibilities. This ties directly into my next issue.

Interaction of product markets

The second development has been the growing breadth of the product market over the past few years, and here once again I am focusing on the government bond market. In the 1970s, the UK had only a cash market in government securities; in the 1980s, we saw the rapid growth of a derivatives market;

in the latter part of the 1990s, the third leg of the market was put in place with the legal and fiscal changes needed to facilitate repo.

Given the interrelationship of these three markets – and in particular the fact that abuse may well involve all three markets – a major issue for the FSA has been to ensure regulatory co-ordination across all three markets, and both on-exchange and OTC. Despite regulatory integration, the UK still has eight official agencies with some form of responsibility that impacts on the gilts market. The UK Government has an obvious interest as the issuer of gilts and this is done through the DMO which took over responsibility for the actual issuance of gilts in June 1998.

We, the FSA, have an interest both through the supervision of the firms involved in the gilt market and also through our responsibilities for maintaining market confidence. The Bank of England, whilst no longer responsible for debt management, has a role in ensuring continued financial stability and also an interest in the implications for monetary policy of movements in the gilt markets. Four other bodies (LSE, LIFFE, CRESTCo, LCH) have a formal role that impacts on the gilt market. The LSE is responsible for listing and trading rules and LIFFE has an interest arising from their gilt futures contracts. CRESTCo is the clearing and settlement vehicle for gilts and finally LCH is the central counterparty for the gilt futures contracts and will also be offering to act as the central counterparty for gilt repo contracts later this year.

Given so many official agencies with varying but important roles, communication is essential. In the UK we have established a forum in which all parties meet on a regular basis to ensure that we all have a clear understanding of each other's roles and are aware of the type of information each party is interested in.

Screen-based trading

The next development I want to touch on is the progressive and accelerating shift of the trading process from bilateral telephone dealing to multilateral screen-based trading. In the government securities markets, this trend is more apparent in the trading of government debt within the Euro-zone than it currently is in UK government debt. But several brokers have screen-based systems for the cash market and the expectation is that the bulk of trading will move to the screen in the medium term. This is recognised both in the market and by the DMO, which in January published a consultation paper seeking market views on how this process should evolve.

As the government's debt manager, the DMO obviously has a particular interest in market structure given the implications it may have either for the willingness of primary dealers to offer certainty of new issues take-up, or, more generally, on the implications for market liquidity and any consequentials for the cost of funding.

From a regulatory viewpoint, we have a rather wider interest in the changing shape of the debt markets generally. Broadly speaking, it seems to us that the shift to screen-based trading has many pluses to offer – from higher degrees of transparency, to greater scope for market monitoring, to much better audit trails.

That said, I am sure that in some respects we are still on a learning curve. As a generalisation, bonds are dealt in larger size than equities and lack their liquidity. We have yet to see how this will play out in screen trading. Will low costs and transparency create the virtuous circle for bonds that not only rapidly draws a critical mass of liquidity to the screen but also encourages greater participation in the market? To what extent will screen-based bond trading systems operate better with committed liquidity providers than relying on natural liquidity? Will splits between screen and non-screen trading increase the temptation of manipulation by moving the screen price? How rapidly will competition reduce the number of electronic trading facilities, creating more centralised markets and greater dependence on the quality of the technical systems underlying them?

As I have suggested, from a UK perspective, there are still a number of interesting, unanswered questions out there. To the extent that we are looking primarily at wholesale markets, we can perhaps stand back rather more and take more time than we might in the equity markets. But we will need to be aware that the new Act sets us, for the first time, a number of statutory objectives – the first of which is the maintenance of market confidence.

Systemic risk

Finally, I want to turn briefly to risk -- a topic close to the heart of both firms and regulators. Clearly, we are now moving fairly quickly down a road in which wholesale market participants who have seen capital strength as a major competitive advantage becoming increasingly interested in moving risk into central counterparty systems. Regulatory capital costs, netting effectiveness and the desire for anonymity in screen-based trading are all major drivers.

In many markets, central counterparties are now coming both for the main cash and repo markets. In the UK, the LCH last year launched 'Repoclear', a central counterparty netting system for government repos. The system enables the participating banks to novate their trades at the close of each day with the LCH. In substituting the original counterparty for the LCH, the participants ensure not only that their inter-bank credit lines do not become blocked over long periods of time, but also that their balance sheets remain free from unnecessary risk. There are currently 14 members of Repoclear and the number of trades per day is rising with the majority of the repos being of relatively short duration. In the longer term it is envisaged that banks should be able to net positions held in LCH in both swaps and repos. In the US the introduction of netting saw an enormous growth in the volume of transactions undertaken in the market and there is no reason to believe that Europe will be any different.

From a regulatory perspective, this is all good. What it does, of course, is to shift the regulatory focus rather more to the clearing houses and the adequacy of their risk management systems. It also leads us into the question of the consequences of concentration of risk in a smaller number of global clearing houses. But that's a topic for another Roundtable!

Transparency in the U.S. Debt Market

by
Mr. Stephen Williams

G-12
G-18 G-24

Introduction

The views expressed herein are my own – not necessarily those of the Commission or the Commission staff. I will begin with a little background material. First, on the way bond markets are organized in the U.S., and how bonds trade. Bond markets are organized rather differently than equity markets in the U.S. Second, I'll recount a bit of the history of the Commission's involvement and Congress's involvement in earlier efforts to bring greater transparency to the bond markets. Finally, I'll describe the developments of the past year and a half, as the Commission, and Congress, have sought to extend transparency to the market for corporate bonds.

Background

Organization of Markets

All of the U.S. debt markets share certain structural similarities. First, nearly all trading is over-the-counter. Unlike equities, there is almost no trading of bonds on registered securities exchanges. Dealers, interdealer brokers, and large institutional investors are principal participants in all markets. Dealers also act as underwriters or distributors. Trades between dealers are normally effected anonymously through the interdealer brokers or IDBs.   Most transactions are done by telephone, but electronic trading is growing rapidly and is expected to continue to grow over the next few years.

We sometimes divide the bond market into five segments by product:

- US Treasury and Federal Agency Bonds

- Mortgage Backed Securities and other asset backed debt securities.

- Corporate Bonds

- Municipal Bonds

- Foreign Bonds, including "Emerging Market" Bonds

These segments roughly reflect the way most dealers and inter-dealer brokers are organized to trade, with a different trading desk for each market segment.

The process of finding an appropriate price for a transaction, which we call *price discovery,* is a very different process in the debt markets than in the equity markets. The "fair" value of a bond is the present value of its expected cash flows. So, if we know the cash flows and we know the right interest rates, we could easily calculate the right value for a bond. Unfortunately, the cash flows are probably uncertain and the appropriate interest rates usually have to be derived from other market prices, so you can't just *calculate* the right price for most bonds from a couple of pieces of readily available information. Nevertheless, pricing bonds involves a degree of computation that pricing equities ordinarily does not, and the value of most bonds is closely related to the value of other -not necessarily similar - bonds. This fact has implications for transparency, of course, because it means that if you are interested in the *value* of one particular bond, you are interested in the *prices* of lots of other bonds as well.

Historical Perspective on Transparency

For purposes of the discussion today, it may be useful for me to say exactly what I mean by "transparency" or a "transparent market". It means a market that is "open to view", in which the prices of bids, offers and transactions are readily available to all participants. The advantages of transparency include the confidence generated by open processes. For this discussion, however, I am more narrowly focused on the value of transparency for *fair and efficient price discovery*. When markets aren't transparent participants, with better information have clear advantages over those who lack that information. That's one reason why the Commission likes transparent markets. Another reason is that we believe that investors with good information make better decisions, and that leads to more efficient markets.

Historically, the debt markets have been slow to move toward transparency. While the stock ticker was well established in the U.S. in the 1920s, there was no organized distribution and display of bond prices, even in the Treasury markets, until the 1970's when several IDBs developed screen-based distribution systems to display current bids and offers to their dealer clients. At first, these IDB systems were provided only to primary dealers, that is, dealers who were recognized by the Federal Reserve System's open market operations desk. All others need not apply. Later, one IDB arranged to sell "indicative prices" through a single vendor in an exclusive arrangement. Still later, a major primary dealer made a similar arrangement to distribute its prices through a vendor of which it was a part owner. By the middle 80's, some prices for Treasury bonds were available, but not in an open and competitive market. Over the next five years or so there were two Congressional studies and a growing consensus that government intervention to compel transparency was justified. At that point, the industry was able, in 1991, to organize a response in the form of GovPX, a private information vendor that distributes both quotation and transaction information for U.S. Treasury bills, bonds, and notes, as well as other information. The quality and timeliness of GovPX information is extremely good, and we now regard the Treasury market as highly transparent.

And so transparency of this extremely large and liquid market was achieved without actual government intervention, but only under the threat of it.

Since then, the Municipal Securities Rulemaking Board, with the encouragement of the Commission, has adopted rules and developed systems for collecting reports of transactions in municipal bonds. The MSRB now publishes, on a next day basis, all transactions in actively traded municipal bonds. The MSRB intends to speed up reporting with the goal of being near real time.

The municipal debt market is actually the smallest major segment of the U.S. debt markets, but it happens to be the only one in which individual investors are a major factor. As a result, transparency of that market has been considered especially important from a fairness standpoint since individuals have clearly been at a disadvantage.

Recent Developments

Commission Review of Debt Markets 1998

In the spring of 1998, the SEC's Division of Market Regulation undertook a review of the markets for debt securities with emphasis on the state of price transparency. Some of our principal goals were:

- – to identify inadequacies in the availability of pricing information, and

- – to recommend improvements as needed.

Overall we found the debt markets to be functioning well, and far more transparent in most segments than they had been 10 years before. Specifically, we found improved transparency in the Treasury market as I just described. Of course, the MSRB, after a couple of years of effort was at that point just beginning to report transactions in municipal bonds. We also found that pretty good prices were widely available for certain mortgage-backed securities. It is perhaps worth mentioning in passing that there are literally hundreds of thousands of mortgage-backed bonds, but that most originate as one of several standardized products. Prices for many of those standardized products are reasonably available.

For U.S. domestic bonds, the only category that lacked almost any transparency was that of corporate bonds. Accordingly, we recommended steps to remedy the situation.

Chairman's Call for Corporate Bond Transparency

In September 1998, Chairman Arthur Levitt, in a speech in New York, called for increased transparency in the corporate debt market. He said, "We are doing so for one simple reason: investors have a right to know the prices at which bonds are being bought and sold. Transparency will help investors make better decisions, and it will increase confidence in the fairness of the markets. Simply put, it's in everybody's interest."

Specifically, the Chairman asked the NASD to do three things:

First, to adopt rules requiring dealers to report all transactions in U.S. corporate bonds, and redistribute prices on an immediate basis;

Second, to develop a database of transactions for regulatory purposes; and

Third, to create a surveillance program for the corporate debt market utilizing the transactions database.

In response to the Chairman's request the NASD began to plan a comprehensive approach to corporate bond transparency. I'll come back to the NASD plan in just a minute.

Congressional Hearings

Following the Chairman's speech, there were Congressional hearings on bond market transparency. Many organizations participated in the testimony, including dealers, major investors, industry associations and others. Almost everyone supported transparent markets in principle, but there were objections to the idea of immediate and comprehensive trade reporting mandated by the SEC or the NASD. Principally, these objections revolved around two points: one, fear of a negative impact on liquidity, and two, a preference for an industry sponsored system such as had been done earlier for government bonds.

The liquidity argument, in particular, deserves some explanation. On the one hand, the fear of a negative effect is based on the belief that if a dealer who buys a large position in an infrequently traded bond is forced to disclose the price he paid to the world, his ability to resell the bond will be materially hurt. This is not implausible, and therefore not easily dismissed, but there is another side to the argument as well. The other side says that transparent markets attract more participants generally, which adds to liquidity, and also that it will attract more participants specifically when they are confident they are being offered a bond at a reasonable price. Even some dealers have said that they will be *more,* rather than less, willing to commit capital when they are confident they know the right prices.

In any case, although the hearings didn't reveal a consensus of opinion, they did lead to a bill being passed by the House last year, though not, at least not yet, by the Senate.

House Bill

The House bill, if it becomes law, would extend the requirement for transaction reporting to a much larger group of securities than we have yet considered. The NASD proposal would cover about 30,000 to 40,000 bonds issued by U.S. corporations and a few foreign corporations. The House bill would potentially extend that coverage to nearly all of the approximately 1 million taxable bonds. The difference, some 900,000 instruments, is primarily made up of mortgage and asset-backed instruments of all kinds, issued or guaranteed largely by public and quasi-public corporations such as GNMA and FNMA. It's my impression that the prospects for this bill becoming law are not considered good.

TBMA/GovPX – Corporate Trades I

In the meantime, both NASD and the industry have been moving forward. There is now an industry-sponsored system that collects reports of trades done between dealers, in investment grade bonds. The trades are published at the end of the day on at least two web sites and are available free of charge to anyone who has access to the Web.

The quality of the information provided is quite good, and includes price, yield, spread to treasuries (at the time of the trade), volume in broad categories, and ratings. Limitations, however, include:

- The limited scope of coverage, only interdealer trades in investment grade bonds,

- The fact that participation is voluntary,

- The lack of timeliness, reporting only at the end of the day, and

- The very small number of transactions reported on a daily basis, typically less than 100.

For purposes of comparison, we know that there are usually more than 5000 trades in investment grade corporate bonds between institutions and dealers ona daily basis. We don't know how many retail trades there are.

Although we acknowledge the value of the information produced by the industry system, because of those limitations, we believe that it is not yet an adequate response to the need for comprehensive, and timely, transparency.

NASD Proposal

On a much slower track, the NASD has developed a much more comprehensive proposal. Let me describe some of its major features briefly.

The NASD proposal covers most ordinary corporate bonds issued in the U.S., including some issued by foreign corporations, but excluding asset and mortgage backed securities. All NASD members will be required to report transactions with non-members and sales to other members.

The scope is much more comprehensive than the industry effort described before, and in particular, it includes all institutional and retail trades.

If approved, implementation will begin sometime later this year, and would be phased in over a seven-month period.

In addition to its transparency aspects, the NASD proposal also involves providing a new method of bond trade comparison for interdealer trades, which itself is controversial for some participants.

This proposal is in the middle of the review process. At this point we have published the proposal for public comment and have received comments back. Among the principal suggestions have been calls for a more carefully structured phase-in period to reduce liquidity risks, and for a more open, competitive approach rather than a regulatory monopoly. We are now considering those comments and working with industry representatives to try to find appropriate solutions.

Concluding Remarks

In conclusion, I want to thank the organizers for inviting me. I would be pleased to answer, or try to answer, any questions you may have.

THE ROLES OF SECURITIES LAWS AND SECURITIES MARKET REGULATORS FOR THE SOUND DEVELOPMENT OF BOND MARKETS: AUSTRALIA

by
Ms. Claire Grose

G21 G12
G28 G18

Trends and Issues in the Australian Bond Market

The current state of the Australian bond market is due in large measure to two main trends:

- the impact of the process of financial deregulation which began in the 1970s and finished in the mid-1980s; and

- Commonwealth and State government budget surpluses in the late 1990s.

The Impact of Financial Deregulation

Key steps in deregulation of the Australian Financial System were:

- gradual removal of controls over bank interest rates;

- removal of other controls on banks;

- freeing up of interest rates on government securities;

- floating the exchange rate; and

- opening up the banking system to foreign competition.[1]

- This contributed to four key financial developments over the past 15 years:

- strong growth in the size of financial markets and in their sophistication;

- an increase in the overall size of the financial sector relative to the economy;

- a tendency towards disintermediation – i.e. for borrowers and lenders to bypass financial intermediaries and deal directly with each other; and

- increased efficiency in the financial system, with competitive pressure (eventually) reducing interest margins and putting downward pressure on costs.[2]

In the period from 1985 to 1999 the average annual growth in the physical bond market was 14 percent and the bond futures market was 35 percent.[3]

This growth in activity in the financial markets has been assisted by improvements in the financial infrastructure, in particular the high standards of efficiency and reliability of Australia's electronic settlement systems -- Austraclear, the Reserve Bank Information and Transfer system ("RITS"), the Australian Stock Exchange's Clearing House Electronic Sub-registry System ("CHESS") and Options Clearing House ("OCH") and the Sydney Futures Exchange Clearing House. Australia's real-time gross settlement ("RTGS") system for high value inter-bank payments complies with the highest international standards.[4]

The Impact of Budget Surpluses on the Supply of Government Bonds

Net public service debt in Australia in 1999 was estimated at around 18 percent of GDP, compared with 31 percent in June 1994.[5] This reduction was the result of a combination of fiscal consolidation and proceeds from privatisations.[6] This trend is likely to continue into the foreseeable future.[7]

Commonwealth government bonds on issue fell from A$95 billion in 1996/97 to $80 billion in 1999.[8] State government bonds on issue fell from A$50 billion in 1994/95 to A$40 billion in 1999.[9] This trend has been accompanied by a fall in turnover in the OTC market for government debt securities from A$1,387 billion in 1996-97 to A$1,054 billion in 1998/1999.[10] This loss of liquidity was reinforced by a shift in retail investment in the bond market from direct holdings to holding through funds under management, particularly superannuation funds, which caused the average holding period for government issues to increase.[11] The trend for fiscal consolidation and privatisations is likely to continue to reduce outstanding government bonds on issue.[12]

The Reserve Bank has moved to preserve liquidity in the Commonwealth government bond market by consolidating government debt into a relatively small number of benchmark series. The State Treasury Corporations have indicated that they will adopt a similar approach to maintaining liquidity in the markets for their bonds.

Growth in the Repo and Non-Government Bond Market

The fall in the supply of government bonds on issue and the increasing demand from funds under management, in particular superannuation funds, has resulted in strong growth in the repurchase market and the non-government bond market.

Annual turnover for repurchase agreements, principally repurchase agreements for government bonds, grew from A$1,484 billion in 1995-96 to A$3,918 billion in 1998/99.[13]

Non-government bonds on issue have trebled from A$22 billion to A$66 billion in the past three years.[14] Moreover, in contrast to the trend prior to the 1990s for Australian corporates to issue in offshore markets, two-thirds of non-government bond outstandings were issued in local rather than offshore markets.[15] Corporate bonds on issue increased from A$10 billion in December 1995 to A$20 billion in December 1998.[16] Turnover in non-government bonds has increased from A$64 billion in 1996-97 to A$150 billion in 1998-99.[17] Turnover in corporate debt securities doubled between 1997/98 and 1998/99 to A$61 billion and turnover in bank debt securities increased by 90 % to A$43 billion in the same period.[18]

Retail Participation in the Fixed Interest Market

Retail investors have increasingly tended to invest in bonds through managed funds.[19] Only a small number of broking firms specialise in dealing in government and non-government bonds on behalf of retail clients. In addition, unlisted finance companies conduct over-the-counter style retail primary markets for debentures issued by them.

Interest in generating greater retail participation in the secondary bond markets appears to have gained some currency. In late October1999 the Australian Stock Exchange ("ASX") launched an Interest Rate Market ("IRM"), which involved providing a special SEATS screen for the trading of debt and debt like securities for retail and institutional investors.

Structure of Regulation of the Australian Bond Market

The Australian secondary market for government and non-government fixed interest securities is essentially an over-the-counter market conducted by a group of 13 large investment banks who conduct an interbank market between themselves and offer two-way prices to their wholesale clients. Two brokerage firms (Tullett & Tokyo and Garban International) provide electronic communication networks to the interbank market which quote prices at which participants in the market are willing to buy or sell government and semi-government bonds and very liquid bank, corporate and foreign bonds. Execution of transactions occurs over the phone.

The regulatory issues that arise in respect of that market can be summarised as:

- pre-and post trade price transparency and the integrity of the price formation process;

- agreement on and compliance with market trading rules and conventions; and

- standards of conduct, training and competence of dealers in the market.

The possibility of retail participation in the fixed interest market through electronic facilities is being considered by participants in those markets.

Greater retail participation in bond markets raises questions of the content and level of detail required in disclosure documents related to the bond issues. Such consideration will have to take into account the relatively low level of understanding Australian retail investors currently have about the risks of investing in debt securities through secondary markets as compared with their understanding of the risks in investing in equity securities through secondary markets. Retail investors may not presently have sufficient understanding of the risk that the capital value of fixed interest securities may fall. Experience has shown that because of the illiquidity of fixed interest securities traded on Australian secondary markets, they have tended to trade at prices that do not reflect what would be expected from orthodox bond pricing theory.

The Corporations Law and the Role of ASIC

Government and non-government bonds fall within the definition of securities in the Corporations Law.[20] Entities or individuals who carry on a business of dealing in bonds are required to be licensed as securities dealers.[21] Facilities by means of which government and non-government bonds are bought or sold meet the definition of stock market and are required to be authorised as exchanges or declared to be exempt markets.[22]

Because dealers in the over-the-counter fixed interest market regularly offer two-way prices, many dealer's activities amount to the conduct of a stock market.[23] In Policy Statement 100: *Stock Markets* ASIC has indicated that on the basis of its discussions with industry bodies, the Australian Financial Markets Association ("AFMA") in particular, about proposals that may result in more formal arrangements for supervision of the fixed interest market and its participants, ASIC does not propose to take action to enforce the prohibition on conducting unauthorised stock markets against dealers in the over-the-counter fixed interest market.[24]

Issues of debt securities are subject to the disclosure provisions of the Corporations Law.[25] However in practice most bond issues do not need disclosure because offers are made to the wholesale market such that they fall within the disclosure exception for sophisticated investors.[26] Disclosure is needed when the offer is made to retail investors.

It has been argued that the disclosure obligations have deterred issuers from large retail bond issues. However, the debenture prospectuses for unlisted finance companies are a case in point of short prospectuses (in some case around four pages) being used for debt issues. Rather, the problem appears to be that issuers who are accustomed to enjoying the benefit of the sophisticated investor exclusion are reluctant to go to the extra trouble of issuing a prospectus to accommodate a retail market which represents only a small percentage of potential demand.

Recent amendments to the Corporations Law have clarified the extent to which issuers can issue shorter and less repetitive disclosure documents.

The amendments require that disclosure documents must contain all of the information that investors and their professional advisers would reasonably require to make an informed assessment of, amongst other things:

- the rights and liabilities attaching to the securities; and

- the assets and liabilities, financial position and performance, profits and losses and prospects of the issuer.

However the prospectus must only contain this information to the extent it is reasonable for investors and their professional advisers to expect to the find the information in the prospectus, and only if a person whose knowledge is relevant actually knows the information or in the circumstances should have obtained the information by making inquiries.[27]

The amendments also provide for profile statements as an alternative to a prospectus at point of sale provided a prospectus is available if requested, although the relevant industry bodies have not sought for policy about the operation of these provisions to apply to debentures.[28] Further, the amendments facilitate electronic lodgement of disclosure documents.[29]

The amendments have clarified provisions of the Corporations Law that allow for the issue of short form transaction specific prospectuses and the incorporation by reference in the prospectus of information disclosed by the issuer as a disclosing entity subject to reporting and disclosure obligation under the Corporations Law and the listing rules of a relevant exchange.[30]

If retail participation in the fixed interest market does grow, ASIC may need to provide guidance to issuers on the question of the required level of disclosure for fixed interest securities.

The prohibitions on insider dealing and market manipulation in sections 1002G, and 997 and 998 of the Corporations Law apply to trading in government and non-government bonds to the same extent as they apply to trading in equity securities. However the prohibitions on insider trading in futures contracts does not apply to trading in futures contracts over government bonds.[31] The prohibitions on market manipulation in the futures market includes trading activities in the government or non-government bond market or the government bond futures market.[32]

Because there is no formal self-regulatory organisation or formalised market structure that establishes trading rules and provides for their effective monitoring and enforcement of the over-the-counter dealer market in fixed income securities, ASIC has no formal mechanism for identifying potential contraventions of the insider dealing and market manipulation provisions of the Corporations Law occurring in that market. However because of the sophisticated and concentrated character of the market, the market participants are better placed to protect their own interests than is the case in more dispersed, retail markets. Market participants are also likely to complain about suspicious trading to ASIC or AFMA, or in the case of Commonwealth Government Bonds, the Reserve Bank of Australia or in the case of State Government Bonds, the relevant State Treasury Corporation or in the case of activity impacting on the futures market, the Sydney Futures Exchange.

The role of self-regulatory organisations: AFMA

ASIC's regulation of the over-the-counter fixed interest market has been greatly facilitated by the role played by the industry association, AFMA. In many respects, AFMA have acted as a policy clearing house for issues related to regulation of the fixed interest market.

Partly as a consequence of the dialogue between ASIC and AFMA in the early to mid-1990s in formulating "Policy Statement 100: *Stock Markets*" and partly as a consequence of some work done on behalf of AFMA and the Markets Practices Group on the potential liabilities of participants in the fixed interest market, AFMA have taken a number of self-regulatory initiatives applicable to the participants in the fixed interest market.

These initiatives included:

- The establishment of market committees to address issues associated with the orderly conduct of the OTC fixed interest market. These committees include the Fixed Interest Committee, the Repo Committee and the Compliance Committee.

- The development of a code of conduct for participants in the fixed interest market.

- The formulation of accreditation standards for dealers in the fixed interest market and the development of training programs to meet those accreditation standards. These accreditation standards are pitched at the level of international best practice.

- The development, in consultation with market participants, of protocols for debt securities and the debt capital market which include dealing conventions, confirmation conventions and settlement conventions. Unless the parties to a transaction agree otherwise, these protocols will apply to transactions entered into by participants in the fixed interest market creating greater legal certainty for market participants.

- The collection from fixed interest market participants of information about the volume and prices at which transactions in the fixed interest market were executed and end of the day reporting of those transactions.

In addition ASIC and AFMA have undertaken a number of co-regulatory initiatives including arrangements between ASIC and AFMA for capital adequacy requirements for fixed interest dealers.

These measures have gone a long way to address the issues identified by ASIC as important to the regulation of the OTC dealer market for fixed interest securities.

ASIC considers that the timeliness of trade reporting and the dissemination of that price information for the fixed interest market could be improved further. End of the day price reporting and dissemination is of limited benefit to price formation. Real time price information would result in improved price transparency and lower spreads. ASIC is also concerned to improve its ability to identify suspicious trading activity and to reconstruct the audit trail for transactions conducted in the over-the-counter market.

The Role of the Reserve Bank of Australia in Bond Markets

The role of the Reserve Bank of Australia in the bond markets is:

- To advise the Commonwealth Government on Commonwealth Government debt issues;

- To conduct government debt issues;

- To maintain the registry for Commonwealth Government Bonds (RITS); and

- To provide a small sales and purchase facility to manage liquidity and imbalances in supply and demand for Commonwealth Government Bonds.

Future Developments in the Australian Bond Market

Electronic Trading Systems and the Financial Services Reform Draft Bill

As noted above, two electronic communication networks service the interbank fixed interest market and the ASX has recently introduced electronic retail exchange trading of fixed interest securities. ASIC is aware of other proposals for the development of electronic facilities:

- which automate the process by which market makers quote two way prices to their wholesale clients; and

- for retail investors to trade directly with market makers.

Change in the structure of the Australian fixed interest market will be given greater impetus by foreshadowed amendments to the Corporations Law contained in the *Financial Services Reform Draft Bill*. The amendments will abolish the current legal distinction between securities and futures markets by introducing the concept of financial products market to include markets for everything from insurance, superannuation and managed investments to securities, futures contracts and other derivative products.

Furthermore, the definition of financial products market excludes:

- a facility created by a dealer through which it alone acts as a market maker; and

- over-the-counter transactions, not through a facility, in which the parties to the transaction accept counter party risk.

Another significant change will be greater flexibility in the regulatory obligations imposed on financial product market licence holders as compared with the existing requirements for regulation as a securities or futures exchange. This will allow regulatory requirements such as operating rules, the need for clearing and settlement facilities, conditions on the licence and supervisory arrangements to be tailor-made to the market in question taking into account the financial products to be traded on the market, the size of the market, the participants in the market, the nature of the activities conducted on the market and the technology used in the operation of the market.

The draft bill will also change existing arrangements for regulation of clearing and settlement facilities for financial products. The Minister and ASIC will have regulatory responsibilities for clearing and settlement of securities and derivatives but the Minister will have power to declare that the Payments System Board of the Reserve Bank will have the responsibility for those facilities which are declared to be of systemic importance to the payments system.

The Australian government's timetable for introducing these reforms is short. It is intended to introduce the Bill into the parliament in the winter sittings with a proposed commencement date of 1 January 2001. The rapidly changing environment in the Australian Bond Market is set to continue and is likely to hasten as electronic trading systems develop and domestic law reform takes shape. These initiatives give rise to new challenges for ASIC as oversight regulator of the Australian financial markets. ASIC will be taking steps to develop policy, educate retail investors in market risks, encourage issuers to adopt best practice in disclosure and take necessary enforcement action to ensure integrity in the Australian markets is maintained at their current high levels.

NOTES

1. Ric Battelino, Assistant Governor (Financial Markets) Reserve Bank of Australia, *Australian Financial Markets: Looking Back and Looking Ahead,* Talk to the Australian Finance and Capital Markets Conference, The Westin Hotel, Sydney, 24-25 February 2000, ["Battelino February 2000"] page 1.

2. Ibid.

3. Ibid page 2.

4. Ibid page 3.

5. Mr R Battelino *"Australian Financial Markets,"* Reserve Bank of Australia Bulletin, March 1999, pp 1-12 ["Battelino March 1999"] at page 2.

6. Ibid.

7. Ibid.

8. Ibid.

9. Ibid.

10. 1999 Australian Financial Markets Report, An AFMA SIRCA joint study, ["AFMR"]at page 6.

11. Battelino March 1999 at page 2.

12. Ibid.

13. AFMR at page 6.

14. Battelino February 2000 at page 5.

15. Mr R Battelino *"Australian Financial Markets,"* Address to 'The Futures of the Australian Debt Market Beyond 2000' Conference, Canberra, 27 August 1999, Reserve Bank of Australia Bulletin, September 1999, pp 10-19 at page 16.

16. Battelino March 1999 at page 3.

17. AFMR page 6.

18. AFMR Highlights at page 2.

19. In 1998/99 fund manager investment in government debt securities increased by 17 percent to A$333 billion while other investment in government debt securities, which would include retail investors,

decreased by 8 percent to A$73.3 billion. In 1998/99 fund manager investment in non-government debt securities increased by 162 percent to A$55 billion while other investment in non-government debt securities, which would include retail investors, increased by 45 percent to A$29 billion.

20.   Section 92.

21.   Section 780.

22.   Section 767.

23.   Paragraph 100.110 of PS100.

24.   Paragraphs 110.113 to 100.115 of PS100.

25.   Part 6D.2 of the Corporations Law.

26.   Sub-section 708(8) of the Corporations Law provides that an offer of securities does not need disclosure if, among other things: (a) the minimum amount payable for the securities on acceptance of the offer by the person to whom the offer is made is at least $500,000; or (b) the amount payable for the securities on acceptance by the person to whom the offer is made and the amounts previously paid by the person for the body's securities of the same class that are held by the person add up to at least $500,000.

27.   Section 710

28.   Sections 714.

29.   Section 720.

30.   Section 712-3.

31.   Section 1253 only applies to futures contracts concerning a body corporate.

32.   Section 1259 (Futures Market Manipulation) applies to transactions (whether a dealing in a futures contract or not) and section 1260 (False Trading and Market Rigging) applies to creating, causing to be created or doing anything which is calculated to create a false or misleading appearance of active dealings in futures contracts or with respect to the market for or price for dealings in futures contracts.

Session 5

THE VIEWS OF RATING AGENCIES AND RESEARCH INSTITUTES

G21 G28

BANK REFORM: AN ESSENTIAL ELEMENT OF CAPITAL MARKET DEVELOPMENT

by
Dr. Julia Turner

By now, it must surely go without saying that Moody's supports financial market reform. We have said so often that the allocation of financial capital at prices that reflect the riskiness of an investment is at the heart of healthy, sustainable economic development. Recently, our sovereign analysts noted that restructuring and reform were critical elements for any further upgrade of the ratings on several sovereign credits in Asia. This is not a moral issue. We simply believe that unless the returns that investors earn on their capital are adequate to support accumulation of capital and therefore expanded reinvestment, wealth will be destroyed and markets will founder.

We believe that regulation is important to sustainable capital allocation. We have long and often argued that financial disclosure and transparent practices are two of the most potent tools that regulators have at their disposal. They are far more effective, to that end, than regulations designed to direct either the source or user of financial capital.

However, bond market reforms alone are inadequate to spur capital market development. We have observed a number of regulatory regimes evolve that were, and are, designed to promote a domestic bond market. In some countries, the monetary authorities and economic managers are anxious to develop an alternative source of financial capital, having watched the damage done to their banks by the last financial crisis.

Nonetheless, in most countries, banks continue to be the primary source, and in some cases still the only source, of debt capital. And, as long as borrowers have the option to borrow at uneconomic rates from their bankers, without disclosing the true state of their financial health, not even the most enlightened reform of capital market regulation will be sufficient to motivate them to borrow in the public debt markets.

For that reason, Moody's believes that the proposals from the Basle committee are a large step in the direction of a more durable market financial framework. As the barriers between market sectors are inevitably, if slowly, destroyed, we believe that motivating bankers to reflect on the relationship between risk and return will increase the opportunities for a broader array of non-bank lenders to enter the markets at more realistic prices.

We expect this process to work slowly, since we believe one can hardly underestimate the resistance to change that characterizes these economic and financial systems. Not necessarily change to a Western system, just any change. Since these borrowers and lenders, and their governments, have operated successfully, in their view, for decades and perhaps centuries, a two-year financial crisis may not seem sufficient reason to abandon the system. However, if regulators can change lending practices at the heart of the financial system for redistribution of capital, the change in approach may support more realistic expectations on the part of borrowers and lenders in the non-bank financial sectors.

So, I would like to focus today on our view of the implications of the Basle accords for banks, and the markets in which they operate. Moody's sees the Basel Committee's Proposal as another step forward in the development of an efficient and globally consistent approach to bank supervision. The proposed new framework recognizes that credit risk management practices are undergoing a technology-driven transformation and that each regulated bank has a unique pattern of risks and capabilities.

I must note that in Moody's view regulatory capital is not the key determinant of capital strength or credit quality. However, to the extent that national regulators implement the proposals in such a way as to strengthen economic capital, banks' systemic credit quality should improve. Not only will their capitalization be stronger, their profitability should be less volatile because of fewer earnings surprises. This will not apply to all banks within a given system. However, we expect that banks with strong management, strong credit cultures, good asset quality and adequate profitability will be the beneficiaries of the proposed accords, emerging as winners over the banks, whose lending practices have depended on regulatory forbearance.

Moody's agrees with the Committee's position that an internal ratings-based regime can provide a more accurate assessment of risk for sophisticated banks than the current Basel capital adequacy framework. We appreciate that the supervisors' responsibilities will be particularly challenging, given the Committee's desire to achieve consistency across a wide variety of banks and nations. In this regard, we expect that external risk assessments such as Moody's credit ratings and related risk management services from a growing number of providers will prove valuable as both direct inputs to banks' internal rating systems and as tools for bench-marking and validating those systems.

The proposal also sets challenges for the bankers, who need to develop and/or demonstrate to investors and regulators a system for loan risk evalution that:

- Is clear, coherent and credible to regulators in all the jurisdictions in which a bank operates;

- Doesn't place a wholly uneconomic burden on risk underwriting costs; and

- Reflects a given bank's specific approach to its target market.

This may be one of those scenarios where "what doesn't kill you makes you stronger." In fact, our expectation that stronger banks will emerge from the effects of the proposals reflects our belief that the future of risk-adjusted regulatory capital lies with internal risk scoring and credit assessment technology, rather than with external ratings.

Nevertheless, not all banks or regulators are yet ready to put an internal ratings-based system into operation. While it seems feasible to design an external ratings approach that, in transition to a fully internal system, would represent an improvement over the current regulatory capital framework, Moody's believes the external ratings approach has a number of shortcomings that first need to be addressed.

- At present, external credit ratings cover only a small portion of most banks' portfolios. Nor are they economically practical. While the economics of individual ratings work in the context of syndicated loans or bonds, its seems pretty evident that they are, shall we say, less than compelling for the smaller assets that comprise a significant percentage of bank portfolios in the region. Moody's quality ratings represent a high value-added exercise, and are priced accordingly.

- Implementation could raise moral hazard in the rating industry. Frankly, we believe that relying solely on external rating agencies to fulfil regulatory requirements would encourage rating shopping.

To allow market discipline to increase the consistency among ratings, Moody's recommends that:

- ratings eligible for use in regulation should be made public and subject to market scrutiny;
- regardless of whether an issuer requested a rating, regulators should consider all ratings that have been assigned to a given issuer by recognized agencies.

Regulators have to somehow reconcile the advantages of internal ratings with the claims of smaller banks that haven't yet developed them. A regime that clearly and systematically discriminates in favor of large and/or multi-national banks is likely to be politically unpalatable for most national bank regulators.

The world's more sophisticated financial institutions have been, for some years, developing a battery of tools, such as scoring models for the extension of consumer credit in the form of credit cards, car loans, and home mortgages. In recent years, an increasing level of analytic technology and expertise has been focused on credit risk management. The financial crisis raised the level of awareness among market participants, some of whom really didn't seem to believe that such a risk still existed.

The regulatory changes proposed in the Basle accords have intensified the interest, and it seems likely that third-party providers will accelerate the process by which the technology spreads to a broad array of banks, large and small, sophisticated and less sophisticated. Moody's Investors Service is, in fact, participating in that process through our subsidiary, Moody's Risk Management Services, by developing and validating public and private default models against different loan and financial accounting systems.

Such validation provides useful information to all participating banks on default probabilities and expected loss for a particular market. This in turn enhances their capabilities in asset management, securitization, provisioning, and risk-adjusted pricing capacity. It also allows regulators to use a credit benchmark in reviewing individual banks' asset quality.

We believe, therefore, that

- Improved risk management techniques are likely to support what we regard as the primary goal of capital market reform, which is efficient allocation of capital.
- Risk management technology is available, will improve rapidly, and will spread to a wide array of users.
- By improving asset quality and supporting sound lending practices, they will strengthen bank capital and profitability of well-managed banks.
- We expect winners and losers among the banks in this process, but we believe that, overall, banking systems will be strengthened.
- And, since banking systems remain a critical component of financial markets, we believe the Basle accords may, if sensibly implemented, contribute significantly to capital market reform and development.

339

341- 46

(Thailand)

A DOMESTIC CREDIT RATING AGENCY IN AN EMERGING ASIAN COUNTRY:
THE TRIS EXPERIENCE

016
G12
G18

by
Dr. Warapatr Todhanakasem

1. Introduction

Credit rating agencies have been established in many emerging economies during the last decade. At present, nearly all Asian developing countries have at least one rating agency. India and Korea each has three rating agencies. Malaysia has two. Indonesia, the Philippines and Thailand each has a rating agency. The importance of domestic credit rating agencies to the development of capital markets is generally accepted and well-recognized by financial communities in Asia.

The Asian economic crisis of the last nearly three years brought a great deal of attention to credit rating agencies, those operating internationally as well as those operating in a single country. The role of major credit rating agencies in global financial markets and their influence on international capital flows have been studied. Responding to the last crisis, some major credit rating agencies have reviewed and fine-tuned their rating methodologies. Domestic credit rating agencies in emerging countries can learn from their own experiences during the crisis and from the lessons of major rating agencies to enhance their skills for the future development of their financial markets.

This paper presents the experience of one credit rating agency, Thai Rating and Information Services (TRIS), to gain insight into the development of domestic credit rating agencies in Asia. The paper will also offer some relevant information about other Asian credit rating agencies, particularly those that are members of the ASEAN Forum of Credit Rating Agencies (AFCRA).

The issues this paper will examine include: the impact of economic crisis on the volume of credit rating business, questions about the transparency and reliability of rating assignments and processes, and impacts of the crisis on the development of domestic rating agencies. The paper will also consider the potential of joint ventures and cooperation among credit rating agencies and future challenges that will affect the performance of domestic credit rating businesses in the globalized and fast moving financial world.

2. Impacts of the Economic Crisis on Domestic Bond Markets and Credit Rating Agencies

The development of local credit rating agencies relates closely to the development of domestic bond markets. The bigger the domestic bond market grows, the more local credit rating customers increase. To show this relationship we can take AFCRA as an example. By the end of 1998, Rating Agency Malaysia Berhad (RAM) had more than 220 customers, the largest client list among AFCRA members. TRIS, even during its best year in 1996, had just 61 rating clients. One reason for this difference is that Malaysia has the biggest bond market in AFCRA. Malaysia's outstanding bonds at

341

the end of 1998 were valued at USD 46 billion or 123% of GDP, while the Thai bond market was just USD 25 billion or about 20% of GDP.

Apart from investors in larger capital markets tending to be more aware of risk than investors in smaller ones, government incentives and statutory requirements regarding credit ratings also have significant influence on the demand for credit ratings. Requiring all corporate debentures in Malaysia to be rated significantly increased the demand for credit ratings since the measure was implemented in 1992.[1] Thailand did not implement such regulations until 3 April 2000. Before this date, private placement corporate debentures did not have to be rated.

The Asian economic turbulence that erupted in mid-1997 hit credit rating businesses hard. Credit ratings were rarely initiated during the crisis, because almost all new investment plans were postponed and few financial instruments were launched. Investor confidence was hurt badly. Domestic interest rates in many Asian countries hit record highs. After successive negative alerts followed by rating downgrades, almost all Asian credit rating agencies saw the number of rating clients significantly reduced. This was particularly true in countries with immature capital markets where no statutory rating requirements existed to limit ratings avoidance and withdrawals. Most AFCRA members recorded substantial declines in customers during 1997 and 1998.

In Thailand, the heart of the Asian crisis, TRIS could not avoid the difficulties sweeping the region. The Thai financial crisis left TRIS with merely 10 company ratings and 12 issue ratings in 1997, compared to 23 company ratings and 38 issue ratings by the end of 1996. Struggling with a paralyzed financial market, extremely high interest rates, and lack of investor confidence, Thai companies suspended their investment plans. Few corporate debt securities were launched. In 1998, the value of outstanding Thai corporate bonds shrunk 5% from 1997 compared to 55% growth in 1995 and 36% in 1996.

TRIS encountered economic turmoil in 1998 with no new credit rating clients. At the end of that year, after 12 downgrades and 12 withdrawals, TRIS had merely 11 rating clients which was the same level of business as the first year it opened. This was the darkest time for Thai companies, and TRIS was no exception. In just two years (1997 and 1998), TRIS lost 56 rating clients (22 company ratings and 34 issue ratings). However, TRIS took this crisis as an opportunity to review and develop its rating process and methodology to prepare for future development. New rating services were studied, including a rating methodology for structured finance securities and mortgage-backed securitization. In the meantime, TRIS staff participated in the development of institutional financial infrastructure in Thailand. TRIS staff joined with other financial experts to provide technical assistance to start up the Financial Sector Restructuring Authority. A representative from TRIS also participated in the development of the state-owned Secondary Mortgage Corporation (SMC).

By the end of 1998, it appeared that the Thai economy was beginning to recover. GDP contraction lessened in the third quarter. Liquidity in the money market eased, and interest rates dropped. Commercial banks were among the first institutions returning to the capital market to increase their funds to meet with stricter capital requirements. In January 1999, Thai Farmers Bank issued the first hybrid equity-debt instruments in Thailand, called SLIPS, for Stapled Limited Interest Preferred Shares. This was followed by a series of bond issues by commercial banks and major companies. Yet, all were issued on private placement basis and needed no rating.

In October 1999, TRIS announced the rating for its first new customer since 1997, a satellite company. Two more companies, one a former client that cancelled a rating-contract in 1997, signed contracts with TRIS at the end of 1999. Business has been picking up since then.

---

[1]   Bank Negara Malaysia Annual report 1993.

3.   Transparency and Reliability of Local Credit Ratings

The Asian economic crisis put credit rating agencies in the spotlight. A number of international rating agencies made sharp adjustments of sovereign credit ratings for many emerging markets. Concerns were raised about the transparency of the credit rating process and the accuracy of rating assignments by the major international rating agencies.

Domestic credit rating agencies were also criticized. Many were in worse situations than their international counterparts because of their short track records. Most of them are younger than 20 years old. TRIS just celebrated its sixth anniversary last July. Yes, we are young. But being young does not necessarily mean being incapable. In fact, local rating agencies are closer to local companies and have greater access to a wider variety of industry and market information. Operating in the country with local staff, domestic rating agencies are more familiar with the people and business practices of local companies. Many times domestic rating agencies are able to detect problems in local industries in their early stages. TRIS in 1996 issued a credit alert for the property industry, several months before the actual collapse of that industry the following year.

Just like international credit rating agencies, domestic rating agencies must build their reputations for independence and capability. A key factor is the necessity to safeguard their rating activities from intervention of any party. To ensure independence, regulators often require domestic rating agencies to have no individual majority shareholders. Particularly to be avoided are shareholders with business activities that could benefit from inside information of rating clients or that would interfere in the rating process to benefit their interests. TRIS's equity is held by government related entities (such as the Ministry of Finance, the Stock Exchange of Thailand and the Government Saving Bank), international organization (namely the Asian Development Bank), finance companies, commercial banks and securities firms. No single private company holds more than 5% of TRIS shares.

For transparency sake, major international rating agencies typically disclose their rating methodologies and processes to the public. Some local rating agencies include their rating methodologies and processes with relevant information on their company's website. TRIS always presents its rating methodology and process to potential clients and interested parties.

It is also important that credit rating agencies be transparent to their rated customers. It is normal practice after a rating is determined for the rating agency to notify the company of the rating assigned and the rationale before they are publicized. Many rating agencies allow their customers to appeal within a certain period. TRIS allows the issuer to appeal the rating decision within five days of being informed. Moreover, TRIS's clients can choose to keep rating results private, unless they issue public debentures covered by the Securities Exchange Commission's (SEC) rating requirements.

Transparency and reliability depend very much on the quality of analytical staff. Moreover, the integrity of analysts is crucial to ensure that rating analysis is fair and professional. Regarding this issue, TRIS has established a strict code of ethics that must be followed by all employees from managers to junior staff. The code of ethics includes a statement on client privacy. All information received from customers has to be kept strictly confidential until the customer decides to make public the information.

TRIS's employees also have to declare their securities holdings and inform the company of any changes to their asset values while they work at TRIS. An analyst who would use rating information for his or her financial gain would be in serious breach of TRIS's code of ethics and would face the strongest disciplinary action.

4. Cooperation with International Rating Agencies

International rating agencies have important roles in the development of local credit rating agencies. Relationships between local and international agencies take many forms. Some are merely marketing partnerships, some receive technical training in return for some kind of compensation, and some participate as equity shareholders. Analytical support and capital from the big credit rating agencies are important reasons that local credit rating agencies need co-operation with international agencies.

International rating agencies have shown interest in domestic credit rating businesses. Major credit rating agencies have established branches in a number of emerging economies mostly Latin American countries. Examples of local credit rating agencies that are subsidiaries of major rating agencies include FitchIBCA Argentina S.A., Standard & Poor's Argentina Branch, FitchIBCA Chile, and FitchIBCA Mexico.

In ASEAN, cooperation with international rating agencies is mostly in the form of technical assistance and joint ventures. For example, Rating Agency Malaysia Berhad (RAM), has a portion of shares held by FitchIBCA Limited. The Malaysian Rating Corporation Berhad (MARC) has a technical cooperation agreement with Thomson BankWatch and technical advisory from Wetton Ratings Limited. PT PEFINDO of Indonesia formed a strategic alliance with Standard & Poor's in 1996.

TRIS is a wholly Thai company. Nonetheless, during its initial three years of operation (1993 to 1996), TRIS received technical assistance from Standard & Poor's. In mid-1997, it formed a strategic partnership with Fitch Investors Service. However, the economic crisis in Thailand two months later affected the development of the capital market and nullified benefits that might have occurred from this agreement.

In the meantime, TRIS has made internal developments to its rating process and methodology in response to the recovery of the Thai bond market. Currently, TRIS has the capability to rate structured securities and amortization bonds. TRIS's clients range from agricultural exporters and property developers to high technological industries such as satellite and mobile phone companies.

5. Factors that Determine Domestic Credit Rating Agency's Performance

Domestic rating agencies need to improve analytical techniques to catch up with financial innovations. The future performance of local credit rating agencies depends on many factors both external and internal. The major external factors are the countries' cultures, quality of information and disclosure standards, and size of the bond market. Internal factors are the quality of rating analysts and rating methodology.

Socio-cultural context can be an obstacle or a support to the development of credit rating agencies. It is difficult for local rating agencies to grow in Asia where people like to maintain anonymity and avoid evaluation. Asian companies are not accustomed to disclosing information or being rated by a third party. It is difficult for a company to accept that its credit worthiness is being compared to other companies, sometimes competitors. Unless companies are sure that their ratings will be favorable or are subject to rating requirements, Thai issuers typically try to avoid being rated or choose to keep their unfavorable ratings private. During the crisis in 1997 and 1998, TRIS's customers were so upset at being downgraded that they did not want to repeat the rating experience. Accordingly, domestic credit rating agencies can find it difficult to develop new rating services because few issuers want to have their relative credit worthiness evaluated.

The quality of information that a rating agency gathers is an important factor determining the relative accuracy of its ratings. Asian rating agencies struggle with the problems of inadequate and unavailable information. Because of varying disclosure standards, Asian rating agencies cannot rely solely on formal sources of information about companies and industries that in developed countries would be sufficient to evaluate the risk potential of those companies and industries. For these reasons, domestic rating agencies may also need to include in their ratings information from informal sources and opinions of experts in specific areas.

In Thailand, the lack of reliable and transparent information has been cited as a major cause of the recent crisis. Realizing this problem, TRIS has been actively promoting transparency and good corporate governance in Thai businesses. In 1998, TRIS was one of the very first companies in Thailand to publish its guidelines for corporate governance. At the present, TRIS is fully implementing this system in its business operations.

The disclosure standards in Thailand have improved significantly. Accounting standards have also been reviewed. The Bank of Thailand now requires financial institutions to disclose details about their debts and investment positions in other businesses and the level of non-performing assets of banks and finance companies. This information now regularly appears on the BOT website. Good corporate governance is becoming part of the business practice of many Thai companies. All firms listed on the stock exchange are required to set up audit committees. Most state enterprises now tie employee compensation to performance. Government–related agencies must comply with the Information Disclosure Act. All of these advances will help improve the nation's information infrastructure, which is essential for the development of the credit rating industry in Thailand.

Another difficulty for domestic credit rating companies is *the small size of domestic debt markets*. Without actual practice, it is hard for analysts to develop their rating skills. An example of this is the development of mortgage-backed securitization (MBS) ratings in Thailand. TRIS studied a rating methodology for this type of securities for more than a year. The laws allowing the establishment of special purposed vehicles (SPV) and setting up a Secondary Mortgage Corporation (SMC) have been enacted since 1997. To date, however, no actual MBS debenture has been issued in the Thai bond market because of the unfavorable property sector in Thailand and remaining problems about tax matters.

The key internal factor leading to the successful operation of a credit rating business is *the quality of human resources*. During the boom period, rating agencies had to compete for high quality and experienced financial analysts with securities firms which were generally able to pay much higher salaries and compensations than a newly established rating company could offer. Domestic rating agencies, therefore, were often staffed with many new graduates who were bright but had little experience. However, since the crisis has changed the labor market, rating agencies can better recruit more experienced financial professionals.

Currently, TRIS staff members average more than five years of experience in financial professions from well-known companies. In addition to their MBAs, some have other credentials, such as CPAs and CFAs, which are useful for credit rating analysis. TRIS's business plan has provisions to ensure that its analysts are always well trained.

To improve rating services, domestic rating agencies have formed *regional co-operations*. For example, AFCRA was established on 5 November 1993 to enhance the effectiveness of credit rating services via a series of joint training sessions for rating analysts from member agencies.

TRIS believes that rating agencies working together is useful and will benefit all parties and the capital markets. Domestic credit rating agencies, like TRIS, can provide details and insight into local situations to international agencies that have not yet established a branch in a particular country. International rating agencies can be valuable sources of technical know-how for new rating agencies in developing/emerging economies.

6.   Looking Ahead

As the emerging Asian economies begin their recovery, Asian credit rating agencies are expecting the number of customers to return to pre-crisis levels. The recovery raises questions: ***Will the Asian bond market return to growth rates seen prior to the crisis? Will the growth be sustainable?   Will domestic credit rating agencies benefit from the potential bond market?***

In 1999, the Thai bond market had a sudden recovery. Outstanding values grew almost 50% from a year earlier. Government bonds took a major part, around 50% of outstanding issues. Corporate debt instruments sharing 30% of the market, however, grew much faster.   The value of private debt securities issued in 1999 alone surpassed the combined value of private bonds issued between 1993 and 1998. Many factors explain this rapid growth including drastically low domestic interest rates, the contraction of commercial bank credits, and substantialy increasing demand for capital, mostly from financial institutions that have to comply with new capital requirements. However, many of these are considered temporary factors, and government policy is needed to ensure that actual development takes place.

The recovery of the Thai bond market has yet to have dramatic impact on TRIS. It is noteworthy that, given the large amount of corporate debt instruments issued in 1999, only a few were rated by TRIS. Instead, many issuers tried to avoid ratings by placing the issues with limited institutional investors that did not require credit rating. By the end of 1999, TRIS had only 16 rating clients; nine were new customers. 2000 seems to be a more promising year for TRIS. Three new ratings were issued in the last three months and more are lining up. Clients are seeking out TRIS for various reasons. Some customers planned huge public bond issues and were subject to rating requirements. Other customers were required by investors to be rated. Customers believed credit ratings would enhance their access to capital. Some knowing that regulators would implement compulsory ratings in April 2000, wanted to be prepared before the requirements took effect. Of these reasons, the requirements of investors are the most powerful factors motivating issuers to the rating agencies. The future of credit rating agencies, thus, depends on the fact that they are established to protect investors' interests. To survive in the credit rating business, it is crucial that domestic rating agencies maintain their credibility and reliability in the eyes of the investors.

CURRENT CONDITIONS AND DEVELOPMENTS IN ASIAN DOMESTIC BOND MARKETS AND FURTHER STEPS

by
Mr. Fumiyuki Sasaki

1.   Importance of developing domestic bond markets

The main reason for promoting domestic bond markets is to provide another channel for funding in the capital market. It enables private sectors to tap the market even in financial turmoil. From the standpoint of investment measures, government securities are a kind of risk- free benchmark, enhancing the corporate bond market. Short-term government securities provide sort of cash position, waiting for shifts for allocation, as well as major vehicle for foreign central banks' management of foreign reserves.

2.   Current situation

Bonds are not popular as equity in developing countries, especially for individual investors. Though it takes time to developthe bond market, steps should be taken to steadily strengthen capital and financial markets. It is a well-known issue that bond markets in Asia are relatively smaller than other sources, such as bank borrowing and equity markets. Table 1 shows the relative size of those sources against nominal GDP. This table shows that local bond markets are undeveloped, with small outstanding. Main funding sources have been bank borrowing and equity markets.

Table 1 **Funding Sources by Types**

	1996			1997			1998		
	Loan	Equity	Bond	Loan	Equity	Bond	Loan	Equity	Bond
U.S.	32.0%	114.6%	158.0%	32.9%	138.7%	158.7%	34.9%	156.9%	165.6%
Japan	106.1%	71.7%	99.8%	105.7%	56.6%	99.8%	107.9%	56.5%	107.9%
Hong Kong	328.5%	291.6%	27.5%	311.1%	241.8%	26.1%	260.7%	210.0%	30.8%
Korea	42.3%	28.0%	34.5%	44.2%	15.7%	36.0%	44.6%	30.7%	52.5%
Singapore	191.2%	201.6%	57.2%	191.9%	233.4%	56.3%	209.6%	187.9%	63.1%
Indonesia	118.6%	40.6%	5.3%	130.1%	25.6%	3.6%	114.6%	18.7%	6.1%
Malaysia	85.9%	31.5%	47.9%	98.0%	75.0%	49.1%	100.5%	76.0%	54.4%
Philippines	79.2%	97.7%	34.9%	86.9%	51.7%	35.5%	77.4%	51.5%	31.1%
Thailand	154.0%	56.0%	11.3%	173.1%	24.3%	11.6%	170.5%	27.6%	20.0%

Note: as of nominal GDP. Loans are through banks.
Source: mofs, central banks, statistical offices and others

Table 2 illlustrates that the outstanding of bonds issued has been increasing. Hong Kong and Singapore have been providing more issues, even with budget surpluses. They have gradually been forming risk-free yield curves. Furthermore, they have tried to extend maturities up to 10 years. I'd like to mention the case of Hong Kong. Looking at the balance sheet of the foreign exchange fund, it is seen that foreign reserves are on the asset side, invested mainly in Treasury Bills and notes in the U.S. Those yields are just above 6%. On the other hand, it issues Exchange Fund Bills and Notes on the liability side. Those (Source) central banks reports and otherscoupons are 7,8,9%. Regarding only these assets and liabilities, they have to enjoy negative spreads, that are cost. Even with this cost, Hong Kong has decided to issue bills and notes to stabilize financial and capital markets, that provide Hong Kong with benefits as a total. Later, I discuss the implications of the case of Hong Kong.

Table 2 **Outstanding of Asian Bond Market**

					(10bil Won)
Korea	1995	1996	1997	1998	1999(Oct.)
National Debt Management Fund Bond	2,959	4,869	6,320	18,183	31,883
Treasury Bills	----	----	----	----	----
Foreign Exchange Stabilization Fund Bond	4,200	4,200	4,200	3,900	4,400
Grain Securities	4,871	4,871	4,871	4,871	4,871
National Housing Bond	10,046	11,377	12,974	13,898	15,638
National Investment Bond					
Seoul Metropolitan Subway Bond	2,454	2,826	3,050	3,005	3,044
Monetary Stabilization Bond	25,825	25,030	23,471	43,926	53,260
Industrial Finance Debenture	13,286	15,117	18,242	23,408	21,961
Long Term Credit Debentures	9,293	9,002	10,986	9,704	
Corporate Bond	61,287	76,327	90,102	121,271	123,161
Total	134,221	153,619	174,216	242,166	258,217

					(bil. HK$)
Hong Kong	1995	1996	1997	1998	1999(Sep.)
Exchange Fund Bills and Notes	58.73	91.85	101.65	97.45	100.36
Exchange Fund Bills	44.33	70.25	72.85	63.85	66.26
Exchange Fund Notes	14.40	21.60	28.80	33.60	34.10
HK$ debt instruments other than EFBN	138.33	187.56	243.86	292.66	313.89
Floating rate	86.26	125.97	167.97	159.53	155.16
Fixed rate	52.06	61.59	75.89	133.13	158.73
Total	197.06	279.41	345.51	390.11	414.25

				(mil.S$)
Singapore	1995	1996	1997	1998
Registered Stocks and Bonds	59,702	67,854	73,306	80,667
Treasury Bills and Deposits	5,750	5,990	6,920	8,540
Total	65,452	73,844	80,226	89,207

				(mil RM)
Malaysia	1995	1996	1997	1998
T-Notes	64,719	66,910	66,262	75,012
T-Bills	4,320	4,320	4,320	4,320
GIC	5,050	4,150	2,750	2,750
Malaysian Savings Bonds	1,131	1,092	918	0
Khazanah Bonds	----	----	794	3,526
Total	75,220	76,472	75,044	85,608
Cagamas Bonds	9,312	13,227	16,756	15,064
PDS(Private Debt Securities)	22,321	31,962	46,543	54,411
Total	31,633	45,189	63,299	69,475
	106,853	121,661	138,343	155,083

Indonesia	1995	1996	1997	1998	(bil. Rupiah) 1999(Nov.)
SBI	11,850	18,553	7,034	42,765	71,439
Bonds	7,056	9,897	15,605	14,505	15,609
Total	18,906	28,450	22,639	57,270	87,048

Thailand	1995	1996	1997	1998	(bil. bahts) 1999 (Sep.)
Government	43.0	18.0	13.8	411.9	583.4
State enterprize	238.3	278.4	293.8	300.6	331.7
-Guaranteed	208.7	239.7	247.3	255.7	284.4
-Non-guaranteed	29.6	38.7	46.5	44.9	47.3
BoT/FIDF/PLMO	9.5	40.5	51.6	36.2	22.1
Corporate	133.6	182.4	187.6	177.6	367.6
Total	424.4	519.3	546.8	926.3	1,304.8

Philippines	1997	1998	(mil pesos) 1999(Nov.)
Total	772,073	721,335	949,300
National Government	713,689	714,150	
Government Corporations	8,356	6,940	
Guaranteed	5,035	4,785	
Non-Guaranteed	3,321	2,155	
Monetary Institution	28	245	

Korea has also issued 3-year government bond as a benchmark. Before the financial crisis occurred in 1997, 3-year corporate bonds were the benchmark because they were guaranteed by commercial banks. However, after the financial crisis, over 90% of the bonds issued by private enterprises are non-guaranteed. So, markets need benchmark issues provided by the government.

Other Asian countries have also issued more government securities, as you know.The graph shows the current outstanding of government bonds by remaining periods to maturities. Relatively speaking, Hong Kong's outstanding seem to be smooth up to 10 years. Other countries also have tried to smooth outstanding. Smooth outstanding can contribute in forming smooth yield curves. Therefore, you can find that benchmark yield curves in Asia have gradually been formed recently, looking at Graph 2.

Graph 3 illustrates the estimated yield curves in the cases of Hong Kong, Singapore, and the Philippines. Using all yields traded in secondary markets, it is possible to estimate yield curves more smoothly than before. We need more issues to estimate yield curves with more statistical reliance in the future. Technically, it is hard to estimate yields curves smoothly, but, it is needed to provide more yields to enable market players to try to estimate, leading to a more efficient bond market.

Graph1 **Outstanding of Asian Government Bond**

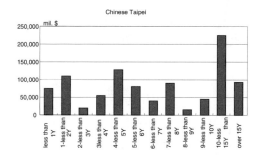

Chinese Taipei

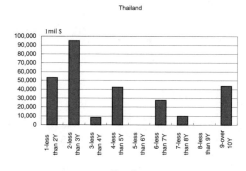

Thailand

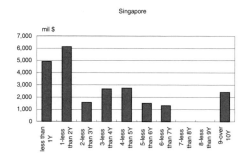

Singapore

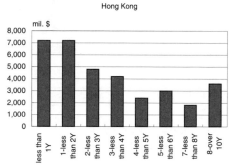

Hong Kong

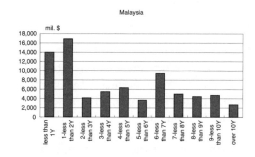

Malaysia

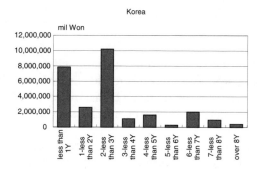

Korea

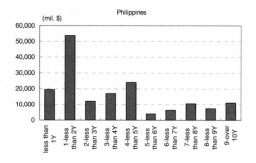

Philippines

Source: Bloomberg

Graph 2 Benchmark Yield and Swap Curves in Asian Bond Markets

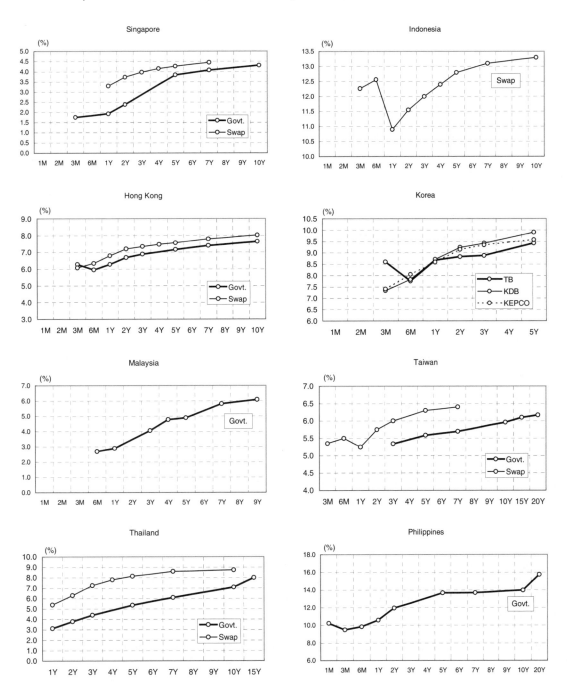

Source: Bloomberg

Graph 3 **Estimated Yield Curves**

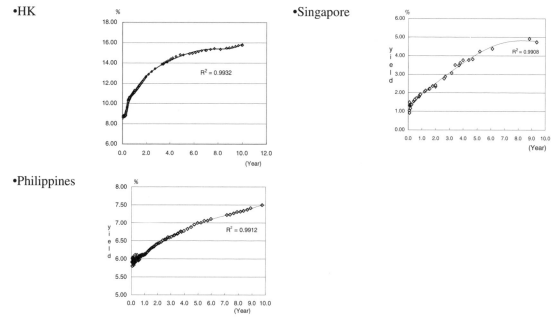

•HK

•Singapore

•Philippines

Note: Approximated by 5 polynominal
Source: Bloomberg

4. Further steps

Local bond markets should be promoted in terms of macro structures. First of all, I'd like to discuss supply side issues.In the medium- and long-term, I think that one of most significant issues is to maintain the amount of outstanding. In Asia, there seems to be a fiscal discipline to keep the budget balanced. I think that there seems to be a big controversy about whether to go back to maintaining a balanced budget or not after the economic recovery. What are the benefits in issuing government bonds?

I suppose that even in the case of a balanced fiscal policy, you can provide sovereign issues to some extent, and maintain outstanding. Consolidating all sovereigns' funding into a single account, you can have a "quasi-government bond market". In order to prevent moral hazard, government should analyze financial statements of public enterprises when deciding guarantee fees, depending on the extent of their financial strengths and soundness.

On the other hand, you need sources to finance infrastructure projects and so on. In Table 3, you can see the potential demands for funding for projects estimated by the World Bank.

To develop secondary markets, you should lift the regulation that requires liquidity ratios for financial institutions holding large part of bonds to some extent. That regulation squeezes up the bond market, because as soon as new issues are released, financial institutions purchase them to clear those standards. And then they try to hold them up to maturities under the situation that eligible issues provided are limited.

Table 3 Investment Requirements, 1995-2004 (in US$ billion)

Country	Power	Telecom	Transport	Water and Sanitation	Total	Percent
China	200	141	302	101	**744**	43.2
India	101	27	102	17	**247**	14.3
Indonesia	54	25	62	20	**161**	9.3
Korea	101	32	132	4	**269**	15.6
Malaysia	17	6	22	4	**49**	2.9
Philippines	19	7	18	4	**48**	2.9
Thailand	49	29	57	10	**145**	8.4
Others	25	18	14	4	**61**	3.9
Total	**586**	**285**	**709**	**162**	**1723**	**100.0**
Percent	32.8	16.6	41.2	9.4	**100.0**	

Source: Infrastructure Development in East Asia and the Pacific; World Bank, September 1995 and The India Infrastructure Report; Export Group on the Commercialization of Infrastructure Project, June 1996

When and how you shift direct monetary adjustment measures to indirect ones is controversial. However, as financial and capital markets develop, you should better be able to gradually shift to indirect monetary operations. These measures can also contribute in promoting bond market microstructures.

I would like to emphasize the role of credit agencies. To promote corporate bond markets, it is clear that you need ratings with enough financial disclosures. To estimate risk premium, timely and frequent review of ratings are required.

Table 4 Indirect Monetary Measures in Asian Countries

	Reserve Requirement	Discount Window	Open Market Operation	
			Measures	Market
Korea	2.0%	CP discount and window lending	TB, MSB(Monetary Stabilization Bonds), FESB (Foreign Exchange Stabilization Bonds), KDIC Bonds KAMCO Bonds	mainly primary gradually on secondary
HK	25% as of liquidity ratio	lending on base rate through LAF Liquidity Adjustment Facility	Exchnage Fund Bills and 2Y 3Y 4Y Notes	primary
Singapore	20% as of liquidity ratio	discount trade bills and TB direct lending and borrowing in interbank market	182days 273days 364days TB	mainly primary
Malaysia	4.0% liquidity requiremaent on each financial institution basis	direct lending and borrowing in interbank market		
Indonesisa	3.0%	discount window lending and borrowing	SBI, SBPU	SBI on primary and secondary SBPU on primary
Philippines	8.0% requirement of holding 7% of government securities as of requirement ratio	discount window lending	TB	mainly primary gradually on secondary
Thailand	6.0% as of liquidity ratio	direct lending and borrowing in interbank market		

(Source) "The Emerging Asian Bond Market June 1995" , World Bank and central banks'

Table5 Rating Agencies in Asian Countries

Countries	Rating Agency	
Korea	Korea Investors Services	(KIS)
	National Information and Credit Evaluation	(NICE)
	Korea Management and Consulting Corp	(KMCC)
Malaysia	Rating Agency Malaysia	(RAM)
	Malaysia Rating Corp	(MARC)
Taiwan	Taiwan Ratings	
Thailand	The Thai Rating and Information Service	(TRIS)
Indonesia	Pefindo Rating Agency	

Finally, I would like to mention demand side issues. To develop bond markets, you should mobilize domestic institutional investors. That also contributes to stabilization of financial and capital markets, fewer dependents on international market. I feel that this issue looks like a conflict where the demand side decides the short-term economic growth rate and the supply side decides long-term one. I think that main reason why capital and financial markets in the U.S. have been dynamic and efficient is that they can provide many types of financial products. Of course, I understand that a combination of them is needed. But, in the short-term, it may be better to promote the demand side more in order to develop the bond market.

Table 6 contains the asset sizes of institutional investors in Asia. The demography of Asia is so young that there is less incentive for pension plans.I think that most benchmarks of pension funds and mutual funds are almost fixed Rates, such as time deposits. In this case, there is less incentive to trade funds actively, Leaving the secondary market undeveloped.

In the case of Hong Kong, they are going to introduce the Mandatory Provident Fund as the 401k scheme in the U.S. this December. I believe that this will lead the debt market in Hong Kong to be more active.

You could introduce some kind of incentive schemes for saving that are market-oriented, such as benchmarks tracing financial and capital markets' movements. In order to beat benchmarks, those funds try to trade actively in the secondary market. That increases trading volumes and promotes microstructure of bond market.

5.   Conclusion

Finally, I would like to express my thanks for hearing my presentation, and I'm sure that you will successfully develop your domestic bond markets in the future. Thank you very much.

Table 6 Institutional Investors in Asia

Korea

(bil. Won)

	Total Assets	%
Deposit Money Banks	576,777	35.8
Nation-Wide Commercial	393,143	24.4
Local Banks	42,339	2.6
Foreign Banks	33,799	2.1
Industrial Banks	38,753	2.4
National Agricultural Cooperative	53,296	3.3
National Federation of Fisheries	7,189	0.4
National Livestock Cooperative	8,259	0.5
Others	986,036	61.2
Korea Development	124,662	7.7
Export-Import Bank of	24,455	1.5
Trust Accounts of Banks	369,757	23.0
Mutual Credits	75,041	4.7
Credit Unions	20,801	1.3
Mutual Savings & Finance	31,631	2.0
Investment Trust	214,980	13.3
Securities Finance	8,419	0.5
Life Insurance	92,891	5.8
Postal Savings & Postal Life	13,584	0.8
Securities Corporation	9,816	0.6
National Pension Funds	47,680	3.0
Total	1,610,493	100.0

Note End of 98. National Pension Funds : End of January,
Source BOK Monthly Bulletin and other

Hong Kong

(mil. HK$)

	Total Assets
Licensed Banks	6,466,149
HK$	2,491,839
Foreign Currency	3,974,310
RLB	247,473
HK$	136,332
Foreign Currency	111,141
DTC	71,651
HK$	53,665
Foreign Currency	17,986
Financial Institutes Total	6,785,273
HK$	2,681,836
Foreign Currency	4,103,437
Unit Trust	US$183,092
	(HK$1,425,243)

Notes   RLB=Restricted License Bank, DTC=Deposit Taking Companies
End of 99, Unit Trust : End of March,99
Source   HKMA Monthly Statistical Bulletin and other reports

Indonesia

	Total Assets	%
Commercial Banks	815,108	90.0
Finance Companies	43,629	4.8
Insurance/Re-insurance	32,000	3.5
Pension Funds	15,000	1.7
Total	905,737	100.0

Note Commercial Banks: : End of 99, Finance Companies : End of
Insurance/Re-insurance ; End of
Source BI Report for The Financial year 1998/99 and other

Singapore

(mil. SG$)

	Total Assets	%
Commercial Banks	326,295	62.0
Merchant Banks	57,122	10.9
Finance Companies	20,743	3.9
Life Insurance	28,512	5.4
Non-Life Insurance	3,914	0.7
Unit Trust	1,109	0.2
CPF	88,562	16.8
Total	526,257	100.0

Notes   Life insurance and property and casualties insurance are
operated under same entities. So, above assetes are each
sections'.
CPF : Outstanding of saving
End of 99. CPF : End of September, 99. Unit Trust : End of 95
Source MAS Monthly Statistical Bulletin and other reports

Malaysia

h.m. Ringgit

	Total Assets	%
Banking	6,298	76.8
Commercial Banks	4,747	57.9
Finance Companies	1,159	14.1
Merchant Banks	392	4.8
Non-Banking	1,907	23.2
EPF	1,602	19.5
Insurance	305	3.7
Total	8,205	100.0

Note End of 99. EPF, Insurance : End of September,99
Source   BNM Monthly Statistical Bulletin and other reports

Thailand

(bil. Bahts)

	Total Assets	%
Commercial Banks	6,973	73.7
Finance Companies	245	2.6
Government owned banks	1,722	18.2
Saving bank	861	9.1
Agricultural bank	279	2.9
IFCT	187	2.0
Housing bank	338	3.6
Export-Import Bank	57	0.6
Investment Trust	311	3.3
GPF(Gov Pension Fund)	70	0.7
PPF(Private Provident Fund)	137	1.4
Total	9,458.0	100.0

Note End of 99, GPF and PPF : End of
Source BOT Quarterly Bulletin and other reports

Philippines

(Bil. Pesos)

	Total Assets	%
Banking	3,022	83.7
Commercial Banks	2,740	75.9
Savings Banks	220	6.1
Rural Banks	62	1.7
Non-Banking	590	16.3
GSIS	121	3.3
SSS	144	4.0
Total	3,612	100.0

Note Commercial Banks : End of 99, Non-Banking : End of 97.
Source BSP Selected Philippine Economic Indicators and other rep

Annex I

COUNTRY NOTES

CAPITAL MARKET DEVELOPMENT IN INDIA

by

Mr. Devendra Raj Mehta

1.   Overview of the Indian Economy

The Indian economy is expected to grow by 5.9 percent in 1999-2000. More importantly, an industrial recovery seems finally to be underway from the cyclical downturn of the previous two years. Growth of GDP from manufacturing will almost double to 7 percent in 1999-2000 from 3.6 percent in 1998-99. The growth in GDP from the construction sector is expected to accelerate to 9.0 percent in 1999-2000 from 5.7 percent in 1998-99. The performance of infrastructure sectors improved markedly. The inflation rate dropped to international levels of 2 to 3 percent for the first time in decades. The balance of payments survived the twin shocks of the East-Asian crisis and the post-Pokhran sanctions with a low current account deficit and sufficient capital inflows. This was demonstrated by the continuing rise in foreign exchange reserves by over US$2.4 billion during the year until the end of January 2000 coupled with a relatively stable exchange rate. Export performance has improved on par with the better performing emerging economies. The restoration of confidence in industry has been best reflected in the rise in the stock market during 1999. Primary issues have increased by almost half during the first nine months of 1999-2000.

Exports showed a strong recovery in 1999, growing by 12.9 percent in April-December 1999 in US dollar value. Despite a 57.8 percent growth in US dollar value of oil imports in April-December 1999, overall import growth remained at a manageable 9.0 percent. As a result the trade deficit was lower in value (US $) during April-December 1999 as compared to April-December 1998. The current account deficit, which defied gloomy forecasts based on the presumed after-effects of the Asian crisis and the economic sanctions, ended at 1 percent of GDP in 1998-99.

The fundamental objective of the economic reforms undertaken by the government since 1991-92 was to bring rapid and sustained improvement in the quality of life of the people of India. Central to this goal was the rapid increase in incomes and productive employment. Such growth in turn required productive investment in farms, industry, infrastructure and people, since sustained and successful development can only be achieved through continuous increase in the productivity of the economy's capital, land and labour resources.

It was with these set of objectives in mind that the government has continued to undertake economic reforms since 1991-92. Critical elements of the reform package include :

1.   A reversal in the trend of growing fiscal imbalances by reducing fiscal deficits

2.   Reforms in industrial policy by removal of extensive bureaucratic controls over choices which should ideally be left to entrepreneurial decision making

3.   Reforms in trade and exchange rate policy

4. Reforms in foreign investment policy which recognise that foreign investment has an important role in supplementing internal efforts and industrial development

5. Tax reforms to simplify the tax structure and to bring about improvement in tax collections

6. Financial sector reforms to increase the efficiency of the financial system and securities markets so that larger savings could be channeled for productive uses

7. Reforms in the public sector to increase productivity and profit of public sector enterprises and their economic structuring through disinvestment.

These reforms have been continued by the various governments with differing ideologies over the past years. The government's Budget for 2000-01 also signalled the continuing commitment of the government towards the process of liberalisation and reform. The Budget has reduced and simplified indirect taxes and reduced tariffs, increased incentives and enhanced competition. Several other measures have been introduced which are aimed at facilitating the development of the financial sector. Most importantly, while pushing for growth and investment, the Budget reinforced the government's commitment to reducing its fiscal deficit to under 5% of its Gross Domestic Product.

Table 1: **Key Indicators of the Indian Economy**

Indicator	1996-97	1997-98	1998-99	1999-00
		% Change over previous year		
Gross National Product (at 1993-94 prices)	7.8	5.1P	6.8Q	5.9A
Gross Domestic Product (at 1993-94 prices)	7.5	5.0P	6.8Q	5.9A
Industrial Production Index (1)	5.6	6.6	4.0	6.2#
Wholesale Price Index (2)	6.9	5.3	4.8	2.9*
Imports at current prices	6.7	6.0	0.9P	9.0#
Exports at current prices	5.3	4.6	-3.9P	12.9#
Foreign Exchange Reserves	21.8	11.1	10.6	7.4
				Absolute Values
Gross National Product (Rs. Billion, At 1993-94 prices)	9537	10025P	10707Q	11343A
Gross Domestic Product (Rs. Billion, At 1993-94 prices)	9644	10128P	10818Q	11454A
Industrial Production Index (1)	129.1	137.6	143.1	148.2#
Wholesale Price Index (2)	320.1	337.1	353.3	364.9*
Imports (US$million)	39133	41484	41858P	34458#
Exports (US$million)	33470	35006	33659P	27419#
Foreign Exchange Reserves (US$million)	26,423	29,367	32,490	34,900*

(P–Provisional Estimate, Q – Quick Estimate, A – Advance Estimate)
April – December 1999, *As on 29.1.2000 (Provisional, ## As on 14.1.2000)
1. Index of industrial production 1993-94 = 100
2. Index with base 1981-82 = 100 at the end of fiscal year
Source: Economic Survey 1999-00 and RBI Annual Report 1998-99

Major Economic Reforms

Financial Sector

- The Insurance Regulatory and Development Act (IRDA) passed by Parliament in December 1999, seeks to promote private sector participation in the insurance sector, permits foreign equity stake in domestic private insurance companies upto a maximum of 26 percent of the total paid up capital.

- Banks allowed to operate different PLRs for different maturities.

Capital Market

- The Securities Laws (Amendment) Bill, 1999 passed by the Parliament incorporating derivatives and units of Collective Investment Schemes (CIS) in the definition of securities in the Securities Contract Regulation Act, 1999.

- CIS Regulations were notified in October 1999.

- Rolling Settlement has been introduced in 10 select scrips.

- Companies given freedom to determine par value of shares issued by them.

Infrastructure

- New telecom policy allows multiple fixed service operators and opens domestic long distance services to private operators. It also allows existing license holders of basic and cellular services to "migrate" to revenue-sharing arrangements.

External Sector

- Foreign Exchange Management Act, 1999 enacted. The new Act replaces the old FERA. It provisions are in conformity with a liberalised market in foreign exchange.

- Indian companies free to access the ADR/GDR markets, through an automatic route subject to the specified norms and post-issue reporting requirements. Such issues would, however, need to conform to the existing FDI policy.

Industry and Services

- The information Technology Bill to create the legal framework for facilitating electronics commerce in the country, has been introduced in the winter session of the Parliament.

1.1   Recent Trends

Economic developments in India have to be viewed against the backdrop of an exceptionally turbulent and unfavourable international economic environment. The past two years saw significant declines in the GDP of a number of East Asian countries, continuing recession in Japan, severe financial crisis in Russia, unusual volatility in capital and forex markets of industrial countries, continuance of drought in capital inflows to developing countries and a sharp devaluation in Brazil in January 1999. The extension of East Asian crisis to countries in other continents slowed down the world growth to 2 percent in 1998, with little chances of recovery in 1999. India was not only immune to these unfavourable developments but exhibited significant growth. According to the Economic Survey of the government for 1999-2000, the initial spurt of reforms from 1991-92 to 1993-94 was very successful by all accounts, resulting in a jump in economic growth to 7.2% in 1994-95 (in terms of GDP at factor cost). The growth decelerated from a high of 7.8 percent in 1996-97 to 5.0 percent in 1997-98. The economy, however, recovered to an estimated growth of 6.8 percent in 1998-99. This trend would have been firmer but for the crisis and its impact on the world import demand and on international capital markets.

Table 2: **Receipts and Expenditure of the Central Government in Rs. billion**

	1995-96	1996-97	1997-98	1998-99(P)	1999-00 (B.E.)
1. Revenue Receipts	1101.30	1262.79	1339.01	1505.32	1828.40
2. Revenue Expenditure	1398.61	1589.33	1803.50	2161.62	2369.87
3. Revenue Deficit (1-2)	297.31	326.54	464.49	656.30	541.47
4. Capital Receipts	483.48	508.72	824.35	1045.09	1010.42
Of which					
(a) Recovery of Loans	65.05	75.40	83.18	101.46	110.87
(b) Other Receipts (Mainly PSU Disinvestment)	13.97	4.55	9.12	58.71	100.00
(c) Borrowings and Other Liabilities	404.46	428.77	732.05	884.92	799.55
5. Capital expenditure	284.24	314.03	359.86	388.79	468.95
6. Total expenditure	1682.85	1903.36	2163.36	2550.41	2838.82
7. Fiscal Deficit (1+4(a)+4(b)-6)	502.53	560.62	732.05	884.92	799.55
(As percent of GDP)					
1. Revenue Receipts	9.3	9.3	8.8	8.5	9.5
2. Revenue Expenditure	11.8	11.7	11.9	12.3	12.3
3. Revenue Deficit	2.5	2.4	3.1	3.7	2.8
4. Capital Receipts	4.1	3.7	5.4	5.9	5.2
Of which					
(a) Recovery of Loans	0.6	0.6	0.5	0.6	0.6
(b) Other Receipts (Mainly PSU Disinvestment)	0.1	0.0	0.1	0.3	0.5
(c) Borrowings and Other Liabilities	3.4	3.1	4.8	5.0	4.1
5. Capital expenditure	2.4	2.3	2.4	2.2	2.4
6. Total expenditure	14.2	14.0	14.3	14.5	14.7
7. Fiscal Deficit (1+4(a)+4(b)-6)	4.3	4.1	4.8	5.0	4.1

P – Provisional and unaudited
B.E. Budget Estimate

However, the budget of 2000-2001 has heralded the era of a second generation of reforms, which would further integrate India with the other economies. Reform initiatives have been introduced or strengthened in almost every critical infrastructure sub-sector. There have also been new policy measures in several areas such as industrial de-licensing, foreign investment, trade policy, financial sector and capital markets. With the growing participation of virtually the entire spectrum of political opinion in the reform process, there is a good prospect that a higher growth rate will become a permanent feature of the economy.

Table 3: **Inflation Rate {Wholesale Price Index (Percent)}**

	End of Year (point-to-point)	52 week Average
1995-96	4.4	7.7
1996-97	6.9	6.4
1997-98	5.3	4.8
1998-99*	4.8	6.9
1999-00	2.9P	3.3P

*P – Provisional as on January 29, 2000
Base Year for Wholesale Price Index 1993-94 = 100
Source : Economic Survey 1999-00

Table 4: **Foreign Exchange Reserves (US$Million)**

	As on 31 Mar 1998	As on 31 Mar1999	As on 29 Jan 2000
Total Reserves of which :	29,367	32,490	34,900
(a) Foreign Currency Assets	25,975	29,522	31,940
(b) Gold	3,391	2,960	2,945
(c) SDRs	1	8	15

Source: Economic Survey 1999-00 and RBI Annual Report 1998-99

1.2 *Savings and Investment*

A sharp slump in investment had a deflationary impact and countered part of this stimulus. Total investment (at 1993-94 prices) declined by about half a percent in 1998-99, after increasing by over 13 percent the year before. There was a deceleration in manufacturing and a slump in agriculture in 1997-98. Average real interest rates, as measured by the cut-off yield on 364-day treasury bills (adjusted by the WPI inflation), declined by 1 percent point in 1998-99.

Gross domestic saving declined sharply in 1998-99 to 22.3 percent of GDP. The 2.4 percent points of GDP decline in the saving rate resulted from a 1.4 percent point decline in public saving and a 1 percent point decline in household saving in physical form (i.e. direct investment). The corporate saving rate also declined to 3.8 percent of GDP in 1998-99 from 4.3 percent in GDP in 1997-98. Though household financial saving increased as a proportion of GDP, the overall private saving rate declined by 1 percent of GDP. The decline in saving rate of the government and households is a counterpart of the higher consumption growth during 1998-99.

Real gross domestic capital formation in 1997-98 at 26.9 percent of GDP (constant price) was only marginally less than the previous peak rate. However, it declined in 1998-99 to 25.1 percent of GDP, marginally less than the five-year average. About half of this decline was due to a fall in household investment, as it reverted back to its earlier trend after a sharp rise this previous year.

1.3 Banking and Finance

The recent East Asian crisis has underlined the critical importance of undertaking reforms to strengthen the banking sector. In recent years, RBI has been prescribing prudential norms for banks broadly consistent with international practice. To meet the minimum capital adequacy norms set by RBI and to enable the banks to expand their operations, public sector banks will need more capital. With the government budget under severe strain, such capital has to be raised from the public, which will result in reduction in government shareholding. To facilitate this process, government has decided to accept the recommendations of the Narasimham Committee on Banking Sector Reforms for reducing to 33% the requirement of minimum shareholding by the government in nationalised banks.

The government has decided to consider recapitalisation of the weak banks to achieve the prescribed capital adequacy norms, provided a viable restructuring programme acceptable to the government as the owner and the RBI as the regulator is made available by the concerned banks.

1.4 Capital Market

In earlier millennia, India was an intellectual leader. Today history is repeating itself as young Indian entrepreneurs are at the forefront of the infotech revolution, whether in Silicon Valley, Bangalore or Hyderabad. They have shown how ideas, knowledge, entrepreneurship and technology can combine to yield unprecedented growth of income, employment and wealth. Companies unknown five years ago have become world leaders. We must do everything possible to promote this flowering of knowledge-based enterprise and job creation.

1.5 Disinvestment / Privatisation / Public Sector Restructuring

The government's policy towards the public sector is clear and unambiguous. Its main elements are to:

– Restructure and revive potentialy viable Public Sector Undertakings (PSUs);

– Close down PSUs which cannot be revived;

– Bring down Government equity in all non-strategic PSUs to 26% or lower, if necessary; and

– Fully protect the interest of workers.

(Source: Taxmann's Budget 2000-01)

1.6 Infrastructure

Infrastructure services remain a key bottleneck to rapid and sustained growth in our economy. We have made substantial progress in encouraging private infrastructure services providers and in establishing independent regulatory frameworks in most infrastructure sectors. We have also sought to give greater operational and commercial autonomy to existing public entities in these sectors

In order to give a fillip to the reform process in the power sector and to undertake investments for renovation and modernisation of old and inefficient plants, and to strengthen the distribution system, a new scheme for providing assistance to State utilities will be introduced.

2.0   International Developments

2.1   *Asian Crisis*

By all accounts, the performance of the Indian economy, has been impressive both in terms of growth and stability. During the period 1992-97, the annual average real GDP growth rate was 6.8 percent. Our annual average growth rate during this period was higher than the 6.4 percent average for developing countries. Our inflation during the period 1992-97 was 8.7 percent, which compares favourably with the average for developing countries. Our current account deficit as a percentage of GDP was only 1.3 percent during this period. Foreign exchange reserves went up from US$9.2 billion in 1991-92 to US$26.4 as end-March 1997.

The above figures show that India's fundamentals are strong making it less vulnerable to contagion, and this is clear from our performance over the last two years. GDP growth has been maintained at a high of 5-7%, the rate of inflation as measured by the wholesale price index had fluctuated between 5-8% and the current account deficit continued to be low at around 2 percent of GDP. The economic indicators of the current and previous years were provided in the initial part of this note. The real interest rates in India, which were relatively higher, have started coming down after the most recent budgetary measures.

Policy Implications

The reason as to why India escaped the contagion can be analysed in terms of the policies that the country has been pursuing in areas where serious concern has been expressed in the context of the Asian crisis. Investments as a percentage of GDP have been reasonably steady in the recent past at around 27 percent on average. About 95 percent of this was financed by domestic savings. In managing our external accounts, we ensure a sustainable current account deficit, strictly control reliance on short-term external debt, limit access to external debt, and emphasise productive use of such debt. We encourage Foreign Direct Investment and portfolio investments through foreign institutional investors as the main sources of non-debt creating capital inflows. Also, the exchange rate is market determined, which the RBI closely monitors, and, when warranted, makes purchases and sales of foreign currency to ensure orderly conditions in forex markets. Early in the reform period, we undertook financial sector reforms, especially banking reform, which included strengthening the regulatory framework, imposing prudential norms and reducing non-performing assets. We discourage banks' investments in real estate and stock markets. Corporates' exposure to debt, especially external debt, is within reasonable limits. As compared with other central banks, there is widely recognised transparency in operations of the Reserve Bank of India. There is, therefore, reason to believe that it is not just chance but sound macroeconomic management which saved us from the South East Asian contagion.

Effect on Securities Markets

The Indian securities markets have withstood the onslaught of the Asian crises. The fall in the valuations in India are comparatively much less than what was witnessed in other countries. The foreign portfolio investments were slightly negative towards the end of 1997 and for some period of 1998. However, the magnitude of these outflows have had minimal effect on the stock markets in 1997 and 1998.

Despite excessive volatility and even closure of some of the Asian and other countries markets, the Indian markets have never been closed on account of the crises. There have been no major defaults, as strict margining systems were imposed and administered.

SEBI's role is to ensure that all material information that is likely to be of relevance to investors, and is likely to help them make an informed investment decision, is disclosed. SEBI has also prescribed a code of conduct for advertisements of primary market issues, which require risk factors related to the particular issue to be stated, and disallows misleading statements and symbols, such as movie stars or sports personalities or any other celebrities or public figures.

Issuers are not under the direct regulatory purview of SEBI, but are regulated primarily by the Department of Company Affairs under the Companies Act of 1956. SEBI, therefore, has been enforcing its disclosure and investor protection norms in the primary market through primary market intermediaries that are under its regulatory purview, and are registered with it. Merchant bankers have been required to carry out due diligence of issues that are lead managed by them, and failure to carry out adequate due diligence has been made a violation of the conditions of their continued registration with SEBI. While the case for developing responsible intermediaries remains strong, SEBI has been further strengthened in its efforts to regulate and take actions against violations by issuing firms. Various powers have been delegated to SEBI under the Companies Act, which allow SEBI to prosecute issuers for delays in transfer of securities, making refunds of application moneys and payment of dividends, in addition to taking action against fraudulent inducements to invest in securities. Since March 1995, SEBI has been granted the power to frame regulations relating to the issue of capital, and to issue directives to companies, enabling SEBI to regulate issuers more effectively.

SEBI has instituted a mechanism for redressing investor grievances related to issuers. These grievances are in the nature of delays extending beyond the legally permitted time frame by issuers or their agents in transfer of securities, in dispatching certificates to allottees, in making refunds of application funds and in paying dividends. SEBI also uses several indirect means for redressal of investor grievances. These include public exposure and requiring disclosure of details of investor grievances pending redressal in future prospectuses issued by the same firm. Also, 1% of the issue proceeds are required to be deposited with stock exchanges, to be released only upon redressal of investor grievances arising from that issue to SEBI's satisfaction.

The sale of securities in the primary market

A firm making an issue of securities appoints a lead manager and / or co-lead manager to the issue, who is a registered intermediary with SEBI. Only body corporates have been allowed to function as merchant bankers. The lead manager is responsible for making all arrangements such as tying up of underwriting, appointment of a registrar to the issue and bankers to the issue (both SEBI registered intermediaries) who act as collecting banks for subscription moneys received. Subscriptions are invited through application forms which are circulated to prospective investors through direct marketing by the lead manager and his consortium, or through a network of stock brokers. Up to 75% of the issue may be sold to institutional investors such as public financial institutions, mutual funds and foreign institutional investors through "firm allotment". The remaining securities have to be offered to the public, and the issue is allotted to investors in the "public" category on a proportional basis.

Book Building

Securities of the companies can be sold on the basis of the book building process. Better price discovery is achieved through the book building process. Time and costs are cut and efficiency is achieved.

Underwriting is optional, subject to the provision that if an issue that was not underwritten is unable to collect more than 90% of the amount offered to the public, the entire amount collected is to be returned to investors. Issuers are allowed to indicate a price band of up to 20% of the floor price at the time of submission of the offer document to SEBI. The actual price is required to be determined only at the time of filing the offer document with the Registrar of Companies or with the stock exchange.

The proportional allotment of securities to applicants in the public category is finalised in consultation with the stock exchange on which the securities are to be listed. Refunds are made to applicants in the "public" category in case the portion of the issue that has been offered to the public has been oversubscribed. Trading in the security on the stock exchange is required to begin after 70 days of the issue opening for subscription. For the BSE and the NSE, the minimum listed capital for a company is required to be Rs.100 million. On the other stock exchanges this level is Rs.30 million.

3.2   *Primary Market Indicators*

Growth of the primary market

Since 1991, the primary market has grown significantly as a result of the removal of investment restrictions in the overall economy and as a result of the repeal of restrictions imposed by the Capital Issues (Control) Act. In 1991-92, Indian issuers raised Rs.62.15 billion. In 1994-95, this figure had gone up to Rs.276.21 billion. In 1995-96 and 1996-97 the funds raised are lower on account of the overall downtrend in the market and tighter entry barriers introduced by SEBI. The annual data on funds raised from Indian securities markets is summarised in Table 5 below.

Table 5 : **Funds raised from Indian securities markets (Rs.billion)**

	Public Issue		Rights Issue		Total	
	Number	Amount	Number	Amount	Number	Amount
1995-96	1,426	142.40	299	65.64	1,725	208.04
1996-97	751	115.57	131	27.19	882	142.76
1997-98	62	28.62	49	17.08	111	45.70
1998-99	32	50.19	26	56.75	58	55.86
1999-00 (Apr – Jan)	43	44.13	25	14.42	68	58.55

Table 6 : **Primary Market Intermediaries**

	31 March 1999	**29 February 2000**
Merchant bankers:	251	173
Registrars to an issue and share transfer agents:	196	170
Debenture trustees:	34	38
Bankers to an issue:	72	67
Underwriters:	16	
Portfolio Managers:	15	23

A large number and variety of primary market intermediaries have been developed over the past decade. We have world class investment bankers who not only manage domestic issues but also participate in some of the international issues such as GDRs, ADRs, and ECBs. Many Indian investment bankers formed joint ventures with reputed international investment bankers. For a well-developed capital market it is necessary to have skillfull and capable intermediaries such as bankers, underwriters, portfolio managers. The preceding table provides numbers on all these intermediaries.

3.3   *Disclosures*

There are several schools of thought on the content and extent of disclosures to be made to investors. One of these believes that if the information is made fully available on a real -ime basis and then the investor himself can protect his interests in the capital market. Here it is assumed that investors have private incentives to protect. SEBI continues to make sustained efforts in every sphere of capital market activity for higher and better disclosures. Offer documents such as prospectus, letter of offer and other documents provide information on par with some of the most developed markets in the world.

Several reforms have been undertaken to facilitate the growth of the primary market. SEBI has been granted the necessary powers to ensure investor protection in the primary market. SEBI has issued Guidelines for Disclosure and Investor Protection which must be complied with for the issue of securities which are to be listed on the stock exchanges. The prospectus accompanying such an issue of securities is required to be filed with SEBI, in order to ensure adequacy of disclosure. SEBI no longer vets this prospectus. The prospectus which is filed with SEBI becomes a public document and the issuer and the lead merchant banker are responsible for ensuring compliance with SEBI Guidelines on Disclosure and Investor Protection. SEBI seeks to ensure full and fair disclosure by issuers through these guidelines which are required to be complied with by issuers and intermediaries. These guidelines specify that risk factors associated with the issue be prominently displayed in the prospectus or offer document, specify disclosure on certain financial data including financial information about the issuing company, background of the promoters, objectives of the issue, minimum contributions by promoters, and specify different lock-in periods for such contributions.

4.0   Secondary Market

Securities markets in India have a long history. The Stock Exchange, Mumbai (Bombay) (BSE), the country's oldest exchange has its origins in the informal trading in stocks that flourished in the 1850s and 1860s. Formal trading on the BSE began in 1875, making it one of the oldest stock exchanges in Asia (there are 23 stock exchanges in India today).

Enacted inn 1956, the Securities Contracts (Regulation) (SCR) Act brought stock exchanges, and their members, as well as contracts in securities which could be traded, under the regulation of the central government, through the Ministry of Finance.

In spite of a long standing history of the Indian capital market, some of the practices followed in India were very archaic. Trading settlement and processes of securities trading required modernisation. The trading and settlement infrastructure remained poor. Trading on all stock exchanges was through open outcry. Settlement systems were paper based. Market intermediaries were largely unregulated. Disclosure requirements were inadequate and of an *ad hoc* nature. The regulatory structure was fragmented and administered by different agencies. There was no comprehensive legislation or apex regulatory authority for regulation of the securities markets. Box 1 below gives a description of Indian securities markets before 1990-91.

Box 1: Indian Securities Markets before 1990-91

– Fragmented regulation; multiplicity of administration.
– Primary markets were not into the mainstream of financial system.
– Poor disclosure in prospectus. Prospectus, balance sheet not made available to investors.
– Investors faced problems of refund delays, transfer delays, etc.
– Stock exchanges regulated through Securities Contracts (Regulations) Act. No inspection of the stock exchanges undertaken.
– Stock Exchanges run as 'brokers clubs'; management dominated by brokers.
– Merchant bankers and other intermediaries unregulated.
– No concept of capital adequacy.
– Mutual funds - virtually unregulated with potential for conflicts of interest in structure.
– Poor disclosures by mutual funds, NAV not published; no valuation norms.
– Private sector mutual funds not permitted.
– Takeovers regulated only through Listing Agreement between the stock exchange and the company.
– No prohibition of insider trading and fraudulent and unfair trade practices.

SEBI took several initiatives and modernised Indian capital market so that the Indian market has become an efficient fair and transparent one. In the following lines we provide a list of regulations, rules and changes brought in by SEBI.

4.1 Developments in Indian Securities Markets Since 1992

– The Securities and Exchange Board of India, set up in 1988 under an administrative arrangement, given statutory powers with the enactment of the SEBI Act, 1992

– Capital Issues(Control) Act, 1947 repealed and the Office of Controller of Capital

– Issues abolished; control over price and premium of shares removed. Companies now free to raise funds from securities markets after filing letter of offer with SEBI

– SEBI introduces regulations for primary and secondary market intermediaries, bringing them within the regulatory framework

– The SEBI has set up a Committee under the chairmanship of Shri Kumar Mangalam Birla on Corporate Governance and accepted the recommendations contained therein. The recommendations have been grouped as mandatory and non-mandatory.

Primary Market

– Reforms by SEBI in the primary market include improved disclosure standards, introduction of prudential norms and simplification of issue procedures. Companies required to disclose all material facts and specific risk factors associated with their projects while making public issues. Disclosure norms further strengthened by introducing cash flow statements

– Listing agreements of stock exchanges amended to require listed companies to furnish annual statement to the stock exchanges showing variations between financial projections and projected utilisation of funds in the offer document and at actuals, to enable shareholders to make comparisons between performance and promises

– SEBI introduces a code of advertisement for public issues for ensuring fair and truthful disclosures

– To give the companies flexibility to issue shares at any amount and to extend free pricing to its logical conclusion and to benefit the investors; to abolish the current requirement for issuing shares with a fixed par value of Rs.10 or Rs.100 for companies whose shares are dematerialised

– To help lower issue cost and time for making public issues and also to simplify procedures, the ceiling of issue size of Rs.100 crore for book-building reduced to Rs.25 crore.

– To encourage the mobilisation of capital by new companies, the entry norms for IPOs further relaxed by substituting the requirement of actual payment of dividend in three out of five preceding years, with the ability to pay dividend as demonstrated by distributable profits in accordance with the provisions of the Companies Act in at least three out of five preceding years.

– To improve the liquidity and to encourage entrepreneurs to raise capital through public issues, the requirement of the lock-in period of promoters' contribution in full reduced to only 20% of the total capital of the company.

– To help investors make informed investment decisions, credit rating by approved credit rating agencies made mandatory for all public and rights issues of debt instruments irrespective of their maturity or conversion period as against exemption granted for 18 months.

– To facilitate floatation of issues by public and private sector banks, relaxation made in the Disclosure and Investor Protection guidelines of SEBI for the issue of capital, subject to the approval of the issue price by the RBI, as banks are under the regulatory purview of RBI.

– The Board decided that a company in the IT sector going for IPO/offer for sale shall have a track record of distributable profits as per Section 205 of the Companies Act in three out of five years in the IT business/from out of IT activities. If it does not fulfil this criterion, it can access the market through the alternative route of appraisal and financing by a bank or financial institution.

Dematerialisation of Securities

– To eliminate the risks associated with trading in physical securities such as delay in transfer, bad delivery, theft, fake and forged shares, several new, and far reaching initiatives were taken by the SEBI to accelerate dematerialisation and electronic book entry of securities -

Compulsory trading in dematerialised form introduced for the first time for all investors starting from 4 January 1999 in a phased manner in shares of a selection of most actively traded companies

The list of companies whose shares are to be compulsorily traded in dematerialised form by institutional investors expanded to cover almost all the actively traded shares accounting for more than 90 percent of the trading volume

The market lots abolished for shares of companies compulsorily traded in dematerialised form by all investors

Derivatives Trading

- To provide the facility of hedging and enhance the liquidity in the market, the committee appointed by the SEBI on derivatives recommended phased introduction of trading in derivative products beginning with trading in stock index futures, accepted by the SEBI. The amendment of the SCR Act was also completed and GOI's approval also obtained. The trading on Index Futures will commence soon.

  The recommendations of the J.R. Verma Committee for risk containment measures for derivative trading including margin system are implemented.

Buy-back of Securities

- To help increase the liquidity in the securities and to enable companies to enhance the wealth of shareholders, the facility of buy-back of securities by listed companies introduced for the first time.

Employees Stock Option Scheme

- J.R. Verma Committee was constituted by the SEBI to formulate the Guidelines for Employee Stock Options and Employee Stock Purchase Scheme. The recommendations of the Committee and the Guidelines are being issued.

Facilitating the Development of Infrastructure

- To facilitate increased raising of funds by infrastructure companies, the SEBI granted several relaxations and exemptions from the existing requirements. These are given below:

  Exemption from fulfilling eligibility norms

  Exemption from meeting profitability norms for free pricing of issues – subject to fulfillment of certain conditions.

Exemption from the requirement of offering at least 25 percent of securities to the public

Exemption from the requirement of the minimum number of 5 shareholders for every Rs.1 lakh of capital issued.

Exemption from the requirement of a minimum subscription of 90 percent of public offer

Relaxation from the requirement of a minimum financial participation by an appraising agency – a minimum participation of 5 percent of the project cost can be made either jointly or severally by the specified institutions, irrespective whether they have appraised the project or not.

Continuing Disclosures

- To improve the continuing disclosure standards for companies for quicker dissemination of information to investors, quarterly disclosure of financial results by listed companies made mandatory for the first time by the SEBI through the amendment of the listing agreement, thus taking India to the select list of countries with similar continuing disclosure requirements.

Credit Rating Agencies

- To strengthen the credibility of the ratings of credit rating agencies and enhance the transparency in their reporting and information system, the recommendations of the SEBI appointed Committee accepted. As a result, the credit rating agencies have to register with the SEBI and follow the guidelines as specified.

Collective Investment Schemes

- Following the Central Government's decision to treat the schemes, through which instruments like agro bonds, plantation bonds etc. are issued, as Collective Investment Schemes (CIS), coming under the provision of SEBI Act, 1992, SEBI constituted a Committee under the Chairmanship of Dr. S.A. Dave to examine and formulate the Regulations in order to streamlining their activity, provide production to investors and introduce transparency. The SEBI Board has approved the draft Regulations for Collective Investment Schemes.

Secondary Market Transparency

- To enhance the transparency in the secondary market, automated screen based trading which was introduced in all 23 stock exchanges.

- To enhance transparency of negotiated deals, stock exchanges directed to ensure that all negotiated deals result in delivery and deals of value of Rs.25 lakh or volume of 10,000 shares are reported on the screens within 15 minutes of transaction and disseminated to the market.

- SEBI reconstituted the governing boards of the stock exchanges, introduces capital adequacy norms for brokers and issues rules for making the client/broker relationship more transparent, in particular, segregating client and broker accounts

- Over-the-Counter Exchange of India (OTC) set up with computerised on-line screen based nationwide electronic trading and rolling settlement in 1992.

- National Stock Exchange of India (NSE) set up as a stock exchange with computerised on line screen based nation-wide electronic trading in 1994.

- System of mark to market margins introduced on the stock exchanges

- "Revised carry forward" system introduced in place of "badla"

- The SEBI advised Stock exchanges to set up either Trade Guarantee Fund or Settlement Guarantee Fund to eliminate counter-party risk to meet the need for a safe and efficient market.

- Upper limit for gross exposure of member brokers of a stock exchange was fixed at 20 times the base minimum capital and additional capital of the member broker.

- All Stock Exchanges are directed to set up independent Clearing House / Corporation.

- Chandratre Committee on delisting of securities recommended exchanges to collect listing fees from the companies for three years in advance. companies opting for voluntary delisting should mandatorily provide an exit route to investors by offering a buy-back facility to them.

- Brokers are permitted to warehouse trades for firm orders of the Institutional Clients only.

- The SEBI constituted a committee under the chairmanship of Shri G. C. Gupta to study the concept of market making and to revive the institution of market makers.

- R. Chandrasekharan committee had recommended adequate safety & security features like use of watermarks, hologram, bar coding, ultra-violet ink etc. Also, section of the printers and paper manufactures for printing of share certificates with the above safety features.

- All stock exchanges are required to set up funds, namely, Investor Protection Fund and Investor Services Fund. They are advised to provide a desk for attending investor complaints and a dummy terminal for showing the on-line trades of the exchanges.

- SEBI has exempted infrastructure companies and municipal corporations from the requirements of Rule 19(2)(b) of Securities (Contract) Regulation Rules, 1957, allowing them to list their debt instruments on the stock exchanges without the pre-existing requirement of equity being listed first.

- Amendments to regulations for merchant bankers have been made. Only body corporates have been allowed to function as merchant bankers. Also, merchant bankers have been prohibited from carrying on fund-based activities other than those related exclusively to the capital market.

– SEBI (Registrars to an Issue and Share Transfer Agents) Regulations have been amended to provide for an arms length relationship between the issuer and the Registrar to the Issue. It has been stipulated that no registrar can act as such for any issue of securities made by any body corporate, if the Registrar to the Issue and the Issuer are associates.

– Many SEBI regulations such as stock brokers, registrars to an issue, portfolio manger, underwriters, debenture trustees, bankers to an issue, custodian of securities, depositories, venture capital funds were amended to provide that applicant should be a 'fit and proper person'.

– B D Shah Committee on Short Sales discussed regulations on short sales. It has now been decided that each stock exchange will announce scrip-wise net outstanding single side position for the top two hundred scrips traded on that stock exchange. However, in the cases of those exchanges where the scrips traded are less than two-hundred, information regarding all scrips traded on that Exchange will be announced.

– The Board decided that exchanges would now be free to set up terminals any place in the country.

– The Board examined OTCEI's proposal to provide a trading mechanism and price discovery for securities of public limited companies which are not listed or traded as permitted securities in any exchange.

– Based on the recommendations of the Committee, rolling settlement would be introduced in the ten scrips from the settlements in those scrips commencing on any day in the week beginning 10 January 2000.

Increase in Market Access

– To increase market access for investors across the country, the Stock Exchange Mumbai and the National Stock Exchange (NSE) further expanded their terminals through VSAT to cover more than 250 cities and towns.

– To increase the access of the Indian securities market to NRIs, OCBs and FIIs, the Indian stock exchanges be permitted to set up their trading terminals overseas subject to regulatory requirements of the host countries.

– Based on the recommendations of the Committee on Internet based securities trading, internet trading can take place in India within the existing legal framework through use of order-routing systems.

Mutual Funds

– SEBI frames regulations for mutual funds. Private mutual funds are permitted and several such funds have already been set up. All mutual funds allowed to apply for firm allotment in public issues – aimed at reducing issue costs.

–   In order to strengthen the disclosure by mutual funds, standard offer document and abridged offer document introduced .

–   Several mutual funds directed by the SEBI to honour their commitment to the investors in assured return schemes thus benefiting millions of investors. By the end of 31 March 1999 the total amount paid to investors was Rs.1350 crore.

–   To ensure that the Trustees discharge their responsibilities more effectively, the report of the Committee under the chairmanship of Shri P.K. Kaul, submitted to the SEBI.

–   The Securities and Exchange Board of India (Mutual Funds) Regulations of 1996 were amended to bring greater clarity to the existing provisions of the regulations and to address certain issues that are important for investor protection.

–   Aggregate investments by a mutual fund in listed or to be listed securities of group companies of the sponsor shall not exceed 25% of the net assets of all schemes of the fund.

–   Securities transactions with associate brokers shall not exceed 5% of the quarterly business done by the mutual fund.

–   Unitholders' approval will no longer be required for rollover of schemes and for converting close-ended schemes into open-ended ones, provided the unitholders are provided with an option to redeem their holdings in full at NAV based prices.

–   Independent trustees who are not associated with the sponsor shall now constitute 75% of the Board of Trustees instead of earlier provision of 50%.

–   SEBI has set up a committee under the chairmanship of Shri.B.G.Deshmukh to advise SEBI on matters relating to the development and regulation of mutual funds in the country.

–   SEBI constituted a working group to frame the guidelines for domestic funds to invest in overseas markets. The group recommended that initially Mutual Funds may be allowed to invest in overseas securities including ADRs/GDRs issued by Indian companies.

Market Safety and Risk Containment Measures

–   SEBI strengthens surveillance mechanisms in SEBI and directs all stock exchanges to have separate surveillance departments.

–   SEBI strengthens enforcement of its regulations. Begins the process of prosecuting companies for mis-statements; issue show cause notices to merchant bankers; ensure refunds of application money in several issues on account of mis-statements in the prospectus.

–   To ensure that settlements take place without failure and to reduce counter party risk, 10 major- and medium-sized stock exchanges have set up trade / settlement guarantee funds.

- To protect market integrity, especially under conditions of abnormal price movement, and to contain extreme volatility, the margin system strengthened by the SEBI in consultation with the stock exchanges by introducing additional volatility margin, incremental margin for carry forward transactions and concentration margin coupled with reduction of daily price bands from 10 percent to 8 percent and abolition of weekly price bands.

Monitoring, Surveillance and Effective Prevention of Market Manipulation

- To help ensure real time monitoring of price movements and broker positions and to generate real time alerts, 4 major and medium sized stock exchanges implemented the first phase of the Stock Watch System.

- Several enforcement actions taken against intermediaries for various violations of the provisions of SEBI Act and rules and regulations and also for market manipulation and unfair trade practices.

Consolidation of Smaller Stock Exchanges

- To help sustain the activities of smaller stock exchanges, the Inter Connected Stock Exchange of India set up by 14 regional stock exchanges, and commenced with limited trading operations.

- Small stock exchanges may be permitted to promote a subsidiary which can acquire membership rights of a larger stock exchange viz. NSE/BSE/CSE/DSE or any other exchange subject to usual conditions applicable to the other members.

- Indian companies permitted to access international capital markets through Euroissues

- Foreign Direct Investment allowed in stock broking, asset management companies, merchant banking and other non-bank finance companies

- Foreign Institutional Investors (FIIs) allowed to access to Indian capital markets on registration with SEBI

- FIIs permitted to directly participate in the public offers in takeover and buyback offer of companies.

- Procedural simplification introduced for registration and operations of the FIIs and the Sub-accounts.

- The SEBI Board approved amendment of SEBI (Foreign Institutional Investors) Regulations 1995, so as to relax the broad based criteria for registration of sub accounts from an existing level of 50 investors to 20 investors and the maximum holding of a single investor to 10 percent from the existing level of 5 percent.

- SEBI introduces regulations governing substantial acquisition of shares and take-overs and lays down the conditions under which disclosures and mandatory public offers are to be made to the shareholders

- To further protect the interest of investors in takeovers and to enhance equity, fairness and transparency in takeover transactions, acceptance of the interim recommendations of the reconstituted Committee under the chairmanship of Justice P.N. Bhagwati, former Chief Justice of India accepted.

   The threshold limit for mandatory public offer increased from 10 percent to 15 percent of the voting rights of a company.

   The creeping acquisition limit raised from the earlier level of 2 percent to 5 percent of the voting rights and also made applicable to persons holding above 51 percent of voting rights up to 75 percent.

Venture Capital Funds

- Guidelines for Offshore Venture Capital Funds announced by the GOI

- The SEBI constituted a committee headed by Shri K.B. Chandrasekhar on Venture Capital with an objective to identify various regulatory issues as well as developmental relating to the functioning of venture capital industry in India. The Board considered the report of the committee and approved the recommendations in principle.

4.2   Stock Exchanges

All the 23 stock exchanges in the country trade securities by using computerised screen based trading system. Most exchanges follow an electronic limit order book position, order-driven system. Investors from more than 300 cities and towns can trade in securities on a real-time basis. Volumes traded on the Indian stock exchanges on certain days reach almost US$4 billion. The market capitalisation and other figures are provided in the following table.

Table 7 : **Statistical Details of the Secondary Market as on 29 February 2000**

No. of Stock Exchanges	23
Exchanges with Automated Trading	23
Exchanges with Settlement/Trade Guarantee Fund	23
Spread of Stock Exchanges	
Cities with BSE Terminals	192
Cities with NSE Terminals	307
Registered Members	9069
Corporate Members	3173
Registered Sub-Brokers	4589
Listed Companies (31.3.99)	9877
All India Market Cap as on	
January 31, 2000 *(NSE Estimates)(Rs. crore)*	*9,33,031*
Annual Turnover at all Stock Exchanges (Rs. crore)	
1997-98	9,08,681
1998-99	10,23,382

4.3 Clearing Corporation

The stock exchanges which earlier had a 14-day trading cycle have reduced their account period settlement to 7 days (effectively 5 days because of 2 intervening no-trading days on Saturday and Sunday). The exchanges netted obligations over a five-day account period, and completed settlement on the 15th day from the commencement of a trading for an account period. Further, after the introduction of dematerialised trading, rolling settlement of T+5 has been made mandatory in the exchanges where trading in dematerialised securities has been available since 15 January 1998. Indian securities market already moved towards rolling settlement and we introduced compulsory rolling settlement in 10 scrips starting in January 2000. The list will be expanded so that we will cover most of the scrips in a year.

SEBI has also pushed the concept of Trade and Settlements guarantee. Most of the big stock exchanges have already put in place either a Trade Guarantee Scheme or a Settlement Guarantee Fund.

Streamlining of physical settlement

In recognition of the reality that even with the successful implementation of the depository system physical certificates are still likely to remain for some time to come, and investors will continue to be affected by the problems associated with trading and settling physical certificates, SEBI has taken several steps to streamline the settlement process for physical securities:

Uniform "good-bad delivery" norms have been prescribed which are required to be followed by all stock exchanges. A time bound procedure has been prescribed for resolution of "bad deliveries" through "Bad Delivery Cells" that have been set up in the stock exchanges. A committee is prescribing model procedures for registration of shares. The implementation of its recommendations is expected to lead to uniform service by registrars and transfer agents and to significantly ease registration delays.

4.4 Depository

In India, certificates of securities, whether government or corporate, are registered with the issuer. In the case of government securities, the record of ownership is kept by the Reserve Bank of India, which maintains a Subsidiary General Ledger in its Public Debt Office. Transfer of ownership takes place through book entry transfer in this ledger. In the case of corporate securities, the issuer maintains a register of members or holders of the securities, and the issuer or his registrar or transfer agent has to physically receive a security from a transferee accompanied by a transfer deed signed by the transferor before transfer is affected. There are no bearer securities in India.

Settlement of transactions in the securities markets continues to be based on physical movement of certificates. The physical movement of paper results in delays, bottlenecks and an increase in transaction costs, besides creating various types of risks for market participants.

The enactment of the Depositories Act, 1996 allows for dematerialisation of securities in depositories and the transfer of securities through electronic book entry. Already, two depositories are functional in India. The statistics presented below speak of the achievement in the move towards total dematerialisation.

Table 8 : **Dematerialisation** **As on February 29, 2000**

No. of Cos. signed for Demat:	756
Market Cap. of the above Cos. (US$bn)	187
No. of Depository Participants	125
No. of Beneficiary A/c Holders	22,10,570
No. of Shares dematerialised (mn)	14,453
Value of demat shares (US$bn)	124

One of the greatest achievements of the Indian capital market is that of introduction and coverage of a dematerialised process of trading and settlement in securities. As of now, more than 80 percent of securities are settled in the demat form on the Indian stock exchanges. All this has been achieved in less than 2 years time. Table 8 provides some of the information on dematerialised activity.

4.5   *Market Indicators*

The National Stock Exchange (NSE) and The Stock Exchange, Mumbai (BSE) are the two largest exchanges in India. The indices of these two exchanges are S&P CNX Nifty (of NSE) and Sensex of BSE. Detailed statistics on these two are presented in the following table and graph. The movement of the indices in the year 1999 and some relevant parameters are given below:

Table 9 : **Index Movement**

Month	Index*	Index*	Price to Book Ratio*		Price to Earnings Ratio*		Average Daily Turnover (Rs billion)		Market-capitalisation** (Rs billion)	
	Nifty	Sensex	Sensex	Nifty	Sensex	Nifty	NSE	BSE	NSE	BSE#
Jan –99	966.20	3315.57	2.39	1.36	12.95	10.71	23.51	17.11	4492.21	5024.51
Feb –99	981.30	3399.63	2.40	1.46	12.99	11.26	21.43	14.83	4520.81	5042.33
Mar –99	1078.05	3739.96	2.69	1.93	14.59	13.88	26.06	20.71	4911.75	5453.61
Apr –99	978.20	3325.69	2.55	1.79	13.77	12.99	17.97	14.21	4453.80	4882.29
May -99	1132.30	3963.56	2.91	2.03	15.76	14.70	23.93	17.25	5039.11	5609.65
Jun -99	1187.70	4140.73	3.06	2.10	16.53	15.35	18.40	15.11	5294.68	5847.88
Jul -99	1310.15	4542.34	3.40	2.36	18.40	17.15	25.21	21.20	5936.51	6489.32
Aug-99	1412.00	4898.21	3.47	2.57	19.87	20.88	24.41	22.72	6681.87	7109.56
Sep -99	1413.10	4764.42	3.48	2.67	20.41	22.63	26.60	22.18	6867.40	7045.68
Oct-99	1325.45	4444.56	3.56	2.74	21.01	24.12	34.39	28.85	6700.62	6734.62
Nov-99	1376.15	4622.21	3.32	2.67	19.99	23.35	31.59	24.56	7264.19	7096.13
Dec-99	1480.85	5005.82	3.45	3.05	20.91	26.80	44.81	35.65	8529.85	8033.53

* Monthly Closing Price   ** As on the last trading day of the month.   # Estimated (A+B1+B2)
Source: BSE and NSEIL

The stock markets recorded a consistent rising trend in the current year with the market indices including the broad based ones showing an uptrend. The BSE Sensex which opened at 3064.95 on 1 January 1999, closed at 5005. on 31 December 1999 recording a rise of 63 percent, or an increase of 1940 points.

Movement of SENSEX (May 1997 – December 1999)

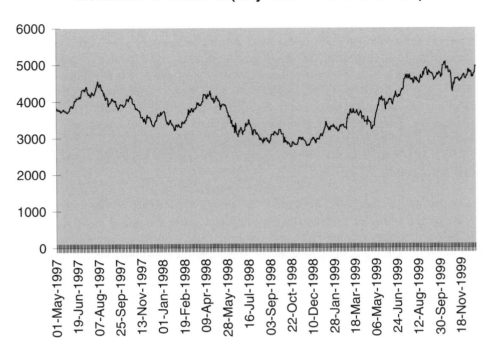

4.6 *Surveillance and Enforcement*

The strong and effective enforcement against violations by intermediaries is vital for ensuring that the integrity of markets is maintained. The SEBI Act of 1992 gives powers to SEBI to call for information from, undertake inspections of and to conduct inquiries and audits of stock exchanges and intermediaries. SEBI's enforcement powers have been further strengthened through the 1995 amendments to the SEBI Act. SEBI was granted powers of a civil court in respect of discovery and production of records and documents and summoning and enforcing the attendance of persons and examining them on oath. SEBI was given powers to levy penalties for a wide range of violations and defaults by registered entities and other persons; through an adjudication procedure that has been prescribed. The amendments also require the setting up a Securities Appellate Tribunal for hearing appeals against an adjudication order. In addition, SEBI was given powers to issue directions in the interest of investors in the securities markets to intermediaries and other registered entities, to companies in respect of the issue of securities, or to persons associated with the securities markets. SEBI has also been given powers to prohibit insider trading as well as fraudulent and unfair trade practices.

SEBI has set up an elaborate system of surveillance and monitoring. The stock exchanges have been asked to implement uniform norms for imposition of circuit breakers and trading suspensions in cases where price manipulation is suspected. Special and penal margins have also been introduced. All the exchanges have set up surveillance departments, and have begun to co-ordinate with SEBI. Daily settlement and pre-issue monitoring reports have been prescribed for submission to SEBI by the exchanges. A trading database has been created within SEBI for trades on the National and Mumbai stock exchanges, which is being expanded to other exchanges. Where price manipulation has been detected, auction proceeds have been frozen, and in several cases impounded, so that they do not accrue to manipulators. SEBI has taken up investigation of a large number of cases for investigation for price rigging and market manipulation. The stock exchanges have also been checking price rigging and market manipulation through their surveillance cells.

SEBI now inspects each exchange and mutual fund at least once every year, and it is in the process of increasing the coverage of inspection of other intermediaries such as stock brokers and merchant bankers. In addition, intermediaries are also inspected in the process of investigation. On the basis of these inspections, action has been taken in the case of a wide variety of violations, and penalties ranging from monetary fines to suspension for different periods of their registration have been imposed. SEBI has also launched prosecutions against issuers for various violations.

Volatility in the Indian context

Excessive volatility in the securities markets is a cause of concern for regulators, corporates and investors. When prices swing at extreme levels, they can have a number of adverse consequences. First, such volatility increases trading risks and requires market intermediaries like jobbers to charge more for their liquidity services, thereby reducing the liquidity of the market as a whole. Second, if such volatility persists, securities firms are less able to use their available capital efficiently because of the need to reserve a larger percentage of cash-equivalent investments in order to reassure lenders and regulators. Third, greater volatility can reduce investor confidence in investing in stocks. As a result of these effects, increased price volatility could in the long run, impact the securities markets adversely.

World over regulators have experienced that curbing volatility is an elusive policy target. It is not clear why volatility rises and falls, and policies directed at reducing it are sometimes unlikely to succeed and may also have harmful effects. However, regulators across the world, remain concerned about excessive price volatility.

SEBI, through its Market Surveillance Division, oversees the surveillance activities of the stock exchanges. Strict implementation of margin mechanism and price caps have proved to be very useful in containing volatility and ensuring safety as seen from the actual experience during such periods. This is borne out by the fact that despite several instances of market volatility, coupled with sharp and erratic fluctuations in prices and volumes, the Indian securities markets have remained secure.

In the background of rising prices in the scrips in general, SEBI took several steps for the integrity and safety of the markets, which are discussed in detail at the later part of this note.

Integrity of markets and containment of risk

Several measures have been taken by SEBI to improve the integrity of secondary markets. Legislative and regulatory changes have facilitated the corporatisation of stock brokers, so that there is an incentive to retain capital in the business, and broking firms are able to access bank and other finance. Capital adequacy norms have been prescribed and are being enforced. A mark to market margin and a margin based on concentration of business are also collected. Further, the stock exchanges have put in place circuit breakers which are applied at times of excessive volatility. The stock exchanges have been recently required to monitor short sales and long purchases. The disclosure of short sales and long purchases is now required to be made at the end of day. SEBI has recently introduced volatility based margins, which have further enhanced the integrity of the secondary markets.

4.7 Globalisation of Markets

Foreign Institutional Investors (FIIs) have been invited to invest in Indian securities markets since September 1992 when the Guidelines for Foreign Institutional Investment were issued by the government. In November 1995, the SEBI (Foreign Institutional Investors) Regulations, 1995 have come into effect, which are largely based on the earlier Guidelines. The Regulations require FIIs to register with SEBI and to obtain approval from the Reserve Bank of India (RBI) under the Foreign Exchange Regulation Act to buy and sell securities, to open foreign currency and rupee bank accounts and to remit and repatriate funds. SEBI registration has been obtained, an FII does not require any further permission to buy or sell securities or to transfer funds in and out of the country, subject to payment of applicable tax.

Investment in Indian securities is also possible through the purchase of Global Depository Receipts, Foreign Currency Convertible Bonds and Foreign Currency Bonds issued by Indian issuers which are listed, traded and settled overseas and are mainly denominated in US Dollars. Foreign investors, whether registered as FII or not, may also invest in Indian securities outside the FII route. Such investment requires case by case approval from the Foreign Investment Promotion Board (FIPB) in the Ministry of Industry in the central government and the RBI, or only by the RBI depending the size of investment and the industry in which this investment is to be made.

Foreign financial services institutions have also been allowed to set up joint ventures in stock broking, asset management companies, merchant banking and other financial services firms along with Indian partners. The foreign participation in financial services requires the approval of FIPB.

4.8 Trends in FII Investment

As on 31 December 1999, 505 FIIs were registered with SEBI. As per the available figures for the portfolio investments, the cumulative net investment made by these FIIs in the Indian capital market till date, is US$10.21 billion.

Till October 1997, FII investment in Indian securities markets had been positive in every month since FIIs began investment in India. Net FII investment stayed positive, even in the months following the large currency and equity price depreciation in South East and East Asian Markets. This uncertainty affected markets in the US, Japan and Europe. Foreign portfolio flows into Indian markets were also affected in this period.

Monthly Net FII investment turned negative for the first time in the month of November 1997. This trend accelerated in the year 1998, and the net investments by the FIIs for the whole of the year 1998 turned negative. The sales in this year were higher than the purchases by an amount equivalent to US$338.2 million. The year witnessed worsening of the South East Asian crises. The economic sanctions against India also depressed the overall sentiments.

The current trend in the investments, however, has again turned positive. The FII net investments in the whole of 1999 have been positive.

Monthly trends in FII investment are given in the figure below.

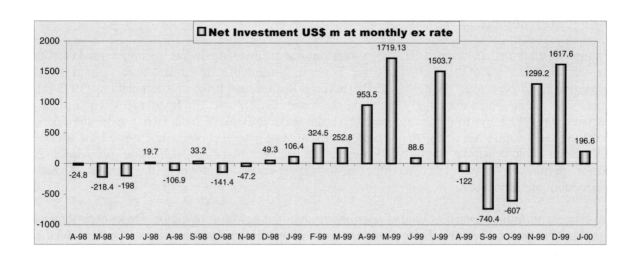

Table10: **Trends in FII Investment as on December 31**

	Net Investment US$million at monthly exchange rate	Cumulative Net Investment US$million at monthly exchange rate
1995	1191.4	4183.4
1996	3058.2	7241.6
1997	1746.7	8988.2
1998	-338.0	8650.0
1999	1559.9	10209.9

CAPITAL MARKET DEVELOPMENT IN INDONESIA

by
Mr. Herwidayatmo

383-87

053 G12 G18
016 G28
019 E44

Macroeconomic Developments in Indonesia

As a result of the Asian economic crisis of 1997, severe damage was done to the Indonesian economy, resulting in the collapse of the banking system, widespread loan defaults, unemployment, and political instability. The following table indicates key economic statistics during this period.

	1997	1998	1999
GDP (Rupiah – trillions)	433.6	376.0	376.9
GDP (Nominal growth)	4.6%	-13.3%	0.2%
Inflation	11.0%	77.6%	2.0%
Interest, 3-month time deposits (annual %)	23.9%	49.2%	28.5%*
Exports (billion US$)	56.3	50.3	49.7*
Imports (billion US$)	46.2	31.9	30.2*
Rupiah per US$	5,402	8.000	7,100
Balance of Payments (billion US$)	3.9	10.0	9.9*

*Notes: Interest rates for 1997-1998 are weighted averages; interest rate of 1999 is the June 1999 figure; Export-Import statistics for 1999 are nine-month figures, annualized; Balance of Payment figure for 1999 is an estimate.
Source: Bank Indonesia, Central Agency of Statistics (Bps-Indonesia), APBN 1999/2000.

In July 1997, the Rupiah-US$ rate was Rp 2,600. The rate rose to a high of Rp 14,950 following civil disturbances in May 1998, recovering to Rp 7,440 by March 2000. In real terms, GDP fell to half of pre-crisis levels as a result of the crisis, causing economic distress and hardship to a large part of the population. Although the situation has been stabilized, economic activity is still far below pre-crisis levels.

The immediate cause of the crisis was the use of short-term foreign loans by private enterprise to finance long-term capital needs. This was aggravated by misuse of the banking system, whereby loans were often granted to affiliated or favored persons, rather than on the basis of credit-worthiness. Despite the drastic fall in the exchange rates, exports did not respond because of the poor credit standing of producers. The government has attempted to restore the banking system by massive equity increases that were paid-in with government bonds. However, the lack of a market for these bonds, together with insolvent condition of many potential borrowers, has hindered these measures from having a significant positive impact on economic recovery.

In 1999, as the result of democratic elections, the reform government of President Abdurrahman Wahid was installed. Since the crisis, the country has followed the recommendations of the International Monetary Fund. The improving political situation is favorable for economic recovery.

Capital Market Development

The Indonesia capital market is one of the newest in the world. Significant trading activity only began in 1989 with the opening of the market to international portfolio investment. As a result of a heavy influx of foreign investment, the market quickly developed. From 24 issuers in 1988, the number of public companies grew rapidly to 132 by 1990 and to 324 today. Since 1988, the total value of new issues now stands at Rp 216.1 trillion. During the same period, total bond issues reached Rp 23.1 trillion.

Average daily trading of equities on the Jakarta Stock Exchange (the largest market) averaged Rp 598 billion in 1999. Daily trading of equities on the Surabaya Exchange averaged Rp 59 billion in 1999. In January 2000, the market capitalization of companies listed on the Jakarta Stock Exchange was Rp 410 trillion, of which 25% was equity of state-owned enterprises.

Before the crisis of 1997, foreign portfolio investors usually accounted for more than half of the trading on the Jakarta Stock Exchange. Until 1997, foreign investors were net buyers from domestic investors. During 1997 and 1998 this pattern was reversed and the participation of foreign investor fell off, dropping to 29% in 1998, 27% in 1999, and 14% in January 2000. In 1999 foreigners again became net buyers.

Soon after the market became active in 1989, the government took steps to establish a proper legal and regulatory framework. In 1990, the Minister of Finance issued Decree 1548 which established a regulatory structure similar to that of the US SEC, based on principles of disclosure. In 1995, this Decree was used as the basis for the Capital Market Law that gave greater enforcement powers to BAPEPAM, the securities regulator. Until now, the securities regulator has been an administrative unit in the Ministry of Finance. In the Central Bank Law of 1999, a provision calls for separation of BAPEPAM from the Ministry and the establishment of an independent agency.

The regulatory structure established by the Capital Market Law and implemented in over 300 BAPEPAM rules is quite sophisticated and generally considered to be on a par with international standards. However, due to lack of independence of the regulator as well as general permissiveness in the business culture, enforcement has lagged significantly behind rulemaking. We are now attempting to correct this situation by stepping up enforcement activities.

The Capital Market Law calls for direct licensing, registration, or approval of all securities exchanges, clearinghouses, central depositories, transfer agents, securities companies, bank custodians, trust agents, investment fund managers, and capital market professionals, such as lawyers, accountants, appraisers, and securities salespersons.

Securities companies, banks, and the central depository are authorized to act as custodians. BAPAPEM rules strictly regulate internal controls and capital adequacy of custodians, with comprehensive accounting standards for broker-dealers and mandatory daily net adjusted working capital reporting. BAPEPAM has also regulated investors' rights and protections with respect to securities accounts, beneficial ownership, and securities transactions. BAPEPAM is currently in process of preparing comprehensive regulations on securities transfer modeled after the US Code on Investment Securities. Investor protection with respect to securities accounts includes mandatory segregation of securities, and establishment of cash escrow accounts for free credit balances. Broker dealers are required to either get customer securities under their direct control within fifteen days or to buy-in the missing securities on the market.

BAPEPAM has issued rules with regards to margin trading, including the financing of short sales. Margin requirements are changed from time to time and are restricted to actively traded securities. Margin financing is restricted to high net worth individuals.

This year, the securities exchanges will commence trading in dematerialized securities with transfer and settlement by means of book-entry in a central securities depository. The clearing guarantee corporation will not only perform the usual clearing and settlement functions, but also will guarantee settlement. The legal basis for scripless trading and book-entry settlement was established by the Capital Market Law of 1995 and is supported by a series of sophisticated regulations issued by BAPEPAM.

The securities exchanges have operated order-driven electronic trading systems since 1993. These systems guarantee client price-time priority and facilitate electronic surveillance.

Trading contracts approved for the scripless environment call for settlement on T+4, T+1, and T+0, with settlement by offsetting trades permitted. All transactions are to be settled by the clearinghouse on settlement day, with fails to deliver automatically resolved by an alternate cash settlement provision equal to 125% of the highest price of trades settling on that day. The Clearing Guarantee Corporation intends to offer securities borrowing facilities as an alternative form of settlement. Netted transactions are all settled with the guarantee of the clearinghouse by debit or credit of cash and securities to brokers' accounts with the central custodian.

BAPEPAM does not approve or disapprove the issuance of securities. Rather, like the US SEC, its function is to supervise disclosure. All public offerings, including tender offers, must be preceded by the submission of a registration statement to BAPEPAM. Registration statements are public documents and the Capital Market Law requires delivery of a prospectus at the time of sale of a public offering. If 45 days pass without request for additional information from BAPEPAM, an offering automatically becomes effective and sales may commence. BAPEPAM may also, at the request of the issue, declare the registration effective, but this does not signify approval.

Accounting and disclosure standards are equivalent to international standards. Financial statements audited by international auditors accompany most public offerings. BAPEPAM has licensed two credit rating agencies, both associated with reputable international counterparts. BAPEPAM requires that bond issues be rated.

In addition to high disclosure standards, BAPEPAM and the Capital Market Law also protect investors against undue dilution of equity through a preemptive rights rule. Preemptive rights must be given to existing shareholders in proportion to their holdings for all capital increases by issuance of equity, warrants, or convertible bonds. In the case of companies in financial difficulties, the preemptive rights rule may be waived.

Independent shareholders, not associated with the interested parties, must approve transactions that involve conflict of interest between directors, commissioners, major shareholders, and the general interests of the corporation. Conflict of interest transactions require not only approval by independent shareholders, but also special disclosure by non-affiliated experts.

Issuers may elect to list their securities on any stock exchange, in Indonesia or abroad, but this is not required. The Indonesian exchanges are self-regulatory institutions, with management elected by their members. The exchanges are free to set their own trading, membership, and listing rules, subject to BAPEPAM approval. The exchanges are expected to inspect their members regularly, conduct surveillance of trading activities, and be generally responsible for the conduct of a fair, orderly, and efficient market.

In addition to stocks and bonds, BAPEPAM also regulates other types of securities. In 1996, rules were issued with respect to open-end mutual funds and the market now has 82 funds, with 24 thousand unit holders and total assets of Rp 2.8 trillion. Each fund has specific fundamental investment policy stipulated in the management contract, the main classifications being: equity funds, bond funds, money market funds, and mixed equity-bond funds. Some funds are denominated in US dollars.

Considering the fact that the population of Indonesia exceeds 200 million, the number of unit-holder in mutual funds, an investment specifically targeted for the mass market, indicates that there are still significant problems in creating public acceptance for this product. The major difficulty seems to be competition from interest bearing bank deposits that now are guaranteed by the government. Of the 82 funds operating, half have less than 100 unit holders and only four (with an emphasis on bonds and money market instruments) have more than 1,000 unit holders. The average fund investor holds about US$26,500, which, considering the per capital income in Indonesia, suggests a lack of progress in selling this product at the retail level. The concentration of ownership also creates liquidity problems for these open-end funds --- about three-fourths of the funds have over 80% of their assets owned by the ten largest unit-holders. BAPEPAM has regulations with respect to diversification of portfolios and unit-holders, but reports on compliance indicate a need for improvement. There is no tax for unit-holders of investment funds, but certain types of income of the fund itself are subject to tax, creating undesirable leverage.

In 1998, BAPEPAM issued rules with respect to asset-backed securities, but because of the crisis, this type of instrument has not yet been used, except through offshore vehicles. These rules provide for the use of the "collective investment contract" as the appropriate vehicle for asset-backed securities in Indonesia. This is the same legal structure used for open-end mutual funds, buy modified for the special needs of asset-backed securities. The securities regulator does not have jurisdiction with respect to tax matters on the various investment instruments. In the case of asset-backed securities this has resulted in the domestic form of these instrument being less attractive to domestic issuers than offshore vehicles.

The Capital Market Law includes criminal provisions for some capital market offenses, with sanctions of up to ten years in prison. Securities fraud, market manipulation, and insider trading are all crimes in this category. The insider trading rules prohibit directors, commissioners, and principal shareholders from buying or selling shares of a company with respect to which they are insiders, if they are in possession of inside information. The Capital Market Law requires all public companies to disclose material information of interest to investors within 48 hours. Non-disclosed material information is considered to be inside information.

BAPEPAM is empowered to conduct criminal investigations with respect to capital market crimes and to present the cases to the Attorney General for prosecution. BAPEPAM may also, prior to initiation of a criminal investigation, come to a settlement with a suspect that may involve disgorgement of profits and other remedies. No criminal cases have as yet been tried under the Capital Market Law, although BAPEPAM has reached settlement agreements with substantial fines in cases involving possible insider trading and market manipulation.

In general, considering the fact that the Indonesian capital market has been active for less than 12 years, considerable progress has been made. However, participation of domestic investors in the market is still very small. There has not been substantial development of the bond market. Many securities companies are still small, with inadequate back offices and systems, and with weak marketing structures. It is estimated that less than one-half of one percent of the population is involved in the securities market.

Since the crisis of 1997, BAPEPAM has conducted a number of studies, with the assistance of World Bank financed international experts, on the development of the stock and bond markets. These studies show that the prevalence of relationship-driven banking has been the major factor in holding back the development of the capital market. When issuers find it easier, quicker, and less expensive to raise money from an affiliated bank than to go to the capital market, development of the market suffers. In addition to the problem with the banking structure, over-complexity in the financial structures of economic groups has hindered adequate disclosure. Many issuers still lack proper attitudes with respect to corporate governance that merit investors' confidence. Furthermore, problems in the judicial system give investors reason to doubt the rule of law and the effectiveness of recourse against delinquent issuers and debtors. Finally, there are no significant tax advantages for open capital companies or public investors, such as are common in more developed markets.

With respect to bond market development, consultants have identified the following problems:

- Generalized defaults on bank loans as a result of the crisis, together with a perception of lack of adequate remedies in the judicial system, have reduced the market acceptance of bond issues.

- Government guarantees on short-term interest bearing bank deposits have placed non-guaranteed private long-term bonds at a competitive disadvantage.

- Conservative, long-term fixed-income investors in Indonesia generally prefer dollar denominated (or indexed) obligations. This is common practice in real estate contracts and life insurance.

- Lack of market acceptance for an extremely large government bond issue related to the bank-restructuring program is a negative influence on private bond issues.

For these reasons, development of a bond market in the current crisis faces obstacles that are not easily overcome.

The reform government is aware of these problems and is addressing some of the issues. However, with the many political and economic challenges facing the nation, capital market development matters are generally of lesser priority compared to restructuring the banking system and restarting the economy.

CAPITAL MARKET DEVELOPMENT IN MALAYSIA

by

Mr. Ali Abdul Kadir

A. Macroeconomic Developments

The shape of Malaysia's economy has changed significantly in the last 20 years. Although there has been a decline in traditional mainstays—Malaysia's share of world rubber production is now behind that of Thailand and Indonesia, while its tin output is lower as a result of depleted reserves—new strengths have emerged. Starting in the 1960s, a policy to diversify industry and foreign trade has hastened the shift away from a traditional reliance on tin and rubber and directed it towards manufacturing. And this has made for a fast-growing and resilient economy, in spite of the crisis of 1997–98. Real gross domestic product grew by 5.4 % in 1999 (4.1% in Q299; 8.2% in Q399; 10.6% in Q499) after having contracted by 7.5 % in 1998 as a result of the crisis. Economic recovery has taken place on the back of, among other things, strong export and manufacturing growth.

Gross domestic product (GDP) at purchasers' value

Year	% change from previous year
1993	8.3
1994	9.3
1995	9.4
1996	8.6
1997	7.7
1998	-7.5
1999	5.4

Source: Bank Negara Malaysia

Inflation (% increase of Consumer Price Index)

Year	% change from previous year
1993	3.5
1994	3.7
1995	3.4
1996	3.5
1997	2.7
1998	5.3
1999	2.8

Source: Bank Negara Malaysia

Budget balance (RM million)

Year	Revenue	Expenditure	Balance
1993	41,691	32,217	9,474
1994	49,446	35,064	14,382
1995	50,953	36,573	14,380
1996	58,280	43,865	14,415
1997	65,736	44,665	21,071
1998	56,710	44,585	12,125
1999	58,675	46,999	11,676

Source: Bank Negara Malaysia and Ministry of Finance

External balance of payments and Bank Negara Malaysia reserves (US$ million)

Year	Overall balance	Reserves
1993	7,695	20,115
1994	-2,174	17,940
1995	-1,159	16,782
1996	1,643	18,425
1997	-2,866	15,559
1998	10,606	26,168
1999	Not available	30,859

Source: Bank Negara Malaysia

Exchange rate

Year	Ringgit per unit of US$
1993	2.30
1994	2.55
1995	2.54
1996	2.53
1997	3.88
1998	3.80
1999	3.80

Source: Bank Negara Malaysia

B.   Historical Development of the Capital Market

(i)   The Stock Market

Although the history of KLSE can be traced to the 1930s, the exchange, in its current form, was established in 1973 to provide a central market place for buyers and sellers to transact business in the shares, bonds and various other securities of Malaysian listed companies. A strong link existed between the KLSE and Stock Exchange of Singapore (SES) at that time as Malaysian incorporated companies were also listed and traded through the SES, and vice-versa for Singapore incorporated companies. A significant milestone for the KLSE came in 1990 which saw the delisting of Singapore incorporated companies from the KLSE and vice-versa for Malaysian companies listed on the SES. This move heralded the growth of the KLSE as a stock exchange with a truly Malaysian identity.

One of the first steps to be implemented after the enactment of the Securities Industry Act in 1983 was the formation of the clearing house, Securities Clearing Automated Network Services Sdn Bhd

(SCANS). The computerisation of the clearing system took away the manual clearing and settlement functions from the brokers, thereby facilitating more efficient trading activities.

In 1986, the KLSE Composite index was launched. The index offers a cross-sectoral analysis of companies listed on the main board of the exchange. In 1987, real-time dissemination via MASA (acronym for Maklumat Saham which means "share information") was introduced. In 1994, Winstock which is a more integrated information system, replaced MASA.

In November 1988, the KLSE launched its Second Board to encourage smaller companies with good growth prospects to gain access into the capital markets. By January 1991, the KLSE launched a Second Board index to provide investors with a performance indicator for Second Board companies and to assist these smaller companies to attract investor attention. Today, companies are listed either on the Main Board or Second Board of the KLSE, and are classified into a range of diverse sectors reflecting their core businesses. The Fixed Delivery and Settlement System (FDSS) was introduced to bring about a more efficient clearing and settlement system.

An order driven market, trading on the KLSE was fully computerised in 1992 with the full implementation of the System on Computerised Order Routing and Execution (SCORE). SCORE has eliminated the need for a trading floor at the Exchange's premises. Trading is facilitated through the Exchange's sixty-two member stockbroking companies located all over the country. These stockbroking companies are equipped with the KLSE's enhanced broker front end system, WinSCORE, whereby each dealer operates from an integrated terminal providing real-time market information dissemination as well as order and trade routing and confirmation. WinSCORE also enables better credit control and risk exposure management by the stockbroking companies.

The Central Depository System (CDS), implemented in 1993, is the automated clearing and settlement system of the KLSE. The CDS has replaced the practice of holding and moving physical scrip of quoted shares with a safe and dependable computerised book entry system.

The various types of securities traded on the KLSE include ordinary and preference shares, loan stocks, property trust units, rights (provisional allotment letters), warrants, transferable subscription rights (TSR).

The need for small– and medium–scale enterprises to seek competitive forms of financing prompted the approval and subsequent establishment of the Malaysian Exchange of Securities Dealing and Automated Quotation (MESDAQ) in May 1997. MESDAQ is targeted to meet the funding needs of technology–based start–ups and high growth companies. One of the main features of MESDAQ is that it orperates in a full disclose-based regulatory environment. The exchange began operations in 1998.

See section D below for the most recent developments concerning the exchange.

Market activity and size

Year	Turnover (billions of shares)	Market cap (RM billion)
1995	36.6	565.2
1996	72.7	806.8
1997	82.3	375.8
1998	60.9	374.5
1999	88.8	552.7

Source: KLSE

Shareholders by nationality (%)
(latest available data)

	1998
Foreigners	4.7
Non-bumi	79.0
Bumiputra	16.3

Source: KLSE

Equity held by nationality (%)
(latest available data)

	1998
Foreigners	22.2
Local	77.8

Source: KLSE

Equity held by type of investors (%)
(latest available data)

	1998
Institutions	39.7
Individuals	16.5
Nominees	42.5
Others	1.4

Source: KLSE

Share issued on the KLSE (RM million)

	1995	1996	1997	1998	1999
Public issues	1,156	1,778	2,929	346.2	634.3
Special issues/restricted offers/private placements	2,436	8,075	4,038	245.0	1,072.6
Rights issues	5,594	7,402	9,362	421.9	6,108.3
Offer for sale	3,091	3,060	2,788	698.5	364.8

Source: KLSE

(ii)   *The Bond Market*

Malaysian Government Securities (MGS) were introduced in the 1960s to meet investment needs of the Employees Provident Fund (EPF). As the Malaysian economy developed, the MGS market was increasingly used to fund public sector development plans. Mandatory investments in MGS, however, left the secondary market underdeveloped with many of the subscribing institutions holding the securities to maturity.

In order to promote secondary trading in MGS, a number of regulatory and operational reforms have been introduced over the years. Measures included are:

- Tax and stamp duty exemptions on income and transactions in MGS

- Higher commission to brokers for transactions in MGS

- Trustee status accorded to MGS

- Ability to include MGS as secondary liquid assets in meeting liquidity requirements

In 1983, Islamic private debt securities were introduced. These were Government Investment Certificates (GIC) which was non-interest bearing to comply with the tenets of Islamic banking.

The establishment of Cagamas Berhad by the government in 1986 was the first stage to develop another sector of the PDS market. Cagamas purchases housing loans from loan originators and repackages them into fixed rate bearer bonds.

The success of Cagamas prompted Bank Negara to introduce guidelines for the issue of private debt securities (PDS) for corporates in December 1988. Lack of response from corporates, however, led to the revision of the guidelines a year later.

- Other measures introduced from the mid-1980s onwards to liberalise and to provide more liquidity in the MGS market included:

- Expansion of permitted market participants to include large finance companies

- Adoption of Kuala Lumpur Interbank Offered Rate (KLIBOR) as the official indicator of conditions in the interbank money market

- Greater flexibility in the calculation of banks' liquidity and statutory reserve ratios

With effect from 1988, an auction system for MGS with maturities of up to 10 years was established. This bidding system enabled MGS to be priced at the market value and did away with the practice of advance subscriptions, which was originally introduced in the 1960 except from the National Savings Bank and EPF.

To further promote a secondary market, a system of principal dealers, first introduced for Cagamas bonds in October 1989, was implemented on 1 January 1989. These designated financial institutions alone are authorised to underwrite and make markets on MGS in the primary and secondary markets.

Operational efficiency of funds and securities transfer was enhanced with the introduction of SPEEDS, a computerised scripless trading system which actually comprises two different systems: the Inter-Bank Funds Transfer System (IFTS) which expedites the transfer of funds was launched on 15 December 1989 and Scripless Securities Trading System which records the book entries for the transfer of scrips on 2 January 1990.

As a stimulus for the PDS market, all non-government bonds were exempted from stamp duty in 1989. Another step towards the development of a liquid secondary market for MGS came with the liberalisation of base lending rates (BLR) on 1 February 1991. This enabled financial institutions to determine their own BLR, thus creating better market-driven rates.

In 1992, Cagamas began to issue floating rate bonds. In February 1993 Bank Negara issued Malaysian Savings Bonds to the investing public. These bonds were discounted with a five-year maturity.

An important milestone in the PDS market was reached in November 1990 when RAM was incorporated. The emergence of an independent rating agency provides investors with important decision-making information. Two years later, it became mandatory for issuers to have a minimum accepted rating before they could gain access into the debt market.

More recent efforts to develop the domestic bond market have included the introduction of a programme by Khazanah Nasional Berhad, the investment arm of the Ministry of Finance, to issue a series of bonds aimed at providing a benchmark for the domestic bond market. The first of these bonds, which complied with Islamic principles, was launched in September 1997. Other efforts included amendments to the Companies Act 1965 to widen the institutional investor base, and tax exemptions on interest income received by unit trusts and listed closed-end funds from specific bonds. (Please see section D for a description of the most recent development initiatives in relation to the bond market).

Total Value Of Outstanding Private Debt Securities

Listed					
	1995	1996	1997	1998	1999
Convertible bonds	1695.9	9491.11	11740.94	-	
Straight bonds	233.00	233.00	233.00	350.00	350.00
Bonds with Warrants	2,180.05	5,741.67	5,584.48	4,524.16	3,683.2
ICULS	1,808.56	2,775.54	4,720.92	4,700.92	3704.99
Others	1,725.90	740.90	1,202.54	1,103.21	803.21
Islamic bonds	-	300.00	300.00	300.00	-
Unlisted					
	1995	1996	1997	1998	1999
Convertible bonds	54.564	54564	25616.5	-	
Straight bonds	7,445.14	8,603.60	12,230.59	25,201.09	59,600.90
Bonds with warrants	5,864.10	8,158.32	11,190.10	10,708.97	9,390.78
ICULS	-	170.00	-	-	-
Others	1,099.03	3,169.42	2,195.80	2,414.61	14,094.93
Islamic bonds	-	3,625.00	9,866.50	13,011.50	19,325.50

Source: SC Annual Reports and Bank Negara Malaysia

Total Value of New Issues Of Private Debt Securities

Listed					
	1995	1996	1997	1998	1999
Straight bonds	-	-	-	50	-
Bonds with warrants	135	3,645.57	1,165.25	-	462
ICULS	660.9	966.98	2,103.18	-	142
Others	0	-	-	-	-
Islamic bonds		-	-	-	-
Unlisted					
	1995	1996	1997	1998	1999
Straight Bonds	3,089.74	2,597.6	3,514.6	14,055.1	14,517.00
Bonds with warrants	3,313	2,134.22	2435	100	555.00
ICULS	-	170	-	-	-
Others	369.79	662.67	56.46	98.78	19.00
Islamic bonds	-	2,350	6,266.50	3,195.00	6,014.00

Source: SC Annual Reports and Bank Negara Malaysia

(iii)   ***The Derivatives Market***

Malaysia's derivatives market began in July 1980 when the Kuala Lumpur Commodity Exchange (KLCE), a company limited by guarantee was established to trade commodity futures. The introduction of the commodity futures market in Malaysia in 1980 was against the background of increasing production of primary commodities, particularly palm oil, cocoa, rubber and tin. Just like the objective of futures exchanges in other countries, the KLCE was established to provide modern hedging or risk management facilities and a better pricing for commodities produced in the region.

The contracts that have been offered to market participants include palm oil futures, rubber futures, tin futures and palm oil futures contracts. However, due to a lack of interest from the industry, all of the futures contracts, with the exception of the palm oil futures, have ceased trading the exchange.

In 1985, the exchange went through a major restructuring exercise involving changes in its membership, trading system, and clearing and guarantee arrangements. This followed a major default in the crude palm oil futures in 1984 due to excessive speculation and the failure of a number of brokers to meet their obligations to the clearing house. A new clearing house was also set-up where the exchange and its clearing members own 73 per cent of the equity and the balance is owned by a consortium of banks. The current market structure in the commodity futures market reflects the changes that were made in 1985.

In December 1990, laws were introduced that allowed the establishment of a financial futures market in Malaysia. By the early 1990s, a consortium of large companies decided to form an exchange to trade financial futures. This led to the formation of Kuala Lumpur Options and Financial Futures Exchange (KLOFFE). The establishment of KLOFFE prompted KLCE to make a similar application to the government to trade financial futures. However, due to the potential conflict of jurisdictions between the different market regulators, i.e. Ministry of Finance (for financial futures) and the Ministry of Primary Industries (for commodity futures), KLCE had to set up the Malaysian Monetary Exchange (MME) for the purpose of trading financial futures.

Both MME and KLOFFE have different underlying products and trading systems, and apply different business philosophies. The differences are summarised as follows:

MME	KLOFFE
• A non-profit making organisation	• A profit making organisation
	• A screen-based trading system
• Open outcry trading system	• Participants mostly mixture of retail investors and fund managers
• Participants mostly financial institutions and large corporations	• Contracts offered:
• Contacts offered	- index futures
- interest rate futures	- stock options
- bond futures	- options and index futures
- options on interest rate futures	
- options on futures	
- currency futures	

In order to minimise potential systemic risks arising from the domestic derivatives industry, the Securities Commission encouraged the establishment of a common clearing house for the derivative exchanges, which led to the formation of the Malaysian Derivatives Clearing House (MDCH).

The industry has undergone some consolidation recently. In November 1997, the two futures clearing houses, Malaysian Futures Clearing Corporation Sdn Bhd (MFCC) and MDCH merged their clearing operations to form a common clearing institution. As a result, MDCH now acts as the single clearing house for the Malaysian derivatives market. Furthermore, in January 1998 the KLSE completed the acquisition of KLOFFE Capital Sdn Bhd, the holding company of KLOFFE Berhad, the operator of KLOFFE. In December 1998, KLCE merged with MME to form Commodities and Monetary Exchange of Malaysia (COMMEX).

KLOFFE

Year	Turnover (no. of contracts)	Open interest (as at year end)
1995	672	69
1996	77,281	1,312
1997	382,974	7,614
1998	771,244	1,650
1999	436,678	2,432

Source: KLOFFE

Market demography (% of volume traded)

	1996	1997	1998	1999
Foreign Institutions	49	45	40	14
Local Institutions	2	2	1	4
Foreign Retail	1	1	2	2
Local Retail	24	31	38	51
Local Members	16	17	17	26
Proprietary Trading	8	4	2	3

Source: KLOFFE

Malaysian Monetary Exchange (MME)

Year	Trading volume (no. of contracts)	Open interest (as at year end)
1996	40,933	3,162
1997	76,382	1,946
1998	24,738	3,092
1999	28,994	7,107

Source: Commodity and Monetary Exchange of Malaysia

C   Regulatory Framework of the Securities Industry

(i)   Background

Before 1993, responsibility for overseeing the Malaysian securities industry fell on the following authorities:

- The Registrar of Companies (ROC)

- The Capital Issues Committee (CIC)

- The Panel on Take-over and Mergers (TOP)

- The Foreign Investment Committee (FIC)

- Bank Negara Malaysia (BNM)

- The Ministry of Trade and Industry (MITI)

- The Kuala Lumpur Stock Exchange (KLSE)

However, with this arrangement regulation developed on an ad hoc basis to meet the specific needs or crises facing the industry and, as a result, regulatory costs tended to be high. In addition, the government recognised that capital market regulators needed to keep abreast of international developments, with a view to the changing needs of investors and issuers.

Hence, efforts were made to create a more streamlined regulatory framework and, importantly, a single regulatory body with a broad overview of capital markets. On 1 March 1993, the Securities Commission (SC) was established under the Securities Commission Act 1993 to fill two main roles: (1) as a single regulatory body to promote the development of the capital market; and (2) with responsibility to streamline the regulations of the securities market and speed up the processing and approval of transactions.

The SC is responsible to the Minister of Finance, and tables its annual report and accounts to Parliament. It is empowered to investigate breaches of securities regulation, enforce rules and regulations, and prosecute securities offenses.

Regulatory consolidation has meant that oversight of the securities industry now falls on four bodies, namely the SC, Bank Negara, FIC and the ROC. Legislation governing the securities industry consists of the Securities Industry Act 1983, the Securities Industry (Central Depository) Act 1993, the Companies Act 1965 and the Futures Industry Act 1993. Each of these Acts has subsidiary legislation (regulations, codes etc.) to further define the law. Furthermore, the SC also comes out sporadically with its own guidelines on the running of certain sectors of the industry.

(ii)   *Regulatory and Developmental Initiatives*

Regulatory and development initiatives in relation to capital markets in Malaysia have been taking place for the better part of two decades. During the 1980s and early 1990s, significant improvements were made to the microstructure of capital markets. Much of this focused on building the capacity of the equity market, which saw a rapid succession of structural improvements, especially in its trading, and clearing and settlement systems. The KLSE introduced computerised settlement via the Securities Clearing Automated Network Services (SCANS) in 1983, followed by real-time price and information dissemination four years later. In 1989, trading was automated under the System on Computerised Order Routing and Execution (SCORE), which paved the way for a fixed delivery and settlement system in 1990 and the immobilisation of share scrips in the Central Depository System (CDS) soon after.

The first half of the 1990s saw efforts to streamline regulation, which resulted in among other things, the establishment of the SC in 1993 (as described in section 1). Major capital market initiatives and measures in the first two years of the SC's existence included improving the efficiency of the primary equity market from the standpoint of both investors and of issuers; clarifying, and where necessary, establishing the regulatory framework concerning corporate finance activity and securities transactions; embarking on a review of the role of collective investment schemes in capital mobilisation; and facilitating the expansion of market breadth by introducing guidelines for the issue of new capital market instruments. From the start, research and development had been identified as core functions of the SC, alongside regulation and supervision.

In 1995, the SC prepared and released its first business plan for the period up to 1997, consisting of initiatives aimed at boosting the depth, breadth and international profile of the Malaysian capital market. That pre-crisis period witnessed a series of major developments covering a wide range of markets, institutions and processes, and which represented a major shift in the direction of regulatory approach. These included:

- Further streamlining of the regulatory structure, involving, among other things: the merger of the Commodities Trading Commission (CTC) with the SC , which came into effect in 1997; the vesting of powers to issue securities and futures licences[1] with the SC; and the decision to place sole responsibility for the regulation of the unit trust industry with the SC.

- Embarking on a programme to move away from merit-based regulation towards achieving a full-disclosure based regulatory environment (DBR), with the release of Policies and Guidelines on Issue/Offer of Securities in late 1995. Due to the challenging nature of effecting this shift, the programme spans a period of several years under three distinct phases. The shift to DBR started in 1996 and is expected to be completed in 2001 with the implementation of the full DBR. Under Phase 1 of the shift, the SC no longer sets pricing of securities offer under initial public offerings.

- The establishment of a financial reporting framework, following the introduction of the Financial Reporting Act 1997, consisting of the Malaysian Accounting Standards Board (MASB) and the Financial Reporting Foundation (FRF) in March 1997. Under the provisions of the Act, the FRF performs the function of a trustee body responsible for overseeing MASB, whose role is to provide for a technically independent authority with responsibility for developing accounting and reporting standards in Malaysia.

- The start of trading in KLCI futures contracts on KLOFFE on 15 December 1995 marked the launch of exchange-traded financial derivatives in Malaysia. This was followed by the start of trading on 28 May 1996 in three-month KLIBOR futures contracts on MME. The establishment in 1995 of the Malaysian Derivatives Clearing House (MDCH) as an independent clearing house for the two exchanges was aimed at lowering the costs of trading in both futures products and minimizing systemic risk.

- Efforts in support of the development of the fund management industry in Malaysia. This included the release of Guidelines on the Establishment of Foreign Fund Management Companies in August 1995 to facilitate foreign participation in Malaysia, with the intention that increased participation by foreign fund managers would act as a catalyst to raise the level of activity and expertise in the industry. In 1997, the SC released a revised set of Guidelines on Unit Trust Funds aimed at liberalising and deregulating certain aspects of the guidelines, enhancing skills and professionalism within the industry, improving disclosure and emphasising regulation and compliance by the industry. In addition, amendments were made to the SIA to incorporate provisions on accounts to be kept and operations of trust accounts for fund managers.

– Further improvements to market structure, in both the equity and bond markets. This included the shortening of the settlement period from T+7 to T+5 in August 1997, the advent of fully-scripless trading on the KLSE on 1 January 1997 following the immobilisation of all KLSE-listed securities into the Central Depository System (CDS); the introduction by BNM of scripless trading in all new issues of unlisted corporate bonds was introduced in 1996, as well as of a bond information and dissemination system one year later to enhance the transparency of the secondary market.[2]

– A push to develop the Islamic capital market. Initiatives included the establishment of the SAC of the SC. The SAC's functions are to advise the SC on matters relating to instruments, modalities and institutions necessary for the development of the Islamic capital market.

– The introduction of new securities market guidelines and regulations in relation to, among other things: the public offering of securities of infrastructure project companies, property trust funds, call warrants, the public offering of securities of closed-end funds, securities lending and a framework for regulated short-selling, the public offering of securities of foreign-based companies with listing and quotation on the KLSE, and share buy-backs by listed companies.

These programmes required major changes to the prevailing regulatory framework, which the SC undertook through a substantial programme of law reform. A major part of this programme involved amendments to the SCA and the FIA, which came into force through the Securities Commission (Amendment) Act 1995 and the Futures Industry (Amendment) Act 1995 in September 1995.

Amendments to the SCA related, on the whole, to the primary market, especially capital market proposals and take-over and merger submissions. In particular, they provided a catalyst for the move towards disclosure-based regulation; expanded the scope of capital market proposals that would require the SC's approval; introduced due-diligence and criminal liability provisions, as well as new statutory functions for the SC. Amendments to the FIA addressed conceptual issues and the need for changes in both market and regulatory structures to facilitate the introduction of exchange-traded derivatives on KLOFFE. They also facilitated the establishment of a common clearing mechanism for the newly-formed financial derivative exchanges. Other major law reform efforts came through the Securities Industry (Amendment) Act 1996 and the Securities Industry (Central Depositories) (Amendment) Act 1996, amendments to the Securities Industry (Central Depositories) Act 1991; promulgation of a host of subsidiary legislation; and the drafting of a new Financial Reporting Act 1996.

Following the satisfactory completion of the first business plan, the SC embarked on its second business plan, for the period 1998–2000. The launch of the plan was all the more timely, if not challenging, given that it coincided with the onset of financial and economic turbulence in the region. In many respects, the second plan built on many aspects of the first. Development of the capital market continued to be a major thrust, with the application of technology in the capital market being added to efforts to promote the conventional as well as Islamic capital markets, instruments and processes. The rationalisation and strengthening of market institutions was also a major strategy. However, a particular feature of the plan was that it accorded an important emphasis on strengthening the capital market regulatory framework, which turned out to be all the more imperative in light of the financial crisis that ensued. The key strategies in this respect included the continuing shift towards disclosure-based regulation, the promotion of front-line regulation, the improvement of corporate governance standards and practices, and the enhancement of the SC's enforcement capabilities. The next few paragraphs will describe some of the major initiatives in relation to these areas.

Disclosure, transparency and investor protection. At the end of 1999, the SC announced amendments to the Policies and Guidelines on Issue/Offer of Securities that would facilitate the progress of the disclosure-based regulation programme. In effect, the revisions marked the start of the second phase of the implementation of the programme. Changes focused on deregulating the requirements on securities pricing, asset valuation and the use of proceeds. The guidelines now allow for the market-based pricing of securities for all types of corporate proposals, not just initial public offerings, while the SC's approval is no longer needed for the revaluation of assets, except under certain circumstances, or on the use of proceeds. In addition, the SC would no longer assess the utilisation of proceeds raised from the issue of securities as long as the proceeds are utilised for core-business activities of the issuers. In April that year, the SC had revised the guidelines' requirements over the listing on the KLSE and for reverse takeovers/backdoor listings, and had introduced a certain amount of flexibility to the pricing of warrants and the issuance of replacement warrants.

At the same time that the SC has worked on the deregulation of the primary market, it has also introduced measures to enhance disclosure and accountability in order to ensure that investor protection is not compromised. Measures have included a strengthening of rules on related-party and interested-party transactions. Previous episodes of abuse of such transactions led the SC to review the relevant rules and subsequently direct the KLSE to make several changes to its listing requirements. These changes involved, among other things, a widening of the scope of rules, enhancing disclosure, and concerned issues such as voting rights, the appointment of corporate advisers and directors' responsibilities. In addition, there must now be an independent corporate adviser to advise minority shareholders. Steps have also been taken to improve the regulation of takeovers and mergers. In January 1999, the SC introduced a new takeover code, supported by comprehensive practice notes, aimed at giving minority shareholders fair opportunity to consider an offer. The new regulatory framework accompanying the new code includes provisions imposing certain criminal liabilities and discouraging "creeping" control of company. In addition, the KLSE has introduced the quarterly reporting requirements where listed companies must now provide quarterly reports that include information on their balance sheets, income statements and explanatory notes in order to enhance content and frequency of corporate disclosure.

Corporate governance. Efforts to enhance standards of corporate governance in Malaysia had been on-going even prior to the crisis but had been piecemeal in nature. The formation of a high-level Finance Committee on Corporate Governance in July 1998, with the SC as the secretariat to the committee, was a watershed, bringing together top-ranking members of the government, the corporate sector, industry organisations and regulatory agencies to undertake a comprehensive review of corporate governance in Malaysia. Its work culminated in a report, released to the public on 25 March this year after a period of consultation, providing 70 explicit recommendations on

- strengthening the statutory and regulatory framework for corporate governance;

- enhancing the self-regulatory mechanisms that promote good governance; and

- the need for training and education programmes to develop the corporate culture in relation to corporate governance and to ensure the necessary availability of human and institutional capital in the industry.

The report's recommendations includes the formulation of a Malaysian code on corporate governance. The main aims of such a code is to establish a set of principles and best practices for good governance aimed at increasing efficiency and accountability of boards by making their decision-making processes independent. The code is based on the principle of self-regulation, which, in our case, is seen as more enduring. The report's recommendations also cover the reform of laws, regulations and rules, with a view to

- clarifying the responsibilities of key corporate participants

- enhancing obligations of those participants especially in related-party transactions

- improving the accuracy and timeliness of disclosures

- enhancing the value of general meetings

- enhancing the efficiency of shareholder redress for grievances

- enhancing the enforcement of good corporate conduct

The SC has been tasked with overseeing the implementation of the recommendations and securing approval from the government. The detailed implementation of the recommendations is being undertaken by a project team consisting of representatives from the SC, ROC, BNM, KLSE, MESDAQ and the Federation of Public Listed Companies.

Enforcement and supervision. Efforts to strengthen enforcement and supervision included improving regulation and enforcement in relation to insider trading and market manipulation. The SC amended the SIA to address weaknesses in current rules and to introduce civil enforcement powers. These came into force in April 1998, and ensure that legislation facilitates the policy objectives of protecting market integrity, promoting proper conduct, suppressing illegal and improper practices, maintaining investor confidence and enhancing investor protection. With these amendments:

- The definition of an insider has been expanded to include a person who possesses information not generally available to others, and not necessarily just a person who has a fiduciary relationship with a corporation. Furthermore, both tippers and tippees now fall under the definition of an insider.

- It is now an offence to trade or procure a trade using insider information or to communicate such information for the purpose of trading. The penalty for doing so carries a fine of not less than RM1 million and imprisonment of up to 10 years.

- A victim of insider trading and market manipulation can now bring civil action to seek full compensation, regardless of whether an offender has been convicted, or even prosecuted for the offence.

- The SC is also allowed to bring civil action against an offender for disgorgement of up to three times the profit made by the offender or loss avoided, or a civil penalty of up to RM500,000.[3]

- As these provisions affect a broad range of activities, including some legitimate commercial undertakings, certain statutory defences have been established to prevent legitimate commercial transactions from being auctioned.

The amendments also give the SC greater clout to deal with directors and chief executive officers, including the power to compel them to make required additional disclosures. Directors and CEOs must now disclose their interests in securities of a listed company and any associated company. The SC can also apply to the High Court to remove a CEO or director who has been declared bankrupt, has contravened provisions of securities laws, or has been convicted of a criminal offence. Moreover, it can investigate nominee accounts relating to dealings in securities of listed and unlisted public companies. The amendments extend the enforcement powers of the stock exchange, as well as providing the clearing house with powers to enforce its rules. The penalty for breach of the rules or listing requirements of the stock exchange as well as the rules of the clearing house has been increased. The SIA also has new provisions that extend enforcement within and outside of Malaysia on offences such as false trading and market rigging, market manipulation, providing false and misleading statements, and fraudulently inducing persons to deal in securities.

Amendments to the SCA enhance and extend the SC's powers of examination and investigation. The Act now distinguishes between the powers of inspection and the powers of investigation, and extends these further. For instance, the SC can now conduct examination on licensed entities, including the stock exchange, the clearing house and the central depository, without prior notice, while its investigating officers can now require suspect offenders to surrender their travel documents to the SC. New provisions also protect the identities of persons giving information or making a complaint to the SC to encourage public assistance. However, to prevent its abuse, the SC can take action against anyone providing false information. In line with its enhanced powers, the SC has boosted the strength and quality of its enforcement staff.

Front-line regulation. The SC continues to drive a front-line regulation programme aimed at (a) redefining the roles and responsibilities of market institutions such as the exchanges and clearing houses in their capacity as front-line regulators (FLRs), and (b) enabling FLRs to take on more initiative and responsibility for formulating and enforcing their respective rules and regulations. The programme has at least four areas of focus. First, the programme aims at enhancing the governance structure and management capabilities of FLRs. Second, in relation to securities issuance and disclosure of corporate activity, it requires FLRs to take on primary responsibility for regulating primary market activities relating to issue, offer and listing of securities; playing a more active role in supervising disclosure, corporate governance and due diligence in secondary market; and raising standards of surveillance, investigation and enforcement. Third, it focuses on the need for improvements to market surveillance and enforcement, especially in the areas of information sharing and co-operation, prudential regulation, client asset protection, audit and examination, and the conduct of business. Fourth, the programme looks at market development, including the introduction of new products, innovation and technology, and training and education.

Market intermediaries. The financial crisis of 1997–98 highlighted the importance of having strong market intermediaries. The SC is implementing a restructuring scheme to resolve the problems faced by the stockbroking industry arising from the crisis. A special task force involving the SC, KLSE and Danaharta, the national asset management company, is overseeing the acquisition of non-performing loans of the stockbroking industry from the banking sector by Danaharta. Among other things, the scheme is expected to facilitate recapitalisation and regularisation, as well as possible consolidation, within the stockbroking industry.

In the area of prudential regulation, the SC has driven the establishment of a risk-based system of capital adequacy requirements to replace the current system of minimum liquid-fund requirements. The new framework brings domestic prudential requirements more closely in line with international standards. The KLSE business rules governing the new requirements were approved by the SC and brought into effect on 1 December 1999. The SC is also taking steps to improve client asset protection, even though the regulatory structure in Malaysia addresses this issue through both statutory requirements and exchange rules. Efforts are aimed at strengthening the existing requirements in line with international best practice. Recent events have reaffirmed the need to review and, where possible, enhance client asset protection arrangements. With this in mind, the SC is in the process of formulating a comprehensive client asset protection framework.

Market institutions. The last few years have also seen consolidation of market institutions, beginning with the merger of MDCH, the clearing house for KLOFFE and MME, with the Malaysian Futures Clearing Corporation, which clears for what was then the Kuala Lumpur Commodities Exchange (KLCE), in December 1997. This was followed by an announcement in July 1998 by the KLSE that it had reached an agreement in principle to acquire KLOFFE Capital for RM35 million, the holding company of the futures exchange. This move was seen as a major step towards enhancing efficiency and facilitating greater co-operation between the two exchanges. On 31 December 1998, KLOFFE was bought over by the KLSE. With similar aims in respect of efficiency, the MME announced on 2 July 1998 that it would be merging with KLCE later in the year. The Commodity and Monetary Exchange of Malaysia (COMMEX) officially commenced operations on 7 December 1998.

D.   Moving Forward

In going forward, the SC is aware that there are several important strategic issues concerning Malaysia's capital markets and their role within the economy that require urgent attention. These include:

- **Financing economic growth**. Malaysia's long-term economic development agenda, embodied in the country's Third Outline Perspective Plan for 2001–10, which encompasses the Eighth Malaysia Plan for 2001–5), is likely to require substantial financing. In addition, economic recovery measures as recommended by the National Economic Recovery Plan of 1997 will also need to be financed.

- **Further diversification and development of Malaysia's real economy**, in particular through the increased contribution of its services sector. At 48% of gross domestic product (GDP), the services sector is relatively underdeveloped compared to those of industrialised and newly-industrialised economies (65%-70% of GDP). It has been recognised that capital markets have an important role to play in making a direct contribution to the real economy through generating activity in the services sector.

These issues have prompted a major effort to focus on the strategic positioning of Malaysia's capital markets as a whole. The advantages of having a comprehensive approach to develop and position the country's capital markets are clear: an explicit strategy provides certainty and gives the industry an incentive for business development. Moreover, it ensures consistency across individual projects. With this in mind, the SC is in the process of formulating a capital markets master plan (CMP), whose key objectives are to determine the strategic and competitive positioning of the Malaysian capital market and to formulate a comprehensive plan with specific recommendations. The CMP aims to produce a capital market that is, among other things: efficient and competitive; financially sound; technologically advanced; and integrated and balanced, in terms of the share each component or sector has in the overall capital market.

Notwithstanding the formulation of a capital markets master plan, specific efforts are being directed to the development of the Malaysian bond market. In August 1999, the government announced a major decision to consolidate the regulatory framework for corporate bond market, which involved the SC taking sole responsibility for regulating the market. The financial crisis of 1997–98 had focused attention on the underdevelopment of bond markets, which had resulted in an over-reliance on the banking sector, problems arising from maturity mismatch of liabilities and a limited opportunity to diversify portfolio risk. In light of the urgency of these issues, the government decided to establish a

National Bond Market Committee to expedite development and growth of the bond markets. The committee, which is chaired by the Ministry of Finance, consists of representatives from the SC, BNM, ROC and the KLSE. Its key areas of focus are legal and regulatory reform, market infrastructure and operations, and product and institutional development.

NOTES

1. The classes of licences relate to Dealers, Investment Advisers, Fund Managers, Futures Brokers, Futures Trading Advisers, and Futures Fund Managers, as well as their respective representatives.

2. Trading still carried out "over-the counter" by telephone and fax but indicative buy-sell quotes and historic price information from executed trades are made available to market through BIDS.

3. After deducting its own cost, the Commission will then distribute the amount recovered to the victims of insider trading.

CAPITAL MARKET DEVELOPMENT IN THAILAND

by
Mr. Prasarn Trairatvorakul

A.   Macroeconomic Development

GDP Growth Expected at 4.5% with the Inflation Rate of 2.5%-3% in 2000

After two years of economic downturn with the contraction of GDP in 1997-1998, the economy began to show signs of recovery in manufacturing, consumption and export, contributing to the preliminary estimated GDP growth of 4% in 1999. Owing to stable exchange rates, decreasing world commodities price, and the initial recovery of domestic demand, which has not put substantial upward pressure on prices, inflation rate for 1999 is projected at a low level of 0.3%. The continuing expansionary fiscal policy, the eased monetary condition and the progress in the financial sector reform help supporting the GDP to grow by 4.5% in 2000 while inflation rate is estimated at 2.5%-3%.

Expansionary Fiscal Policy

To stabilize and stimulate the economy, the government has implemented the fiscal stimulus measures including expenditures, tax reductions, and energy price reductions. The government cash balance recorded a deficit of Bt 133.8 billion in 1999, equivalent to 2.9% of GDP. The consolidated public sector deficit is estimated at 5.5% of GDP in the fiscal year 1999 and is targeted at 5% of GDP in the fiscal year 2000.

Eased Monetary Condition

On the monetary front, liquidity has been eased to the point that money market rates stand at their historic lows over the past decade. The one-year fixed deposit rate decreased from 6% at the end of 1998 to 4%-4.25% at the end of 1999 while the MLR declined from 11.5%-12% to 8.25%-8.5% over the same period.

To pursue an appropriate monetary policy in the environment of the floating exchange rate system, the Bank of Thailand (BOT) plans to adopt inflation targeting as its main focus. This new policy requires a revision of the Bank of Thailand Act, which will permit the establishment of an independent monetary policy committee responsible for executing monetary policy to achieve the inflation target.

Continuing Surpluses in Current Account and Balance of Payments

The current account surplus is expected to decline slightly from US$14.3 billion in 1998 to US$11.3 billion in 1999. Exports have begun to pick up by recording the preliminary growth of 7.4% in 1999 after a decrease of 6.8% in 1998. In line with the economic recovery, imports have also increased by 17.7% after a sharp drop of 33.8% in 1998. The repayment of external debts has mainly contributed to the net capital outflow estimated to be US$6.5 billion. In total, the balance of payments recorded a surplus of US$4.6 billion, adding to the international reserves which stood at US$34.9 billion at the end of 1999.

In 2000, it is expected that the economic recovery and rising domestic demand will lead to import growth of 19% while the government stimulus measures, the regional recovery, and expanding world trade will boost exports growth of 9.6%. As a result, the current account and balance of payments are projected to register smaller surpluses of US$7.7 billion and US$0.2 billion respectively.

Stable Exchange Rates

The measures to revive the economy and reform the financial sector coupled with the strength of external position have restored the confidence in the economy and resulted in the stability of exchange rates. The baht strengthened from the average of Bt 41.37/US$ in 1998 to Bt 38.18/US$ in 1999. Moreover, the exchange rate also moved within a more narrow range of about Bt 36-40/US$ in 1999, compared with Bt 36-54/US$ in 1998.

B.   Capital Market Development

1.   *Development of Capital Markets*

Thai businesses have traditionally relied on internally generated cash and bank loans as their primary sources of funds. As can be seen from Figure 1, bank loans accounted for the highest portion of funding sources. The outstanding value of loans rose continually during 1994-1997; on the contrary, the stock market capitalization dropped substantially during 1995-1997 after the peak of the index in 1994. The bond market is very small compared with other funding channels but has recorded very rapid growth as can be seen from the outstanding value in 1996 which more than doubled that in 1994.

However, after the crisis unfolded, banks were reluctant to provide new financing. As shown in Figure 2, in 1999, the repayment amount exceeded the value of new loans, thereby resulting in a decline in outstanding loans. Instead, corporations turned to direct financing by issuing equities and bonds. Equities were issued primarily by financial institutions to meet their provisioning needs and regulatory capital requirement while the bond issuance became more attractive due to low interest rate. The increasing use of direct sources of financing is viewed as a positive trend since the deepening and widening of the capital market can lessen the reliance on the banking sector and create a more balanced structure of capital mobilization.

Not only is the banking sector the main source of financing for businesses, it is also a safe-keeper in which people put the majority of their savings. As shown in Figure 3, bank deposits constituted almost 90% of total household savings while investments in the stock market accounted for just 0.25%, a negligible percentage of the total. Therefore, the capital market has strong growth potential from the retail investor base and one channel for these retail investments is through many types of collective investment funds, which are strongly promoted. The details about the promotion of institutional investments will be covered in section 2.3.

405

Figure 1 : Thai Corporate Sources of Funds

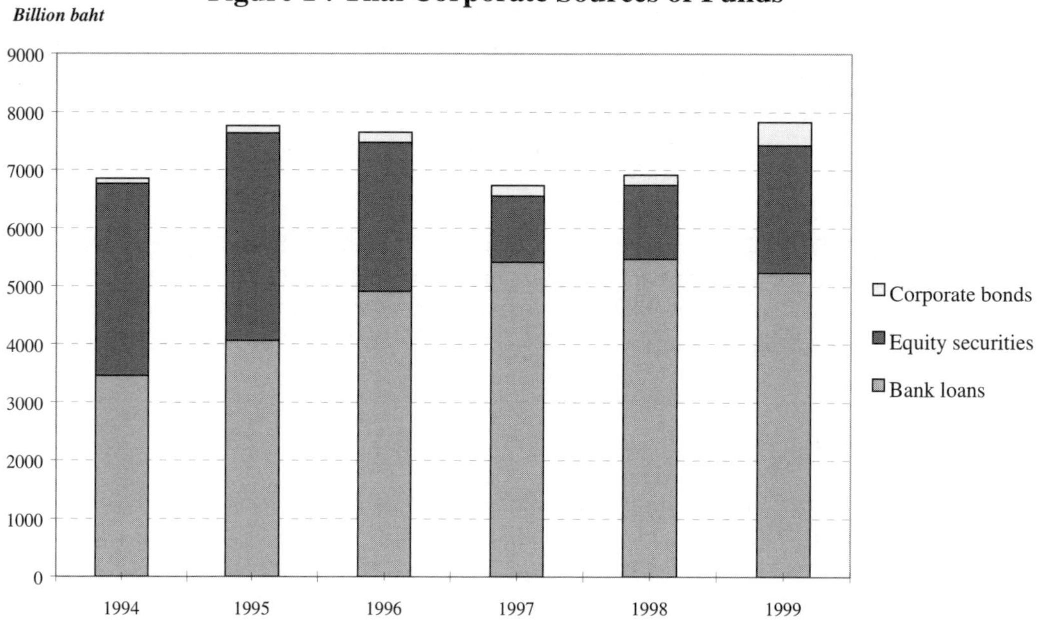

Billion baht

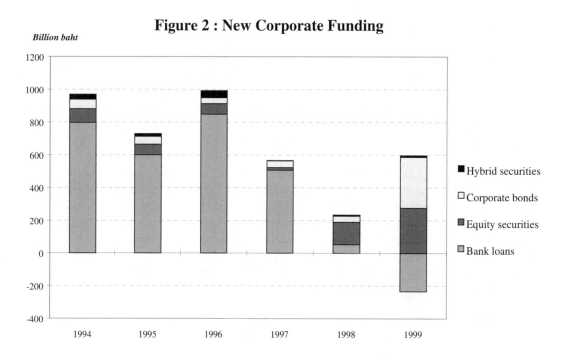

Source: Bank of Thailand, Securities and Exchange Commission, Thai Bond Dealing Centre

Figure 2 : New Corporate Funding

Billion baht

Source: Bank of Thailand, Securities and Exchange Commission, Thai Bond Dealing Centre

Figure 3 : Components of Household Savings

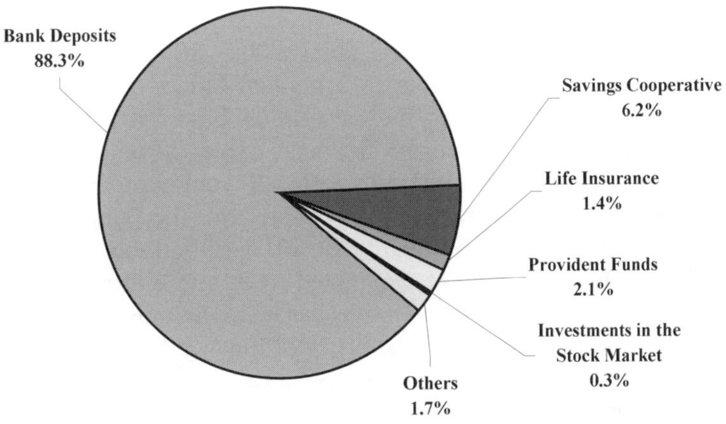

Bank Deposits
88.3%

Savings Cooperative
6.2%

Life Insurance
1.4%

Provident Funds
2.1%

Investments in the
Stock Market
0.3%

Others
1.7%

Source: Socioeconomic Survey by National Statistical Office in 1998

1.1   Activities in the Markets

(i)   Equity Securities Market

Primary Market

The equity securities market has still served its very useful function of capital mobilization. It began to show signs of recovery after having experienced an economic downturn and financial market turbulence for the last two years. The year 1999 witnessed a dramatic increase in the issuance of equity securities. The value of stock issued doubled from Bt 136.3 billion in 1998 to Bt 276.1 billion in 1999. Most securities were issued domestically in private placement. Commercial banks shared approximately 65.79% of total equity offering value to support their recapitalisation schemes in compliance with the provisioning requirement while building materials and finance sectors recorded 10.18% and 7.50% of the total value, respectively.

Secondary market

Trading activities on the Stock Exchange of Thailand (SET) recovered considerably throughout 1999, reflecting investor sentiment that the worst for the economy was over and corporate performance would improve. Efforts by government to stimulate economic growth through tax incentives and fiscal programs eased pressure on listed companies. Falling interest rates, low inflation and stable baht also gave companies room to cut their expenses as well as restructure debt and operations.

At year-end 1999, the SET index closed at 481.92 points, up by 126.11 points or 35.44% higher than year-end 1998. Total turnover volume was recorded at 96.32 billion shares with total turnover value of Bt 1,609.79 billion and an average daily turnover of Bt 6.57 billion. These figures indicated an increase of 35.98%, 88.24% and 87.47% respectively from 1998. Market capitalization also increased 72.93% from the previous year. A total of 395 companies and 450 securities were listed on the SET at year-end, including 19 new securities whose total offering value was Bt 111.35 billion.

(ii)   Fixed Income Securities Market

Primary Market

Before the economic problem reached a critical point in July 1997, the government had experienced several years of budget surplus, contributing to a gradual fall in the supply of government bonds. After passing the period of economic crisis, the government has issued significant amount of bonds to support the budget deficit and to finance the financial sector cleanup. High liquidity in financial market throughout the year 1999 caused interest rate to fall continuously and stay at low level, which made bond issuance become more attractive. In this regard, the outstanding value of government bonds increased from Bt 65.4 billion in 1997 to Bt 463.1 billion and Bt 630.2 billion in 1998 and 1999, respectively. The newly issued bonds amounted to Bt 455 billion and Bt 410.7 billion in 1998 and 1999 respectively compared with no new issues in 1997. The most important issues of government bonds at present are loan bonds issued by the Ministry of Finance (MOF). Because of their large issue sizes and trading volume as well as various maturities, the market can derive risk-free benchmarks, which are now available for maturities of up to 14 years.

Apart from the government loan bonds, state enterprises bonds guaranteed by the MOF could also be regarded as risk-free. However, each issue is quite illiquid so their yields are often higher than the benchmarks. Government-guaranteed bonds have been issued quite often over the past few years. There was Bt 309.1 billion of outstanding value in 1999 compared with Bt 247.3 billion and Bt 255.7 billion in 1997 and 1998, respectively. The amount of new issues was Bt 32.5 billion in 1999 compared with Bt 41.3 billion and Bt 46.7 billion in 1997 and 1998 respectively. There was no new issue of non-guaranteed bonds for the last two years.

The very high interest rates in early 1998 had affected the corporate bond market. It was only in December 1998, after interest rates had fallen sharply, that companies began to consider raising funds by bonds issuance. Most corporate bonds were issued domestically in private placement. The outstanding value in 1999 totaled Bt 402 billion compared with Bt 187.6 billion and Bt 177.6 billion in 1997 and 1998, respectively. The amount of new issues were Bt 311.2 billion in 1999 compared with Bt 40.9 billion and Bt 37.1 billion in 1997 and 1998 respectively.

Secondary Market

In 1999, the secondary bonds market showed a sign of improvement from the previous year. Major positive factors included a downtrend of interest rates in money market, more stable Baht, and additional listings of government and state enterprise bonds which have increased the number, volume and total turnover of listed bonds.

At year-end 1999, total turnover value was recorded at Bt 431.2 billion, almost five times the value in 1998. Of the total, the government bonds value accounts for 90% and the remaining value is comprised mainly of corporate bonds.

1.2   Major Products

(i)   Equity Securities

There was a diversification of products listed on the SET, covering more choices of equity securities, hybrid debt-equity instruments and unit trusts among others. The year 1999 marked the creation of a market for small-cap listings (Market for Alternative Investment) and key preparations for the introduction of index options, both as alternative choices of investment and risk management tools for investors. In line with the government's efforts, the SET in 1999 also continued to actively support the debt restructuring of listed companies through revision of relevant criteria and reduction of fees for new types of products, namely: derivative warrants, transferable subscription rights and unit trusts of mutual funds investing in debt instruments.

(ii)   Fixed Income Securities

Prior to the crisis in 1997, corporate bonds dominated the Thai debt market. The combined issue of bonds by the property and financial sectors was about 60% of the total market. However, during 1998-1999, the Thai corporate bond market became very inactive. Instead, government bonds issued to finance budget deficit and to solve problems in the financial sector began to play an increasingly important role. Financial institutions are becoming more interested in purchasing government bonds, which can also be used as company reserves. Moreover, institutional investors such as pension fund and insurance companies invest more in government bonds given the prevailing low bank deposit rates.

1.3   Investor Structure

(i)   Equity Securities

Equity securities trading by investor type can be summarized into three main categories, local individual investors, foreign investors, and local institutional investors. In 1999, transactions of local individual investors recorded the highest percentage of 66% of total turnover while those of foreign investors and local institutional investors accounted for 29% and 5% of total turnover respectively.

(ii)   Fixed Income Securities

According to the classification of the Thai Bond Dealing Centre (Thai BDC), bonds trading transactions are divided into inter dealer-member transactions and dealer to client transactions. In 1999, trading volume of inter dealer-member transaction accounted for 55.5% of total turnover. Of the remaining transactions between dealers and their clients, pension funds were the most active players sharing 32.5% while mutual funds and insurance companies shared the rest of 15.8% and 5.6%, respectively. Foreign investors were not active in bonds trading as shown by their slight trading turnover recorded at 0.86% of total transaction value.

1.4   Foreign Participation

Foreign investments have a significant impact on the trading volume and the direction of the SET index of the Thai stock exchange. The current regulations do not restrict trading activities or investments of foreign investors, including proprietary trading and hedge funds. The greater foreign participation can be expected as the revised Alien Business Law, which has recently become effective since March 2000, revokes foreign ownership limit in many of the previously restricted industries.

2. Measures for Fostering Market Development to Date

2.1 Operational Infrastructure

(i) Equities Securities Market

Promotion of Small and Medium-sized Enterprises (SMEs)

One of the government's measures to stimulate economic recovery is to encourage private investments especially in small and medium-sized enterprises (SMEs) as the driving force for the sustainable economic growth. In this regard, the SME Promotion Act has been enacted in February 2000 to unify responsibilities for promoting SMEs in a new entity named the "SME Promotion Office" and to foster the effective implementation of the promotion plan.

Moreover, the government has set up venture capital funds to invest in competitive SMEs and enhanced the effectiveness of SME financing by restructuring specialized financial institutions, the Small Industry Finance Corporation and the Small Industry Credit Guarantee Corporation. Both institutions are injected with additional funds to be able to expand their financing and credit guarantee to the SMEs.

To support the government's SME promotion plan, the SET has established a market for small-cap listings named "Market for Alternative Investment" (MAI). Previously, the Bangkok Stock Dealings Center (BSDC) was planned to be the market for the SMEs not qualified for listings on the SET. However, the unfavorable tax treatment for trades in the BSDC together with the image of being the second-class stocks hampered its success and the BSDC finally closed down its operations in May 1999.

On the other hand, the MAI, which is considered a part of the SET's organization, will enjoy the good image from association with the SET as well as the same tax treatment for its trades as that of the main board. For example, capital gains taxes are exempted for individual investors. Furthermore, the shift of public offering criteria from merit-based to disclosure-based with the emphasis on good corporate governance will facilitate the mobilization of funds especially for the SMEs. The MAI plans to begin trading within the third quarter of 2000 and expects to have 6-10 listed companies within 2000.

Internet Trading

To keep up with technological advances and enhance the attractiveness of the stock market, the SET has just launched the regulations on internet trading in January 2000. According to the rules, securities companies with computer support and information security systems can start offering internet trading services immediately once obtaining approval from the SET. The Securities and Exchange Commission (SEC) is also going to set up minimum standards for securities firms providing services through the internet.

At present, the extent to which internet trading is permitted is limited to the use of internet technology for communication between brokers and their clients as well as the exchange, rather than the creation of an alternative market.

To provide legal framework to support the growing volume of electronic commerce and use of internet technology, electronic commerce and electronic endorsement laws have been drafted and expected to be enacted in 2000 .

Liberalization of Commissions

To cope with the downward pressure on the commissions from the internet trading and to enhance the competitiveness of the Thai capital market, the SEC and the SET plan to liberalize commissions to the fully negotiable basis from September 2002 onwards. In the meantime, commission rates will be negotiable with the floor of 0.25%, starting from September 2000, except rates for sub-brokers which are now fully negotiable.

(ii)   Fixed Income Securities Market

Compared with developed markets, the Thai bond market is still quite small and thus has strong potential to play an increasingly important role in mobilizing funds to support the economic recovery. In this regard, the authorities have made significant progress to foster market development.

Issuance of Government Bonds to Create Benchmark

The consecutive budget surpluses over 1994-1997 resulted in the absence of bond issuance and consequently the lack of benchmark in the market. However, in 1998-1999, the government issued bonds totaling Bt 500 billion to restructure the liabilities of the Financial Institutions Development Fund from short to long-term, enabling the market to construct the benchmark rates. Realizing the importance of the benchmark, the government also plans to issue bonds on a continuous and consistent basis. In this regard, the Debt Management Office has been set up to centralize the duties of debt management of the country which were previously divided among many government units.

Establishment of the Primary Dealer System

The central bank has begun the primary dealer system by initially designating nine financial institutions as recognized market makers to be its counterparties for the conduct of open market operations. .

Introduction of Inter Dealer Broker

Having realized the lack of a collector of real-time quotations and a center of market information as a problem in the present market making system, the SEC has proposed that the MOF issue licenses for inter dealer brokers (IDB) which will be regulated as another type of securities business. The IDB will function as a wholesale broker to facilitate trades between dealers by collecting real-time quotations and matching trades between dealers on an anonymous basis. As a result, the IDB could enhance liquidity and transparency of trading in the secondary market. The draft regulations for the IDB are now under the consideration of the MOF and are expected to be launched in this year.

New Trading Platform of the Thai Bond Dealing Centre

The Thai BDC plans to launch a new screen dealing system to facilitate bonds trading. The new system will be equipped with two features, the auto matching system for liquid bonds and the electronic person-to-person system for illiquid bonds and repo transactions. The coexistence of the Thai BDC's trading system and the IDB is not deemed undesirable as these two systems will have to compete to provide the best services to their clients to promote bonds trading, thereby benefiting dealers and other participants in the market.

Reporting Requirement for Dealers

Starting from the second quarter of 2000, dealers and IDBs will be required to report their daily transactions of debt instruments to the Thai BDC so that the Thai BDC will be a center for the collection and dissemination of trade data to the public. Furthermore, financial institutions with the dealing license in debt instruments will be required to register their traders with the Thai BDC, who will enforce the codes of conduct and industry standard of these traders.

Removal of Tax Impediments for Bond Trading

Tax treatment on debt instruments is currently one of the authorities' key concerns to ensure it does not impede active trading of government and corporate bonds. The main tax problem of bond dealers is related to the Special Business Tax (SBT) which is imposed on capital gains received from bond trading on a gross basis, i.e. the deduction of capital losses is not allowed. Therefore, such tax treatment tends to increase transaction costs to dealers and could hinder market liquidity.

The SEC has coordinated continually with the Revenue Department to remove tax impediments on financial transactions. Some problems have recently been solved to increase the effectiveness of liquidity management tools such as income tax for securities borrowing and lending as well as repo transactions.

To further solving the remaining problems and plan for tax treatment of derivatives transactions, the MOF has received technical assistance from the World Bank in conducting studies, which aim at analyzing the present status of the Thai tax law system regarding financial instruments with particular emphasis on debt and derivatives instruments, and equipping the Revenue Department with analytical tools to make appropriate judgments and take definitive actions necessary for reforming the existing system.

Promotion of Credit Rating

Since 1 April 2000, the SEC has required compulsory credit rating for private placement issues in addition to public offering issues to promote credit rating as well as rectify a loophole in the former regulations. Since the definition of institutional investors qualified for private placement sales includes individual investors with minimum investments of Bt 10 million, issuers attempted to evade the compulsory credit rating, which was limited to only public offering issues, by pooling many individual investors to meet the above definition.

Moreover, the establishment of a second credit rating agency is also strongly encouraged to motivate the existing single credit rating agency, the Thai Rating Information Services, to improve its efficiency and promote the competition in this industry.

(iii)   Clearing and Settlement System

Risk Management System of the Securities Clearinghouse

The Thailand Securities Depository Company (TSD), a central clearinghouse and depository for transactions on the SET has continually improved its operational systems to meet the international standard. For example, the depository has begun its scripless system since 1992.

The developments in 1999 therefore emphasized risk management measures. First, the settlement cap, which limits the settlement volume of each member based on its net capital, was imposed in the first quarter. Second, the early warning system has been launched to monitor the impact of market risk from volatility of securities prices on the pending settlement value. In case a member trades above the settlement cap or is expected to pose excessive losses than the designated warning level, TSD will enforce him to place collateral to cover the risk. If the member cannot place the collateral within appropriate time, TSD will consider terminating the defaulter's membership.

Development into Delivery-Versus-Payment for Bonds Settlement

At present, the clearing and settlement system for government securities is a Real Time Gross Settlement (RTGS) semi-automated delivery-versus-payment (DVP) system in which funds can be transferred automatically through the BOT's electronic payment system named "Bahtnet" while securities transfer still requires the submission of evidence of ownership to the BOT. The BOT will then check to ensure that a buyer's funds and a seller's securities are available before making transfers to both sides simultaneously.

Though the electronic payment system is available, the fact that banks and their customers prefer to use cheques, which take time for clearing, hinders the DVP and poses settlement risks to counterparties. To address the problem, the BOT requires inter-bank payments be made by transfers through the Bahtnet system instead of using cheques from March 2000. Moreover, the BOT will provide the intra day credit facilities to users of the Bahtnet system provided that a borrower places sufficient collateral.

In terms of securities transfers, the majority of holdings are still in the scrip form though the BOT provides scripless depository services. The presumption under the current SEC Act, which provides legal certainty for the beneficial ownership of securities in the muti-tiered holding structure, applies only to the SET or a depository center which is a SET's subsidiary, not other depositories including the central bank. Therefore, the SEC has proposed the amendment to the Securities and Exchange Act (SEC Act) to remove the legal impediment to the multi-tiered holding structure for government securities deposited with the BOT to encourage scripless holdings.

These measures are the preparation before the upgrading of the current system to the full DVP status under the Bahtnet2 system where funds and securities transfers can be made electronically after the availability of both sides is checked electronically by the system. It is expected that the Bahtnet2 system will be launched within the first half of next year.

2.2   Legal Infrastructure

Draft Derivatives Bill

As financial instruments to hedge against price risks and create exposure to underlying assets, derivatives are deemed very essential for the effective functioning of the financial market. Therefore, the SEC drafted the Derivatives Bill to create legal certainty for derivatives contracts and provide regulatory framework for derivatives markets and intermediaries. The Draft Bill has been approved in principle by the Cabinet in March 1998, and after the review by the Council of State is expected to go to the Parliament this year.

In the meantime, the SET is preparing to acquaint investors with derivatives products by launching derivatives warrants and index options. Trading of derivative warrants began in May 1999, attracting substantial investor interest. In 2000, the SET will allow trading of index options. In this regard, the SET has continuously provided knowledge, information and training on such instruments to brokers, listed companies, investors, and other relevant parties to prepare all market participants for the full-fledged derivatives trading in the future.

2.3   Cultivation of Institutional Investors

More Flexible Portfolio Management for Mutual Funds

As mentioned earlier, a substantial demand for stock investments could come from the strong retail investor base. To attract these investors, the SEC has revoked minimum requirements for types and characteristics of securities permitted for investments of mutual funds, thereby giving more leeway to asset management companies to set up new types of funds with various risk-return profiles. For example, venture capital funds can be established with an objective of investing in high-risk assets provided that the investment policy and risks have been adequately and clearly disclosed to investors. Moreover, the SEC also supports long-term investments in retirement mutual funds by proposing the Revenue Department to provide tax benefits to the investors.

Supervisory Authorities of Provident Funds Transferred from the MOF to the SEC

According to the revised Provident Funds Act and the revised SEC Act, the supervisory authorities of provident funds will be transferred from the Fiscal Policy Office, the Ministry of Finance, to the SEC in March 2000 to integrate the oversight of collective investment funds management into a single body, the SEC which currently supervises mutual funds and private funds. This will create a uniform standard for funds management since provident funds managers will need the private funds management license under the SEC Act and be regulated accordingly.

2.4   Investor Protection

Improvement of Risk Management and Customer Protection Measures of Securities Firms

Regulations on risk management and customer protection measures of securities firms have been continually improved to reflect the changing market environment. For example, the net capital rule has been revised to reflect risks from new types of businesses and instruments such as derivatives. The segregation rule has been modified to be more comprehensive to provide protection for all kinds of customer assets.

Moreover, the proposals have been made to revise the SEC Act to improve the enforcement mechanisms and provide better investor protection. For example, the definition about unfair trading practices will be more clarified and the enforcement mechanisms will be improved to facilitate the prosecution processes.

Supervision of Sales Representatives of Mutual Funds

The SEC plans to launch regulations to supervise sales representatives of mutual funds within the second quarter of 2000. In this regard, the staff of assets management companies or their selling agent firms have to get approval from the SEC to be sales representatives. The sales representatives have to follow codes of conduct including the advisory and disclosure guidelines to upgrade the industry standard and protect individual investors.

Supervision of Investment Advisors

The SEC is working to set up a new supervisory framework to give appropriate guidelines for investment advisors. Under the new framework, analysts will have to comply with a professional standard when dealing with investors. Their advice has to be free from bias and supported by an acceptable explanation.

In principle, the new framework will help to clearly define the scope of responsibilities which investment advisors will have to take into account when advising investment strategy to the investors. There will be certain limitations on the scope of investment commentary. It is expected that the new framework will help improve the professional standard of investment advisory practice in the Thai capital market.

3. Regulatory Reforms

3.1 Listing Standards

To promote the number and quality of products available on the exchange, the SET started implementing the new securities listing criteria effective from 16 December 1999 onwards. Revised in line with the current economic environment and the disclosure-based screening policy, the new listing criteria are aimed at facilitating new listings of promising companies which may be temporarily affected by the economic downturn, promoting corporate information disclosure and fostering good corporate governance to enhance investors protection.

The SET also promoted good corporate governance of existing listed companies by firstly requiring them to establish audit committees within 1999. Secondly, the Committee on Good Corporate Governance was set up to set out a framework and provide advice with regard to the development of good corporate governance for listed companies, state enterprises, and other interested private companies. The SET has also established guidelines for shareholders' meetings of listed companies as a further measure to protect shareholders' rights. Lastly, the SET also established the Thai Institute of Directors Association to promote awareness of the roles and responsibilities of company directors and raise their professional standards.

3.2 Enterprise Accounting

The SEC works very closely with the Thai accounting association for setting the accounting standards to ensure that the Thai GAAP conforms to the International Accounting Standard (IAS). In addition, the SEC and the SET have become more stringent in reviewing financial statements of listed companies. The statements that are not in compliance with GAAP are rejected for correction. Moreover, auditors are closely monitored and sanctioned to ensure that their performance meets the high professional auditing standard.

3.3   Disclosure Requirement

The SEC has already approved, in principle, a gradual shift from the quantitative merit-based system of screening new offerings of securities to a much more disclosure-based system by amending the public offering rules. The greater emphasis is placed upon the improvement of corporate governance and disclosure standard.

In terms of good corporate governance, companies making public offering of securities have to clearly delineate authorities and responsibilities of their directors and set up effective management control mechanisms which are subject to annual reviews by their audit committees or independent directors.

With regard to the disclosure standard, risk assessment, both from financial and operational perspectives, must also be disclosed in greater details with mandatory comments through management discussion and analysis which must also be endorsed by financial advisors. Large financial exposure must be highlighted in great detail with accompanying explanation and assessment of their impact on the company's financial position. In the well-developed market with a disclosure-based environment, it is believed that institutional investors can help raise the standard of corporate disclosure and market discipline.

C.   Current Situation and Future Development

1.   Current Situation of the Capital Market

Recent progress in financial and economic reforms together with the low interest rate environment has helped boost investment sentiment and increase opportunities for Thai corporations to issue new securities. Investors have shifted their funds from low-return bank deposits to debt and equity securities with the hope for higher yields. On the issuers' side, several large corporations have reentered the capital market to mobilize funds given the low interest rate and the restoration of public confidence from economic recovery.

The financial turmoil caused the financial system to be more liberalized. Banking and securities sectors, which were a stronghold of Thai domestic companies, have now been largely taken over by overseas financial conglomerates as more new funds were injected into the ailing financial institutions. Taking Thai securities firms as an instance, they are no longer stand-alone corporations. Most of them are now subsidiaries of securities companies or commercial banks whose shares are held by large foreign financial conglomerates. A few of them also hold controlling shares in foreign financial institutions. This poses a new challenge to regulators of the financial market to foster strong cooperation and open exchanges of information in the supervision of these financial conglomerates.

2.   Challenges and Future Development

2.1   Quality and Diversity of Products on the Exchange

Owing to the recent financial crisis, many listed companies have had to go through the rehabilitation process and some others have experienced deteriorating performance, thereby dampening the attractiveness of the exchange in the eyes of investors. To help troubled companies weather the economic downturn, the authorities have strongly encouraged the debt restructuring process by revising the bankruptcy law to enable the rehabilitation of companies under financial distress.

Moreover, tax benefits are provided and fees for transfers of collateral are reduced for both creditors and debtors, who can jointly reach an agreement on debt restructuring.

To facilitate the debt restructuring of listed companies, the SET has relaxed criteria regarding listing, delisting, acquisition and sales of assets, related transactions, and mergers. For example, the SET will resume trading of companies, which have made significant progress in debt restructuring.

While the above effort may help alleviate product problems in that it allows listed companies in distress some time to cope, instead of being immediately delisted, in the long run it does not solve the exchange's problem of lack of attractiveness. The Thai authorities look to privatization of major promising state enterprises for their long-term solution.

The Corporatization Act became effective in December 1999 to facilitate the privatization process and allow state enterprises to raise capital directly from the capital market without adding burden to the government. According to the government's privatization plan, five state enterprises -- Thai Airways International, Ratchaburi Power Plant, Airport Authority of Thailand, Petroleum Authority of Thailand and Bangchak Petroleum -- are on track to be privatized within this year.

In line with the plan, the SET has encouraged listings of privatized companies by relaxing the listing criteria. The listing of more privatized companies will not only enhance the supply of large-capitalized and quality stocks but also lessen the sensitivity of the index to the performance of banking and finance sector, which currently represents the highest weight of almost 30% in the index.

2.2   Investor Education

While the overall Thai financial market faced the problem of overreliance on the banking sector, the capital market itself depended to a great extent on foreign funds, resulting in the vulnerability to capital flows.

One way to cushion the market against rapid capital mobility is to strengthen the domestic base of investments. As mentioned before, there is substantial room to penetrate the strong retail investor base and enhance their investments in the capital market, either directly or indirectly, through various types of funds.

During the period of economic downturn and the slump in the stock market, many people withdrew their investments and turned to put their funds in bank deposits, which previously offered very attractive rates. However, the continual fall in interest rates to a very low level has encouraged retail investors to reenter the capital market with the hope for higher returns.

The challenge is how to draw their investments without their misunderstanding about the risk-return feature of securities investments. Among these wrong expectations are the belief that the authorities will intervene and bail out their investments whenever problems arise, and the misconception that mutual funds are safe investments and will not bring in losses.

Regulations on better disclosure of information and codes of conduct for sales representatives of mutual funds and investment advisors could ensure that investors receive adequate and correct information. However, these measures are not enough. Regulators and related parties need to educate investors more about the role of regulators as well as risk and return features of financial instruments.such as bonds and derivatives so that investors have sufficient knowledge to analyze and understand possible outcomes of their alternative investments.

(i)   Securities Companies

After the revocation of foreign ownership limit in the financial sector, many banks and securities companies have been taken over by their foreign counterparts who also bring in new technology and customer base.   This factor, coupled with new technology, has thus intensified competition in the industry and motivated companies to continually increase their operational efficiency.   As the authorities attempt to lay down the sound infrastructure to promote a freely competitive market, they face a challenge to balance, on the one hand, the timely response to the globalization trend to keep up with other markets and the attention to the structural problems of local companies on the other hand. For example, the action plan and timeframe to move to the fully liberalized commission structure underwent extensive discussion and negotiation among related parties before they were finalized.

Since many securities companies are subsidiaries of commercial banks whose shares are held by foreign financial firms, financial market regulators need close cooperation and open exchanges of information both domestically and internationally to effectively supervise these financial conglomerates.

(ii)   Stock Market

With the advent of new technology, a growing number of alternative trading systems (ATSs) have been developed as low-priced choices for securities trading in competition with traditional stock exchanges.   These ATSs blur the distinction between broker-dealers and exchanges, thereby raising questions among regulators about how they should be regulated.   Facing increasing competitive pressure from these ATSs, exchanges throughout the world including the SET are conducting studies to improve their efficiency and to find out appropriate structure and strategy to adapt to the changing market environment.

The SET has also formed strategic alliances with other exchanges to exchange information, technology and expertise as well as facilitate cross-border listing and cross-border trading in the future.   As for the SEC, our role is to ensure that our regulatory framework does not pose unnecessary obstacles to players (brokers as well as exchanges) in their attempt to cope with the new environment.

516 544
853 612 618

THE LATEST DEVELOPMENTS IN THE SECURITIES MARKETS IN CHINESE TAIPEI

(Taiwan)

by
Mr. Kuang-Wha Ding

Due to globalization and liberalization of financial markets and the introduction of new financial instruments, securities regulators need to keep themselves abreast of the on-going changes in both domestic and international markets. This is especially true in the wake of the regional financial crisis, by which many economies were affected. In order to address the problems, the Securities and Futures Commission in Taiwan has initiated several new measures to meet the challenges. Let me briefly introduce them as follows:

1. Market developments during the past year:

a) Continued to expand the market size by encouraging companies to tap the capital markets. Total listed companies has grown from 437 in 1998 to 462 in 1999; OTC quoted companies from 176 in 1998 to 264 in 1999; publicly held companies from 1,810 in 1998 to 2,018 in 1999.

b) Total market capitalization exceeded US$ 390 billion as of the end of 1999 and is about the same size as Australia. The stock market constitutes 110% of our national GDP last year as compared to 96.24% in 1998.

c) The annual trading value (or turnover) in 1999 reached US$ 917.3 billion, ranking Taiwan Stock Exchange the 4th largest stock exchange in the world, only after New York, London and Tokyo.

2. Significant market events during the past year.

a) Excessive cross-holding of shares, misappropriation of company's funds and poor financial management by some listed companies at the end of 1998 and early 1999 resulted in severe problems. In light of the situation, the Commission amended relevant regulations to restrict companies from creating investment vehicles to hold the shares of the parent companies. The Commission has also strengthened mechanisms to monitor the internal control of publicly held companies. It also enhanced the responsibility of CPAs in auditing both their financial statements and internal control systems. These efforts should be able to improve the corporate governance standards of public companies.

b) In order to better protect the interest of minority shareholders and creditors of affiliate companies, the Commission issued guidelines for the preparation of consolidated financial statements and operational reports to enhance the transparency of the business and financial operations of the controlling company.

c) The Commission promulgated the "Criteria for Mergers and Acquisitions among Securities Firms" with a view to expanding their operating size and improving competitiveness of securities business.

d) In the wake of the massive earthquake that occurred on September 21 last year, the Commission quickly took a series of measures, including closing down the market for four trading days and adjusted the price-down limit from 7% to 3.5%, to reduce volatility. The measures proved to be effective, and fortunately, no default was reported after the natural disaster.

3. Significant measures that have been instituted during the past year.

a) The Commission has decided to launched a second board market for the shares of smaller firms to be traded on the OTC market. It is expected that many small- to medium-sized enterprises, and start-up technology & Internet firms will be interested in floating their shares on the second board, or Taiwan Innovative Growing Entrepreneurs, "TIGER". Listing procedures and requirements for such companies will be significantly relaxed. In the meantime, the Commission will require a high standard of information disclosures, place more responsibility on the part of sponsoring underwriters and CPAs, and require company directors, supervisors, managers, and major shareholders to deposit their shares with the central depository.

b) In order to better protect investors, the Commission has drafted the "Securities Investors/Futures Traders Protection Bill". The bill, currently under legislative review and if enacted, will create a fund to compensate the losses of investors in case of defaults by securities firms or futures commission merchants. The law will also introduce the system of class legal action.

c) The Commission has encouraged the Taiwan Futures Exchange to increase its product line by introducing contracts on electronic sector and financial and insurance sector indices. Products on TAIEX options and short-term interest rate futures contracts are under consideration. And in order to increase the trading of futures contracts, the Commission has allowed futures brokers to take orders through the Internet. The Commission also publicized relevant regulations to safeguard the security of on-line trading.

d) The Commission raised the ceiling of share ownership of any listed/quoted company by foreign investors to 50%. It is expected that by January next year, the ceiling will be lifted. The Commission has also raised the maximum quota for each Qualified Foreign Institutional Investor to invest in Taiwan's securities markets from US$ 600 million to US$ 1.2 billion. As of the end of February, this year total net remitted-in amount by foreign investors amounted to US$ 27 billion, or 7.2% of our market capitalization

e) The Commission has proposed to amend Article 171 of the Securities and Exchange Law to increase civil and criminal penalties on corporate directors, supervisors, managers and employees in the event of insider trading and price manipulation. The draft article is being reviewed by relevant committees of the Lgislative Yuan (the Parliament).

f) The Commission required all securities and futures related organizations and public companies to step up their preparation in solving the Y2K problem. The efforts proved to be successful. No damages were reported.

g) Because the securities markets in Taiwan are retail-driven and are highly liable to the impact of non-economic factors, a stabilizing mechanism, or the National Stabilization Fund, was created by law to deal with the situation.

4. **Latest developments in our markets:**

a) In order to encourage merger of listed or OTC quoted companies, to safeguard investor interest and to ensure markets order, the Commission has issued "Rules governing merger of listed or OTC quoted companies" in February this year

b) The Commission has instructed the Taiwan Stock Exchange to revise rules for after-hour-trading. New rules will allow investors to trade stocks after the market closes at 12:00. The after-hour-trading will start at 12:30 and ends at 13:00, and the reference price will be fixed at the closing price of the same trading day.

c) To meet the trend of on-line trading across international securities markets, the Commission is considering extending daily trading hour from the present three hours in the morning to the afternoon. Details of the modification are still under review. It is expected that longer trading hours will attract more interest and meet the demand of global institutional investors.

My dear colleagues, my Commission has been working hard to improve investor protection and promote market development. We are also committed to working closely with regulators in other markets and in abiding by the rules or guidelines of international organizations such as the OECD and IOSCO. I believe our open discussion will be beneficial for all participants of this Round Table. I look forward to your comments and suggestions. Thank you very much.

Annex II

AGENDA

Tuesday, 11th April

9:00 a.m.   Welcome remarks by **Mr. Seiichi Kondo**, Deputy Secretary-General, OECD

Welcome remarks by **Dr. Masaru Yoshitomi**, Dean, Asian Development Bank Institute

Introductory remarks by the Moderator, **Prof. Anthony Neoh**, Peking University

9:40 a.m.   **Part I: Progress in Capital Market Reforms in Asia**

Progress in Capital Market Reforms in Hong Kong and the Activities of the Implementation Committee of IOSCO Principles: **Mr. Andrew Procter**, Member of the Commission and Executive Director, Securities & Futures Commission, Hong Kong and Chairman of the Implementation Committee of IOSCO Principles (15 minutes)

Presentation on India: **Mr. Devendra Raj Mehta**, Chairman, Securities and Exchange Board of India (10 minutes)

Presentation on Indonesia: **Mr. Herwidayatmo**, Chairman, Capital Market Supervisory Agency, Indonesia (10 minutes)

Presentation on Malaysia: **Mr. Ali Abdul Kadir,** Chairman, Securities Commission, Malaysia (10 minutes)

10:45 a.m.   Presentation on the progress of macroeconomic stability and capital market reforms in the Asian economy: **Mr. Kunio Saito**, Director, Regional Office for Asia and the Pacific, International Monetary Fund (15 minutes)

Capital Market Reform in Japan: **Mr. Masamichi Kono**, Director, Planning and Legal Affairs Division, Financial Supervisory Agency, Japan (10 minutes)

Presentation on Thailand: **Mr. Prasarn Trairatvorakul**, Secretary-General, Securities and Exchange Commission, Thailand (10 minutes)

The Latest Development in Taiwan's Securities Markets: **Mr. Kung-Wha Ding**, Vice Chairman, Securities and Futures Commission, Chinese Taipei (10 minutes)

Q & A Session (20 minutes)

12:00 p.m.   Lunch: Luncheon speech: **Mr. Haruhiko Kuroda**, Vice Minister for International Affairs, Ministry of Finance, Japan

2:00 p.m.   **Part II: Development of Bond Markets in Asia**

Session 1: Introduction

Overview presentation, **Prof. Eisuke Sakakibara**, Keio University, Former Vice Minister for International Affairs, Ministry of Finance, Japan (15 minutes)

Developing a Viable Corporate Bond Market Under a Bank-dominated System: Analytical Issues and Policy Implications: **Prof. Shinji Takagi**, Visiting Scholar, Asian Development Bank Institute (15 minutes)

Q & A Session (20 minutes)

Session 2: Experience in Asia and Policy Issues to be Addressed

Strategy to Develop Domestic Bond Market - Case of Thailand - : **Mr. Noritaka Akamatsu**, Principal Financial Economist, Capital Markets Development Department, World Bank (15 minutes)

Presentation on the view points of Singapore, **Ms. Yeo Lian Sim**, Assistant Managing Director, Capital Markets, Monetary Authority of Singapore (15 minutes)

Singaporean Experience in Bond Market Development: **Mr. Toshio Karigane**, Senior Executive Advisor, Daiwa Institute of Research (15 minutes)

3:55 p.m.   Debt Market in China: **Dr. Gao Jian**, CFO and Chief Economist, China Development Bank, China (15 minutes)

Presentation on the view points of Hong Kong, **Mr. Norman Tak-lam Chan**, Deputy Chief Executive, Hong Kong Monetary Authority (15 minutes)

Presentation on the Issues to be Tackled for the Development of Bond Market: **Mr. Lawrence Fok**, Senior Executive Director, Stock Exchange of Hong Kong (15 minutes)

Experience of bond market development in Malaysia: **Mr. Ranjit Ajit Singh**, General Manager, Economic Analysis & Financial Policy, Securities Commission, Malaysia (15 minutes)

Policy Agenda for Bond Market Development in Asia: **Dr. Yun-Hwan Kim**, Senior Economist, Asian Development Bank (20 minutes)

Presentation on the development of regional bond markets in the context of the New Miyazawa initiative: **Mr. Toshio Kobayashi**, Director, International Finance Division, International Bureau, Ministry of Finance, Japan (15 minutes)

Q & A Session (20 minutes)

Wednesday, 12th April

9:00 a.m.   **Part II Session 3: Lessons from the Experience in OECD Countries and other Emerging Economies**

The Development of Fixed Income Securities Markets in Emerging Market Economies: Key Issues and Policy Actions: **Mr. Hendrikus Blommestein**, Senior Economist, Financial Affairs Division, Directorate for Financial, Fiscal and Enterprise Affairs, OECD (15 minutes)

Developments in European Bond Markets: **Dr. Hans-Dieter Hanfland**, Division Chief, Ministry of Finance, Germany (15 minutes)

The Reforms of the Japanese Government Securities Market: **Mr. Masaaki Shirakawa**, Advisor to the Governor, Financial Markets Department, Bank of Japan (15 minutes)

Further Reforms After the <Big Bang>: The Japanese Government Bond Market: **Prof. Ghon Rhee**, University of Hawaii (15 minutes)

Corporate Bond Markets Development: **Mr. Tadashi Endo**, Senior Capital Markets Specialist, Capital Markets Development Group, Financial Markets Advisory Department, International Finance Corporation (15minutes)

Q & A Session (20 minutes)

10:55 a.m.   **Session 4: The roles of securities laws and securities market regulators for the sound development of bond markets**

The Role of Regulators in the Development of Government Securities Markets: an Overview: **Mr. Giovanni Sabatini**, Head of Market Regulation Office, Commissione Nazionale per le Societa e la Borsa, Italy, and Chairman of the WP 2 of the Technical Committee of IOSCO (15 minutes)

Developing Bond Futures Markets: **Mr. Rick Shilts**, Acting Director, Division of Economic Analysis, Commodity Futures Trading Commission (15 minutes)

Mr. David Strachan, Head of Department, Market Conduct and Infrastructure, Financial Service Authority, UK (15 minutes)

Transparency in the U.S. Debt Markets: **Mr. Stephen Williams**, Senior Special Advisor, Securities and Exchange Commission, US (15 minutes)

The Roles of Securities Laws and Securities Market Regulators for the Sound Development of Bond Markets: Australia: **Ms. Claire Grose,** Director, National Markets Unit, Australia Securities and Investment Commission (15 minutes)

2:00 p.m.   **Session 4 (continued)**

Q & A Session (20 minutes)

2:20 p.m.   **Session 5: Tour de table**

Development of Local Currency Markets in the Asia Pacific Region: **Mr. Kevan Watts**, Executive Chairman, Asia Pacific Region, Merrill Lynch International Inc. (15 minutes)

Ms. Julia Turner, Managing Director, Moody's Asia Pacific Ltd. (15 minutes)

A Domestic Rating Agency in an Emerging Asian Country: the TRIS Experience: **Dr. Warapatr Todhanakasem**, President, Thai Rating and Information Services (15 minutes)

Current Conditions and Development in Asian Domestic Bond Markets and Further Steps: **Mr. Fumiyuki Sasaki**, Senior Economist, Economic Research Department, Nomura Research Institute (15 minutes)

3:40 p.m.   Discussant:
Dr. Takatoshi Ito, Deputy Vice Minister for International Affairs, Ministry of Finance, Japan (Former Professor of Hitotsubashi University) (15 minutes)

3:55 p.m.   Tour de table (110 minutes)

5:45 p.m.   **Concluding Session**

Round Table concludes at 6:00 p.m.

Annex III

SUGGESTED POINTS FOR DISCUSSION

Part I: Progress in Capital Market Reforms in Asia

The development of capital markets since the first Round Table will be discussed, with particular emphasis on the progress of policy initiatives and their effects on the market. Policy initiatives that each country is planning to implement will be introduced as well.

− Following the severe turbulence of 1997-98, both fixed-income and equity markets in Asia staged a strong recovery during 1999. While foreign banks and investors reduced their exposure to emerging markets in 1997-98 a sharp reversal of this trend became visible in 1999. To some extent this reflects the unexpectedly strong recovery from recession in Asian countries which gathered momentum throughout the year.

− Although the volume of new issues of debt by Asian countries did not recover strongly in 1999, spreads on debt declined appreciably especially later in the year. Throughout 1999, yields on Asian sovereign bonds have been sharply compressed as investors have bid aggressively, partly in anticipation of expected future upgrades. Spreads on some Asian countries are considerably narrower than in 1997. This improvement in conditions for Asian borrowers occurred despite steadily rising world interest rates, which have usually been a sign of impending trouble for emerging markets.

− There are some doubts as to the extent to which the sharp gyrations in equity prices in the past two years can be explained in terms of fundamentals. It can be argued that with declines in Asian exchange rates and equity indices in 1997-98 and with some signs of structural reforms, investors sought to build up positions in those markets that appeared to be clearly undervalued. However, it is equally credible that the wide swings of the past three years have been out of proportion to actual changes and to the implementation of the reforms in Asian markets.

− How do participants interpret the strong recovery of Asian Markets in 1999? Have any particular kinds of investors been most prominent in driving markets to higher levels?

− What is the current situation of financial sector reform, and particularly capital market reform? Are the items to be pointed out as causes of the crisis, such as a weak banking sector, inappropriate risk management, insufficient supervision, being addressed in a proper manner?

− To what degree is the sharp recovery in equity markets reconcilable with only modest progress in introducing structural reforms?

–   Is there a real danger that the ease of obtaining external financing will lead to a slacking in efforts to persevere with reforms? Will improved market conditions for Asian countries and economic recovery make it more difficult to maintain the momentum in structural reforms, especially financial sector reforms?

–   In what ways are the Asian countries less vulnerable to a reversal of investor sentiment than before the 1997 crisis? How would additional increases in world interest rates or a major correction in the stock markets of OECD countries affect the Asian markets?

–   There were a number of policy initiatives on securities market reforms and market intervention during the period of the crisis. It seems that the evaluation of the international community on market intervention and market regulation taken during the crisis has somewhat changed and favourable arguments dealing with those measures have been increasing. On the other hand, there is still a strong argument against the introduction of capital control, especially on capital outflow. They claim that such measures have a negative effect on investors' sentiment in the medium term and can adversely affect the development of financial markets. Taking these various views into account, what are participants' current evaluation of these market interventions and regulations?

–   What is the current situation of the implementation of the IOSCO Principles in Asian countries? What is the self-evaluation of each securities commission on this issue? Are there any specific characteristics in Asia in comparison with other parts of the world? What is the action plan of each securities commission in order to further progress the implementation?

–   What are the participants' evaluation on the new phenomenon of demutualisation and mergers of various exchanges in the region and the challenges these changes will bring to the regulators?

–   Corporate governance is now regarded as a main basic issue to be addressed in Asia for the future development of the economy, including financial markets. In this respect, what is the participants' evaluation on the situation of corporate governance of each respective country and what policy measures are they going to take to tackle this issue?

Part II: Development of Bond Markets in Asia

A.   *Overview*

–   The development of liquid, sound and deep bond markets has become one of the most important policy issues in the financial sector in Asian countries. In fact, though this issue has been discussed for a while now, the Asian financial crisis re-emphasised its importance, and it is worth discussing this issue in the framework of the post-crisis landscape.

–   Actually a mature and liquid bond market can improve resource allocation by effectively channelling both local and foreign savings into domestic investments and can diversify the investment channels for investors. Greater diversification of financing and investment channels is beneficial to the stability of financial markets.

– This issue has to be discussed from the following four viewpoints of the market:

    (1) Demand Side, especially Institutional Investors, including pension funds
    (2) Issuer, Supply side
    (3) Regulator, securities laws
    (4) Market operator (Stock exchange), rating agencies and the securities industry

– The description of the issue of bond market development owes much to "Compendium of Sound Practices ---Guidelines to Facilitate the Development of Domestic Bond Markets in APEC Member Economies ---", APEC Collaborative Initiative on Development of Domestic Bond Markets, September 1999

B. *Issues related to Domestic Bond Markets*

The following issues will be discussed from the viewpoint of the development of domestic bond markets in Asia. The lessons from the experience in OECD countries and other emerging economies including Latin America will also be discussed.

(1) *The situation of bond markets in each country*

– Though the Asian domestic bond markets have been growing steadily, they are still generally underdeveloped. In fact judging from the ratios of market capitalisation to GDP, there is plenty of room for further improvement in this field in Asia.

– Supply side (1) --- In Asia, bonds were issued mainly by governments to finance budget deficits and infrastructure developments. There is and will be a massive amount of issues of government bonds in Asia to fund the capital injections to financial institutions and other fiscal demands, including infrastructure development in the coming years. In several countries the supply of bonds has increased as fiscal policy turned more expansionary. How does this affect the development, structure and functioning of government bonds markets?

– Supply side (2) --- In some Asian countries there is growth in asset-backed securities and mortgage backed securities.

– Demand side --- The necessity of well-developed bond markets for sound fund management of institutional investors, especially pension funds ---

– Banks and financial institutions are the major buyers of Asian bonds. However, with increasing income and aging populations, most countries are in the process of establishing funded pension schemes. Collective investment instruments are also expanding aggressively in Asian as people have more money to invest for their future. Therefore, the demand for Asian bonds is likely to increase in the coming years. However, considerable institutional strengthening will be necessary in the institutional investor sector.

– What policy measures have governments in the region been taking for the development of bond markets? Is there consensus to develop domestic bond markets among different parties concerned, such as government, central banks, regulators, facilitators and issuers? In this context, what roles have securities market regulators been taking on this issue?

– Private sector bond issuance was not active in Asian countries. The reason is that Asian corporations are usually assigned lower public credit ratings, which makes private sector bonds less attractive to investors. After the crisis, however, banking sectors still have serious problems on non-performing assets and have difficulties in their lending activities. What are the prospects for sound companies to issue corporate bonds in view of the lack of ability of banks to sustain adequate lending volumes at present? How rapidly will corporate bond markets be able to adjust to these new capital demand requirements? What interrelations can be expected to influence the development of a corporate bond market with that of government securities markets?

(2)   *Bond market development in the analytical framework of the development of financial markets in Asia*

– What are the determinants of the development of financial market in Asia? Given the fact that in many countries the financial system is banking sector-led, how could any reform measures or incentives be best sequenced to develop financial markets, especially the bond market?

– In this respect should the model of the development be different for each country by the stage of economic development and institutional capability? Or are there core economic principles that hold true generally?

(3)   *The necessity to develop sound institutional investors*

– On the demand side of securities markets, it is necessary to develop sound institutional savings: mutual funds, insurance companies and pension finds. In general, research indicates that the interaction between institutional investors and financial markets works in both directions: institutional investors contribute to the growth and development of financial markets, but, in order for these institutions to operate efficiently, they are themselves dependent on the presence of a supportive securities market infrastructure.

– Though there are some institutional investors in Asia, they tend to adopt a buy-and-hold strategy due to their long-term investment horizons. There are a small number of institutional investors who actively trade Asian bonds. One of the reasons why institutional investors remain in an undeveloped stage, is that Asian people tend to hold a very large share of assets in bank deposits, though they have high savings rates.

– Foreign institutional investors may play an important role in promoting the fund management industry in the region by introducing the experience and the technology developed in other regions in regards to improvements in products and on the architecture of a market.

– What policy measures are needed to promote the growth of the institutional savings and to activate the investment activities of institutional investors in Asia?

(4)   *Development of an effective primary market*

- The development of an effective primary market is an important element of bond market development. Emphasis should especially be placed on a primary market for government securities. Various auction models can be explored with a view to adopting the appropriate model, which can serve to enhance efficiency of bond issuance.

(5)   *Establishment of benchmark yield curves*

- Most Asian economies have maintained government benchmark yield curves up to about 10 years. In exceptional cases corporate bonds are used as the yield curve benchmark. In fact it is difficult to maintain a reliable yield curve because of the buy-and-hold strategy of pension funds and long-term investors. Without an active secondary market, the yield curve would not be accurate or credible.

- Most yield curves are below 10 years. This has made pricing for corporate debt securities in the secondary markets difficult, especially for long-maturity bonds. A number of measures could help to build up an accurate and reliable benchmark yield curve. These include, (a) regular issuance of bonds at appropriately spaced benchmark maturities along the entire yield curve in order to build up liquidity, (b) large volume issuance of bond issues to maintain liquidity, and (c) issuance of new bonds of long maturity to maintain the length of the yield curve. In this regard governments should have a plan to issue government bonds to maintain the reliability and accuracy of the yield curves. What are the attitudes of governments in this regard?

- A benchmark yield curve is also essential for the sound risk management of financial institutions in order to evaluate their asset on a mark-to-market basis. This would also attract more institutional investors to bond markets.   Therefore financial market regulators have to push the establishment of a reliable yield curve from the viewpoint of promoting appropriate risk management of financial institutions.

(6)   *Development of secondary market of bonds: Primary dealer, size of issuance*

- The development of a secondary market is essential for the development of a bond market. However, secondary markets of bonds in Asia are generally inactive and lack liquidity. There are a number of reasons for this. The attitude of institutional investors mentioned above is one. Another reason is that Asian bonds are often issued in small sizes. Due to low liquidity and inactive secondary market trading, the bid/offer spreads are often very wide, and this makes trading very costly.

- There is a lack of committed market makers. Committed market makers are important for active secondary trading. Due to the volatility of Asian bonds relative to the bonds issued in developed countries, financial institutions and securities houses are not keen to make prices on bonds. In this regard is the primary dealer system useful and viable in Asian countries? What are the lessons to be learned from the experience in OECD countries in the primary dealer system?

- Having taken the above-mentioned points into account, what policy measures are involved in the sound development of secondary markets?

(7)   *Credit rating agency*

–   Credit rating agencies have to play a very important role for the development of bond markets. They should be encouraged to maintain and improve their credibility and reputation by avoiding conflict of interests in their ownership, staffing and decision-making processes. They are also requested to allow issuers to comment on draft rating opinions when possible; maintaining the highest possible level of transparency and objectivity in the rating processes; and publicly disclosing their policies on unsolicited ratings.

–   In several Asian countries joint ventures with foreign credit rating agencies have been formed and the domestic rating business has started its development.

–   In what respect can rating agencies be expected to improve their performance in the future? What role are 'domestic' rating agencies likely to perform?

(8)   *Credit Guarantees (New Miyazawa Initiative)*

–   In the "Resource Mobilization Plan for Asia --- The Second Stage of the New Miyazawa Plan" (May 1999) Mr. Miyazawa, Minister of Finance of Japan, announced that Japan stood ready to provide assistance to mobilize domestic and foreign private-sector funds for Asia through such measures as credit guarantees by the "Export-Import Bank of Japan" (now "Japan Bank for International Cooperation"). How has this scheme been operating so far? What kind of effect will it have on financing by Asian countries and by the private sector in Asia?

(9)   *Others*

–   'Improvement of securities clearing and settlement system' and 'Development of derivative markets for the enhancement of investment strategy and better risk management for investors' are the topics we should also need to address for the development of bond markets.

C.   *Issues Related to Regional Bond markets in Asia*

(1)   *The necessity of the development of the regional bond market*

–   An Asian regional bond is a bond issued by an issuer in the region in markets in the region. The idea of regional bonds is to facilitate direct financing within the region.

–   What do the participants think of the idea of regional bonds? In this context in what currency should regional bonds be denominated?

(2)   *Cross border placement and trading of bonds in Asia*

–   What are the impediments to cross border placement and trading of bonds in Asia? What measures should be taken to address them? What are the major obstacles for Asian investors to purchase Asian regional bonds? In this context what do the participants think about the following ideas?

-- Regionalized trading system

-- Regionalized listing requirements

-- Regionalized clearing and settlement system

–   In this respect it is proposed that Asian countries should develop bilateral or multilateral linkages between their securities settlement systems, with a view to promoting efficient clearing and securities settlement system, which can reduce transaction cost as well as settlement risk. What initiatives may be required to facilitate the cross border linkage of the clearing system of bonds?

(3)   *Regulatory harmonisation*

–   In this context is regulatory harmonisation on the regional level a prerequisite for the development of regional bond markets?

(4)   *Lessons to be learned from the experience in other regions*

D.   *The roles of securities law and securities market regulators for the sound development of bond markets*

Securities market regulators have responsibilities to implement appropriate regulations not only on the equity market but also on the bond market. Securities laws have to be suitable to the sound development of bond markets.

In fact, an effective regulatory and supervision framework for bond markets, intermediaries, institutional investors and other market participants is essential for adequate investor protection and sound business practices that reduce systemic risks.

(1)   *The role of securities laws*

–   What role should securities laws have to take in the regulation of bond markets, particularly laws concerning issue and continuing disclosure to bond holders, as well as laws relating to market malpractice, such as insider trading and market manipulation? Are the existing securities laws paying due consideration to these aspects?

–   Regulation should promote transparency in trading and price reporting and deter manipulation and unfair trading practices. What is the participants' evaluation on the current regulation in this respect? What further policy measures, if any, should be taken in this respect?

–   The legal and regulatory framework should clearly differentiate between bank deposits, money market instruments and debt instruments and set out the respective applicable regulatory regime. What is the current legal and regulatory framework in this regard?

(2)   Disclosure

–   Investors need full, timely and accurate disclosure to make investment decisions. In the absence of adequate accounting, auditing, and financial reporting, it is not possible for the investors and the securities markets to properly value securities. Greater emphasis is now being placed on the adequacy of accounting, auditing and disclosure standards. Disclosure requirements of debt issuers should be enhanced. More financial information would give confidence to bond investors. How do participants evaluate the current situation in regards to full, timely and accurate disclosure of information material to investment decisions? What policy measures, if any, have to be taken in this regard in the future?

(3)   Transparency in the primary and the secondary markets, including listing standards

–   Transparency in secondary market price reporting and trading activity is important to the valuation of securities. It contributes to pricing efficiency and thereby aids in establishing a market-based yield curve. The appropriate level of disclosure of large exposure and position concentration, with due consideration to ensuring anonymity of market participants, can be useful for enhancing market transparency and stability. These measures will deter manipulation and unfair trading practices.

–   Where bonds are listed on stock exchanges, objective criteria have to be established and adhered to for the listing and de-listing of debt securities on the stock exchange. This contributes to an increase of confidence in the market.

–   Measures should be taken to enhance transparency in the primary and secondary markets to promote market participation, and hence market liquidity. For example, disclosure of information about the general issuance strategy could help market participants formulate their investment strategies.

–   What are the regulatory frameworks on these points in Asian countries and their future prospects? How should the activities of SROs be assessed in this regard?

(4)   Private Placement

–   There should be a clear differentiation of private placement and public offering to assess the appropriate level of regulation required. For applications for exemption of securities from the public offering disclosure requirement, there should be objective criteria to differentiate between public offering and private placement and to distinguish sophisticated investors from other investors.

(5)   *Regulatory framework*

- In view of the diversity of bank and non-bank participants in the bond market, defining roles, responsibilities, and objectives of the relevant regulatory authorities is essential for a well-organised market. The existence of financial conglomerates engaged in banking, securities, and other financial services as well as serving both dealers and brokers in bond markets, may complicate the job of regulators. Co-operation with SROs is important as well.

- The legal and regulatory framework should clearly differentiate between bank deposits, money market instruments and debt instruments, and set out the respective applicable regulatory regime. It is important to define instruments carefully to avoid the creation of potential regulatory gaps or unequal regulations of similar financial products.

- There must be a clear legal mandate for the government or the regulatory authorities to exercise appropriate and adequate oversight in order to ensure that self-regulatory organisations are performing their duties in a fair and transparent manner.

- Having taken the above-mentioned points into account, what is the participants' evaluation of the current regulatory framework? What further measures have to be taken in this respect and what are the impediments to doing so?

(6)   *Regulatory framework for the instruments for hedging in the bond markets*

- As many sophisticated products are introduced to the markets, it is imperative that regulations and compliance standards be developed to protect the investors' interests.

- For example, the development of repo and futures markets may also provide some participants with opportunities for squeezing the cash market. This possibility requires the monitoring of cash, repo and futures markets and entering the markets as necessary. Measures may include limiting the short selling of financial instruments through increasing margin requirements and preventing short selling below the best offer price. What are the lessons from the experience in the OECD countries as well as in emerging economies in this respect? What regulatory and risk management structures are needed with regards to the development of combined debt-equity instruments and derivative instruments for hedging in the bond markets?

(7)   *Others*

- Appropriate regulation of institutional investors is also necessary for promoting institutional investors and thus the development of bond markets.

Annex IV

LIST OF PARTICIPANTS

CHAIRMAN

Prof. Anthony Francis Neoh
Professor
Shao Yuan, Block 5, Room 206, Peking University
Haidian District, Beijing, China
Chief Advisor, China Securities Regulatory Commission
Jin Yang Plaza, 16 Jin Rong Street,
Beijing 100032 PRC
Tel: 8610 8806-1383. 8806-1018
Fax: 8610 8806 1028
Email: tonyneoh@pacific.net.hk

OECD Countries

GERMANY

Dr. Hans-Dieter Hanfland
Division Chief
Ministry of Finance
Grautheindorfer Str. 108
53117 Bonn, Germany
Tel: 49 228 682 1525
Fax: 49 228 682 4646

AUSTRALIA

Ms. Claire Grose
Director, National Markets Unit
Australian Securities and Investments Commission
Level 18, 1 Martin Place
Sydney, NSW 2000 Australia
Tel: 612 9911 2069
Fax: 612 9911 2138
E-mail: claire.grose@asic.gov.au

AUSTRIA

Mr. Paul Maier
Deputy Head of Division
Österreichische Nationalbank
Otto Wagner Platz
A 1090 Vienna, Austria
Tel: 431 404 20 3201
Fax: 431 404 20 3299
Email: Paul.Maier@oenb.co.at

CANADA	Mr. John C. Sloan Counsellor (Finance) Embassy of Canada, Tokyo 7-3-38 Akasaka Minato-ku, Tokyo 107 Tel: 813 5412 6294 Fax: 813 5412 6260 Email: john.sloan@dfait-maeci-gc.ca
KOREA	Mr. Chang-Kuk Ahn Deputy Director Securities Policy Division Ministry of Finance and Economy Chhong-Ang Dong 1 Kwa-Chon, Kyoung-Ki Do 247-760 S. Korea Tel: 82 2500 5063/5 Fax: 82 2503 9265 Email: zest88@mofe.go.kr
	Mr. Hyun-Chol Park Deputy Director Market Monitoring Division Financial Supervisory Commission 27 Yoido-Dong, YeungDungPo-Gu Seoul, Korea Tel: 82 2 3771 5209 Fax: 82 2 3771 5163 Email: hcpark@fsc.go.kr
	Mr. Doo Yong Yang Research Fellow Korea Institute of International Economic Policy (KIEP) 300-4 Yomgok-dong, Seocho-Gu Seoul 137-747 Korea Tel: 82-2 3460-1227 Fax: 82 2 3460 1212 Email: yangdy@kiep.go.kr
UNITED STATES	Mr. Rick Shilts Acting Director Division of Economic Analysis Commodity Futures Trading Commission Three Lafayette Centre 1155 21st Street, NW Washington DC 20581 USA Tel: 1 202 418 5275 Fax: 1 202 418 5527 Email: rshilts@cftc.gov
	Mr. Stephen Williams Senior Special Advisor Securities and Exchange Commission 450 Fifth Street, NW Washington, DC 20549 USA Tel: 1 202 942 0071 Fax: 1 202 942 9643 Email: WilliamsSt@sec.gov

Prof. S. Ghon Rhee
K.J. Luke Chair of International Finance and Banking
Univeristy of Hawaii, College of Business Administration
2404 Maile Way, C-304
FEI/CBA
Honolulu, Hawaii 96822 USA
Tel: 1 808 956 2535
Fax: 1 808 956 2532
Email: RheeSG@Hawaii.edu

Mr. Hiroshi Yoshida
Visiting Scholar
Asia-Pacific Financial Markets Research Center
Univeristy of Hawaii, College of Business Administration
2404 Maile Way, D-308
Honolulu, Hawaii 96822-2223
Tel: 1 808 956 8418
Fax: 1 808 956 8729
Email: hyoshida@cba.hawaii.edu

FRANCE

Mr. Sebastien Clanet
International Banking Systems Specialist
Banking Commission
115 Rue de Réaumur
75002 Paris, France
Tel: +331 42 92 6616
Fax: +331 42 92 20 15
Email: sai@banque-france.fr

Mr. Jean-Yves Marquet
Financial Attaché
French Embassy, Japan
PMC Bldg, 8F
1-23-5 Higashi Azabu Minato-ku
Tokyo 106-0044 Japan
Tel: 813 3582 7432
Fax: 813 3582 0490
ely^. This is because investment of long-o.or.jp

HUNGARY

Mr. Béla Teremi
Director and Chief Representative
National Bank of Hungary
Tokyo Representative Office
1-7-1 yurakucho Chiyoda-ku
Tokyo 100-0006 Japan
Tel: 813 3201 2811
Fax: 813 3216 0430
Email: nbhtyo@gol.com

ITALY

Mr. Giovanni Sabatini
Head of Market Regulation Office
Commissione Nazionale per le Societa e la Borsa
Via Mantova, 1
00198 Rome, Italy
Tel: 39 06 8477327
Fax: 39 06 8477487
Email: g.sabatini@consob.it

Mr. Alberto Cogliati
Deputy Chief Representative
Bank of Italy, Representative Office for Japan, Hong Kong,
Singapore
ARK Mori Building, West Wing 27 fl., 1-12-32, Akasaka,
Minato-ku, Tokyo 107-6027 Japan
Tel: 813 3588 8111
Fax: 813 3588 8008
Email: bitokyo@mx.miinet.or.jp

JAPAN

Dr. Takatoshi Ito
Deputy Vice Minister for International Affairs
Ministry of Finance
3-1-1 Kasumagaseki, Chiyoda-ku
Tokyo 100-8940 Japan
Tel: 813 3581 4720
Fax: 813 5251 2144
Email: takatoshi.ito@mof.go.jp

Mr. Toshio Kobayashi
Director
International Finance Division
International Bureau, Ministry of Finance
3-1-1, Kasumigaseki, Chiyoda-ku
Tokyo 100-8940, Japan
Tel: 813 3581 4111(Ex 2860)
Fax: 813 5251 2170
Email: toshio.kobayashi@mof.go.jp

Mr. Masayuki Tamagawa
Director, Research Office
Financial System Planning Bureau, Ministry of Finance
3-1-1, Kasumigaseki, Chiyoda-ku
Tokyo 100-8940, Japan
Tel: 813 3581 7636
Fax: 813 5251 2213
Email: sem04scu@mof.go.jp

Mr. Yasushi Kanzaki
Director for International Affairs
Financial System Planning Bureau
Ministry of Finance
3-1-1, Kasumigaseki, Chiyoda-ku
Tokyo 100-8940 Japan
Tel: 813 3581 7636
Fax: 813 5251 2213
Email: yasushi.kanzaki@mof.go.jp

Mr. Toru Shikibu
Director, Securities Business Supervision
Financial Supervisory Agency
3-1-1 Kasumigaseki, Chiyoda-ku
Tokyo 100-0013 Japan
Tel: 813 3506 6107
Fax: 813 3506 6117
Email: t-sikibu@fsa.go.jp

Mr. Masamichi Kono
Director
Planning and Legal Affairs Division
Financial Supervisory Agency
3-1-1 Kasumigaseki, Chiyoda-ku
Tokyo 100-0013 Japan
Tel: 813 3506 6040
Fax: 813 3506 6113
Email: m-kuono@fsa.go.jp

Ms. Ginko Sato
Chairperson
Securities and Exchange Surveillance Commission
3-1-1, Kasumigaseki, Chiyoda-ku
Tokyo 100-0013 Japan
Tel: 813 3581 7868
Fax: 813 5251 2136

Mr. Masaaki Shirakawa
Advisor to the Governor
Financial Market Department
Bank of Japan
2-1-1 Hongoku-cho
Nihonbashi, chuo-ku
Tokyo 103 8660 Japan
Tel: 813 3277 1442
Fax: 813 5203 7187
Email: masaaki.shirakawa@boj.or.jp

Mr. Atsuo Takahashi
Managing Director
Japan Securities Dealers Association
Tokyo Shoken Building
1-5-8 Kayaba-cho, Nihonbashi, Chuo-ku
Tokyo 1030025 Japan
Tel: 813 3669 1657
Fax: 813 3667 6691
Email: a_takahashi@wan.jsda.or.jp

Mr. Takaaki Okada
International Liaison, Japan Securities Dealers Association
Tokyo Shoken Building
1-5-8 Kayaba-cho, Nihonbashi, Chuo-ku,
Tokyo 1030025 Japan
Tel: 813 3669 9817
Fax: 813 3249 3020
Email: t_okada@wan.jsda.or.jp

Mr. Mitsuo Sato
Senior Advisor,
Daiichi Life Research Institute Inc.
1-13-1 Yurakucho, Chiyoda-ku
Tokyo, 100-0006 Japan
Tel: 813 5221 4500
Fax: 813 5219 8323
Email: msato@dlri.dai-ichi-life.co.jp

Prof. Eisuke Sakakibara
Professor
Keio University
1-14-5-801 Akasaka Minato-ku
Tokyo 107-0052 Japan
Tel: 813 3568 2970
Fax: 813 3568 2971
Email: sakakiba@gsec.keio.ac.jp

Mr. Toshio Karigane
Senior Executive Advisor
Daiwa Institute of Research, Ltd.
15-6 Fuyuki, Koto-ku
Tokyo, 135-8460, Japan
Tel: 813 5620 5416
Fax: 813 5620 5869
Email: t.karigane@dir.co.jp

Mr. Sadakazu Osaki
Head
Capital Market Research Unit
Nomura Research Institute, Ltd.
Shin Otemachi: Bld: 2-2-1, Ote-machi
Chiyoda-ku, Tokyo 100-0004, Japan
Tel: 813 5203 0431
Fax: 813 5203 0639
Email: s-ohsaki@nri.co.jp

Mr. Fumiyuki Sasaki
Senior Economist
Economic Research Department
Nomura Research Institute, Ltd.
Shin Otemachi: Bld: 2-2-1, Ote-machi
Chiyoda-ku, Tokyo 100-0004, Japan
Tel: 813 5203 0421
Fax: 813 5203 0498
Email: f1-sasaki@nri.co.jp

CZECH REPUBLIC

Mr. Jiri Kulis
Head, Economic and Trade Unit
Embassy of the Czech Republic, Tokyo
12-16-14, Hiroo, Shibuya-ku
Tokyo 150 0012 Japan
Tel: 813 3400 8122/3; 3400 8125
Fax: 813 3400 8124

Mr. Ludek Niedermayer
Member of the Board and Chief Executive Director
Czech National Bank
Na Prikope 28
11513 Prague 1 Czech Republic
Tel: 4202 2441 2084
Fax: 4202 2441 3448
Email: Ludek.Niedermayer@cnb.cz

UNITED KINGDOM

Dr. Ruben Lee
Director
Oxford Finance Group
25 Mugo Road
London N195EU, United Kingdom
Tel: 44 20 7700 2917
Fax: 44 20 7700 2201
Email: rubenlee.ofg@btinternet.com

Mr. David Strachan
Head, Market Conduct and Infrastructure
Financial Services Authority
25 The North Colonnade
Canary Wharf
London E14 5HS
Tel: 44 171 676 5840
Fax: 44 171 676 9728
Email: david.strachan@fsa.gov.uk

TURKEY

Mr. Levent Özyürek
Head of Section
Foreign Relations Department
Central Bank of the Republic of Turkey
T.C. Merkez Bankasi Idare Merkezi
Dis Iliskiler Genel Müdürlügü
06100 Ulus, Ankara
Turkey
Tel: 90 312 310 26 58
Fax: 90 312 310 91 15
Email: levent.ozyurek@tcmb.gov.tr

Mr. H. Ersen Ekren
First Economic Counsellor
Turkish Embassy, Japan
2-33-6 Jingumae, Shibuya-ku
150-0001 Tokyo, Japan
Tel: 813 3470 2395
Fax: 813 3470 6280
Email: turkiye@crisscross.com

Targeted Countries

CHINA

Dr. Jian Gao
CFO and Chief Economist
China Development Bank
29 Fuchengmenwai Street
Xichend District
Beijing China 100037
Tel 8610 6835 8507
Fax: 8610 6830 7759
Email: gaojians@homeway.com.cn

HONG KONG, CHINA

Mr. Andrew Procter
Commission Member & Executive Director
Securities and Futures Commission
12/F Edinburgh Tower
The Landmark, Central
Hong Kong SAR
Tel: 852 2840 9313
Fax: 852 2526 5304
Email: aprocter@hksfc.org.hk

Mr. Norman Tak-lam Chan
Deputy Chief Executive
Hong Kong Monetary Authority
30/F Citibank Tower
3 Garden Road
Hong Kong
Tel: 852 2878 8128
Fax: 852 2878 8130
Email: Norman_TL_Chan@hkma.gov.hk

Mr. Lawrence Fok
Senior Executive Director
The Stock Exchange of Hong Kong Ltd.
11/F One International Finace Centre
1 Harbour View Street, Central
Hong Kong
Tel: 852 2840 3050
Fax: 852 2868 5028
Email: lawrencefok@sehk.com.hk

Mr. Siu-tsun Francis Lau
Head, External Relations Division
Hong Kong Monetary Authority
30/F Citibank Tower
3 Garden Road
Hong Kong
Tel: 852 2878 8137
Fax: 852 2509 0651
Email: Francis_ST_Lau@hkma.gov.hk

INDIA

Mr. Devendra Raj Mehta
Chairman
Securities and Exchange Board of India.
Mittal Court, 'B' Wing, 1st Floor
Narimam Point, Mumbai, 400 021
Tel: 91 22 202 8221/285 1596
Fax: 91 22 285 5585
E-mail: chairman@sebi.gov.in

Mr. Schanunathan Sundareshan
Minister (Economic and Commercial)
Embassy of India, Tokyo
2-2-11 Kudan-Minami
Chiyoda-ku, Tokyo 102-0074
Tel: 813 3262 2391
Fax: 813 3261 0723

INDONESIA

Mr. Herwidayatamo
Chairman
Indonesian Capital Market Supervisory Agency (BAPEPAM)
New Building, Ministry of Finance, 5th Floor
Jalanl. Dr. Wahidin Raya No. 1
Jakarta, 10710, Indonesia
Tel: 6221 385 7902
Fax: 6221 385 7917

MALAYSIA

Mr. Ali Abdul-Kadir
Chairman
Securities Commission Malaysia
No. 3 Persiaran Bukit Kiara,
50490 Kuala Lumpur, Malaysia
Tel: 603 654 8514
Fax: 603 651 5058

Mr. Ranjit Singh
General Manager
Securities Commission Malaysia
No. 3 Persiaran Bukit Kiara, Bukit Kiara
50490 Kuala Lumpur, Malaysia
Tel: 603 654 8531/559
Fax: 603 653 3451
Email: ranjit@seccom.com.my

SINGAPORE

Ms. Yeo Lian Sim
Assistant Managing Director, Capital Markets
Monetary Authority of Singapore
MAS Building
10 Shenton Way
Singapore 079117
Tel: 65 229 9461
Fax: 65 229 9697
Email: lsyeo@mas.gov.sg

Ms. Bee Bee Tay
Senior Assistant Director
Securities & Futures Industries, Financial Supervision Group
Monetary Authority of Singapore
#23-00 MAS Building
10 Shenton Way
Singapore 079117
Tel: 65 2299856
Fax: 65 2299697
Email: bbtay@mas.gov.sg

Mr. Nam Sin Ng
Director (Marketing)
Financial Promotion Department
Monetary Authority of Singapore
MAS Building
10 Shenton Way
27th Floor
Singapore 079117
Tel: 65 2299164
Fax: 65 2279786
Email: nsng@mas.gov.sg

Mr. Kok Chuan Chew
Industry Development Manager
Monetary Authority of Singapore
MAS Building
10 Shenton Way
27th Floor
Singapore 079117
Tel: 65 2299187
Fax: 65 2279786
Email: justinchew@mas.gov.sg

CHINESE TAIPEI

Mr. Kung-Wha Ding
Vice Chairman
Securities and Futures Commission
85, Sec. 1, Hsin-Sheng S.Road
Taipei, Taiwan ROC
Tel: 886 2 2774 7109
Fax: 886 2 8773 4143
Email: ViceChairman-Ding@sfc.gov.tw

THAILAND

Mr. Prasarn Trairatvorakul
Secretary-General
The Office of the Securities and Exchange Commission
16th Floor, Diethelm Towers B,
93/1 Wireless Road, Patumwan, Lumpini,
Bangkok 10330, Thailand
Tel: 662 256 7782
Fax: 662 256 7722
E-mail: prasarn@sec.or.th

International Organisations

ADB

Dr. Yun-Hwan Kim
Senior Economist
Asian Development Bank
PO Box 789
Manila, Philippines
Tel: 632 632 6625/5790
Fax: 632 636 2360
Email: yhkim@adb.org

IFC

Mr. Tadashi Endo
Senior Capital Markets Specialist
International Finance Corporation
2121 Pennsylvania Ave., N.W.
Washington DC 20433
Room No. 6P-150
Tel: 1 202 458 1800
Fax: 1 202 974 4373
Email: tendo@ifc.org

IMF
Mr. Kunio Saito
Director
Regional Office for Asia and the Pacific
International Monetary Fund
21F Fukoku Seimei Building
2-2-2 Uchisaiwai-cho, Chiyoda-ku
Tokyo 100-0011, Japan
Tel: 813 3597 6700
Fax: 813 3597 6705
E-mail: ksaito@imf.org

WORLD BANK
Mr. Noritaka Akamatsu
Principal Financial Economist
Capital Markets Development Department
World Bank
1818 H Street, N.W.
Washington, DC 20433 U.S.A.
Tel: 1 202 473 5832
Fax: 1 202 522 7105
E-mail: Nakamatsu@worldbank.org

Private Sector

MERRILL LYNCH
INTERNATIONAL
Mr. Kevan Watts
Executive Chairman, Asia Pacific Region
Merrill Lynch International, Inc.
17/F Asia Pacific Finance Tower
3 Garden Road
Central, Hong Kong
Tel: 852 2536 3311
Fax: 852 2536 3312
E-mail: kevan_watts@hk.ml.com

MOODY'S ASIA PACIFIC, LTD.
Ms. Julia Turner
Managing Director
Moody's Asia Pacific, Ltd.
Room 2510-2514
International Finance Centre Tower One
One Harbour Street View
Central, Hong Kong
Tel: 852 2916 1155
Fax: 852 2509 0165
Email: juliat@moodys.com

THAI RATING AND INFORMATION
SERVICES
Dr. Warapatr Todhanakasem
President
Thai Rating and Information Services
Silom Complex Building , 24th Floor
191 Silom Road
Bangkok, 105000 Thailand
Tel: 662 231-3033/662 231 3011 ext. 111
Fax: 662 231 3034/662 231 3012
Email: suwanna@tris.co.th

OECD Secretariat

Mr. Seiichi Kondo
Deputy Secretary-General
General Secretariat
OECD
2 rue André Pascal
75016 Paris
Tel: 331 45 24 80 30
Fax: 331 45 24 79 31
Email: seiichi.kondo@oecd.org

Mr. Hans Blommestein
Senior Economist
Division of Financial Affairs
Directorate for Financial, Fiscal and Enterprise
Affairs
OECD
37 bis Bd. Suchet
75016 Paris
Tel: 331 45 24 79 90
Fax: 331 45 24 78 52
Email: hendrikus.blommestien@oecd.org

Mr. Fujiki Hayashi
Head of Unit
Outreach Unit for Financial Sector Reform
Directorate for Financial, Fiscal and Enterprise
Affairs
OECD
37 bis Bd. Suchet
75016 Paris
Tel: 331 45 24 18 38
Fax: 331 45 24 18 33
Email: fujiki.hayashi@oecd.org

Ms. Dina Nicholas
Assistant
Outreach Unit for Financial Sector Reform
Directorate for Financial, Fiscal and Enterprise
Affairs
OECD
37 bis Bd. Suchet
75016 Paris
Tel: 331 45 24 78 59
Fax: 331 45 24 18 33
Email: dina.nicholas@oecd.org

ADBI Secretariat

Dr. Masaru Yoshitomi
Dean
Asian Development Bank Institute
8th Floor, Kasumigaseki Building,
3-2-5, Chiyoda-ku, Tokyo 100-6008
Tel: +81-3-3593-5541
Fax: +81-3-3593-5571
Email: myoshitomi@adbi.org

Mr. Hitoshi Nishida
Director
Administration Management & Coordination
Asian Development Bank Institute
8th Floor, Kasumigaseki Building,
3-2-5, Chiyoda-ku, Tokyo 100-6008
Tel: +81-3-3593-5502
Fax: +81-3-3593-5571
E-mail: hnishida@adbi.org

Mr. Suay Bah Chua
Director
Capacity Building & Training
Asian Development Bank Institute
8th Floor, Kasumigaseki Building,
3-2-5, Chiyoda-ku, Tokyo 100-6008
Tel: +81-3-3593-5511
Fax: +81-3-3593-5587
E-mail: sbchua@adbi.org

Prof. Shinji Takagi
Visiting Scholar
Asian Development Bank Institute
8th floor, Kasumigaseki Building
3-2-5 Chiyoda-ku, Tokyo 100-6008
Tel: 813 3593 5517
Fax: 813 3593 4270
Email: stakagi@adbi.org

Dr. Ramesh Adhikari
Senior Capacity Building Specialist
Asian Development Bank Institute
8th floor, Kasumigaseki Building
3-2-5 Chiyoda-ku, Tokyo 100-6008
Tel: 813 3593 5508
Fax: 813 3593 5587

Mr. Megumi Araki
Senior Administrative Officer
Asian Development Bank Institute
8th floor, Kasumigaseki Building
3-2-5 Chiyoda-ku, Tokyo 100-6008
Tel: 813 3593 5516
Fax: 813 3593 5571
E-mail: maraki@adbi.org

Ms. Eiko Kitamura
General Coordination Assistant
Asian Development Bank Institute
8th floor, Kasumigaseki Building
3-2-5 Chiyoda-ku, Tokyo 100-6008
Tel: 813 3593 5539
Fax: 813 3593 5571

Ms. Ruri Fujihata
Program Assiastant for Reasearch Group
Asian Development Bank Institute
8th Floor, Kasumigaseki Building,
3-2-5, Chiyoda-ku, Tokyo 100-6008
Tel: 813 3593 5550
Fax: 813 3593 4270
E-mail: rfujihata@adbi.org

Ms. Michiko Yoshida
Progam Assistant for Capacity Bulding/Training
Asian Development Bank Institute
8th Floor, Kasumigaseki Building,
3-2-5, Chiyoda-ku, Tokyo 100-6008
Tel: 813 3593 5543
Fax: 813 3593 5587

Ms. Tomoko Doi
Program Assistant for Capacity Bulding/Training
Asian Development Bank Institute
8th Floor, Kasumigaseki Building,
3-2-5, Chiyoda-ku, Tokyo 100-6008
Tel: 813 3593 5544
Fax: 813 3593 5587

OECD PUBLICATIONS, 2, rue André-Pascal, 75775 PARIS CEDEX 16
PRINTED IN FRANCE
(14 2001 05 1 P 1) ISBN 92-64-18629-8 – No. 51757 2001